1995

HISTORY OF MEDIEVAL ART

980-1440

GEORGES DUBY

HISTORY OF MEDIEVAL ART

980-1440

SKIRA

RIZZOLI
NEW YORK

First published in three volumes 1966-1967
New edition in one volume 1986

© 1986 by Editions d'Art Albert Skira S.A., Geneva

Published in the United States of America in 1986 by
RIZZOLI INTERNATIONAL PUBLICATIONS, INC.
597 Fifth Avenue/New York 10017

Printed in Switzerland

Library of Congress Cataloging-in-Publication Data

Duby, Georges.
    History of medieval art, 980-1440.

    1. Art, Medieval.   2. Cathedrals.   3. Christian
art and symbolism—Medieval, 500-1500.   4. Civilization,
Medieval.   I. Title.
N5970.D798   1986   709 02   85-43525
ISBN 0-8478-0710-X

I

THE MAKING OF
THE CHRISTIAN WEST

980-1140

CONTENTS

THE AWAKENING

Western Europe was thinly, very thinly, populated in the year 1000. Great tracts of waste-land extended west, north and east, growing ever larger until they covered the entire face of this part of the continent: a seemingly endless wilderness of fens and forests, moors and winding rivers, bogs and copses, and the ragged undergrowth that springs up after forest fires and the operations of nomadic charcoal burners. At long intervals were clearings where, exceptionally, patches of land had been brought under cultivation, if only to a limited extent: shallow, irregular furrows cut in a stubborn soil with wooden plough-shares drawn by half-starved oxen. Even in the food-producing areas there were still large empty tracts, fields left fallow for a year, two years, even three, so that the soil could rest and gradually recover its fertility.

The men who worked the land lived in ram-shackle huts made of stone, mud or branches, surrounded by thorn fences and gardens. Some-times in the center of a group of huts protected by a palisade was the residence of a chieftain, with a wooden hall, granaries, sheds for the serfs and, a little way off, the hearth for cooking. Cities were few and far between and where one existed all that remained was the gaunt anatomy of a Roman town, mostly in ruins and ploughed over, a crumb-ling city wall, stone buildings dating to the Empire converted into churches or strongholds, and alongside them a huddle of vine-growers' huts and private houses occupied by priests and warriors, by weavers and the blacksmiths who manufactured weapons and articles of personal adornment for the garrison and the local bishop; also some families of Jewish money-lenders. Along the roads, now little more than cart-tracks, moved long files of carriers of merchandise and along the waterways whole fleets of boats. Compared with Byzantium or Cordova, the "cities" of the West cut a humble figure in the year 1000; poverty-stricken, fallen on evil times, haunted by the spectre of starvation.

Scanty though it was, the population was still, economically speaking, too large. The peasantry had to struggle, almost with their bare hands, against the enmity of nature, whose laws held them in thrall, and with a soil unrewarding for lack of expert tendance. For each grain of wheat he sowed no peasant expected to reap many more than three: just enough to provide his daily bread till Easter. After that he had to fall back on herbs and roots, the makeshift food procurable in forests and on the river banks. In the period of most arduous toil, the summer, the countryfolk had to work themselves to the bone, on empty bellies, nursing frail hopes of a plenteous harvest. But if it was a bad season—and many seasons turned out bad—there was a still earlier shortage and the bishops were constrained to relax ecclesiastical discipline and waive the rule against eating meat in Lent. Sometimes, too, when an exceptionally heavy rainfall had made the earth too sodden for autumn ploughing, or storms had laid low and spoilt the crops, shortages of this kind developed into those widespread famines whose horrid consequences are described with brutal candor by so many chroniclers of the period. "People hunted each other, devoured one another, and many cut the throats of their fellow-men and gorged on human flesh, like wolves."

Were they exaggerating when they spoke of piles of corpses in the charnel-houses, of starving men with empty bellies who took to eating earth and even, on occasion, digging up the bodies of the dead to allay the pangs of hunger? If these writers, all of them clerics, were at such pains to describe these tragic happenings and the great epidemics which decimated an undernourished populace and led to outbreaks of mob violence, the reason surely was that such calamities brought vividly home to them both the fragility of human life and the enigma of God's ways to man. To eat one's fill all the year round was a privilege reserved to members of the nobility and to a handful of priests and monks. All the others were enslaved to hunger and these writers saw in hunger an ineluctable concomitant of the human condition. Man, they thought, is born to suffering; he has a feeling of being naked, bare to the buffetings of fate, doomed to death, disease and daylong apprehension because he is a sinner. Since Adam's fall he has been the prey of hunger and no one can hope to be rid of it any more than of original sin. The men of that age lived in constant fear, not least of their own shortcomings.

Yet for some time already this early medieval world had been involved in an almost imperceptible movement that was delivering it little by little from abject poverty, and the eleventh century witnessed the gradual emergence of the peoples of western Europe from a state of barbarism. They were becoming less exposed to famine, achieving one by one a place in history, making steady headway towards a better mode of life. This was a period of awakening: the childhood of our civilization. For this part of the world—and this was to be its distinctive privilege, the mainstay of its growing ascendancy—was gradually entering on a period of immunity from invasions. Until now, for many centuries, wave after wave of migrant races had swept across the West, playing havoc with men's lives, destroying everything that lay on their path. True, the widespread conquests of Charlemagne had succeeded in restoring for a while a semblance of peace and order, but after the Emperor's death there was no resisting the hordes of invaders pouring in on all sides; from Scandinavia, from the eastern steppes, and from the Mediterranean islands overrun by the hosts of Islam, all of whom harried and pillaged Latin Christendom. The rude beginnings of what is known as Romanesque art make their appearance at the very time when invasions of this kind came to an end, in the regions where the Norsemen settled and developed an ordered way of life, where the King of Hungary installed the Christian faith, and whence the Count of Arles expelled the Saracen marauders who controlled the Alpine passes and had recently held to ransom the Abbot of Cluny. After 980 we hear no more tales of plundered abbeys and bands of terrified monks roving the countryside, carrying with them their relics and treasures. From now on, when flames were seen rising on the outskirts of the forests, these had been kindled by peasants reclaiming land for cultivation, not by pillagers.

That some progress in agricultural skills had been made in the "dark age" of the tenth century seems certain (though we know little about it). Initiated in the vast domains of the monasteries, these improvements had begun to take effect in the surrounding countryside; from now on they gathered speed and thanks to them the peasants of the feudal period were equipped with more effective implements, better ploughs, better harness and, above all, iron ploughshares capable of turning up the ground more efficiently, rendering it more fertile, and coping with heavy soil hitherto left untilled. As a result the cultivated area gained on the waste-lands, old clearings were enlarged, new ones opened up, and the improvement in farming methods led to more abundant harvests. No explicit mention of these improvements is made in extant records of the period, but there are many indications of them and they lay at the origin of all the cultural developments of the eleventh century. The famine of 1033 whose harrowing tale is told in the *Historiae* of Rudolph Glaber, a Cluniac monk, was in fact one of the last of the great famines; thereafter food shortages were less disastrous and took place at longer intervals. Thanks to the extension of the cultivated areas and increased productivity the land could easily support a larger population and these men were more robust, less vulnerable to epidemics. Calamitous though it was in many ways, the year 1000 witnessed, we can see, the upsurge of a new, active and enterprising generation, forbears of those who for three crowded centuries were to pioneer the ascent of Europe. As Thietmar, Bishop of Merseburg, in Saxony, observes in his *Chronicon* for the period 908-1018, "when came the thousandth year after the birth of our Saviour Jesus Christ by the Blessed Virgin, a radiant dawn flooded the world with light."

But that dawn did not rise for all; a vast majority were to live for a long while yet in darkness, destitution, constant anxiety. Whether free men or serfs, the peasants still had nothing of their own and, though they suffered less from hunger, were oppressed, denied any hope of escaping some day from their hovels and bettering themselves—even if they succeeded in accumulating, penny by penny, over ten or twenty years, just enough to buy a small patch of land. For in that age the landed nobility held them in close subjection; as a result of the rights of exploitation and privileges possessed by the rulers, the social order formed a pyramid of several tiers, sealed off from each other, with at the apex an all-powerful élite. A few families, friends and relations of the monarch, owned everything: the soil, the oases of cultivation, the waste-lands around them, the hosts of slaves, the taxes and corvées due from the tenant farmers on the great estates, the means of making war, the rights of judging and condemning, all the highest posts in the Church and State. Clad in rich garments, bedecked with jewels, attended by a mounted escort, the nobles roved the countryside, laying hands on the few chattels of any value owned by the impoverished inhabitants. The nobles alone benefited by the influx of wealth due to improved methods of cultivation. This rigorously hierarchic social order, the centralization of power and prosperity in the hands of the nobles and a favored few provide the explanation of how it was that, despite the extremely slow growth of this rudimentary material culture, we find, nonetheless, a surprisingly rapid expansion of so many activities in so many fields during the last quarter of the eleventh century: the development of de-luxe industries, the urge to conquest that sped the warriors of the West in all directions, and last but not least the rebirth of western culture. Had the supreme authority of a small group of nobles and churchmen pressed less heavily on the masses of powerless workers, the forms of art illustrated in this volume would never have come into being in those vast empty spaces among a peasantry so primitive and backward, so poverty-stricken, so totally devoid of even the vestiges of a culture.

What is perhaps most remarkable in these works of art is their diversity, the exuberant inventiveness of the men who created them, and none the less their fundamental unity. Latin Christendom extended over an immense area; months were needed to traverse it from end to end, intersected as it was by obstacles of all descriptions and huge empty tracts isolating the populated zones from each other. Each province lived a life apart, free to cultivate its ethnic idiosyncrasies. For in the flux and reflux of the great migrations, when empires were founded and soon fell to pieces, cultural layers of very different natures were deposited in various parts of Europe—some of them still quite novel in a whole group of regions, and intermixing or superimposed along their frontiers. Moreover the tenth-century invaders had ravaged the West to an extent that greatly varied

from place to place, and here we have another reason for the remarkably large number of local variants existing in the year 1000.

Nowhere were these differences more noticeable than on the confines of the Latin world. North, west and east the Christian lands were encompassed by a zone of barbarism, where paganism still flourished. These were the regions which had formerly been overrun by Scandinavians, Danish and Norwegian sea-venturers and traders from Gotland. There was still an abundant maritime traffic plying on the rivers and along the estuaries. Though piratical attacks on shipping still were frequent, the feuds between rival tribes and clans were tending to die out, giving place to commercial dealings of a peaceful order. From the Saxon strongholds in England, from the banks of the Elbe, from the forests of Thuringia and Bohemia and from Lower Austria missionaries were sallying forth, destroying idols and erecting crosses. Many died a martyr's death, but the princes of these lands, whose inhabitants were leading now more settled lives, building villages and installing farms, encouraged their subjects to be baptized and with the Christian faith to acquire a modicum of civilization. But the outlying, still semi-barbarian regions contrasted sharply with the southern marches, those of Italy and the Iberian peninsula, where contacts with Islam and Byzantine Christendom, far from primitive cultures, were operative. In the county of Barcelona, in the small kingdoms that had struck root on the mountains of Aragon, Navarre, Leon and Galicia, by way of the centers of culture in the Po delta, at Ferrara, Comacchio, Venice and above all Rome—frontier city between Hellenism and Latinity, always eyeing Constantinople with jealous admiration—a ferment of progress was creeping in. Along with new skills and new ideas, finely wrought objects were finding their way into these lands and, no less alluring, the gold coinage which testified to the material supremacy of the cultures on the frontiers of the southern zone of Latin Christendom.

Even in the heart of the vast area of Europe that Charlemagne had succeeded in incorporating in his empire, we find a great diversity. The most radical divergences, those that affected even the tenor of daily life, were determined by the greater or less extent to which Roman influences had made good their ascendancy. In some places, as in northern Germany, they seem wholly absent. Elsewhere they had been partially but not completely wiped out long ago by the inroads of barbarians, as was the case in Bavaria and Flanders. Elsewhere, again, they still were active and effective, as in Provence and, south of the Alps, in those lands where the towns were less dilapidated and where the native languages had a definitely Latin accent. Other contrasts, too, derived from the imprints left here and there by various races which during the early Middle Ages had settled in the West. The names of the lands they occupied betray their presence—Lombardy, Burgundy, Saxony, Gascony—and memories of the conquests of their ancestors in earlier times had developed a sense of nationality, premature in this age, among the provincial aristocracy. Associated with this was that rooted antipathy for "foreigners" which led the Burgundian chronicler Rudolph Glaber to mock the Aquitanians when one day he saw their troops escorting a princess. In the tangled pattern of the map of western Europe in the year 1000, the chief points of interest for the present-day historian are the regions where divergent cultures came in touch with each other, exchanged ideas and pooled discoveries, to the advantage of all concerned. Among these favoured regions were Catalonia and Normandy, the district of Poitiers, Burgundy, Saxony and the great plain stretching between Ravenna and Pavia.

More remarkable, however, is the deep-seated unity which prevailed at all cultural levels—notably that of creative art—in a civilization so widely scattered over an area so hard to bring under any uniform control. One reason for this underlying kinship was the extreme mobility of the population. For the most part it was congenitally nomadic, and this applies particularly to its higher ranks. Kings, princes, nobles, bishops and the large retinues which always accompanied them were continually on the move and made a point of visiting all their domains in the course of the year so as to consume their products on the spot and to hold their courts; moreover, hardly had they arrived than they set out to visit some local shrine or to lead a military foray. They lived on horseback, on the roads, and ceased their peregrination only in the dead of winter. Probably the worst privation for the monks was that of being confined, year in, year out, in a cloister; many of them found this unbearable and were accordingly permitted to move about, to change from abbey to abbey. Naturally enough these migra-

tory habits of the privileged élite on whose patronage all creative art depended led to fruitful contacts, rewarding exchanges of ideas.

No true frontiers existed in this part of Europe, divided up into small compartments. Once a man quitted the village where he had been born and bred, he was conscious of being a stranger everywhere and as such a suspicious character, in daily peril of robbery or worse. Adventure began on his doorstep and life was equally dangerous whether he settled a stone's throw from home or went to some remote country. Can one even speak of a frontier separating Latin Christendom from the rest of the world? In Spain no clear-cut barrier had ever existed between the zone in Moslem occupation and the regions ruled by Christian kings. The area of these latter fluctuated greatly as a result of the changing fortunes of war. In 996 Al-Mansur sacked Compostela, but fifteen years later the Count of Barcelona entered Cordova. Many petty Moslem princes were bound to the kings of Aragon and Castile by treaties under which they were assured protection and required to pay tribute. Conversely, a great number of active Christian communities flourished under the domination of the caliphs. Strung out in a continuous line along the Mediterranean coast then in Moorish occupation, from Toledo to Carthage, Alexandria and Antioch, these communities acted as connecting links between the western empire and Byzantium. All these factors must be taken into account when we seek to understand why Coptic themes proliferated so extensively in Romanesque iconography, and whence came the curious idiom of the illuminations in the Saint-Sever *Apocalypse* or the colonnettes and arches of Saint-Michel-de-Cuxa. For in point of fact eleventh-century Europe was less divided into water-tight compartments than it might seem at first sight to have been, and lent itself to exchanges of aesthetic ideas from country to country, race to race.

Among the various factors of cohesion operative at the higher cultural levels the Carolingian "cement" still played a vital part. For some decades practically all the West had been united under a single political domination, that of an homogeneous group of bishops and legislators, all of whom were members of the same families and had been educated under the aegis of the royal household. They held periodical meetings presided over by their common master, the monarch, and their many ties of kinship were strengthened by shared memories of their collective studies. This is why, widely scattered though it was, and despite natural obstacles, the aristocracy of the eleventh century formed a coherent whole, a body of men united in the same faith, by the same rites, the same language and the same cultural heritage. United, too, by abiding reminiscences of Charlemagne, that is to say of the immemorial prestige of Rome and the Roman Empire.

Yet even the most deep-seated affinities, those which did most to ensure a close cohesion between the various manifestations of art, were conditioned above all by the single *purpose* of that art. For in that age the sole mission of what we now call art was to offer to God worthy images of the visible world, His creation, and by such gifts to appease His wrath and win His favor. Thus every work of art was essentially numinous, not to say sacrificial, less concerned with aesthetics than with magic. Here indeed we have the most distinctive feature of the creative art of the period 980 to 1140. The expanding economy of this period, leading as it did to progress in many fields, provided Latin Christendom with the material means of creating less uncouth, far more advanced works of art, though this advance had not yet been carried far enough wholly to override the mental attitudes and primitive comportment of the past. The eleventh-century Christian always felt himself overwhelmed by the mystery of things, a helpless puppet of the unseen, elemental, terrifying forces of the world that lay behind appearances. Even the best thinkers were haunted by phantasms of the irrational. This is why at this turning point of history, this brief interval in which, without yet being delivered from his dread of the unknown, man set to forging weapons to overcome it, there emerged the greatest and indeed the only truly sacred art of Europe.

Since this art was, as set forth above, an act of cult, a "sacrifice," it was under the exclusive control of those members of the community whose function it was to parley with the unseen powers governing life and death. In virtue of an ancient tradition this function had been vested in the king. But Europe was becoming feudalized; the power of the kings was disintegrating, passing into other hands. As a result, superintendence of the work of art was ceasing to be a royal prerogative. It was the monks who took it over, since in the existing climate of culture they were the most trusted intermediaries between man and the divine. And practically all the changes that came over the art of the West during this period reflect this gradual transference.

I

DESTINY
OF IMPERIAL ART

CROWN OF THE EMPEROR OTTO I. REICHENAU (?), ABOUT 962. KUNSTHISTORISCHES MUSEUM, VIENNA.

I. 14

THE KINGS OF THE EARTH

"One alone reigns in the Kingdom of Heaven, He who hurls the thunderbolts; it is but natural that there should also be one alone who, under Him, reigns on earth." And in the eleventh century the world of men was commonly regarded as an image or reflection of the City of God, a city governed by a king. In fact feudal Europe could not dispense with monarchs, and when the crusaders, perhaps the most undisciplined army that has ever existed, swept down on the Holy Land, they promptly made of it a kingdom. Paragon of earthly perfection, the *persona* of the monarch invariably figured at the summit of all the mental diagrams which aspired to illustrate the order of the visible universe. Arthur, Charlemagne, Alexander, David—all the heroes of chivalric culture were kings, and it was with the king that every man, priest, warrior, even peasant, sought to identify himself. This permanence of what might be described as a mystique of royalty must not be lost sight of, for in it we have one of the predominant characteristics of medieval civilization. The conception of the work of art, in particular, was closely bound up with the idea of kingship, its functions and prerogatives. That is why, when seeking to elucidate the relations between the social system and creative art, we must begin by examining attentively the then accepted concept of royal power and the manner in which it functioned.

Kingship was a legacy of the Germanic past, brought by the races whom perforce the Romans had incorporated in their empire, without in the least subtracting from the powers of their rulers. The principal duty of these rulers was to lead their armies in battle, and every year when winter ended the young warriors mustered for some military exploit under their command. Thus throughout the Middle Ages the sword was chief of the emblems of sovereignty. But these barbarian kings had another prerogative, more numinous and still more vital to the common good: the magical power of interceding between the people and their gods; the welfare of the race depended on their mediation. This power came to them directly from the All Highest; divine blood ran in their veins and "the custom of the French was always, on the death of their king, to chose another member of the royal line." In this capacity the king presided at religious ceremonies and the chief sacrifices were made in his name.

An event momentous for its bearing on the "royal" art of Europe in the years to come took place in the middle of the eighth century. From then on the crowning of the mightiest of the monarchs of the West, accepted by all as the dominant figure of Latin Christendom, was a religious ceremony, like the coronations of the petty kings of northern Spain. In other words, he no longer owed his charisma to a mythical kinship with the obscure powers of the heathen pantheon; it was conferred on him directly by the Christian God, in the rite of sacring. When the priest anointed him with the holy oil he was invested with otherworldly powers and something of the sanctity of godhead. The king himself became a priest, ranking beside the bishops, who were consecrated with the same rites. *Rex et sacerdos*, he was given the ring and staff, insignia of a pastoral mission. By the hymns of praise chanted in the coronation ceremony the Church installed him in the heart of the celestial hierarchy. She defined his function, not merely that of a leader in the battlefield, but also that of a dispenser of peace and justice. Last and not least, since in the eighth century the art traditions stemming from the golden age of Rome survived in the West only under the aegis of the Church, and since all the architectural and decorative activities which hitherto had glorified the cities celebrated the glory of God—since in short all great art was now liturgical—it followed that the king, who by reason of the Christianization of his talismanic powers had become the leading figure in Church ritual, initiated and directed the major artistic enterprises. The rite of sacring had in effect transposed art into the royal domain.

The art forms due to monarchical initiative were given a more specific shape when, after 800, the restoration of the Empire had enlarged the scope of royalty. Imperial authority now became another divine institution ranking somewhat higher than before in the hierarchy of powers, midway between the kings of the earth and the celestial principalities. A pope had made obeisance to Charlemagne and on St Peter's tomb hailed him "Augustus." A Constantine redivivus and a new David, the Emperor of the West was charged with the task of guiding Latin Christendom on the path of salvation. On a page of a liturgical book, illuminated at Regensburg in 1002-1014, a painter depicted the Emperor Henry II in the center of a cruciform composition, i.e. at the "crossroads" of the universe, with angels coming down from heaven to invest him with the emblems of his sovereignty. St Ulrich and St Emmeram are uplifting his arms as Aaron and Hur held up the hands of Moses in the battle with the Amalekites and, throned in glory as in the Apocalyptic visions, Christ Himself is placing on his brow the diadem. Even more unequivocally than the kings who bowed down to them, the new emperors of the West saw themselves as God's vicegerents on earth. But they also knew themselves to be the successors of Caesar and in the acts of consecration they were called on to perform and which gave rise to works of art they were mindful of their forerunners, those whose largesse had embellished the cities of classical antiquity. Therefore they wished the objects presented to God at their bidding to bear the mark of a distinctive aesthetic, that of the Empire, in other words of Rome. Henceforth, and more deliberately than in the past, the artists who carried out their orders and those employed by the other sovereigns of the West drew inspiration from the masterpieces of Antiquity. All that in this eleventh-century art still shows affinities with the classicism of ancient Rome stems directly from the second rebirth of the western Empire.

For, two centuries after the coronation of Charlemagne as Emperor, creative art was still to a large extent oriented by the convergence of all temporal powers on the person of a sovereign, the Lord's Anointed, whose authority had a supernatural source and whose ministry, as set forth in the *Laudes Regiae*, signified the alliance of the two worlds, seen and unseen, the "cosmic harmony" between the earth and heaven. In the year 1000,

though the process of feudalization was steadily gaining ground, Europe continued to delegate to its emperor and its kings, its spiritual guides, the duties of rendering to God the homage of the people and of distributing among them the favors He bestowed. Similarly, there fell to them the task of tending the major offerings of the community, the churches, and providing the altar decorations, the reliquaries and the illuminated books in which God's words were enshrined. All agreed that these services befitted their high estate; that liberality, generosity, magnificence were attributes of kingship. By common consent the sovereign was *ex officio* a giver—to God and man—and works of beauty should flow from his open hands. Since, in the highly primitive social conditions of the age, the chief object of the gift was to dominate its recipient, to subject him to the donor, it was by making offerings that the monarch procured for his people the good will of the heavenly powers, and by his benefactions that he won the love of his people. When two kings met, each wished to prove himself the greater by the peculiar excellence of his gifts. This is why the leading artists of the eleventh century attached themselves to the monarchs—so long as these retained their power. The art of the age is essentially aulic, because it is a sacred art. Its best exponents operated in workshops under the patronage and control of the royal courts; indeed a geographic survey of eleventh-century art gives us an accurate idea of the respective eminence of the various kings of Europe.

In the year 1000 the most active creative centers in the West were to be found—as at Byzantium and in the Islamic lands—in the propinquity of the man who was regarded as the religious leader: in the case of Latin Christendom the Emperor. Reduced to a mere shadow of itself by the swift collapse of Charlemagne's successors, the imperial power had recovered substance and driving force in the land that the Carolingians had shaped with their own hands and civilized throughout its length and breadth: in Germania. This rejuvenation had begun in Saxony, most barbarous but also most vigorous of the German provinces, the one which had been spared by the hordes of marauders then scouring Europe, by reason of its extreme poverty, but also of the courageous resistance put up by the population. It was in Saxony that the fugitive monks took refuge, bringing with them their sacred relics and their skills. In the early tenth century the Saxon Dukes built fortresses at the foot of the Harz mountains, which proved an effective barrier against the onsets of the heathens, and the Germanic peoples chose one of these sturdy warriors to be their king. One of them won an epoch-making victory in Hungary which put an end to the invasions. Hailed as the saviour of Christendom, Otto soon became the protector and reformer of the Holy See. He was crowned emperor by the pope in 962 and, for the second time, the Empire was restored.

The Ottonian empire was more "Roman" than the Carolingian had been. In 998 Otto III, fourth of the line, decided to make his residence in a palace he had built on the Aventine and, though the *bulla* he used to seal his decrees still bore the effigy of Charlemagne, it had on the other side an image of the Eternal City, Roma Aurea. When speaking of himself and citing the long list of his titles, it was the honorific "Roman" that he placed in the forefront. And in pursuance of this *renovatio imperii romani* he spoke of Rome as "capital of the world." For the reborn Roman Empire boasted of its universality, and even more insistently than their predecessors its new masters claimed to be lords of the universe. Moreover there were now no clashes with Byzantium; the western emperors married "Greek" princesses and made no secret of their admiration for the Constantinople of the year 1000 where, too, a renaissance was in progress. It was from the Basileus that they took their new conception of imperial authority and the emblems of their power: the golden cope and the globe that fitted perfectly into the emperor's hand and signified a sovereignty embracing the entire world. At the chief State ceremonies Henry II (the "Saint") wore a great cloak whose embroidery invested his body with the constellations of the cosmos. As for the imperial crown (the one in the Vienna Museum may be that of Otto I), its eight sides, resembling the eight walls of the palatine chapels, signified eternity and symbolically evoked the heavenly Jerusalem, in other words the realm of perfection which would take form on the Last Day. Indeed it may well have seemed that the reign of the new Caesar prefigured that of Christ when at the end of Time He would return to take His throne on earth as King of Kings. The Ottonian emperors dreamed of making theirs once more a worldwide empire like that of God, and when giving their court painters commissions

for illuminated liturgical books, often asked them to portray a group of large female figures, signifying the nations of the West, and they were shown bowing their heads in token of submission at the foot of the imperial throne.

Yet, in practice, the Emperor was unable to hold his own in Rome, where the old nobility entrenched in its ruined ancestral homes retained its ascendancy. He was king of Italy, and soon became king of Burgundy and Provence as well. But he reigned effectively only over the Germanic lands and Lotharingia, home of the lineage of Charlemagne. In the year 1000 Otto III went to Aachen where, "being unsure of the exact spot where the bones of Charlemagne rested, he had the pavement of the church torn up in secret at the place where he supposed they were, and continued digging until he found them, sealed in a royal sarcophagus. Then the emperor took for himself the cross of gold hung round the dead king's neck and such parts of his vestments as had not decayed, and after this set all back in place, with the utmost reverence." According to another chronicler the remains of the first restorer of the Empire were exposed to public view, like the relics of saints, and "proved their potency by signs and wonders and noteworthy miracles." Thus the restored imperial power was grafted on to the Carolingian trunk, around which already legends of strange happenings had gathered. Nominally, it was Roman and worldwide; in reality it had become almost entirely Germanic and as a result of this far-reaching change in the structure of the Empire the seminal centers of creative art in the eleventh century were to be found in Saxony, in the Meuse valley and on the shores of the Lake of Constance. It was the German lands that propagated to most effect the Frankish traditions of monarchical art, of architecture, of the pictorial and plastic forms in which was fructified the heritage of the workshops of the year 800, reinvigorated by Byzantine models and a return to Roman sources. But since the Emperor's real power was restricted to a few provinces and he was not the only monarch, "royal" art was no longer concentrated at a single point as in Carolingian times, and we find it operative in other kingdoms, far from the seat of empire.

For other kings were competing with the Roman and Germanic Caesars for the imperial title, to begin with those in the regions which Charlemagne had never subjugated. The English king styled himself "Totius Albionis Imperator Augustus." When in the early eleventh century Canute had extended his dominion over all the coasts of the North Sea and "five kingdoms had been brought under his sway: Denmark, Anglia, Brittany, Scotland and Norway," he had become an emperor. Similarly the kings of León, consecrated guardians of the shrine of Santiago de Compostela, after their many victories over the princes of Cordova, spoke of their *imperium* over the other Iberian kings. Lastly, in the very heart of Carolingian territory there still existed a king, but only one, whom his biographers thought fit to invest with the rank of an Augustus. For them the true Imperator Francorum was not the king of Germany but the ruler of West Francia, the king of France. In the year 1000 he was universally esteemed the chief rival of the Teutonic emperor; his bishops reminded him that "the Empire itself had been constrained to bow to his predecessors." Moreover the king of Germany treated him as an equal; when in 1023 the Emperor Henry II and King Robert of France met on the frontier of their respective dominions to discuss affairs of State, they greeted each other as brothers. By common consent the western world was split between two great kingdoms, one governed by the "Caesar," the other by the legitimate descendant of Clovis, the king who had been crowned at Reims beside that baptismal font at which in earlier days the people of the Franks had solemnized their pact with God. "We see that the Roman Empire has been, in the main, destroyed, but so long as there are Frankish kings with a vocation to preserve it, its glory will not wholly fade, since the kings will sustain it." Was it not clearly in favor of the Franks that the transfer of the *imperium* had taken place and was not the Ile-de-France the true Francia? Like Charlemagne, the Capetian monarch in the year 1000 held conclaves surrounded by bishops and counts, he embellished churches with his gifts, and the illuminations of sacred texts were made at his behest in abbeys under his patronage, at Saint-Germain-des-Prés and Saint-Denis in France. And since he felt himself heir to the Empire, the artists he employed (like those of Germany) used as their models the imperial works of the ninth century.

The *imperium*, the power of dispensing peace and justice, the sacred task of intercession and the cultural prerogatives allied with it were thus divided in the West in 1000. The effect of this was the rapid emergence of two Europes. One, that of the South, was kingless; for in the region beyond the Loire, including Catalonia, the French king's writ did not run. The authority of the Emperor as well was purely illusory at Lyons and in Provence, and in Italy, too, it was waning. Hence the opportunity in these southern provinces for the development of an art untrammelled by monarchical control. The European kingdoms were all located in the North, except for those in the highlands around León and Jaca in Spain, ruled by Christian sovereigns. On the fringes of the Europe of the kings, in the Scandinavian hinterlands and the isolated regions hemmed in by marshes where the first cathedrals of Poland, Bohemia and Moravia were now being built alongside the princely residences, serf artisans were continuing to employ for the personal adornments of the chieftains of tribes, who scarcely knew even the name of Christ, an art language stemming from the prehistoric past. Yet even here, thanks to progressive Christianization, the renown of a royalty consecrated by the Church was encouraging them to draw on reminiscences of the Carolingian aesthetic. This was what happened at Winchester under the approving eye of the Anglo-Saxon kings. And the Capetians made still more brilliant use of Carolingian art at Reims, Orléans and Chartres. But its true home was Germany. This was the chief source of all the forms of royal art which kept nearest to the spirit of Antiquity; they flourished in the forests of Saxony and most vigorously around Aachen, at Liège, on the banks of the Rhine, at the heart of what had been the Carolingian domain, and under the auspices of Henry II Bamberg (in Franconia) became their chief seminal center. The Teutonic emperors' frequent progresses through their dominions made that art known as far afield as Rome. These, in fact, were the places where, on the eve of the eleventh century, north of Tours, Besançon and the Alpine passes, the tradition of the Augustan patronage of art and the last traces of classical antiquity still survived, converted henceforth to the service of the Christian God.

THE EMPEROR

The Empire was the myth whereby the West, disrupted by the rise of feudalism, regained the basic unity of which it dreamt and which it deemed agreeable to God's plan. Under the imperial government, it became a united body, a brotherhood which, under the banner of Christ, advanced in serried ranks towards the promised bliss of the Heavenly City. This conception was bound up with the eschatological mystique which bulked so large in Christian thinking of the period. The end of the world and "the consummation of the Empire of Rome and of the Christians" were to take place conjointly when an emperor, last monarch of the age, came to Golgotha to offer his insignia to God—after which would come the reign of Antichrist. The imperium envisaged in the eleventh century was a combination of three notions. Under its spiritual aspect it was a divinely appointed institution; the All Highest selected a ruler, gave him victory and by the same token filled him with his grace: that numinous power (felicitas, Königsheil) which set him above all other monarchs and made him the sole guide of God's people. It was on the battlefield, after their crushing defeats of the Hungarians, that first Henry the Fowler, then his son Otto I was acclaimed emperor by his troops, and both kings regarded themselves as Charlemagne's successors. Enduring memories of the Carolingian triumphs and the aura investing Aachen formed the second element of the "imperial idea" and this gave rise to a third: a belief that the defunct Imperium Romanorum had been reborn in the West. For the imperial myth was tied up with the Roman myth. The liturgical rites of the emperor's coronation could be solemnized only in the Eternal City, in the church erected on St Peter's tomb, and by the Bishop of Rome, and the sovereignty thus bestowed purported to be universal.

This universality and its divine bestowal were given visual expression in a host of images: the dais (the throne on which Otto II took his seat as ruler of the nations of the world); the constellations and signs of the zodiac, signifying the firmament, woven on the cloak of Henry II; and the octagonal crown of the Holy Roman Empire. As "Servant of St Peter," the Emperor fulfilled an evangelical mission and by means of the missionaries he sent forth, sought to increase the number of believers. Before him was borne the Holy Lance containing one of the nails of the Cross. He led his people to the final triumph of good over evil, of resurrection over death. One symbol summed up all, a truly imperial symbol since it stood for victory, and that symbol was the cross: the cross that Otto III took from Charlemagne's neck, to hang it on his own; hence the countless crosses made by the court goldsmiths for the emperors, who distributed them as tokens of their invincible power.

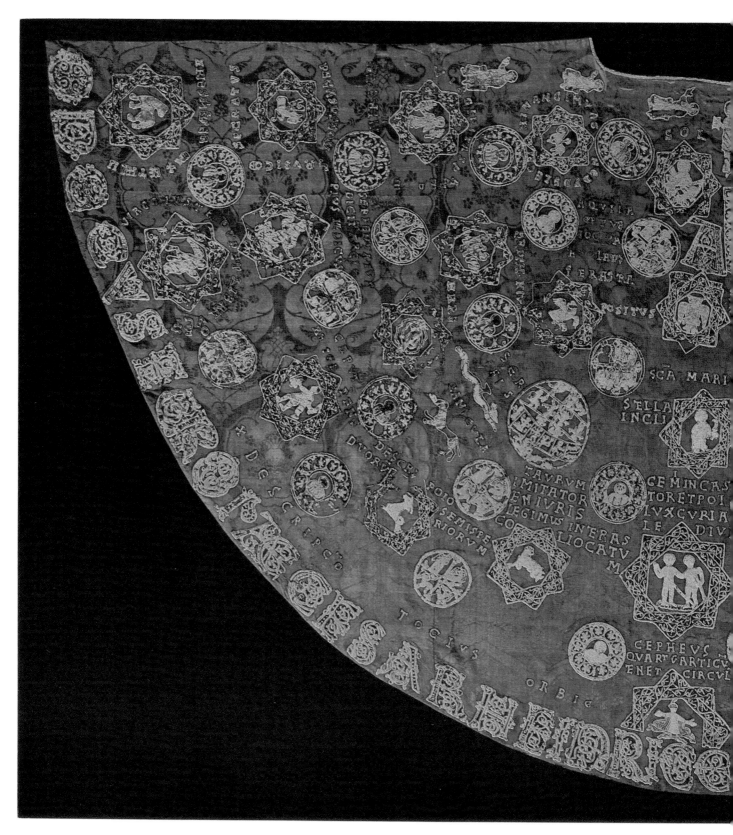

THE STAR-PATTERNED CLOAK OF THE EMPEROR HENRY II.

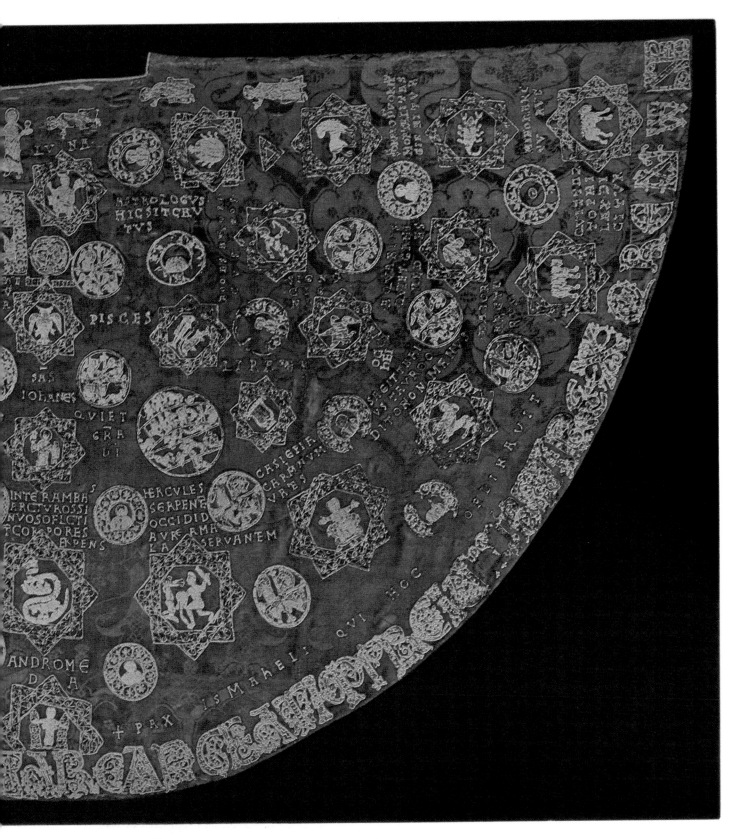

NORTH ITALY OR GERMANY (?), ABOUT 1020. DIOCESAN MUSEUM, BAMBERG.

LAMBERT OF SAINT-OMER, LIBER FLORIDUS: AUGUSTUS, RULER OF THE WORLD.
ABOUT 1120. FOLIO 138 VERSO, MS 92, UNIVERSITY LIBRARY, GHENT.

SO-CALLED CROSS OF LOTHAIR. COLOGNE, LATE 10TH CENTURY.
CATHEDRAL TREASURE, AACHEN.

MASTER OF THE REGISTRUM GREGORII: THE EMPEROR OTTO II WITH THE SYMBOLS
OF THE FOUR PARTS OF HIS EMPIRE. TRIER, ABOUT 983. MUSÉE CONDÉ, CHANTILLY.

I. 24

The imperial administration did not make an end of kings; royalty was an older institution and no less sacrosanct. The king, too, believed himself a Christ. Like the bishops, shepherds of the people and successors of the apostles, he owed his rank to an intervention of the Holy Ghost, was acclaimed by an assemblage of churchmen and warriors in a cathedral and anointed with holy oil which bestowed on him the power of vanquishing evil. Describing the coronation of the German king, Bishop Otto of Freising wrote as follows: "On the same day and in the same church, the elected bishop of Münster was consecrated by the same prelates who had anointed the king, so that the presence of both the king and the supreme prelate at the ceremony might be regarded as a favorable presage for the future, since the same church and the same day witnessed the unction of the two persons who, as enjoined in the Old and New Testaments, are the only persons sacramentally anointed, each alike entitled Christus Domini." *The king, that war-lord whose* potestas *ended once age or infirmity had made him incapable of riding a horse, was also a member of the priesthood. The one man in the Christian community whose power lay at the junction between the spiritual and the temporal, on the border of the seen and unseen worlds, he was minister of both the sacred and the secular. Helgaud of Saint-Benoît-sur-Loire, who wrote the life of King Robert of France, describes him as "a man of God" whose chief function, like the monks', was praying for his people. "So devoted was he to the Scriptures that never a day passed without his reading the Psalms and beseeching the Most High in the words of St David." The vow made on the day of his sacring imposed on him the duty of protecting "God's people" (the priests and the poor) against the powers of darkness. When the members of his court were seated at his feet, he occupied the same place as Jesus, whom the age envisaged primarily as a crowned judge. Like Jesus, the king had a miraculous power of curing diseases. "By the will of God," Helgaud continues, "this perfect man had so wonderful a gift of healing that if he laid his very pious hand on the place where a disease was lurking, he cured it then and there." Despite the fact that Henry IV, King of Germany, had been excommunicated, peasants flocked to him, when he was traveling through Tuscany, so as to touch his garment, believing this would ensure for them better harvests. Thus "the king holds a place above the common herd of laymen, for being anointed with the holy oils he participates in the sacerdotal ministry," and in the eyes of God is the supreme sacrificer. This explains the part he played in creative art, always envisaged in this age as an offering to God and an act of consecration.*

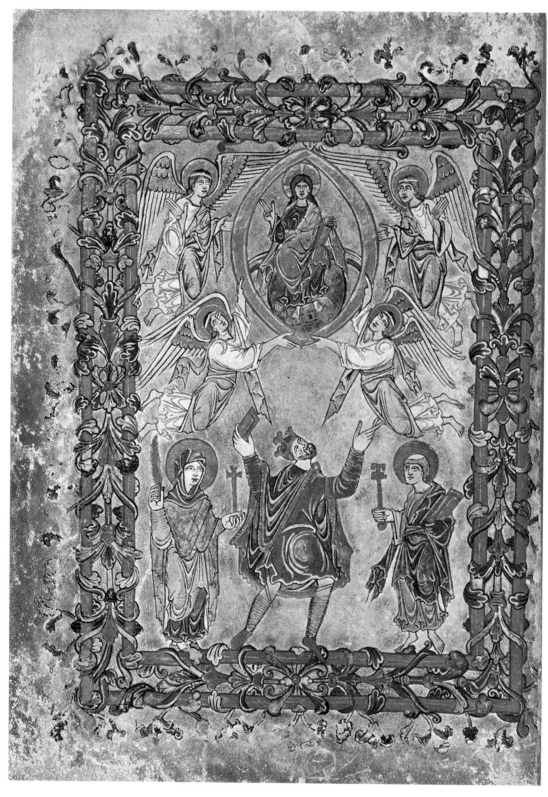

NEW MINSTER CHARTER: KING EDGAR OF ENGLAND (957-975) PRESENTING THE CHARTER TO GOD.
WINCHESTER, 966. FOLIO 2 VERSO, COTTON VESP. A. VIII, BRITISH MUSEUM, LONDON.

IVORY COVER OF THE GOSPEL BOOK OF ABBESS THEOPHANU OF ESSEN (1039-1056): THE CRUCIFIXION.
MID-11TH CENTURY. CATHEDRAL TREASURE, ESSEN.

GOSPEL BOOK OF OTTO III: THE SERMON ON THE MOUNT. REICHENAU, 1010.
FOLIO 34 VERSO, CLM. 4453, STAATSBIBLIOTHEK, MUNICH.

CHRIST THE KING ENTHRONED IN THE CITY OF HEAVEN. FIRST HALF OF THE 12TH CENTURY.
FRESCO IN THE VAULT OF THE NARTHEX, CHURCH OF SAN PIETRO AL MONTE, CIVATE, NEAR COMO.

ANGLO-SAXON SACRAMENTARY: THE NATIVITY. ELY, 1006-1023. FOLIO 32 VERSO, MS Y.6, BIBLIOTHÈQUE MUNICIPALE, ROUEN.

I. 30

The Carolingians had decreed that every cathedral and church in the Empire should have a school attached to it. During the eleventh century the schools in northern Christendom remained very much as they had been when Alcuin and his disciples established them two hundred years before. As a matter of fact the relative prestige of the educational centers was determined by the personality of the bishop of the diocese or the abbot of the local monastery. A stable element in almost every school was its collection of books, a source of knowledge that the scholasticus, *canon or monk in charge of studies, could consult for the courses he delivered. As it so happened, Carolingian copyists had stocked these libraries with classical works and they served to keep alive the humanist tradition.*

There was a natural link between the school proper and the scriptorium, the place where the copies of ancient texts were made. But in this period all books were regarded quite as much as adjuncts of the liturgy as vehicles of knowledge. And since the book played a not unimportant part in Divine Service it had to be decorated, like the altar, the sacred vessels and the walls of the church. It became an "object of art" in which the connection between the written culture and the image was given its most intimate expression. So it was that the tradition of ancient art was transmitted most effectively by the decorative work done in scriptoria. In the eleventh century prayer books, lectionaries and Bibles illustrated in the reigns of Louis the Pious and Charles the Bald were still to be found in all the monastic and cathedral libraries, and the aesthetic qualities of these works were appreciated and admired by clerics and laymen alike. The paintings in them were almost without exception imitations of Early Christian models. The plastic vigor of the evangelist portraits and the simulated architecture in which the figures were located, all the ornaments surrounding calendars and canon tables were attuned to the humanist ideal of the Latin poets and historians. Since these works, it seemed, transmitted the message of Augustan Rome and, like the teaching of the grammarians, inculcated the pure Latinity of an earlier age, untouched by barbarian solecisms, the images in Carolingian books inspired the same respect as the classical writers. They were copied, just as the texts of Virgil, Suetonius and Terence were copied. The artists who were commissioned by the emperor at Reichenau or Echternach and at Saint-Denis by the kings of France, to make paintings for the Gospel Books, drew freely on the imagery of the ninth-century illuminators so as to produce decorations appropriate to the dignity of their royal patrons. But they did not copy slavishly, their figurations tended to diverge from the Carolingian prototypes. Though given plain gold grounds signifying an abstraction from the temporal akin to the sense of the eternal conveyed by the liturgic rites, these images still conformed to the aesthetic of the Late Empire. Resolutely figural, they represented the human body as the eye sees it, located in space, without deliberately modifying its proportions.

A bolder forward step was the revival of relief work. True, Carolingian artists had drawn inspiration from Roman sculpture but usually in a somewhat timid manner; in the ninth century paganism was still a peril to be reckoned with. If statues of Our Lord and, more especially, of saints were publicly exhibited, was there not a risk of encouraging a rebirth of idolatry? This is why figures carved in ivory or moulded by goldsmiths were always placed beside the altar where they would be seen only by initiates and the officiating priests, by those whose faith and culture immunized them against temptation. But at the end of the tenth century this danger had ceased to exist; the wooden idols once worshipped by the tribes had long since been demolished, the Cross had triumphed, the Church had nothing to fear from pagan gods. So there was now no obstacle to placing representations of sacred personages, given the convincingness of full plasticity, on the doors of churches. First to make a move in this direction was, it seems, Bernward, Bishop of Hildesheim. A man of learning, he was employed by the Emperor as tutor to his son, but his biographers speak of him also as an architect, an illustrator of manuscripts, and a skilled metalworker. For the monastery of St Michael which he had founded near his cathedral to serve as his burial place, he had two bronze doors cast, piece by piece, in 1015. In this he was following the example of Charlemagne and high prelates of the Carolingian Church. But he was the first to adorn church doors with images. Those at Hildesheim are covered with them. There are sixteen scenes set out one above the other in two parallel columns. On the left are Old Testament figures spanning the period from the Creation to the slaying of Abel; they illustrate the Fall. On the right is an ascending sequence of Gospel figures, from the Annunciation to the Resurrection, illustrating the process of redemption by which humanity rises to the celestial heights.

The Hildesheim doors marked a rebirth of large-scale relief work, and this took place, surprisingly enough, in one of the outlying, least civilized parts of the West. They were imitated in the Rhineland and the Meuse region. Thus the trail was blazed which, from the reliefs on the gold altar of Basel, led to the perfectly classical forms of those made by the bronze-founder Renier de Huy in 1107 on a baptismal font at Liège. Whether this wonderful renascence may have inspired the large-scale sculpture at Cluny is a moot point, but there is no question that it pointed the way to the revival of monumental statuary in the twelfth century, first at Saint-Denis, then at Chartres.

GOSPEL BOOK OF OTTO III: JESUS WEEPING OVER JERUSALEM. REICHENAU, IOIO.
FOLIO I88 VERSO, CLM. 4453, STAATSBIBLIOTHEK, MUNICH.

I. 33

THE CRUCIFIXION. LATE 11TH OR EARLY 12TH CENTURY. IVORY.
TREASURE OF THE CATHEDRAL OF SAINT-JUST, NARBONNE.

BRONZE DOOR OF BISHOP BERNWARD, UPPER LEFT HALF: SCENES FROM GENESIS. 1015.
CATHEDRAL OF HILDESHEIM.

"THE BASEL APOSTLES." FIRST QUARTER OF THE 12TH CENTURY. FRAGMENT OF AN ALTAR RELIEF.
BASEL CATHEDRAL.

GOLD ALTAR FRONTAL FROM BASEL CATHEDRAL. FIRST QUARTER OF THE 11TH CENTURY.
MUSÉE DE CLUNY, PARIS.

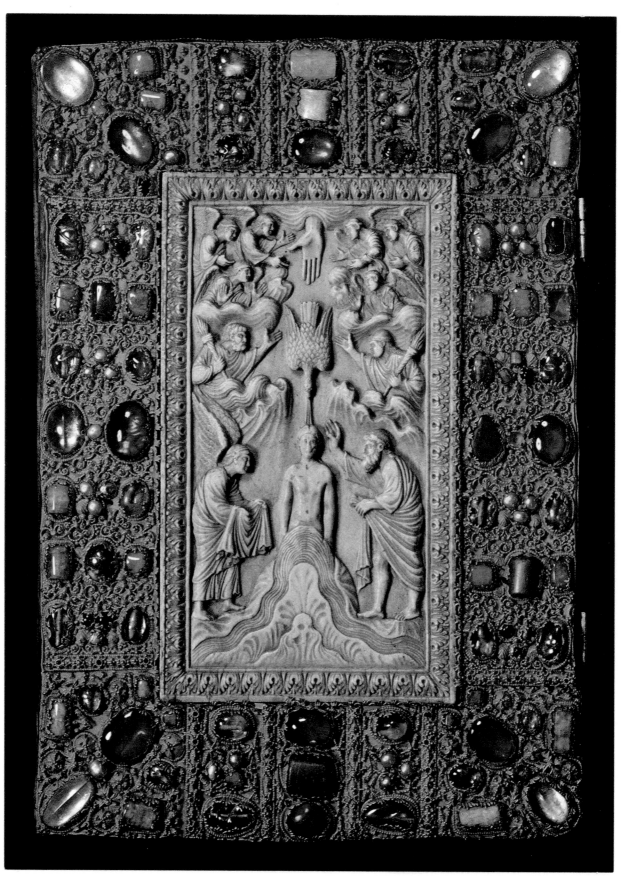

IVORY COVER OF A GOSPEL BOOK: THE BAPTISM OF CHRIST. WESTERN GERMANY, ABOUT 960-980.
CLM. 4451, STAATSBIBLIOTHEK, MUNICH.

I. 38

BAPTISMAL FONT OF RENIER DE HUY. 1107-1118.
CHURCH OF SAINT-BARTHÉLEMY, LIÈGE.

ST AUGUSTINE, DE CIVITATE DEI: TITLE PAGE. CANTERBURY, ABOUT 1100.
FOLIO 2 VERSO, PLUT. 12, COD. 17, BIBLIOTECA LAURENZIANA, FLORENCE.

I. 40

1

THE BASILICA

Europe in the year 1000, for the building of her churches, had inherited from Carolingian culture two types of edifices, both of which claimed to conform to the Roman tradition at its purest. For more than any other kind of architecture the churches were treated as royal buildings since, for one thing, God was regarded as the crowned sovereign of the world seated on his throne to judge the living and the dead; and, secondly, because every place of worship was under the direct patronage of the king, Christ's vicegerent on earth. And since the kings of Europe regarded themselves as heirs of the Empire, it seemed right and proper that monuments due to their munificence and the peace reigning in their dominions should take inspiration from ancient Rome.

Charlemagne had wished his oratory at Aachen to resemble the imperial chapels, an example of which he had seen at Ravenna: a round church. The circular plan purported to symbolize the king's specific mission of interceding between his people and God, between the temporal and the spiritual, nature and supernature. For the design of this type of church embodied the connection between the square (sign of the earth) and the circle (sign of heaven); and in the symbology of numbers the octagon, which effected the transition between them, signified eternity. In Rome the Early Christians had given their baptisteries this form, since in them took place the rites whose numinous virtue freed man from the shackles of the earth and enabled him to soar to the celestial heights where angels hymn eternally the praise of God. Clearly a similar plan was needed for the churches whence the sovereign launched prayers of intercession to the Almighty. Ottmarsheim, consecrated in 1049 by Pope Leo IX, imitated Aachen, as did so many churches then built in the Empire, even at its confines on the Slav frontier where Christianity, backed by the imperial army, was gaining ground. The central plan, with two superimposed elevations, also derived from an existing tradition, that of the martyrium or reliquary-tomb, transmitted by the builders of crypts. When at their journey's end pilgrims to the Holy Land came to Jerusalem, they entered a round church, built in the same manner as the Emperor's chapel.

However, once the Church had triumphed and Christianity, coming out of hiding, had invaded Rome and taken possession of its most official edifices, almost all Roman churches—especially the outstanding ones, those which were built above the tombs of St Peter and St Paul—were basilicas, that is to say "royal courts," large oblong buildings of the type used for judicial proceedings, with rows of arcades supporting a light wooden roof and dividing the interior into three parallel aisles. There was an apse equivalent to the seat of the Judex in pagan times, and ample lighting was provided by the tall windows of the central aisle. In fact, the internal arrangement of the House of God had much in common with an ancient forum. During the Carolingian period, owing to changes in the ritual, the church entrance had been modified, and the atrium roofed over so that it became a sort of vestibule or antechurch two storeys high, with a sheltered porch at ground level and a room for prayer above. Were these alterations intended to detain the crowds of pilgrims in the forepart of the church and prevent them from disturbing the services? Or to provide a special place for the worship of Christ the Saviour, who shared the patronage of the church with a local saint? Or was this enlargement of the portal due to the recent extension of funerary rites? Whatever the answer to these questions, it certainly lay at the origin of that solid mass of masonry which, throughout the Empire, gave the basilicas a second apse at the west end corresponding to the belfry-porches at the entrance of churches in the Ile-de-France.

THE BASILICA

1. Jumièges (Normandy), church of the Benedictine Abbey. 1040-1067.

2. Bari (South Italy), basilica of San Nicola. 1087.

3. Saint-Benoît-sur-Loire (near Orléans), narthex of the church. 1004-1030.

4. Caen (Normandy), church of Saint-Etienne or Abbaye aux Hommes. Founded in 1064.

5. Caen (Normandy), Trinity Church or Abbaye aux Dames. Founded in 1062.

6. Caen (Normandy), interior of Trinity Church or Abbaye aux Dames. Founded in 1062.

7. Cérisy-la-Forêt (Normandy), interior of the abbey church, looking towards the apse. Late 11th century.

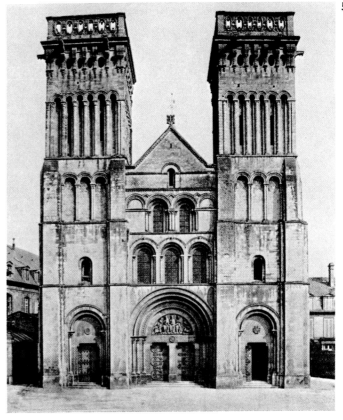

In the eleventh century these royal types of architecture prevailed in the north of western Europe, where monarchy best resisted the encroachments of feudalism. That is, north of the Alps, in all the provinces where the king of Germania had the bishops under his control: in Lotharingia, homeland of the first line of Christian "Caesars" in the West (the Carolingian princesses were buried in the crypt at Nivelles), and in Saxony, cradle of the second restorers of imperial dignity. The basilica at Gernrode, begun three years after the imperial coronation of Otto I, and St Michael's at Hildesheim, founded by Bishop Bernward, tutor of Otto III, where the bishop was buried (in the Chapel of the Cross) show complete fidelity to Carolingian models. These were also copied in Champagne, at Vignory, at Montier-en-Der, and the region of Reims provided a connecting link between the art of the Ottos and that of the Capetians. However, at this time little building was being done in the Ile-de-France, the only churches built shortly after 1000 being those for which King Robert had a special veneration: Orléans, Saint-Benoît-sur-Loire, Saint-Martin of Tours. Later, the art of Neustria came to florescence in the most prosperous, most solidly organized of the feudal States: the Duchy of Normandy. Its rulers had a predilection for the monasteries reformed by William of Volpiano; in 1037 the building of a new basilica began at Jumièges. On the eve of his conquest of England Duke William, to atone for a marriage condemned as incestuous by the Church, provided jointly with his wife the funds for building two abbey churches at Caen: that of the Trinity, begun in 1062, and St Stephen's, begun two years later. The innovations of the Neustrian architects were perfected in the Norman workyards; in the apse a line of radiating chapels flanked the ambulatory, the towers of the façade were prolonged by buttresses. These methods were propagated far afield in the wake of the great expeditions launched by the Norman knights. Not, however, as far as Bari, where the basilica was built in the Roman style. But in conquered England Norman architecture flowered, and Abbot Suger took inspiration from it when at Saint-Denis he built what was to be the prototype of the Gothic cathedral.

ROME: AN ABIDING PRESENCE

Eleventh-century man visualized his king as a horseman, sword in hand, dispensing peace and justice to his people. But he also saw in him a sage, and assumed he was capable of reading books. Once the western world had come to regard the monarchy as a *renovatio*, a rebirth of the imperial power, sovereigns could no longer remain illiterate, as their barbarian ancestors had been. The ruler was now expected to conform to the ideal image that Rome had built up of the "good emperor," paragon of knowledge and fount of wisdom. "In his palace he has a multitude of books, and when he chances to have a respite from warfare, he devotes it to reading them, spending long nights in meditation on their contents, until sleep seals his eyes." This commendable habit is attributed by a chronicler hailing from Angoulême to the Duke of Aquitaine, when he seeks to convince his reader that the Duke was the peer of kings. Before this, Einhard, friend and biographer of Charlemagne, had spoken of the emperor's persistent efforts to learn to write; King Alfred had had the Latin texts in monastery libraries translated into Anglo-Saxon so that the nobles of his court could understand them; and Otto III, emperor in the year 1000, had presided in person over the debates of men of learning and summoned the most famous, Gerbert (later Pope Sylvester II) to his court.

Nevertheless it was the coronation ceremony that did most to seal the alliance between the monarchy and erudition. For in virtue of this rite the sovereign was invested with a sacerdotal function, and it was the bounden duty of a priest to familiarize himself with books, now that the Word of God was inscribed in written texts. Thus the king had to be a "man of letters" and he saw to it that the son who was to inherit the crown received the education of a bishop. Hugh Capet, though he had not yet ascended the throne (but hoped to do so), put Robert, his eldest boy, to study under Gerbert, ablest pedagogue of the day, asking him to impart to Robert "sufficient knowledge of the liberal arts to make him acceptable to Our Lord by the practice of all the holy virtues." But it was also incumbent on the sovereign, responsible as he was for the salvation of his subjects, to see that the clergy, of which he now formed part, was qualified for its high vocation, in other words that it was well-educated. Hence his active support of institutions which, in a social order whose aristocracy, wholly militarized, had turned its back on studies, shaped ecclesiastics for their sacred calling. If today Charlemagne is pictured as a fatherly patron of schools, reprimanding bad pupils, patting the heads of good ones, this is because more than any other he applied himself to carrying out the duties of a Christian monarch. All reigning sovereigns of around 1000 followed his example. They saw to it that monasteries and cathedral churches were well supplied with books and teachers, and tried to establish in their residences the best possible educational centers. For among the many young scions of the aristocracy attached to the royal court, those who were not destined to a military career but to the Church had to be provided with the intellectual pabulum needed to qualify them for holding the highest posts, worthy of their rank, in the ecclesiastical hierarchy. The powers that God had delegated to his vicegerent, the sovereign, made this one of the latter's most immediate and urgent duties. Education was always closely involved with the monarchy in the eleventh century. And for two reasons: because the king regarded himself as the successor of the Caesars, and even more because, in St Jerome's translation of the Scriptures, God expressed Himself in the language of Augustus, the culture diffused by the royal schools was neither contemporary nor vernacular. That culture was, in fact, a heritage that successive generations had piously safeguarded through the darkness and decadence of the early Middle Ages: the heritage of a lost golden age, that of the Latin Empire. Essentially classical, it kept alive the memory of ancient Rome.

How many were there to benefit by this education? Some hundreds, possibly thousands, in each generation, and of these only a privileged few, perhaps several dozen in all, had access to the highest grade of knowledge. Though scattered all over Europe at very great distances from each other, these schoolmen knew each other, exchanged letters and manuscripts. They were the makings of the medieval "school"—they and the books they had copied with their own hands or been given by colleagues—and they attracted to them small groups of auditors, men of all ages who had often traveled half way across Europe, sometimes even risked their lives, to sit at the feet of the masters and hear them read or lecture. All were churchmen, all cultivated learning not for its own sake but so as the better to serve God and understand His words. The mother tongues of members of these groups differed completely from the language of the Bible and the liturgy. So a study of Latin words, their meanings and usages—the acquisition of a knowledge of the lexicon and grammar—was an essential part of the curriculum. The pedagogues of Late Antiquity had formulated seven ways to the getting of understanding, the seven so-called liberal arts, all of which figured in the scholastic program. But the eleventh-century teachers gave serious attention only to the first and most elementary, an initiation into the language of the Vulgate. "Students," wrote Abbon of Fleury in 1000, "must begin by learning to swim expertly in the deep, tumultuous, treacherous ocean of Priscian's *Grammar*; next, to make them grasp the meaning of Genesis and the Prophets, the teacher should read out to them and make them in turn read out such models of good Latinity as Virgil, Statius, Juvenal, Horace, Lucan and Terence." True, these writers were heathens, but they had handled the Latin language to perfection. That is why after the catastrophic end of Roman culture their works were rescued from oblivion. Parts of them had escaped destruction and, in view of their educational value, intensive search was made for these in the libraries that had suffered least—those of Italy—and these fragments were collated in the scriptoria attached to every teaching center. Young priests and novices copied out long extracts from these books and memorized them, and *disjecta membra* of classical poems came constantly to their lips, mingled with verses from the Psalms. As a result of these methods of education the highest dignitaries of the Church developed into humanists, bent on imitating the best classical writers, and discreetly plagiarizing them. A German abbess, Hrosvitha, "adapted the plays of Terence so as to make them suitable reading for the sisters of her convent." Born in the purple, the Emperor Otto III was given the education of a cleric; he dispatched his scribes to Reims and the Abbey of Bobbio with orders to make copies of the works of Caesar, Suetonius, Cicero and Livy, so as to have a complete record of the glories of Republican and Imperial Rome, the Rome he dreamed of making once again the center of a worldwide empire, and at Pavia he spent long hours studying and musing on Boethius' *De Consolatione Philosophiae*. This, to his thinking, was one of the obligations of kingship. Thus the methods of teaching practised in the ecclesiastical schools, the whole trend of scholastic culture and its unflinching championship of Roman literary values maintained, at the dawn of the feudal age, a close association between the monarchical institution and ancient literature, the masterworks of Antiquity which the kings, as students, had been trained to revere and imitate. This explains why that part of the art activity of the eleventh century which emanated directly from the person of the sovereign drew so tenaciously on the classical heritage.

It was the taste for well-turned Latin poems and the cult of Antiquity resulting from it that led such a man as Bernward, Bishop of Hildesheim, and tutor of Otto III, to commission an imitation of Trajan's Column, to give his church bronze doors and to have their decorations made in a thoroughly classical style. For the heads of schools of which the sovereigns were patrons did not salvage merely classical texts, but all that had survived of ancient Rome. Its monuments were falling in ruins, but its cameos, ivories and the remains of its statues were reverently preserved. One day Abbot Hugh of Cluny received a poem celebrating the discovery at Meaux of a Roman bust. For the old mistrust of a taint of paganism lingering on in these stones and images was gradually dying out. The Christian faith was now so solidly established that it had nothing to fear from the idols which early missionaries had felt a compulsion to destroy and eleventh-century art lovers had no need to feel qualms about admiring these collectors' pieces evidencing the highly developed culture which had given birth to them. The teaching of the schoolmen dispelled illusions of their intrinsic "wickedness"; the Christian could take over the beauties of the pagan world provided he dedicated them to God. With the sovereigns' approbation grammarians took their examples from the classics and the creators of the new royal art drew inspiration from the same source.

This antiquizing tendency of the new monarchical art was encouraged by the fact that its workshops always functioned in the neighborhood of a church or palace treasure. The king, so lavish of gifts for the welfare of all his subjects, and thanks to whose munificence all the places of worship under his control were provided with precious stuffs and jewels, clad himself in rich garments, bedecked with ornaments, when he showed himself to his people. Since he was in God's image, was it not fitting he should thus adorn his person? This display of gems and gold invested his form with glory, and made visible to all the aura of divinity surrounding a Christian king. On the material side, these precious objects were tokens of his earthly power, they impressed his rivals; also, this parade of the wealth on which the sovereign could draw to reward his friends was a stimulus to loyalty. No king without a treasure—and when its lustre dimmed it meant that the royal power, too, was dwindling. Such collections had been gradually amassed over a long period, perhaps centuries. Some of the finest pieces were dynastic heirlooms, handed down generation by generation; others were gifts from eastern potentates. Nearly all bore the stamp of Rome; of the bygone Rome whose wonders barbarian kings had looted to adorn their pomps and ceremonies; or of the new, rejuvenated Rome at Byzantium where a renaissance, accompanied as it so happened by a revival of the ancient style, was now in progress. Lastly, these collections were by no means "dead"; they had nothing in common with a modern museum. They were put to daily use and since each object in them had a specific function in a culture where ceremony played a major part, all was conveyed by way of rites or symbols, each decoration, every adornment, every detail, was meaningful. Exchanges of gifts were constantly adding new pieces to the treasure. One of the principal duties of the artists attached to the royal household was to keep the king's treasure in good condition, to renovate old ornaments so that they could figure as accessories at religious or secular ceremonies, to perform such tasks as setting a cameo in the binding of a Gospel book or transforming an ancient cup into a chalice. Another of their duties was to modify newly acquired objects so as to bring them into line, as far as possible, with the other pieces in the treasure. In this mass of goldsmith's work classicizing trends predominated. So, naturally enough, with an eye to harmony no less than out of deference to an aesthetic tradition whose chief repositories were the royal residences, the palace artists did their best, in their renovations and adaptations, to achieve the technical perfection of ancient works of art. It was above all the stylistic principles of these works that they studied and adopted.

The same spirit prevailed in the libraries annexed to the study centers patronized by the sovereign; also in the sumptuous ornaments which proclaimed his wealth and power at the coronation festivities. For in the embellishments of Christian ceremonies use was often made of ancient motifs, examples of the beauties of a golden age of art, and objects on which these figured were carefully preserved or faithfully reproduced. Doubtless the artisans working for the kings in the eleventh century copied these prototypes less slavishly than their predecessors had done in the days of Charlemagne and during the first renaissance of imperial culture. For since Antiquity was now remoter by two centuries, and Carolingian copies were often all they had to go on, memories of it were losing precision and more latitude was allowed to the artist's personal inventiveness. However, the fact remains that basic to the best culture of this period was a thorough-going deference to the past, due to a keen sense of the relative barbarism of the present age. This discouraged any attempts at originality, any hope to vie with a perfection that had long since left the world. Like the prelates-to-be, like the kings who in their nightly vigils tried to learn to read, the goldsmiths, painters, artificers employed by the court saw themselves as the merest tyros; their one ambition was to assimilate their work as far as possible to Roman models and keep to the safe and beaten track of tradition. So it was that in the heart of a countryside covered with dense forests, in towns where herds of swine were the only scavengers, the kings were still surrounded by memories of the great age of Rome. Hence an aesthetic attuned to the prosody of the *Aeneid* and Lucan's *Pharsalia*: an art that ruled out imagination, the tortuous geometric abstractions of Germanic jewelry, the distortions of human and animal forms found on barbarian ornaments. It was essentially an art of words, discourse and dialogue, not of symbols or free fancy; an art of monumental forms, not of line and incised images, and its true exponents were architects and sculptors. Such in fact was the art of the "pericopes" that the Reichenau painters illuminated for the emperors; of the Saint-Denis scriptorium; of the baptismal fonts at Liège.

Reichenau, Saint-Denis and Liège were not capitals; the kings of that time had none. They were always on the move; their military duties forced them to be continually on horseback. However, their religious function obliged them sometimes to call a halt, when, like the bishops, they were due to take part in solemn celebrations of the chief festivals of the Christian year in the great churches. Nor was there ever any question of displacing the cultural centers, whose formation and activities they encouraged. The art schools and workshops were established in the great abbeys patronized by the monarch, under the aegis of the royal churches, and in the bishoprics on which his power largely reposed. Thus it is possible to draw up a map of the centers of education, a map that does not precisely coincide with the geographical distribution of the kingdoms, but, combined with this, accurately indicates the domain in which during the period we are dealing with the classical spirit continued to predominate.

This domain hinges on a region extending from the Loire to the Main, covering exactly the same area as that of the Carolingian renaissance. It was in the Frankish provinces, and in the entourage of the royal palaces, that Alcuin's work bore fruit and the teachers who sought to restore in ecclesiastical circles the usage of correct Latin, labored to best effect. Further east, Germania was a far less promising field for such endeavors. In the zone of German influence the only really active centers of learning were still, as in the days of Charlemagne, the monasteries of Franconia and those on the banks of the Rhine, Echternach, Cologne, St Gall; above all, the churches of the Meuse valley. On the borders of the provinces which had been wholly barbarized by the invasions of the early Middle Ages, and of those where the Roman imprint had survived somewhat better, the masters and artists of Liège were brilliant exceptions to the prevailing mediocrity. Similarly in the French kingdom the only really active schools flourished in the regions which the

Carolingians had always regarded as conquered territories, to be exploited to the best advantage —in other words, in the South. All the centers of monarchical culture were concentrated in Neustria. In the year 1000 the best masters were at Reims (where the kings were crowned and anointed with oil from the Holy Ampulla)—in the monastery of Saint-Benoît-sur-Loire near Orléans, where the relics of St Benedict were preserved, where the panegyric of Robert the Pious was written and where, later, Philip I had himself buried—and, lastly, at Chartres. A century later the best teachers were still to be found at Chartres; also at Laon, Tournai, Angers, Orléans and Tours.

Outside these truly Frankish lands, traversed by the Rhine, the Meuse and the Seine, only two notable cultural developments call for mention. One of them, grafted on to the Neustrian branch, ramified little by little into the countries conquered by the Normans. First affected was Fécamp, next the Abbey of Bec, and before long Canterbury, York and Winchester followed suit—when in 1066 on both sides of the Channel a dynamic monarchy held sway and activated all the ferments that the Vikings had inseminated in this part of Europe in earlier times. Other, more venturesome developments were in progress in Catalonia where, in that furthest outpost of Christendom, bishops and abbots of the year 1000 welcomed the exotic skills coming from the Islamized lands. Such novelties as algebra, astronomy and the science of numbers particularly appealed to them. It was to Catalonia that the youthful Gerbert went to learn the technique of making astrolabes. This province, however, like Germany, had been entirely remolded by the Carolingians. Here the sense of the Arab peril, more instant and compulsive than elsewhere, kept alive the memory of Charlemagne, hero of the Islamic wars, precursor of the crusades, but also an enthusiastic patron of classical literature. So it was that in the cathedral of Vich, the abbeys of Ripoll, Cuxa and Montserrat, the masters kept to the traditional educational methods practised by Alcuin and Hrabanus Maurus, and enraptured their pupils with readings from the poets of Antiquity.

Poor masters, poor schools, and even poorer science—but at least true to their ideals and therefore capable, in a civilization that had sunk into almost complete barbarism, of keeping afloat an art pointing to better things. This much is clear: that the trickle of classical culture took its rise in royal palaces and the places of worship where the kings were anointed with the holy oil; and that the chroniclers who collated memories of their exploits treated the sovereigns as being at once men of God and avatars of Caesar. At first sight it may seem absurd that the flowers of classical rhetoric should have been lavished on mere tribal chiefs who tricked themselves out with strings of beads and dissipated their energies in futile forays. But these schools of learning, these libraries, these treasures whose finest cameos bore the profiles of Trajan and Tiberius, had anyhow the merit of ensuring, in a series of naive but fervent renaissances, the survival of a certain type of humanism. The roots of Suger's aesthetic, of the erudition of St Thomas Aquinas, of the whole Gothic efflorescence and the new creative freedom it engendered, were struck in these oases of culture that held their ground, undaunted, in a wilderness of semi-savagery.

But after 1000 the centers of classicism lost much of their lustre—coincidently with a decline in the personal power of the kings—and this change had a decisive effect on the evolution of art in the course of the eleventh century. By 980 these kings made their presence felt only in a limited part of their dominion and in the following decades their authority continued to dwindle throughout the western world, soonest and most rapidly in the kingdom of France. The sovereign lost nothing of his spiritual prestige, but prelates and provincial magnates ceased putting in an appearance at his court. In 1100 the only persons who attended its sessions were country squires living near Paris and some officers of the household. Feudality wound its way parasitically around the trunk of royalty; the throne was still its necessary prop, but little by little the overgrowth strangled the parent stem and soon the crown was no more than an ineffectual symbol. The real powers, the regalia, attributes of kingship—among them the upkeep of the churches, the task of decorating them, in short the control of art activities—were soon dispersed among a number of hands. In the second half of the eleventh century the greatest church-builder in northern France was no longer the king, but his vassal, the Duke of Normandy.

The authority of the German monarch did not disintegrate so rapidly; before 1140 the Germanic lands cannot be said to have become truly feudalized.

In Italy, however, the emperor was forced to recognize that the rights remaining to him were gradually passing from his hands. The main reason was that his personal power was being challenged by another, markedly in the ascendant: that of the Bishop of Rome. As early as the year 1000 Abbot William of Volpiano stressed this fact. "The might of the Roman Emperor to which heretofore all monarchs bowed throughout the world is wielded now in the various provinces by several sceptres; but the power of binding and loosing in heaven and on earth has been granted by an inviolable gift to the *magisterium* of St Peter." A hundred years later the Pope had gathered most of the Churches of the West under his sole sway, he boldly reprimanded kings and even in Germany made a bid to wrest his prerogatives from Caesar. Between 980 and 1140 two tendencies were strongly operative: one of them was the gradual collapse of monarchical authority in all the western lands, the other, more uniformly distributed throughout Latin Christendom, developed into a movement to reform the structure of the Church and, with this in view, to transfer *auctoritas* to the prelates, to bring them into close association with the Holy See and to limit the freedom of action claimed by the kings. These were the causes of the great divide in the evolution of western art that developed between the reigns of the Emperor Henry II and of St Louis of France: the break of continuity in the evolution of the major forms of art sponsored by royalty.

The reflux of the royal aesthetic synchronized with the decline in the institution of kingship. This movement began in that part of Europe in which from 980 on royalty was becoming, for all practical purposes, a dead letter: in the southern provinces. Here either the schools were languishing or the teaching in them was given a different orientation. Thus free scope was allowed to these distinctively "Romanizing" tendencies which had always been alive and active in the culture of the South of Europe.

For what was in process of emerging as a result of the ebbing of monarchical power in Provence, Aquitaine and Tuscany was in reality another visage of Rome. Not the one that had fascinated Charlemagne and still charmed Otto III and Abbon of Fleury: a visage whose features had been petrified as it were by recurrent phases of archaization and, for all their charm, now seemed elegant but "dead" as a line of Virgil. This other visage had nothing

II

FEUDALISM

THE THREE ORDERS

In the eyes of God—and in the eyes of his servants, the ninth-century churchmen—all men formed but a single people. They differed of course in race, sex, birth and social status. Yet, as Agobard, Archbishop of Lyons, had written in the time of Louis the Pious, "the one thing all insist on is a kingdom." Under the aegis of the king, in whom were vested both priestly and military functions, who both wielded temporal power and shouldered the collective responsibilities of the people towards the celestial principalities, all alike joined in an ordered progress towards the Light. Needless to say the people was divided; age-old barriers existed between laymen and churchmen, clerks and monks, and above all, in this age of serfdom, between freemen and those who were used like beasts of burden. Nevertheless, in the early Middle Ages, a small élite of high-ranking prelates, the only men capable of constructing an ideology, whose views alone are handed down to us by records of the period, pictured all God's children as "of a kind," and this notion of unity linked up with another leading idea, that of the stability of the social edifice and the monarchical institution. The Latin word *ordo* signified the immutability of the conditions of man's earthly existence. This "order" was imposed by God at the Creation; to every man He allotted his appointed place in a scheme of things that assigned him certain rights and specific duties in the gradual edification of the Kingdom of God. Anyone who tried to step outside the state to which God had called him did so at his peril; any act of this kind was sacrilege. On the day of his coronation the king gave a solemn pledge to accord to each of the social orders its due prerogatives. Thus the highly primitive world of the ninth century may well give an impression of having been impervious to change, determined for all time by the tempo of rural life in which the sequence of the seasons never varies and time moves in a cycle constant as that of the heavenly bodies. No one in that social system could nurse a hope of getting wealthy enough to improve his status and enter the higher grades of the temporal hierarchy. All the rich were heirs, owing their fortune and prestige to legacies handed down, generation after generation, from an immemorial past. And the poor were humble tillers of the soil that their ancestors had made fertile by the labors of their hands. Any change in their lot seemed accidental, any thought of it preposterous. God—like the kings, like the emperor—reigned supreme at the heart of things, sovereign of the immutable.

So it seemed; but actually the world was changing, if imperceptibly, and to a rhythm that was very gradually speeding up. As the year 1000 drew near and, to begin with, in the most highly evolved of the western provinces—the kingdom of France—new social structures were beginning to take form. The seeming "modernity" of the eleventh century comes from this new trend, so far-reaching as to affect all the aspects of civilization, most notably the manner in which power and wealth were distributed, the conception of man's relation to God and, as a result, the whole orientation of creative art. It is impossible to understand the emergence of the Romanesque and the forms it assumed without taking into account this change: the growth of what is known as the feudal system. The cause of this mutation was not economic; by and large the economy stagnated or progressed much too slowly to effect any considerable changes in the social structure. Its origin was rather of a political order, the steadily increasing impotency of the kings. Today the unity of power, when it lay in the hands of the great Carolingians, may well seem miraculous. How, one wonders, did these kings, little more than tribal chieftains, manage to keep under effective control a State so far-flung, so lacking in communications, so heterogeneous as was the Empire around 800? How did they succeed in reigning simultaneously over Friesland and Friuli, on the banks of the Elbe and at Barcelona; how was it that their word was law in townless, roadless territories where even the king's messengers had to travel on foot? Their authority was founded on a permanent state of war, an ever-extending range of conquests. Charlemagne's forbears had sallied forth from Austrasia at the head of a small troop of kinsmen, friends and faithful retainers who followed and obeyed them simply because they were victorious, shared out the booty of each campaign and were free to pillage to their hearts' content. The Carolingians had ensured the loyalty of these comrades of early days, their sons and nephews, by marriages, ties of kinship and those of vassalage. Every spring, when the grass began to grow and companies of mounted men could count on forage for their horses, they mustered all their friends, counts, bishops, abbots of the larger monasteries. Then there began the "open season" for forays, massacres, rape and rapine, with the king riding once again at the head of his troops towards the profitable thrills of some new campaign.

But already, as early as the ninth century, in the intervals between campaigns and in the autumn, when each of the sovereign's lieges was back on his ancestral domain, with his family, concubines, serfs, dependents, he was promptly freed from royal tutelage and, the roads being blocked, needed obey no law but his own. At these times the noble held unchallenged sway over all the cultivated lands around his castle and ruled despotically over a peasantry, aware indeed that a king existed but seeing him only as a shadowy figure, inaccessible and invisible as God Himself. For the countryfolk peace and prosperity depended entirely on the will of the local lord. In time of famine they could count on a dole of a few handfuls of wheat from his granaries and if he abused his powers, to whom could they complain? But soon after the revival of the Empire there came a moment when the kings ceased being war-makers; there were few if any military expeditions, no more lootings, no more spoils of war. Why then should the great of the land endure the hardships and perils of never-ending campaigns for the good pleasure of a ruler who had ceased to give them anything in return? Accordingly they spaced out their visits, fewer and fewer nobles attended the royal courts, and the State whose unity was based on periodical reunions of this kind gradually fell to pieces.

Its disintegration was speeded up by the Nordic, Saracen and Hungarian invasions. The Continent and the off-shore islands were attacked by new enemies and fighting no longer took place outside the pale of Christendom but at its very heart. The effects of this were calamitous; heathen hordes swooped down on defenceless cities, burnt and looted, then retreated in boats or on horseback carrying off their plunder. Equipped for planned campaigns, slow to mobilize, the king's armies were quite incapable of forestalling these attacks and resisting them. In the constant onslaughts to which all Western Europe was exposed the only war leaders capable of restoring order were the petty princes of each region. They alone could muster all the able-bodied men at a moment's notice, maintain and equip a permanent force to garrison their strongposts, the castles, and the large fortified enclosures in which all the peasants of the region took refuge with their flocks and herds. It was to these local rulers, no longer to the ring, that the population looked for its defence. It was now that the power of royalty underwent a real decline. The notion of it lingered on in men's minds, but only as a legend having no contemporary validity, no bearing on everyday life or concrete reality. All prestige, all effective power, came to be vested in local chieftains, dukes and counts, hailed as the true heroes of the Christian Resistance. Armed with miraculous swords, helped by angelic hosts, they forced the invaders to turn tail, empty-handed. In the assemblies of warriors minstrels hymned in rousing strains the exploits of these gallant lords and openly derided the supineness of the sovereigns.

The West and South of Latin Christendom, regions which the Carolingians had never brought fully under control, and which had suffered most from inroads of marauders, were the starting point of parallel developments affecting the two chief sectors of society: the Church and the body of laymen. The men who had hitherto recruited the troops of each province under their banner, at the bidding of the king, their kinsman and their lord, broke completely with the sovereign. They still professed to be his loyal subjects and on occasion placed their joined hands between his, sign of homage; but they now treated as a heritage the judicial and executive powers which he had delegated to them. These they exploited freely and transmitted to their eldest sons. The greatest princes, the dukes, to whom fell the task of defending large areas of the kingdom, were the first to make good their autonomy (in the early tenth century). This political fragmentation did not make headway in the north and east of the former Carolingian empire; here the kings asserted their rights more vigorously and the age-old tribal institutions were more firmly rooted. But elsewhere it continued, and soon the counts, in turn, emancipated themselves from the dukes. Then, as the year 1000 approached, the principalities under the sway of counts followed suit and each of the barons who, in a region of forests and small cultivated tracts owned a stronghold, built up a little independent State around it. On the eve of the eleventh century new "kingdoms" were established everywhere, their rulers were crowned with all due pomp and ceremony, and no one called in question their status as God's lieutenants. Henceforth the central military and judicial power became more and more dispersed, broken up into an archipelago of isolated units, small and large.

Each had a master entitled "seigneur" or "sire" (equivalent to the Latin *dominus*, he who truly dominates). This title ("lord" in English) was the same as that assigned to "God" in Christian ceremonies. For the lord claimed the prerogatives of which, formerly, the king had the monopoly; his word was law. Like the sovereign he was well aware of belonging to a dynasty whose roots had been struck by his ancestors in the regions under his sway, and in the stronghold where he held assemblies of his vassals, and he also knew that his offspring would continue to draw sustenance from the same soil, century after century. In short the dynasty was a tree with a single stem, since like the royal crown the local lord's *auctoritas* was transmitted, indivisible, from father to son. Like the king, again, each lord felt it was his divinely imposed duty to maintain peace and justice in his domain, and the complex of rights enabling him to perform it converged on his castle. The tower, formerly a symbol of royal majesty under its military aspect, was now regarded as an affirmation both of personal power and of the prestige of a dynasty. "Men of noble birth and affluence," a chronicler of the early twelfth century tells us, "spend most of their time in warfare, on the battlefield; so as to guard himself against his enemies, to vanquish his equals and subjugate the weak, each makes a point of building the highest possible embankments and digging a broad, deep moat surrounding them. Crowning these fortifications is a rampart of squared treetrunks solidly nailed together." Such was the castle of the period and though built on highly rustic lines, it served its purpose well, given the primitive nature of military skills. Secure behind his ramparts, the lord could snap his fingers at his rivals, even defy the king himself. The castle was the core, the vital center of political power and the new social structure that was emerging.

The changes in this structure reflected those that had recently taken place in the art of warfare. For it had become clear that the old-fashioned royal army, consisting of a mob of poorly equipped footsoldiers, was quite incapable of repelling the invaders of the ninth and tenth centuries. Only well-armed mounted troops protected by cuirasses could hold their ground, move promptly to threatened points and effectively pursue aggressors. So there was no longer any question of mobilizing the peasantry whose only weapons were staves and stones and who, in any case, lacked the spare time needed for training them in cavalry warfare. Thus military service was confined to a limited number of professional soldiers. The residents around the fortress, who fled to it for refuge in times of danger and therefore took orders directly from their lord, were by reason of the military specialization which had become indispensable divided into two well-defined classes, treated differently by their master, the owner of the castle. All alike were "his men," but the poor, the "yokels," who took no active share in the defence of his land, were treated by the lord as mere supernumeraries whom he protected but exploited without compunction. All these people belonged to him; they had ceased to be truly free, if no more slaves. All shared alike the burden of *corvées* and levies—the price they had to pay for the security assured them by the great landowner.

Unlike them, the few young men who still had the privilege of bearing arms enjoyed a real freedom. They escaped exploitation and oppression by the lord of the land since they took turns to garrison his castle; public safety had come to repose on the courage of this little band of mounted warriors, and they gallantly risked their lives defending it. Their duty towards the "master of the tower" was summed up in some honorable services deriving from the oath of vassalage and the homage they had paid to the owner of the castle. They were horsemen, "knights," and mustered as a squadron under the banner of the local lord, just as the large armies of eighth-century kings had enrolled under his banner for some foray. They formed in fact a replica, but on a smaller scale, of the royal court.

This new system of political and social obligations was an adjustment to the concrete realities over which the Carolingian sovereigns had temporarily triumphed, but which persisted beneath the surface in the social order of the day. Among the realities which had to be allowed for were the enterprise and energy of the aristocracy, the vastness of the great domains, too remote to be effectively controlled by the central power. The decentralization due to the feudal system was appropriate to a rural world split up into a host of hermetically sealed-off compartments. Master of all he surveyed, the lord of the castle cut the figure of a petty king, though he lacked an essential of kingship: he had not been consecrated. Hence a second development: the reaction of the Church to the new order.

The power of kings in the early Middle Ages had not trespassed on what, in this world, pertained to God: his sanctuaries and the rights of those appointed to His service. The sovereigns protected the Church and were careful not to exploit it too flagrantly. All the bishoprics and great monasteries were given charters whose terms forbade the levy of taxes by government officials on their domains and the requisitioning of their men. These privileges were imperilled by the disintegrating effect of feudalism and the increasing independence of the local authorities. Dukes, counts and lords of castles ensured the defence of the territory they controlled and claimed the right of judging, punishing and exploiting all its inhabitants (except the knights), even if they were representatives of the Church. This was a first infringement of the *status quo*. Moreover, being at a safe distance from the king and secure behind the walls of their castles, the strongest of these local lords usurped another royal prerogative; they claimed to be the guardians and patrons of the cathedrals and monasteries and, as such, to have the right of nominating bishops and abbots. Now, though the Church tolerated the selection of its dignitaries by the sovereign since he had been anointed and thus invested with spiritual power, it could not countenance high-handed conduct of this kind on the part of a duke, or count, who had only might, not right, on his side.

But in the conflict that ensued the Church lacked the backing of the king. The decline of royal executive power led the ecclesiastical authorities to claim for themselves the chief of the king's functions, that of maintaining peace. In former times God had delegated to the king, by the rite of coronation, powers that the sovereigns had now become incapable of exercising. Thus it was left to God to withdraw them from the king and to exercise them Himself, through the intermediary of His servants. The first claim to this right was voiced in southern Gaul, in Aquitaine and the county of Narbonne, a region in which, more keenly than elsewhere, the absence of a king had made itself felt. Solemn declarations of the overlordship of the Church were made in the late tenth century at great assemblies presided over by the bishops. Next, the idea made its way northwards by the valleys of the Rhone and the Saone and by 1030 had reached the northern frontiers of the kingdom of France. It did not cross them; beyond them lay the territory of the Emperor, still quite capable, unaided, of keeping peace and order in his dominions. But throughout France "the bishops, abbots and all those dedicated to our holy religion began to convene the people in Councils, to which were brought bodies of saints and countless shrines containing relics. Prelates and princes from all the land gathered together for the re-establishment of peace and the institution of our holy Faith. On a placard divided into chapters a list was drawn up of the acts that were prohibited and of the Christian's duties, accepted in the oath he swore to his Creator. Chief of them was the duty of maintaining an inviolable peace."

The Peace of God ensured special protection (like that formerly given by the kings) to the weakest, most vulnerable members of the community. God Himself ordained the immunity of places of worship and their precincts, of the churchmen and, lastly, of the poor. Any man who violated these sanctuaries and laid hands on the weak was to be anathematized and excluded from the community until he made due repentance. For he had incurred the wrath of God, invisible and dreadful Judge, who, unless He took mercy, would set loose on the offender all the powers of terror in this world and the next. "I will not force my way into a church in any manner since it is under God's protection; nor into the storerooms in the precinct of the church. I will not attack a monk or churchman if he be unarmed with earthly weapons, nor any of his company if he be without lance or buckler. I will not carry off his ox, cows, pig, sheep, goats, mare or unbroken colt, nor the faggot he is carrying. I will not lay hands on any peasant, man or woman, sergeant or merchant; nor take away their money or constrain them to pay ransom. I will not mistreat them by extorting their possessions on the ground that their lord is making war." These are among the vows solemnly enacted at one of the assemblies of the knights; to break them was tantamount to flinging oneself headfirst among the demons.

The first effect of this legislation was to mark out for reprobation a specific group of the community which, in the eyes of the Church, was constantly waging aggressive wars and responsible for the prevalent disorder of the age. A group that had to be guarded against and whose nefarious activities must be checked by ecclesiastical coercion, by inspiring it with terror of God's wrath. This class of men, treated as public enemies which, viewed from the angle of the naive dualism prevalent in the religious beliefs of this sadly unenlightened age, seemed an embodiment of the hosts of evil, was none other than the nobility, more exactly the body of mounted knights. It was the knights of his diocese whom Bishop Jordan of Limoges excommunicated, hurling anathemas at their weapons, even at their horses, instruments of their misdeeds, and at the insignia of their rank. Thus from now on the provisions of the Peace of God delimited more strictly still the warrior caste, which the waning of the king's authority and the redistribution of executive power were tending to isolate from the rest of the lay populace by assigning to it a specific function and certain privileges.

So it was that at the close of the tenth century the image of the social system was modified in the more cultivated circles of ecclesiastics. The notion of the division of the Christian community into categories or "orders" was still regarded as immutable. This was part of the scheme of things, established for all time. But henceforth it was posited that God had ordained the separation of mankind into three clearcut classes. "Human law recognizes but two classes; in practice the noble and the serf are not dominated by the same statutes. The nobles are warriors, defenders of churches, protectors of the people, great and small alike, themselves included.

The other class consists of serfs. But the city of God, commonly thought to be a single whole, has in reality three Orders: the men who pray, the men who fight and, thirdly, they who work. All three Orders coexist; none can dispense with the others; the services of each enable the others' tasks and each in turn assists the others." This passage in a political poem by Adalberon of Laon dedicated to King Robert of France is echoed in the remarks of another bishop, Gerard of Cambrai, of about the same date (c. 1030). "From its very origin the human race had been divided into three classes, all of which aid each other: the men who pray, the fighting men, the tillers of the soil." These latter were the enslaved mass of food-providers, "common folk," contrasting with the two élites, priests and warriors. Such was the notion of the social order which, inaugurated in the early eleventh century, was to be accepted throughout the western world for several centuries as a law of nature. It had at least the merit of putting an end to that involvement of the spiritual with the temporal, exemplified in the persona of the Carolingian kings, survivals of which can still be seen in the monarchies of around 1000. The break-through of the forces of feudalism put an end to this confusion, under their impact the veil fell from men's eyes and the basic cleavage between the spiritual and the temporal authorities became apparent. The feudal war-lords were not vested with religious functions or any other-worldly powers, while the churchmen took over all the charismatic missions hitherto reserved to royalty.

This point has its importance when we seek to trace the effect of the changed social conditions on the development of art. For in the course of the eleventh century the lay lords dispossessed the king to some extent of the resources he could freely draw on in the past; deprived of the emoluments enabling him to practise a luxurious way of life, he had less to spend on large-scale works of art. From now on any small surplus earned by manual workers passed almost entirely into the hands of the landed nobility, who spent much of it on their incessant wars and squandered what remained on elaborate festivities in which the leading knights indulged their taste for display. Nevertheless, even in the regions where the forces of political dissolution were most active and where the power of the monarchs was most drastically curbed—that is to say in southern Europe—money was still available to finance great works of art. For a slow but steady improvement in methods of agriculture, bringing larger crops, constantly increased the income of the feudal lords. Some part of it was diverted from worldly ostentation and devoted to a worthier purpose, the service of God, in which creative art participated. For the feudal nobility were God-fearing men and, as the kings had done, gave generous alms to the monks and clergy. So it was that the gifts of the high nobility replaced those of the monarchs; their pious donations provided the wherewithal for building, sculpture, painting. However, unlike the sovereigns, the feudal lords did not attempt to supervise and orient the activities of artists. They were not well-read men as the kings were (or aspired to be), nor like them did they have a personal liturgic function, for they had not been consecrated. Thus the aesthetic functions of royalty reverted to the Church, as did that other royal duty, the duty of maintaining public peace. But—and this was another outcome of the political and social upheaval—this ecclesiastical art took shape in a world crushed and brutalized by the dominance of the warrior caste. Hence the stamp it bears of an age of violence, of the culture of a class of men who, never having learnt to read or write, were incapable of reasoning and responsive only to gestures, rites and symbols: the culture of the knights.

THE POWERS OF EVIL

In the provinces south of the Loire and the Alps, where kingship was a dead letter and the Carolingians had failed solidly to establish the educational system reconstituted by Alcuin, eleventh-century artists did not employ the disciplined art language which reflected the teaching of the schools under the patronage of royalty. Put to the service of monasteries where to read the classics was regarded as a misguided, not to say pernicious hobby, and in which it was hoped to solve the mystery of things by mental processes as remote from reality as the stuff of dreams, art was identified with an exploration of the invisible. It was not concerned with representing what the eye sees; the data of visual experience were considered unworthy of serious interest, since the world of concrete things was imperfect and soon to pass away. The function of art was to figure forth the true reality concealed behind the veil of appearances, that ultimate reality of which the liturgical rites gave premonitory glimpses, pending its total revelation at the resurrection of the dead on the Last Day. The work of art was called on to lift the veil, and what it revealed to the beholder was not man, nor a God in the likeness of man, but the dark, secret forces which pervade and activate the cosmos.

Many of these forces were ambivalent. To eleventh-century man, even to a scholar who had pondered deeply on the Scriptures and the writings of the Fathers and thanks to them had cleared his mind of the gross superstitions of the people, it often seemed that the interventions of the unseen world in man's affairs were at once beneficent and maleficent. However, the progress in religious enlightenment was tending to dispel this ambiguity and to make it possible in speculations on the Other World to distinguish more surely between good and evil influences, light and darkness. Clearly the chief task of architect, sculptor, painter was to create visible counterparts of the powers of light, and so to build up an image of the Kingdom of God. But it was no less needful to represent the hostile forces lying in wait for man, laying traps for him, barring his path, forever seeking to lead him astray and hinder his progress to salvation. For the Christian soul must never relax its vigilance, it must be always on its guard, unsleeping, quick to detect the multifarious perils threatening it at every step. Committed as it was to a spiritual warfare, the whole monastic community had to be ever on the alert and the figurations of Evil were intended to remind the monks of the enemy at the gates.

In the symbolism of sin two "perverse" natures—that of woman, that of an animal, the serpent—are combined. In this age when so high a value was assigned to chastity, then regarded as the supreme virtue of the man of God, and extolled as one of the surest paths to salvation, there was a tendency to assimilate Eve to the serpent that tempted her. Though on the metopes of Modena cathedral she is still an innocent young woman and keeps at a safe distance the insidious reptile, at Autun it is otherwise; under the sculptor's chisel her body is beginning to acquire something of its sinuosity. And in the siren figures human and animal forms are frankly merged.

In the Garden of Eden there had been a pact, ordained by God, between man and the animals, who willingly submitted to his rule. This ended with the Fall; the beasts became a rebellious, dangerous mass of creatures, without speech or reason, sunk a degree deeper in the mire of brutish sensuality. It was admitted that domestic animals whose services were useful to man might have certain "virtues." As for creatures that crept and crawled, obviously they were Satan's allies. Even more sinister were the strange monsters described in medieval teratologies and seen in dreams. They were usually hybrids, half bird, half serpent, combining the forms of beasts of the air and beasts of the earth. Such was the basilisk, king of the creatures of the infernal regions, also the dragon of the Apocalypse, agent of chaos and destruction, against whom the archangels of the Lord—like the ancient heroes, founders of cities—would wage war on equal terms. Hell itself was given the look of a monster with huge gaping jaws. And it was in the guise of a raging beast that a painter represented the storm-tossed boat in which Jesus lay sleeping. This creature, with its horrific face, was an embodiment of the fears that haunted the minds of peasants huddled round their meagre fires in the dark night of the medieval world, or roving among the crowded charnel-houses where bodies of men and beasts, dead of hunger, lay rotting.

GIRL AND WINGED SNAKE. ABOUT 1130-1135. METOPE FROM MODENA CATHEDRAL.
MUSEO LAPIDARIO, MODENA CATHEDRAL.

GISLEBERTUS (ACTIVE FIRST THIRD OF THE 12TH CENTURY).

THE TEMPTATION OF EVE. ABOUT 1120-1130. MUSÉE ROLIN, AUTUN.

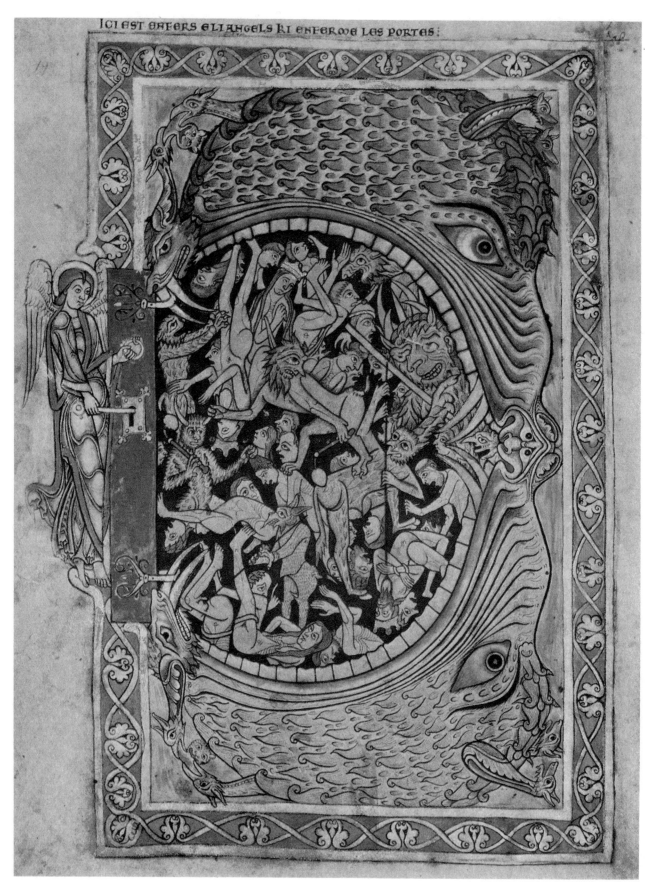

PSALTER OF HENRY OF BLOIS: ANGEL LOCKING THE DAMNED IN HELL.
WINCHESTER, MID-12TH CENTURY. FOLIO 39, COTTON MS NERO C.IV, BRITISH MUSEUM, LONDON.

THE DESTRUCTION OF THE WORLD. ABOUT 1130. UPPER PART OF A SCULPTURED DOOR PILLAR.
ABBEY CHURCH OF SOUILLAC, PÉRIGORD.

BEATUS OF LIEBANA, COMMENTARIES ON THE APOCALYPSE: THE FLOOD. SAINT-SEVER, GASCONY, MID-11TH CENTURY.
FOLIO 85, MS LAT. 8878, BIBLIOTHÈQUE NATIONALE, PARIS.

GOSPEL BOOK OF HITDA OF MESCHEDE: CHRIST AND THE DISCIPLES IN THE STORM ON THE SEA OF GALILEE. ABOUT 1020.
FOLIO 117 RECTO, MS 1640, HESSISCHE LANDES- UND HOCHSCHULBIBLIOTHEK, DARMSTADT.

2

THE ENEMY

Eleventh-century Christianity was of its very nature Manichaean. These men, who hunted heretics and haled them to the stake so that the germs of corruption they disseminated should be consumed by fire, regarded the City of God as a beleaguered citadel in which the heavenly garrison withstood unsleepingly the onslaughts of the Satanic hosts. These latter did not fear the Lord, any more than the knights respected the interdicts of the Church, or wolves spared the peasants' sheep. In the provinces which had relapsed into anarchy, where there was no longer any central power capable of defending the populace against gangs of young swashbucklers who pillaged, burnt and destroyed for the sheer joy of destroying—how could the inhabitants fail to regard the world, indeed the universe, as split up in two parts, divided against itself? Anathemas and excommunications notwithstanding, the Peace of God had failed to establish itself on earth; nor, indeed, did it prevail in the world invisible. At the very foot of God's throne Michael and the devil joined combat, like champions in the tiltyard. No one supposed that at the end of time Good would wholly triumph over evil; all the Scriptures promised was a segregation: on the Judge's left yawned open for all eternity the bottomless pit of Evil.

God's almighty power was forever challenged by a determined adversary, Satan, the arch-enemy.

Hitherto he had not figured often in religious art. But he now acquired a prominent place in the Christian world-picture. Not, it is true, in the sector given a relative clarity by the educational centers; rather, in the vast domain then being taken over by the monastic rites and liturgy; a domain which, to strengthen its control over the masses, was welcoming popular superstitions that till now the clergy had tried their best to suppress. This involved the acceptance of much of the folklore relating to death: belief in the continued presence of the dead and apparitions of souls in Purgatory. Men were plunged into a nightworld full of the terrors that walk in darkness. Thus devils came to haunt the cloisters, to trouble the sleep of chaste and healthy men. To keep away these spectral presences, the Rule of Cluny enacted that lamps should be kept burning all night in the dormitory. But this did not prevent their "appearing by night at the hour when the bell is rung for Matins." Three times Rudolph Glaber saw the devil, the hideous being, his head ringed with a cone of leaping flames described in the Psychomachia and the Apocalypse. At the monastery of Saint-Léger, in the dim light of daybreak, he saw "rising up at the foot of his bed a sort of little man horrible to see, of low stature (it seemed), with a thin neck, haggard face, jet-black eyes, peaked, puckered brows, a narrow nose, a prominent mouth, blubber lips, a mean, receding chin, a goatee beard, hirsute, pointed ears, a shock of touseled hair, dog's teeth, a tapered skull, a bulging chest, a hump on his back, flapping buttocks, filthy clothes." At Saint-Bénigne in Dijon, then at Moûtiers, he was visited by "a very similar devil, probably the same one." Now Rudolph was far from being an ignoramus or particularly gullible. Which of the monks of Cluny had not had experience of these visitations from the underworld? Such encounters were of course exceptional. "We must not forget that when manifest prodigies meet the eyes of a man still in the flesh, whether the prodigies are the work of good or evil spirits, this man has not long to live on earth, after seeing such things."

How was one to know whence come these unearthly visitants? For Glaber the world of appearances and that of dreams still had the ambivalence with which the primitive mind invests them. In this respect the dualism latent in monastic thought marked an advance, since it essayed to draw a clearcut distinction between the good and evil powers.

THE ENEMY

1. Urnes (Norway), portal of the stave church. 11th century.

2. The Destruction of the World. Sculptured pillar, portal of the abbey church, Souillac. About 1130.

3. Capital, cloister of San Pedro de Galligans, Gerona. 12th century.

4. Capital, cloister of Santo Domingo de Silos, near Burgos. 12th century.

5. Capital in the apse of Trinity Church or Abbaye aux Dames (founded 1062), Caen.

6. Man-Eating Devil. Capital in the church of Saint-Pierre at Chauvigny, Poitou. 12th century.

7. St Gregory, Moralia in Job: Fight against the dragon. Cîteaux, 1111. Folio 4 verso, MS. 168, Bibliothèque Municipale, Dijon.

8. The Temptation of Christ. Capital in the church of Saint-Andoche at Saulieu, Burgundy. 12th century.

9. Profane Music and Woman. Capital in the nave, church of the Madeleine at Vézelay, Burgundy. About 1120-1150.

I. 76

For those who reflected seriously on the subject and tried to master their instinctive dread, Satan had not the seductive aspect he was to be given in the psychologically more advanced thirteenth century. He was for them a figure out of a nightmare, utterly devoid of charm, and there are curious resemblances between Glaber's vision of him and the wild creatures armed with claws on the capitals of Saint-Benoît-sur-Loire and Saulieu, half concealed by the tempting objects they are handling, almost all of them being women. To represent the Enemy artists employed two styles. One was linear, sinuous, directly stemming from certain barbarian images and characteristic, it seems, of the sea peoples of the northwest, Irish, English, Scandinavians. In these lands there was no Roman substratum and the Church had not been affected by the return to classicism promoted by the Carolingians. Christianity had crept into the indigenous culture-pattern without greatly disturbing it, adopted its stylistic formulas and mental figurations. On the portals of the stave churches of Norway, as in the illuminated manuscripts of Winchester, Satan had quite naturally found a place among the fantasies of Nordic folklore, with their overtones of magic and wizardry. Whereas in the cloisters of Catalonia, Castile and Rouergue, the image of Evil was adapted to the solid, well-knit forms of the fabled monsters of antiquity. The hunting scenes (conceived in a quite different spirit) which had adorned Late Roman sarcophagi were used to represent the struggles taking place in a human soul. We see centaurs and chimeras disporting themselves in a scrollwork of stylized flowers and foliage. But the artists in these provinces also sought to body forth less familiar beings, the bizarre winged creatures invented in the East which figured on the embroidered textiles used for wrapping relics. The man who carved the capitals at Chauvigny took inspiration from the Apocalypse when he made the image of the Great Whore, symbol of all erotic taboos. But it was on the deepest level of the collective psyche that he found the figure of the demon that feasts on human flesh, the werewolf. Using all the resources of plasticity, he offered to God a living image of man's terrors, so that by His grace He might dispel them.

THE KNIGHTS

Little by little in the eleventh century a term came into common use—in France to start with—as a synonym for a member of the aristocracy. In its Latin form "caballarius," it had designated merely a soldier who fought on horseback. But in the French-speaking lands the connotation of "chevalier" was narrowed down; it became equivalent to the English "knight." In French parlance the men who, mounted on their warhorses, lorded it over the common herd and terrorized even the monks, were referred to as "chevaliers." All these men had been formally initiated into the profession of arms. Some came from the old nobility many of whom were affiliated by family ties to the royal family during the early Middle Ages. Others were petty local lords, mere countryfolk just wealthy enough not to have to work with their hands and to maintain the equipment needed for active service in wartime. There were also members of a still poorer class, the henchmen whom the lords gathered round them in their castles, who slept near their masters in huge wooden halls and lived on their munificence; and, finally, a host of nondescript adventurers who voluntarily enrolled under a young leader, to fight under his standard, share with him the fortunes of war and join with him in bold, often remunerative forays. Medieval "chivalry," at first a body of men of very different origins, became a well-defined, united whole, thanks to its privileges, to its place at the apex of the political and social structure, and above all to the fact that all these men followed the same way of life, had the same hopes and qualifications—those of "specialists in warfare."

It was an essentially masculine society. The culture of the eleventh century shut its eyes to woman and gave her little or no place in its art. There are no effigies of female saints; only, on occasion, strange, shadowy figures with wasp-like eyes and a wandering gaze that disconcerts the observer. The few feminine figures with a certain charm that found their way into the imagery of the churches were the crowned Allegories, representing the months and the seasons, flotsam of the bygone classical aesthetic, with Latin verses in keeping with the theme appended—figures as unreal, as artificial as flowers of rhetoric. Very occasionally the Mother of God makes an appearance in group scenes from the Gospels, but she is a mere supernumerary, kept discreetly in the background, like the lord's wife in the assemblies of the warriors. Usually woman is given a sinuous, serpentine form like that of some malignant tare that has crept into the good wheat in order to taint it. For is she not lasciviousness incarnate, the germ of corruption denounced by preachers, Eve the temptress, responsible for the Fall and all the sins of the world?

The knighthood was not only purely masculine but a sodality of heirs, held together by bonds of kinship. The power of the living lord was founded on the prestige of his forbears, the wealth and renown bequeathed by them to the clan, a sacred trust that each generation transmitted to the next. When dukes, counts and lords replaced the kings and took over their prerogatives, they justified this by the fact that their lineage was linked up with the sovereign's in a tangled skein of kinships. "The titles of the nobility," wrote Bishop Adalberon, "come from the blood of the kings from whom they are descended." This is why the concept of ancestry played so large a part in the social system. Even the most bare-faced adventurer boasted of his blue blood, every knight was spurred to action by a cohort of the valiant dead who had brought glory to the family name and to whom he would have to render account in the Hereafter. Though the rank and file were for the most part forgotten, every noble knew the names of the great men of his House, for the jongleurs in their songs kept alive the memories of these eponymous heroes. Thus they won a place in the annals of the race, and an undying fame. Their bodies lay side by side in the family vault built in ancient times by the founder of the lineage, and the chief religious rites centered on these tombs. Indeed, the Christianity of the year 1000, conditioned as it was by the mores of the aristocracy, gives an impression of being concerned primarily with a cult of the dead. This strong family feeling shared by the members of a line, which led them to hasten to the rescue when one of the clan was attacked and, if he fell, to join in taking vengeance on the relatives of the aggressor, may have persuaded the Church authorities to endorse the view that after a man's death living members of the family could help him on the path of salvation and purchase indulgences on his behalf. Almost all the alms given by the knights, who more than any others provided the wherewithal for artistic creation, were intended to ensure the well-being of dead members of the line in the after-world.

In this social order it was the so-called "young" who set the tone. Actually they were men in the prime of life, who had undergone their training and made proof of skill and valor in the public ceremony of initiation whereby they qualified as full-fledged members of the knighthood. None the less for a long while yet—so long as the young knight's father lived and he had not yet received from his hands the management of the estate—he chafed at the feeling of dependence, inevitable in a purely agrarian economy, so long as he stayed at home. So he left home at the earliest opportunity, roved the world with friends of his own age, in quest of pleasure, plunder and adventure. Hence the qualities most valued in the "perfect knight" were courage, physical strength, pugnacity. The hero whom all wished to emulate, whose exploits were recounted in the vulgar tongue at the gatherings of warriors, was an athlete of the stature suitable for combat on horseback: stalwart, thick-set, steady as a rock. Only the body counted, the heart as well, but not the mind. For the embryo knight did not learn to read, study might cramp his mettle, the knight was, purposely, illiterate. His proper sphere was warfare, real or mimic —the only activity that seemed worth while, that gave existence its savor, the great game in which a man stakes all, his honor and his life, but from which, also, those who succeed come home rich, triumphant, haloed with a glory worthy of their forbears, a fame whose echoes will go on resounding through the ages. The culture of eleventh-century Europe, shaped so largely by the warriors, was almost wholly based on a thirst for conquest, rapine, feats of derring-do.

But fighting took place only in fine weather and the "virtues" of the knight were not solely of a military order. Caught up in the elaborate network of loyalties and moral obligations which, when the king's power had ceased to function, enforced at least a semblance of discipline on the Western aristocracy, the chivalric hero was at once a lord and a vassal. He had to prove himself as generous as the best of lords, loyal as the best of vassals. Like the king, lord of lords, his model, the good knight was expected to be open-handed; *noblesse oblige,* and he felt bound to distribute all he had to those he cherished. After discarding his entire estate piecemeal, giving it to his "men," a Duke of Normandy announced: "I shall make over to you all my chattels: brassards, swordbelts, breastplates, helmets, leggings, horses, battleaxes and these fine, richly adorned swords. Always when dwelling in my house shall you enjoy my benefactions and the glory won by chivalrous exploits if you devote yourself with a good heart to my service." First, then, came largesse, cardinal virtue on a par with loyalty. No man could hold his head up in gatherings of the warriors if ever he broke the fealty he had sworn to. At this level of the social order the solidarity of the community hinged on a system of personal and collective oaths and on the mutual obligations they entailed. Boldness, energy, generosity, fidelity—these were the facets of that master value "honor," forever at stake on the battlefield and in the rivalries of the feudal courts.

Some familiarity with these conventions and the mental attitudes from which they sprang is needed for an understanding of the specific qualities and directives of the works of art produced during this period. Needless to say they were not made under the orders of the warriors, nor for their own use. True, these men had a passion for personal adornment; the hilts of their swords were made by skilled artisans; their wives and daughters richly embroidered the garments they wore on State occasions and the fabrics draping their great halls and the walls of seignorial chapels. But, flimsy or fragile for the most part, these things were by-products, mere excrescences of the domain in which architecture, sculpture and painting reigned supreme. In those days the work of art *par excellence* was a church; the one great art was sacred art. As in the past, it was the king and the churchmen who supervised and tended it, to the exclusion of all others. Yet—and this was something new—the spirit of chivalry was gradually invading this domain, and striking deep. Now that their power was faltering under the onslaughts of feudalism, the kings of France and England and soon the emperor himself came more and more to have a feeling that they, too, were becoming knights. How, indeed, draw any clear distinction between their status and that of a private *seigneur*? The ethic of the warrior caste was coming to impose its standards on their way of life. As for the Church, it was now under the rule of laymen—meaning, here too, the knights.

For every church was situated at the center of a seigniorial domain which provided the priests-in-charge with their sustenance. Like any feudal baron, every bishop, every abbot, every canon "owned" a host of peasants over whom he exercised judicial powers. When he held sessions, he was surrounded by vassals, he built towers, and when he entered the cloister was attended by a bodyguard of turbulent retainers, fighting men. Knights came and knelt, bare-headed, before him, placed their hands between his to signify they were "his men," and after swearing on the sacred relics to keep fealty were invested with a fief. These servants of God were also "bonny fighters." Was it not their duty to defend the property of their patron saints against aggressors and to risk their lives in campaigns for the enlargement of their Master's kingdom? When a bishop came to visit the Cid, El Campeador, he said: "Today I said Mass on your behalf; I have left my land and come to join you, for I desire to kill some Moors. I wish to do honor to my rank and, so as to deal more doughty blows, to be posted in the forefront of the fray." When they sallied forth, helmeted, at the head of a band of young prelates attached to their church, the virtues of honor, loyalty and courage meant as much to them as to the knights, their rivals. Though they knew it their duty to maintain the Peace of God, this did not mean they had to refrain from warfare; on the contrary, the Pax Dei had to be won by the sword —it was an aftermath of victory. As for the spirit of poverty, there was no trace of it in the Church of the year 1000. Given an assured place in the feudal system and by reason of their wealth and eminence ranking beside royalty (and indeed aspiring to dominate it, the more the prestige of the throne declined), the high ecclesiastical dignitaries took for granted that God desired the Church to wield temporal power and that wealth was a necessary mainstay of its domination. When the churchmen inveighed against the knights and called them Satan's henchmen, this was often because they saw in them rivals of their own seigniorial power, dangerous competitors whose activities might lessen the profits made by exploiting the workers. Characteristic of the Church of this period was a will to power, coupled with a taste for fighting.

All great prelates and most of the monks came of noble families. So long as the right of nominating bishops and abbots rested with the king he kept to the practice of his Carolingian predecessors and chose persons of high birth. In a society whose structure was so rigorously determined by ties of blood, all the virtues—above all, perhaps, a gift for leadership—could stem from one source only, a man's ancestry. To assign the highest posts in the Church, those that gave the holders wide authority, to other than high-born men would have seemed like flouting the divine plan of reserving governance, and all seigniorial powers, to a certain breed of men. As for the feudal lords, when they had succeeded in wresting from the sovereign the patronage of a church, they regarded and treated it as a personal asset and exploited it like any other part of their belongings. Sometimes they kept to themselves the titular right of an abbacy and gave it to one of their sons or to some vassal as a reward for faithful service. And exactly the same rite as that of feudal investiture, the transfer of a symbolic object from the patron's hand to the beneficiary's, was employed by the emperor, by kings and barons for the granting of high posts in the Church. Ritual gestures of this kind had so much importance that ecclesiastical benefices came to be commonly viewed as fiefs constraining their holders to service and transforming them into vassals. Thus the Church became more and more tied up with the feudal system, the intrusion of temporal into spiritual affairs ever more pronounced. The services of the lay lord tended to take precedence over the service of God, priests to become less and less distinguishable from laymen. How, indeed, could this have been prevented? Knights, their brothers and cousins, forgathered with the canons and these latter no longer led the coenobitic life prescribed by the ancient Rules. They administered like other lords the estates which were their prebends; they hunted, rode the best horses, wore fine accoutrement, and many lived with women. Their only signal difference from laymen was the result of a special type of education and a veneer of scholarly culture, possessed by all high-ranking ecclesiastics and disdained by the knights. But even this veneer was disappearing. Under the feudal prelates the schools stagnated and in the diminution of the educational facilities provided by the Carolingians in monasteries and cathedrals, along with the progressive decline of humanistic values that can be traced in all the works of art produced in the eleventh century, we see one and not the least striking of the effects of the intrusion of the knightly spirit into the mores of the clergy.

It had an even deeper influence on the structure of religious thought and, as a result, on the trends of sacred art. Mixing freely as they did with members of the feudal courts, in which the nobles flaunted their social superiority by luxurious living, squandering and ostentation, clerics and monks gradually came to adopt their standards, to set store on gaudy ornaments, on objects that sparkled, made of the costliest gems and metals. Like the feudal princes and with a similar purpose—to prove her eminence in the hierarchy of powers ordained by the Will of God—the Church of the eleventh century decked herself with gold and jewels. She convinced the nobility of their duty to contribute some of their wealth to the service of God, and to set forth around the altars and, before dying, to hang around the necks of the reliquary "idols" the goldware and gems they had amassed in their forays. The kings set the example. To Cluny Henry II of Germany bequeathed "his golden sceptre, his golden globe, his imperial golden vestment, his golden crown and crucifix, weighing in all one hundred pounds." The monk at Saint-Benoît-sur-Loire who wrote the biography of King Robert describes in detail all the valuable objects that the churches at Orléans had been given by the king, stating their weight and value: in one case sixty pounds of silver, in another one hundred sols of gold, also an onyx vase bought for sixty livres. "He had the table of St Peter to whom the church is dedicated entirely covered with fine gold; after the death of the very holy king, Queen Constance, his widow, had seven livres of this gold withdrawn from the table and gave it to God and St Aignan for the embellishment of the roof of the convent she had built." All the nobles, according to their means, emulated the king's largesse. The Duke of Aquitaine presented the church of Saint-Cybard at Angoulême with "a cross of gold adorned with

precious stones weighing seven pounds, and some silver candelabra weighing fifteen pounds, wrought by Saracens." This last item evidently formed part of the loot, after some combat with a Moslem host on the frontiers of Christendom. "The booty they took came to an enormous weight of metal; for it is a custom of the Saracens to deck themselves for the fray with plaques of gold and silver. Mindful of the vow they had sworn to God, the knights made haste to send all this gold and silver to the monastery of Cluny, and with it the Abbot, St Odilo, made a most beauteous ciborium for the altar of St Peter." All the glittering jewelry that pagan kings in former times had caused to be buried with them in their tombs was now accumulated in the House of God, making it more resplendent than the thrones of the greatest princes of the earth. In the midst of a half-starved peasantry the knights squandered their resources light-heartedly, but the Church guarded its wealth in order to enhance the splendor of its rites and make them even more sumptuous and spectacular than the great feudal fêtes. For was it not fitting that God should manifest Himself in the most gorgeous of "glories," surrounded by that blaze of light ineffable which the sculptors of the Romanesque apocalypses figured forth symbolically as an almond-shaped nimbus enveloping His body? Was He not entitled to own a treasure more magnificent than that of all the great ones of the earth?

For He is God the Lord. The image of His authority all men conjured up was in the spirit of the age: feudal through and through. When he described the Almighty enthroned in the world invisible, St Anselm placed Him at the summit of a hierarchy of personal dependencies; the angels held fiefs granted by Him and behaved as His vassals —His "thegns," as the Old-English poet Cynewulf called them. All the monks pictured themselves as fighting for Him on much the same terms as the domestic warriors, the lord's "men," who as of right counted on a reward for their loyal service; on recovering, for example, a lost heritage, or a tenure confiscated in days gone by as a punishment for some misdeed of their forbears. As for the ordinary layman, the church relegated him, in respect of divine grace, to the abject condition of the enslaved peasant. Bishop Eberhart went so far as to describe Christ as his Father's vassal. The subjection of mankind to the Lord God was assimilated to the relationship between the vassals as a body and their feudal lord. The Christian promised fealty and service to his God; thus it was that the posture of the vassal doing homage, bending his knee to his lord, bare-headed, his hands clasped, became in this period the attitude of Christian prayer. But just as the contract of vassalage engaged both parties to aid each other, just as the feudal lord was obliged to succor "his man," provided the latter carried out his duties, just as the owners of great domains felt obliged in time of famine to distribute food to their peasants and, lastly, just as generosity was regarded as the cardinal virtue of the man of property, so the Christian, vassal of his God, looked to receive from Him protection from the dangers of this world and, crowning all, that eternal fief—his meed of paradise.

The lords' best gifts went to the bravest warriors, as rewards for valiant exploits. And it was by his exploits that a man hoped to win God's especial favor. This cult of knightly values gave eleventh-century Christianity an heroic cast; the greatest saints of the time were fighters. Like St Alexis, one of whose poems (datable to about 1040), composed in the vernacular for a princely court in Normandy, glorifies the feats of asceticism, these heroes of the faith were paragons of chivalry, muscular young Christians who dedicated to their Lord's service not only their stamina but also their physical sufferings. It must have been an effort for a community whose standards were set by a group of swashbuckling horsemen to hearken to the Gospel message of humility, compassion, loving-kindness. So, in order to appeal to a congregation of young knights and bring them back to God, the priests (who like them had grown up in the shadow of the lord's castle and like them were his servitors) stressed the idea of a Church Militant, led to the fray by Jesus brandishing banner-wise the Cross. They dilated on the lives of warrior saints like Maurice and Demetrius, urging their hearers to display an equal courage in their fight with that invisible but formidable foe, Satan's army. Such was the hold of the idea of chivalry that even mental activities were pictured as a sort of combat. Did not even the heavenly bodies battle with each other? Had not the monk Adémar de Chabannes seen one night "two stars in the sign of the Lion jousting with each other, the small one rushing at the big one, furious but fearful, and the big one hustling it with its mane of rays towards the west"? Christians faced up to the mysterious forces of the universe as they faced the enemy in feudal warfare. Virtue entailed constant watchfulness, a series of pitched battles with treacherous assailants. Every man pictured his individual life as a beleaguered tower which he was in honor bound to defend and hand back intact to his Lord. At the Last Day his courage and his failings would be weighed in the scales. Some Romanesque frescoes show us a warlike Christ gripping between clenched teeth the sword of justice and of victory.

The vocation of the knight was in a sense equivocal. The weapons God placed in his hands—those long swords which in the legends are always miraculous, sometimes inset with relics so as to enhance their magic power, and to which during the eleventh century a priestly benediction was often given—were used by the knight for the defence of the people. In this duty he had divine assistance, for the knighthood was the bulwark of Christendom against the pagan hordes. In practice, however, he often wielded his sword for selfish ends, to gratify his predatory instincts. And by so doing he enlisted in the hosts of evil.

The monks of the West saw in the knight an embodiment of evil; militia, malicia—*did not the very tongue in which God expressed himself, classical Latin, point to an equivalence between maleficence and knighthood? Such ambivalences—not to say contradictions—in the functions of a social group were tokens of the cleavage in the created world, in which the heavenly hosts waged endless combat with the emissaries of Satan. The tower, symbol of peace and of the mission of protection that, now the king was powerless, had passed into the hands of the warrior class, had also come to seem a symbol of armed aggression, of the violence and rapine in which the aristocracy delighted. A place of refuge to which the countryfolk could resort in time of trouble, the castle was also a lair from which troops of mounted men poured forth from time to time to rob the common people of their meagre gains. The foursquare castle tower had the same structure as the heavenly Jerusalem, citadel of just men made perfect. But when the painter of the Saint-Sever Apocalypse encircles it with the baneful Serpent, it evokes Babylon, corruption, city of Evil, at once alluring and alarming.*

Eleventh-century chivalry did not create; it destroyed. What of its culture has survived? A mere handful of charming songs, some of which, after 1100, seemed worthy of being committed to writing. Almost all the castles were built of wood and no trace of them remains except the mounds on which they stood. However, soon after the year 1000, the feudal lords of Anjou, influenced no doubt by the current vogue for rebuilding churches, took to replacing the wooden towers with large stone edifices. Between these fortresses and the towers built on the fronts of Norman abbeys, there was a marked family likeness, due no doubt to the association in religious symbolism of scenes of combat with the image of God triumphant over the powers of Evil. It was for the adornment of a cathedral (at Bayeux) that about 1095 Norman princesses embroidered on a band of linen, 231 feet long, a design in the Scandinavian manner representing episodes of the conquest of England. Had not Duke William crossed the sea as a soldier of Christ to punish a perjurer and to amend the evil ways of the English church?

SCENES FROM THE BAYEUX TAPESTRY. ABOUT 1095. MUSÉE DE LA REINE MATHILDE, BAYEUX.

THE CASTLE TOWER AT LOCHES (INDRE-ET-LOIRE). 11TH CENTURY.

THE TOWER OF LONDON: INTERIOR OF THE NORMAN CHAPEL OF ST JOHN IN THE WHITE TOWER. AFTER 1078.

BEATUS OF LIEBANA, COMMENTARIES ON THE APOCALYPSE: BABYLON. SAINT-SEVER, GASCONY, MID-11TH CENTURY.
FOLIO 217, MS LAT. 8878, BIBLIOTHÈQUE NATIONALE, PARIS.

I. 90

SALVATION

God the Lord, this terrible God wielding a sword —how was one to render Him the services He required, how win His favor? Was it a matter of obeying His laws? But what were those laws? There can be no knowing what glimpses of the Gospel message were imparted to the peasants massed at the portal of the church when services were being held, who had to watch the priest's gestures from a distance, and heard snatches of hymns which, sung in Latin, were incomprehensible to them. What could these simple folk get from a clergy recruited among the serfs of the domain, from the village priest who, in order to support a wife and children, had to push the plough himself and soon forgot what little he had learned at school? One wonders how these priests themselves pictured the Saviour and what they really understood of His teaching. Hardly more is known of the religion of the knights, except that for them it was essentially a matter of rites, gestures, mechanical responses—to the exclusion of all else. For reading and writing had no place in their culture; theirs was a religion based on spoken words and images, that is to say on formalism. When a warrior came to take his oath what really counted, to his thinking, was not the dedication of his soul but the touch of his hand on a holy object: the cross on which he placed it, the Bible, or a bag of sacred relics. When he stepped forward to become his lord's "man," it was once again an attitude that counted, a special position of his hands, a string of words prescribed by use and wont, and the mere fact of uttering them sealed the compact with his lord. Likewise, on entering into possession of a fief he made a significant gesture, took in his hand a symbolic object. Submerged by the dark powers of nature, trembling at the thought of death and all that followed it, the knight clung to rites, his only safeguard. For they, he felt assured, would win God's mercy. He might solemnly confess his sins, but what saved him was a cultic gesture: his act of homage when he proffered to God his right-hand glove, symbol of fealty that the archangel Gabriel, coming from heaven, would carry aloft to the Ruler of the Universe. The highest eulogy King Robert the Pious was given by his biographer was for the exceptional care he gave to ceremonies, "ordering them so minutely that in them God did not seem to be greeted by another's pomp but to be hallowed with the very glory of His own majesty." During his long death-agony this king, following the monks' example, sang psalms unceasingly and when his last moment came "he made again and again the sign of the cross on his eyelids, lips, neck and ears."

Basic to all these rites, physical counterparts of mental images, was a certain conception of God. This was twofold, as was the concept all men had first of the king, then of the feudal lord, when he took over the monarchic attributes. Arbiter of war and peace, he wielded both the sword and the sceptre. The eleventh-century God differed but little from the war-lords who laid ambushes in the marshlands to trap and wipe out the last Nordic pillagers in the year 1000. Every man was called on to join His army and share in the attack on those malignant powers which make their presence known from time to time in premonitory visions of death, by eerie rustlings after nightfall, but which—as was common knowledge—were the rulers of a world behind the world, of which men saw but the outer husk. These hidden powers were held to be infallible and invincible; hence the belief in judgment by ordeal. If two men were suspected of a crime the culprit could be distinguished from the innocent man by applying a piece of red-hot iron to both, and the nature of the scars would reveal which was guilty. Or else they could be thrown bound into water, which receives the innocent and rejects the guilty. None questioned the magical powers of the elements and in such ordeals their verdict was final. For sometimes in God's war with sin, whose issue the Christian could not help regarding as precarious, difficult cases arose, in which the All Highest had need of men to aid Him.

None the less, for the eleventh-century Christian the power of God was manifested most clearly in acts of justice, just as the power of the owner of his tenement was for the peasant, and that of the master of his fief was for the knight. God was He who punished; the most familiar image of Him was the majestic figure posted by Romanesque sculptors of the late eleventh century at the gates of monasteries, showing Him on the judgment seat, attended by His vassals. These "barons" His assessors were not as yet the Apostles, but the Elders of the Apocalypse and the Archangels, *duces* of the heavenly hosts. One of them, St Michael, took his stand in front of the throne, like a seneschal; his function was to keep order and perform the duties of a "clerk of the court." For God administered justice in the same manner as the feudal lords. The accused man, when he appeared before one of the many assemblies convened to reconcile knights and settle disputes between warring clans, was never alone. He was supported by friends who swore to his innocence and he could count on seeing among the members of the court men who were bound to him by family ties or reciprocal vows of fealty and would speak up for him, perhaps sway the verdict in his favor. This is why, dreading the prospect of the Last Judgment, so many of the men of this age were at such pains to earn the good will of the saints. These heroes of the faith composed God's tribunal, it would give ear to their pleadings, they would allay the divine wrath. So it was possible for everyone to make sure of an intercessor, to enlist "a friend in court" by the same method as that which made a good impression on an earthly court: by gifts. "Make to yourselves friends [in heaven] with the mammon of unrighteousness": this precept often figures in the records placed in the storerooms of monasteries, listing offerings made by the nobility. Saints existed everywhere; though their true abode was the unseen world, one might get in touch with them on earth, in certain places, for instance in churches dedicated to them, some of which housed their mortal remains. Through the intermediary of the priests officiating in these churches the saints could receive alms, the gifts which, it was assumed, would dispose them favorably to the giver. It was by generous donations distributed among a number of religious foundations that the eleventh-century knight, unable to curb his appetite for violence, even to discern what the Master expected of him, but haunted by a sense of guilt and a dread, whatever amends he made and however contrite he might be, of punishment, took steps to become a *persona grata* with the celestial court before which he must one day come to trial.

In the practices of terrestrial justice giving also served a purpose—to regain the favor of the lord. The feudal courts very rarely inflicted corporal punishments and the sentence usually took the form of a money payment. The object was to restore the social tranquillity that had been ruptured by the offender and to do away with a desire for revenge on the part not only of the injured party but also of his kinsmen and of the lord responsible for public order. For he regarded the conduct of the man who by an act of violence had broken the peace whose guardian he was as a personal affront. Therefore the guilty party was condemned to pay a fine in addition to a monetary compensation awarded to the family of the victim. This fine was to make amends for the damage that the king, the count or the lord of the castle—all responsible for public order—had suffered as a result of the crime committed. In the same way God's pardon could be bought. "Alms wash away sin as water extinguishes fire" was a dictum that often recurred in cartularies. A donation to God was by common consent the fundamental act of piety in this highly primitive Christendom still laboring under a sense of ineradicable guilt.

Giving to God did not mean giving to the poor. Who indeed but the lord did not cut the figure of a pauper, given the scanty yield wrung from the soil? Poverty was the common lot; its only remedies lay in the normal functioning of the seignorial institutions and the generosity natural to the men of high estate. True, Robert the Pious kept open house to the poor. On Maundy Thursday "kneeling on the ground, he delivered with his holy hands into the hands of each of them fish, vegetables, bread and a penny"; twelve of them always accompanied him on his travels and "to replace the ones who died he always kept a large reserve, so that their number never declined." But the symbolic side of these acts of charity must not be overlooked; they were not prompted only by compassion, but were also a ritual evocation of the Gospel narrative. The twelve men who accompanied the king played the part of the twelve Apostles, the distribution of food was a recall of the Last Supper. In practice all the donations made to appease God's wrath went to the churches.

It was to them that the men and women who had not won a place in the closed ranks of God's servants and were exposed to the onslaughts of Satan and his host offered their most precious possessions. Some even gave their persons and their offspring; hence the increase (especially within the Empire) of the host of "servants of the altar" as they were called, those who every year at the festival of the church's patron saint, whose "man" they had become, lined up in Indian file to lay on the stone of sacrifice the symbolic penny, token of their voluntary servitude. But everyone without exception was called on to donate a moiety of his worldly goods, his jewels and, more frequently, his land, the only real form of wealth. Donations were given whenever expiation had to be made for a specific sin, but it was above all on a man's deathbed that alms were most needed and most salutary.

The representations of the pains of hell that, following the revival of monumental sculpture, were systematically placed on the forefront of Cluniac basilicas in the last decades of the eleventh century were the end-product of a form of propaganda, some elements of which had made their first appearance around 1040. Striking fear into the hearts of all beholders, they led to a further increase in the number of donations *in articulo mortis*. These gifts did not merely serve the turn of the man who made them; he had in mind not only his personal salvation but that of the members of his family. When he divested himself of his property and drew on the wealth bequeathed by his ancestors, it was as much to benefit the souls of his dead forbears as for his own salvation. And he hoped on the Day of Judgment to pass as it were unnoticed in the midst of that undying entity, the race, which shouldered, collectively, the responsibility of each individual. This steady flow of pious gifts certainly did much to stimulate what was in effect the most active economic movement of an age only just emerging from complete stagnation. It implemented the only considerable transfers of wealth that took place, those arising out of successional partitions. These gifts impoverished the lay aristocracy and enriched the Church. They largely outweighed the extortions of the knights, at whose expense they enlarged the resources of the ecclesiastical power. But for the huge influx of new property and money, added year by year to the patrimony of the saints and providing their servitors with steadily increasing funds, there

could hardly have developed that creative urge which between 980 and 1140 gave rise to such remarkable achievements in European art. The flowering of Romanesque was nourished by the gradual progress of agriculture, but there would never have been this amazing spurt of energy had not the knighthood so gladly dedicated to God so large a portion of its wealth.

There was another means of making oneself acceptable to God and to His powers and principalities, another way of stripping oneself of worldly goods, but it asked more of one's body and one's soul—and this was a pilgrimage. What better offering could a man make to God and to the saints whose tombs he proposed to visit than the act of quitting his family and the safety of his home and launching out into the sea of troubles awaiting the medieval traveler once he had crossed his threshold? Pilgrimage was the most effective form of asceticism which eleventh-century Christianity, imbued with the heroic ideal, proposed to the knight concerned for his soul's salvation. It was an act of penitence which bishops habitually enjoined as a means of purifying the soul. It was also a symbol; in his wayfaring the pilgrim felt he was imitating the long, slow journey of the chosen people to the Promised Land and wending his way to the heavenly Jerusalem. And, lastly, pilgrimage was a pleasure; traveling, especially in the company of friends (as was usually the case), was the most enjoyable experience one could hope for. While they made their way on foot or horseback along forest tracks or sailed up the rivers, these bands of dedicated travelers differed little from the bands of young knights errant riding out in quest of adventure, and even less from the troops of vassals who, at the bidding of their lord, went to attend sessions of his court. For the pilgrims, too, were performing an aulic duty, that of gathering on an appointed day to pay homage to the saintly bodies enshrined in golden reliquaries studded with gems. Unseen forces emanated from these sacred objects, they healed bodies, ministered to troubled souls. And all were convinced that the mysterious beings whose mortal remains lay in these reliquaries would bestow their help and loving-kindness on those who had come so far to pay their respects to them. Such books as *The Miracles of St Foy* and *The Miracles of St Benedict* furnished lists, compiled by monks, of miraculous cures proving the efficacity of these pilgrimages.

The pilgrims usually made their devotional journeys in successive stages, with a halt at each of the shrines containing relics. Wishing to prepare for death King Robert with his court set out in Lent to pay his respects to all the saints "conjoined with him in the service of God." His long wayfaring took him to Bourges, Souvigny, Brioude, Saint-Gille-du-Gard, Castres, Toulouse, Sainte-Foy-de-Conques and Saint-Géraud-d'Aurillac. It is interesting to observe that he followed exactly the same route as anyone interested in Romanesque art today would choose. For during the eleventh century, and particularly in the southern provinces where the king's power was declining, the most advanced architecture was to be found in the vicinity of the miracle-working tombs. Here it was that the creative imagination which engendered the boldest inventions and innovations of monumental sculpture was given fullest scope. This upsurge of creativity was largely due to the vast sums of money donated by the crowds of pilgrims flocking to the shrines. Here, for example, is an account of one of the treasures then drawn on for the decoration of altars and the renovation of religious edifices. "What above all contributed to its increase was the tomb of St Trond where every day new and wondrous miracles took place. Such was its fame that for a good half mile around the little town all roads leading to the tomb and even fields and meadows were daily crowded with pilgrims of all classes, ranging from the nobility to the humblest peasants, above all on feast-days. Those who, because of the great press, could not find lodgings made shift to dwell in tents or shelters hastily put together with branches and curtains. One would have thought that they had gathered round the town to lay siege to it. They were attended by a whole host of merchants whose horses, carriages, carts and beasts of burden were kept busy all day supplying the pilgrims with food. Words fail to enumerate the offerings placed on the altar. Nor can we give an account of all the beasts, horses, oxen, cows, pigs, sheep and ewes brought thither, in number like the sands of the sea. Nor can we assess the quantity and value of the fine linen, wax, bread and cheeses. To gather in all the silverware and the pieces of money which poured in without cease until nightfall several sacristans had to labor without a moment's respite."

In the eleventh century the most cherished dream of every fervent Christian who hoped to win the divine mercy by a pilgrimage was that some day it would be given him to pray at the three most famous tombs: of St Peter, St James and Christ Himself. William, Duke of Aquitaine, "had formed a habit in his youth of going to Rome, seat of the apostles, every year and if perchance he could not do so made up for it by a devotional journey to St James's tomb in Galicia." Shortly before his death (in October 1026) the Count of Angoulême joined a group of several hundred knights who, so as to arrive in time for the next Lent, traveled post-haste to Jerusalem. They were not the first, others had preceded them; and Rudolph Glaber tells us in his *Historiarum Libri V* that as the year 1033 drew near "a countless multitude from all parts of the world flocked to the sepulchre of Jesus in Jerusalem; first men of low estate, then men of the middle class, then the great ones of the earth: kings, counts, bishops, prelates. And lastly—this had never been seen before—ladies of the high nobility made their way thither, in the company of people of the humblest rank. Many desired to die before returning to their own land." And, in fact, many did perish on the way. For when these pilgrims set out on that arduous and perilous journey, they hoped it would serve their turn at the moment when the greatest offerings were most needed, in other words when they felt their end approaching. But some of them perished because on their way to the Holy Sepulchre they had to go through countries where Christians of the West were not always welcome. Was it because of the risks involved that pilgrim knights tended to join in armed bands, constantly ready for the fray? Or was it not rather a sign of the combative instinct of a new generation eager to take the measure of its rising strength? In any case this was a decisive moment in the evolution of chivalry vis-à-vis religion.

Until now the Church had shielded herself against the aggressive instincts of the warrior caste, had set up barriers against their intrusions, built ring walls around certain holy places and those groups of the community which most needed protection: clerics, monks, the poor. Now she embarked on a more ambitious plan, that of converting the knights themselves, weaning them from their evil ways, canalizing their restless energy into God's service. A practice developed of fixing Whitsun, the festival commemorating the descent of the Holy Spirit, as the date for the ceremony of initiation into the profession of arms, hitherto a purely pagan rite.

Priests attended it, blessed the young men's swords and assigned to them the tasks which hitherto had been the king's: of protecting the weak and also waging war on the heathens. The first Peace of the Church synods did not prohibit the warriors from fighting; if God had placed them at the apex of the social hierarchy, this was to carry out a military function. But around 1020 some churchmen boldly asserted that "the joys of war" were sinful, that God approved of him who turned his back on them. Thus to the proscriptions of the Pax Ecclesiae were added those of the Truce of God. "From Lent to Easter, I vow never to molest a knight who is unprovided with a weapon of attack." For in the season of penitence it behooved the Christian to abstain from war, no less than from all other carnal pleasures. When, towards the middle of the century, the pilgrimage to St James of Compostela was getting more and more to resemble an armed campaign in Moslem territory, the councils presided over by the bishops went so far as to condemn all acts of violence between Christians. "Let no Christian slay another Christian, for assuredly in so doing he sheds the blood of Christ." Where then were the knights, dedicated as they were to warfare by Divine Providence, to go forth to battle? Surely to lands outside the pale of Christendom, peopled by enemies of the Faith. Thus only a Holy War was lawful. In 1063 the pope urged the knights of Burgundy and Champagne, who were about to make the pilgrimage to Spain, to launch an attack on the infidels; if any of them fell in battle, he, successor of St Peter, guardian of the keys of heaven, promised a plenary indulgence. Fired with holy zeal, the knights took by storm Barbastro, a Saracen town "rich in gold and women." Thirty-five years later another pope proposed a loftier aim to the ardor of the knights: the deliverance of the Holy Sepulchre. To each of the pilgrims-in-arms who rallied to his call he presented the pennon of Christ, emblem of victory. The crusades, indeed, were an outcome of the insistent pressure brought to bear by Christianity on the feudal mentality. What were the first crusaders but the trusty vassals of a jealous God who led the war into the camp of his foes and by dint of mighty blows bent them to His yoke? Among the attributes of divine power figuring in religious sculpture were leather, metal-studded jerkins, hauberks, helmets, shields, a sheaf of lances pointing towards the hosts of darkness.

VIEW OF CONQUES (AVEYRON) WITH THE ABBEY CHURCH OF SAINTE-FOY.

PILGRIMAGE

It was about the middle of the tenth century that the Christians in Gaul formed a habit of traveling to Galicia to visit the Roman tomb said to contain the remains of James the Apostle. Henceforth this shrine had an extraordinary attraction for Christian pilgrims, stronger in certain provinces and indeed operative earlier than the appeal of the Holy Sepulchre itself. On the Autun tympanum, recognizable by the shell on his wallet, the pilgrim to Compostela precedes the crusader figure. Along the various roads through the French kingdom converging on this shrine there was an incessant stream of pilgrims which by stimulating exchanges of cultural ideas did much to shape the mentality of eleventh-century man. Though these pilgrimages did not (as once was thought) originate the chansons de geste, *they helped to co-ordinate the subject matter of these verse chronicles, and the masterworks of Romanesque art are to be found along the main pilgrim routes.*

These roads were studded with monasteries where pilgrims could rest on their journey and were lodged according to their social rank in specially equipped "pilgrim-refuges." On leaving, each was given a viaticum. In every abbey on the route they worshipped the relics in it, less highly esteemed no doubt than those of St James, but none the less beneficent. An organized publicity, in which the monasteries excelled, vaunted the specific virtues of these holy objects and drew attention to the frequent miracles attesting their magical power. Compiled under the aegis of Cluny about 1135, the Pilgrims' Guide *advised, for example, "all who go to St James by the Tours route to turn back to venerate at Orléans the wood of the Cross and the chalice of St Euvertius, bishop and confessor, in the church of the Holy Cross; in this same town they must also visit the church of St Samson and see the knife which was undoubtedly the one used at the Last Supper. Also, while on this route the pilgrim must go to the place on the Loire bank where he can gaze on the much-revered body of St Martin, bishop and confessor. There he rests, this most holy saint who miraculously brought back three dead men to life and restored to health lepers, cripples, madmen, demoniacs, and victims of many other diseases. The shrine near the city of Tours which contains his most holy remains glitters with a profusion of gold, silver and precious stones and constant miracles attest its potency." In fact the true divinities of the age were the relics of holy men hidden from the eye under a scintillating mass of goldsmiths' work in the dim religious light of crypts. God—Father, Son and Holy Ghost—remained invisible, but these relics could be touched, they were known to repel the powers of evil, to ward off demons or drive them out of persons possessed by them, and to counteract the latent infections which covered a man's body with pustules. They were often "mobbed" by wildly excited crowds. At Limoges, for example, "in mid-Lent such a press of people filled the sanctuary for the night services, jostling each other around the tomb of St Martial, that over fifty men and women were crushed to death inside the church."*

After a devious path across the Aubrac mountains, pilgrims coming from Notre-Dame-du-Puy arrived at Conques, an abbey that had enjoyed the patronage of the Carolingian kings. Some of its monks had succeeded in a perilous venture, that of securing the relics of St Foy, virgin and martyr, and the fame this brought the monastery was so skilfully exploited, that in the second half of the tenth century a larger church was needed. Odolric, abbot from 1039 to 1065, supervised the building of the new basilica, whose interior layout and decorations made it particularly suitable for the reception—and edification—of large congregations. They gazed in awe at a statue, having the exotic glamour of an African fetish, glittering with gold and gems, within which was contained the skull of the martyred saint. It was reputedly made shortly before the year 1000. "There then prevailed a long-established custom in the regions of Auvergne, Rouergue and Toulouse, and in all nearby lands, of fashioning in each locality, according to its means, a statue of the local saint, reproducing with all due reverence in gold, silver or some other metal the saint's head or some other part of his or her body." These effigies were reminiscent of the anthropomorphic deities which from time immemorial the peasantry had venerated and whose succour they invoked in times of need. These "idols" shocked the master of the cathedral schools of Angers; indeed when he saw them in 1013, this learned man, imbued with the best traditions of Carolingian culture, was startled by this glimpse of another form of Christianity, knowing nothing of intellectual disciplines and all too ready to adjust the Christian ritual to the local superstitions racy of the soil. He even remarked that the decorations of the crypts looked like "reflections of the rites of adoration formerly addressed to pagan gods or, rather, to demons. Ignorant though I am, it seemed to me highly perverse, contrary to all Christian tenets, when for the first time I saw the statue of St Geraldus placed on an altar and given the form of a human face. To most of the peasants who gazed at it in wonder, it seemed to be observing them with an understanding eye and by the impact of its gaze to betoken its acceptance of their prayers."

CHURCH OF SAINTE-FOY, CONQUES (AVEYRON): VAULTING OF THE TRANSEPT CROSSING. 1039-1065.
(CHURCH FINISHED IN THE 12TH CENTURY).

THE BLACK VIRGIN. 11TH CENTURY (?). POLYCHROME WOOD. CHURCH OF DORRES (FRENCH PYRENEES).

OUR LADY OF GOOD HOPE. 11TH CENTURY. POLYCHROME WOOD. CHURCH OF NOTRE-DAME, DIJON.

RELIQUARY STATUE OF SAINTE FOY. 983-1013. ABBEY TREASURE, CONQUES (AVEYRON).

3

THE SAINTS

The monastery churches were nearly always built over a funerary monument erected in Early Christian times, the tomb of the monastery's patron saint, a bishop, confessor or martyr. The Carolingian lands, where the emperors imposed the liturgical usages of the Church of Rome, had adopted the type of church which gave rise to the structural system of the Romanesque choir and apse. This type of design was derived from the two-storey structure that Pope Gregory the Great had raised over the tomb of St Peter, consisting of two superimposed altars: at floor level, the altar shrine erected on the tomb itself; and immediately above it, in a space flooded with light from the windows, the main altar where church services took place. Conforming to this model, the choir of the pilgrimage churches stood over a crypt. At Tournus and at San Salvador de Leire the crypt has a basilical plan; that of Saint-Bénigne of Dijon, built in the time of Abbot William of Volpiano, has the central plan of a martyry. In this subterranean chamber were buried the sacred relics of men and women who had once lived on the earth but who now in heaven formed part of the choir invisible and from time to time manifested their power by laying low those who offended them and shielding from evil those who feared and honored them. Through the dim light of the crypt the monks led processions of awe-stricken pilgrims, and there, beside the sacred relics of the patron saint, miraculous cures and resurrections took place. Often the relics were surrounded by the tombs of lesser saints, of prelates and princes who had served the monastery well.

The crypt was not only a burial place but a treasure chamber. Amassed around the tombs and relics was a hoard of gold and silver, coins from far-off lands, trinkets, jewels offered by kings of long ago. At the very center of the piety and anxieties of the eleventh century—at the very heart of Romanesque art—stood that masterwork of the goldsmith's art, that gem which the church itself was built to house: the reliquary. A simple box or casket, the reliquary shrine had the form of a sarcophagus whose sides were often discreetly adorned with images in the figural tradition of the imperial workshops. Sometimes it took the form of a tabernacle; such is the small cupboard-like shrine in which Abbot Begon of Conques enclosed the relics received in 1100 from Pope Paschal II. Often, too, the shrine was shaped like the part of the saint's body which it contained; the goldsmith employed by Archbishop Egbert of Trier hammered the metal into the shape of a foot. Its decorations, however, were exclusively classical, for in the late tenth century the episcopal workshop was at the service of the Ottonian emperors, and the influence of the Byzantine renascence made itself felt through the Empress Theophano and her retinue. Finally, in southern Gaul, the reliquary took the form of a statue.

As an instrument of divine grace, the relic was the all-powerful element in the religion of the people. When secular princes presumed to lay violent hands on a church, there was no surer way to subdue and humble them than by taking away the holy relic which gave the church its sacred virtues. The Abbot of Saint-Martial made his way into a church by night: "he took the body of St Vaulry and brought it back with him from Limoges; he kept the relics of this holy confessor until the wicked lords recognized and proclaimed the rights of St Martial; when the saint was restored, not without a heavy payment, to the full possession of his prerogatives, the abbot returned the body to the church from which he had taken it." In times of famine and pestilence, to allay the wrath of God the nobles and the people compelled the priests to bring forth the relics from their underground shrine and parade them to conjure away the evil spell. Relics were sent from place to place for this purpose and, like princes,

THE SAINTS

1. Dijon, crypt of the cathedral of Saint-Bénigne. Early 11th century.

2. Shrine of St Hadelin. 12th century. Champlevé enamels of the school of Godefroid de Huy. Church of Saint-Martin at Visé, near Liège.

3. Godefroid de Huy: Head-shrine of St Alexander. Stavelot, 1145. Musées Royaux d'Art et d'Histoire, Brussels. Silver chased and gilt, inlaid with champlevé enamels. Overall height 17½ in.

4. Foot-shrine of Egbert, archbishop of Trier (977-993). Cathedral treasure, Trier.

5. Christ Pantocrator. Silver-gilt cover of a Gospel book. 12th century. Abbey treasure, Conques.

6. Martyrs commended by Christ. Ivory book-cover from St Gereon, Cologne. Shortly after 1000. Schnütgen Museum, Cologne.

7. Shrine of Paschal II. About 1087-1107. Abbey treasure, Conques.

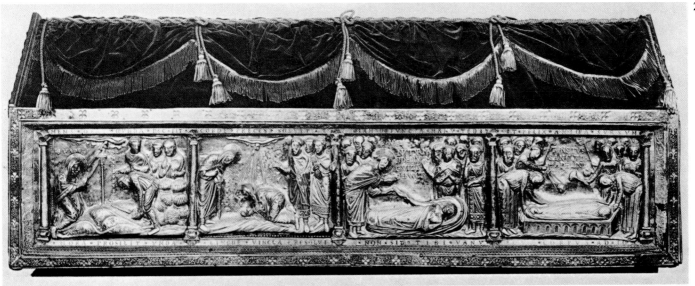

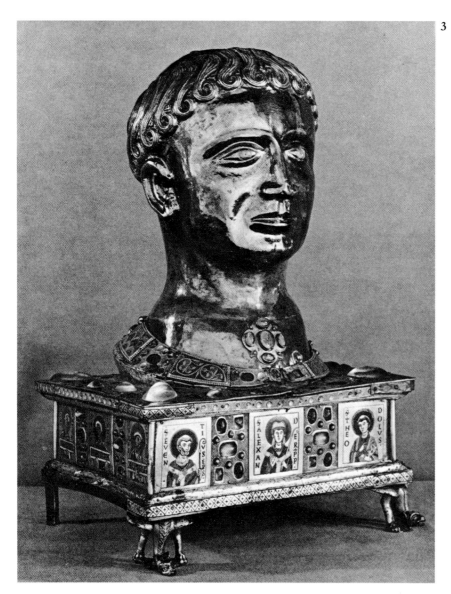

3

4

I. 106

paid each other visits; with pomp and ceremony they were transferred to a new building erected to house them. King Robert, who had just built a new church for St Aignan, "took up on his shoulders the remains of the saint, with the co-operation of his whole people and all were filled with joy and gladness; he carried them, praising the Lord and St Aignan, to the sound of drums and human voices, organs and hurdy-gurdies."

Relics multiplied miraculously, new ones turning up everywhere, and they largely account for the sudden outbreak of popular superstition in the early eleventh century. At Angély "the head of St John was found in the basilica, stored in a coffer shaped like a pyramid." Nobody knew how it came to be there. "Princes hastened thither, the King of Navarre, the King of France, and the latter offered a silver plate weighing thirty pounds, with stuffs woven of silk and gold, to decorate the church." "When the whole world was draped in a white robe of new churches, a time came, in the eighth year after the thousandth anniversary of our Saviour's incarnation, when divers tokens led to the exhumation, in places where they had long been hidden, of the relics of saints. It was," adds Rudolph Glaber, "as if they had been awaiting this moment of a glorious resurrection and, at a sign from God, had arisen in the sight of the faithful, to assuage their hearts with a mighty solace." The shrewder clerics knew that many relics were not genuine. In a treatise on saints and relics, Guibert de Nogent reprimands the monks of Saint-Médard of Soissons for claiming to preserve one of the teeth of Christ. But as the millennial anniversary of the Passion drew near, this sudden profusion of sacred relics appeared to ordinary men like a further sign of that new springtime of the world towards which Latin Christendom seemed so surely to be moving. The West had been poor in relics, and travelers coming back from the East were full of wonder that so many of them had survived. Surely God in His goodness was now revealing them everywhere, so that the West too, in its progress towards the light, should have an abundance of these vessels of divine grace and miraculous powers.

III

THE MONKS

THE WRATH OF GOD

Bristling with weapons, shielded against attack, the western world of the eleventh century lived none the less in a constant state of fear. How be sure that Nature, of which so little was known, might not at any moment unleash her forces against man? While there is no clear trace in any records of a wave of panic in the millennial year, it is certain that Christians felt a very real anxiety as the thousandth anniversary of the Passion approached, the year 1033. The year of God's death counted for more than that of His birth in a society so mindful of the cult of the dead and visits to their tombs. This anniversary, according to the chronicler Rudolph Glaber, was preceded by a series of catastrophes. "Men thought that the order of the seasons and elements which had reigned since the beginning of time had been destroyed, chaos had come again and the knell of man had tolled." In any case there is good evidence that during this period the undernourished, superstitious peasantry was liable to sudden accesses of terror which, starting in some remote region, spread like wildfire, sending whole villages in headlong flight across the countryside.

At the source of the rankling disquiet leading to these panics lay a belief in the imminence of the Last Day. "The world is growing old"—these words often figure in the preamble of deeds of gift to religious foundations. But everyone wished to know in advance the date assigned to this dreadful happening when the world would "shrivel like a parched scroll." With this in mind schoolmen searched the Scriptures. In the Book of Revelation (Chapter XX) they read that Satan was to be loosed from his prison and the horsemen of the Apocalypse would spread havoc in the four quarters of the earth "when the thousand years are expired." On this text was based the forecast of the preacher who, towards the middle of the tenth century, "announced to the congregation of a church in Paris that Antichrist would come at the end of the year 1000 and that shortly after his coming the Last Judgment would

take place." Nevertheless many clerics discouraged speculations of this kind; it was most unseemly, they said, to pry into the secrets of the Most High, nor was it lawful to forecast the day and hour He alone had ordained. No explicit mention of a date was to be found in the Gospels; only of premonitory signs. "Nation shall rise against nation, and kingdom against kingdom: and there shall be famines and pestilences, and earthquakes in divers places. All these are the beginning of sorrows." Then will be the time for men to make ready to confront the dazzling brightness of the face of Christ, coming down from heaven to judge the living and the dead. And in the millennial year the whole Christian world kept anxious watch for these premonitory signs.

What did men know of the structure of the physical universe? They saw the stars keeping strictly to their courses, dawns and springtimes endlessly recurring, all creatures moving irreversibly from birth to death. This convinced them that everywhere in the scheme of things God had imposed an order, that stable order exemplified in the walls of Romanesque churches, which their builders took such pains to body forth. Yet sometimes there was a break in these appointed rhythms as if something had gone "out of order." This was the case with such phenomena as meteors and comets (whose orbits were not circular like those of the other celestial bodies), or the monsters seen by mariners, such as the whale "huge as an island which made its appearance at dawn one morning in November, and was seen proceeding on its way until the third hour of the day." What was one to make of cataclysms, unseasonable gales, volcanic eruptions or that dreadful dragon many men saw in the skies of Gaul one Saturday evening before Christmas, "breathing forth vollies of sparks and heading for the South"? Wonders in the air, in the depths of the earth, at sea —descriptions of these happenings fill pages of the chronicles kept up by medieval monks. If they recorded them, it was because they believed these "signs and wonders" were of high significance, celestial warnings of impending doom. During the 1033 eclipse "every man was white as a sheet, all were stricken to the heart with a terror no words can express; for well they knew it to be a portent of some terrible disaster that would soon befall mankind." In his description of a comet, Glaber remarks that "as for knowing if this was a new star sent by God or simply a heavenly body whose lustre He had increased so as to strike fear into the hearts of men, these matters concern Him alone whose wisdom rules all things better than words can say. Nevertheless this much is sure: every time men see a portent of this sort on earth or in the heavens, something strange and fearsome soon befalls them." For in the world-view common to all, even the erudite, the universe was pictured as a gigantic forest, trackless, "measureless to man." To penetrate it, to ward against its hidden perils, the wisest course was to act like the skilled hunter: to follow a winding path, to study faintly indicated traces and take guidance from a pattern of seemingly haphazard coincidences. Was it not clear that the order of the scheme of things rested on a network of slender links charged with magical properties? Anything perceptible to the senses—a word, a gesture, a noise, a lightning flash—might be a sign. Only by patiently unraveling the tangled skein of phenomena could man hope to make a little progress, to blaze a trail in the dark forest of the natural world.

At the very heart of the mystery he had glimpses of strange events that needed skilled interpretation. The great thing was to trace their origin: which of the unknown, stealthy forces lurking behind the veil of appearances had given rise to them? Were they the work of chthonic powers, those furtive emissaries of Satan, hordes of which, to the thinking of medieval man, lay in wait beneath the earth and in the undergrowth, seeking whom they might devour: those hideous creatures—half snake, half woman—conjured up to such grim effect by the Romanesque artists? "It is common knowledge that wars and whirlwinds, pestilences, all the evils that afflict the human race are the work of devils." Christianization had imposed on the complex of ideas inherited by eleventh-century man a certain number of images and tenets, but had never really succeeded in effacing the belief-patterns of the past: that mythological deposit in which for untold generations men had sought to find an explanation of the unknowable.

These mental images tended towards a crude manichaeism envisaging the universe as the scene of an endless duel between Good and Evil, between God and rebel hosts that resented His order and disarranged it. Hence the belief that all catastrophes, sudden breaks in the divinely ordained rhythm were defeats of the friendly forces, victories of man's arch-enemy, the devil, whom an angel had held captive "for the space of one thousand years" and who was now breaking loose, attacking and spreading ruin, like the wanton knights who galloping across the fields trampled down the rising crops.

But why not take the opposite view: that God Himself, not Satan, sent these signs? An irascible God, prone to fly into a rage, like the kings of the earth when they felt themselves braved or betrayed, yet a God who loved His children, who preferred to warn them in advance rather than strike them unexpectedly, and to give them breathing-space in which to prepare themselves for His hardest blows. All his life long man is crushed by the Almighty's power, but he must never lose heart. His Creator has given him eyes to see and ears to hear, and speaks to him as Jesus spoke to the disciples, in parables. He uses obscure metaphors and it is the Christian's duty to seek out their meaning. By the startling deviations He introduces into the normal course of events He does humanity the service of putting it on its guard. These are preliminary warnings of the sterner punishment to come. The manifold disasters that befell the peasantry in the year 1000—floods, war, plague and famine—were natural enough in a still extremely backward civilization always at the mercy of the weather, epidemic disease, outbreaks of demented violence. All these inexplicable phenomena were taken to be the great tribulations spoken of by St Matthew as heralding the Son of man's "coming in the clouds of heaven" for the Last Judgment, and as such a call to repentence.

Admittedly the only data telling us of the climate of opinion in the eleventh century are furnished by documents which, written in monasteries, were given a didactic slant. They were recorded by men whose vocation inclined them to pessimism and to regarding renouncement of the world as the ideal rule of life. Naturally enough the monks exhorted others to undergo the privations they had imposed on themselves, and their preaching was fortified by the signs and wonders taking place in ever greater numbers: tokens of God's displeasure. In fact there was every indication of the nearness of Christ's Second Coming and the Last Day. To enter the banqueting hall to which the heavenly King would shortly summon them all men must don in haste the "wedding garment," and woe to him who was not thus attired! Let each man, then, cleanse himself of the taint of sin and, willingly rejecting carnal pleasures, earn God's indulgence. There is every indication that the widely attended gatherings whose ostensible purpose was to make good the Peace of God in southern Gaul were in reality penitential assemblies convened with a view to collective purification. An epidemic of ergotic poisoning in Aquitaine was regarded as a manifestation of God's wrath. At Limoges "the bodies and relics of saints were brought in from all directions and the body of St Martial, patron saint of Gaul, was exhumed from its sepulchre. All men rejoiced exceedingly, everywhere the disease abated, while the Duke and the nobility joined in a pact of peace and justice."

This will to peace and concord had a part in the movement towards austerity activated by the premonitory signs of the Last Day. For the vows to keep the Peace of God bade all good Christians eschew the "joys" of combat. And at the same time as the Church was imposing on the knights, as the penitence most befitting their estate, the periodical abstention from warfare known as the Truce, she stiffened the rules of fasting. For surely the priests whose duty it was to provide a model of the Christian life should set the example by practising purity and chastity, renouncing the luxuries indulged in by the knights, and above all getting rid of their concubines—in short behave like monks. To win God's mercy, to be made ready for the Second Coming, all taints of sin must be wiped out, more heed be given to the basic prohibitions. Satan keeps his votaries in thrall by playing on men's lusts: for gold, for war, for rich food and for women.

Let all, now that the hour of Judgment is at hand, resist these four temptations. The renunciation of wealth, the laying down of arms, a life of continence, the custom of fasting—none of them was new, the monks had practised these abstentions for centuries. So the Church now bade every Christian imitate the monks, observe the same rules of poverty, chastity, peace and temperance and turn his back on all things carnal. Thus, at last united in the Faith, the whole human race would make its way to the New Jerusalem clad in the austere habit of the coenobites.

Convinced that the End of the World was at hand, the eleventh century took for its ideal —an ideal which works of art were called on to evoke—the way of life obtaining in the monasteries. Situated in the heart of great empty spaces where only a few acres had been rescued from the forest, surrounded by a peasantry bowed down by endless toil and the prey of atavistic fears, and built beside castles manned by the rude warriors of medievaldom, the monasteries too were strongholds, but strongholds with a difference: oases of hope and piety against which the powers of evil launched their attacks in vain. To the thinking of the age the Christian community had two lines of defence and was guarded by two allied orders: the order of those who carried arms and the order of those who prayed. And where could men pray better than in the refuges of purity protected by the cloister walls? Day after day in all the abbeys of the West a host of worshippers offered, like Abel, to God the only sacrifices to which, as to Abel's, the Lord "had respect." The monks had more power than the enfeebled kings of Europe, than bishops and priests, of averting the divine wrath; in the domain of religion they were clearly paramount. The knighthood, firmly entrenched in Latin Christendom, might have the upper hand in worldly affairs. But in the affairs of the spirit, in the domain of religious fears and supernature—and by the same token in creative art—the monks held unquestioned sway.

"Let nothing be ranked higher than the divine service" : the Benedictine Rule gave a central place in monastic life to the ceremony of praise to God. Its choral prayers, processions and elaborate ritual fell into two concentric cycles. The intoning of the psalms never ceased throughout the day. In the hours of darkness a bell summoned the monks for the night service; this was followed successively by Lauds, a hymn to God chanted at daybreak, and Prime, said when the sun was rising. In the hours of daylight, when the monks had their daily tasks like other men, the canonical hours—Terce, Sext and None—were shorter. But collective prayers began again at the approach of night; at Compline all the monks joined in prayers for protection against the perils of the night.

The other cycle, covering the year, centered on Easter. One of the main duties of the sacrist and precentor, the monks responsible for the conduct of the services, was to compile the Calendar for the Year, to distribute the books appointed to be read and to organize the services enjoined on special days. Thus the life of prayer involved a constant awareness of the unbroken course of Time, whose cyclic rhythms it observed punctiliously, and by refusing to countenance any interruption in them the monastic community lived already in eternity. The monks could truly say that, for them, death was vanquished. There was no break of continuity; the living friars prayed for the dead, as if they were still present at their sides. The eternal return of the daily and yearly prayers did away with any notion of a personal destiny, of youth or age. This explains why the symbolism of the movements of the heavenly bodies was given a central place in monastic art.

The Gerona tapestry, like the Bayeux tapestry, belongs to a type of monumental decoration very few examples of which have survived, but which, none the less, had a major role among the accessories of divine worship. The walls of Romanesque churches have come down to us bare of any decoration, and we like them thus. But, when new, they were embellished with frescoes, oftener with figured textiles. In the eleventh century Amalfi owed its wealth wholly to the importation of silk fabrics from the East. These were not used as yet for personal adornment, except by kings and high-ranking prelates who wore them at public ceremonies in which they sought to evoke for the edification of the populace the hieratic splendors of the celestial world. They were mostly used for draping walls. When Pope Celestine II made his state entry into Benevento, "the whole town was clad in purple," and as a gift to the Emperor Henry IV, Desiderius, Abbot of Monte Cassino, bought from traders at Amalfi "twenty pieces of most rare, truly imperial silk."

THE FLIGHT INTO EGYPT. 1004-1030.
CAPITAL IN THE NARTHEX, CHURCH OF SAINT-BENOÎT-SUR-LOIRE, NEAR ORLÉANS.

NOLI ME TANGERE. 12TH CENTURY. CAPITAL IN THE CHURCH OF SAINT-ANDOCHE, SAULIEU, NEAR DIJON.

THE SIGNS OF THE LION AND THE RAM. FIRST HALF OF THE 12TH CENTURY.
MARBLE FIGURES FROM THE CHURCH OF SAINT-SERNIN, TOULOUSE. MUSÉE DES AUGUSTINS, TOULOUSE.

THE DESCENT FROM THE CROSS. 12TH CENTURY. RELIEF ON THE NORTHEAST PILLAR,
CLOISTER OF SANTO DOMINGO DE SILOS, NEAR BURGOS.

FULDA SACRAMENTARY: THE MONTHS (CALENDAR PAGE). LAST THIRD OF THE 10TH CENTURY.
STAATSBIBLIOTHEK, BERLIN (ON LOAN TO THE STAATSBIBLIOTHEK, TÜBINGEN, THEOL. LAT. FOLIO 192).

GERONA TAPESTRY: THE CREATION, DETAIL. ABOUT 1100.
CATHEDRAL TREASURE, GERONA, SPAIN.

4

THE MONASTERY

Western Europe in the eleventh century still had
its hermits, men who elected to live a solitary life of
penance in remote caves and fens, after the manner
of the anchorites of the Greek Church; and many
of them were to be found in out-of-the-way corners
of Italy. But most monks lived together in fraternal
communities, like the apostles. Under the Rule of
St Benedict, the bond of brotherhood was even
closer than ties of blood among high-born knights,
and the monastery was like the domain of a large
and prosperous family with a vast estate and many
servants. It had contacts with the outside world:
on its threshold stood buildings set aside for hospi-
tality and charity, where pilgrims and the poor were
housed and fed; near the hostelry were quarters for
the servants charged with the menial tasks which the
monks, devoting themselves entirely to their liturgical office, no longer had time to perform; and to the
gate-house of the monastery came peasants with
the produce of their labors in the fields, and the
surplus of their abundant contributions was stored
away in the cellars and granaries. But very few
monks were to be seen at this point of contact with
the outside world and its temptations. As a rule
they lived in cloistered isolation, cut off from the
world by a wall which they had vowed never to
cross. The monastery was a closed community, self-
sufficing and self-contained.

Of that renunciation which was the first principle of the religious life, the cloister was a symbolic representation. It was a place of retirement and seclusion. Its proportions were so designed as to body forth perfections which are not of this world. A quadrilateral co-ordinated with the four cardinal points and the four elements of the cosmos, the cloister was a small space shielded from the evils to which human life since the Fall has been a prey, and recreated in terms of the "divine quaternity," paragon of perfection, spoken of by Rudolph Glaber. For the man who withdrew to the cloister, everything around him breathed intimations of the life to come in the Other World.

The church itself communicated directly with the dormitory, since the monks held divine services during the night. St Benedict thought of the monastery church as a private oratory. "After divine service, all the friars will file out in profound silence and they will show to God the reverence which is His due; so that if a friar should wish to tarry and spend a while in solitary prayer, he will not be troubled by the importunity of others. Likewise, should a monk at any other time desire to say his orisons in private, let him be free to go in and pray." The monastery church was originally intended for the exclusive use of the monastic community; as a rule no outsiders were admitted. But in fact the abbey churches had opened their doors to pilgrims during the eleventh century. This was in response to the pressure of the masses, eager for miracles and initiation into the secrets of the Other World. Moreover, as a result of ecclesiastical reforms, new monasteries were being created around the older basilicas which, founded on the tombs of saints and staffed by teams of prelates, the canons, had been and now continued to be centers of popular worship. Finally, as the cult of relics spread, the Benedictine abbeys themselves acquired holy relics and became shrines to which the faithful flocked. The role of the monastery was thus gradually being changed—until Cîteaux reacted against this tendency.

Hardly any trace remains today of the monastic buildings erected in the eleventh century; like the homes of even the greatest lords, they were flimsily constructed. In most cases only the church still stands. For at this time the monks, whenever possible, rebuilt their churches in stone. From about 1000 on, building projects were in progress in all parts of Christian Europe, and the monks and churchmen, with their master-masons, proceeded to

THE MONASTERY

1. Cluny (Burgundy), the abbey church seen from behind the apse. From a lithograph by Emile Sagot (after 1798). Cabinet des Estampes, Bibliothèque Nationale, Paris.

2. Pomposa (near Ferrara), façade and tower of the monastery church. 10th-12th century.

3. Abbey of Saint-Martin-du-Canigou, Pyrenees. Built between 1001-1009 and 1026.

4. Monastery of San Pedro de Roda, near Gerona, Catalonia. 10th-11th century.

5. Moissac (near Toulouse), cloister of the church of Saint-Pierre. Finished in 1100.

6. Payerne (Switzerland), nave of the abbey church. 10th-12th century.

3

4

5

devise a new style of religious architecture. The boldest innovations were made in the eastern Pyrenees and in Burgundy. Oliva, abbot of Ripoll and Cuxa, seems to have been the moving spirit of the new Catalan architecture, from which stemmed the church of Saint-Martin-du-Canigou, begun in 1001, and the admirable ensemble of San Pedro de Roda, consecrated in 1022. Their counterparts in Burgundy were Tournus, Saint-Bénigne of Dijon, and above all Cluny. As early as 955 work had begun on a church that was to replace the first oratory of Cluny. Consecrated in 981, this edifice was given a barrel vault that improved its acoustics, enhancing the rich sonorities of the liturgic plainsong. In the second half of the eleventh century the builders of Payerne and Romainmôtier (now in Switzerland, but then part of the kingdom of Burgundy) drew inspiration from it, as did the Norman monks whom William of Volpiano had recently reformed, also the German monks of Hirsau. But this second Cluny church was soon torn down to make place for another, still larger and more grandiose, the third church of Cluny.

This last was destroyed early in the nineteenth century (it had gradually fallen into complete ruin), but enough has survived to demonstrate the immense size of the monastery, built to house a very large religious fraternity. In 1088, when the abbot St Hugh started work on it, the community numbered over three hundred monks. At first building proceeded rapidly, for alms flowed in abundantly from many sources. In 1095 Pope Urban II, a former Cluniac monk, consecrated the high altar, in the course of the missionary journey which took him to Clermont to preach the first crusade. But then work slowed down and the vault collapsed in 1125. Six years later Pope Innocent II solemnized a rededication, but for many years the abbots lacked the funds needed to complete the church. The truth is that Abbot Hugh had "seen big," had made plans for a building some 600 feet long with exceptionally high vaults, so that his sons, escaping from the prison-like seclusion of the cloister, could let their thoughts soar freely towards the celestial heights. An image of heaven, the basilica had better lighting than any other Romanesque church. "Full of the glory of God, it was like a gathering place of angels."

THE FUNCTIONS
OF THE MONASTERY

A society that attributed so much value to set formulas and gestures and lived in constant apprehension of the unseen world needed rites to still its ghostly fears and to make its peace with the supernatural powers; it called for sacraments and, therefore, priests. Still more necessary seemed the duty to "pray without ceasing." These prayers took the form of liturgical chants rising in clouds of incense towards the throne of God, sounding His praises and entreating His mercy. Hence the need for monks.

Their primary function was to pray for the community as a whole. For at that time the individual did not count, he was a mere unit in a group, all personal initiatives were merged completely into the activities and collective obligations of the community. Just as the vengeance of a family was a joint enterprise in which all its members took part and reprisals were directed not only against the offender but also against all his kinsmen, so the whole body of believers felt responsible, in God's eyes, for the acts of each of its members; tainted by the crime that one of them committed, purified by the holiness of others. For most men saw themselves as too paltry or too ignorant to achieve salvation by their unaided efforts. Or, rather, they hoped to win redemption by a sacrifice performed by others, whereby the whole community benefited and whose merit succored all alike. The agents of this communal redemption were the monks. The monastery acted as an intermediary in spiritual matters; it procured God's pardon and dispensed it to others. True, the monks were the first to benefit by these direct dealings with their heavenly Lord; by prayer and fasting they staked a personal claim on the celestial fief which was to reward their loyal service; nevertheless other men shared in the divine favor thus acquired—and the more abundantly, the closer were their contacts with the monastic community. In their devotions the monks gave priority to intercessions for their next-of-kin. This explains why so many scions of the nobility were dedicated

to the service of God in early youth and sent to an abbey where all their life they would pray for the spiritual welfare of their kinsmen who had remained in the outside world. But the monks also labored for the salvation of all their "brothers in the spirit" and this is why so many laymen affiliated themselves to a monastery, by the donation of their persons, by an act of vassalage, or by joining one of the many pious confraternities which sprang up around every church. And, finally, the monks made a point of doing their utmost for the salvation of their benefactors; hence the frequency of gifts made to the monasteries. These are among the reasons why so many monasteries were founded and prospered at this time; most of them for men (there were few nunneries) as was to be expected in a culture so thoroughly masculine, in which the question was often asked, "Have women a soul?" Such being the primordial functions of the monasteries, we can understand why a large part of their income was devoted to decorative enterprises. For the praises of the Lord are not celebrated by prayers alone; they call for offerings of things of beauty, of ornaments, of the types of architecture most suitable for bodying forth the omnipotence of the Lord God. So it was that the decline of monarchical power and changes in the social system led to a transference to the abbeys of the hitherto royal function of consecration and that of sponsoring artistic ventures. Indeed the flowering of sacred art in the eleventh century was largely due to monks and their desire to embellish the offices of the church.

Moreover, the monasteries had now become repositories of relics. No layman had dared as yet to keep in his possession these remains of sacred bodies, charged with such tremendous power: numinous manifestations of the supernatural in the world of men. Only the king, or else those holy men, the monks had the right to lay hands on them. The edifice housing them was always the property of a saint, their patron; he would not suffer any ordinary mortal to touch them, the fires of God would strike down any man who trespassed on his rights. Christ himself was physically present in some of these relics, vestiges of His earthly sojourn; thus they created a link between the everyday world and the mystery of the unseen. It was close beside the relics of a saint or martyr that the Christian best paid homage to him, could feel certain of his miraculous protection, and count most surely on his help in an hour of need, for any of the maladies whose course he governed, or on the brink of death. Many abbeys were built above the tombs of martyrs or famous missionaries, heroes of the incessant war with the powers of darkness. On one tomb, or on several. At Saint-Germain of Auxerre, "in the small church there were no less than twenty-two altars," and Rudolph Glaber when renovating the epitaphs of the saints "adorned in like manner the sepulchres of certain religious notables." Supervisors of the cult of relics, celebrated in shadowy crypts among sarcophagi, the monks served as mediators between the underground world of the dead and the world of the living. This, their basic function, had a marked effect on art. For it involved the disposition around the relics of ornaments worthy of their virtues. The monastery church itself became a monumental reliquary invested with all the splendor feasible in that age. And, being concerned with the relics of dead saints, it naturally had affinities with funerary art.

This preoccupation with death characteristic of eleventh-century Christianity testifies to the continuing vigor of certain beliefs which, long current in the lower strata of the populace, had been reactivated by the triumph of feudality. By encouraging their adoption by the Church the feudal lords elevated these beliefs to the highest cultural level and they were given a new lease of life. All the legends basic to the medieval verse chronicles took their rise in the vicinity of cemeteries, such as the Alyscamps at Arles and at Vézelay (tomb of Girart of Roussillon) at the time when Christian burial rites were undergoing a modification. Formerly these had simply entrusted the dead man, with all his sins upon him, to the mercy of God. Now, however, the knighthood bade its priests take steps to sanctify the corpse; hence the insertion into the funeral rite of the act of censing and formulas of absolution —implying that the priest himself had the power of remitting sins. For the dead body's sojourn until the day of resurrection no place could be more salu-

tary than one in the vicinity of sacred relics and of the choir where constantly the priest voiced supplications to the God of Judgment. This is why graveyards proliferated around the monasteries, the most favored and costliest places in them being those adjoining the church wall. Funeral services held on the graves came to bulk ever larger in the liturgy and day after day an ever-lengthening list of names of those for whom a special mass was to be celebrated figured in the obituary notices. Last but not least, the monastery welcomed men on the point of death. A practice grew up among the knights of being "converted," i.e. changing their way of life on their deathbed and donning the Benedictine habit. Thus in the hour of death they joined the community of monks and won a place in that spiritual lineage which would never end and, mindful of the salvation of all its members, would pray for them year in, year out. At the Last Judgment, it was hoped, the resurrected man, closely surrounded by his brothers the monks, might, if all went well, succeed in concealing from the divine Judge's eyes a garment less immaculate than theirs. Envisaged as collective graveyards forming a halfway stage between the drab reality of earth and the splendors of heaven, the abbey churches were bedecked with all the beauties of the world.

Shrines, cemeteries, founts of indulgences, monasteries were so essential that more and more were built. But for their ministrations to take full effect, assurance of their complete integrity and independence was indispensable. Now, as it so happened, monachism had suffered greatly in the troubles of the ninth and tenth centuries. Stocked with treasures but ill defended, the abbeys were the first points attacked by bands of pillagers. They had been looted and burnt by Northmen, Saracens and Hungarians and the monks compelled to take to flight. Violently expelled from their seclusion, they had been abruptly cast adrift in the outside world, domain of the Evil One, and exposed defencelessly to the temptations of the age. Most of them ended up by establishing new foundations, in provinces less liable to heathen attacks. Thus, after long wanderings the community of Noirmoutier, driven on and on by the Vikings, succeeded in carrying to Tournus, on the Saône, the relics of St Philibert, their patron, and in building at this peaceful spot one of the finest abbey churches in the "new style." But in the same period the monasteries were forced to bow to another yoke.

The kings, once their patrons, were losing hold of them. In the year 1000, in the diocese of Noyon, close though it was to the royal residences of the Capetians, only one of the seven abbeys was still under the patronage of the king of France; all the others had gradually come under the personal control of local princes. Meanwhile numerous members of the high nobility, and others less highly placed, mere castle-owners, founded monasteries in which to "place" some of their sons, bury their dead, and have prayers said for their well-being in this world and the next. And since the founder of a monastery regarded it as his private property, the monks soon came to be treated by him like the serfs included in a family inheritance. They were under the strict control of a master who ruthlessly exploited them and kept to himself the offerings made by worshippers at the shrines. Often, too, he squandered the treasure of the monastery church, drew on it for feeding his packs of hounds and paying the upkeep of his concubines, and compelled the friars to make do with the crumbs that fell from the great man's table. Even where better treated the monks were obliged to transfer in fiefs to their patron's knights much of the monastery's domain and feed his henchmen in their refectory. However independent he might seem, every abbot, every prior was harassed by temporal problems, constrained to lodge complaints against nearby lords who were challenging the saint's rights. Sometimes he had no choice but to make war on them and enterprises of this kind, coupled with the turbulence of the feudal age, led to frequent lapses from the Christian's proper path. How, then, apply the Rule, maintain respect for the cloistered life and save the monks from the taint of bloodshed common to warriors, their greed for gold, their fleshly lusts? How keep up the monastic standard of erudition in these conditions?

Once the West had emerged from a state of chaos and spiritual darkness, its rulers applied themselves to restoring the instruments of collective prayer; this was to their mind the most urgent task. Some members of the nobility took the lead. Anxious, at the close of their lives, to win the favor of heaven, they strove to restore order in the monasteries founded by their ancestors, or those whose patronage they had taken over from the kings. In 980 the reform movement, which had begun in the early years of the tenth century, was in full swing and by 1140 it had achieved its object. The functions then assumed by the monastic communities show that this spirit of reform developed, primarily, in the abbeys. Until the beginning of the twelfth century the official Church remained tied up with temporal affairs; this explains why in the period we are here concerned with abbots were more esteemed than bishops, and the monks triumphed everywhere. Because they led holier lives and the services they rendered God were clearly of a higher quality. This was the underlying reason for the success of monachism that Adalberon, Bishop of Laon, deplored in a conversation with Robert the Pious. Until 1140 the great centers of Western culture, the places where the new art was given form, were not cathedrals but monasteries. For the latter were built in the heart of the country at the center of some great domain that, having benefited by the steady advance in agricultural methods, was better adapted to the acquirements and activities of an essentially rural society. But the chief reason for this primacy was that the monastic institutions had been renovated much earlier, cleansed of the blemishes that for a while had marred their spiritual health. In western medievaldom abbots were canonized sooner than bishops, quicker to provide educational facilities, less inclined to squander the ever increasing wealth provided by almsgiving, and devoted it to rebuilding and adorning abbey churches.

The reformer of a monastic establishment was usually some highly gifted man, famed for the strictness of his morals and his energy, whom feudal princes, wishing to have the best type of monks in their domains, called in to eradicate indiscipline. This man of God moved from place to place in his crusade for better morals in the monasteries. To safeguard his reforms he retained control of several of the houses he had reorganized. They formed a united group under his orders and, by reason of their union, were better able to resist any recrudescence of the evils with which they had been afflicted and, more important still, any attempts by the secular power to intermeddle in their affairs. Thus the reform gave rise in the natural course of events to the "congregation," that is to say a structure which henceforth determined many of the traits of sacred art. Until recently art historians dealing with Romanesque productions divided them up by provinces and spoke, for example, of a Provençal or a Poitou school. But the notable resemblances between certain eleventh-century monuments were much less due to proximity than to certain spiritual affinities that in all parts of Christendom linked together the monasteries which, having been reorganized by the same reformer, had subsequently kept in close touch with each other. Often their abbots demonstrated these affinities by building churches of the same type and similarly decorated.

There were many groups of this kind. Among them mention may be made of the one which took form in Lorraine on the initiative of Richard of St Vanne and of the Mediterranean foundation which affiliated under the aegis of the church of Saint-Victor at Marseilles a number of Catalan and Sardinian monasteries. Another group was formed by William of Volpiano, abbot of Saint-Bénigne at Dijon, when in 1001 the Duke of Normandy asked him "to set on the right path" the monks at Fécamp; in 1003 he founded Fruttuaria in Lombardy. This abbot owed his success to his extreme severity, he was said to be punctilious *super regulam*, demanding even more than the Rule required: "mortification of the flesh, abjection of the body, squalid garments, scanty nourishment." He imposed on the monks a strict asceticism calculated to keep them in a state of the utmost purity and to make their prayers "more agreeable to the Lord." Along the axis of his original ministrations—running from northern Italy to the English Channel—branches proliferated; the reform movement spread from Fécamp to the abbey of Saint-Ouen at Rouen, to Bernay, Jumièges, Saint-Michel-au-péril-de-la-mer (invoked by Roland at the hour of his death, since to the archangel Michael fell the task of weighing souls on Judgment Day) and a number of monasteries on which William the Conqueror and Lanfranc drew after 1066 in order to provide England with good bishops, and where the most eminent divines of the year 1100, among others St Anselm, were trained. The influence of Dijon made itself felt in Bèze, Septfontaines, Saint-Michel of Tonnerre and Saint-Germain of Auxerre (where Rudolph Glaber was a monk); that of Fruttuaria extended to the monastery of Sant' Ambrogio at Milan and Sant'Apollinare at Ravenna. When he died in 1031 William was abbot in sole control of no less than forty houses and over twelve hundred monks.

But towering above all other congregations of the eleventh-century was the Order of Cluny. Founded in 910, the abbey enjoyed complete independence, neither the temporal powers nor even bishops were permitted to meddle in its affairs. With this in view its founder had linked it directly to the Church of Rome, whose patron saints, Peter and Paul, it shared. It was certainly to this total autonomy—the monks had the right to elect their own abbot, unaffected by any outside pressure—that the success of the Cluniac Order was due. In 980, though already vastly respected, it still was modest in its ambitions; Maieul, its abbot, refused to reform Fécamp and Saint-Maur-des-Fossés and delegated this duty to one of his disciples, William of Volpiano. The Cluniac "empire" was created by St Odilo around the year 1000. He induced a great number of smaller houses to place themselves under the control of a single abbot and to adopt the Cluny style of monachism, the *ordo cluniensis*; the Holy See directly encouraged this move by granting to all the daughter houses special privileges: immunity as regards the lay lords and exemptions vis-à-vis the bishops. The Order steadily gained ground on both sides of the frontier between the French kingdom and the Empire, ramifying into Burgundy, Provence and Aquitaine. Then it established itself in those parts of the West which were most emancipated from the domination of the monarchs, that is to say where the process of feudalization had been carried furthest and the stabilizing factor was the Peace of God; and in the provinces where latinity had not been grafted on to the prevailing culture by Court archaeologists, but was a natural growth deeply rooted in the soil—in other words the true domain of Romanesque aesthetic. By way of the pilgrim route of Compostela the Cluniac system penetrated Spain and its establishment in the great royal monastery of San Juan de la Peña led the Spanish Church to adopt the Roman rites. In 1077 the King of England installed a Cluniac foundation at Lewes and two years later the King of France founded another in Paris, the monastery of Saint-Martin-des-Champs. Not only did the congregation have branches in countries where monarchical art held sway, but it also won favor with the greatest sovereigns of the West. The King of Castile presented it with the Arab gold coins that circulated freely south of the Pyrenees; the King of England with the silver that was pouring into the North Sea ports thanks to the prosperity of seaborne trade. These precious metals helped to rebuild the abbey church and to adorn it on a scale worthy of the huge organization over which Cluny had control. The Cluniac system owed allegiance neither to a king nor to the emperor; it was self-sufficient. And though the monks of Cluny saw in Alfonso of Castile and Henry of England the true founders of the Order, its moving spirit was Abbot Hugh, friend of the Emperor, adviser to the Pope, and by general consent the guiding spirit of Christendom.

The reformed monks of Lorraine accepted the rule of their bishops and these prelates, who were selected by the Emperor, were then the best—or should one say "the least bad"?—to be found in Europe. On the other hand, in the provinces where Cluny had a foothold the inroads of feudalism had thrown the secular Church administration so completely out of gear that the Cluniac movement had to make an open stand against the bishops. It disintegrated the dioceses at the same time as the growing insubordination of lords of castles was disintegrating the countships. Thus the triumph of Cluny coincided with the decline of the episcopate and a progressive deterioration of the Carolingian system in which the reins of government had been held conjointly by the bishop and the count, under the guidance of the sovereign. This triumph also involved a setback of the cathedral schools, a weakening of the humanistic tendencies due to a study of the Latin classics, and by the same token a retrogression of the "royal" aesthetic. On the intellectual plane, in the domain of religious thought and artistic creation, the conquests of Cluny parallel-ed those of feudalism; indeed they joined forces in destroying the tradition of the previous age. This widespread renovation which, starting from Cluny and the region of its earliest successes, gradually spread all over Europe (it coincides exactly with the extension of the forms of art we now call Roman-esque) submerged the Carolingian heritage. Little by little it became obliterated, leaving the field free for indigenous forces, welling up from the Roman substratum, to make their full effect.

Together with the less spectacular but very real advance of rural economy, the success of Cluny was an epochal event in eleventh-century European history, far-reaching and complete. Bishop Aldabe-ron wrote a whole poem devoted to proving to the king of France that the victories of the "black-habited militia" were undermining his power. Cluny owed its success to the exceptional ability of four abbots whose administration of the great monastery

demonstrated that a religious institution could per-fectly fulfill the duties the lay world expected of it. "Know," wrote Rudolph Glaber, "that this House hath not its equal in the Roman world, above all in the task of rescuing souls that have come into Satan's clutches... In this monastery, as I have seen with my own eyes, so great is the number of monks that it is customary for masses to be said without an instant's break from the peep of day until the hour of sleep, and such was the dignity, such the piety pervading them, one could well believe that the officiants were not men but angels." For concomi-tantly with its insistence on asceticism (all the more necessitated by the imminence of the end of the world) Cluny stressed the need for thorough-going purity, and combined the administration of the sacraments, function of the priesthood, with the austerities of the monastic life. By contrast the world-liness, not to say frivolity, of the ordained priests became yet more glaring. The triumph of Cluny held out hopes of that universalization of monachism of which the bishops of Aquitaine dreamt when the year of the millennium of the Passion approached and the world was racked by calamities and epide-mics. But Cluny also succeeded—and this was per-haps the chief reason of its immense influence—in meeting the desires of a populace haunted by the fear of death. Nowhere to finer effect than in the great Burgundian abbey were celebrated the funer-ary rites, the masses for the dead and the memorial repasts at which the whole community of monks joined in celebrating the memory of a dead man and making propitiatory libations. To the Cluniac abbots was due the practice of combining in one service, the second of November, the commemoration of all the dead. They declared that souls would be deli-vered sooner from the pains of purgatory if certain specified prayers were made on their behalf. They also carried out an extensive program of thoroughly Christianizing the naive, semi-pagan beliefs touching the future life that had lingered on among the lower classes, all the daughter houses of the Order being enlisted in this missionary enterprise. This is why so many of the greatest princes of Europe desired to be buried in the graveyard of the parent monastery. The basilica of Cluny, which undoubtedly repre-sented all that was best in eleventh-century art and whose elements and ornaments were devised to sig-nify the resurrection of the dead to the sound of the trumpets of the Second Coming, in a blaze of light, rose from a soil fertilized by a multitude of graves.

THE SACRED EDIFICE

The art we know as Romanesque found its supreme expression in architecture. For the chief concern of artistic creation in the eleventh century was the building of churches, edifices in which divine service could be celebrated with the utmost splendor and in whose very structure the major symbols of the Faith were embodied. Combined with the art of music that of architecture sought to make perceptible to the human senses the order of the universe and the attributes of God. Painting and sculpture could never give more than intimations of the supernal world, whereas the edifice could body forth its entire significance. Its function was to co-operate in the revelation of the divine and, like the liturgy, like close study of the Scriptures and meditation on them, to help the monks gradually to apprehend the inexpressible by its structure, an organized arrangement of meaningful elements. For the church purported to be a plenary representation both of the cosmos and of man the microcosm: in other words of all Creation. Thus it conveyed an image of God Himself, since by His will there existed a resemblance between Him and His creatures.

This image had already been provided in the Romanesque cathedral by the manner of its disposition in space. Oriented eastwards, it caught the first sunbeams marking the ending of the night and the terrors that walk in darkness, and this reassuring light of daybreak was greeted in the cycle of the liturgy by a hymn of praise to the Creator. Thus the church was turned, symbolically, towards a realm of hope, that of a glorious resurrection, and the position it occupied relatively to the four cardinal points imposed on the processions of monks a direction towards the blaze of light announcing the Second Coming. The ground plan, too, was a sign. It was largely determined by exigencies of the ritual; the parallel aisles, staircases, ambulatories and the exits provided by the transepts—all were designed to facilitate the ritual, the access of pilgrims to the relics, the movements of the monks from their cells in the cloisters to the places where they prayed. Thus the layout of the church was functional, its structure adapted to the program of the collective worship taking place in it. But it was also symbolic. The crossing, forming one of the axes of the basilical plan, and the incurvations of the chevet carried suggestions for the understanding worshipper. For they reminded him of the cross: of both the plain cross of Calvary and the crook of the shepherds of the people. At a deeper level they conveyed an image of man, and of God who created man in His own image, and of the Son of Man in whom the two substances were united. Of man both temporal and spiritual, his arms outspread in the bays of the transept, his head framed in the apse, and the most vital part of his body occupying the choir. The center of the crossing forms a square, as does the cloister. Its shape signifies the four elements of the terrestrial world and the four evangelists, symbolic figures of whom were often placed at the four corners in the supports of the vaulting. This part of the church celebrates the God of the Ascension and from it rise the prayers of the congregation towards the heights, where a cupola presents a circular image of celestial perfection.

Lastly, the edifice conveys ideas of the divine order of the cosmos in all its parts, notably in the numerical relations between them which determine their proportions. In monastery schools arithmetic was placed on an equal footing with the science of music. But it was also regarded as an instrument of divination. For according to an ancient tradition each number had an esoteric import knowledge of which was essential for an understanding of the divine plan. For the initiated, in other words the clergy, four was the number of the world, five that of man, and the numeral ten, sum of all the numbers (described by Pythagoras as an expression of the perfect) was the sign of God. Both the most complex monastic basilicas, as at Tournus and Saint-Benoît-sur-Loire, and the simplest churches of the country priories, as at Chapaize and Barberá, conformed to a mathematical schema. For their builders wished them to be, like Gregorian chants, meaningful representations of the harmony of the spheres. To this "scientific" planning they owe that perfect balance which delights us today, but whose hidden meaning we are now unable to decipher.

Of the monk Gunzo who planned the great church of Cluny, we are told that he was "an admirable precentor." And it is clear that in designing this church he had recourse to structural methods resembling those used by the polyphonists of a later age for the composition of motets and fugues. Using as his module a unit measuring five Roman feet, he built up an intricate system of arithmetical relations. Implicit in these numerical values were a host of symbols, charged with other-worldly intimations. The proportions of the apse were based on the number seven; those of the great porch on the progression one, three, nine, twenty-seven. Much importance was assigned to the "perfect numbers" of Isidore of Seville and to the Pythagorean theory of harmonic numbers—an eminently musical conception, appropriate to the order of the universe, mirrored in the balanced structure of the edifice. This network of numerical relations was intended to enwrap the mind and draw it nearer God. For the abbey was dedicated to Peter, fisher of men, and Abbot Hugh of Cluny saw his church as a great net spread out for catching souls.

CHURCH OF SANT'ANGELO IN FORMIS, NEAR CAPUA: VIEW OF THE INTERIOR. LAST QUARTER OF THE 11TH CENTURY.

CHURCH OF SANTA MARIA IN COSMEDIN, ROME: VIEW OF THE INTERIOR. 11TH AND EARLY 12TH CENTURY.

CHURCH OF SAINT-MARTIN AT CHAPAIZE IN BURGUNDY. BEFORE 1020.

CHURCH OF SANTA MARIA AT BARBERÁ, NEAR BARCELONA. LATE 11TH OR EARLY 12TH CENTURY.

CHURCH OF SAINT-PHILIBERT AT TOURNUS, BURGUNDY: THE NARTHEX. 11TH CENTURY.

CHURCH OF SAINT-PHILIBERT AT TOURNUS, BURGUNDY: GROUND FLOOR OF THE NARTHEX. 11TH CENTURY.

5

VAULTING

Eleventh-century churches are remarkable for the variety of their design. The men who built them were free to adopt the forms of their choosing. These men were the prelates themselves, like Bernward of Hildesheim, or Hervé of Saint-Martin de Tours who, "filled with the idea of God, set out to rebuild from top to bottom the church in his keeping, making it vaster and higher; under the inspiration of the Holy Spirit, he showed the workmen where to lay the foundations of this admirable edifice which he himself brought to completion just as he had planned it." Neither the abbots nor the bishops knew anything of architectural theory. They worked empirically, trying to reproduce the forms of some building they had admired, or copying from memory some other which had close ties with their own church. The art of church-building thus progressed by a series of random experiments until the ground had been prepared for the magnificent achievements of around 1100.

This progress, whose results were noticed and commented on by Rudolph Glaber, was made possible by the economic expansion which, around 1000, was beginning to raise Europe from the slough of poverty and barbarism. For these walls were erected by whole armies of salaried quarrymen, carters, stonecutters and masons. It was not by forced labor or volunteers that these mighty stones were hewn and fitted together to build the House of God, but by workmen whose wages had to be paid. Chroniclers sometimes attribute the rebuilding of a church to the chance discovery, as if by miracle, of a buried treasure. Bishop Arnoul of Orléans wished his new church to be built with the utmost speed. "One day when the workmen were making soundings, in search of solid ground for the foundations of the new basilica, they discovered a large amount of gold." They handed it over to the bishop and it was said that an earlier prelate, when building the original cathedral, had laid by this hidden reserve to provide for future renovations. Actually that gold came from the cathedral treasury. Many religious communities were then capitalizing on the valuables so long stored away in their treasuries, and also turning to account the precious metals made over to them by Western knights fresh from their campaigns on the confines of Islam. The wealth swallowed up in the building operations at Cluny was enormous. Behind the masterpieces of Romanesque art lay the first economic upsurge of the new Europe in the making.

The chief innovation in the architecture that flourished in southern Gaul, in the area where triumphant feudalism had swept away the Carolingian aesthetic, was a systematic use of vaulting. Architects of the previous age had on occasion resorted to vaulting, using it to roof those parts of the church which, from the eighth century on, had been added to the Frankish basilicas as a result of the development of the liturgy and the cult of relics. The entrance porch and the chevet had accordingly become two-storey units, with large ceremonies taking place on the upper floor. It had thus been necessary, in the crypt and the entrance of the church, to substitute pillars for columns and vaulting for timber-work. The nave, however, remained timber-roofed throughout the eleventh century in all regions where the imperial tradition had maintained itself: Germania, Lorraine, the Ile-de-France, Norman Neustria, and even Italy. It was probably in the smaller monasteries in the mountains of Catalonia that the vaulting was first extended to cover the entire church. This was a significant innovation, made in a province strongly influenced by Mozarabic culture and invigorated, round about 1000, by thriving trade. The abbots of Cuxa, Canigou and Ripoll were enlightened, open-minded men. They were well versed in mathematics and, in Spain, well placed to benefit by the

VAULTING

1. Marseilles, dome of the former cathedral of La Major.

2. Ennezat (Auvergne), nave and south aisle of the church. Late 11th century.

3. Cardona (near Barcelona), dome of the collegiate church of San Vicente. Consecrated in 1040.

4. Périgueux, cathedral of Saint-Front, dome of the main bell-tower. 1125-1150.

I. 148

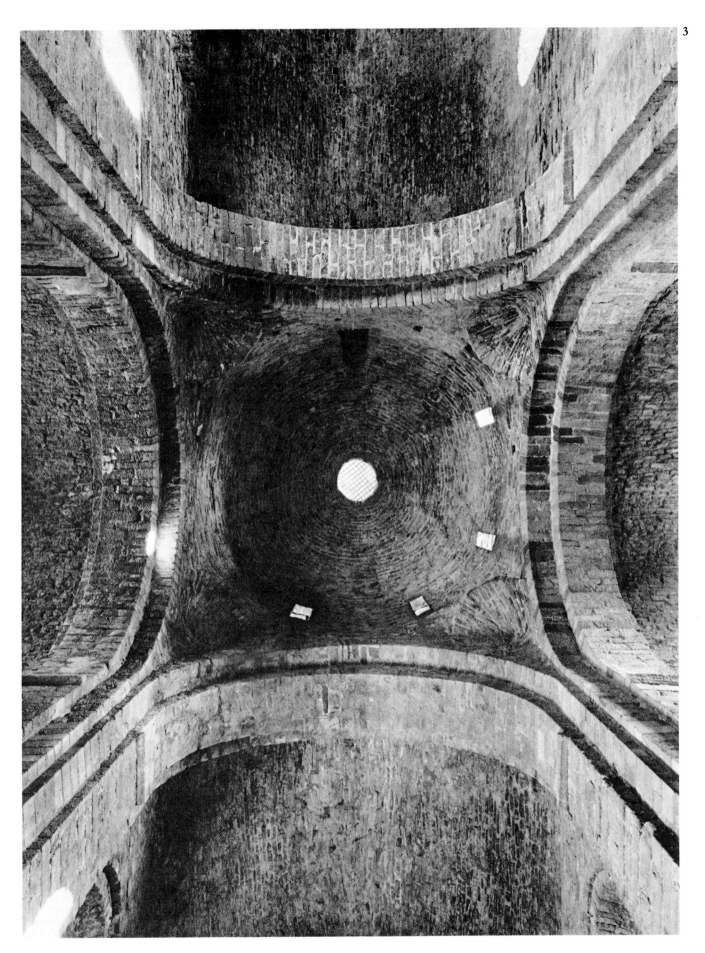

advances made in building techniques by Islamic architects. The methods they experimented with were carried northwards along the trade routes and pilgrim roads into Provence and the Toulouse area, from there to Tours, then into Burgundy and so to Cluny, which diffused them far and wide.

The new, vaulted nave at Vézelay was erected about 1135 to replace a timber roof destroyed by fire. The churchmen who created the Romanesque aesthetic had, however, higher aims in view than merely fireproofing the House of God. That was but an incidental advantage of their immense and arduous venture, their persevering efforts in the face of mishaps and setbacks to throw a barrel vault across the main nave, to absorb the thrust by groined arches in the side aisles, to extend the galleries, to stabilize the domes. For vaulting was one of the cardinal elements of the architectural style created by the medieval churchmen—a style which they intended to be an expression of the visible and invisible worlds, and a means of uplifting man to an apprehension of transcendental realities. Possibly too, at a time when the monastic Church was enlarging its funerary functions and thus coming into favor with the mass of laymen, the Benedictine abbots may have aimed at shrouding the whole church in that dim religious light of crypt and vestibule in which the burial rites, prelude of a glorious resurrection, could be most tellingly celebrated. It is certainly true that by the substitution of a stone for a wooden roof the church gained a unity of atmosphere which made it an apter symbol of the One World created by the divine will. Vaulting, moreover, greatly improved the acoustics of a building whose primary function consisted largely in vocal and musical ceremonies. Finally, and above all, vaulting introduced the circle into the architectural rhythms—an image of the cycle of Time, a perfect, never-ending line, the clearest symbol of Eternity and of that heavenly reward to which the monastic church sped the shriven believer on the day of his death.

IV

QUEST OF THE INVISIBLE

LITURGY

In the eleventh century the monks of Europe made their way to God by two distinct routes. One group kept to the trail blazed long before by Byzantine Christendom and the axis of its greatest successes lay along the neutral zone spanning central Italy and dividing Latinism from Hellenism. Needless to say its sphere of influence was not limited to this narrow area; it extended into Sicily and the tip of the peninsula, which Norman lords were gradually conquering at the expense of both Byzantium and Islam, annexing it to the West, and where they soon built (in Bari) a Romanesque cathedral. In these lands the monk truly withdrew from the world and made his abode in the wilderness. In Sinai and in Cappadocia he lived in solitary squalor in a cavern, naked, covered with vermin, treating his body with scorn and living on what God in His goodness accords to the lilies of the field and the birds of the air. The mountains of Latium, Tuscany and Calabria teemed with anchorites and there were many little groups of hermitages where, under the guidance of a master, a band of disciples mortified their flesh for the salvation of their souls. As time went on, these colonies of solitaries joined forces in organized communities such as the Order of Camaldolesi founded by St Romuald. Not only Italians adopted this sternly penitential way of life. The emperor Otto III betook himself to St Nilus, another champion of mortification; accompanied by Francon, Bishop of Worms, "he made his way in the utmost secrecy, barefoot and wearing a hair-shirt, to a cave near the Church of Christ, and there they abode fourteen days, fasting, keeping vigil and saying prayers." This style of monastic life, involving a renunciation of the world, total poverty, seclusion in a cell and silence, ruled out any artistic activity —except when, as for instance at Pomposa, the foundation was a worldly success. One of the reasons why in the eleventh century the prestige of the monasteries steadily increased was doubtless its appeal to the knighthood who could appreciate the physical heroism, the feats of endurance, required of the monks. Monachism proliferated everywhere; it took root in the heart of the West when St Bruno founded the Grande Chartreuse, and St Stephen of Muret the Order of Grandmont. To it was due the tinge of austerity which began to invade the Romanesque aesthetic and prepared the way for the technical and visual achievements of Cistercian art. But its real triumph came after 1140. During the period we are here concerned with western monasticism for the most part took another path, the one that St Benedict of Nursia had traced in the sixth century. Diffused from Monte Cassino, from the abbey of Saint-Benoît-sur-Loire (which claimed to possess the relics of the founder) and above all by England which had been evangelized by the Order, the Rule of St Benedict had been imposed by the Carolingian reformers on all the monasteries of Europe.

The new Benedictine way approximated to the earlier one since it, too, called for abstinence and reclusion and dispensed with missionary activities. But it differed from its predecessor in two respects; it instilled moderation and the spirit of confraternity. Each Benedictine monastery housed a community resembling a family firmly governed by a "father," the abbot, having all the powers and responsibilities of the paterfamilias in ancient Rome. All were brothers and the laws prohibiting any individual monk from acting independently were even stricter than those of the consanguinity binding together children of the same father. St Benedict stressed the monastic virtue of obedience. "Prompt and positive obedience," he said, "is the first step in our practice of humility. Renounce your own will and gird on the noble and potent weapon of obedience for your battles under the banner of Christ, our true King." Weapons, battles, a banner—the community of monks was envisaged as an army pledged to obey the orders of a military commander. They could indeed be described as enlisted men, for all of them had to sign a written undertaking like the one signed by soldiers of the Late Empire. They practised the team spirit in the fullest sense and none had a moment's solitude, not even the abbot of the monastery. He took his meals, slept and prayed among his "sons" and comrades, and the bond between them was far closer, even more irrevocable, than that between the vassal and his lord.

Among the other cardinal virtues in the Benedictine ethic was stability, there was no longer any question of wandering from place to place and the monk spent all his life in the monastery of his profession. Like the feudal families, the community established itself permanently in a domain which supplied it with the necessaries of life. None of its members owned any private property and each could honestly describe himself as poor. But in point of fact his poverty differed little from that of a knight's son who, though his father might be wealthy, had no resources of his own. And it was even more like that of the "domestic" warriors incorporated in the households of the greater lords: men whose weapons were their only personal possession. For like the common soldier, the monk participated in a collective source of wealth which provided him with his sustenance and with the rough-and-ready but substantial amenities then enjoyed by the rural nobility. Since it had so many of the characteristics of the establishments of the feudal lords, the Benedictine monastery fitted quite readily into the culture-pattern of the early Middle Ages and could welcome within its walls both young scions of the nobility and ageing knights anxious to spend their last days in a place dedicated to God's service. This was all the more understandable since the monastery was pervaded by the spirit of moderation inculcated by St Benedict's precepts: the habit of a well-tempered life, discretion, a sense of measure and a sound commonsense—the qualities to which this "little Rule for the beginner" owed its success. "We trust we are not enjoining anything onerous or over-stringent." For St Benedict disapproved of extreme asceticism; he limited the periods of fasting and, discouraging indulgence in mysticism, advocated a simple, forthright morality. To his mind, Christ's soldiers, if they were to win the day, should be allowed proper clothes, sufficient food, a reasonable amount of sleep. The monk, he held, did better to forget his body than persist in fighting it down; let him cultivate to good effect the land around his House so as to wean from it more copious harvests and offer to God more abundant sacrifices.

Cluny kept to the Benedictine Rule, but interpreted it in its own way, and from the inflexions that the Cluniac *consuetudines* gave the master's teaching derived undoubtedly some of the basic characteristics of the Romanesque aesthetic. From the start the Cluniac Order occupied that place in the hierarchy which from the earliest period of Latin Christendom had been assigned to God's servants: the highest rung of the social ladder. It felt no qualms about utilizing the great wealth that accrued from the steady flow of alms into each of its Houses. For the abbots felt sure that by no other hands could that wealth be expended on a worthier purpose. Did not the Order devote these alms wholly to the service of God? Why, then, refuse them? And since the Order of Cluny constituted as it were an earthly vanguard of the hosts of heaven, surely her sons, like the knights, were justified in "living like lords" and being supported by the labors of the peasantry which, by God's will, provided both fighting men and monks with their sustenance. St Benedict had wished the monks to be self-supporting, to till their fields and reap their harvests. Cluny, however, surrendered to the spirit of the nobility who thought it quite natural for free men to lead a leisured life, and regarded manual labor as dishonorable and degrading, of the nature of a punishment; surely it was God's will that some men should be slaves. So the monks of Cluny performed only symbolic tasks and, like the nobles, were served by tenants cultivating their domains and left all menial duties to a staff of domestics. Though men of leisure, the monks were not men of learning. St Benedict took no interest in intellectual pursuits, he was concerned with men's souls, not with their minds, and in terms of his Rule quite illiterate persons had an equal right with the best educated of entry to the monastery. The Anglo-Saxon Benedictines, however, whose recommendation inspired the reform that took place in the eighth century had thought differently and seen in the abbey school a mainstay of the monastic life, and, Latin being to them an unknown tongue, they made a point of studying it, even reading Virgil. This is why the Germanic and Gallic monasteries had developed into flourishing centers of culture in the Carolingian period. In 1000 many such still existed in the lands most deeply marked by the imperial imprint: Bavaria, Swabia, Catalonia. The best libraries, the ablest teachers of the eleventh century were to be found at St Gall and Reichenau, at Monte Cassino, Bec and Ripoll. But not at Cluny.

For a movement against all intellectual pursuits was in progress in the Cluny congregation, a movement that had begun in certain abbeys of the Empire on the eve of the ninth century. It had not gone to the point of closing the school or locking up the bookcases, but there was a tendency to reduce the mental pabulum of the monks to readings from the Fathers, particularly St Gregory the Great. After 1000, Cluniac abbots did their best to discourage studies of the pagan classics and warned their monks of the spiritual danger incurred by surrendering to the charms of Latin poetry. The fact that this mistrust of the *auctores* of Classical Antiquity prevailed in the circles in which the Romanesque aesthetic took its rise helps us to understand why it differed so markedly from the imperial aesthetic and from all the "renaissances" motivated by a will to humanism. Of the three subjects of the Trivium the monk confined himself to the third, the art of grammar. What use could Rhetoric be to a man who seldom spoke and usually expressed himself by gestures? Equally useless was Dialectic, weapon of argument; in the cloister there was no occasion for discussing or persuading. So only grammar remained. But that was no justification for exposing the monk to the lures of pagan literature. He could learn the meaning of Latin words quite well enough from textbooks such as the *Etymologiae* of Isidore of Seville. With the aid of reference books of this kind, in which the gist of the great works of the past was set forth in a matter-of-fact manner stripped of any pernicious "glamour," the sons of St Benedict could peruse in the seclusion of the cloister a few sacred texts and gradually memorize them. For surely it was not by dint of reasoning, still less by a surrender to the magic of fine writing, that the Christian could acquire the true knowledge needful for his spiritual well-being. The monk had dedicated himself to silence and a long pilgrimage towards the light divine. He would obtain that ultimate enlightenment more speedily if he gave free play to remembered words and images, welling up unsummoned from the depths of consciousness; flashes of intuition would leap forth from associations of these words and from the symbols they evoked. Such was the mental climate in which the sacred painting, sculpture and architecture of the eleventh century came to florescence. There was no question here of logic or method, and allusions to the classical writers were few and far between. The one thing needful was a full and faithful memory of Holy Writ, each word

being regarded as a God-given sign and therefore treasured, pondered on, turned over in the mind, manipulated, until a chance contact with another term struck out a sudden, new illumination. A train of thought, illogical in substance, a compound of vagrant reminiscences, it none the less became coherent in the ordered symbolism of the liturgy.

For basic to the Cluniac way of monastic life was its convergence on the great act of service, the *opus Dei* (as St Benedict called it): the public celebration of the canonical office. All the modifications made by the *ordo cluniensis* combined to elaborate and multiply these services. St Benedict had already treated communal worship as an essential function of the monastery; it was, he said, the "specific vocation" of the monks to hymn the praises of God, and twelve of the chapters of his Rule dealt with the Administration of the Rites and Ceremonies of the Church. What indeed, he asked, was the purpose of the monastic life if not collective prayer and supplication for the spiritual welfare of Christendom at large? When a school was included in the monastery its only object was to train men for this service, a service best performed by those who had accepted wholeheartedly the vocation of obedience and humility. In it the sense of a collective life—the team spirit, as we now would call it—was intensified by the liturgy into which were interwoven all the flowers of thought and speech the monks had culled from their daily reading and solitary meditations. But in this respect Cluny asked far more of the monks than had the founder of the Order. To begin with, by prolonging the duration of the services. The monks were expected to devote as much time every week to the recitation of the Psalms and to the intoning of passages from sacred texts as to all other occupations. So it was that in the Cluniac *consuetudines* divine service lasted seven hours on ordinary days and still longer on special occasions. To chant continuously for so many hours was physically exhausting; hence the abandonment of manual labor and the relatively comfortable way of life adopted by the Order. Cluny, moreover, made a point of diverting to church ceremonies, for the greater glory of God, the taste for luxury and rich adornment characteristic of the age of chivalry. What was to be done with all the wealth that was pouring in from the great estates in an ever-increasing flow now that they were better managed, and much of which all good Christians, as in duty bound, were making over to the abbey: the pieces of gold, ingots of silver that the knights of Christ, vanquishers of Islam, were constantly donating to the great monastery? Surely they could not be better employed than for enhancing the splendor of its ceremonies. So it was that the Cluniac monasteries combined to form as it were one gigantic workshop in which all who had any skill in the arts devoted their talents to adorning the House of God. Rudolph Glaber had this in mind when he spoke of "the friendly rivalry which led each community to seek to have a church more beautiful than those of its neighbors" and caused the world "to shake itself, cast off its ancient garment and clothe itself everywhere with a white robe of churches." But these edifices, their lavish decorations and the profusion of goldsmiths' work around the altars were only the outer husk, a tegument perfectly adjusted to contain it, of a work of art far vaster than they and renewed day after day in the elaborate ritual of the Cluniac liturgy.

Throughout the year these rites enacted a sort of ballet in very slow motion, miming man's lot on earth, his destiny and the march of Time from the Creation to the Last Day. The physical participation of the community of monks in this celebration of the divine plan began with a procession, signifying the progress of God's people led by Moses to the Promised Land; thereafter by Christ to the heavenly Jerusalem. In the Carolingian period this fundamental rite had determined the layout of the new abbatial foundations. At Saint-Riquier, for example, three separate churches were built at some distance from each other and in the course of the procession the monks visited each in turn, and by an instinctive response to a symbolic analogy the thoughts of all were drawn to another triad, that of the Persons of the Trinity. Similarly, the exigences of the processional liturgy determined the structure of the Romanesque basilicas; new side aisles were added to the central nave, and these were prolonged by an ambulatory circling the choir, frequent openings being provided at appropriate points. The growing tendency to increase the length of the church was due to the same cause. In the third church at Cluny St Hugh, its builder, with a view to suggesting more emphatically the long road man must follow to attain salvation, arranged for a wide gap between the entrance, place of initiation into the divine light, and the central point where the sacrifice was solemnized and where the monks' collective prayers rose

towards God—the part of the church where the soaring movement was intensified by the upward thrust of columns and vaults: the choir.

The liturgic act was, first and foremost, musical; the spiritual fervor of the eleventh century found its most complete expression in chants sung in unison by a male choir. They voiced that unanimity which pleased God in the praises of His creatures. Seven times daily the monks made a processional entrance into the church to sing the Psalms and the "psalm-tones" used by them had the distinctive qualities of Benedictine plain chant as opposed to that of Oriental monachism: restraint, decorum, an interpretation ruling out any touch of individual fantasy. For at Cluny the practice of humility and obedience applied equally to the precentor to whom the abbot had delegated his functions of training, conducting and leading the choir. We must not assume, however, that originality was completely excluded in the monasteries of the West. Several great eleventh-century abbeys, such as St Gall and Saint-Martial of Limoges, took an active part in developing the major art of the age, liturgic art, and devising new, happier associations of words and melodies. In the technical language of the day the verb *trouver* ("finding") meant just this: arranging and adapting new texts to the modulations of the plain song. The men who specialized in this fully realized that in so doing they were often bound to modify—for a religious end—the accepted grammar. This called for much ingenuity, since it was no easy task wedding the vocabulary of prayer to the vast, simple rhythms of Gregorian melodies, perfectly adjusted to those of the cosmos, *ergo* to the divine mind. No easy task, but a noble one, for were they not sublimating forms of human speech to those of the hymns of praise chanted forever by the angels? In eleventh-century schools the Quadrivium, second cycle of the liberal arts, consisted almost entirely of music and to this the other subjects—arithmetic, geometry, astronomy—were subordinated. By common consent the art of music was the climactic point of the grammatical studies composing the Trivium. Since no one read in a speaking voice, since all public reading was vocalized in the manner of a recitative, and since, if it was to be faultless, the singing of the psalms called both for a knowledge by rote of the sacred text and an understanding of its meaning, the study of Latin vocables and that of musical sounds marched side by side. In this culture the logic of musical consonances ranked as the only perfect logic. When Gerbert proposed "to make fully perceptible the various notes by marking them off on the mono-chord, dividing their consonances and symphonies by tones, half-tones and sharps, and distributing them according to the intervals of the scale," he was anticipating the scholastic analysis of sounds made two centuries later. But what most of all he hoped for was to gain thereby an insight into the underlying order of the universe.

Music and, through it, the liturgy were undoubtedly the most potent instruments of knowledge known to eleventh-century culture. By reason of their symbolical significance and the mental associations evoked by them, the words of the liturgy enabled the Christian to plumb the mysteries of the cosmos; they led him towards God. And music led to Him more directly still, since it revealed the transcendent harmonies of the created world and by its instant action on the human heart led man to participate, indeed to merge himself, in the perfection of the divine plan. In Chapter xx of his Rule St Benedict had quoted a line from the Psalms "I shall sing to thee in the presence of the angels." In the choir of monks he saw a prefiguration of the choirs of heaven; overleaping the barriers between this world and the next, it gave the earthbound mortal access to the supernal realm and to the uncreated Light. "When we join our voices in these chants," St Benedict had said, "we stand in the very presence of God and His angels." For then the whole man—body, soul and spirit—is flooded by that divine illumination; he attains the *stupor* and the *admiratio* told of by the twelfth-century mystic Baldwin of Ford, and is rapt in contemplation of the eternal splendor. Monasticism made no attempt to rationalize its faith; rather, to stimulate it by the collective emotion of the congregations in the daylong services. Unconcerned with causes and effects or logical demonstration, it entered into communication with the unseen powers, the most

direct avenue to which was the choral singing of the liturgy. When week by week, at the same hour, the monk sang the same verses to the same melodies, did he not by the very act of joining in the plain song participate in depth in an experience of the ineffable, unattainable by any other means? "The rites which, as prescribed in the Calendar for the Year, take place in the divine service are signs of the highest realities, contain the holiest sacraments and all the majesty of the celestial mysteries. They were ordained for the glory of Our Lord Jesus Christ, Head of the Church, by men who understood the sublimity of the aforesaid mysteries and made it known by spoken words, by writings and by rites. Among the many spiritual treasures with which the Holy Spirit has enriched his Church, we should cultivate devoutly that one which aids to an understanding of what we say in prayers and chants." And Rupert of Deutz adds: "This is nothing short of a manner of prophesying."

In the social order of the eleventh century the monks were ministrants of a ceremony of constant praises of the Lord, a rite invested with all the creative powers of a work of art. Thus this work, closely connected with the liturgy, was even more intimately bound up with the art of music. St Hugh of Cluny thought fit to install in the center of the new basilica, on the capitals of the choir, a representation of all the tones of music since, for him, they equated a cosmogony in virtue of those occult correspondences which, according to Boethius, linked the seven notes of the scale to the seven planets and gave a key to the harmony of the spheres. But it was most of all as a sort of diagram of the divine mystery that the abbot proposed them to the contemplation of the monks. *Tertius impigit Cristumque resurgens fingit*; in this inscription beside the figure was defined the function of the third tone. By the emotion it arouses it enables the soul, better than any words or imagery could do, to sense the true significance of the Resurrection of Our Lord.

Very few could read. For the great majority speech and gestures were the only means of communication. Each time he uttered certain words of power a man established contact with the mysterious world around him. There were formulas of exorcism which expelled evil spirits from possessed persons; of oaths calling God to witness to a compact entered into; of anathema bringing down divine reprisals on the head of an offender; of the sacraments which opened the doors of heaven to the believer. If the prayers chanted by the assembled monks had such efficacy, this was because they were a collective invocation. While they rose heavenwards the barriers between God and mortal man fell one after another—like the walls of Jericho. The word, then, triumphed over the invisible; captured it; enlisted its powers and bent it to its use.

God Himself spoke through His prophets; His utterances are enshrined in the Scriptures and man has no better weapon in his fight against evil than the words recorded there. Dark words in many cases, and the aims of all the teaching in the monastery and the cathedral schools was to make their meaning clear. The churchmen tried to do this by collating the vocables employed in the Scriptures and seeking to detect the occult links between them. "To elucidate a word by means of another word," was the function assigned to the gloss by Conrad of Hirsau. These words were inscribed in the phylacteries which, carved in stone or ivory, were upheld by prophets and apostles. Painters and sculptors, too, used these texts, for their chief task in the eleventh century was to illustrate the Word of God.

In or about 810 Charlemagne had founded, above a martyry and a graveyard, the monastery of Saint-Savin. The church was built in the second quarter of the eleventh century, then adorned with frescoes. Each part of the edifice was given images appropriate to its religious functions, those of the life of the patron saint being placed in the crypt (where the relics were housed) and those of the Apocalypse in the porch. A long barrel vault in the nave provided a large space for painting, uninterrupted by ceiling beams and here the tale of mankind, as recorded in Genesis, from the Creation till the time of Moses, up to the giving of the Law, was represented. The history of the race, as here depicted, revealed the divine plan governing the lot of individual man and heralded the coming of the Messiah and Christ's return on the Last Day. The narrative comprises thirty-six scenes in which earth colors, white and yellow ochres, predominate. But the semicircle of the vault, like the canopy of heaven, enframing the successive episodes, translates them into the world eternal.

ABBEY CHURCH OF SAINT-SAVIN-SUR-GARTEMPE, POITOU: VIEW OF THE NAVE WITH CEILING FRESCOES. 11TH CENTURY.

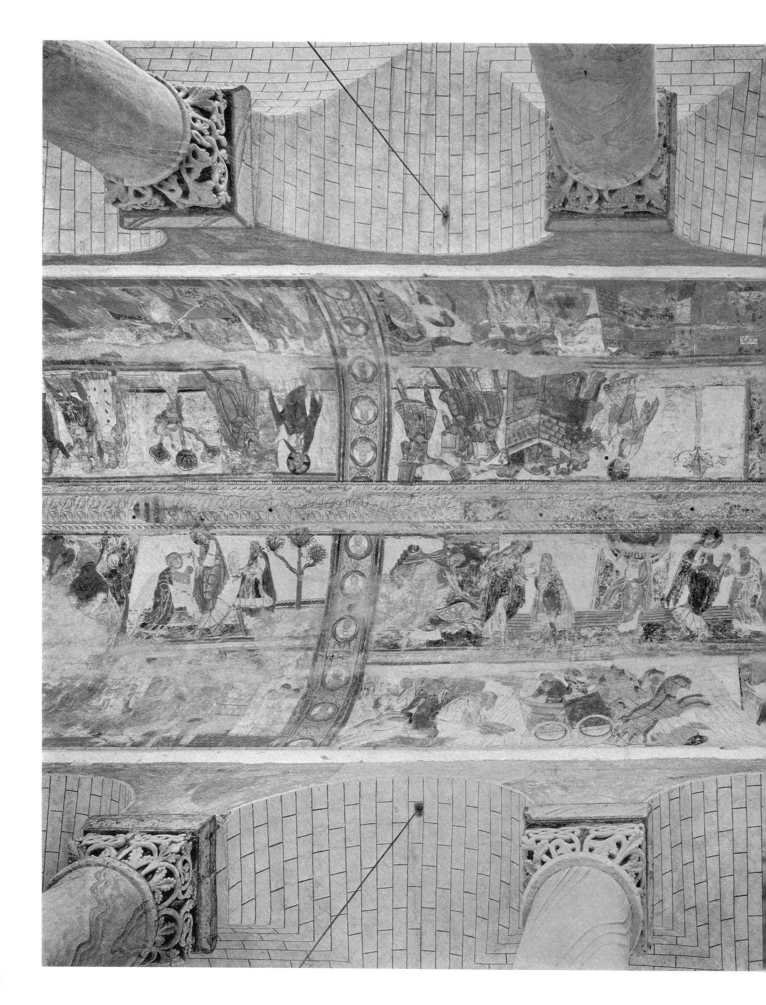

SCENES FROM THE OLD TESTAMENT. IITH
CENTURY. FRESCOES ON THE VAULT OF THE
NAVE, ABBEY CHURCH OF SAINT-SAVIN-SUR-
GARTEMPE, POITOU.

I. 163

THE PROPHET ISAIAH. ABOUT 1130.
SCULPTURE FROM THE PORTAL OF THE ABBEY CHURCH OF SOUILLAC, PÉRIGORD.

ST PETER AND ST PAUL. ABOUT 1120-1150. DOOR-JAMB OF THE NARTHEX.
CHURCH OF THE MADELEINE, VÉZELAY, BURGUNDY.

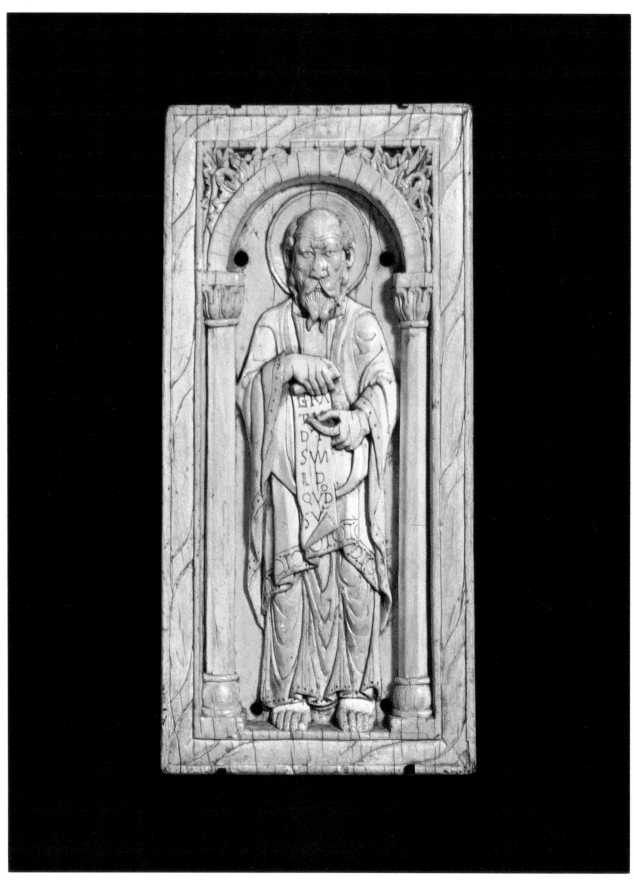

MASTER OF ECHTERNACH (?). ST PAUL. ABOUT 1000. IVORY BOOK-COVER. MUSÉE DE CLUNY, PARIS.

In the Old Testament God speaks through the mouths of the prophets; in the Gospels He speaks in person. Jesus, the Word incarnate, delivers His message directly. It was the duty of every monk, if he wished to follow Christ and to identify himself with the disciples who heard the Master speaking in the hills of Galilee, to make himself familiar with the sacred text, "full of true words and wonders"—to hearken to it, read it or, best of all, copy it with his own hand.

To write down the words of God, to shape each letter slowly, like a graver, on that stubborn material, parchment—an exacting task that Peter the Venerable likened to the ploughman's toil ("in each furrow you trace on the page sow the good seed of God's word")—this was, like the discipline of the liturgical plain song, to dedicate one's labors to God. The work done in the scriptorium ranked among the practices of monastic asceticism. For like prayer and fasting, Abbon of Fleury pointed out, it helps to drive away evil thoughts, to escape the thrall of the flesh and to open the mind to higher things. Since they were receptacles of the word of God, these books were given the aspect of a shrine, were lavishly adorned, bound in finely wrought leather or in gold, and made resplendent, like the sides of reliquaries, with carved ivories and precious stones. For the same reason illuminations supplement the text in the transmission of the divine message. Indeed the making of each book was regarded as an act of consecration. The two monks at Stavelot who in the eleventh century copied a text by Josephus, employed the same formula that the priest used in the dedication of the Host. "Receive, Holy Trinity, the offering of this book." Both the readers of the book and those who were to preserve it till the end of time participated in this offering and in its talismanic virtues. For, like relics, like even the Holy Sacrament, these objects in which words and images were combined were regarded as intermediaries to which men could resort with a view to obtaining God's favor and a passport to eternity. No distinction, in fact, was drawn between the making of a book, in which the patience of the scribe, the commentator's learning and the talent of the painter co-operated, and an act of thanksgiving. When the Germanic emperors commissioned, at Reichenau or Echternach, a Gospel Book or a Book of Pericopes; when Henry III presented to Speyer Cathedral the Codex Aureus, *they were not so much thinking of adding to their glory by an act of high munificence, as conscious of "officiating." They were fulfilling the sacred, priestlike function enjoined by the state to which God had called them.*

MASTER OF MONTE CASSINO. THE SONS OF ZEBEDEE. LAST QUARTER OF THE 11TH CENTURY.
FRESCO, CHURCH OF SANT'ANGELO IN FORMIS, NEAR CAPUA.

BOOK OF PERICOPES OF HENRY II: CHRIST TAKING LEAVE OF THE DISCIPLES.
REICHENAU, ABOUT 1010. FOLIO 136 RECTO, CLM. 4452, STAATSBIBLIOTHEK, MUNICH.

MISSEL OF SAINT-DENIS: CHRIST IN MAJESTY. ABOUT 1050.
FOLIO 15 VERSO, MS LAT. 9436, BIBLIOTHÈQUE NATIONALE, PARIS.

6

THE LIFE OF JESUS

The art and culture of the eleventh century were rooted in a dark forest of primitive beliefs. It was taken for granted that only by magical operations, by incantations and sorcery, could man free himself from the grip of the unseen, elemental forces lurking behind the veil of appearances. The cult of relics, the sacramental rites and the liturgy belonged to the same non-rational universe as amulets and wizardry. They operated in the same manner, had the same purpose: that of bending the sacred to a human will. The work of art had a like function; it explored the unknowable, it provided clues through the labyrinth of the spiritual world and attempted to lift the veils, one by one. Like the churchmen, the medieval artist aimed at clarifying two great mysteries: the realm of nature and the text of Holy Scripture.

The architect's commentary on them is cast in an abstract form. He does not speak in images properly so called, but by signs less easily grasped, by the arrangement and harmony of masses, and by a mathematical formula implicit in the overall structure of the edifice. He formulates a complex of symbols which act imperceptibly on the minds and souls of those who live and pray in the ordered space which he creates. The painter, obviously, keeps closer to visual reality, he depicts, and, unlike the architect's, his language is that of allegory. Painting in general, and especially manuscript illumination (which seems to have furnished most of the themes used in large-scale monumental decoration), was strongly influenced by the arts of the goldsmith and the jeweler which, well represented in the church treasure, preserved the traditions of the art of classical Antiquity. Even when it decorated a wall, painting remained closely related to a text, which its purpose was to illustrate. Of each word, each verse, each paragraph, it gave a visual equivalent which, like the glosses of the school, helped to elucidate and clarify the text. The painter used quite simple images, very close to what the eye perceives; all he did was to record the normal data of perception and fit them into an ordered pattern.

Still, some of the texts he illustrated relate to signs and wonders and here the artist could exercise his imagination, indulge in fantastic visions, notably when his themes were taken from the Book of Revelation. The Gospels, on the other hand, tell of everyday things and people, of inns and robbers, of kings following a star, of caves and fishermen, figtrees, lances, thorns, a storm-tossed lake. Doubtless the narrative contains references to the world invisible, but these are relatively rare; almost all the action takes place on earth, among human beings. This explains why the life of Jesus has so small a place in eleventh-century iconography. To men who saw the world around them as a prison and were always groping to find a fissure in its walls, an escape from the perils and privations of daily life, and who tried to forget their present afflictions by dreaming of a splendid Hereafter, the text of the synoptic Gospels may well have seemed too drab and colorless. They wanted to be told of the glories to come, not reminded of present hardships. For their priests and monks, too, what counted was not the story of Christ's humble life on earth, but visions of the Eternal Life.

None the less, readings from the Gospels formed part of the liturgy and these texts were illustrated. Pictures of Christ preaching, His miracle of the loaves and fishes, His triumph over the temptations of the devil and His converse with the disciples bulk large in the pages of illuminated manuscripts, Gospel Books or Books of Pericopes in which passages from the New Testament were collated for use at divine service. Scenes of Christ's childhood and Passion adorned the capitals of certain cloisters, intermingled with images symbolizing the powers of evil. They also figure at the top of the long lines of pillars

THE LIFE OF JESUS

1. The Nativity. Trier or West Germany, about 1000. Ivory book-cover by the Master of the Registrum Gregorii. CLM. 4451, Staatsbibliothek, Munich.

2. The Presentation in the Temple. About 1120. Bas-relief in the south transept. Church of Sainte-Croix, La Charité-sur-Loire.

3. Episodes of the death of John the Baptist. 12th century. Capital from the former cloister of Saint-Etienne, Toulouse. Musée des Augustins, Toulouse.

4. The Kiss of Judas and the Arrest of Christ. 12th century. Capital from the cloister of La Daurade, Toulouse. Musée des Augustins, Toulouse.

5. The Crucifixion. 12th century. Bas-relief on the northwest pillar. Cloister of Santo Domingo de Silos, near Burgos.

6. The Way to Emmaus. 12th century. Bas-relief on the northwest pillar. Cloister of Santo Domingo de Silos, near Burgos.

7. The Supper at Emmaus. About 1080. Ivory plaque of an altar frontal from Salerno Cathedral. Staatliche Museen, Berlin.

3

4

I. 176

flanking the processions of the monks towards the Light. For each episode of the life of Jesus marks a stage of man's journey to the Last Judgment and his resurrection. Yet during the eleventh century —and this is noteworthy—in none of these images is Jesus represented, as yet, as a brother; always He is the Master, the Lord, the Judge. For most of the monks of Europe the incidents of His life on earth were primarily metaphors of the sacred, signs in the secret vocabulary of man's heavenly guides, symbols he was invited to interpret. For the monks the Gospel narrative described a long ascent at whose summit stood Christ in glory, clad in the splendors of God's kingdom. This is why the painters represented the apostles on the gold grounds of the Pericopes as beings outside Time and the human situation. Who in this age could have pictured as fishermen or paupers St James or St Paul, those all-powerful saints whose tomb was the scene of miracles, who launched thunderbolts and fell diseases on those who belittled their authority. No wonder, then, that Christians of the year 1000 were indisposed to think of the human side of Christ. Romanesque art pictured the apostles as denizens of the invisible world, that of the Lord Jesus who, risen from the dead on Easter Day, forbade the Holy Women to touch Him and returned to heaven in the Ascension: the Pantocrator lording it in the apses of Cluny and Tahull.

Nevertheless it is in these images of the living Son of Man, present in this world, that we find the source of the ideology which was later to make the Gothic cathedral a hymn of praise to the Incarnation. For was not the very act of carving in stone, as in the cloister of Santo Domingo de Silos, the figures of men and women grouped around the dead Christ's body, or St Thomas laying his hand on the wound, tantamount to introducing the divine essence into dead matter and creating a concrete figuration of the mystery that the ablest theologians in Europe were seeking to elucidate?

THE WORLD ORDER

"God cannot be seen directly. The contemplative life which begins on earth will reach perfection only when God is seen face to face. The meek and simple soul, when, soaring on the wings of speculation and breaking its carnal fetters, it gazes at things celestial, cannot stay long above its terrene self; ineluctably the weight of the flesh drags it back to earth. It is dazzled by the blinding light of heaven, but is soon recalled to itself. Nevertheless the little it has tasted of the divine lovingkindness has greatly refreshed the soul and soon, fired by abounding love, it hastens to resume its flight." In these words John of Fécamp has well described the monastic ideal. By wholehearted penitence, obedience, humility and a life of brotherly love the monk aspired to break free from the prison-house in which his senses, and his extreme difficulty in subduing them, held eleventh-century man captive. He was engaged in a never-ending struggle to overpass the limits of normal perception and human understanding, to glimpse the splendors of that new world of light which, after the resurrection on the Last Day, will be revealed to all mankind, and even now to gain admittance to that other part of the universe whose stupendous possibilities could be surmised but not perceived as yet. A thirst for God—that is to say for mystery.

For, however learned they might be, the clergy were still unable to intellectualize their faith. Their reasoning powers were in fact as feeble as the wooden ploughshares drawn by half-starved oxen in the farmlands. They could not read Greek and the philosophy of the ancients was, to them, a dead letter. The few scientific treatises bequeathed to them by moribund Rome—a Rome that in any case set little store on intellectual acquirements—did nothing to free their minds of the illogical ways of thinking current among the peasantry. Like the hunters and warriors, their kinsmen, who always felt uneasy when they ventured into strange country or the perils of war, the men of God were constantly on their guard, apprehensive of what might lie in wait

for them. Gerbert, whose culture was so widely admired in the year 1000, had the reputation of being a magician, not a philosopher. He, too, laid snares for the invisible and sought to propitiate the dark powers of fate by spells and ruses. The men of that age had a feeling of being lost in a dark forest. God lurked somewhere in that forest but His presence could be detected only by vague, half-hidden imprints, traces of His handiwork. These made it possible to follow up His trail, and by dint of infinite patience and persistence, not indeed to have sight of Him, but perhaps to catch fleeting gleams of His passing.

The collective rites enabled men, by means of chants and cultic gestures, to share in the mystery of the divine, to quit their earthbound selves, to come in touch with the transcendent and, as Rupert of Deutz put it, themselves to become "prophets," in other words harbingers of God. This is why music and the liturgy ranked highest as a means to grasp the inapprehensible. No one as yet believed this could be done by logic. But exegesis could help, and to this all the mental activities of the time were directed. For from the hidden God came signs, mysterious as Himself, and the first thing needful was to learn to decipher them. Since the revival of education in the Carolingian monasteries all the methods of teaching tended to this end. The Benedictine monk Hrabanus Maurus, *Praeceptor Germaniae* (educator of Germany), who was Abbot of Fulda in the second quarter of the ninth century, was a pioneer in this field. "It occurred to me," he wrote, "to compile a small work dealing not only with the nature of things and the proper usage of words but also with their mystical significance." As things stood, words and nature constituted the two domains accessible to the human mind in which God deigned to manifest Himself. The primary study of the monk was the Scriptures, and the chief function of the teaching of grammar was to train him to make the transition from the textual to the underlying connotation, the mystical significance, of each word. He also scrutinized the created world, searching for the analogies whose unbroken chain could guide him towards enlightenment. "By the manifold differences of figures and forms which the Creator has established between His creatures, He willed that the soul of the man of understanding, by way of what the eyes perceive and the mind apprehends, should attain to a simple knowledge of the divine. For," Glaber continues, "these undeniable relationships between things tell us of God in a silent testimony, at once clear and elegant. There is a continuous progression whereby each thing reveals within itself the other thing; and, after making known the Principle from which it proceeds, tends to revert to its primal entity."

The methodology of the age was based on these assumptions. Since it was God who created the universe perceived by our senses there exists an identity of substance between the Almighty and His creature, or at least some fundamental union, that *universitas* of which John Scotus Erigena spoke. Thus it is possible to discern God by contemplating the world He has made and progressing step by step *per visibilia ad invisibilia*, from things seen to things not seen. The whole creation bears constant witness to the divine purpose and tells us all we need to know. But just as we can arrive at a true understanding of Holy Writ by studying the relations between words, lines and passages in the Old and New Testaments, so a wise study of the infinite diversity of forms and figures in the visible world will lead to the discovery of interrelations, harmonies, an order. For the universe is (as William of Conches and Gero of Reichersberg were later to describe it) "an ordered assemblage of creatures" and, in fact, resembles a *magna citara*, a large zither of many strings. This being so, surely it was natural to see in music a royal road to knowledge, since music depends *par excellence* on a just perception of rhythms and consonances and their orderly arrangement. The science of numbers enjoyed equal favor, since the underlying relations between things, insight into which helped to an understanding of the divine plan, were of an arithmetical order. Hence the high place given the symbolism of numbers in the intellectual disciplines of the age. Glaber, for instance, wrote a long dissertation on "the divine quaternity," the mystic significance of the number four, as exemplified by the Evangelists, the natural elements, the virtues, man's senses, the rivers of paradise, the ages of the world. Thus "quaternity" not only pointed to correspondences between them but also, in the last analysis, reduced the entire universe to a simple formula, symbolic expression of its quintessential unity.

As for art, its sole function was to give visible form to the harmonic structure of the universe, to set out in their due places a certain number of signs, *semata* of the secret language of the inaccessible, by which expression could be given to facts beyond our ken. In short it transposed into simple forms, easily understandable by Christians still in the early stage of initiation, the fruits of the contemplative life. Art was, in fact, a discourse on God, as were music and the liturgy, both of which closely linked up with it. Like them, it aimed at pruning away the tangled overgrowth of appearances and bringing to light the basic values immanent in nature and in the often perplexing text of the Scriptures. Its task was to reveal the underlying structure of the edifice built by the divine architect at the beginning of Time. With this in mind the artists drew on texts recording the words of God, on the images they evoked and on a schema of numbers measuring and defining the rhythms of the universe. Like music and the liturgy, art had recourse to symbols, to novel juxtapositions of discordant values from whose clash a truth flashed forth, and to the rhythms whereby the world is attuned to the breath of God. In their structure, in the positioning of their parts and in the numerical relations between those parts, as in the images they body forth, all the monuments, the gold- and silverware and carvings acted as visual glosses, commentaries on and elucidations of the Scriptures. Concurrently with the development of polyphony and the beginnings of scholasticism, the art language of the period 980-1140 aimed at providing an intuitive understanding of the numinous "something behind everything." More directly than listening or reading, more profoundly than reasoning, the work of art made it possible to apprehend the substantial reality of the universe and learn something of its meaning.

Thus, like music and the liturgy, the architecture and visual arts of the eleventh century were in the nature of an initiation. This is why their forms made no concessions whatever to popular taste. Not in the least intended to appeal to the masses, they catered for a small, restricted élite, for men who had set foot on the ladder of perfection—that is to say primarily for the monks. None the less it was hoped that works of art could take a share—the same as the early type of stage performance then being tried out by the Benedictines at Saint-Benoît-sur-Loire and at St Martial's at Limoges—in the instruction of the common people. In 1025 it was declared at the Synod of Arras that "with the aid of certain painted images the unlettered can perceive what they are unable to get from writing," and the large monumental figurations provided by the "new art" could be seen, on occasion, by the whole Christian community. It was a forthright way of teaching, and some of the largest groups of Romanesque sculpture figuring on the entrances of abbey churches were obviously meant for the edification of the masses and treated, for this reason, in a manner all could understand. (An example is the tympanum at Conques.) But this didactic function was always marginal to creative art, practically all of which emanated from the monks and like the literary, liturgical and musical creations was with few exceptions intended exclusively for them. True, the monastery did not shut its doors against the public, the monks were hospitable folk and on certain days laymen were allowed to attend the services. But they took no real part in them; like the cloister itself, a place of retreat closed to the public, the monastic aesthetic was likewise a "closed" one, introverted, appropriate to men who, turning their backs on the world and all its vanities, headed the pilgrimage of Christendom towards the truth.

For the universe was not static, but subject to the motion God, the Prime Mover, had imposed, and every venture of the spirit was seen as an advance, a progress onward and upward. This progress was made evident and guided by music and the liturgy; and architecture and sculpture, though of their nature unmoving, were called on to implement it. This universal movement took two forms. Firstly, cyclical; the cosmic rhythms, the courses of the stars, the changes of the seasons, day and night, the birth and rebirth of nature—all moved in their appointed orbits, and these continual recurrences were interpreted as symbols of eternity. But in the act of Creation God had stepped forth from His eternity so as to place man, His creature (and even Himself, in virtue of the Incarnation) in Time, and Time ran straight ahead, like a javelin from the hand that

hurls it. Henceforth, all things human, the march of history, individual lives, were given a set direction and the work of art, too, needed to be directed towards a precise point in space, if it was to interpret faithfully the divine plan.

The widespread unrest prevailing in western Europe in this momentous century stimulated the idea of progress, of an advance towards some distant goal. In the code of chivalry the quest of adventure had a leading place; indeed it had become almost an obsession with the younger knights, and it was this that sent them post-haste to the four corners of the known world. The first impression given by a reading of the chronicles of the year 1000 is one of a perpetual departure: of pilgrims flocking to shrines, boatmen speeding to fairs to sell cargoes of wine or colored textiles, hordes of peasants, urged on by a vague hope of better things, setting forth under the lead of some half-crazy fanatic to a promised utopia—soon followed by the crusaders and that strange band of fallen women whom Robert d'Arbrissel, founder (about 1100) of the Order of Fontevrault, mustered and led towards redemption. The monks, however, had vowed to stay in their monasteries and, now that the reform of ecclesiastical mores was taking effect, were rarely be to seen on the roads. Even so, shut up in their cloisters, they applied themselves to studying the movements of the world at large and trying to interpret them.

One of their specific functions was the writing of history. This propensity for chronicling contemporary events and recalling those of the past reflected *inter alia* a desire to maintain a venerable tradition, that of the great prose writers of Antiquity. For the teaching of classical Latin in the cloisters was based on a study of the pagan historians, less attention being given to the poets. Sallust seemed less "unsettling" than Virgil from the Christian viewpoint, and the works of Livy figured in the Lenten readings of the monks of Cluny. But this predilection for historical works (which led to the recopying of those of Gregory of Tours in several scriptoria) accorded with one of the chief concerns of monastic culture. For what, in fact, was history but an "inventory" of the Creation? It presented an image of man, and was not man in the image of God? Orderic Vitalis, himself a Benedictine monk and one of the best historians of the period stressed this point. "We should 'sing' history like a hymn of praise to the Creator and just Ruler of all things." Thus history, "a canticle of glory," was given a place in the elaborate liturgy which was regarded in the monasteries as being both an exemplar of the perfect life and a foretaste of the glories of heaven. Moreover, history helps us to trace within the maze of Time the path that man has followed on his way to salvation, to note successive stages of his progress and to discern its orientation. The panoramic view we get from history makes it easier to choose the surest route and set our course to best advantage. Begun on the day of his creation, man's progress has been continuous, and it will remain so until the end of time. The Holy Bible (and what is the Bible but a book of history, divinely inspired?) represents man's gradual advance towards perfection as falling into three parts or phases. In the first, previous to the Incarnation, he was groping in the dark for enlightenment; then the New Testament opened his eyes to better things. But even so, as compared with what he will be after the Second Coming, man is still in the same "under-developed" state as were the worthies of the Old Covenant vis-à-vis the apostles. Early medieval historians were fond of pointing out that the world was growing old and the end of time drawing near. Eleventh-century man lived in constant expectation and terror of the Day of Judgment on which a wrathful God would soon descend in a blaze of light which would be as it were a final baptism of mankind. Prefigurations, then grace and at last glory—such were the three ages of humanity. To all the men of prayer, and particularly to the monks, placed as they were in the heart of a community racked by apprehensions of the Last Day, befell the duty of pointing out the path to follow and making it smooth. The constant processions in the abbey churches symbolized the march of history seen as an ordered progress timed to the rhythms of eternity. But these processions were charged with even loftier intentions; they mimed the entrance into the Kingdom, into the world invisible. All monastic meditation, all monastic art aspired to solve the mystery, rend the veil and glimpse the pure white light of heaven behind it.

Henceforth it seemed less urgent closely to scrutinize the visible world of nature; what was most needed was to advance beyond it. It was in the Bible, more specifically in certain parts of Holy Writ, that images of truth, intimations of the things to come could be discovered. Since in the year 1000

western man had been living in constant anticipation of the end of the world and, taking guidance from the monks, trying to imagine what was soon to meet his gaze—and since all human history was a record of ephemera counting for next to nothing as against Eternity—the Acts of the Apostles, given their "factual" content, were less closely studied than the Old Testament and the Apocalypse. For the former told of the confidence of the righteous man in the beneficence of God and held out hopes of the coming of the Messiah and the attainment of a Promised Land, after a phase of fears and hopes akin to that through which the world was passing now. As for the Book of Revelation, where find a better image of man's future? Does it not describe "the holy city, new Jerusalem" where the wall "was of pure jasper; and the city was pure gold like unto clear glass... and the city had no need of the sun, neither of the moon to shine in it, for the glory of God did lighten it, and the Lamb is the light thereof." These descriptions of the strange and wonderful city seen by the Apocalyptist were incessantly commented on and illustrated in the cloisters. It was observed that, for all its supramundane splendor, the world St John the Divine saw in his vision did not altogether differ from the visible world—which tended to show that according to the divine plan there existed correspondences between the earthly and the heavenly realms. "As I understand it, that mighty Jerusalem is but a reflection, an aspect of the sublime serenity of God. It is governed by the King of Kings, the Lord reigns over it, and this is why he divides its dwellers into grades. None of its shining gates is panelled with metal, the walls are not of stone, stones as we know them do not enter into its walls. It is built of living stones, and living is the gold that paves the streets, whose sheen is brighter than that of the finest earthly gold. Though built to be the city of the angels, it also welcomes hosts of mortals within its walls; one group of its inhabitants rules it, the other lives and breathes in it." There is, in fact, common ground between the cities of men and the Celestial City.

Therefore, when the heavens roll open, we shall be bewildered, yet not feel quite lost in our new abode. Indeed it is possible for man in his life on earth, helped by what he sees, to picture his existence in the after-life. This was done by all the painters who, in Mozarabic Spain, in Aquitanian monasteries, or for the Ottonian emperors, illustrated the text of the Apocalypse itself and the commentaries on it written by Beatus of Liebana. None of them could have wished for a better stimulus to his creative powers, and none of the monks for a theme more apt to launch them on the "successive soarings heavenwards, winged by the love of God" described by John of Fécamp.

Eleventh-century art interpreted the hopes of men who despaired of ever finding in the world they lived in—a hostile, iron-hearted world—the happiness for which they craved. And since they knew this world was transitory, doomed to pass away (perhaps quite soon), and also because the Church aimed at delivering them from its thrall, the art the age needed was not figural. But neither was it abstract—for the good reason that the two worlds corresponded in essentials, nature was a true reflection of the invisible. So the artist drew inspiration from the forms of nature. But he purified them, stripped them of the grosser elements that would be out of place in the glorious after-life, and tried to find equivalences of the gleams of the transcendent glimpsed in moments of illumination. What he wished to depict was the absolute, an aim that corresponded with the aspirations of the monastic milieu which, indeed, was the source of all the art of the period. For the function of the monastery did not consist solely in offering to God the communal and constant praises which were His due, but also in guiding mankind towards salvation. Thus the monks were expected to take the lead, to precede the rank and file of Christendom in their progress to the Light.

The brotherhood of monks had already broken with the temporal world, was sheltered from it by the cloister, had accomplished half the journey and climbed the mountain-top whence, across the mists, they could see, if dimly as yet, the wonders of the Promised Land. The choir of monks joined forces with the choir of angels and the whole culture, all monastic art, was drawn heavenwards by the love of God.

"Who will give us wings like the wings of a dove, so that we can fly across all the kingdoms of the world and make our way to the courts of heaven? Who will lead us into the city of the Great King, where all that we now read in books and see in a glass darkly shall be made visible to our eyes by the grace of God, in the nearness of God, filling our hearts with joy?" Study perhaps, music and the liturgy assuredly, and with them art would point the way. "Let us, then, lift our hands and hearts towards them [the Blessed], and transcend all the passing shows of earthly life. Let our eyes feast unceasingly on the joys that are promised us and rejoice in all that has been already consummated in the believers who, yesterday, were fighting for Christ and reign with Him today in glory. Let us also rejoice in what has been said to us, infallibly; we shall go to 'the land of the living.'" This lyrical apostrophe penned by an anonymous disciple of John of Fécamp gives an admirable idea of the function then assigned to sacred art. It broke the chains of human bondage and it was on the mystery of God that the portal of the cloister opened.

In the eleventh century sacred art was still attempting to condense the teaching of the Gospels into a few signs serving, like the pillar of fire in the wilderness, to guide God's people to the Promised Land. Some of these figurations are highly complex and reflect the intricate symbolism pervading the teaching of the Doctors of the Church. This applies to one of the compositions painted by a deacon under the supervision of Bishop Bernward of Hildesheim on a Gospel Book, to serve as a commentary on the Gospel of St John. His task was to represent the mystery of the Incarnation and reveal in an image how the Word became flesh; to make plain the conjunction between the eternal and the temporal, nature and supernature, God and man. This is why the scene —like the Ascension in the Limoges Sacramentary which depicts a similar conjunction—is laid out in two registers, one above the other. In the upper one Christ sits in glory, holding two symbols, the Lamb of Redemption and the Book of Life. In the lower we are shown the temporal world. The natural forces, sources of evil but under God's control, are represented in two allegories inspired by classical antiquity: Oceanus riding on Leviathan and the Earth Mother holding in her lap Adam, Eve, the Tree of Knowledge and the Serpent—in other words the personages and setting of the Fall. The irruption of the divine into the affairs of men is signified by five rays striking down through the boundary between the supernal and the terrestrial worlds and alighting on the newborn Babe of Bethlehem. There are few works which illuminate to such remarkable effect the way in which the figural methods of classical art were used to body forth ideas wholly concerned with the world ineffable.

In the apse of San Clemente in Rome and in the tympanum of Jaca Cathedral, the symbolism is much simpler; the Incarnation and God's presence in the created world are conveyed by the sign of the cross. The arms of the cross extend in four directions, in the four dimensions of matter, towards the four winds, the four rivers, the four virtues. The cross seals the universe and sanctifies it. It is also an emblem of the peace God promises to man, of His victory over the turbulence of the age, and in the battle ever raging between Good and Evil. At this time crosses were set up on roads to demarcate the zones around monasteries which served as sanctuaries, and in which acts of violence and pillage were strictly prohibited. The badge worn by the crusaders on their garments proclaimed to all that they were on their way to Golgotha, but it meant more than this. It imprinted on their bodies the mark of the paschal sacrifice, of their alliance with the angelic hosts;

it signified that they belonged to the company of the Blessed and already had an appointed place in the Kingdom of Peace to come on the Last Day. Abbot Odilo of Cluny bade his monks see in the cross a promise of universal salvation, a sign of purification enabling all the human race to follow Christ, their Saviour, into the glory of the celestial realm and by the same token a symbol of the two cardinal virtues of monachism: humility and poverty.

At the close of the tenth century the bishops of Germania—great princes whom the emperor had invested with temporal power over their cities and the surrounding country—united in their person the royal function of administering peace and justice with their pastoral charge. They it was who broke with the tradition of refraining from figuring forth the cross as an instrument of torture. A thousand years after the death of Christ the great wooden crosses erected in the center of the basilicas showed the people, for the first time, not a man wearing a kingly crown, but a suffering victim. The apparition of these crosses marked a turning point in the evolution of religious sensibility in the West. Yet, since Romanesque Europe was expecting at any moment the end of the world and since all the relations of men amongst themselves and with the mysterious powers above were envisaged in terms of hierarchies modeled on those of the feudal system, eleventh-century monks and priests preferred epiphanies of Christ in majesty to effigies of Christ crucified. Theirs was above all the Christ of the Apocalypse.

"Behold, a throne was set in heaven, and one sat on the throne. And he that sat was to look upon like a jasper and a sardine stone: and there was a rainbow round about the throne, in sight like unto an emerald. And round about the throne were four and twenty seats: and upon the seats I saw four and twenty elders sitting, clothed in white raiment; and they had on their heads crowns of gold... And in the midst of the throne, and round about the throne, were four beasts full of eyes before and behind. And the first beast was like a lion, and the second beast like a calf, and the third beast had a face as a man, and the fourth beast was like a flying eagle... And they were full of eyes within: and they rest not day and night, saying, Holy, holy, holy, Lord God Almighty, which was, and is, and is to come." Inspired by this resplendent vision, ablaze with jewels, many artists conjured up an image of it in the dimly lit crypts where the choir of monks could gaze at it when they assembled for their chants; then at the entrances of abbey churches, where it could catch the rays of the setting sun.

BOOK OF PERICOPES OF ABBESS UTA OF NIEDERMÜNSTER (1002-1025): THE CRUCIFIXION.
REGENSBURG, FIRST QUARTER OF THE 11TH CENTURY. FOLIO 3 VERSO, COD. LAT. 13 601, STAATSBIBLIOTHEK, MUNICH.

GOSPEL BOOK OF BISHOP BERNWARD OF HILDESHEIM: THE INCARNATION. ABOUT 1015.
FOLIO 174 RECTO, COD. 18, CATHEDRAL TREASURE, HILDESHEIM.

THE LAST JUDGMENT. TYMPANUM OF THE PORTAL OF THE ABBEY CHURCH OF BEAULIEU-SUR-DORDOGNE
(BEGUN BEFORE THE MIDDLE OF THE 12TH CENTURY).

THE MONOGRAM OF CHRIST FLANKED BY LIONS. LATE 11TH TO MID-12TH CENTURY.
TYMPANUM OF THE WEST PORTAL, CATHEDRAL OF JACA (HUESCA), SPAIN.

APSE MOSAIC IN THE LOWER CHURCH OF SAN CLEMENTE, ROME
(REBUILT IN 1108 BY POPE PASCHAL II).

SACRAMENTARY FROM THE CATHEDRAL OF SAINT-ETIENNE, LIMOGES: THE ASCENSION.
ABOUT 1100. FOLIO 84 VERSO, MS LAT. 9438, BIBLIOTHÈQUE NATIONALE, PARIS.

CROSS OF QUEEN GISELA OF HUNGARY. REGENSBURG, ABOUT 1006.
SCHATZKAMMER DER RESIDENZ, MUNICH.

In the portal of the oratory reserved for celebrations of the praise of God, the skies roll open; for it was here that illustrations of the text of the Apocalypse, initiations into the mystery of the Hereafter, were placed. At Saint-Benoît-sur-Loire they adorn the capitals of the gate-tower. At Saint-Savin painters represented Christ within the globe, His arms outspread, in the vestibule of the church. Two angels beside Him hold up the instruments of the Passion and he is attended by the strange beings peopling the vision of St John the Divine. No place could be better fitted for unveiling the mysteries of the invisible to the man who, turning away from the world, came to the church door so as to draw near to God; and for making known to him the divine event prefigured by the church in its entirety—the return of Jesus in power and glory—before he made his way into the flooding light of the chevet. The porch, a perfect cube, had the same dimensions as the holy Jerusalem seen by the Apocalyptist, "foursquare, and the length is as large as the breadth... Having the glory of God... her light was like unto a stone most precious, even like a jasper stone, clear as crystal." It had a wall great and high pierced with wide gates "and the foundations of the wall were garnished with all manner of precious stones... and the twelve gates were twelve pearls."

But before the light of the Lamb rose on the world, the four angels "holding the four winds of the earth" would raise their trumpets to their lips and sound the end of all things. Therefore it behooved him who entered the church to begin by destroying the seeds of corruption in his soul, stripping himself of his wealth, his weapons, his family, even his personal volition, as did the monk when he made his profession. Then and then only he could join the great procession faring to Jerusalem. "The nations of them which are saved shall walk in the light of it [the City] :and the kings of the earth do bring their glory and honour into it. And the gates of it shall not be shut at all by day : for there shall be no night there. And they shall bring the glory and honour of the nations into it. And there shall in no wise enter into it any thing that defileth, neither whatsoever worketh abomination, or maketh a lie : but they which are written in the Lamb's book of life." Romanesque art was the creation of a group of men who, fired with the love of God, sought to transcend in the cloisters the sordid mediocrity of the world around them, and, fascinated by these visions of the heavenly Jerusalem, set their course to the celestial heights. There at last, in those imagined splendors, their yearning for perfection would be satisfied. To make its earthly simulacrum they assembled all the treasures not to be found in their native land : gold, lapis lazuli, strange perfumes brought from the East. The monks by their daylong liturgy, the groups of pilgrims braving the perils on the way and, soon, the bands of crusaders—all alike advanced, side by side, towards this visionary goal.

BEATUS OF LIEBANA, COMMENTARIES ON THE APOCALYPSE: THE COMING OF THE END OF THE WORLD.
SAINT-SEVER, GASCONY, MID-11TH CENTURY. FOLIO 141 RECTO, MS LAT. 8878, BIBLIOTHÈQUE NATIONALE, PARIS.

BEATUS OF LIEBANA, COMMENTARIES ON THE APOCALYPSE: HORSEMEN OF THE APOCALYPSE. 1086.
FOLIO 151 RECTO, COD. I, CATHEDRAL OF BURGO DE OSMA (SORIA), SPAIN.

MORTVVSAGNVS
DIGNVSHABETVR
SVMERELIBRVM
ILLIVSATQVE
SOLVERESEPTEM
NEMPESIGILLA

HICSACERAGN
VNDIQ:SEPTVS

MILITECAELI
EMITETALBVS

AECCLESIA ECCE

CER   NVA
QVIP   PE
SVSCI   PIT
AG   NI
DIG   NA
CRV   OREM

FULDA LECTIONARY: THE ADORATION OF THE LAMB. LAST THIRD OF THE IOTH CENTURY.
FOLIO I VERSO, MS 2, HOFBIBLIOTHEK, ASCHAFFENBURG.

SACRAMENTARY FROM ST GEREON, COLOGNE: CHRIST ENTHRONED. 980-990.
FOLIO 15 VERSO, MS LAT. 817, BIBLIOTHÈQUE NATIONALE, PARIS.

CHRIST PANTOCRATOR. 1123. FRESCO FROM THE CHURCH OF SAN CLEMENTE, TAHULL.
MUSEO DE ARTE CATALAN, BARCELONA.

CHRIST. ABOUT 1000-1020. CENTRAL PART OF THE GOLD ALTAR IN AACHEN CATHEDRAL.

THE THRESHOLD

Christ Himself had said "I am the door," meaning a portal opening on the celestial world beyond our ken. Throughout the eleventh century an idea gained ground, *sub rosa* to begin with, that the terrible God of the Moissac porch, presiding a tribunal of judges, the God who showed His wrath by visiting mankind with pestilences, famines, wars and the cruel hordes of invaders who had but recently swept in from the East, leaving devastation in their wake—this God was after all not different from the Son; in other words, from man. Hence a tendency to stress the doctrine of the Incarnation, a tendency that was perhaps more active among the populace than in the cloisters.

This much is certain: that a spirit of unrest developed among the masses, setting them against the Church and moving them to lend a readier ear to the discourses of itinerant preachers, laymen and the hermits who, always abundant in Italy, had now taken to roving the countryside of France. These illuminati spoke of a poor God who took no pleasure in the gold heaped round Him by the priests; an inflexible God who disdained the prayers of a worldly, pleasure-loving clergy. For the rank and file of Christians the sacramental rites opened the door of salvation, and the reform movement in progress in the Church quickened their desire to see these propitiatory gestures made by purer hands.

This was what the townsfolk of Milan had in mind when they demanded that their priests abstain from women and revolted against their simoniac archbishop. They were infuriated by the moral decadence of the priesthood, whose task it was to ensure a "magical" communication between man and the divine. But what, one wonders, can it have been that incited the peasant from the Champagne region whom Rudolph Glaber describes as a madman to an iconoclastic frenzy, to tear down crucifixes and smash images of the Saviour? What attribute of divinity was specially revered by those thirteen

canons at Orléans "who seemed purer than the others" and whom King Robert in 1023 condemned to be burnt as heretics? And when the group in Aquitaine who "denied the virtue of the Cross, the efficacy of Holy Baptism, all the doctrines of the Holy Church, abstained from certain kinds of food, had the air of monks and feigned chastity," were suspected of leanings towards Manichaeism, was it not because they over-emphasized the conflict all men sensed between the God of the Bible and the powers of darkness and, in anguished expectation of the End of Time, rejected over-drastically all things carnal? Maybe they were also protesting against an excess of ritualism, and, tormented by the problem of the existence of evil in the world, perplexed by the mystery of the Incarnation, asked to be given more than mere ceremonial—a clearer explanation of the true nature of Christ and how it was that this divine essence should have dwelt among men and "saved their souls alive."

It was certainly the spiritual malaise of the age, this dissatisfaction with the *status quo*, now manifesting itself with ever-increasing intensity, that gave rise to the two movements which developed after 1050, within the Church itself. One was a tendency to discuss, using the apparatus of reasoning and dialectic, those central mysteries which were giving pause to the "plain man's faith": the Trinity, the Eucharist and indeed the whole question of the intervention of God in the affairs of men. Already in the reformed monasteries of Normandy John, a nephew of William of Volpiano, who in 1028 became abbot of Fécamp, had scrutinized the text of the Synoptic Gospels, seeking to discover means of delivering man from his condition, from the world of sin which held him in thrall. He saw in Jesus the Way, leading us to the light of Godhead. "He was circumcised so as to cut us free from the vices of the flesh and the mind; presented in the temple so as to bring us, pure and sanctified, towards God; baptized so as to wash us clean of our offences; tempted, so as to defend us against the onslaughts of the devil; made captive to free us from the power of the Enemy; mocked so as to rescue us from the derision of the demons; crowned with thorns so as to extricate us from the thorns of the primordial curse; raised on the cross to draw us to Him; given to drink of vinegar and gall so as to lead us to a land of endless joy; sacrificed, a lamb without blemish, on the altar of the cross so as to take away the sins of the world." John of Fécamp's theology followed the winding roads of the anagogical method; images and words join forces, all being oriented towards a theophany, a manifestation of the blinding light of God. It told of a mysterious alchemy whereby base matter is transmuted into the pure gold of the unknowable. But it also pointed the way to St Anselm's major work *Cur Deus homo*? Italian by birth, Anselm too was abbot of a Norman monastery; then, from 1094 to 1098 Archbishop of Canterbury. In *Cur Deus homo?* he answered the question asked in this title on scholastic lines and thus inaugurated the doctrine of the Incarnation which was to be bodied forth on so many Gothic monuments.

Meanwhile, finding the Apocalypse less inspiring than the rest of the New Testament, some monks began preaching against the ceremonial pomp and splendor of the Cluniac liturgy, and advocated a way of life that did not seek to imitate the glory of the seraphim, the grandeur of the New Jerusalem, but following in the footsteps of the Master, converted God's servants into true apostles, poor and humble. In 1088, the very year when Abbot Hugh installed the workyard of the new basilica, the great days of Cluny were over. A new type of monachism, all for austerity, was setting in. Priests were now disposed to lead a communal life like that of the monks, but without ceasing to go forth and preach the Gospel to the people, the body of canons was amending its ways, conforming to a stricter Rule, and, thanks to the activities of the Gregorian reformers, there was a revival of the dignity of the episcopate.

Thus the soil was prepared for the flowering of great cathedrals in the near future and, as the result of an intensification of the religious sensibility, less importance was attached to the ceremonial of the liturgy. What all thoughtful Christians wanted was a religion that no longer focused attention on the promised glories of the celestial Jerusalem but stressed the humanity of the Son of God.

This change in the spirit of the age was also promoted by the religious movements that led to the crusades. When, instead of descending into dark crypts to venerate relics of tutelary saints whose talismanic power had replaced that of the heathen gods, pilgrims elected to travel to the tomb of Christ, and when the penitential rites imposed on knights anxious for their soul's salvation diverted the aggressive instincts of these warriors towards a pious journey to the Holy Sepulchre, the Cross began to have a new significance. Hitherto it had been but one of many symbols of God's power over the universe. A cosmic sign conjoining Space and Time, a Tree of Life, it stood for the entirety of the cosmos, and if God had chosen it to be the instrument of his Son's death, this was by reason of its esoteric values. When Christ's body hung on it, He was not shown racked by pain, but as a crowned king, living and triumphant. The cross was in fact an emblem of victory and kings made much of it; King Robert even played the part of Jesus in the passion play of Holy Week. But gradually, after the year 1000, the symbol was given more actuality and, in the process, a new orientation. Thus when in 1010 a monk of the Abbey of Saint-Martial at Limoges saw "an enormous cross hovering in the sky with Our Lord's body hanging on it and an abundant rain of tears streaming from His eyes," this vision brought to his mind the sufferings of Christ. It was a similar emotional response that led the knights to observe the Truce of God every Thursday and Friday "in memory of the Last Supper and of the Passion of Our Lord." The ordering of golden crosses from the artificers working for the royal household and their distribution to churches had long been a privilege reserved to emperors and kings. Now, however, they lost this monopoly—as they were losing all their regal powers, which were passing into the hands of the feudal nobility. In the eleventh century more and more people wore crosses. In 1095 all who embarked on a journey to the Holy Land had the sacred sign sewn on their garments. Thus they too became avatars of Christ, as hitherto only anointed kings had been. It was the earthly life of God incarnate they were going to relive in Palestine. When in the year 1000 some learned clerics were asked "what such a great concourse of people at Jerusalem could signify," they replied that in their opinion it was a portent of "the coming of that son of perdition, Antichrist" and the imminence of the Last Day. Had it not been foretold that one premonitory sign would be that all the nations "made smooth the road of the East," by which he (the Antichrist) was to come and the nations prepare to go forth to meet him? But the pilgrims came back full of pregnant memories. Was it because he had visited the Holy Sepulchre so recently that the Count of Angoulême hoped to die "adoring and kissing the wood of our Saviour's cross"? This much is certain: that the many devout travelers who were to be seen in those days hastening like swarms of bees or migratory birds towards the Promised Land, prompted in many cases by the eschatological apprehensions of the age and fascinated by the prospect of setting eyes on the Holy City, returned to their villages, castles, cathedrals (if they had not died en route) with a new awareness of the living Jesus.

Did they already identify the Son of Man at whose tomb they had worshipped with the transcendent image of justice and domination that sculptors of the year 1100 were placing on portals of the abbey churches in which the "new" art was coming to fruition? In Carolingian times an important liturgical function was assigned to the church porch, for it was there that certain funerary rites were solemnized. Hence the emphasis on Christ the Saviour, and the placing in the porch of scenes of the Second Coming and the Last Judgment, pivot of the entire iconography of the age. The porch represented the celestial Jerusalem but also a way of access to the world of light awaiting the Christian on the day of resurrection. Suger was the creator, about 1140, of what we call the Gothic. But he was a member of the Benedictine Order and his theology, like that of all eleventh-century monks, was based on an elaborate system of analogies whose sequences and associations were thought to lead the questing spirit of the recluse to an understanding of the mysteries of godhead. He therefore adopted *in toto* the symbolism of Romanesque art, which may be said to culminate in his great Abbey of Saint-Denis. For its portal he composed dedicatory verses (which can be interpreted in various ways) setting forth the purport of the "noble work" he had in mind. "Of that which shines herein"—that is to say, within the edifice but also in the heart of the world, the heart of Time, the heart of man, the heart of God—"this golden door gives an intimation." Art, in other words, prefigures the transcendent realities which will be revealed to the human soul once it has crossed the barrier of death and seen the heavens opening to reveal the *verum lumen* (the True Light) on the Last Day. "For by way of material beauties the mind is elevated to true Beauty and by the light of its splendors raised up from the earth in which it lay buried, and enters into heaven." It is no overstatement to say of eleventh-century art that it makes God a visible presence, that it illuminates and aspires to proffer man the noblest means to rebirth in the world of light beyond the grave.

Among the many discoveries, inventions and changes in the field of creative art to which the making of the Christian West gave rise, none was more remarkable and unexpected than the deliberate return to monumental sculpture. Imbued with memories of classical antiquity, imperial art had for several centuries exalted the values of the free-standing figure realized in three dimensions of space, which gradually superseded the incised design and the tendencies to geometric abstraction and plant forms of barbarian art. The first bold forward step was taken by prelates of the Ottonian renaissance when they commissioned sculptures of sacred figures: Christ crucified and bronze reliefs of Biblical scenes. But the truly revolutionary move was made towards 1100 when in the Romanesque part of Christendom, in the provinces where Latinity had never wholly died out, sculptors were called on to make divine figures having the full plasticity of Roman statues. Benedictine monks had no qualms about placing them in the portals of the churches, no longer near the altar where they were almost hidden from sight during the services, but publicly, where all could gaze on them at leisure.

We have no means of ascertaining in what monastery this new departure, this triumph over the Christians' age-old mistrust of the evil lures of pagan statuary, originated. Which is the oldest Romanesque tympanum, that of Moissac or that of Cluny, is an open question. For the chronology of works of art in this period is highly conjectural. These carved figures were solemn offerings to Almighty God; they belonged to Eternity, not to Time, and no one thought of dating them. True, we have good reasons for believing that when St Hugh of Cluny undertook to embellish the edifice whose building he had undertaken, and whose every element he wished to decorate as soon as it was set in place, he summoned to the mother abbey the most skilled artisans in Christendom. Can it be assumed that the best of these sculptors had already carved the stone portals of the small churches in the Brionnais region whose adornments may be equally well regarded as belated reflections of the great Cluniac art? It seems safer to assume that the artists called on to devise the grandiose ensemble that about 1115 came into being at Cluny on the threshold of the largest basilica in the world —and, before this, to carve the capitals in the choir—took inspiration from models found in the ornamental work produced by the Mosan metalworkers, in which the classical traditions of Ottonian art continued to have an active part.

CHURCH OF SAINT-PIERRE AT MOISSAC, NEAR TOULOUSE: SOUTH PORTAL. 1110-1115.

CHURCH OF THE MADELEINE AT VÉZELAY, BURGUNDY: PORTAL OF THE NAVE. ABOUT 1120-1150.

CATHEDRAL OF SAINT-LAZARE AT AUTUN, BURGUNDY: MAIN PORTAL. ABOUT 1120-1130.

There can be no question that both Gislebertus, who signed his work at Autun, and the Vézelay master derived their skill perhaps, in any case their inspiration, from the famous workyard of Cluny. From the viewpoint of an historian of the culture and aesthetic sensibility of the age, all the large-scale works of this order, contemporary with the First Crusade and the wave of religious fervor that ensued, marked an important stage in the evolution of western Christendom. Hitherto images of Christ had never been located in the visible world. Even when they were not purely abstract, esoteric symbols in the form of the Cross, Alpha and Omega, or the sacred monogram were always given (as on the illuminated pages of Ottonian liturgic manuscripts) a completely unrealistic setting. The figures, too, without weight or thickness, remind us of Rudolph Glaber's description of the souls in Purgatory. All, in fact, belonged to that unseen realm whose underlying order was embodied in the architecture of the Romanesque church.

Thus at the very time when dialecticians in the chapter schools of Neustria were beginning to discuss the nature of the three Persons of the Trinity and trying to discover how God made Himself man, monumental sculptors were transposing these images from the supernatural world, bringing them down to earth and embodying them in the hardest, most durable material. In so doing they anticipated that trend of religious thought which was soon to replace the fantasies of the Apocalypse with the human virtues of the New Testament in the cathedrals of the Ile-de-France, virtues of which these images were incarnations.

True, one feels that the sculptor of the Moissac Christ, a despotic figure surrounded by the tetramorph and twenty-four music-making elders, was still poles apart from this humanized conception of Our Lord. But already in the Autun porch this distance is reduced; we see Jesus seated among the apostles, terrestrial beings, whose faces express love rather than numinous awe. We see these same apostles caught in the graceful swirling movement of the Vézelay tympanum, which evokes not the world invisible, but, for the first time, the world of man, the world whose time is measured by the twelve months of the year, and whose space extends to the confines of the world, peopled by strange races. It is as if, on the brink of the twelfth century, the Romanesque dream-world was fading out and the Gospel message at long last being diffused everywhere, freeing man from his atavistic fears and urging him on to conquest. On the threshold of Vézelay, where St Bernard was soon to preach a crusade before the King of France, there then arose the most majestic figure of the living God that Christendom had seen.

CHURCH OF THE MADELEINE AT VÉZELAY, BURGUNDY: CHRIST, DETAIL OF THE PORTAL OF THE NAVE. ABOUT 1120-1150.

INDEX OF NAMES

LIST OF ILLUSTRATIONS

PHOTOGRAPHS BY

Alinari-Anderson, Florence (pages 44 top, 126), A.C.L., Brussels (pages 105 bottom, 106 top), Archives photographiques, Paris (pages 147, 148), Maurice Babey, Basel (pages 20/21, 36, 37, 44 bottom, 66/67, 69, 76 left and right, top and middle, 77 upper right and bottom, 78, 88, 96, 99, 101, 102, 107 lower left, 108, 117 top and bottom, 119, 121, 127 upper right and bottom, 128, 140, 141, 143, 149, 150, 161, 162/163, 164, 165, 166, 173 bottom, 175, 176 upper left, 188 top and bottom, 194, 197, 203, 204, 205, 207,) B. Henry Beville, Alexandria, Va. (pages 34, 118), Bernard Biraben, Bordeaux, by courtesy of the Commissariat Général au Tourisme de France (page 127 upper left), Robert Braunmüller, Munich (page 191), Claudio Emmer, Milan (page 29), Foto Fuchs, Aschaffenburg (page 195), Marc Garanger, Paris (page 142), Photographie Giraudon, Paris (page 45 left and upper right, 76 lower right), Atelier Niko Haas, Trier (page 106 bottom), A. F. Kersting, London (page 89), Raymond Laniepce, Paris (pages 24, 30, 87 top and bottom), Louis Loose, Brussels (pages 22, 39), Erwin Meyer, Vienna (page 14), Umberto Orlandini, Modena (page 65), Karl H. Paulmann, Berlin (page 176 lower right), Studio R. Remy, Dijon (pages 77, 105 top), Herbert Rost, Darmstadt (page 71), Jean Roubier, Paris (pages 43, 45 lower right, 46), Guido Sansoni, Florence (page 40), Oscar Savio, Rome (pages 139, 189), Scala, Florence (pages 138, 168), Schmölz-Huth, Cologne (pages 23, 198), Studio für Fotografie, Tübingen (page 120), Hermann Wehmeyer, Hildesheim (pages 35, 187), Yan, Toulouse (pages 100, 174 top and bottom), and the photographic services of the following libraries and museums: Bergen, Universitetet, Historisk Museum (page 75), Cologne, Kölnisches Stadtmuseum, Rheinisches Bildarchiv (page 107 upper right), London, British Museum (pages 26, 68), Munich, Bayerische Staatsbibliothek (pages 28, 33, 38, 169, 173 top, 186), Paris, Bibliothèque Nationale (pages 70, 90, 125, 170, 190, 193, 196). Photographic material for the illustration on page 27 kindly lent by Verlag Fredebeul & Koenen KG, Essen.

II

THE EUROPE
OF THE CATHEDRALS

1140-1280

CONTENTS

THE ART OF FRANCE

The meaning of the term "cathedral" is a bishop's church, containing his *cathedra* or throne, and since this was always located in a city, the art of the European cathedrals reflects the revival of urban life that took place in the twelfth and thirteenth centuries. During that period towns grew steadily larger and wealthier, proliferated their suburbs along the main roads and, north of the Alps, became the chief centers of the most advanced culture of the time. But they drew their vitality almost entirely from the neighboring countryside. Many noblemen preferred town to country life and it was to the towns that the produce of their domains was carted; hence the ever increasing prosperity of the merchants trading in wheat, wool and wine. The town owed its affluence to the country and, by the same token, the art of the cathedrals thrived on the wealth of the rural areas, and it was brought to fruition, if indirectly, by the labors of innumerable peasants, wheat and vine growers, builders of dikes and watercourses, who exploited indefatigably the resources of the soil. That plenteous crops and prolific vineyards lay at the origin of the towers of the noble cathedral of Laon was frankly recognized by the architects when they placed at the summit the effigies of plough-oxen, and on the capitals clusters of vineshoots. Similarly the cycle of the seasons was represented on the façades of the cathedrals of Amiens and Paris by images of rustic labors. A well-earned tribute, for it was that peasant sharpening his scythe, and those others planting and layering vines whose humble toil gave rise to the great churches. Throughout the period the new zest for intensive husbandry was nowhere more pronounced than in northwestern Gaul, and the most fertile regions of the world were brought into full production in the plains surrounding Paris. This is why the art which now arose was commonly described as "the art of France." It came to its full flowering in the province which then bore this name, where Clovis had died and which lay between Chartres and Soissons, its seminal center being the city of Paris.

First city of medieval Europe to become a real—and royal—capital (which Rome had long ceased to be), Paris was in fact the capital not of an empire, nor of Christendom, but of a realm, the Kingdom of France. The urban art which matured in Paris under the forms we now call Gothic was an essentially royal art, and its leading themes celebrate a sovereignty, that of Christ and the Virgin. For in the Europe of the Cathedrals the power of the kings was gaining ground, freeing itself from the shackles of the feudal system. Before formulating, for his church of Saint-Denis, the rules of his new aesthetic, Abbot Suger had built up in the service of the Capetians the image of a suzerain king, apex of a hierarchical pyramid, vested with and concentrating all the powers that had hitherto been dispersed among the feudal overlords. Of all the States then in process of reconstruction, the largest and best organized was the kingdom whose monarch had his seat in the city of Paris. Throughout Latin Christendom no other ruler had more renown and wealth than Louis IX (St Louis). And this wealth flowed in through all the channels provided by seignorial dues and the financial obligations of vassalage, levies on cultivated land and vineyards.

Moreover Louis IX, a deeply religious man, did not regard his function as being merely temporal and secular; he felt himself, and wished, to be above all a faithful servant of the Church. From Joinville's *Histoire de Saint Louis* we learn how, after a light-hearted youth, St Louis decided to forsake all worldly vanities, "to love God with all his heart," and to do his best to live as his friends the Franciscans told him Christ had lived. Fifty years earlier much of the wealth of the richest monarchs, such men as Henry II of England and Richard Cœur de Lion, had been squandered on mundane pleasures and the recreations of the knightly caste. To the mind of St Louis, austerity befitted the King of France whom the rite of coronation had made the Lord's Anointed, and in a sense an avatar of Christ.

Had it not given him the miraculous power of healing sick men by the laying on of hands and an equal place among the bishops consecrated with the same rites? Thus the king devoted his wealth to the service of God, to works of piety, and built not palaces but churches. True, like the bishops, St Louis clad himself on occasion in fine raiment, but he did not adorn his residences and in the whole tenor of his life observed a strict simplicity. When administering justice he sat under an oaktree at Vincennes or on a terrace. It was he, rather than the German emperors, who inherited the fabled glory of Charlemagne, theme of the medieval verse chronicles. When, again like Charlemagne, he drew freely on the royal treasury for the building of a chapel, he was following in the footsteps of his ancestors who by reason of their lavish donations to the bishops, could rank as the true builders of the new cathedrals that had sprung up in France.

Sponsored as it was by royal patronage, the art of France was basically liturgical; though it is known to have included non-religious works, these were of a minor, perishable nature and none of them has survived. Its major forms were devised by a small group of wealthy prelates in direct contact with the king, a group that represented, on the intellectual level, the most advanced thinking of the day. Holding positions of the highest rank in the feudal hierarchy, the bishops (and the canons who shared with them the worldly goods of Mother Church) owned the best lands and enormous barns which the tithes exacted at each harvest filled to repletion. They levied taxes on urban fairs and markets and part of the profits from trade and agriculture found its way into their coffers. The other part went to the lay nobility, much of it being absorbed by the festivals which bulked so large in the age of chivalry. But the nobility, mindful of their immortal souls, also made substantial offerings to God, that is to say to his representatives on earth. Moreover the social order of the time was so constructed that peasants and middle class were expected and enjoined to deliver a large part of their earnings to the military and ecclesiastical authorities. The poor were systematically kept on the brink of destitution, the wealth accruing from the development of agriculture was used to provide for the luxury of a favored few, and crowning the pyramidal structure of the State was the king who, conscious of being himself a priest, was surrounded by bishops when he made his deci-

sions. In short the French cathedrals, an apanage of royalty, were an outcome of the new prosperity of the countryside.

Under the auspices of a stable and enlightened monarchy the art of France acquired a fine serenity and little by little sculptors mastered the expression of the smile, token of a new-found joy in life. And since the sacred and the secular were combined in the *persona* of the king, the temporal entering into a mystical conjunction with the eternal, this joy was not only of a mundane order. The art of the cathedrals culminated in the celebration of a God incarnate, in figurations of an inviolable union between the Creator and his creatures. It sublimated to a transcendent plane and, so to speak, sacralized the careless rapture of a young knight galloping across the flower-strewn fields of May and trampling down light-heartedly the growing crops.

But it would be a mistake to read into the moral climate of the thirteenth century the serene joy expressed in the faces of the crowned Virgins and smiling angels. For life was hard, not to say barbarous. It was an age of storm and stress, ravaged by internecine conflicts and social unrest. The bishop of Laon who planned the new cathedral could not forget that his predecessor had been brutally massacred in a revolt of the townsfolk. In 1233, infuriated by the exactions of another prelate, also a cathedral builder, the citizens of Reims rose up against him, forced him to close down the workyards for a time and to dismiss the masons and sculptors in his service. Such troubles were only incidental and sporadic. But they throw light on the latent fissures in the structure of the feudal social order, firmly established though it was. In it three groups were constantly at odds: the priesthood, the nobility, and the oppressed, exploited, submerged masses. For even the knights were in conflict with the Church, with its rigid moral code, with everything that tended to restrict the free exercise of their favorite activities: fighting and lovemaking. And artistic creation, too, was hampered by this nexus of conflicting purposes.

Still, there is no denying the relative stability of this social system in the period from 1140 to 1280. The "underground" movements which gradually modified its structure hardly affected the closed circle of clerics which commissioned artists and directed building operations, and in practice had little effect on the process of artistic creation itself. Its evolution coincided, by and large, with the progress of religious thought. We have, then, to give more attention to the theology than to the sociology of the period if we wish to understand its art.

During this phase of European history, marked by a steady increase in production and commercial activity, men's minds were the prey of conflicting emotions: on the one hand an urge for amassing wealth and profiting by the new prosperity, and, on the other, an idealization of the life of poverty and chastity enjoined on the true Christian as the surest means to the salvation of his immortal soul. In this age, when the great European kingdoms were taking form, there was another problem that weighed heavily on the minds of the Christian community: which of the two establishments spiritual and temporal—Pope or Emperor, Church or King— should wield sovereign power and regulate the conduct of society. And both these conflicts tended to merge into a wider, more fundamental issue, the antagonism between orthodox faith and the deviations of heresy. A prime concern of every bishop and, soon, of every monarch, was to combat the "false prophets," to refute their arguments and to hound down their sectaries. An equally urgent need was felt to rid the Christian faith of the uncertainties of its early, prelogical phase, to formulate a comprehensive, clear-cut body of doctrine, to make its tenets known and acceptable to the public at large, and by demonstrating the fallacies of heresy to lead back to the fold all who had strayed from the Christian's proper path. The outbreaks of heresy so frequent at this time were symptomatic of the growing pains of Western culture as a whole—hence their violence. During the twelfth and thirteenth centuries an awareness of the prevalence and perils of heresy played a leading part in the development of an art that claimed to be an exposition of the truth.

No portraits were made in this period. It costs an effort to discern behind the Angel's smile a reminiscence of the drunkard's leer, the hollow cheeks of the mendicant, the set lips of the inquisitor. None the less these elements are latent under the mask of ritual serenity. Gothic statuary aimed at presenting an ideal image of man made perfect. But we must never forget that the men of the time lived in a world where brutality and rapine were the order of the day: also that the rest of Europe was far from accepting in their entirety the canons of Gothic art. For the Western world was still divided up into watertight compartments, and many regions stubbornly refused to conform to a program initiated in France and enacted by French kings. Attempts were made to enforce it in certain provinces, but there were always marginal areas of resistance in outlying regions. When we seek to ascertain the true relations between the early manifestations of a new creative art, the structure of the social order and the prevailing climate of opinion, we must never lose sight of this geographical factor. For the horizons of European civilization were greatly modified in the years between 1140 and 1280. Not as the result of a gradual mutation, but by leaps and bounds. Here chronology acquires a determinant value. In this essay we propose to chart the successive stages (and also the permanent elements) of the various forces which confronted and reacted on each other throughout this period.

I

GOD IS LIGHT
1140-1190

UPPER FRONT OF THE PORTABLE ALTAR OF STAVELOT: SCENES FROM THE LIFE OF CHRIST, ABOUT 1175.
MUSÉES ROYAUX D'ART ET D'HISTOIRE, BRUSSELS.

SAINT-DENIS

In 1140 the most royal of churches was not a cathedral but an abbey: Saint-Denis-en-France. After the reign of Dagobert, Clovis's successors chose this sanctuary to be the royal mausoleum and the three dynasties which ruled successively the kingdom of the Franks used it as their burial place. Charles Martel, Pepin the Short and Charles the Bald were interred in the royal vault beside Hugh Capet, his ancestors the dukes of France and his descendants the Capetian kings. Compared with Saint-Denis and its series of royal tombs, Aix-la-Chapelle (Aachen) plays a secondary, not to say adventitious role in the annals of European royalty. It was in the crypt of Saint-Denis that the genealogical tree of the French monarchy, which Clovis had founded with God's aid in virtue of his baptism, had its roots and there, beside the tombs of their forbears, that successive kings of France laid their crowns and the emblems of their power. It was there, too, that they went to take the oriflamme (the sacred banner of red and yellow silk) before starting on their campaigns; there that they prayed for victory, there that the chronicles of their exploits were recorded. This "master abbey" figured prominently in the legends of medieval France and furnished many of the themes of the epic *chansons* which, centering on the heroic figure of Charlemagne, hymned the praises of *la douce France*, her monarchs and their deeds. Thanks to royal benefactions, the abbey became extremely wealthy. It had control of the great Parisian vineland and the big annual Foire du Lendit, where the Seine boatmen loaded casks of wine for export to England and Flanders. That on the brink of the twelfth century its wealth was constantly increasing was due to the rising prosperity of trade and agriculture, and its prestige, too, increased along with that of the kings in Paris. On Saint-Denis converged that slow movement which had been gradually orienting the driving forces of Christianity away from the Empire, which the Ottos had reintegrated in Germany, towards the kingdom of the fleur-de-lys. Neustria was having its revenge on Teutonic hegemony. Taken over by the Capetians, the Carolingian tradition reverted here, beside the tombs of Dagobert and Charles the Bald, to its place of origin, the true "land of the Franks," i.e. the plain of France (not Franconia). And the new art that came to birth at Saint-Denis clearly demonstrated this reversion.

It was due to the efforts of a single man, Abbot Suger. Though born of poor parents, he was a schoolfellow of the king and thanks to their lifelong friendship rose to a position of great eminence. On his appointment as abbot of Saint-Denis, he gave deep thought to the symbolic values of the abbey of which he was in charge. He saw in his post an honor of the highest order calling for the pomp and dignity befitting it. For he was a Benedictine, and his conception of the monastic way of life did not involve any idea of poverty or withdrawal from temporal affairs. Suger kept to the Cluniac path and, like St Hugh of Cluny, believed that the office of abbot ranked high in the terrestrial hierarchy and that it was his duty to embellish Saint-Denis by all the means in his power, for the greater glory of God. "Everyone is entitled to his own opinion," he wrote. "Personally I deem it right and proper that all that is most valuable should be employed, exclusively, to celebrate the Holy Eucharist. If golden pouring vessels, golden phials, little golden mortars were used, according to the word of God and at the Prophet's bidding, to collect the blood of goats and calves and red heifers, how much more must golden vessels, precious stones, and whatever is most valued among created things, be laid out with continual reverence and full devotion for the reception of the blood of Christ! True, there are some who disagree and say that all that is needed for this celebration of the Eucharist is a saintly mind, a pure heart; and we, too, explicitly affirm that it is these that chiefly matter. But we maintain that we must do homage also through the outer ornaments of sacred vessels, more particularly in the service of the Holy Sacrifice;

that the purity of their content may be seconded by noble exteriors." With these "noble exteriors" in mind, Suger devoted the great wealth of his abbey to creating a magnificent setting for the services taking place in it. In the period 1135-1144, despite violent opposition from the partisans of "total poverty," he rebuilt and adorned the abbey church. He was working, he declared, for the honor of God and the kings of France, the dead kings who were his guests and the living king, his friend and benefactor. Proud of his achievement, he described it at length in his *Liber de rebus in administratione sua gestis* and its supplement, *Libellus de consecratione ecclesiae S. Dionysii*. From these we gather that he saw this royal monument as a synthesis of all the aesthetic innovations he had admired in the course of his travels in southern Gaul. But he also wished to excel them and aimed at creating something new, at bringing Aquitanian and Burgundian procedures into line with the imperial, Carolingian, truly Frankish tradition. With this in view he imported into Neustria the Austrasian aesthetic and the sophisticated artistry of Aix-la-Chapelle and the Meuse region, and fused them into the Romanesque art which had made a bid to replace them. But it was above all as an *œuvre théologique*—a sermon in stone—that he envisaged the rebuilt abbey. And, naturally, the theology he had in mind was that of St Denis (Dionysius), the abbey's patron saint, first Christian martyr in the land of France.

The kings of France were buried near the earliest tomb in the royal abbey, that of the martyred saint, the Apostle of the Gauls. Suger and all his monks, like the abbots who had preceded him, identified this heroic missionary with St Paul's disciple, Dionysius the Areopagite mentioned in the Acts of the Apostles, reputedly the author of several treatises on Christian mysticism which had an enormous influence on medieval thought. Actually, however, these famous books, which were devoutly preserved in the royal monastery, were written by an unknown author in the very early Middle Ages. In 758 the pope had presented a Dionysius manuscript to Pepin the Short, King of the Franks, who had been educated at Saint-Denis; next, in 807, Louis the Pious, emperor of the West, was given a second copy by the East Roman emperor, Michael the Stammerer. The original Greek text of the works of the Pseudo-Areopagite was translated into Latin by Hilduin, an abbot of Saint-Denis,

and from now on the *Theologia Mystica* was closely studied at Saint-Denis, notably by Suger who derived all his ideas from it. Dante assigned a high place in the *Paradiso* (XXVIII) to

> Dionysius [who] with so great desire
> To contemplate these Orders set himself,
> He named them and distinguished them as I do.
> (Translation by H. W. Longfellow)

For the texts attributed to Dionysius (*Concerning the Celestial Hierarchy*, *Concerning Ecclesiastical Hierarchy*) present the universe as a structure whose orders are disposed in a precise hieratical gradation. Suger clearly derived his conception of the social order with the king at its apex from these writings. Basic to the teaching of Dionysius is the principle: God is Light. Of this initial Light, uncreated and creative, every creature has a share. He receives and reflects the divine illumination according to his capacity, that is to say according to the place assigned him in the scale of things and the level to which the ultimate divine Source has appointed him. Born of the *vera lux* of Godhead, the universe is one vast field of light, streaming down from that Source which gives each created thing its being and its place in the universal hierarchy. This light pervades the whole material universe, visible and invisible, binds all the orders of existence together in their Maker's love and, since every object reflects light to some extent, this "first radiance" starts a chain of reflections that, after striking down into the heart of darkness, sets up a counterflow of light, returning to its Source. Thus the primal act of Creation—"let there be light"—called forth *per se* a reciprocal upward motion towards the invisible and ineffable Being from whom all proceeds. Everything reverts to Him, using as stepping stones those visible things which at successive levels of the hierarchy reflect better and better His transcendent light. The created ascends to the Uncreated by a ladder of analogies and concordances. Each rung of this ladder brings man a step nearer to an apprehension of God and a perception of that superessential light which is more or less veiled in every earthbound creature in so far as it is refractory to His illumination. Yet every created being reveals to some extent, proportionate to its love of the Creator, the spark of light within it. Here we have the key to that "new art," the art of France, of which Suger's church is the perfect paradigm: an art of clarity, of progressive illumination. "The dull mind rises to truth through that which is material. And, seeing the light, is resurrected from its former submersion." Suger had these lines inscribed on the portal of his church, to act as an initiation and explain its function.

Suger began work with the porch. Built in the Carolingian tradition and including portions of the ancient basilica, this part of the earlier church still gives an impression of massiveness and gloom. One reason for this is that it stands for the first stage of the Christian's journey out of darkness towards the light. Another, that it befitted the entrance of the royal monastery to produce an effect not only of compelling power and regal majesty, but also of military efficiency, since in those days the king was primarily a war lord—an effect that is heightened by two crenellated towers included in the façade. None the less these towers are pierced by a series of arches and the light of the setting sun enters the interior of the edifice through the three portals, above one of which is a rose window facing west, first of its kind in any Christian church. Its light falls on the three lofty chapels dedicated to the celestial hierarchy, to the Virgin, St Michael and the angels. On the forefront of his church Suger gave visible form to his theology and created what was to be the prototype of the façades of the cathedrals of the West.

But it is in the new transparent choir that we find the greatest aesthetic innovation. Here, at the far end of the church, terminal point of the liturgical progress towards the rising sun, he installed a source of light untrammelled, a dazzling approach to the divine presence, by doing away with walls. With this in mind he bade his master-mason exploit all the architectural possibilities of what had hitherto been no more than a crossing composed of pointed vaults. Thus between 1140 and 1144 there arose "a series of chapels set out in a semicircle, thanks to which the whole church was flooded with an all-pervasive light pouring through marvelously translucent windows." In the early twelfth century it was found necessary to provide abbey churches with a great number of chapels. These were needed because every monk now held the rank of priest and was called on to celebrate daily masses. The plan of an ambulatory equipped with radiating niches had already been employed in Romanesque churches and Suger applied himself to making these niches pervious to light. This he did by modifying the structure of the vaults in order to open out bays, and by replacing long stretches of walls with columns; this enabled him to realize his dream of imposing unity on the liturgical ceremony, by means of omnipresent light. All the worshippers were gathered together so as to form a united body both by their semicircle and, above all, by the unifying illumination. When this was implemented by a simultaneity of gestures, the effect was that of an unanimous celebration—a symphony of prayer. On the day of the consecration of the choir the Mass was solemnized "in such a festal atmosphere, in a manner so joyous and so corporate, that their euphonious singing, with its concord and harmonious unity, composed a sort of symphony more angelic than human."

Here we may see the influence of Dionysius, who particularly insisted on the unity of the universe. From the choir to the entrance of the church no obstacle impeded the flow of light which, filling the whole interior, converted the church into a symbol of the process of Creation. Suger dismantled the old roodscreen which "dark as a wall had cut across the nave, so as to prevent the beauty and splendor of the church from being obscured by any such impediment." Every barrier is laid low, everything that might halt the flux and reflux of the divine effulgence. "Once the new rear part is joined to the part in front/ The church shines with its middle part made bright/ For bright is that which is brightly coupled with the bright/And bright the noble edifice which is pervaded with this new light."

Suger had begun by making additions to both ends of the church. Time failed him to build between the porch and choir the nave uniting them, but we know that he had made plans for this. Adapting the new technique of vault construction to the traditions of Neustrian architecture, he envisaged it as a set of wide, continuous aisles, an anticipation in fact of the plan brought to fruition a century later at Bourges.

The mystique of light implicit in Suger's theological writings and the aesthetic deriving from it were not applied solely to the domain of architecture. For, to the thinking of the ecclesiastics of the twelfth century, there existed also certain objects in which the spirit of the divine was immanent and which could act as stimuli of mystical meditation. Like the subjacent plan of the sacred edifice, they invited the soul to proceed from the created to the uncreated, from things material to things ineffable. Such a power resided in certain precious stones to which mystical thinkers assigned peculiar properties, seeing in them symbols of the virtues which help the soul of man to elevate itself towards the ultimate Perfection. Basing their conclusions on certain passages in the Bible, they pictured the heavenly Jerusalem, destined to be the abode of "just men made perfect" in the fullness of time, as glittering with jewels. When Louis VII laid the first stone of the choir of Saint-Denis, he was given a handful of gems to lay beside it, while the clergy chanted "Thy walls are built of precious stones." Hence the practice of placing objects resplendent with jewels in the central portion of the church, their scintillations kindled by the light which, streaming through the bays, converged towards the choir, focal point of the sacramental rite. The prevailing taste for translucent substances, for enamels and jewelry (which in the past had fascinated the barbarian chieftains) found a justification, both mystical and liturgical, in the precincts of the altar. For, as Suger said, "when my whole soul is steeped in the enchantment of the beauty of the House of God, when the charm of many-colored gems leads me to reflect, transmuting things that are material into the immaterial, on the diversity of the holy virtues, I have a feeling that I am really dwelling in some strange region of the universe which neither exists entirely in the slime of the earth, nor entirely in the purity of Heaven; and that by God's grace I can be transported from this inferior to that higher world in an anagogical [i.e. upward-leading] manner."

In extolling the mediative virtues of finely wrought sacred vessels and jewels, the abbot of Saint-Denis was conforming to a tradition handed down by the great mystics of monasticism. But the special emphasis on light in the doctrine of Dionysius led Suger to assign to it a more precise, more vital function in the ordering of his church. It was in the "illuminated core of the edifice," at the transept crossing, that "the reliquaries of saints adorned with gold and precious stones" were placed "for contemplation by all who visited the church." Thus the basilica ceased to be what until now the Romanesque churches had been—merely a superstructure above a hypogeum or martyrium, an underground crypt to which pilgrims descended: a cellar-like place of awe-inspiring darkness where they had

but glimpses of the holy bodies in the dim religious light of tapers. In Saint-Denis the sacred relics were translated from their cavernous abode and its atmosphere of numinous awe, and brought up into the church itself. Among the reliquaries exposed to the full light of day that of St Denis, flashing with gems, held pride of place in the heart of an uninterrupted light, the very light of his theology. Itself a reflection, mirror of God, it contributed to the illumination of the assembled congregation.

The main altar already had a gold frontal presented by the Emperor Charles the Bald. Suger added three more panels "for it to be resplendent on all sides" and set forth around it the precious vessels belonging to the abbey treasure. "We adapted to the service of the altar a porphyry vase admirably fashioned by the sculptor's and the polisher's hand, converting it from the amphora it was formerly into a vessel shaped like an eagle, adorned with gold and silver. We acquired a precious chalice wrought of a single block of sard, and another vessel of the same substance but not of the same shape, which resembled an amphora, and yet another vessel seemingly of beryl or crystal." Clearly Suger had a fondness for rare substances, their broken gleams and swirls of lambent light, and employed a team of expert craftsmen on giving a functional value to these "collector's pieces." Assisted by "a strange miracle that the Lord vouchsafed us," he gave the finishing touch to his work by setting up in the heart of the church and visible on all sides a cross twenty-one feet high. "I had to stop work owing to the lack of precious stones and had not the means of procuring enough since their rarity made them very costly. Then, lo and behold, from three abbeys of two Orders, from Citeaux, from another abbey of the same Order, and from Fontevrault, there came certain holy monks who entered our little room beside the church and asked us to buy a store of jewels—amethysts, emeralds and topazes—such as I could not have hoped to gather in ten years." (In those monasteries an ascetic interpretation of the Benedictine rule prevailed, more stress being laid on poverty, and the monks refrained from ornamenting their churches.) "They had been given these stones," Suger continues, "as alms by Count Thibaud. Freed from the need for searching for precious stones, I rendered thanks to God. We gave the monks four hundred livres (though the jewels were worth much more), and not only these but many other gems and pearls enabled us to give our church an adornment befitting so holy a place. I remember using some eighty marks of pure refined gold. We employed goldsmiths from Lorraine, sometimes five, sometimes seven, on making the pedestal adorned with the four Evangelists and the column on which stands the holy, delicately enameled image and the story of our Saviour, with all the allegorical figures of the Old Covenant set forth and, crowning all, the death of Our Lord on the topmost capital."

The Great Cross was placed near the altar frontal, a Carolingian work. Suger's feeling for style led him to avoid any discrepancies between the older work and the new. This is why he summoned artificers from the Carolingian province where the old art of the Empire still survived. And by so doing he introduced into the heart of Neustria the aesthetic traditions of Austrasia. At the very time when, to glorify the Capetians, Saint-Denis was welcoming and celebrating the saga of Charlemagne, Suger linked up this artistic heritage with the royal abbey he was creating, and thus speeded up and amplified the cultural mutation of which he was the originator. For the imperial, humanist "renaissance," charged with allusions to antiquity, which was promoted by the Lorrainese craftsmen, was poles apart from the aesthetic of the Cluniac monasteries, whose abstract signs, strange animals and far-fetched imagery it rigorously excluded. It exalted plastic values and gave a central place to the human element in its vision of the world.

When, after radically changing the prevailing idea of architecture by using it to promote a "theology of light," Suger restored, beside the tombs of Pepin the Short and Charles Martel, the forms employed by Carolingian artists for the glorification of their monarchs, he was associating himself with the second "renaissance" of which the regions around the Loire and the Seine were then the seminal center, and with the return to classical prototypes which was then being promoted by the admirers of Ovid, Statius and Virgil, by men like Hildebert of Labardin and John of Salisbury. Associating Charlemagne with his celebration of the triumph of the Capetians, Suger also drew inspiration from the Ada Gospel Book, the Hildesheim gates and the ivories of Reims. In a word, he imposed on the art of France its other specific—anti-Romanesque—traits.

To begin with, in the stained glass he ordered for his "more luminous" windows. Here we have, in fact, a transposition of Mosan enamels and a derivative of the Lorrainese and Rhenish innovations. So disposed as to enrich the light of heaven, to give it glints of amethyst and ruby and "to guide blind spirits into the paths of anagogical meditation," Suger's windows, like Ottonian lectionaries, like Mosan enameled altars and the mosaic pavements of antiquity, framed the human figure in medallions, isolated by successive cloisons. Thus he completely separated it from the architectural context in which Romanesque *imagiers* had deliberately imprisoned it. Suger decided to apply this same procedure, taken over from the goldsmiths and miniature painters of the ninth century, also to monumental statuary. In Burgundy and the Poitiers region he had seen portals adorned with sculptured figures in the façades of abbey churches. He imitated these, and to him were due the first great effigies in stone north of the Loire. In the porch of Saint-Denis, however, these figures flanked bronze doors (those of the Ottonian basilicas) and the modeling of the stone jambs had to be adapted to that of the metal. The result was that here the carved figures did not grow out of the wall like efflorescences of the masonry, but, being separated by a recess and a canopy (like those we see in Carolingian ivories) from the building itself, produce the effect of independent works of art. Displayed in this manner, like pieces from a cathedral treasure or goldsmith's work, the Wise Virgins of Saint-Denis were the first "framed" statues in medieval art. All these images, those in the porch and stained-glass windows, those on the golden cross and those of the treasure around it—all alike bear witness to the central fact of Suger's theology: the Incarnation. "Whoever you may be, if you seek to do honor to these doors, praise not the gold nor the cost of them, but the work and the art. Surely the noble work shines, but that which shines is its nobility; it enlightens men's minds and by these lights guides them to the true light whereunto Christ is the true door." At Saint-Denis the treasures of the world were assembled to glorify the Eucharist; it was by the grace of Christ that man entered the holy light filling the church. This "new art" created by Suger was a celebration of the Son of Man.

Romanesque artists had not disregarded Jesus, but they saw in him God, the Lord. They were still dazzled by the blinding splendor of the Burning

Bush and the apocalyptic visions of the Book of Revelation. But the Christ of Saint-Denis was the Christ of the Gospels, in the likeness of man. For Saint-Denis was built in the mood of exaltation following the conquest of the Holy Land. All the epic chronicles whose themes took form in the regions around the abbey conceive of Charlemagne as a crusader faring to Jerusalem; King Louis VII, too, went on a crusade soon after the completion of the Saint-Denis choir, and instructed Suger to act as his regent during his absence. In the half-century following the deliverance of the Sepulchre of Christ, when hosts of Christians made the pilgrimage to the Holy Land almost every year, all religious-minded churchmen, noblemen, even peasants, were intensely aware of the call of the East, of the places where Christ had lived and suffered, and they shared in that splendid hope which led the Neustrian chivalry and the king of France, earthly representative of the crowned Christ, to embark on the great adventure. A supreme achievement of the crusade was the concrete, conclusive discovery at Bethlehem of the Well of the Woman of Samaria and on the Mount of Olives of the human reality of the Saviour. Around the workyards of Saint-Denis returned crusaders talked of the Holy Sepulchre, and in this context the relics of the Passion, a nail from the Cross, a fragment of the crown of thorns presented by Charles the Bald to the abbey, acquired a profounder actuality. This is why Suger's theology shows a consistent attempt to link up the new image of God, the living Christ of the Gospels, with the old image of the Lord God which till then had dominated monastic thought.

Suger based his theology on principles resembling those which had obtained for several generations in the monasteries of the West and it took the form of an interpretation or "gloss" of Holy Writ. In the ninth century Walafrid Strabo had compiled his *Glosa*, a Biblical exegesis which all monks of a scholarly turn of mind had heard read or copied out for their own use. Starting out from the premise that man is composed of three principles, body, soul and spirit, Walafrid inferred that every verse of the Bible had three significances: literal, moral and mystical. All the intellectual activities of monastic writers were henceforth directed to elucidating the Scriptures on these lines. St Augustine, too, had written that "the Old Testament is but the New

Testament covered with a veil, and the New but the Old Testament unveiled." He held that the life-story of mankind fell into two phases, separated by the birth of Christ. The whole course of Jewish history was to be regarded as a prophetic series of events, in which Christian history was prefigured symbolically. Thus the Old Testament narrative contained a record of premonitory happenings having a spiritual significance whose true purport, St Augustine says, "is to be looked for in reality itself not merely in the words." The New Testament is the decisive, definitive history, adumbrated by the Old, which, though anterior to the truth—the new revelation—is not a cause but an effect of it. Christ "fulfils" the protagonists of the Old Testament and supersedes them. Here we have the doctrinal background of Suger's theology. But he gave expression to it, not in writing, but in images generated by his tectonic handling of light. What he aimed at was to bring out the concordances and analogies between the Old Testament and the Gospels which for his contemporaries, the crusaders, had now become a living reality. Though the iconography of Saint-Denis keeps to the canons of Romanesque symbolism, it deflects them towards the personality of Christ.

These reminders of the correspondences between the Old and New Testaments begin on the very threshold of Saint-Denis, in the porch. Here the imagery also serves the function of a profession of faith, the true faith, and a repudiation of heretical deviations. The portal is triple and at its consecration three priests simultaneously performed the rites. It was a representation of the Trinity, whose image figures explicitly at the summit of the archivolt. For in point of fact the whole system of Dionysius the Areopagite centers on the theme of the Trinity, itself a symbol of the Creation, and moreover the mystery of the Trinity was one of the subjects most ardently discussed by theologians of the period. (Recently, in 1121, the synod of Soissons had condemned Abelard for an heretical interpretation of the Trinitarian dogma in his *De Trinitate*.) Nevertheless the imagery in the portal is tributary above all to the central figure of the Three Persons: Jesus "the true door." This is why for the first time the columns supporting the arches are given the form of statues— of the kings and queens of the Old Testament. Assembled as a triumphal escort celebrating the new age inaugurated by the Incarnation, these figures of the old dispensation body forth the royal lineage of Christ, Son of David—his prefigurations—and also his ancestors in the flesh, those through whom he participated in the created world, the world of men. And, finally, these figures serve yet another purpose as symbols and reminders of the glory of kinghood.

This theme recurs in the center of the church, on the Great Cross, a shining symbol of the Redeemer's victory over the powers of evil and the emblem the crusaders wore on their garments. The Cross served to refute the lurking doubts of men of little faith and challenged the undercover sectaries who denied that man could be redeemed by the death of an enfleshed man. It arraigned that notorious heresiarch Peter of Bruys who at this very time was making a holocaust of crucifixes at Saint-Gilles on the southern frontier of Gaul. It also demonstrated the "concordances" by juxtaposing in the sixty-eight scenes adorning it incidents in the life of Our Lord and their Old Testament prefigurations. The same lesson is conveyed by the stained-glass windows of the three chapels on the east of the church; that of the south chapel shows Moses, *novum testamentum in vetere*, that of the northern chapel, the Passion, *vetus testamentum in novo*, while that of the central chapel shows the Tree of Jesse which, figuring forth the genealogy of Mary, inserts Christ, the body of God, in a human family, "planting" him so to speak at the focal point of human history, in Time and in the flesh. One of the windows, which represents Christ crowning the New Covenant and stripping the veils from the Old, bears an inscription which might be said to epitomize Suger's theology: "What Moses veiled is unveiled by Christ's teaching." And pervading all these analogies we can see an evident desire to combat the temptations of a facile dualism and to signalize, not God's transcendence, but His Incarnation.

A tendency prevailed in ecclesiastical circles to divert attention from the Psalms, the Books of Kings and the Apocalypse towards the synoptic Gospels. So Suger was naturally led to emphasize the human side of Our Lord, to give the Virgin a central place in the iconography of the stained-glass windows, to represent the Annunciation, the Visitation and the Nativity on the main altar, and to locate on one of the windows, framed by the tetramorph, not the image of God the Father as at Moissac, but Christ crucified. At Saint-Denis, as at Conques, the Last Judgment figures on the central tympanum of the portal, but here the imagery is based on the Gospel of St Matthew as well as on the Book of Revelation. The old men making music are relegated to the archivolt and give place to the Wise and Foolish Virgins—symbolizing those who are mindful of God and those who are forgetful. The arms of Christ are stretched out as if crucified and nearby are the instruments of the Passion, while beside him are the apostles, St John (perhaps) on his left and on his right the mediatrix, the Virgin. Thus the glorious event of the Last Day and the scene of Calvary revealed their profound identity, and we have here a clear allusion to the high hopes of the first crusaders, whose minds as they made their way to Golgotha were haunted by a vision of the heavenly Jerusalem bathed in apocalyptic light. Greatly daring, Suger had himself represented just below in the attitude of a donor—the proud gesture, doubtless, of a creator content with his work, but also a reminder of man's presence in the very heart of the Second Coming. For in Dionysius's *Hierarchies* did not even the humblest of men share in the universal immanence of the divine Light? The basilica of Saint-Denis stands for a form of Christianity no longer expressed solely in terms of liturgy and music, but also in those of a theology, a theology whose leitmotif is the Incarnation. This is why Suger's work opened up a new dimension, that of man illuminated by the *verum lumen*.

Situated at a crossroads on the edge of the plain just north of Paris, among workmen's huts and vineyards, Suger's abbey church benefited by its central position in a region of France then in the ascendant both economically and politically. Saint-Denis opened up a host of novel possibilities; all the "new art" of France derived from it. Let us now turn to the first cathedrals, which tended to rationalize its message, to the Cistercian monasteries, which stripped it of its outward splendor, and, lastly, to the heretical movement, which shut its eyes to it.

In the early medieval West a church or palace treasure was not regarded as a luxury but as an obligatory manifestation of power and prestige. It was right and fitting that the form of God and the bodies of saints and kings should be encircled with a blaze of gold and gems. Their luster and beauty made visible to everyone the glory emanating from these bodies and the aura of sanctity with which they were invested, elevating them above earthbound men and assuring the veneration of the populace. In the heart of darkest Europe, amid the forests and waste lands from which famished nomads equipped with rough wooden implements scratched a precarious livelihood, all the wealth of a semi-barbarous age was accumulated at certain favored points, in churches and shrines containing relics and in palaces.

At the bidding of prelates and princes highly skilled craftsmen, utilizing the most precious materials, created gorgeous adornments for altars and royal thrones, vying in delicacy and splendor with those rare objects which, produced in ancient times or in far lands having a high cultural level, had found their way into the hands of their employers. They were often called on to re-employ these "collector's pieces"—relics of Roman antiquity, intaglios, cameos, crystals fashioned in the Byzantine or Islamic East—and to assemble and mount them in the vessels used for divine service or at royal banquets. Their task was to make the adornments of the sacred.

The best of the workshops were the oldest, those which had served the empire of Charlemagne, then that of the Ottos. Since the empire styled itself Roman, it was desirable that the objects which proclaimed the glory of the vital center of Christendom and which imperial munificence distributed to the great churches, should bear the stamp of Rome. Thus the art of the Carolingian and, after them, the Ottonian treasures was deliberately archaistic—in other words, classical. In virtue of its techniques, its feeling for plastic values and all it owed to Mediterranean humanism, it was diametrically opposed to the Romanesque aesthetic. In the time of Suger this artistic tradition was still alive; it persisted in Saxony, cradle of the Ottonian line, and, more vigorously, in cities of the Rhine and Meuse regions and in Lotharingia, most Carolingian of the provinces of Europe. This was the home of the bronze-workers, of the only true statuary art of the age and of the most expert enamellers.

When the abbot of Saint-Denis decided to assemble a treasure worthy of his abbey and the majesty of the kings of France, who were now beginning to feel qualified to take over the heritage of Charlemagne and, in their turn, to lead western Christendom on the pathway of salvation, he called in Lorrainese goldsmiths. The works of art produced by them were costly and extremely fragile. The function of the treasure was not merely ornamental; it also constituted a reserve of wealth which could be drawn on in emergencies. Periodically, when it was proposed to "modernize" the artefacts owned by the royal abbey, the old ones were broken up. This is why so few of the objects commissioned by Suger have survived: only some sacred vessels in sard or crystal, remakes of vessels of antique or Arab provenance. Nothing remains of the Great Cross of Gold which he set up in 1140 above the tomb of St Denis; it is represented, however, on a painted panel of the fifteenth century, and a small-scale replica of its foot is preserved at Saint-Omer. This last was made some thirty years later by another Mosan artist, Godfrey of Claire (or Huy). Its decoration tells us something of Suger's theological program, his wish to demonstrate the concordances between the Old and New Testaments by means of juxtaposed scenes. The base is supported by gilt-bronze statuettes of the four Evangelists, whose writings are fundamental to the Christian faith, and on the shaft are four enamel plaques representing Old Testament prefigurations of the life of Jesus: Moses and the brazen serpent, Isaac carrying the wood for the burnt-offering, Aaron tracing on the brows of the Chosen the Tau symbol (the pre-Christian cross), Joshua bringing back the bunch of grapes from the Promised Land. On the capital figure the four elements of the Cosmos.

Starting from Saint-Denis, this typological symbolism spread throughout the Christian West, then engaged in a bitter struggle with the Cathar heresy; these images testified to the truth of the Redemption. The enamel plates on a portable altar preserved in the treasure of the Abbey of Stavelot, in Lorraine, also bore effigies of Isaac, the brazen serpent, Melchizedek and Abel, and the intricate iconography of the Klosterneuburg ambo, decorated about 1180 by Nicholas of Verdun, another craftsman from the Mosan region, is likewise based on the doctrine of concordances.

GODFREY OF CLAIRE (OR OF HUY). FOOT OF A CROSS FROM THE ABBEY OF SAINT-BERTIN, SECOND HALF OF THE 12TH CENTURY. MUSÉE-HÔTEL SANDELIN, SAINT-OMER.

RELIQUARY SHRINE OF ST HERIBERT, ARCHBISHOP OF COLOGNE (DIED 1021), ABOUT 1160-1170.
CHURCH OF ST HERIBERT, COLOGNE-DEUTZ.

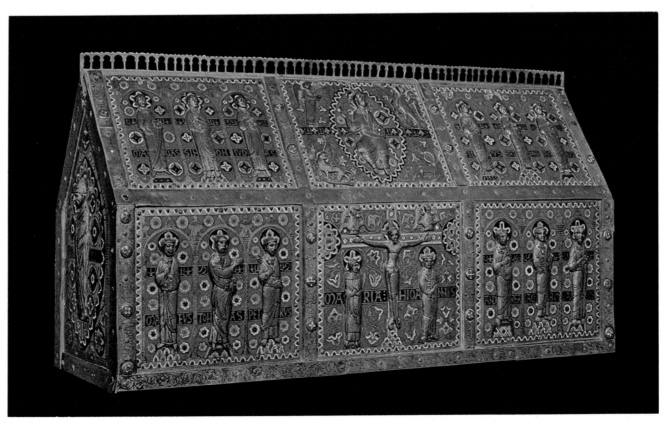

RELIQUARY SHRINE OF ST CALMIN, LATE 12TH OR EARLY 13TH CENTURY.
CHURCH OF SAINT-PIERRE, MOZAC, NEAR RIOM (PUY-DE-DÔME).

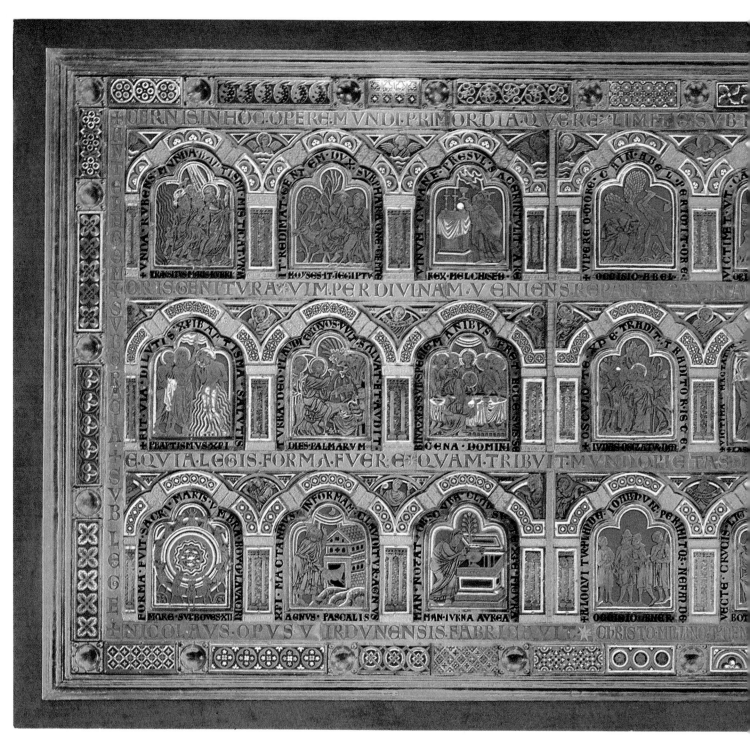

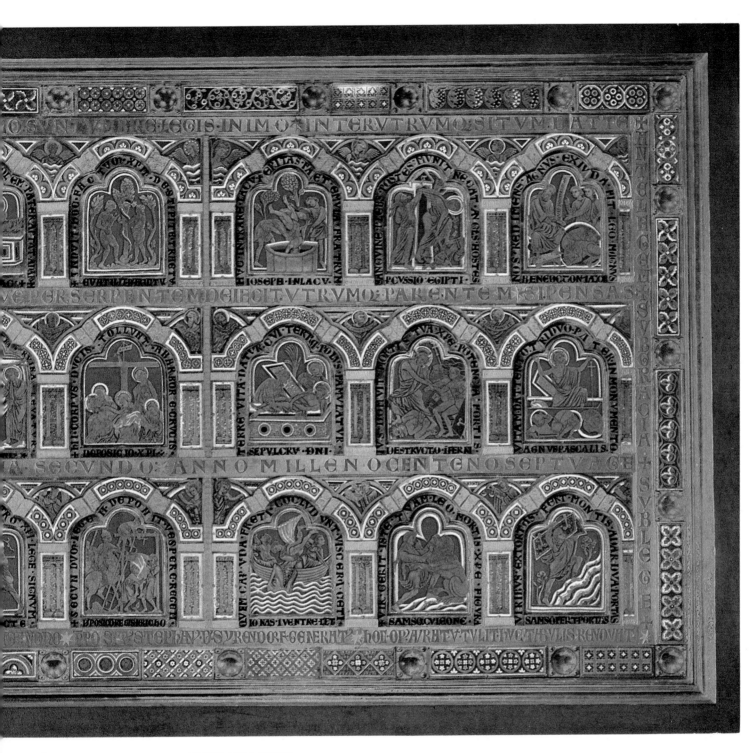

ADVENT OF THE STAINED-GLASS WINDOW

God is Light and the interior of His church prefigures the heavenly Jerusalem whose walls, the Book of Revelation tells us, are made of precious stones. The function of the stained-glass window is to admit the light of day and in so doing to transmute it, embellish it, invest it with the hues of the various gems—rubies, topazes, emeralds, lapis lazuli—which according to the ancients were endowed with magical virtues corresponding to specific properties of the soul. The art of the stained-glass window is bound up with that of the reliquaries and chalices, and of the altar incorporated in the sacred edifice. Playing on these holy objects, the light streaming through it bathes the interior in an iridescent sheen, a splendor heralding the glories of the after-life and creating an atmosphere of ecstatic awe. But, like the enamels on pulpits, crosses and reliquaries, the window also had a didactic purpose, that of a proclamation of the Christian verities. Its imagery set the thoughts of the congregation on the path of holy meditation leading to true belief.

Suger, then, transposed the message of edification, which the officiating priests could "read" at close quarters on the Great Cross of the high altar, on to the windows of the choir so as to make it visible to the entire congregation. As in Ottonian Gospel books and Mosan enamels, this imagery formed a well-ordered sequence, combining all the themes that were henceforth basic to Catholic propaganda and affirmed the validity of the Incarnation as against the doctrines of the heretics. Soon these same themes were transferred from the windows to the illustrated pages of religious books and the sculpture in church portals. The Cross held the central place. The windows of Saint-Denis were a visual equivalent of the homiletics of the monastic schools. They interpreted the Scriptures, revealed their hidden meanings and proved that the Old Testament contained intimations, antetypes, of the New. And to demonstrate the unity of God in Three Persons, Suger showed the Trinity as a group surrounded by the four Evangelist symbols: God the Father upholding Christ crucified, linked to His image by the Dove, the Holy Spirit.

Little by little the symbolism of the Old Testament concordances gave place to themes centering on the Passion; characters from Genesis and Exodus were replaced by images of the participants in the tragedy of Calvary. On the Crucifixion window in the cathedral of Poitiers, Jesus is shown (following a tradition transmitted by the ninth-century ivory carvers) still alive on the cross, with the Virgin, St John, the lance bearer and the man holding the sponge beside Him.

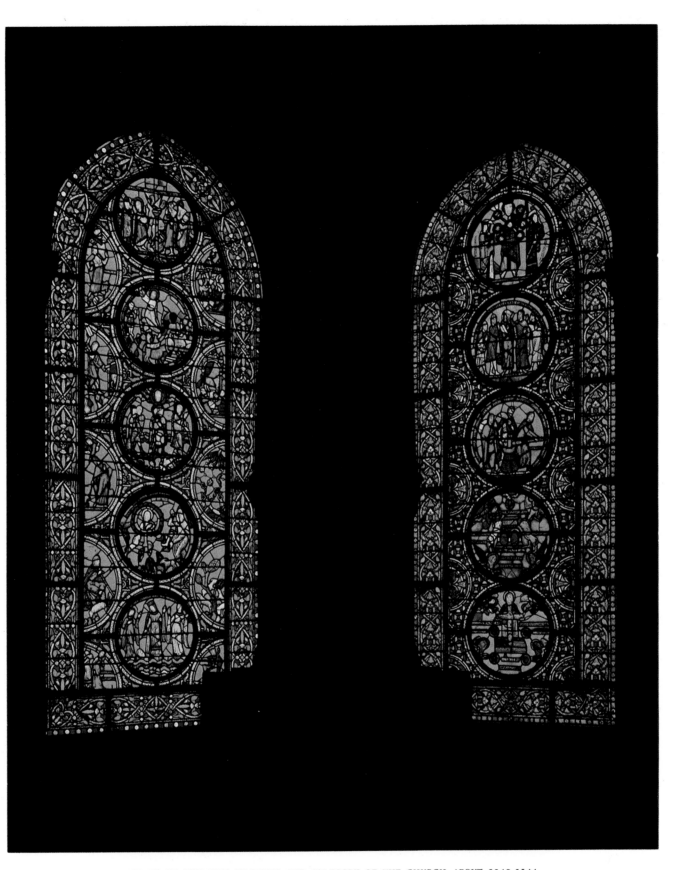

SCENES OF THE LIFE OF MOSES AND ALLEGORY OF THE CHURCH, ABOUT 1140-1144.
STAINED-GLASS WINDOWS IN THE CHAPEL OF SAINT-PÉRÉGRIN, CHURCH OF SAINT-DENIS.

THE CRUCIFIXION, ABOUT 1165. DETAIL OF A STAINED-GLASS WINDOW, CATHEDRAL OF SAINT-PIERRE, POITIERS.

FLOREFFE BIBLE: THE CRUCIFIXION, ABOUT 1170. FOLIO 187, ADD. MS 17738, BRITISH MUSEUM, LONDON.

THE TREE OF JESSE

The high nobility to begin with, then the knights, had set much store on lineal descent. This deep respect for ancestry, basic to the fame and fortune of the aristocratic families and to the prestige of every feudal lord, was undoubtedly the factor which, more than any other, maintained the cohesion of the social order during this period. Every canon, every knight was conscious of his lineage, of being the scion of a noble House, and cherished the memory of his forbears. Hence came the notion of a family tree rooted in the ancestral soil and spreading out across the years in many branches. So when in the twelfth century the Church affirmed its faith in the humanity of Christ and vigorously denounced the heretics who declared it impossible that the divine essence should commingle with the carnal, it illustrated its demonstration with a genealogical symbol, the Tree of Jesse. According to Emile Mâle this image made its first appearance on one of the Saint-Denis windows, and the idea of a tree came from the layout of the text, dated 1100, of a manuscript from the abbey of Saint-Martial at Limoges. The "tree" contains images of all the persons mentioned in the Bible whose words foretold the coming of the Messiah, headed by Isaiah, who prophesied: "There shall come forth a rod out of the stem of Jesse, and a Branch shall grow out of his root" (Isaiah, xi. 1). It is clear that the prophet had a lineage in mind. In its simplified form this motif is composed of three figures, one above the other, rising from the loins of Jesse: King David, Mary, and her Son. Thus the notion of a celestial dynasty was grafted on to that of an earthly dynasty, and sublimated it. In the brilliantly illuminated choir the initial symbol figuring in the porch recurs, but with an added emphasis and greater luminosity. Begun on the threshold of the church with a cortège of stately figures of the Old Dispensation, prophets and the ancestors of Jesus, the sequence of images terminates with the Tree of Jesse.

Thirteenth-century liturgical books and all the objects in the treasure have the air of replicas of the cathedral. Typical is the Saint-Taurin reliquary shrine, decorated in 1240 and 1255. The commission for this, clearly a Parisian work, was given by St Louis and it bears the heraldic emblem of the King of France; fleurs-de-lys and Castilian castles adorn this reliquary, from whose upper part rise stylized ears of wheat. It is given the form of a church with a transept and belfry above the crossing. Like the new cathedrals, it projects skywards a fantastic tangle of pinnacles, finials and gables, the architecture of an imaginary city, symbolizing the heavenly Jerusalem.

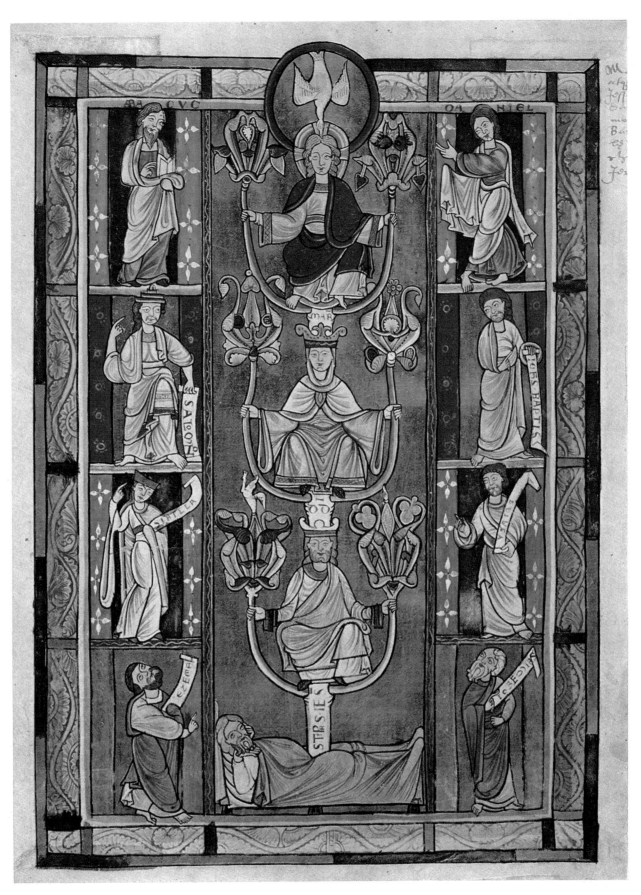

RABANUS MAURUS, "DE LAUDIBUS SANCTAE CRUCIS": THE TREE OF JESSE, SECOND HALF OF THE 12TH CENTURY.
FOLIO 11, MS 340, BIBLIOTHÈQUE MUNICIPALE, DOUAI.

II. 31

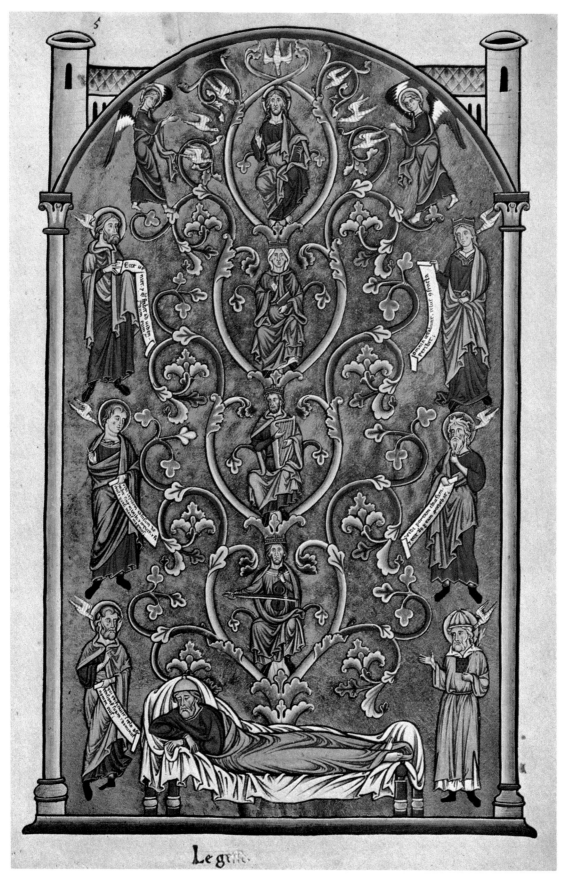

Le griffe

PSALTER OF QUEEN INGEBURGE: THE TREE OF JESSE, EARLY 13TH CENTURY. MUSÉE CONDÉ, CHANTILLY.

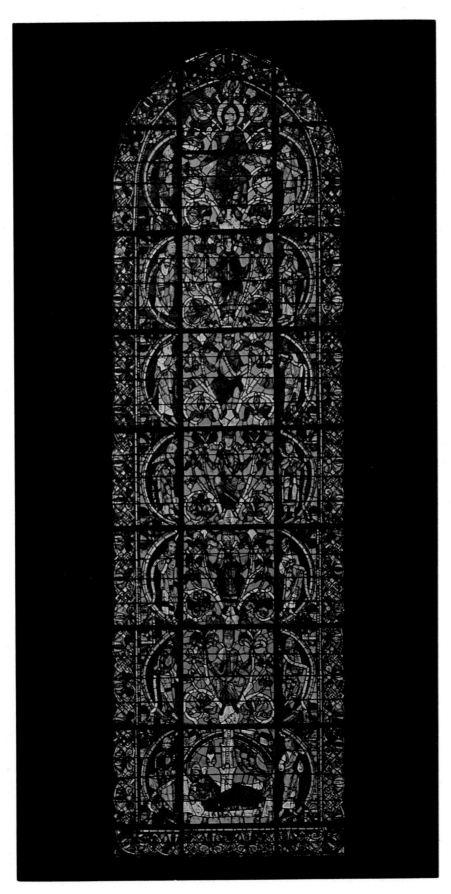

THE TREE OF JESSE, 12TH CENTURY. STAINED-GLASS WINDOW TO THE RIGHT OF THE ROYAL PORTAL, CHARTRES CATHEDRAL.

RELIQUARY SHRINE OF ST TAURIN, 1240-1255. CHURCH OF SAINT-TAURIN, ÉVREUX.

THE CITY CHURCH

A true son of St Benedict, Suger was an abbot and the abbey he built—if in a sense the most "urban" of its kind—was essentially a monastery church. But the men who carried on his work were bishops, prelates of the now renascent towns. From the stained-glass windows of Saint-Denis stemmed, in the mid-twelfth century, those of Chartres, Bourges and Angers, all of them cathedrals; from its column-statues those of Chartres, Le Mans and Bourges. The architectural innovations of Saint-Denis were followed up between 1155 and 1180 at Noyon, Laon, Senlis, Paris and Soissons, all in the lineage of the cathedrals of Neustria. A natural affiliation, since for Suger the power of the consecrated king rested less on the feudal hierarchy than on the Church, and he saw in the bishops, as in the time of the emperors Louis I the Pious and Charles the Bald, the true pillars of royalty. This shift of artistic activity from the abbey to the cathedral was a symptom of the vast changes that were taking place in the social structure and the rapid growth of urban life in northern Gaul.

Towns had been almost completely obliterated in the forests of the Carolingian age. Now that the land was being reclaimed for cultivation, they took a new lease of life. Being a "lord," whether of the Church or of a domain, meant living in luxury and a rank above that of the common people. Every owner of a large estate felt as in duty bound to wear rich garments, and to provide good wine and exotic fare at his banquets. Thanks to the new prosperity of agriculture, the feudal lords could gratify these tastes, and they also enriched the boatmen, known as "marchands de l'eau," who plied a thriving trade on the great rivers—Seine, Oise, Aisne and Marne—and had their headquarters in Paris. The vendors of wine, spices and colored textiles prospered, and by the end of the eleventh century Italian traders were making their appearance on the roads of France. Sixty years later, in Champagne, there developed the great fairs, soon to become the chief centers of international commerce. The merchants of those days were roving adventurers, perpetually on the move, but they had offices and warehouses in the towns, which they thus helped to repeople. In the far north of Gaul the Romans had founded few towns and these few had fallen to pieces irreparably in the dark age of barbarism. So now new towns sprang up at the most promising spots, usually near a castle or a monastery. In the heart of Neustria, however, the old Roman towns were more thickly populated and more active than ever. Merchants built houses at the foot of the walls and a whole new quarter developed along the river bank, at the points where barges were moored, beside the marketplace. As business intensified throughout the twelfth century the marketplace was steadily enlarged. Ramshackle huts with wooden or wattle walls housed negotiable goods of considerable value, no longer the visible produce of the land as in the old days, but now consisting of ingots, spices, bales of merchandise of various kinds, and large sums of money were made available for operations in foreign currency and loans. It was from these hoards, kept secret to evade the tax collector, that the bishop and his chapter of canons, lords of the city and its environs, drew the funds for rebuilding the local cathedral.

For the old cathedral seemed sadly out of date. No building had been done in this part of France during the tenth century, when the region was infested with pirates, Northmen who looted everything they could lay hands on. Nor was any done in the eleventh, the century when the countryside was being slowly reclaimed for cultivation. Now, however, money was pouring in; the canons were taking a hand in trade, selling the wheat and wine of their domains and trafficking in the tithes. They levied taxes on the ports and markets, which despite evasions were extremely fructuous. The townsfolk were their "men," that is to say their subjects, liable to a *taille* and a capitation tax.

The bourgeois was known to be well off and the Church authorities deliberately squeezed him, confiscating on occasion his casks of wine and bale goods. Thus a large part of its wealth was drained off from a section of the population that was steadily becoming larger and more affluent. Sometimes the victims retaliated and in an atmosphere of rioting and violence banded together in a town commune, a fighting force. In the course of these disturbances some of the canons and sometimes the bishop himself lost their lives, but sooner or later a settlement was arrived at. A charter was drawn up giving the townsfolk partial emancipation from their lords and there was a show of regulating taxation. Yet, appearances notwithstanding, the outcome was always in effect a stiffening of the claims of the cathedral chapter on the wealth of the community.

Money flowed in, perhaps even more abundantly, through another channel, that of voluntary alms. For the rich tradesfolk had uneasy consciences; they were told that "no merchant can find favor in the eyes of God," since he enriches himself at the expense of his fellow men. In twelfth-century France the practice of trade was still regarded as a sin. When he felt his end approaching the businessman, feeling qualms about his future lot, tried to free himself from his burden of sin by making a generous donation. This he could do all the more easily because his wealth was his alone and not, like the landed estates of the nobility, the common property of a family whose members saw to it that their patrimony was not dilapidated and sometimes even sought to recover from the Church the legacies of too generous ancestors. Formerly the rural nobility had been lavish givers—the prosperity of the monasteries was due to their largesse—but they were now becoming parsimonious. In the reigns of Louis VII and Philip Augustus a flood of pious donations poured in from the new-rich merchants, most of them no longer in the form of land but in cash, with the result that a large proportion of the money circulating in the shops and on the money-changers' tables found its way into the hands of the bishop and the chapter. Moreover any prelate who embarked on the building of a new cathedral could count on receiving a large sum from the king, always the most generous of donors. This was especially the case when the bishop was a relative, brother or cousin of the king, for then the latter could easily secure lucrative prebendal canonries for sons of vassals or members of the clergy serving in his chapel. Hence the remarkable fact that so many French cathedrals were created almost simultaneously.

Amply supplied with funds from all these sources, the bishop could give free rein to his ambitions, chief of which was the celebration of his power and personal prestige. For he not only ranked as a *grand seigneur* but also wished his name to live on the lips of men. A new cathedral seemed to him an exploit, a battle won. Reading Suger's description of his building activities at Saint-Denis, we feel he is consumed with vanity. This desire for personal renown accounts for the spirit of competition which within twenty-five years came to possess, one by one, all the bishops in the royal domain and later, at Reims, led the archbishop to have himself represented, surrounded by his suffragans, on the large windows of the cathedral, and to reconstruct the portal so that it should be even more sumptuous than the one recently built by his rival, the bishop of Amiens.

The bishop's church, as now rebuilt, signified also the alliance of Melchizedek and Saul, that is to say the effective union of episcopal power and royalty. No less than Saint-Denis, Reims was a royal monument. Here, too, there were engaged towers built into the façade and the same ambivalent column-statues, in which the townsfolk recognized the figures of Philip of France and Queen Agnes rather than those of Solomon and the Queen of Sheba. And, finally, the new cathedral vaunted the prosperity of the town and its inhabitants, of the many shops and workyards all of which had contributed to its erection and above which it towered majestically. It symbolized the pride of a middle class that had come into its own. With a profusion of spires, pinnacles and gables fretting the sky it conjured up visions of the ideal City of God, a sublimation of the earthbound city spread out at its foot. Whenever the communes chose their seals their choice fell on a design showing the profile of the cathedral; there could be no better emblem of their power. Its towers kept watch and ward over their industries and trade, and its nave provided the only covered expanse in the center of a town which elsewhere was little more than a huddle of narrow alleys, drains and piggeries. The cathedral was not only a place of worship; it was here that the guilds assembled and it was the meeting place of the entire population on great occasions.

Moreover the status of being a "man" of the Church ensured certain privileges and exemptions from customs tariffs, of whose value the local merchants were fully conscious. This was one of the reasons why the merchant class regarded this splendid monument, on which they prided themselves and which they had adorned, as theirs. At Amiens the dealers in the dyes used for textiles felt that their renown was enhanced, if indirectly, by the beauties of the cathedral; at Chartres each of the guilds insisted on having its own stained-glass window. Huge sums of money were spent on these edifices which, without exhausting the wealth of the community, dedicated it to God's service, justified the opulence of the city and increased its fame. But it was not the wine merchants or drapers who directed building operations; that was left to experts, men of erudition.

In the twelfth century the only schools that still existed in Neustria, the western kingdom of the Franks, later called Normandy, were the cathedrals. During the dark Carolingian age the kings of the Franks had actively promoted a system of education modeled on Greek and Roman disciplines and founded large libraries and scriptoria. But, as was to be expected in a region whose population was entirely agricultural, where only students of theology and prelates had books at their disposal and where the abbeys were the keystone of the ecclesiastical edifice, these instruments of knowledge were available only in the monasteries. For several centuries education had been almost a monopoly of the monks; they trained novices, and the children of the nobility were their pupils. The king sent his sons to study at Saint-Denis. Even in the eleventh century, after the troubles due to the decline of the imperial power, when the church had lapsed into the comparative rusticity of the age of chivalry, the monastic schools still maintained their prestige as centers of learning in northern Gaul. After 1100, however, their influence rapidly waned, they tended to keep to themselves, to restrict their educative functions to the monastic communities and no longer to diffuse knowledge. For the new impulse to asceticism cut off still more the cloister from the world. The Benedictine's duty was to pray, to seek God in isolation, and teaching was henceforth the specific task of the priesthood. Of the bishop to begin with; but he was too much of a *grand seigneur* to teach in person; too busy sitting in the royal court, passing judgments or, on occasion, clad in armor, leading military expeditions. Most of the time he delegated his administrative duties to the priests attached to his church, to the canons and in particular to the one who was put in charge of the school. The precincts of the cathedral (always called the cloister, though not enclosed by walls) were usually crowded with pupils. This tendency to shift the educational activities of the monastery towards the cathedral was paralleled by a similar movement which led to the formation of centers of creative art in many of the larger towns. Both were due to the changes that were coming over the social structure as a result of improved communications, intensified commercial activity and facilities for traveling —all of which speeded up the innovations taking place in the field of ecclesiastical art.

Thus the teaching in the cathedral schools proceeded on new lines, and became less withdrawn, more accessible to the contemporary world-view. The abbeys had shunned the outside world, secluded themselves from it by walls that the monks were not allowed to cross—they were already half way to their true home in heaven. In the monastery education was seldom given in groups, more usually in pairs: every novice was assigned to the tutelage of a senior monk who supervised his course of reading, initiated him, and led him step by step along the path of meditation. But the cathedral school consisted of classes; groups of disciples sat at the feet of a master who read out to them a set book and commented on it. And these students were not isolated from the world but free to roam the streets of the town and to share in its life. Needless to say all or almost all were destined to a career in the Church; they were "clerks," wore the tonsure and were subject to the bishop's jurisdiction. Learning was of the nature of a religious rite. But the training they were given prepared them for an active life; it was both secular and evangelical, for their mission was to preach, to familiarize the populace at large with the Word of God.

The new world that the march of progress was calling into being after an age of darkness and relative barbarism had need of men capable of thinking clearly and expressing themselves. These youngsters who, turning from the profession of arms and a life at the courts of chivalry, had elected for the service of God knew well that only if they developed their minds would they qualify for the best posts in the Church. So they flocked to the cathedral school, where the number of students was growing. But these numbers fluctuated, increasing or diminishing according to the capacities of the teachers. The word went round that this or that cathedral chapter had a particularly well-stocked library, that the man in charge was more learned, more competent than the average and that students trained by him would have a better chance of advancement. Soon, certain schools eclipsed the others and intellectual activities tended to center in some major institution where the pupils had the choice of several professors, could change from one to the other, and where the disciplines were planned not to overlap. At the close of the eleventh century Chartres and Laon were the cathedral schools which attracted most pupils. That by the time when Suger's work on Saint-Denis was completed Paris was by way of supplanting them was largely due to the prestige of Abelard, most brilliant teacher of the age. In 1150 the royal city was crowded with students who came not only from the countryside of the Ile-de-France but also from Normandy, Picardy, the Germanic lands and, above all, England, to profit by his teaching. This took place in the cloister of Notre-Dame, but there now was also another center on the left bank of the Seine, on the Montagne Sainte-Geneviève. Meanwhile other, more independent teachers the boldness of whose ideas won them a following among the younger men rented booths on the Petit Pont (Rue du Fouarre). In 1180 an Englishman who had studied in Paris founded a school for poor students. South of the Seine a new student quarter, facing the Ile de la Cité (residence of the royal household) and the Pont au Change (the business center), was in process of formation. The great city, which was to be the vital center of the art of France, was now assuming its triple role—royal, commercial, educational—and in the narrow streets of the student quarter a new spirit was coming to birth.

Within the monasteries, and still at Saint-Denis, studying meant a discipline based on contemplation, solitary musings on the scriptures, a graduated progress towards enlightenment by way of symbols and analogies—little different from prayer and choral singing. But at Chartres, Laon and Paris the same dynamism that animated the businessmen in their commercial enterprises urged the young students to intellectual adventures. They did not only read and meditate, they discussed; masters and students confronted each other in wordy jousts, in which the former were not always the victors. Often indeed the classes at the cathedral school had all the air of tournaments, contests of verbal prowess which, like the knightly lists, trained the young men to hold their own in combat. In his youth Abelard had made his name in these open contests and, like a hero of chivalry, had achieved not only fame but triumphs in the lists of love.

Though it covered a wider field, the teaching in the cathedral schools kept to the old curriculum of the "liberal arts" which the scholars of the court of Charlemagne had, long before, unearthed in certain didactic treatises, a legacy of Late Antiquity. The only novelty was that, after the first third of the twelfth century, the elements of the medieval *Trivium* came more and more to be treated as preparatory to what was regarded as the chief function of the clerk: detailed commentation of the Holy Scriptures with a view to clarifying and demonstrating the Christian verities. Students were still required to take a course of rhetoric and grammar. For the commentator of the Bible dealt with words, whose meaning and construction he had clearly to understand, and these were Latin words. With this in mind the masters read to the junior classes the great classical texts—Cicero, Virgil, Ovid—and their beauty was not lost on the more perceptive students. Abelard and many others, even St Bernard himself, retained their early enthusiasm for the Latin poets throughout their lives. This teaching gave the pupils a bias towards humanism and the education provided in the schools of the larger towns did much to instill a taste for the values of Antiquity and a feeling for the human into the minds of those who planned the decorations of the new cathedrals. Now that their eyes were opened, they lost interest in Romanesque forms and tended to prefer Carolingian ivories, the art of the first renaissance, the plastic values of Mosan enamels. It is in the schools of Chartres and Orléans, where more attention than elsewhere was directed to the study of the humanities, that we can trace the source of the renascent current that carried to the portal of Reims Cathedral the classicizing figures of the Visitation.

But this applies only to a preliminary phase. At Laon, and above all in Paris, dialectic soon came to be regarded as the major element of the *Trivium*. And this, the art of reasoning, the exercise of *ratio*, now ranked highest among the faculties of the educated man. Reason, Berengar of Tours (died 1088) had declared, was "the honor of man" and his "specific light," that reflection of the celestial light which is man's prerogative. To the professors and their disciples, the "intellectuals" of the age, intelligence seemed the most effective weapon, the only one capable of defeating error and enabling comprehension of the mystery of the divine. Since all our ideas stem from the mind of the Creator and since they are often set forth imperfectly, in veiled, obscure, sometimes even contradictory terms in the Scriptures, it is the task of logical reasoning to dispel these shadows and resolve these contradictions. The first thing is to examine the *word* and find out its inner meaning, but this must be done by the strict dialectic method and not by a surrender, as in the monasteries, to the vagaries of meditation. Each problem must be tackled with an open mind. "By doubting we are led to inquire: by inquiry we perceive the truth," Abelard says in *Sic et Non*, in which he assembled contradictory statements of the Fathers, with a view to reconciling them. He begins by setting forth the texts separately, brings his mind to bear on them, interprets them from different angles, discusses their possible meanings, weighs these up, then formulates conclusions, "sentences." Many contemporaries regarded this rationalistic approach as presumptuous, perilous, even diabolical. Abelard justified it on practical grounds. "My students," he said, "asked for human and philosophical reasons, intelligible explanations, rather than categorical assertions. They said it was useless to talk if one did not make one's statements meaningful; no one can believe what he has not begun by understanding."

That during the period this dialectical procedure made such rapid strides was largely due to the progressive assimilation of a methodology which western thinkers were discovering in cultural areas lying outside the domain of Latin Christendom and better provided with the instruments of logical exegesis. It now was possible to draw on the philosophic wealth of the Moslem world and through its intermediacy on that of ancient Greece. After vanquishing Islam the Christians pillaged the intellectual hoard of their defeated foe. No sooner was Toledo reconquered than teams of Latin and Jewish scribes started translating Arab texts and versions of Greek writers. While the armies which were gradually driving back the Infidels from the continent were mainly composed of French knights, the intellectual exploitation of their triumphs in the field was the work of the priests of France. The chief gainers by the translations made in Spain were the schools of Neustria, primarily Chartres and to a less extent Paris. Their libraries were provided with the new books, notably the logical treatises of Aristotle. These furnished the masters with a compendium of dialectics of which the western monks had hitherto gleaned only a partial, vague idea by way of the works of Boethius. This is why such a man as John of Salisbury, who had studied in Paris in the years 1136-1148, spoke of Aristotle as "*The* Philosopher" and of dialectics as "queen of the *Trivium*." All intellectual advancement, he said, rested on dialectics, which by the exercise of *ratio* co-ordinates the experience of our senses, then by the exercise of *intellectus* relates all things to their divine Cause and apprehends the scheme of Creation, leading the thinker, step by step, to perfect knowledge, *sapientia*. In Paris Peter Lombard in his *Book of Sentences* developed the first logical analysis of the Biblical text, while Peter of Poitiers boldly asserted that "though surely certitude exists, it is meet for us to doubt the articles of faith, to search and to discuss."

From this doubt, these searchings and discussions, the new theology drew its strength—less emotional but more vigorous and more precisely ordered than its predecessor. Abelard had incurred the wrath of the monks of Saint-Denis by being first to put forward the view that the titular saint of the abbey was not the same person as Dionysius the Areopagite, and he had the courage to propound another *Theologia*, also based on illumination. "The light of the material sun is not the result of our own efforts to apprehend it, but flows over us *per se* so that we may enjoy it. Likewise we come near to God in so far as He himself approaches us, bestowing on us His light and the warmth of His love." For the professors, then, God was Light, and the cathedrals that now were built were even more luminous than Saint-Denis. But they also became more "evangelical," in that the teaching of the schools tended more and more to relate the Old Testament to the New, to lay more emphasis on the Incarnation and to rely more strongly on the first chapter of the Gospel of St John and all the passages describing the Word of God as the *vera lux* by which all things were created, that light of life which illuminates every man when he comes into the world. By the masters of the urban schools, more mindful of strict logic and wishing more clearly to define what their words meant, God was not so often viewed as that nucleus of dazzling light whose supreme effulgence still blinded the eyes of the monastic theologians; they saw Him, rather, in man's image. Like them, Christ was a Doctor who disseminated the light of the understanding; like them, carried a book and, like them was a teacher—their brother.

Their teaching aimed at clarity. It freed man from the thrall of formalism, emphasized the will behind his acts. Did not Abelard, writing to Heloise, affirm that "crime consists in the intention not in the evil deed"? It practised the analytical method, progressively resolving a complex datum into its parts, and asserted that "only the individual exists in its own right." It represented reality as an aggregate whose unity (like that of the new cathedral) was a sum of discrete elements. It directed attention to Nature; for as Abelard pointed out "there are forces operating in seeds and plants, in the essences of trees and stones, which can stimulate or tranquillize your souls." It described—and the sculpture in the cathedrals followed suit—the created world as it presents itself to the eye. Thierry of Chartres made an interpretation of the Book of Genesis, first of its kind to be based not on symbols but on new discoveries in the field of physics. He reduced God's work to the interaction of the basic elements of the cosmos and its concentric spheres. Fire, the lightest element, tended to escape towards the outmost verge of Space; water, in evaporating, gave birth to the stars; heat to life and all existing living beings. Ceasing to be a bewildering complex of signs, the universe became a logical configuration which it was the cathedral's mission to body forth by assigning all visible creatures to their proper places. It was the duty of the geometrician, using the deductive science of mathematics, to translate men's visions of the heavenly Jerusalem, evoked in the previous age by the ethereal, many-colored radiance of stained glass windows, into the concrete reality of stone.

For mathematics (another acquisition from the culture of conquered Islam) now bulked large in the training of professors and reinforced the discipline of logic. In Spain and southern Italy the members of the clergy who accompanied the leaders of the Christian reconquest discovered little by little in Arab treatises not only the philosophy of ancient Greece but her science too. Translations of Euclid and Ptolemy, also of manuals of algebra, were made for use in the schools of Chartres. Geometry and arithmetic were given a leading place in the new revised *Trivium* and in his *Didascalion* the Parisian *scholasticus* Hugh of Saint-Victor ranked the mechanical beside the liberal arts. At Saint-Denis the layout of a building had been for the first time "determined with the help of instruments of geometry and arithmetic" and it seems clear that for the plan of the crypt, where allowance had to be made for ninth-century substructures, recourse was had to diagrams and compasses. Thanks to these methods the new architecture had nothing of the makeshift character of so much Romanesque; logical planning overcame the handicaps of the material employed and made it possible to construct less narrow, less ponderous, more translucent edifices. The new "science of numbers" and the services of competent mathematicians played a large part in these architectural innovations and to them was due the invention in 1180 (in Paris) of the flying buttress which enabled the builders of Notre-Dame to increase the height of the nave. In recognition of their debt to the cathedral schools, French architects and artists often inserted figurations of the seven liberal arts in the basements of their churches. At the end of the twelfth century the art of France was in the hands of logicians; it was soon to become an art of engineers.

Very few pieces of the Saint-Denis treasure have survived, and next to nothing of the sculpture. Chartres, however, to which Suger's team of artists migrated about 1150 is fortunately intact. There, in the Royal Portal, the new art of France can be seen at its best. This art reflects the far-reaching changes which came over the climate of opinion in ecclesiastical circles at the turn of the century. At the schools of Chartres, Laon and Paris the new generation of churchmen had imbibed the teaching of the boldest spirits of the West and gradually learnt to turn away from the abstractions which had meant everything to their predecessors. The writings of Cicero, Ovid and Seneca told them that man is an individual who loves, suffers, pits himself against the coercive power of destiny. They took to analysing human emotions, the description of which was coming into vogue at the time when the Chartres workyard started. For the entertainment of the knights and high-born ladies, poets and troubadours were now composing elegant variations on antique themes, such as the adventures of Aeneas and the Trojan war. But, most important of all, an enlightened study of the Bible was providing them with a new image of God.

For these clerics, as for the artists who gave form to their ideas, the beautiful was that which most resembles God. Dazzled by the transcendent splendor of the God of Moses, Isaac and Jacob—the face whose blinding glory none can gaze on and which, to the human eye, has no apparent features—the monks of the year 1100 had made shift with symbolical equivalents. Their prayers were music and when they transposed them into figures, these did not represent any visual actuality, but intellectual concepts. But the God of the new bishops, canons and professors in the Ile-de-France was the Son of Man. For them he had assumed a human form, the face and body of a man. And so, for the rendering of the divine perfection, the artist no longer needed to take refuge in signs; he had but to open his eyes.

At Chartres, then at Le Mans, at Saint-Loup-de-Naud and Bourges, the statues of the Old Testament kings and the apostles were linked up with the walls and given the proportions of the columns from which they derived. There was no apparent life, no hint of movement, in the stiff, narrow, cylindrical bodies, strictly clad in robes with parallel flutings. Yet their faces were alive and little by little lost the formal symmetry appropriate to denizens of an abstract world. In 1185 when re-presenting angels escorting heavenwards the sleeping Virgin, the Senlis sculptor no longer followed the pattern of the Gregorian antiphonals; he watched the flight of birds.

FAÇADE OF CHARTRES CATHEDRAL. MID-12TH CENTURY.

ROYAL PORTAL (WEST PORTAL) OF CHARTRES CATHEDRAL. 1145-1150.

KING SOLOMON, THE QUEEN OF SHEBA AND KING DAVID, 12TH CENTURY. STATUES IN THE SOUTH PORTAL OF BOURGES CATHEDRAL.

II. 44

KINGS AND QUEENS OF JUDAH, 1145-1150. STATUES IN THE ROYAL PORTAL OF CHARTRES CATHEDRAL.

A KING OF JUDAH, 1145-1150. DETAIL OF A STATUE IN THE ROYAL PORTAL OF CHARTRES CATHEDRAL.

II. 46

A KING OF JUDAH, 1145-1150. DETAIL OF A STATUE IN THE ROYAL PORTAL OF CHARTRES CATHEDRAL.

NAVE OF LAON CATHEDRAL. SECOND HALF OF THE 12TH CENTURY.

1

THE SPACE OF THE CATHEDRAL

The façades of the new churches proclaimed the sovereign might of God, the Lord. Garrisoned by the celestial hosts, the House of God was an impregnable stronghold. The powers of evil, the malignant influences it held at bay, could not prevail against it. This is why its form recalls a castle, or one of the stone keeps the barons built at the end of the eleventh century in the regions of the Loire and the Seine. Foursquare, massive, solidly constructed, the front of the cathedral held a commanding position. Like the crusades, it evidenced the military background of feudal society and reminded its members of their duties as soldiers of Christ. This is why a cohort of the Kings of Judah, who transmitted to Jesus, their offspring, the legacy of worldwide sovereignty, welcomed the Christian congregation on the threshold of a citadel.

In Neustria the structural elements of the building, symbolizing the grandeur of the Church, derived from a very old tradition. In planning the forepart of his basilica, Suger drew inspiration from the gate-towers of the Ile-de-France and, still more, from the tall façades of the Norman abbeys whose governors had served William the Conqueror. As early as 1080, when Normandy teemed with mail-clad warriors eager for adventure, it was usual to flank with towers the entrances of the sacred edifices patronized by the dukes, who drew from them the priests needed to reform the English church and keep it under control. These towers lay at the origin of the lofty walls which the Norman bishops built in conquered England, at Ely and Wells, at the forefront of their cathedrals.

When Suger included two towers like those of the Caen monasteries in the western block of Saint-Denis, he was introducing into the church that vehement upward drive which was to prevail until the close of the Middle Ages. Nevertheless the structure of the fore-church (devised by him), the storey of the high chapel and the rose window illuminating it, brought back the elevation to the horizontal. This interplay of the two dimensions, one stressed by buttresses and pilasters, the other by galleries and friezes, was to be a prime concern of the builders of the façades of Gothic cathedrals. But these façades never lost their original aspect, expressive of strength and victory. This victory of the Faith and the Word made flesh was bound to be of a military order in a community dominated by warriors, whose bishops, ever eager for a chance of leading their troops to battle, were escorted by helmeted vassals and whose ideal hero was the "Knight of Christ." In that age of a belligerent Christianity, the Kingdom of God was envisaged as a supernal stronghold.

Saint-Denis, prototype of the Gothic church, was an abbey church, built to be the scene of monastic liturgies; it adjoined the cloister and was connected with it by the transept. It was the private oratory of a closed community and if at times the public were admitted, they always seemed intruders. The cathedral, however, was the city church; it belonged to the clergy and the people, the bishop being their chosen representative, their "pastor." *Clerus et populus;* the cathedral, an open church, was equally at the disposal of the two orders of the Christian community. Actually, however, at the end of the eleventh century the Gregorian reform had emphasized the gap between the clergy and the congregation and the higher status of the former. Thus of the space within the cathedral walls the better part was reserved to the prelates and the building as a whole so arranged as to answer to the requirements of their sacred function. In practice this did not differ fundamentally from that of the monks; the chief

duty of the cathedral clergy was, like theirs, to chant the praise of God together at all hours of the day. Like that of the monastery church, the floor space of the cathedral was organized around the choir and provided passages for the free movement of ceremonial processions. The congregation occupied the back of the edifice near the entrance, or else (as in the basilicas of the pilgrimage monasteries) was relegated to galleries on the sides, overlooking the central nave. For the ordinary worshipper was, so far, only a spectator and though he attended the service did not take any active part in it.

Nevertheless the space within the cathedral differed in several ways from that of the basilicas attached to monasteries, and this for two reasons. One was that the clergy were far from being as segregated from the populace as were the monks. For in none of the lands specifically French had the cathedral clergy been subjected to the strict corporate discipline imposed by canonic law on priests of the Carolingian period. True, the French canons were an organized body, but they enjoyed a certain liberty and had not to live together between four walls. What was still called the "cloister" in French cities was in fact an open tract of ground near the cathedral, where every member of the chapter had a house of his own. And since there was no collective life there was no transept. This transverse passage crossing the central nave at right angles had ceased to serve any practical purpose; though it survives in Notre-Dame of Paris it does not project beyond the body of the edifice. Thus the space of the cathedral was by way of becoming self-contained, sufficient to itself.

The new theology of the *verum lumen* called for this structural unification; since light was both the manifestation of God Himself and the bond of union between Him and the human soul, it was fitting that the kingdom of God, demarcated symbolically by the walls of the cathedral, should be entirely filled with light. Therefore there were no breaks in the lines of bays, alternations of pillars and columns were abandoned, galleries eliminated, since they impeded the enlargement of the windows. Total unity is achieved in the Sainte-Chapelle—but this is essentially a reliquary shrine. Yet Bourges cathedral with its five naves side by side has no less unity.

THE SPACE OF THE CATHEDRAL

1. Cathedral of Notre-Dame, Paris. 1163-1250.

2. Ely Cathedral. Late 12th century.

3. Laon Cathedral. 1150-1350.

4. Wells Cathedral. 1220-1239.

5. Nave of Salisbury Cathedral. 1220-1320.

6. Bourges Cathedral: rib vaulting of the ambulatory and nave. About 1200-1280.

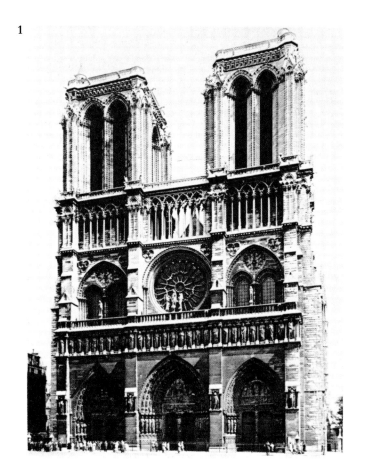

1

3

2

II. 52

4

5

II. 53

THE CISTERCIAN WAY

None the less the ideal of holiness prevailing at the time when the new cathedrals were being built was still essentially monastic in spirit. It was the age of Abelard and the flying buttresses of Notre-Dame that witnessed in the West the culmination of that spiritual trend which, after the triumph of the Christian faith, followed by the plight of Rome in the upheavals of the sixth century, had led to the belief that the surest way to salvation was a rejection of the world, its pomps and vanities. To the mind of the contemporaries of Philip Augustus, King of France (1180-1223), man's best means of escaping from the thrall of sin and saving his soul alive was plenary conversion, and this meant taking the Benedictine habit and retiring to the seclusion of a cloister. Not the open cloister of the canons and schoolmen, but that of the monks.

What was wanted, above all, was a new, reformed type of monasticism. The old interpretation of the Benedictine *regula*, the Rule of Cluny, which had been perfectly suited to the seigniorial structure of early feudalism, now seemed unacceptable. The Cluniac monks were accused of living like lords and yielding too readily to the spirit of the age. Exception was taken to their avoidance of manual labor, to that taste for comfort and display for which Suger seemed to have catered in his reorganization of Saint-Denis. The prosperity of the outside world, the new, unblushing zest for pleasure and easy living, led to a compensatory reaction: an idealization of poverty, withdrawal, self-supporting toil, total asceticism. Those who accepted this doctrine of austerity took for their exemplars the hermits who dwelt in forests and lived on herbs and roots. When, touched by divine grace, a knight decided to cut his earthly ties, to lay down his arms and to give up the pursuit of glory, he no longer entered a Cluniac abbey. That would not have meant a real break with the world of luxury and ostentation from which he wished to escape. He set to working as a charcoal burner. Thus round about the year

1100 several new religious orders were founded. Striking out in a new direction, the Carthusians elected for a monastic life of solitude and silence in the Oriental manner, in some desolate spot where the recluse "ate bread of unbolted meal and took so much water with his wine that it had hardly any flavor left." Other orders, however—and these were more in favor—practised a monachism less drastically opposed to that of Cluny and reconciling the Benedictine rule of communal life with asceticism. The year of the consecration of the choir of Saint-Denis, also the year when work began on the Royal Portal of Chartres, witnessed the triumph of another great monastic order, that of Citeaux. By 1145 there were over three hundred and fifty Cistercian houses in various parts of Western Europe, a Cistercian monk was elected pope (Eugenius III) and St Bernard's authority was everywhere paramount. We may dislike the personality of this violent, aggressive man who so brutally hounded down Abelard, who lashed the Roman Curia with invectives and strove persistently for temporal power. But it was he who launched crusades, counseled kings—and browbeat them—and went to Albi to preach against the heretic Cathars. When offered the archbishopric of Reims, he declined it and preferred to stay a monk. Under his dynamic leadership the White Monks won through to the conquest of the Church, and of the age.

This triumph, St Bernard's work, lasted after 1200; for many years Citeaux was still the alma mater of great bishops, a spearhead in the combat against heresy. Two hundred more abbeys were founded in the thirteenth century, Cistercians held many posts at the court of the French king and figured in the entourage of Blanche of Castile. Royaumont, the monastery that the sainted king preferred to all others, was a Cistercian foundation and he often stayed there, obeying the rule of the order, keeping silence and working with his hands, and he made the whole royal household do likewise.

"When a wall was being built around the Abbey of Royaumont, our sainted king often went there to attend Mass and other services or to inspect the work in hand. And since, observing the rule of Citeaux, the monks went after the hour of Tierce to carry stones and mortar for the wall that was a-building, the king too helped to bear the stretcher laden with stones, walking in front while a monk held it behind. Now and again our holy king had the stretcher carried by his brothers or by other knights of his household, and when sometimes his brothers were minded to talk, to shout or to play, the king admonished them: 'The monks are keeping silence, we should do as they do.' And once when his brothers had overloaded their stretcher and wished to rest on the path half way to the wall, he said to them: 'The monks do not rest, we too should not rest.' Thus our sainted king constrained his household to well-doing." Actually in the reign of St Louis the best days of Citeaux were over; pioneers of the great forward strides being made in agriculture, and profiting by them, the monasteries were becoming too rich, and the target of adverse criticism. Nevertheless the Cistercian mode of thought left a deep imprint on the age that saw the building of the first cathedrals.

Characteristic of the order was its antagonism to the cathedral schools. Cistercians heartily disapproved of the towns they had deliberately quitted, of the urban clergy whom they regarded as inferiors in the spiritual hierarchy, of the scholastic curriculum (futile in their eyes), and above all of Paris, the New Babylon, a hotbed of iniquity, especially pernicious to the young. In 1140 St Bernard himself had visited Paris with the sole aim of "converting" the students, that is to say inciting them to desist from their studies. The address he composed for their benefit, entitled *De Conversione ad Clericos*, counseled an escape from Babylon to the great open spaces, the desert, as the only means of salvation. The teachings of the masters, he said, "set up an uncalled-for screen betwixt the soul and Christ." Why, then, waste time on them? "You will find more in forests than in books; trees and rocks will teach you things no master can make known to you." In St Bernard's opinion any discussion of the scriptural message was a sin. Nothing, he said, is more injurious than dialectics, rational inquiry, vain attempts to make faith seem intelligible. He fiercely attacked the professors *en masse* at the council held

at Sens (1141) before which Abelard was arraigned, and again at the council at Reims where the "logic" of Gilbert de la Porée was similarly censured. Like Pierre de la Celle (the abbot of Saint-Remi of Reims whom Dante momentarily chose to be his guide in his spiritual journey) St Bernard held that "the true school, the one in which the pupil does not pay his teacher, in which there are no discussions" is the school of Christ. In point of fact Citeaux and the houses under Cistercian influence did not altogether prohibit meditation on the text of the Scriptures; they only gave it a new orientation, convinced as they were that the divine element in man consisted not in the reasoning faculty but in love; "understanding is nothing else than love."

In this way, combating the rationalistic approach of the "modern" philosophers, a new mode of religious thought was propagated by St Bernard and the Cistercians. Its fountainhead was the teaching of that pioneer of Latin mysticism, St Augustine, and this stream of thought attracted to itself the masters of certain cathedral schools less committed than the Parisian schools to the discipline of dialectics: notably the masters of the school of Chartres. As early as 1100 these latter had directed their pupils' attention to the few writings of Plato then available, fragments of the *Timaeus*. Suger's way of thinking owed much to them. Diffused by Chartres, these ideas, of Platonic inspiration and less appropriate to logical inquiry than to emotional effusion, found favor shortly after in another city school, in Paris itself. Not at Notre-Dame, but in the Abbey of Saint-Victor, a hermitage that, after being "converted," a learned canon had founded at the gates of the city. His disciples led an ascetic life and, as members of the clergy, continued to perform their religious duties as teachers. But what they inculcated was the Augustinian rule of contemplation. It would seem that the Victorines did not expressly condemn dialectics and philosophy; indeed Richard of Saint-Victor spoke in favor of the humanists and philosophers of Notre-Dame and the Montagne Sainte-Geneviève. The soul, he said, should exercise all its faculties, particularly the reasoning faculty; God is Reason and we can approach Him from this angle. But that is only one approach; nothing but love can elevate us to the highest sphere of knowledge, plenary inspiration. As for Hugh of Saint-Victor, like St Augustine—and like Suger—he declared that every perceptible image is a sign or "sacrament" of the things invisible, those that the soul will perceive when it has cast off its carnal garment. Following St Augustine, Hugh bade his disciples make the spiritual ascent towards this supreme vision, stage by stage. They must begin with *cogitatio*, an investigation of the visible, material world, for this is necessarily fundamental to all abstract thought; next, the inner man must rise higher, to the stage of *meditatio*, in which the soul looks inward at itself; then, finally, it attains the stage of *contemplatio*, intuitive knowledge of the truth. This doctrine was taken over by the Cistercians and it was in their houses, where the monks lived in total poverty, that the rules for this progress towards a contemplative enlightenment were most strictly observed. William of Saint-Thierry, who had dealings with the Carthusians in 1145, extolled the mediative power of love. As a humanist, he had enriched his mind with studies of such works as Cicero's *De Amicitia* and Ovid's *Ars Amandi*, the very works which were being read by the pupils in the cathedral schools of the Loire region. They were also studied by the troubadours in the princely courts, with a view to refining the theory of another, secular form of love, the so-called courtly love. Just as the knight was told to win his way into the heart of his ladylove by acts of martial prowess and by the sublimation of his grosser passions, so the disciples of William of Saint-Thierry were bidden to engage in a mystical ascent which, starting from the body, seat of animal life, moved ever higher to the soul, seat of Reason, and finally to the spirit, crown of all and seat of the sublimest ecstasy of love. By the light of love, true communion with God, "the soul passes from the world of shows and shadows into the full light of noonday, the supreme radiance of grace and truth."

The leading figure of the age, St Bernard, was a fervent champion of this doctrine. It was the pabulum with which he nourished day in, day out, his spiritual sons, the monks of Clairvaux, in one of the bays of the abbey. Profoundly impressed with the oneness of God, St Bernard fiercely resisted the dialecticians who called His unity in question: men like Abelard and Gilbert de la Porée who dissociated the Persons of the Trinity and whose rationalizing approach, incapable of elevating man to the mystical plane, tended to reduce God to the human status—to disaggregate Him. But how was the ineffable to be apprehended in its plenitude? An uncompromising

ascetic, St Bernard believed that, for such an apprehension, complete poverty, that of the White Monks, was an indispensable preliminary. Only after vanquishing his body and climbing the "twelve steps of humility" could man hope to perceive himself as he truly is, an image of God. A faithful mirror, only falling short of the divine perfection by reason of the sin that tarnishes it. All that is needed is the uplift of love—and "the supreme cause of our love of God is God himself." The five Latin words composing this formula sum up the "back and forth movement" which in the *Hierarchies* of Dionysius governs the circulation of light. St Bernard keeps to the metaphor of light so frequently employed in the writings of the Pseudo-Areopagite, but he also uses others taken from the Song of Songs and these are of a nuptial order, for the union of the soul with God in states of ecstasy is of the nature of a wedlock, sealed by "the kiss of the spouse" (the soul). In this supreme moment there is an accord of wills, without confusion of substance, and the soul is "truly deified"; for what it then experiences is entirely divine. The soul is absorbed in this union as air flooded with sunlight is merged into the light, but it can achieve this union only if it is stripped of everything extraneous. "How can God be all in all if there remains in man something of man? True, the substance remains, but in another form, another glory, another power." On his upward way to the empyrean Dante placed his hand in St Bernard's.

Since St Bernard's ideas so closely approximated to the Dionysian theology, they should have led to an art resembling Suger's. But on one capital point the two men differed; St Bernard disapproved of outward show. The art of the Cistercian cloister and the church beside it was one of extreme austerity, eschewing any sort of adornment. Hence St Bernard's stern disapproval of Saint-Denis. "Not to mention the immense height and excessive breadth of your oratories, their sumptuous decorations and alluring paintings whose effect is to draw away the attention of the worshipper and hamper his meditation, and which recall after a fashion the rites of the Jews (for I am quite willing to grant that the purpose of all this is to glorify God), I shall in speaking to you, my fellow monks, use the same words that a pagan poet used, speaking to pagans like himself. 'What has gold to do,' he asked, 'in the temple?' And I, too, ask you, varying the poet's words and not his thought, what is the use for poor people like yourselves—assuming you are truly dedicated to poverty—of all the gold that glitters in your sanctuaries? The statue of a sainted man or woman is exposed to view and it is deemed the holier, the more it is bedecked with colors. Then people flock to kiss it and they are urged to donate alms; but it is to the beauty of the object rather than to its holiness that homage is being paid. Often, too, we see hung in churches what are rather wheels than crowns, spangled with gaudy beads, ringed round with lamps and inset with precious stones whose gleams are even brighter than those of the lamps. By way of candelabra there are veritable trees of brass wrought with wondrous skill, and the sheen of the gems is no less dazzling than that of the tapers they uphold. O vanity of vanities—but rather, I say, folly than vanity! The church is everywhere resplendent, but the poor are left destitute; its stones are clad in gold, but children go unclothed; lovers of beauty find in the church the wherewithal to gratify their taste, and the poor lack means to stave off their hunger."

St Bernard's conception of monasticism precluded ornamentation; there must be no more images in the House of God. Once his influence had taken effect in the Order, the White Monks ceased illustrating their books and the admirable school of painters that had flourished in earlier days came to a sudden end. The same fate befell monumental demonstrations of the Truth, the sculpture that had figured on the portals of the monasteries of Cluny. For the Cistercian abbey had no façade, not even a door; simple and devoid of ornament, it was isolated from the world. "Let those of us who are led by their concern for all that lies within to scorn and disregard what lies without, build for their worship edifices bearing the stamp of poverty, imitating the *sancta simplicitas* and wise restraint of their forefathers" (William of Saint-Thierry). By its very structure, the ordered sobriety of its parts and its symbolic layout, the abbey church, cornerstone and image of Christ, was meant to lead the soul towards the mystic heights. In its quiet precinct the light of day described the circles of the cosmic motion and traced the path of contemplation. No more was needed, for "it is not by a change of place," St Bernard said, "that we approach the Presence, but by successive enlightenments of a spiritual, not a physical order. Let the soul seek the light by following the light." Thus the sacred edifice was planned in terms of the discretion

native to the Rule of St Benedict. There is no straining upwards, no display, but a serene order conforming to the rhythm of the universe. Both in its mystique and in its handling of architectural volumes and their relations, Citeaux carried on the Benedictine tradition and its churches were as sturdy and massive as the Romanesque churches of southern Gaul.

In two respects, however, its art resembled that of Saint-Denis and the first cathedrals. Primarily, in the emphasis given to light and its use of spacious bays adorned with stained-glass windows painted only in grisaille (with non-figurative motifs), giving free access to the light of day. For these openings in the walls of their churches the Cistercians kept to French structural methods, notably the usage of crossed pointed arches. The Order of Citeaux, which originated in the east of the kingdom, began by establishing itself in Burgundy and Champagne, but affiliated abbeys soon sprang up in all parts of Latin Christendom and did much to diffuse the art of France, the *opus francigenum,* throughout the Christian world. It made its way even into the heart of the recalcitrant South; examples of it were to be found at Poblet in Catalonia and at Fossanova in central Italy. St Bernard also did much to promote the cult of the Virgin; he saw in her the "spouse" of the Song of Songs, the patroness of marriage, and under his aegis Cistercian art became a Marian art like that of the cathedrals.

Suger had included the Virgin in his schema of iconographic correspondences; had not the Mother of God participated in the Incarnation? But he assigned to her only a minor place in Saint-Denis. In the cathedrals of France, however, all of which were dedicated to Notre Dame, effigies of the divine motherhood figured in the center of the monumental decorations and on them was focused the devotion of the masses. Given the posture of the gilded "idol" of Romanesque Auvergne, these carved images did not as yet convey the emotion of love, but rather sovereignty and majesty. The Virgin Mother effaced the sins of womankind, put to flight evil spirits, impure dreams and sinful desires, and, in a sense, atoned for them. To her were directed the mystical yearnings of all these men who were striving for chastity, of the canons on whom attempts were now being made to enforce the rule of celibacy and, needless to say, of the monks of Citeaux.

The Virgin made a majestic entrance, escorted by a company of sainted women, into the piety of the twelfth century. The Magdalen, sinner, hope of fallen women, triumphed at Vézelay and in Provence. And as it so happened, at the very time when Christendom was beginning to concern itself with feminine values, the exaltation of woman in the courts of chivalry in the Loire and Poitou regions was getting under way. There songs were being composed extolling the beauty of the great lord's wife, the singer's "ladylove," all the young nobles were trying to win her heart, and dalliance with the rites of "courtesy" was becoming one of the most exciting games in vogue at gatherings of the nobility. The cult of the Virgin and that of the ladylove had of course quite different origins, deep-seated but obscure, of which history tells us little. Yet they certainly had something in common. This much is clear: the note of passion struck for the first time in the West in Heloise's letters to Abelard, the Latin poems that Abbot Baudry of Bourgueil wrote for the Angevin princesses, the songs composed by Cercamont and Marcabru for the boudoirs of the ladies of Aquitaine and all the romances based on ancient themes, on the story of Aeneas and the Fall of Troy—the first tales whose episodes were not only of a military but of an amorous nature—link up with William of Saint-Thierry and the interpolations from Ovid in his *De Natura Amoris*. The same humanist sources, the same vocabulary, the same sequences of "ordeals," the same desires, the same ideals are everywhere apparent in the writings of the age, both sacred and profane; its atmosphere pervades both the statuary of Chartres and the Marian sermons and poems of St Bernard. France was discovering love; both courtly love and love of the Virgin Mary. It was the duty of the prelates and, above all, of the monks to sublimate carnal love and to canalize these emotive trends into the liturgies of the Church. About 1140 Peter the Venerable, Abbot of Cluny, introduced into the traditional hymnal the passages relating to the Nativity. In the soft radiance of lamps and candelabra, in clouds of incense, the sonorous Latin incantations took on the quality of a rite of coronation, the crowning of the Mother of God.

"I hail thee, Virgin Mary, spouse of the All-highest, mother of the gentle Lamb of God, who hast put to flight the powers of evil. Thou reignest in heaven and savest those on earth; men yearn towards thee and the evil spirits fear thee. Thou art the window, the door and the veil, the courtyard and the house, the temple, the earth, lily in thy virginity, rose by thy sufferings. Thou art the closed garden, the fountain of the garden that washes all who are defiled, purifies all who are corrupted and brings back life to the dead. Thou art the mistress of the ages, the hope, after God, of all generations, the king's house of rest and the abode of godhead. Thou art the star which, shining in the East, scatters the shadows of the West; the break of day; the light that knows no darkness. Thou, who didst engender Him who is our begetter, hast the joy of a mother who has well fulfilled her task, reconciled man with God. Pray, O Mother, the God whom thou didst bring into this world to forgive our sins that, after forgiving us, he may bestow on us grace and glory. Amen." The great Benedictine prayers invest the Virgin Mother with the majesty that inspired the art of the cathedrals. For the priests who devised its setting the Christmas festival solemnized in highest heaven, chanted by the choirs of angels, the first coming of Christ the King. And so the woman who had given birth to Him held an exalted place in the celestial hierarchy. It was from the store of symbolic names garnered by Abbot Peter that the first Marian iconology drew its vocabulary, while other metaphors—the garden enclosed, the orchard, the bed of sweet flowers, the tower of ivory—were taken from the Song of Songs. In the prayer that Dante puts into the mouth of St Bernard in the *Paradiso* we find a similar range of symbols.

Thou Virgin Mother, daughter of thy Son,
Humble and high beyond all other creatures,
The limit fixed of the eternal counsel,
Thou art the one who such nobility
To human nature gave that its Creator
Did not disdain to make himself its creature.
Within thy womb rekindled was the love
By warmth of which in the eternal peace
After such wise this flower has germinated.
Here unto us thou art a noonday torch
Of charity, and below, in the world of mortals,
Thou art the living fountainhead of hope.

As champion of the Queen of Heaven, St Bernard, who had entered the lists against the greatest churchmen of the day, now joined issue with the knights of the princely courts. Seeking to "convert" them, too, and lead them back to the way of holiness, he drew up the rule of a new religious order, the Templars. This was composed of converted warriors who, while remaining knights, had become monks, a *nova militia* who directed their arms against the enemies of Christ and their love towards Our Lady. St Bernard urged all the warriors of France to follow their king in a new crusade and enlist their restless energy under the banner of God. Likewise, he tried to orient the emotions celebrated in the literature in favor at the courts—love songs and romances— towards the path of mysticism. Stirred by his passionate appeal, some of the courtly poets underwent a conversion, supreme achievement of which in the field of literature was the famous romance of the Quest of the Holy Grail (c. 1200); the earliest version of it, written some years before the turn of the century, was *Le Conte del Graal* by Chrétien de Troyes. Whereas the heroes of earlier romances had practised a merely conventional religion, the Christianity of Perceval (the tale of whose adventures he composed some time before 1190) was a religion based on love of the Saviour, on penitence and prayer, and it extolled purity as the highest virtue. After the triumph of St Bernard young noblemen underwent the ceremony of dubbing and the ancient rite of initiation into knighthood as if it were indeed a sacrament. They came to it escorted by priests, prepared for it by a night of prayer in the oratory; a bath—a second baptism—washed them clean of sin, and then and only then could they join an order whose members practised the virtues of Christ, or were enjoined to practise them. For the victory of the Cistercian doctrines was only on the surface. It was by no means so easy as St Bernard thought to quell these young men's appetite for profane pleasures, for luxury and high living, for showy exploits in the lists or on the battlefield.

In any case Citeaux itself was following the trend of the times when the century drew to its close. It was common knowledge that the Cistercian abbeys were extremely wealthy. The White Monks had many sources of income—benefices, tithes and rents—while the menial tasks were performed by "serfs" recruited from the peasantry. Like feudal lords, the Cistercians lived on others' labor, and soon, tiring of the seclusion of the cloisters, they mingled in the life of the townsfolk. St Bernard might be outraged at the proposal that he should be an archbishop, but one of his monks had quitted the monastery to ascend the papal throne as Eugenius III. Other friars followed a similar path as the twelfth century ended; they wore the mitre, built cathedrals, took to study, and soon the order founded in Paris a daughter house where instruction was given in the humanities. At Toulouse the clergy chose for their bishop the abbot of Le Thoronet, a Cistercian monastery. This was Folquet of Marseilles, formerly a troubadour, and before long a new bishop's church was erected on the lines of those of the Ile-de-France. And at this same time the fact had to be faced that Citeaux had completely failed in its latest enterprise, the systematic eradication of heresy in the South.

THE CLOISTER

During the twelfth and thirteenth centuries, despite the success of the mendicant orders and of the new ideal of the Christian life they sponsored, retirement from the world and seclusion in a monastery, there to lead a life of prayer and strict austerity, were still regarded as providing the surest path to perfection. Where could one more confidently hope to achieve salvation than in a quiet haven remote from the corruptions of the world? Places of meditation, instruments of collective redemption, which dispensed God's pardon on their bene- factors, the Benedictine foundations attracted the alms and the devotion of the Christian community. Moreover, throughout Southern Europe the eleventh-century reform had led to the organization of the cathedral clergy and canons in a compact, disciplined group on monastic lines. The lives of these self-contained communities centered on the cloister.

Completely enclosed by the monastic buildings, the cloister was the core of this little world apart. Sheltered from the evil of the outside world, it was a "garden close" where the air and sunlight, trees, birds and flowing streams still kept the freshness of the first days of the earth: a sort of paradise regained where all things testified to God's per- fection. Situated at the heart of the monastery, the cloister was the only part of it which, left empty, had no specific function and so lent itself best to meditation. It was here that the head of the community sum- moned his sons for the evening sermon; here that took place the strictly educational courses, readings from set books and rumination on their texts. That is why the capitals carried symbolic images, incentives to a progress, step by step, towards the Truth. Everywhere the cloister was decorated—with sculpture in regions with a strong Roman tradition; with colored incrustations in the south of Italy where an Oriental aesthetic still prevailed; with all the sophisticated elegance of Gothic art on Mont Saint-Michel.

But Cistercian cloisters were bare; the Rule of the Order banned all ornament, proscribed those decorative fantasies which had lent a delicate charm to the pages of its earliest Bibles. Yet even here, in these abodes of total austerity, the cloister, like the church, told of the beauty of the universe, God's handiwork; but it did so only in the harmony of its volumes and the ebb and flow of light in its arcades, determined by the hour of day and the cycle of the seasons.

CLOISTER OF SAINT-TROPHIME AT ARLES. LATE 12TH CENTURY.

CLOISTER OF THE ABBEY OF LE THORONET. FOUNDED IN 1146.

NAVE OF THE ABBEY CHURCH OF FOSSANOVA, SOUTH OF ROME. 1163-1208.

NAVE OF THE ABBEY CHURCH OF SILVACANE, NEAR MARSEILLES. FOUNDED IN 1147.

COUNTER-CURRENTS

By 1190 the art of France had forged a language of its own, a language of clarity, light and logic befitting the quest of a God made man for our salvation. This new aesthetic made good in Neustria, from Tours to Reims, along the very axis of the Carolingian "renaissance," and not only in the great cathedral schools but also in the countryside, throughout the area ruled by the Capetian kings. Under the lead of Cîteaux its influence spread far afield, filtering into Burgundy and Champagne; the choir at Vézelay was rebuilt in accordance with its formulas. This expansion of the art of Saint-Denis kept pace with that of the royal power, for the king of France had recently included in his dominions Mâcon and the province of Auvergne. He traveled widely beyond his frontiers, visited the Grande Chartreuse, the tomb of St James and Jerusalem. Many of the bishops of Germany and England had studied under Parisian masters and new cathedrals in both countries—Bamberg, Canterbury—imitated the Notre-Dames of France; one can detect borrowings, if at a far remove, from these models in the porches of Compostela, Saint-Gilles and Saint-Trophime at Arles. When the goldsmith Nicholas of Verdun designed a pulpit for Klosterneuburg, near Vienna, he utilized an iconography of concordances directly stemming from that of Suger. This breakthrough of the new art thrust Romanesque forms into the background. In the Ile-de-France they were relegated to the darker corners of portals, among the devils of the Last Judgment, and to the tangled imagery on some capitals and the consoles of statues. Here the ancient bestiary stood for evil trampled underfoot, for sin and death. But it was not obliterated everywhere and Romanesque "monstrosities" still flourished, unabashed, in many provinces remote from Chartres and Paris.

For at the four cardinal points the Gothic invasion came up against traditions, beliefs and ways of thinking allergic to those of the properly French provinces. On the north it was challenged by an urge to fantastic forms and figurations stemming from England and Ireland and by that vogue for an emotive line full of capricious spirals and sinuous divagations which Scottish monks were importing to the Continent, even as far south as Regensburg. Within the Empire that Ottonian heritage, the art of the bronze-workers, had lost nothing of its driving force; it was making headway in Italy and, untouched by any French influence, flourishing at Pisa, Benevento and Monreale—no less than at Gniezno. Moreover, under its lead, the Romanesque aesthetic continued to proliferate in all the marginal regions of the south. The decorations at Ripoll and those of Notre-Dame-du-Port at Clermont-Ferrand date to the close of the twelfth century. All are Romanesque, and in this part of Europe contacts with eastern art forms, due to the Christian conquests, furthered a resistance to the allurements of the new Gothic art. The illustrations in the Mozarabic style of the *Commentaria* of the eighth-century theologian Beatus, made about 1190, were a Spanish contribution. But the chief source of inspiration was Byzantine art which, after winning favor in the Bavarian Marches and at the court of the king of Palermo, influenced all the art of the south.

The individual history of each of these "recalcitrant" provinces accounts for the obstacles they set up to the progress of the French aesthetic. In some countries the fact that they clung so firmly to antiquated procedures points to a state of arrested development. For not all of them benefited by the revival of agriculture which, sooner than elsewhere, had given the bishops of the great cities, from Chartres to Soissons, the wherewithal to play the part of generous, liberal-minded patrons of the arts. In the mountains of Auvergne conditions were very different; their ancient churches catering for a simple-minded peasantry continued to distribute, so to speak, the small change of the creations of the eleventh century. Isolated in its backwater from the main stream of progress, Provence stagnated. On the confines of the civilized world, Ireland, Scotland and Scandinavia still were barbarous countries peopled by nomad tribes of hunters and fishermen. England had no towns, nor had the forested parts of Germany. The lands of the Empire, where Charlemagne had now been canonized, were still in process of assimilating little by little Carolingian culture. All these regions lacked schools, or where they existed they had not yet fallen in line with the advanced ideas of the West. They knew nothing of the new liturgies celebrating the Divine Light and the Incarnation, nor had they yet been touched by the spirit of inquiry which led thinkers to seek out the truth and nourish their faith with understanding; choral singing was the main element of the curriculum. In any case the cathedral chapters were composed of members of the feudal nobility; the archbishops and canons of Lyons and of Arles were great lords ever ready for the fray, better trained in wielding arms than in using their brains. In these provinces the monasteries were the chief centers of religious life, but the monks confined themselves to liturgies in the Cluniac mode; when any new idea made its appearance it was usually sidetracked into some innocuous path. When Hildegard, Abbess of Bingen, wrote her *Liber divinorum operum* she took inspiration from an allegorical poem recently composed by a prelate of Chartres, but transmuted what she found in it into a tissue of incoherencies bathed in the apocalyptic atmosphere of the Beatus *Commentaries*. Similarly, when the Calabrian abbot, Joachim of Floris, took over Suger's exposition of the concordances between the Old and New Testaments he handled it in such a way that it dwindled into vague, messianic reveries. Here again we have evidence of a mentality that had failed to keep in step with the spirit of the age.

In other parts of Europe, however, the progressive ideas deriving from the Ile-de-France came up against trends of thought which, prompted by an intellectual evolution quite as active as that of the region around Paris, took a very different course. South of the Loire it was the spirit of the courts of chivalry that came in conflict with Gothic art. Aquitaine had never acquiesced in Carolingian overlordship and had doggedly resisted Pepin, Charlemagne and Charles the Bald. It had never accepted their conceptions of a learned clergy, of church schools, and of the fusion of the spiritual and the temporal *potestas* in the person of the Frankish king, but

had continued to keep religion and life in separate compartments: on the one hand the lofty ideal of the cloister, on the other the pleasures of the fashionable world. During the eleventh century Aquitaine was the region most affected by the ecclesiastical reform promoted by Pope Gregory VII. The religious communities were freed from state control, monks and churchmen differentiated from the lay nobility more sharply than in the past, the former dedicated to chastity, the latter spending their days in feats of arms and love-making. The princes of Aquitaine did not think themselves invested with any sacred function and took little or no interest in their religious duties, while the members of their courts trusted to the prayers of the monks for the salvation of their souls, and hoped by generous alms-giving to earn sufficient merit to justify a life of pleasure-seeking. They enjoyed hunting and warfare no less than did the knights of France, but they lived in cities where the Roman tradition of urbanity had not declined to the same extent and they could still relish the more refined joys of civilized life. About 1100 a Duke of Aquitaine made the first love-songs in the French tongue, adjusting to the melodies of Gregorian chants verses in praise of his ladylove, and all the young men at his court followed suit. They invented the love game in which the young man idolizes his lord's wife and transfers to her the loyalty, services and vassalage he owes his lord. This code of courtly manners developed in an aristocracy whose emotions were less bridled than they were north of the Loire by the Church, which here kept strictly to its cloisters and ritual devotions. It gained ground in the region of Toulouse, in Provence and later in Italy. The nobility of all the provinces that were truly French finished by adopting it, if not without twinges of remorse, in the second half of the twelfth century. King Louis VII had married the heiress of the dukes of Aquitaine, but her frivolity displeased him; the monks in his entourage, Suger to begin with, convinced him that it was of diabolic origin and persuaded him to divorce her.

Eleanor of Aquitaine soon found another husband, Henry Plantagenet, King of England, who was already possessed of the continental inheritance of Anjou and still held Normandy. After his marriage the king extended his domain over a long chain of territories covering about half the kingdom of France. Determined to outdo the Capetian king, he bade the intellectuals of his court devise an aesthetic capable of competing with that of Paris. Indifferent to faith and intellectual problems, this new aesthetic aimed at giving pleasure and stimulating the imagination. Hence its combination of "courtesy," a speciality of Aquitaine, with the *matière de Bretagne*, meaning the English idiom. The royal Abbey of Malmesbury—British equivalent of Saint-Denis—near the Welsh border was the repository of a wealth of legendary lore (including the Arthurian cycle), fructified by the Celtic imagination. From it the writers at the court of Henry II drew the themes of their romances: fabulous adventures of knights errant slaying dragons in the perilous quest of some fair lady. The tragic tale of Tristan and Iseult challenged the French martial epics describing the exploits of helmeted bishops and Charlemagne's valiant knights; challenged, too, the mystic chivalry of Perceval. The art of France came up against a similar resistance in the west. The cathedral of Angers, while utilizing crossed ogival arches, retained the massive structure of the Romanesque churches of Poitou. In point of fact the aesthetic of the Plantagenet domain never achieved an architectural style of its own. Its art was almost always confined to the poetic field and, except in English book illuminations, whose free-flowing line was frankly opposed to the stateliness of the Chartres statuary, rarely found visual expression. The only monumental illustrations of the romances which were written for the princes of western France are to be seen in Italian cathedrals. Characters from the Tale of Troy figure in a mosaic pavement at Bitonto, and the Knights of the Round Table on a tympanum at Modena. These can be accounted for by the fact that the Italian élite were attracted by the culture of the princely courts of northern France and that in Italian cities the cathedral, heir of the ancient basilica, was as much a civic as a religious edifice. For here, far more than in France, the cathedral was the common property of all the citizens, it was quite literally "their" house.

On the southeast of Latin Christendom other factors, perhaps more deeply rooted, in any case more active and stimulated by the growth of commerce in the Mediterranean area, combated the influence of the Ile-de-France. Here the relapse of western Christendom into the barbarism of the early Middle Ages had never quite extinguished the towns and they had soon recovered their vitality. The Germans streaming down through the Brenner Pass were startled to find them so powerful. The communes had driven back the feudal barons into the poverty-stricken castles of the countryside, brought to heel the bishop and his priests, vanquished Frederick Barbarossa and carried back in triumph to Milan the eagles of the Empire. Within their city walls arose a type of culture which, as in Aquitaine, though emancipated from Church control, was tributary to the schools. For the Italian schools were not ecclesiastical, nor did they base their education on theology; any Italian youth who wished to study it went to Paris. In this part of Italy, in Pavia and above all at the University of Bologna, jurisprudence was the chief discipline. It was in Bologna that at the end of the eleventh century Justinian's *Digest* was rediscovered and henceforth this text held the same place in the local curriculum as that of the Scriptures in the *studia* of the Ile-de-France. For its interpretation the same methods of dialectical analysis were applied as those employed for elucidating the Decretals of canon law, and in his *Concordia discordantium canonum* Gratian (c. 1140) took the same intellectual approach as that of Abelard. But this discipline was unconcerned with religion and intended solely to provide a corps of jurists for the service of the Emperor and the cities where they practised. Further south in Italy, around the provinces formerly ruled by Byzantium and Islam, other forms of education emerged; they too were of a temporal order, relating to the body, not the soul. In these schools medicine and astrology bulked large, and, algebra and astronomy being needed for drawing up reliable horoscopes, there was an intensive study of translations of Hippocrates, Galen and Aristotle. Neglecting Aristotle's works on logic, the professors read his *Meterologica* and sought to learn from him what were the links between the four elements of the cosmos and the "humors" of man. In Italy, now that the communes were in the saddle, the curriculum of the schools centered on practical life.

In South European cities the Church no longer sought to base its teachings on logical argument: it did not preach; it chanted. None the less the advance of civilization was taking effect on the mentality of an élite in the larger towns. For soon the rites and ceremonies of church services ceased to satisfy the knights, lawyers and businessmen, all of whom had a feeling of guilt vis-à-vis their Maker. Anxious to save their souls, they sought for spiritual nourishment. No longer finding this in the cathedral, they listened eagerly to the itinerant preachers who delivered sermons at street corners and in public squares. These men, anyhow, spoke their language, they had a message to deliver. Many of them were renegades, former members of the clergy who had left the church, feeling ill at ease among the canons, or else had failed to win admittance to the exalted circles mainly reserved to sons of wealthy parents. Tempted neither by the cloister nor by the hermit's cell, they felt constrained to preach the word of God—usually in an aggressive manner, for the bishops hounded them down remorselessly.

Most of them preached penitence. Behind the heretical movement lay a desire for the reform of the Church and this—the preachers stressed the point—linked up with the reforming zeal of the great Pope Gregory. The cathedral prelates were unworthy, corrupted by worldliness and luxury. What value had sacraments administered by their soiled hands, the chants rising from their tainted lips? The people had need of efficacious rites; let them, then, expel the sinful priests and restore to the Church its spiritual mission. Given the social unrest in the towns, such words had an immediate appeal. Would not the act of stripping the bishop of his temporal power bring freedom to the community? Surely, too, the rule of apostolic poverty justified insurrections of this order. In 1146 Arnold of Brescia, a canon regular who had studied at Paris and one of the leaders of the reformist movement in Italy, set up a commune in Rome, basing his campaign against the wealthy Curia on the poverty of Christ. Nine years later, after being denounced as a heretic for bidding the prelates "lead the life of Jesus," he was hanged and his body burnt. If Arnold's campaign had a political tinge, this gradually died out as the cult of "holy poverty" gained ground in the middle class; the rich merchant of Lyons Peter Waldo was far from being a leader of revolt. Waldo had a translation made of the Gospels into Provençal and learnt from them that as a rich man he was excluded from the kingdom of God. So he sold all his possessions, gave the money to the poor and, with a view to assuring municipal independence for his fellow citizens, took to preaching. But since he was a layman, the archbishop forbade him to speak about religion, sentenced him (in 1180) and had the sentence confirmed by the pope. His disciples, the Waldensians, had to go into hiding. Even so this clandestine sect, in revolt against the established Church, attracted a large following—chiefly of businessmen, cattle merchants and weavers—in the cities, country towns and villages of the Alpine region, Provence and Italy.

Meanwhile, in the Toulouse district, other sectaries were making many converts to a doctrine which, though invoking the name of Christ, differed radically from Christianity. Here the Catholic Church was openly challenged by a rival church, that of the Cathars. The way to this revolt against the establishment had been prepared, early in the twelfth century, by such unorthodox preachers as Peter of Bruys and Henry of Lausanne. They too began by violently attacking the worldly lives of the clergy. The bishops called them Manichaeans, and it is clear that in their championship of poverty and purity they tended to stress the antinomy between the spiritual and carnal principles and to represent the world as the scene of an endless conflict between Good and Evil, sequel of the primal war in heaven. Their teachings were readily accepted in a region where, more than elsewhere, the layman rarely came in touch with the servants of God. The fact that in the latter half of the century this dualism was explicitly formulated and crystallized into a rigid doctrinal system was due both to the influence of the Crusades and to closer contacts with the Balkans by way of trade. The Greek word "Cathar" made its first appearance in 1163, when it was applied to the members of this sect. By this time they were very numerous, probably more numerous than the orthodox Catholics in some districts. Twenty years before, alarmed by their growth, St Bernard had thundered against them—but in vain. The victor on this occasion was not the Cistercian abbot but a newcomer from the East, Nicetas, bishop of the heretical sect of the Bogomils, who installed four bishops in Languedoc and one in northern Italy. It was now that the chapter general of Citeaux received a call for aid from Count Raymond of Toulouse. All his noble vassals, he said, were being contaminated and a whole community in the Albi region had broken with the Church and embraced the rival religion.

Here there was no question of a mere deviation; rather, of a new dogma. We shall never have a clear idea of its tenets, so ruthlessly was Catharism exterminated by the inquisitors of the next century.

They destroyed its records, wiped out all trace of it. However, from the manuals issued for the guidance of the inquisitors we can learn some basic facts. The Cathars were dualists, believing that two supreme powers or principles exist: a god of light and the spirit, a god of darkness and the flesh, perpetually competing for the governance of the world. Man is involved in the combat, and in it his future is at stake. For if he wishes to have access to the light after he dies, instead of being reincarnated in a fleshly body, he must co-operate in the victory of the "light principle," that is to say shun everything in which Satan has a part, reject money, nourish himself with the least impure aliments, eat no flesh and refrain from carnal intercourse. For procreating favors the triumph of the material and adds recruits to the Satanic host. In practice only a few Cathars, the so-called Perfecti, were capable of this total ascesis. These men, "vessels of election," had the power of ensuring the salvation of weaker brethren and, by the imposition of hands, even *in extremis*, of impregnating them with the Spirit. Familiar with intercession of this type, the inhabitants of Aquitaine felt no qualms about delegating to others the vocations of poverty and chastity and entrusting to the ritual gestures of these specialists in salvation the care of their souls, while they themselves enjoyed with a clear conscience the good things of this world. The "Perfects" had this advantage, that in their lives they gave a shining example of self-imposed poverty and that they were less hypocritical and exacted less from the people than the clergy. Hence they seemed far better qualified as intercessors between man and God. Noble troubadours and wealthy merchants often called them in, on their deathbeds, to administer the Cathar rite of *Consolamentum*, or "baptism of the Spirit," and many of the wives of the lords of Aquitaine in their declining years formed "Communities of Perfect Life."

We may be sure that few of these men and women had any clear notion of the radical antinomy between the doctrine of the "Perfects" and orthodox Catholicism. For the exponents of the Bogomil dualism had taken over the terminology and some of the symbols used by the Catholic clergy—to such effect that the transition from the anti-episcopal diatribes of the preachers to the paradoxes of Cathar dogma passed unnoticed. None the less that dogma repudiated the hierarchical orders defined by Dionysius, his theory of progression from the

Source and ultimate return, and indeed the whole idea of Creation. For how could matter, intrinsically evil, emanate from a God who was the principle of goodness? The Cathars also rejected the doctrine of the Incarnation; they saw, it seems, in Jesus only an angel sent on earth by the God of Light, and justified this view by the opening pages of the Gospel of St John. How, they asked, could the divine illumination have submerged itself in the darkness of the flesh and taken form in a woman's womb? How, then, endorse the cult of Mary? They rejected, too, the notion of redemption. How could the God of Light have suffered in his flesh, what value could be assigned to the pangs of a mortal body? Thus the "Perfects" broke completely with the ideas embodied in Suger's Saint-Denis, with the doctrine of the Trinity and the iconography of the cathedrals.

At the end of the twelfth century the addicts of diverse forms of heresy, the Cathars and the Waldensians (also known as Vaudois) who dispensed with priests and practised their purifying rites in secret, the many obscure sects that flourished in the south and in the cultured circles of the courts—all alike set up a solid resistance to the ideology of the schools of Paris and the concepts of the cathedral builders. But heresy went further; it imperilled the unity of Christendom. Expressing as it did the troubled mental climate of the age, it came to be the prime concern of the rulers of the Church. The best of the monks, the Cistercians, had failed in their crusading mission; the Abbot of Cîteaux had to confess defeat. It behooved the Roman Church to use all the weapons in its armory. Why not those of art? It was already used in Italy in the service of orthodox propaganda. In 1138 Guglielmo of Lucca confronted those who doubted the efficacy of His sacrifice with an image of Christ crucified, and in the choir of Santa Maria in Trastevere, in Rome, a mosaic was set up celebrating the triumph of the Mother of God. Both works proclaimed the truth of the Incarnation, just as Benedetto Antelami's *Deposition from the Cross* (1178) affirmed that of the Redemption. At Arles, in the porch of Saint-Gilles, all the arguments for the True Faith were figured forth dramatically. Thus at the end of the twelfth century all the possibilities of visual persuasion were being exploited in the Romanesque art of southern Europe. It was, however, the art of the Gothic cathedrals that now became what was perhaps the Church's most efficacious ally in the war on heresy.

The success of the cathedral schools of Neustria had a profound and stimulating influence on the evolution of twelfth-century culture. All the same the art language based on the transcription of the new theology into visual terms did not hold its own unchallenged. We find signs of an insidious penetration of scholastic values into the world of art, though this process was very gradual and is often hard to trace.

Most of the students in the Parisian schools came from the region between the Loire and the Rhine, and from England. The new aesthetic made headway earliest in these provinces, but never wholly dominated them. Thus the art of the illuminated book was little if at all affected; it formed a domain apart, untouched by the prevailing trend. This was because illumination was a less public art and relatively immune to the pressure of official propaganda. The illustrator of manuscripts was surrounded by much older works and took inspiration from them. Also, during this period, he was more controlled than other artists by the monks, and the abbey schools were becoming more and more conservative, less disposed to welcome new ideas. For them, far longer than in the outside world, God remained "the Invisible" and artists working in monastic scriptoria sought above all to interpret in line and color their inner vision and their reveries.

As a result of the Scandinavian invasions in the tenth century, of the intensification of maritime traffic which had preceded them and continued after them, and, most notably, of the Norman conquest, a close cultural association developed between England and Western France. In this part of Europe the manuscript painters kept to the Carolingian tradition; they modeled their work on books that were illuminated in the Franco-insular style, in which two trends were intermingled. The first, which triumphed about 1150 at Hénin-Liétard, at Saint-Amand and Valenciennes, derived from the "renaissance" spirit active in the palatine school, its purposive revival of the imperial art of Antiquity. This humanist tradition gave rise to monumental figures of Evangelists and Doctors of the Church and Crucifixions stamped with a classical serenity. A second, very different art came from the British Isles, where it had taken refuge in the tenth century. Winchester was the chief scene of the flowering of this art of free fancy. It abounds in pictures of weird monsters, in scenes of hell and the apocalyptic visions described in Revelations, and its line has all the suppleness and emotive dynamism of the drawings in the Utrecht Psalter. In representations of human figures this line is disciplined, quite in the classical spirit; but it runs free in animal and vegetable forms, weaving them into flowing arabesques and geometric convolutions.

GOSPEL BOOK OF HÉNIN-LIÉTARD: ST MATTHEW, 12TH CENTURY.
FOLIO 22 VERSO, MS 14, I, BIBLIOTHÈQUE MUNICIPALE, BOULOGNE-SUR-MER.

II. 74

SACRAMENTARY OF SAINT-AMAND: CRUCIFIXION, SECOND HALF OF THE 12TH CENTURY.
FOLIO 58 VERSO, MS 108, BIBLIOTHÈQUE MUNICIPALE, VALENCIENNES.

UTRECHT PSALTER (COPY): ILLUSTRATION FOR PSALM XLIII. LATE 12TH CENTURY (?).
FOLIO 76, MS LAT. 8846, BIBLIOTHÈQUE NATIONALE, PARIS.

EADWINE PSALTER: ILLUSTRATION FOR PSALM XLIII, ABOUT 1150.
MS R. 17.1, TRINITY COLLEGE LIBRARY, CAMBRIDGE.

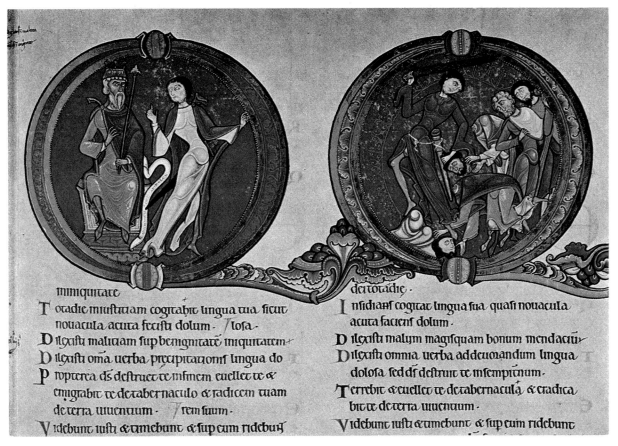

miniquitate

Totadie miuftitiam cogitabit lingua tua sicut
nouacula acuta fecisti dolum · Iosa ·

Dilexisti maliciam sup benignitate miquitatem·

Dilexisti oma uerba precipitationis lingua do

Propterea ds destruet te infinem euellet te &
emigrabit te detabernaculo & radicem tuam
de terra uiuentium · Item suum ·

Videbunt iusti & timebunt & sup eum ridebunt

dei totadie ·

Insidians cogitat lingua sua quasi nouacula
acuta faciens dolum ·

Dilexisti malum magisquam bonum mendaciu

Dilexisti omnia uerba addeuorandum lingua
dolosa sed ds destruit te insempitnum ·

Terrebit & euellet te detabernaculo & eradica
bit te de terra uiuentium ·

Videbunt iusti & timebunt & sup eum ridebunt

BIBLE OF HENRY OF BLOIS: DOEG THE EDOMITE SLAYING THE PRIESTS OF NOB. SECOND HALF OF THE 12TH CENTURY.
VOL. III, FOLIO 16 RECTO, CATHEDRAL LIBRARY, WINCHESTER.

APOCALYPSE: THE DRAGON WITH SEVEN HEADS CAST DOWN FROM HEAVEN. ST ALBANS, ABOUT 1230.
MS R. 16.2, TRINITY COLLEGE LIBRARY, CAMBRIDGE.

ENAMELLED FUNERARY PLAQUE ALLEGEDLY FROM THE TOMB OF GEOFFREY PLANTAGENET (1113-1151) IN LE MANS CATHEDRAL.
12TH CENTURY. MUSÉE DE TESSÉ, LE MANS.

II. 78

In the twelfth century churchmen, knights, merchants, even peasants could travel much more freely than in the past and these journeys, encounters and exchanges of ideas did something to reduce the barriers between the various provinces of Christian Europe. All the same they remained shut up, to some extent, in watertight compartments. If we were asked to make a "map of culture" for the period—an almost hopeless task, given the gaps in our information—we should have to begin by delineating a network of interlocking frontiers, a complex of fragmentated units, refractory in many cases to any outside influence, a many-faceted pattern of regional particularities. It would, however, be possible to discern in this medley of conflicting ideologies and mores a clear-cut dividing line corresponding to the political cleavage of which all the men of the time who gave thought to such matters were acutely conscious. Running north and south this line separated the Kingdom (that is to say France and the western zone of Latin Christendom) from what still survived of the Empire: Germany, Italy and the satellite states, politically and culturally united since the tenth century under a single government.

During this period the king of Germany became as a matter of course Roman Emperor. When Frederick Barbarossa sought to restore the Empire to the position it had occupied in its glorious past, he made a point of asserting the imperial prerogative at Besançon and Arles, in Lombardy and Tuscany, and declared himself the heir of Charlemagne. This may explain the ascendancy of the Carolingian aesthetic in these parts of Europe and its resistance to the blandishments of the royal art of France. For there could be no denying that the art of the emperors, descendants of Charlemagne and Otto the Great, was in the lineage of the art of the Caesars. Thus all the new churches built in Germany, Lombardy, Tuscany and Rome retained the proportions of the ancient basilicas. In the interior there were the same arcades, the same system of lighting, the same timber ceilings. There were also frescoes and often, under the triumphal arch, an image of the Crucifixion, symbol of the triumph of the Church. In most cases the façades were very soberly adorned. However, the new affluence of the Tuscan cities, due to their sea-borne trade, commercial enterprise and the manufacture of costly imitations of Oriental luxury wares, led them to decorate the fronts of their churches. Indeed this desire to flaunt their opulence often gave rise to an excess of ornamentation, an over-lavish use of color, a plethora of sculpture. There are many points in common between the churches of Lucca and the imperial art of Rome and Ravenna: notably the façades with their curtain of tracery fretting the western light, pediments and long colonnades.

FAÇADE OF THE CHURCH OF SAN MICHELE IN FORO, LUCCA. BEGUN ABOUT 1210.

FAÇADE OF BAMBERG CATHEDRAL, FOUNDED BY HENRY II. 1004-1012 (RESTORED ABOUT 1081 AND AGAIN IN 1185).

INTERIOR OF THE ALL SAINTS CHAPEL, REGENSBURG. 12TH CENTURY.

MOSAICS

In the course of the thirteenth century the art of France forced its way into Italy, this incursion being promoted, firstly, by the Holy See, which saw in the aesthetic of the University the most effective vehicle of Catholic theology and, secondly, by the religious Orders, its faithful exponents: the Cistercians and after them the Mendicants. None the less, the scope of this French influence was necessarily limited since it came up against two forms of culture which in the course of many centuries had solidly established themselves in Italy: that of imperial Rome and that of Byzantium.

The Germanic invasions had swept through Italy from end to end, brushing aside the figurative and humanist traditions of Roman art and imposing an art of jewelers and engravers, the barbarous geometry and weird animal forms of the Nordic belt-buckles. But a considerable part of Italy had held out against the intruders and incorporation in Charlemagne's empire. Latium was never more than a weakly held fringe of it; Venice and all the south kept their independence. These regions remained tied up with the East, and this association had been growing closer since the tenth century, now that the sea routes were being swept clear of pirates. That is why at the time when work was beginning on Notre-Dame in Paris the Doges of Venice still elected for a "Greek" decoration in St Mark's, and the Norman kings of Sicily did likewise for the walls of their palaces, oratories and cathedrals.

The Byzantine church was a habitation of the divine. Its façades were left severely plain and the aesthetic effort of its builders was concentrated on the interior, where mosaics spangling the shadows with flakes of living light conjured up visions of the Celestial City. The makers of the mosaics of Palermo and Monreale—and, following them, those of the Baptistery of Florence and the Monastery of the Santi Quattro Coronati in Rome—adopted the narrative form of presentation favored by the Duecento artists, but—this was a new development—couched it in the idiom of the then current Oriental iconography. The subjects are Gospel scenes and tales culled from the Apocrypha. Yet here, too, the logical spirit of the age makes itself felt; the settings of the figures of Christ's childhood and Passion are given a mathematical precision, space is carefully organized and each group of scenes boldly demarcated by a frame.

THE NATIVITY, 1140-1143. MOSAIC IN LA MARTORANA (CHURCH OF SANTA MARIA DELL'AMMIRAGLIO), PALERMO.

THE ENTRY OF CHRIST INTO JERUSALEM, 1143. MOSAIC IN THE SANCTUARY, CAPPELLA PALATINA, PALERMO.

CHRIST PANTOCRATOR AND THE VIRGIN AND CHILD WITH ANGELS, APOSTLES AND SAINTS. 12TH-13TH CENTURY.
MOSAIC IN THE CENTRAL APSE OF THE CATHEDRAL, MONREALE (SICILY).

II. 86

THE VIRGIN AND THE APOSTLES, DETAIL. 12TH-13TH CENTURY. APSE MOSAIC IN THE CATHEDRAL, TORCELLO (VENICE).

2

ROMANESQUE RESISTANCES

There were several factors telling against the rise of Gothic art, most active of them being the monastic tradition. Until the first quarter of the thirteenth century the monastery had played a leading role in the cultural evolution of the West, and the triumph of Citeaux fell far short of eclipsing the ancient Benedictine style. The Benedictine monks held an exalted status in the social hierarchy since it was their sacred task to celebrate day by day and hour by hour the praise of God in rites invested with the utmost pomp and dignity. In England, which had been Christianized originally by the disciples of St Benedict, the monastery still was closely linked up with the cathedral and (as in Carolingian times) it was regarded as the cornerstone of the ecclesiastic edifice in the German provinces and the lands near the Slav frontier. But the regions in which its ascendancy was most pronounced were those which had come under the direct influence of Cluny in its heyday: Burgundy, southern Gaul, Catalonia and the fringe of Christendom which, starting from the Compostela pilgrim road, had widened out into the heart of Spain.

Linked together by a network of confraternities and daughter houses, these abbeys and priories were extremely wealthy. They held a secure place in the feudal system, owned large estates and had troops at their disposal; they levied tithes and land taxes, administered justice, had thriving villages in their domains and, along with the cathedral chapters, the monks who lived in them ranked as the aristocracy of the Church. Aging nobles often retired to them to end their days in peace and preparation for the after-life. They sent there those of their sons who seemed inapt for the profession of arms, so that they could pray for the welfare of the line, without falling short of the high estate of leisured ease to which it had pleased God to call them. However, the feudal barons were always wrangling with these institutions, accusing them of unfair competition and of infringing on their seigniorial rights. They harassed the abbots and priors with all sorts of petty vexations and chicaneries, and made difficulties about handing over to them, without reservations, the lands and peasants that, generation after generation, members of the nobility had donated to the monastery on their deathbeds. But though the barons pressed their claims so vigorously that they usually obtained compensation or a partition of these donations, they still were lavish in their gifts to the monastery. For most knights held land in fee from the abbot or prior, had done homage to him, owed him fealty and rallied round him at sessions of the feudal court. Moreover all of them revered this House of Worship to which they could delegate their chief religious duties; this place where their forefathers were buried and one day they would sleep beside them. On the anniversary of a man's death a memorial service was held in which prayers were made for his soul, ensuring his felicity in the next world. Also, the monastery church contained holy relics to which the populace *en masse* did obeisance on feast-days, which at certain seasons were carried in solemn procession across the country-side to ensure the fertility of the soil, and contact with which cured diseases. The monasteries were in fact organisms of collective intercession on which a whole province depended for its salvation. Every-where, but most persistently in southern Europe, laymen committed their hope of a glorious resurrec-tion to the good offices of the monastic community.

In a largely illiterate world the monasteries were oases of culture, in which books were preserved, studied and copied. But this culture was hampered by a host of antiquated regulations and in the period we are here considering its scope became still narrower. The spirit of monasticism is clearly reflected in its music. Revolving in a closed circle of harmonies and melodies, the chants accompanying the never-ceasing prayers of the monks had a somewhat stupefying effect on the mentality of the congregation. Their thoughts were not encouraged to rove in new directions, and kept to the measured rhythms of the liturgic chants, whose cycle corres-ponded to that of the seasons. The contrast between the rapid tempo of urban life and the stagnation of the countryside was paralleled by that between the venturous cathedral schools of Neustria and the static traditionalism of monastic culture.

Places of collective purification, readying men for the Last Judgment, the abbeys and priories served an eschatological end, for they were always awaiting Christ's Second Coming. This is why visions of the Apocalypse bulk so large in the iconography of their churches and Beatus's *Commen-taria* always figured in their libraries. In these sanctuaries men were trained to face calmly and courageously the great catastrophes which were to precede the End of Time. They contained images of the dreaded Horsemen of the Apocalypse, carriers of the scourge of God, looming up on the horizon. On one of the capitals of Saint-Nectaire the Destroying Angel carries three arrows repre-senting the three things most feared by the peasantry: war, famine, sudden death. Monastic art, however, centers primarily on the figure of the Son of Man, encircled by rays of dazzling celestial light. On the Angoulême façade we see Christ rising from the world of men in His Ascension and descending in glory for His final appearance on earth at the Last Day, proclaiming the death of Time, the triumph of eternal life in a world beyond the world.

In its inquiries into the scheme of things monastic thought was largely guided by visions of the ineffable, and moved in an imaginary realm. Hence the strong vein of fantasy in medieval sculpture, as well as in the illuminated books. Many of the themes relate to myths culled from *Bestiaries*, and are treated so esoterically that their symbolism is as dark to us today as it must have been to their con-temporaries. What is the significance of the fights between men and animals on the portal of San Pietro of Spoleto? Where find a clue to the enigmatic reliefs which the Irish monks who settled in Regensburg in the twelfth century set up on each side of the entrance to their church?

ROMANESQUE RESISTANCES

1. The Destroying Angel, detail of a capital in the church of Saint-Nectaire (Puy-de-Dôme), France. 12th century.

2. Christ in Majesty, detail of the frieze over the door of the church of San Pedro de Moarbes (Palencia), Spain. 12th century.

3. The Trinity, detail of the doorway of the church of Santo Domingo at Soria, Spain. 13th century.

4. West front of Notre-Dame-la-Grande at Poitiers. 11th-12th century.

5. Bas-reliefs on the façade of the church of San Pietro at Spoleto, Italy. 12th century.

6. Dome of the collegiate church of Santa Maria la Mayor at Toro (Zamora), Spain. Begun in 1160.

7. Portal of the church of St James (Schottenkirche) at Regensburg, Germany. 12th century.

2

3

4

5

5

II. 94

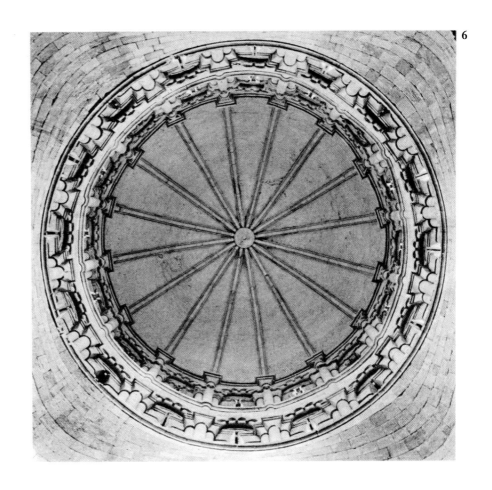

II

THE AGE OF REASON
1190-1250

THE CATHOLIC REPRESSION

At the close of the twelfth century the Church was a beleaguered fortress. Some of the outer bastions had been stormed, the last lines of defence were but precariously held, and the most active and alarming of its enemies was heresy. But this was not the only danger. Another, more insidious threat stemmed from the rapid advance of learning which, in the school of Paris in particular, was giving rise to daring speculations, often of a subversive nature. As a result of closely analysing the works of Dionysius and pondering on the mystery of the Trinity and the Creation, Amalric of Bena, a teacher of philosophy at the university of Paris, came to think and taught his pupils that since "all is one and God is all," every Christian was a member of the body of Christ and as such immune from sin. Knowing himself "possessed" by God, he could indulge in a life of joy and freedom. Needless to say, this doctrine was greatly to the taste of the young noblemen and poets of the courts (hence its prompt success), but it also implied that a priesthood was superfluous (hence its drastic condemnation by the church authorities).

Meanwhile Parisian teachers were turning more and more to the pagan philosophy of Aristotle. In 1205 the pope himself sent some of them to Constantinople to study Greek thought at its source, while at Toledo the teams of translators which had already produced a version of the *Organon* had moved on to the master's *Physics* and *Metaphysics*. The eyes of theological students and teachers were being opened to a body of logically argued and demonstrated theses which provided a rational, coherent explanation of the universe, but nevertheless relied on premises that were patently incompatible with those of Holy Writ. There was, then, a danger that the very men whose duty it was to uphold the dogmas of the Church and to do away with heresy might let themselves be lured from the Faith by the seductions of these pagan works. The first symptoms of doubt, the first deviations, manifested themselves at the very time when the rapid growth of affluence and an urge to make the most of it were tending to undermine, insensibly, the established social order. Based on a monastic ideal of withdrawal, and given form at a time when the population consisted of backward peasants and uncultured warriors, the structure of the Church was ill-adjusted to the contemporary world and its aspirations. If unity was to be regained a drastic revision was obviously called for, the structure had to be tightened up. In the result the Church was given a monarchical, not to say totalitarian form, centered on the Holy See and, specifically, on the personality of a very able pope, Innocent III.

For over a century the papacy had been consolidating and extending its power. It had successfully defied emperors, and the jurists of the Curia had formulated a system of theocracy by which the pope was vested with an *auctoritas* superior to that of any temporal power. He claimed a right of moral jurisdiction over the whole world, sent his legates everywhere and sought to keep the bishops under his direct control. Elected pope in 1198 when he was only thirty-eight, Innocent III brought this long effort to a successful conclusion. Born of a noble family, he was a well-educated man, had studied law at Bologna (in the Italian style), then theology in Paris (Neustrian style). He was the first pope categorically to declare himself not only a successor of St Peter, but Christ's vicegerent on earth—in other words a king of kings, *rex regum*, who ranked above all princes and was their judge. On the day of his coronation he proclaimed: "It is to me that Jesus said 'I will give unto thee the keys of the kingdom of heaven: and whatsoever thou shalt bind on earth shall be bound in heaven.' See him, then, this servant of the Lord for what he is: vicar of Christ, and successor of St Peter. He stands midway between God and man, less great than God, greater than man." The pope accordingly set out to assert his feudal suzerain rights over all the states of Europe

—and he nearly succeeded in this attempt. Assured of his supremacy, he held at the end of his reign an ecumenical council at the Lateran which played the same part in medieval Christendom as the Council of Trent was to play in sixteenth-century Europe. Innocent clearly defined his program: it was "to stamp out heresy and to fortify faith, but also to reform men's morals, extirpate vices, implant virtues, remove excesses. Also to allay disputes, establish peace, repudiate tyranny, and to cause the Truth to prevail everywhere, for all."

So now the Church was mustering its forces, consolidating its position, expelling foreign bodies. A previous Council in 1179 had enacted that all impure persons affected with purulent diseases, madmen and those possessed by devils were to be segregated in lazar-houses, so that good Christians might not be infected. Innocent's Council followed this up by ordering all Jews to wear a distinctive circular badge so that they might not be confused with Christians. Next, the Church, mindful of Catholic unity, launched an attack on schismatics (in 1204 the Crusaders captured Constantinople), but above all on heretics, the major danger. In 1209 the pope proclaimed the same indulgences for a crusade to Languedoc, for the suppression of the Albigenses, as for crusades to the Holy Land. In the struggle to achieve world power, characteristic of Innocent's pontificate, the Church knew it could count no longer on the monks.

For the old monastic orders had fallen into disrepute. They were the targets of ribald jests at the banquets of the knights. The didactic poems written in their language for the French nobility at the close of the twelfth century are full of criticisms of Cluny, Cîteaux and the Chartreuse, where, entrenched in their cloisters, the monks led self-indulgent lives and behaved "like vulgar tradesmen at their junketings." The knightly orders, Templars and Hospitallers, were viewed more favorably. They, anyhow, went out into the world, risked their lives and promoted, after their fashion, one of the ideals of chivalry; they stood for a Church Militant. None the less the religious movements which now were giving rise to new congregations sponsored a life no longer centered on the clash of arms, on knightly jousts and tourneys, but on brotherly love. The Imitation of Christ in his care for the poor was the guiding principle of the new Order of the Holy Ghost, and

the Order of the Trinitarians devoted itself to the liberation of Christian captives. These Orders won the admiration of the populace at large, and they alone challenged with success the heretic sects. Innocent III was well aware of this when he re-admitted to the Church certain sects dedicated to the rule of poverty and some offshoots of the Waldensian heresy. He welcomed into the fold the Pauperes Catholici and the Order of the Humiliati and encouraged laic penances. But it was left to two great evangelists, the two "Princes" of whom Dante speaks, to lead to Christ the Church, his bride; two men whom "Providence ordained in her behoof/ Who on this side and that should be her guide": St Francis of Assisi and St Dominic.

In 1205 the hills of Languedoc had not as yet been scoured by troops of Parisian horsemen slaughtering, in the name of Christ, the Albigensian heretics. This was the year when Innocent III received a visit from the bishop of Osma (in Spain) and Dominic, sub-prior of his chapter. On their way to Rome these two men had traversed the domain of Catharism, then in its hour of triumph, and had met at Mont-pellier the disheartened papal legates. The reasons for the Catholic defeat were evident to them: the lax morals and indecent wealth of the clergy. The Spanish prelates informed the pope that "to shut the mouths of evil men it is needful for churchmen to behave and talk in accordance with the example of their Master, to practise humility, to travel on foot without gold or silver, in short to copy faithfully the apostles' way of life." The bishop and his canons told the pope of their resolve to renounce the pomp and luxury which all the prelates of the West had flaunted since the days of Charlemagne, rich garments and the insignia of temporal power. Their plan was to return to the heresy-ridden lands and preach the Gospel, in truly evangelical fashion, as poor men "without purse and scrip." The pope wished them Godspeed. In the Narbonne region, at Pamiers, Lavaur and Fanjeaux, they engaged in public disputations with the "Per-fects" and everyone could see that the envoys of the Church were, like their adversaries, without weapons, wives or wealth in any form. There were jousts of eloquence, for Dominic and his companions were schoolmen, intellectuals. Heresy had vanquished the men of the cloister and now the men of the schools entered the fray. They had marshalled in advance their arguments, in the *langue d'oc*, the language of the people, and this time Catharism was to be attacked on dogmatic grounds, refuted by theological premises. These debates were attended by members of the nobility and middle class who, as in tournaments, decided on the winner. Dominic alone remained in France and it was now that he founded, at Prouille, near Toulouse, the first nunnery, a refuge for women converted from heresy, as an antidote for the "conventicles" where ladies of the region made retreats under the strict régime of Cathar perfectionism. He imposed on the nuns the rule of St Augustine: total poverty. We know little of his activities during the stormy years of the crusade, but, soon after, he resumed his "holy preaching." The new bishop of Toulouse, his personal friend, welcomed his aid and that of his disciples in this region, ravaged by the bands of Simon de Montfort, where Catholicism was being imposed by force on what remained of a decimated, harassed population, who accepted the change with sullen resentment. The small devoted group of Friars Preachers did its best to overcome this hostility and to effect a change of heart. When Dominic attended the Lateran Council, the Fathers, who were struggling to prevent the multiplication of sects, showed some reluctance to approving of a new congregation. However, Dominic had his way, though the Council instructed him to adopt one of the existing Rules, not to invent one of his own. His choice fell on the Rule he had imposed on the nuns at Prouille, that of the Augustinian canons. But when founding the Order of the Friars Preachers and its Rule he made some small yet signal changes in it.

The fundamental condition of the Dominican way of life was absolute poverty. Not, like that of Cîteaux, factitious; but the real poverty of Christ. The contemporary world had been corrupted by wealth and this was the first thing to attack. Chapter xxvi, entitled "Concerning the Rejection of Property," contains this vital precept: "We shall not accept in any manner either property or a fixed income." Thus in a social order in which land was ceasing to be the only form of wealth, a religious community was established which for the first time did not rely for its maintenance on real estate, which no longer lived on the produce of its own land, but on charity, begging its bread from door to door. The Dominican had no personal possessions, except books. But these were the tools of his trade; his mission was to preach the true doctrine and to combat manfully the demons of unbelief, cunning foes whom only the Light of the Spirit could lay low. Therefore he had to train himself, to develop his reasoning faculty, to read and study. And, as the masters of the schools had shown, studying involved teamwork. So the Dominicans, like the cathedral canons and Benedictine monks, lived a corporate life. Not like these latter to join in chanting hour by hour the praises of the Lord. For the Dominican the ritual was more flexible and simpler; he need not trouble over-much about fixed hours and could, whenever necessary, cut short his devotions. He was not subservient to the cosmic rhythms which for many centuries, in less disturbed ages, had set the tempo of devotion in the monasteries. For the vocation of the Friar Preacher necessitated his entering the lists whenever need arose; the enemy was at the gate. There was no coming to grips with him in solitude, in the desert or even in the fields. No, he must be confronted among men, in the heart of this new world where the countryside no longer held first place; in the towns. Hence the founding of Dominican monasteries in the great centers of population, where their message was most needed. But the Dominican House differed from the cloister since the friars were not secluded in it; it was no more than a rest-house to which, their labors ended, they came to share the food begged in the streets, and to sleep. But like the cathedral cloister the Dominican friary was a place of intellectual activity, indeed its chief function was educational. In each a friar read out passages from the Scriptures and commented on them, and one of the rules was that every Dominican should possess a copy, written in his own hand, of the Bible, also of Peter Lombard's *Sentences*, a compendium of the dicta of thirteenth-century theology, and the *History* of Peter Comestor (the "devourer" of books) which provided concrete themes for preaching. These books were neither bulky nor ornate like those from the monastic libraries used for the celebration of the Mass or for private meditation. They served as manuals ready to hand that the Friar Preacher kept in his wallet so as to verify a detail, if needed; for he had already memorized their substance. "They (the Friars) must not base their studies on the writings of pagans and philosophers—even if they consult them on occasion. Nor should they study the secular sciences or even the so-called liberal arts unless the Master of the Order or the Chapter General makes an exception in the case of certain persons.

The Superior can grant the students a dispensation provided it is of such a nature that their studies will not be interrupted, and they are not handicapped by questions relating to divine service or other such matters." These militants in the doctrinal arena had to be well equipped; so dispensations were frequently granted. For Dominic, we repeat, was a man of learning and the new Order took form at the heart of the scholastic disciplines of the period.

In all the great university towns—Montpellier, Bologna, Oxford and, above all, Paris—Dominican foundations came to take an ever greater part in theological research; indeed they soon became its seminal centers.

After stemming from a cathedral chapter, the Order of Preachers had broken away from it so as the better to adjust to contemporary needs the educational activities of the cathedral, to place them at the service of the Holy See and under its control. The Franciscan Order was composed of different elements; it stemmed from the urban laity and reflected its spiritual frustrations. St Francis, son of a well-to-do merchant, belonged to a commune which had elected a Cathar mayor. In his early days he had led a life of pleasure in the company of "young men about town," had composed love songs and joined in chivalrous exploits. Then he was caught up in the spiritual unrest that was affecting the middle class in the Southern towns. Not that he heard the call of Catharism; it was the voice of Christ he listened to. And when, like Peter Waldo, he stripped himself of his possessions, cast off his clothes and confronted his father, flinging at his feet his personal adornments, the bishop of Assisi covered his nakedness with his cloak. Francis stayed in the Church and he too was a mendicant. But he never ceased singing, he was "God's songster," and, like the troubadours, idolized a mistress, in his case Lady Poverty. He preached not only penitence, but the beauty of the universe, Brother Sun and all the stars. Some young men, friends of his, joined forces with him and, as Christ had done, he sent forth his disciples on the highways, empty-handed, clad in sackcloth. They lived among the poor, worked in the fields to earn their daily bread, and in the evenings these "jongleurs of God" gathered together to sing the perfect joy of poverty. If it so happened that they could not find work they could always beg their bread from door to door; God would not let them die of hunger.

In 1209 Innocent III, who looked with a friendly eye on the mendicant sects, gave his approval to the preaching of Francis and his very simple Rule, based on texts from the New Testament. The "Minors" (as Francis called them) started visiting the larger cities; the first of them reached Paris in 1219. To begin with they were looked askance at, suspected of being heretics, and required to produce their "visa" from the Pope. But by 1233 they had established themselves in all the towns of northern France. This was the time when the status of wives and daughters of the nobility was being ameliorated and women were beginning to form religious associations of their own. Born of a knightly family in Assisi, St Clara founded a community of nuns (the Poor Clares) modeled on the Minors of her friend Francis. And an Order of Tertiaries was formed consisting of women who, without completely breaking with the world, observed an apostolic rule of life appropriate to their condition. Francis, meanwhile, drew ever closer to a true fraternity with Jesus and even identified himself with Him so perfectly that "in the flame of his love" he received on his body "the Stigmata of the Crucified." Everywhere he was venerated as a saint, exemplar of a new perfection in keeping with the urge to poverty which now prevailed among the younger townsfolk: their will to strip themselves of worldly goods, to dispense charity, and to obey the precept of Francis that his followers should be constantly "rejoicing in the Lord," singing hymns of joy. He did not combat heresy with the sword but with the voice of reason and with the example of his life, a life of all-embracing kindness. He did more than any other to make the simple Gospel truths an actuality, to show that the Christian life was feasible. Next after Christ, St Francis is the dominant figure of Christian history and it is no exaggeration to say that what remains of true Christianity in the modern world derives directly from him.

He was not a priest and never dreamt of becoming one; nor did his disciples. But he showed no hostility towards the priests and in his addresses to the people aimed at aiding those whose daily task it was to celebrate the Mass. In its conflict with the Cathars and Waldensians the Church stressed the efficacy of the Eucharist and it was now that the dogma of Transubstantiation was promulgated by the Lateran Council. Representations of the Last Supper were carved on church portals in towns contaminated by heresy, at Beaucaire, Saint-Gilles and Modena, and Jesus was shown giving the morsel of bread even to his betrayer Judas. Thus St Francis labored in the defence of the priests. "If the Blessed Virgin is so greatly—and so rightly—venerated, since she bore Christ in her most holy womb; if the blessed Baptist trembled with awe and dared not touch the holy head of his Lord; if the tomb in which Christ's body lay for several days is treated with such respect, how saintly, righteous and worthy must that man be who takes Christ Jesus in his hand, holds Him to his heart, raises Him to his lips and gives Him as nourishment to others." And again, in his spiritual testament, St Francis wrote: "Even if I find poor priests leading a worldly life, I would not dare—even if I had the wisdom of Solomon—to preach against their wishes in the parishes where they dwell. For these priests too (like all other priests) I am bound to fear, to cherish, and to honor as my masters. So I have no wish to draw attention to their sins, since I discern in them the Son of God, and they are my superiors. The reason why I treat them thus is that in this world I find no perceptible token of that same Son of Almighty God other than His most holy body and most sacred blood, which these men consecrate and which they alone dispense to others. And I desire above all to honor and venerate these very holy mysteries and to situate them in places worthily adorned." A humble and reverent auxiliary of the priesthood, the Franciscan message began by being extremely simple, rather an example of a way of life than a logical exegesis—hence its remarkable success. The cardinals, however, desired to organize it, reinforce it, and the Holy See to give it a sound doctrinal foundation. Despite the efforts of St Francis and some of his disciples, the Order of the Minorites was gradually transformed into a militia of priests and intellectuals on the lines of the Preaching Friars. Established in monasteries, the Franciscans had to abandon their life of poetic vagrancy, their roamings in the gracious Umbrian countryside. They were given books and professors; studia were set up for them in Paris and other educational centers. From 1225 onward they constituted a second "army of knowledge" under the pope's control and, in heretically minded cities, were called on to participate in the clerical campaign of repression.

For Innocent III had decided that henceforth this campaign could be made most effective by a planned co-ordination of parishes in which the priests, aided by the mobile forces of the mendicant orders, would be able to exercise a strict surveillance over their flocks. Throughout Christendom there soon developed an elaborate network of parishes. In the rural districts of France the parochial system was brought into application in the thirteenth century and it became the custom to describe each peasant as a "parishioner" of such and such a place. He was not allowed to partake of the Sacrament elsewhere than in his parish church and attempts were made to regularize his devotions. The Lateran Council bade all laymen communicate and make confession once a year and the local priest was called on to track down those who sought to evade these duties, so as to detect clandestine heretics. Hence the humorous descriptions of "Prospère," village curé and petty tyrant, in the fabliaux, the *Roman de Renart* and the cycles of comic poems. In new districts of the larger towns similar parochial units were established, and the bishop was held personally responsible for this supervision of the mores of the population in all parts of his diocese.

The bishop had two well-defined functions. First of these was the repression of heresy. As a *judex ordinarius* he summarily heard complaints of breaches of ecclesiastical discipline. But there was also a special procedure: the inquisition. This involved preliminary inquiry, and the bishop took action without waiting for the formal laying of a complaint. Enacted by the Lateran Council, this special procedure was soon applied throughout southern France. Persons commonly reputed to be heretics were arrested and questioned in public; means were taken to expedite their confessions. If they persisted in their false beliefs they were made over to the secular authorities, to be burnt at the stake; otherwise the inquisitor imposed on them a penance, sometimes a pilgrimage, oftener the "wall" (i.e. life imprisonment). This repressive function was vested in the bishop. The duty of the priest was to rid his parish of evil-doers, to preserve the Christian community, already segregated from Jews and lepers, from any risk of being infected with the germs of heresy. The bishop kindled the faggots that burnt the heretics; but it was also his task to spread the light of Christian truth. This second mission, that of making known the dogmas of the Church and proclaiming the eternal verities, was traditional; as was that of teaching in person or, anyhow, promoting educational facilities in the city.

As a centralized monarchy, the Catholic Church entrusted directly to the pope the management of the great student centers, the academies of theology in which the tenets of the Church were precisely formulated. Henceforth they were a pivotal element of the machinery needed by a religion seeking to enroll the intelligentsia in its defence.

The chief educational centers were reorganized as more coherent units, the "universities," over which, though they were exempted from the bishops' control, the pope sought to exercise authority. Already for a long time teachers and students had been banding themselves together in guilds (like the trade guilds in the towns), with a view to freeing themselves from vexatious interference by the local authorities and the domination of the cathedral clique. In Paris the guild had wrested from the king and the chapter of Notre-Dame substantial freedoms. Innocent III took official notice and, when his legate drew up the statutes of this *universitas magistrum et scolarium parisientium*, this was to keep a stricter control of its activities and link it more closely to the Holy See. The doctrine of Amalric of Bena was proscribed and ten teachers who persisted in propagating it were burned at the stake. Books with "dangerous" tendencies were banned and in the university of Paris professors were forbidden to acquaint their pupils with Aristotle's *Metaphysics* and the commentaries of Avicenna. Finally, it was decided that the mendicant orders were most trustworthy and members of them were appointed to the senior professorships in theology. The disciplines of logic were the *sine qua non;* no time was to be wasted on aesthetic problems or "vain researches." In the early thirteenth century the university of Paris became one vast "thinking machine" and in the faculty of arts, where theological students took their preliminary courses, dialectics reigned supreme. The "lesson" involving direct contact with an author gave place to organized debates in which young men learned to bandy arguments and to make an expert usage of the syllogism—in short to prepare themselves for the doctrinal disputations of their later years. Ceasing to serve as an approach to the study of literature, grammar became an exercise in practical linguistics and verbal logic; its chief function was to analyse modes of expression with an eye to the handling of language as a vehicle of close reasoning. What, then, was the point of reading Ovid or Virgil, of seeking to get pleasure out of literature, now that words were no more than the machine-tools of constructive argumentation, and dialectics the science of sciences? This way of thinking soon dried up the well-springs of humanism, and scholastic disquisition, stripped of all ornaments, tended more and more towards an arid formalism. Thus in Paris and at the other great universities, at Oxford and Toulouse, whose activities were mobilized to combat heresy, there rapidly developed a theological discipline of an unprecedented rigor and precision.

This theology was paramount in the evangelical preaching in the towns, where the Dominicans and Franciscans took the lead. Specialists in the field of verbal eloquence, they compelled the bishop and his priests to recognize their superior qualifications. Mixing as they did with the people on an equal footing, they were more alive to the stirrings of the new mentality, knew how to hold the interest of large crowds and to touch their hearts. They employed everyday language and homely metaphors, enlivening their discourses with anecdotes adapted to the social status of the audience they addressed. Nor did they fail to note the propaganda value of the miracle play; it was now that Parisians flocked to see the first of the *Miracles de Notre-Dame*. And art, too, was called on to serve, more perhaps than ever before, as an instrument of edification.

During the first half of the thirteenth century the mendicant orders did not, as yet, take any active part in artistic creation. They had hardly "settled down"; so far their monasteries were ramshackle edifices, their oratories mere sheds, and they left the task of adorning places of worship to the clergy. But they advised the ecclesiastical authorities to embellish their churches and provided them with iconographic themes culled from their sermons. Though he banned images from the Cistercian abbeys, St Bernard had agreed that figurative art could have a place in city churches "to enable the bishops who have charge of souls, both the wise and the ignorant, to stimulate by visible images the 'carnal' devotion of the people, when they find themselves unable to do this with spiritual images." St Francis, too, wished churches, sheltering as they did the body of our Lord, to be "finely decorated." Thus in the days of the first Dominican and Franciscan missions a new generation of cathedrals —enduring sermons in stone—arose above the cities and their growth was surprisingly rapid. Work on Notre-Dame of Paris was brought to a speedy close in 1250 (after nearly a century's delays). The rising prosperity of the middle class, a more efficient canalization of alms and the pressing need to instill instant conviction of the Christian verities led to more rapid building. The men who toiled in the cathedral workyards were fired by a holy zeal. Begun in 1191, the new cathedral of Chartres was completed twenty-six years later and work at Amiens progressed even more rapidly. At Reims, where the first stone was laid in 1212, all the essential parts of the cathedral had been erected by 1233. More money was expended on cathedral building, far more workers were employed, than on even the most ambitious secular enterprises of the age. The chapters now left the conduct of building operations to technicians who moved from place to place, wherever their services were required, and the notebooks of one of them, Villard de Honnecourt, have survived. They show that he had a keen interest in mechanical appliances such as cranes for lifting heavy weights, which ensured an economy of labor and speeded up completion of the work in hand. He also had a gift for the practical application of mathematical formulas and for envisaging schematically the overall effect of an edifice. For the architects—entitled *docteurs ès pierre*—had mastered the mathematics taught in the schools and indeed described themselves as "masters." None the less the edifices they were called on to design still embodied, in inert matter, the ideology of the professors and their dialectics. The cathedrals acted, in fact, as visual demonstrations of Catholic theology.

More than ever, this theology identified the essence of God with light. The better to combat the lures of Catharism, the best thinkers of the day reverted to the hierarchies propounded by the Pseudo-Areopagite, but sought to buttress them with more telling arguments, incorporating recent discoveries in the field of physics. Robert Grosseteste, who launched the new schools of Oxford, read Greek, was acquainted with the works of Ptolemy, with the new astronomy and the Arab commentaries on Aristotle's *De Caelo*. He, too, conceived of God as light and the whole material universe as a brilliant sphere radiating from a central nucleus into the three dimensions of Space. All human knowledge sprang from the spiritual effluence of this primal, uncreated light. Sin makes the body opaque; hence our inability to see directly the emanations of the Light Divine. But in the body of Christ, God and man, the spiritual universe and the material universe regained their pristine unity. Jesus and by the same token the cathedral, which was His symbol, were thus regarded as the center from which all proceeds and in which all things are clarified: the Trinity, the Word made Flesh, the Church, mankind, the whole created world. And these ideas pointed the way to a precise aesthetic. "Best of all things, most delectable, most beautiful is natural light; it is light that constitutes the perfection and beauty of all material forms." Grosseteste stated in philosophical terms what was obscurely sensed by the Franciscans in their *laudes* of St Clara. "Her angelic face was brighter and lovelier after prayer, such was the joy resplendent in it. Verily our generous and gracious Lord flooded with his rays his humble little spouse, so that she shed the divine light on everything around her." And the Dominican Albertus Magnus defined beauty as "a resplendence of form."

Thus even more than the edifices from which they originated the second generation of cathedrals were illuminated with the celestial light. The upper part of the Sainte-Chapelle in Paris is a vast net spread out to trap light in its meshes, and the walls vanish into thin air, so that the whole interior is flooded with a radiance more evenly distributed than ever before—which would certainly have delighted Suger. At Reims Jean d'Orbais constructed windows executed in open-work, whose designs Villard de Honnecourt copied in his notebook and which soon came into vogue everywhere. Master Gaucher suppressed all the tympana of the façade and replaced them with stained glass. Everywhere rose windows blossomed forth, sometimes expanding so as to touch the masonry of the buttresses. Forming perfect circles, symbols of the rotation of the cosmos, they also signified the cyclic flux and reflux of light inaugurated by the Creator on the First Day.

Grosseteste's views were set forth in detail in his treatise *De physicis, lineis, angulis et figuris*, and were based on strictly applied geometry. From them derived the luminous precision of thirteenth-century architecture, its clarity and its logic, rigorous as a syllogism. It reflected the approach to knowledge promoted by the Faculty of Arts. Thus the new cathedral gives an impression of being less eloquent than its predecessors; it caters less for the pleasure of the eye, is more concerned with the rational disposition of its parts and aims at perfect cogency, like the proof of a scholastic theorem. For its forms were inspired by schoolmen who, year in, year out, furbished the arms of their intelligence in order to hold their own in the great jousts of Eastertide, public debates in which they nimbly plied the rapiers of their wit. Like them the master-of-works proceeded dialectically, sorting out homologous parts, then the parts of those parts, before reassembling them in a logical catena. Soaring heavenwards in a geometrical progression woven in strands of light, the cathedral owed much of its compelling power to the intelligence of the master mind behind it.

Its adornments were not selected for their charm; their purpose was to give the assembled congregation a visual corroboration of the Faith, a résumé of Christian *sapientia* and an antidote to heresy. Above all to inculcate a theology of the kind approved of by the Church. Intended to appeal directly to the masses, the images were placed well in view. At Reims and Amiens the statues quitted niches and recesses and advanced towards the congregation, silent sponsors of the efficacy of the ritual. Their message was a reminder of the sacred function of the prelacy, of the masters teaching in the schools, of priests who consecrated the bread and wine, of bishop and inquisitor. Melchizedek is shown presenting the Host to Saul accoutred like a medieval knight. In his attacks on the Waldensian heresy the sculptor did not represent Christ as poor, betrayed, alone, but as the founder of a church, escorted like a bishop by his clergy. Since the Cathars denied the Incarnation, the Redemption and even the Creation, the figurations in the cathedrals proclaimed with no uncertain voice the omnipotence of the Triune God: Creator, Incarnate, Redeemer.

A whole community of metal-workers lived in the Austrasian forests and the best weapons in the early medieval world had come from their smithies. It was largely thanks to these that the Franks had succeeded in bringing all the western continent under their sway. When their conquests had reinstated the Roman Empire, and Charlemagne, a new Augustus, was moved to erect monuments like those of the Caesars in his ancestral domain, he gave orders for ancient bronzes to be brought from Rome to Aix-la-Chapelle. Henceforward the craft of bronze-working played a leading part in the new imperial art. Suger, too, when he sought to revive the Carolingian tradition in his reconstruction of the royal abbey of Saint-Denis, which housed the tombs of the kings of France, decided to provide it with bronze doors. But the wide diffusion of this type of ornament in twelfth-century Europe testifies above all to the prestige of the Germanic Empire in the great days of Frederick Barbarossa.

The Slav kingdoms of the East acknowledged his suzerainty. When around 1155 the Bishop of Plock planned to embellish his church he commissioned historiated bronze panels from Saxony (or Lorraine) to decorate the entrance. Unfortunately for him these were stolen en route; they are now in the cathedral of St Sophia in Old Novgorod. This was then a flourishing market town where enterprising German traders bartered cloth for honey, wax and Russian furs. These panels depict, in a somewhat uncouth way, scenes from Holy Writ, and give them the barbarian accent of the paintings in the Rhenish Bibles. The doors of the cathedral at Gniezno, however, are thoroughly classical in spirit. They narrate in the style of the Saxon renascence episodes in the life of St Adalbert, friend of the Emperor Otto III, who shortly before the year 1000 preached the Gospel in Bohemia, died a martyr's death at the hands of the Prussians, and whose remains were preserved in Gniezno, the Polish capital.

During the same period the Empire consolidated its hold on Tuscany and southern Italy, on the old Lombard duchies and on the kingdom of Sicily, the heiress to which married Barbarossa's son. In 1180 at Pisa the bronzesmith Bonannus made figures of angels and shepherds for the entrance of the Grotto of the Nativity; the classicizing influence of the Hildesheim bronzes can be seen in these figures and they have nothing of the barbaric violence of those on the door of San Zeno at Verona. Fifteen years later at Benevento and Monreale other bronzes set the imperial seal, at once Germanic and Roman, of the Hohenstaufens on churches otherwise decorated wholly in the Byzantine style.

BONANNUS OF PISA (DIED ABOUT 1183). BRONZE DOOR (PORTA DI SAN RANIERI) OF PISA CATHEDRAL, 1180

BRONZE DOOR WITH SCENES FROM THE LIFE OF ST ADALBERT, ABOUT 1175. CATHEDRAL OF GNIEZNO (POLAND).

BRONZE DOOR OF BENEVENTO CATHEDRAL, DETAIL. LATE 12TH CENTURY.

BONANNUS OF PISA (DIED ABOUT 1183). BRONZE DOOR OF THE MAIN ENTRANCE OF MONREALE CATHEDRAL, DETAIL. FINISHED IN 1186.

The spate of heresies in southern Christendom, the alarming progress of Catharism and of a host of obscure sects which denied the primacy of Rome made the proclamation of the truth, that is to say of Catholic dogma, a matter of extreme urgency. For the enlightenment of the masses, whom the "Perfects" were discouraging with growing success from attending services conducted in it, the church, it was felt, should body forth on its façade, for all to see, a sermon in stone, easy to grasp and carrying conviction. The sculpture in the portal should no longer have as its leitmotiv a vision of the Last Day, but convey in the simplest possible terms its message that in Jesus God was made man, recount His life on earth and demonstrate the efficacy of His sacrifice.

On the façade of the Ripoll monastery scenes from the lives of Moses, David and Solomon had been displayed in successive, super-imposed tiers, as in liturgical manuscripts. In 1160-1170, however, in the heart of the region most affected by the Cathar schism, the portals of Saint-Gilles were crowded with dramatic antiheretical figurations. We see the apostles, witnesses to the Word incarnate, stalwart athletes of the True Faith, standing between the columns of an ancient temple, vigorously trampling underfoot the powers of evil and the sophistries of the schismatics. The frieze above illustrates the Gospel narrative, culminating on the lintel of the largest portal in a representation of the Last Supper. It affirms the verity of the Eucharist, the sacrament whereby Jesus remains a living presence in this world until His triumphal return at the Last Judgment.

The theme of the Last Supper was also treated in the cathedral of Modena by contemporary artists very close to Benedetto Antelami. At Parma, for the decoration of the ambo of the cathedral, the Gospel pulpit, Antelami was persuaded by the local theologians to revert to the Byzantine image of the Deposition from the Cross. This representation of the dead Christ on Calvary, flanked by soldiers and the Holy Women (Mary is kissing His right hand), made it clear to every beholder that God was not only spirit and light, but took flesh to suffer and to die so as to bring redemption to mankind. But the same artist also had a gift for expressing the joyful side of God's creation. On the front of the church he placed illustrations of an allegorical Carolingian poem ascribed to Alcuin recounting the combat of Winter and Spring. Here Spring, Symbol of the triumph of life, of nature's resurrection and also that of Jesus and all mankind, is given the form of a chaste and simple maiden of high degree. To this simplicity is due the singular grace and winsomeness of the young body.

PORCH OF THE ABBEY CHURCH OF SANTA MARIA AT RIPOLL (CATALONIA). MID-12TH CENTURY.

SAINT-GILLES DU GARD. ABOUT 1160-1170.

KING DAVID, DETAIL OF THE FAÇADE OF THE CATHEDRAL OF FIDENZA (BORGO SAN DONNINO).
1214-1218. (SCULPTURES ATTRIBUTED TO BENEDETTO ANTELAMI)

ANSELMO DA CAMPIONE AND HIS WORKSHOP. THE LAST SUPPER, 1160-1175.
DETAIL OF THE CHOIR SCREEN IN MODENA CATHEDRAL.

BENEDETTO ANTELAMI (ABOUT 1150-ABOUT 1230). THE DESCENT FROM THE CROSS, 1178. MARBLE.
PARMA CATHEDRAL.

THE BAPTISTERY OF PARMA WITH THE NORTH PORTAL (PORTAL OF THE VIRGIN) BY BENEDETTO ANTELAMI. 1196-1200.

3

THE PORCH

"O Thou who hast said 'I am the door, by me if any man enter in, he shall be saved,' show us clearly of what dwelling-place Thou art the door, and who they are to whom, and at what hour, Thou wilt open it... Surely the house of which Thou art the door is the heaven in which thy Father dwells." The French cathedral was a visible, abiding answer to this prayer of the Cistercian William of Saint-Thierry. Jesus is the Way, and the cathedral, body of Christ, has portals opening in many directions. The function of its transept is to provide, on the north and south of the building, porches as spacious and impressive as the one facing west. These entrances gradually developed into complex, almost independent units. The beholder's gaze, intercepted by masses of houses huddling round the edifice which, owing to the absence of broad avenues, cannot be viewed in proper perspective, is limited, as he approaches, to the upper parts of the building. With its portals the cathedral extends a welcome to the townsfolk, on all sides, and their mission is to instruct, to serve in short as schools. Schools that were less cut off from the world than those of the cloisters or the booths where crowds of students sat at the feet of learned pedagogues. The portals did not talk Latin but a language that everyone was, or should be, capable of understanding. Their function was to popularize the teaching of the doctors and this was held to justify the lavish expenditure of money and materials, of art and labor, which absorbed so large a part of the alms and taxes levied on all sides, the huge sums exacted by the bishop and his canons from merchants in the town and the peasants of the nearby countryside. In its porches the cathedral demonstrated its pastoral vocation—of propagating that true faith which had been clarified and consolidated by the schoolmen working in the centers of learning attached to it.

The front parts of the churches which preceded the cathedrals had been used for funerary rites. Thus, they had given prominence to representations of the Last Judgment and visions of man's lot after death, in which the beholder found intimations of a world beyond the grave, beyond Space and Time, and of a glorious hereafter bathed in the white radiance of eternity. The scene of the Last Day still held a prominent place in the cathedral porch, but it was differently arranged and carried new significances. The figure of Christ in Judgment towers above the Portico de la Gloria carved by Master Mateo in 1188 for the cathedral of Santiago de Compostela, but here there is little or nothing of the ethereal transcendency of the Christs of the Second Coming in Cluniac Aquitaine. He has the body of a living man. Yet this Jesus, escorted by angels, has not yet come down to the level of the people; He has, rather, the aspect of a priest celebrating the divine liturgy, or a king who has set forth around him—as at a coronation ceremony—all the richest objects in his treasure. Here they are relics of the Passion, preserved in fine linen, and attendant angels display them to the worshippers, as being the earthly weapons of the divine victory over death, instruments of the salvation of mankind.

The Compostela portal contains many statues and reliefs. But in royal France the cathedral porches sheltered a far greater number of the participants in the divine tragedy. Grouped together, they compose a didactic and dramatic exposition, in visual terms, of the tenets of Catholic dogma. For some time past all the devices of stage performances had been used for making clear to the populace the purport of the liturgic rites, and these "mystery plays" were given static form in sculpture. In those that took place at Christmas actors recited to the audience passages from the Scriptures foretelling the Incarnation, and played the parts of Isaiah, Jeremiah, Moses, David. From these performances derived the statues of prophets, of Simeon, Elizabeth, John the Baptist, the angel Gabriel and all the Biblical characters held to be forerunners or prefigurations of Christ: Adam (first parent in the flesh of the Son of Man), the shepherd Abel, Noah, Melchizedek who "brought forth bread and wine"—paradigm of the Last Supper. So as to make them more convincing the churchmen who drew up the iconographic programs ceased to embody the sacred figures in the architecture; they stepped forth from the wall towards the public. The tympanum was heightened so that the scenes displayed on it could be given wide dimensions and deployed on successive tiers for all to see. The number of free-standing figures increased. In the numerous portals of Chartres the thematic material of the statuary covers an immense field, including not only the entire Old and New Testaments, but also the Creation and all the holy intercessors whose relics were preserved in the Cathedral, with their respective virtues represented for the edification of the sinner.

Jean Le Loup had made plans for an enormous portal in the façade of Reims; the Archbishop, Henri de Braisne, wanted it to be even more grandiose than that of Amiens, whose see was suffragan to his. Work on it was completed by Maître Gaucher, who replaced the tympanum with stained-glass windows and transferred to the gable the scenes which figured on it. Most of the statues had been carved under the supervision of Le Loup. When between 1244 and 1252, Gaucher installed them he rearranged them so as to conform to the new trend of theological thought, in which the cult of the Virgin was taking an ever larger place. It had been intended to place the patron saints of the cathedral—St Nicasius, St Remigius and Pope Celestine—in the center; now they were relegated to the left side-portal on whose arches are scenes of the Passion and the Resurrection. That on the right, devoted to the Last Judgment, housed the figurations of the prophets, while the central portal was occupied in its entirety by the Virgin. None of the statues made in the Reims workyards has the beauty and emotive fervor of the Amiens Visitation and Presentation in the Temple.

THE PORCH

1. Amiens Cathedral: portals of the west front. Second quarter of the 13th century.

2. South portal of Chartres Cathedral. 13th century.

3. Main portals of Reims Cathedral. About 1230-1250.

4. West portal of Bourges Cathedral. Mid-13th century.

5. Portal of the church of Santa Maria la Real at Sangüesa (Navarre), Spain. 12th century.

6. Cathedral of Santiago de Compostela: Portico de la Gloria by Master Mateo. 1188.

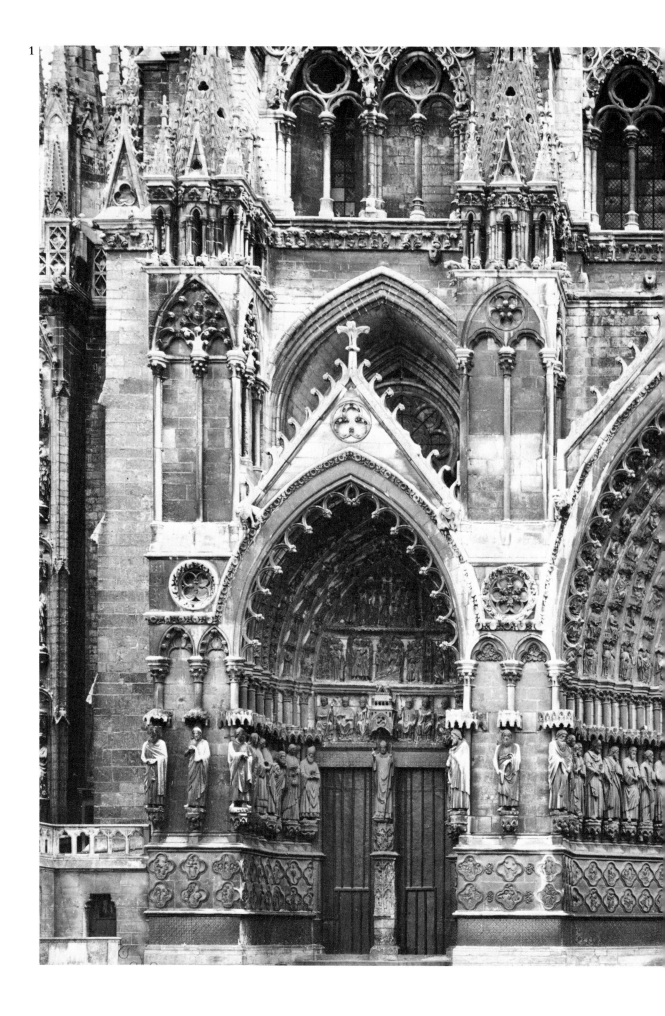

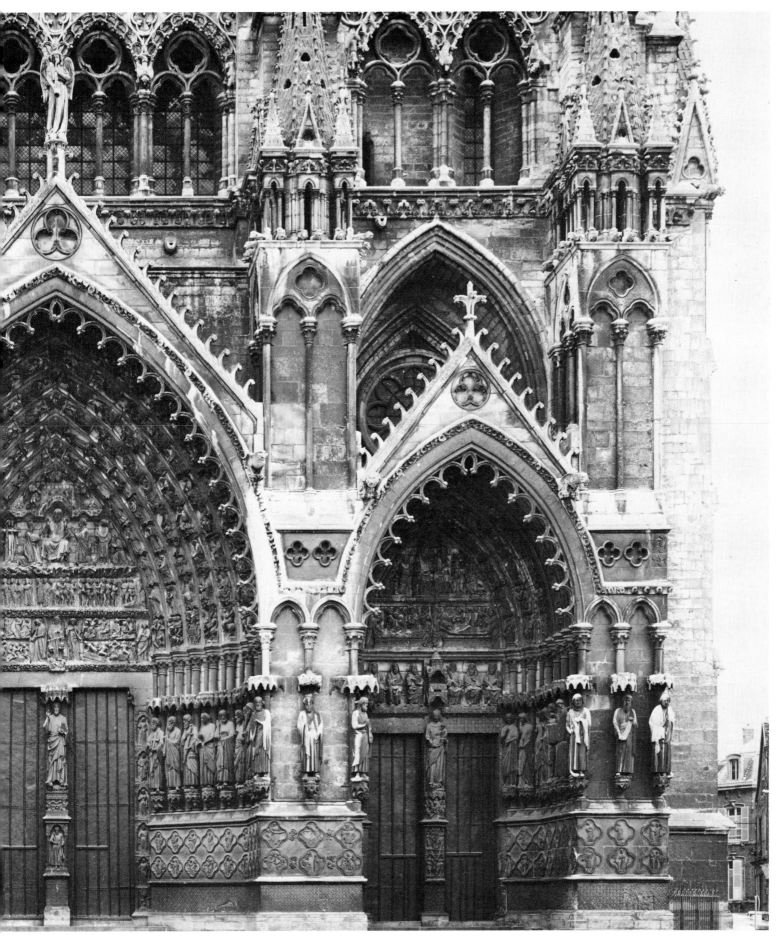

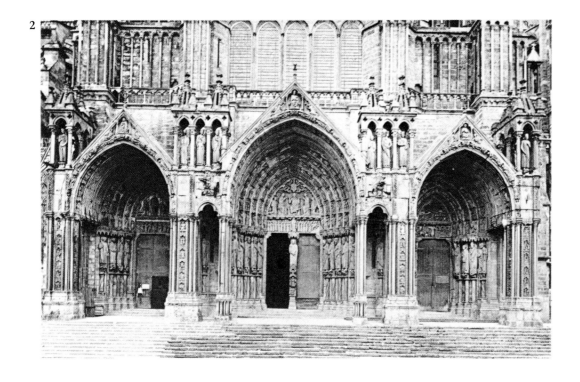

2

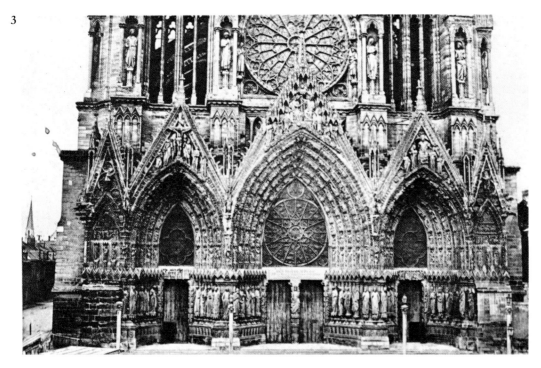

3

II. 124

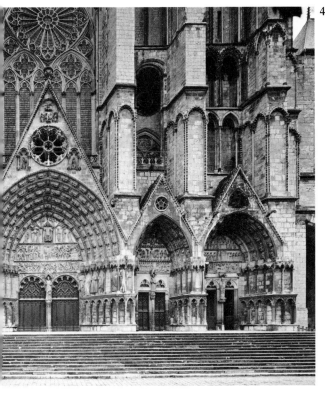

THE CREATION

At the beginning of the century Amalric's heresy had been ruthlessly exterminated; it was clearly necessary for the Christian not to confuse God with his creatures and a clear-cut distinction between the specific values of body, soul and spirit had to be made. Not that matter was to be condemned *per se* as alien to God and pitted against him as a rival, adverse principle; indeed this Manichaean dualism was the greatest peril of the age. Cautiously interpreted, the theology of Dionysius provided a satisfactory solution. For it represented nature as issuing from God and returning to Him, absorbed in His oneness. This flux and reflux was the work of love; God's creatures were envisaged as substances distinct from the godhead which existed independently of them, but conforming in a fashion, like a Platonic "idea," to a divine exemplar. Yet though illumined, filled with Him, they are but reflections of the divine light. According to Dionysius and the orthodox theology inspired by him, all material things participate in God's splendor, celebrate Him, and enable us to know Him.

This was how that joyous optimist Francis of Assisi saw the world of matter. "How describe the emotions that came over him when he found in each created thing the signature of the Creator and tokens of his power and loving-kindness. Even as the Three Holy Children in the fiery furnace bade all the elements praise and glorify the Creator of the universe, so Francis, filled with the spirit of God, found in all the elements, all creatures, good grounds for praising, glorifying, blessing the Maker of the world. When his gaze fell on a meadow gay with flowers he made haste to preach to them, as though they had the gift of reason, and called on them to praise the Lord. Wheatfields and vineyards, flowing streams, verdant gardens, earth and fire, the air and the winds—all these he exhorted, with entire sincerity and simplicity, to love God and gladly to obey Him. He called all created things his brothers and by a gift peculiar to himself could read their inmost secrets, as though already, freed of this mortal coil, he were living in the glorious freedom of the children of God." Brother of Jesus, Francis also felt himself a brother of the sun, wind, birds of the heavens—and of death. As he roved the Umbrian countryside, all its beauties kept him company in a jubilant cortège. This glad communion with all things great and small accorded with the carefree *joie de vivre* of the youth of the feudal courts, and helped to lead back to God the bands of boys and girls who danced around the maypoles. For it was by making much of nature, the wild life of field and forest, the soft sweet air of summer dawns, the bloom of ripening grapes, that the Church of the cathedral builders had the best chance of recalling to the fold the sportive knights, the troubadours and the peasantry still half convinced of the powers of the old nature-gods. St Bernard had said the same thing with his usual bluntness. "You shall see for yourselves that one can get honey from stones, oil from the hardest rocks."

By rehabilitating matter the Catholic theologians struck at the very root of Catharism and it may well be that the Franciscan canticles in praise of all God's creatures did most to vanquish heresy. By stressing the fact that the material universe was God's creation the theologians encouraged the cathedral builders to give a central place to images of the reconciliation of the visible world with the divine. The rose window in the north transept of Reims and the arches of Chartres show God creating light and the heavenly bodies, separating day from night, land from water, molding plants and animals and, lastly, man. They give in fact an imaged résumé of the Creation. Here, moreover, the narrative is not treated symbolically. In his commentary on the Book of Genesis, Thierry of Chartres had sought to harmonize Scripture with the physical science taught in the schools, and it now was possible to represent the incidents of the Creation clearly and realistically. In giving man his senses God had invited him to contemplate and study all his works as they really are—not to evoke them in a sort of waking dream. "The soul," Thomas Aquinas said, "has to get all its knowledge from the perceptible." It is by opening our eyes that we see these forms of God. Hence the tendency of the new school of thinkers to discard the fables, bestiaries, all the bric-à-brac of a more credulous age. Now that traders and missionaries were discovering lands hitherto veiled in mystery, real animals were taking the place of the fabulous monsters which knights errant used to encounter on their quests, and plants and trees seen every day in nearby forests replacing the symbolic flora of the Romanesque illuminators.

In the provinces where the new French art was born we find at the end of the twelfth century a keener interest in the factual; thus the famous *Roman de Renart* cycle has much to say of the avarice of the middle class, the boastfulness of braggart knights. Thomas de Cantimpré's *Book of Nature*, though still professing to give an allegorical interpretation of the phenomenal world, does not insist merely on the links between created beings and the "virtues," moral abstractions, it also dwells on their practical uses in the scheme of things. And, following Aristotle's example, all the theological treatises combine physics with their metaphysics, basing the latter no longer on analogies but on the evidence of the senses. For these epitomes of existing knowledge set out to be scientific; their compilers utilize data furnished by Greek and Arab experts. Optics, seconded by geometry, was given pride of place in these researches. This was, in Europe, the great age of astronomy and it was now that the first attempts were made to determine the exact measurements of the celestial bodies. It was also an age of naturalists. On his arrival in Paris in 1240 Albertus Magnus promptly acquainted his pupils, despite the ban on it, with Aristotle's *Physics*. "In matters of faith and morality," he said, "we must follow St Augustine rather than the philosophers, when they disagree. But when dealing with medicine I take my stand on Galen and Hippocrates, and when dealing with the nature of things I turn to Aristotle or some other expert on the subject." Albertus wrote a lengthy treatise *De Animalibus* in which he analysed in detail the characteristics of the fauna of Germany, where he had lived as a young man. For, like many of their contemporaries, the Dominicans sought relaxation in wild nature and even the towns were not so large or shut-in as to exclude the scents of spring; space

was found for gardens, vineyards, even wheatfields, within their new walls. The material civilization of thirteenth-century man, if still backward, did not cut him off from the outside world. He was still an open-air creature, the tempo and savor of whose life were bound up with the rhythms of nature and the seasons. Even the intellectuals spent more of their time in orchards and meadows than in their rooms, and all the cloisters were built around gardens full of flowers and birds. This intimacy with nature, this feeling that, far from being sinful, it bore the mark of God and revealed his visage, furnished the sap of the vegetation that twined its way around the pillars of Notre-Dame, fanning out in the capitals into a crown of leafage. Here the choir—completed around 1170—was still an intellectual construct, the lines and curves determined by a geometrical schema. But only ten years later, in the first bays of the nave, we find the flowers in the corbels taking less abstract forms, there is less symmetry, more of the diversity of nature, and it is becoming possible to identify each leaf, to distinguish every species. All the same these plants are still essentially signs; life, real life, begins to stir in them only in those parts of the building which were decorated after 1220.

But limits were set to the progress towards realism. Men were being encouraged to investigate the universe, but this was chiefly with a view to defining "types" more clearly and determining the role assigned to them by the Creator. For according to the Scholastics each individual, *qua* individual, belonged to a species whose type form is immanent *ante rem* in the mind of God. The task of the artist adorning the cathedral was to body forth that specific form, not its individual "accidents." He must therefore sort out the visual data and bring his reasoning faculty to bear on them. For God's mind, like man's, proceeds logically and the forms it engenders are precise as rays of light, that is to say geometrically ordered. When Villard de Honnecourt in his sketchbook constructs schematic figures of animals and of men wrestling or casting dice, the figures are built up with triangles, squares and curves, like the architecture of the cathedral as a whole. This rationalizing treatment brings out the underlying form, stripped of accidentals, which for the theologian is the true reality of the individual. Gothic imagery is accordingly subjected, perhaps even more strictly than Romanesque, to geometrical disciplines. The novelty here is that this geometry is applied not to products of the imagination but to objects actually perceived, and that their proportions are respected.

Moreover, these images, if isolated from each other, would have been meaningless. It was, then, the duty of the master-of-works so to arrange them that together, each in its due place, they combined to figure forth the created universe in its entirety. For all nature is one, like the God from whom its emanates, and the cathedral represents it as an organic whole. That is why its decorations are not mere samples or fragments, but a complete inventory, a "summa of creatures." Alan of Lille saw in nature the "vicegerent of Almighty God," a multiple reflection of His Oneness. This implies an affinity of all the parts of creation; harmonies and correspondences between them. The realism aimed at by French medieval art was a realism of essences; not of individuals but of a totality. Logical through and through, this art keeps to the hierarchies defined by Dionysius. It assigns to its due place each heavenly body, each species of the vegetable or animal kingdom, each order of existence; co-ordinates a multiplicity. For, as St Thomas Aquinas put it, "the divine nature keeps all things in their proper order, without confusion, in such a manner that all are linked together in a concrete coherence, each retaining its specific purity, even when involved in reciprocal co-ordinations." Here every word *tells*, and in this typically scholastic formulation we have a key to the Gothic aesthetic. In his *Paradiso* (I, 103-113) Dante expresses and expands the same idea.

> . . . All things whate'er they be
> Have order among themselves, this order being
> [the form
> That makes the universe resemble God.
> Here do the higher creatures see the impress
> Of the Eternal Power which is the end
> Whereto is made the Law set forth above.
> In the order that I speak of are inclined
> All natures by their destinies diverse
> More or less near towards their origins;
> Thus they move towards different ports
> O'er the great sea of being.

Lastly, the artist is told to represent the image of each being in its totality. "When a man subtracts anything from the perfection of a creature, it is from the perfection of God Himself that he subtracts it" (St Thomas Aquinas). All the laws of nature tend to that perfection. But they have to struggle to attain it and it is man's duty to eliminate all that obstructs the free play of nature's rhythms; this indeed is why God has endowed him with reason. Gothic man like Romanesque man was located at the center of the cosmos, linked to it by "reciprocal co-ordinations," and his body was subjected to its influences. His course of life was oriented by the courses of the stars, his "humors" were constantly affected by the elements. But, unlike Romanesque man, he was not overwhelmed by the scheme of things, nor its passive slave. By making him the highest of created beings, setting him at the apex of the hierarchies of the visible world, the Supreme Artist invited him to collaborate in His work. When creating him, He saw in man not merely a product but an agent of the creative process. That urge which lay behind the conversion of waste lands into tillage and vineyards, and the steady encroachment of towns on the countryside; that made the merchants flock to fairs, the knights go forth to battle, the Franciscans conquer souls—all the stirrings of the new spirit of the age were incorporated in the theology and the art of the cathedrals. Creation was still in progress and man called on to join in it with his works. Thus, along with the material world, labor of the hand was rehabilitated. Schoolmen at Paris and Oxford declaimed against the disdain for manual tasks which had prevailed among the aristocracy in periods of stagnation and had survived in Cluniac foundations. And while the Cathar "Perfecti" refused to stir a finger in the service of base matter, Cistercian monks, Premonstratensian canons, the Humiliati of Lombardy and the Little Brothers of St Francis all worked with their hands. They contributed thereby, so far as in them lay, to the continuous creation of the universe—like the humble peasants who at this same time were diverting streams to irrigate their crops and replacing tracts of brushwood with symmetrically ploughed fields. In the new manuals for the use of father confessors every profession based on honest toil was approved of and moralists sought out reasons to justify the profits accruing to it. The images of manual labors which figured in the portals of city churches reflected the rising prosperity of the working class, and when the members of a trade guild presented a stained-glass window to the cathedral they saw to it that the techniques of their craft were accurately represented. The triumph of the all-conquering worker was celebrated even in the House of God.

Central to this creative activity and the iconography of the cathedrals was the effigy of man. And Gothic man was of a new type. He had neither the emaciated face of the ascetic nor the rather bloated features of the prelate (apt to suffer from stone and to die of apoplexy). He bore no mark of the ravages of age or self-indulgence. An emanation of godhead, he is born in the prime of life, at that precise moment when his growth reaches its culminant point without the least hint as yet of the declining years. He might be twin brother of the potter-God we see at Chartres molding man in clay. To make his body misshapen for "realistic" ends or, like the Romanesque sculptors, distort it to fit into a specific setting would have involved "subtracting something" from God's perfection—sacrilege. The rational concordances between man and the cosmos should be perceptible in his effigy, since they determine his configuration. The bodies and faces of Adam and Eve at Bamberg conform to a perfectly constructed paradigm. They are among the Saved, entitled to a "glorious resurrection," washed clean of the taint of sin, the stigma of mortality. Already God's rays are falling on them, drawing them up towards the joys of heaven, and their faces are already lit with the happy smile of the angels.

But Gothic man is also a human individual. At Reims—among the saints and apostles, near the Virgin and Jesus (who is like him)—we see in her humility the maidservant of the Presentation. She is free, responsible for her acts, endowed with self-awareness. For the thirteenth-century Christian, who was learning to confess his sins each year, to look into himself and to trace the intentions behind his lapses, practised the introspection Abelard had counseled in the previous century. The figures which by order of the Doctors of the Church were set up on the fronts of churches were no longer mere symbols, but effigies of adult men and women, not puppets of blind forces but self-controlled, responsible beings. They are filled with that love which, aided by the faculty of reason, gives access to God's world of light. This is why their lips are quivering and their gaze seems held by a vision of enthralling splendor. For through the eyes the Light Divine strikes down to the secret places of the heart and kindles the flame of charity. The gaze, indeed, bulked large in the "light metaphysics" of the medieval theologians and did much to shape the destiny of Gothic man. True, this creature was born, will die, has sinned, lives in a space of time meted out by the courses of the stars. But now the great scholastics showed him that he could break the thrall of circumstance, free himself from the mutability of the sublunary world, shield himself against the powers of corruption and, participating in the moving immobility of celestial time, attune himself, even in earthly life, to his eternal archetype. Like Jesus who, though enfleshed as a time-bound man, none the less was before Abraham was, and lives and reigns throughout eternity.

4

TIME

The savants of the cathedral schools did not visualize God the Creator as "the Most High," a mysterious being, an Idea too transcendent for human minds to comprehend. According to them the universe was created *in principio*, i.e. *in verbo*, by the Word, the Son, incarnate throughout eternity. Thus the God who, in the bends of the Chartres arches, shapes Adam's body with his hand is so much like his creature that he might be Adam's brother. It is, in fact, a man, Jesus, who is making man in his image and imposing his features on all living beings. "Every created thing," Honorius of Autun affirmed, "is a shadow of the Truth and the Life"—in other words, of Christ. Since Christ existed at the first day and was, in his human *esse*, maker of all things, the world which his thought evoked from nothingness was given dimensions on the human scale.

The movement of the celestial spheres, in which we discern the underlying rhythms of the cosmos, is rotatory, and determines the cycle of days and nights and seasons. As the hours pass, the light of the sun moves from bay to bay of the Cistercian cloister, summoning to life its austere volumes and, similarly, the sequences of the liturgy, the choral chants joining in prayer the voices of the community, move in fixed cycles which, completed every day and every year in an eternal recurrence, form closed circles. However, this cyclic movement is much less frequent in the Gothic cathedral than in the Romanesque church. The Gothic mind preferred the straight line, vector of the historical process whose trend the thirteenth-century churchmen were beginning to perceive more clearly, the long straight path taken by the Christian and indeed all life on its way towards eternity. Straight, too, is the ray of light that represents the act of creation and divine grace, the line followed by the reasoning mind in action, by scholastic inquiry and all the intellectual progress of the age. Each proceeds unswervingly towards its terminal point. Only the rose window, symbol of fulfilled creation, in which God's light, issuing from its transcendent source, then converging back towards it, conforms, like the heavenly bodies, to the pattern of a closed circle.

The façade of the cathedral, embodiment in stone of God's omnipotence, figures forth another image of Time. Actually all that the sculptors responsible for it did was to revert to the symbols used in the calendars of Carolingian Gospel books. Figurations of the labors in the fields, coupled with the appropriate signs of the zodiac, they stand for the months of the year. Whereas the occupations of urban workers and even those of the merchants (though these latter were to some extent dependent on the seasons, since the great fairs took place at fixed times of the year) were relatively unaffected by the cosmic rhythms, the peasant observed them faithfully, they governed his way of life. In thirteenth-century Europe the towns, focal centers of all forms of artistic activity, opened widely on the countryside, and the lowlands around them contributed to the wealth of their inhabitants. The townsman usually owned some fields, cultivated a vineyard and kept sheep in sheds beside his house. The prosperity of the lords depended on the success of the crops and the cycle of the customary dues which formed the staple of their income was tied up with the cycle of field labors. Owners of large domains which were the source of their wealth, prelates and canons were far from being recluses; they conferred with their estate agents, marked out the tracts which were next to be cleared for cultivation and chose the sites of new villages. They made periodical visits to their country houses, kept track of the work being done, and at harvest time supervised the gathering of the crops and their storage in the tithe-barns, anxiously scanning the sky for threats of storms which might ruin the vine harvest. There was a feeling among these dignitaries of the Church that their quest of God and their interrogations of the heavenly bodies had an intimate connection with the daily round of agriculture. They contemplated Time, in fact, with a farmer's eye. For these men remained strangely backward by modern standards. Their homes were ill-lit, badly heated and even kings and bishops spent most of their time in the open, in woods, orchards, cloistered gardens. Everyone promptly took notice of the lengthening or shortening of the days, the first frost of the year, the timid awakening of Nature in the month when vines are pruned, and her seeming lethargy at the time of ploughing and that of sowing the early wheat. And all of them pictured the brazen fervor of high summer, the climbing of the sun towards the zenith, in a quite concrete guise: that of a drouthy harvester.

In the early twelfth century Romanesque sculptors had inscribed the sequence of the labors of the months in a half circle around the tympana. They were now set out by the French sculptors in long rows. Successive figures symbolizing the course of nature's time were enclosed in medallions isolating them from the plane surface of the wall. Italy transformed them into statues. In Venice, however, in St Mark's, the Months, arranged in low relief on vertical bands, recall the French iconography. But in the Romagna, at Parma and Modena, in the region where Rome was by way of regaining her true visage and ancient monuments were encouraging sculptors to disengage from the wall the effigies of grape-harvesters, wine-pressers and the cask-makers of the month of August, they took to producing stalwart, free-standing figurines like the bronze effigies of the dark powers of Earth revered by their remote forefathers.

Yet in Italy as in France, the month of May, "dead season" of agriculture, was represented as a horseman. His triumphal progress through the fields is a survival of the rites celebrating nature's rebirth in spring, but he also expresses the joy of the young knight riding forth, once winter's grip was ended, on some heroic foray. At Parma, however, in the heart of the fertile province of Emilia, the horseman brandishes a rustic implement, a bill-hook, used in this season for pruning trees and hedgerows.

TIME

1. Amiens Cathedral: the Labors of the Months and the Signs of the Zodiac. Frieze on the west front, details. Second quarter of the 13th century.

2. Notre-Dame, Paris: July, the Harvest. Sculpture on the door-jamb of the Portail de la Vierge. 12th century.

3. St Mark's, Venice: the Labors of the Months, detail. Bas-relief of the central doorway. 13th century.

4. Santa Maria della Pieve, Arezzo: sculptures on the vaulting of the central doorway. 12th-13th century.

5. Master of the Months of Ferrara (early 13th century). The months of April, July, September and December. Sculptures from the cathedral. Museo dell'Opera del Duomo, Ferrara.

6. Workshop of Benedetto Antelami. The Knight of May. 1206-1211. Baptistery of Parma.

7. Benedetto Antelami (c. 1150-c. 1230). Spring, about 1180. Baptistery of Parma (originally in the cathedral).

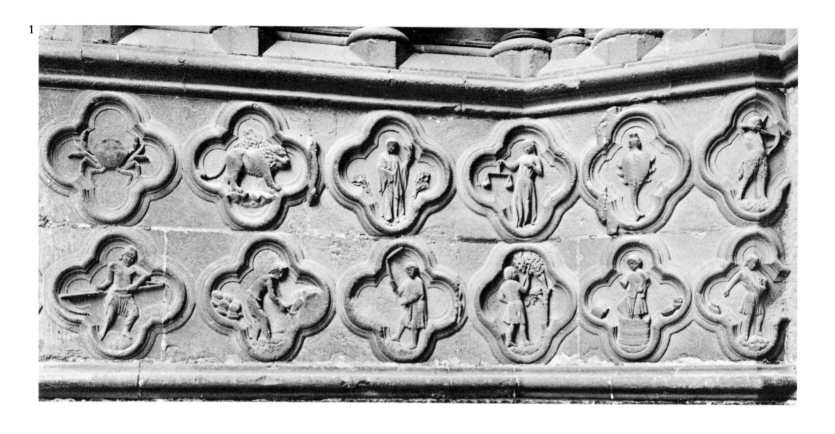

1

2

3

II. 134

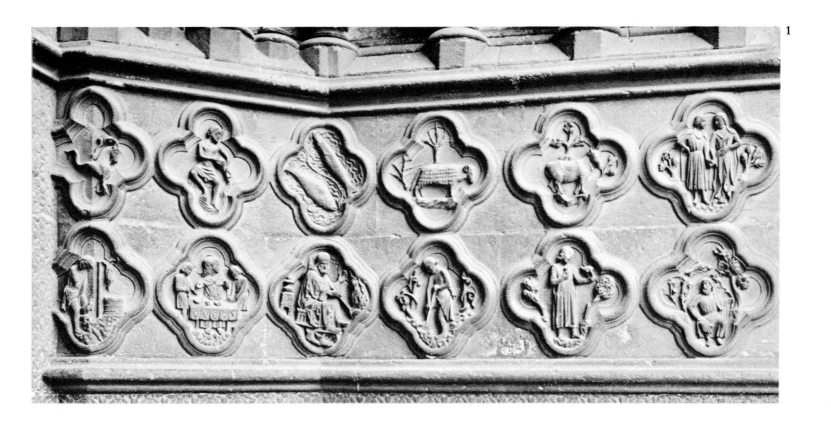

1

4

II. 135

6

7

II. 137

THE INCARNATION

Time plays no part in the recurrent ebb and flow which according to the mystical theology of Dionysius the Pseudo-Areopagite pervades the created universe: a movement oriented by two opposite polarities: God's loving-kindness and the love His creatures give Him in return. According to St Thomas Aquinas God's wisdom and goodness emanate from all His creatures, "but this process may also be regarded as a means of returning to the Supreme End, a return enabled by the gifts which alone unite us with that Supreme End, that is God, these gifts being sanctifying grace and our sense of the divine glory. In this emanation of creatures, which proceeds from their first principle, there is as it were a circulation or a respiration, inasmuch as all created beings tend to return to that from which they proceed, their primal essence. And in so doing they obey certain laws, governing alike their return and their procession." While basing his dialectic on Aristotle, St Thomas bore in mind the mystical doctrine of Dionysius. In the mid-thirteenth century the Dominican and Franciscan masters lecturing in the Paris schools at once achieved lucidity and reconciled the rationalism of Aristotelian thought with St Bernard's appeal to the emotions. Using logical methods, they sought to discover the laws of that creative "respiration," like the act of breathing, of which Aquinas speaks and at discovering the God of the natural world, identical with the God of the supernatural. But their *primum mobile* was love, the love that Dante speaks of in his *Purgatorio*.

> As fire moves, rising to the zenith
> By reason of its very form, made to ascend
> To the place where it lasts best in its substance,
> Even so the living soul is filled with yearning,
> A movement of the spirit, and never rests
> Until it has enjoyed the object of its love.

For at the point of junction between love and reason, at the precise point where the forth-flowing divine light encounters the returning tide, where nature and supernature, time and eternity meet, is Christ, God made man, "light born of light," yet clad in human flesh. From its earliest phase at Saint-Denis on, Gothic art strove to express the Incarnation and elaborated the imagery seen to perfection in the thirteenth-century cathedrals. Inspired directly by the Gospels, it was imbued with the spirit of the underground movements which already in the eleventh century had been gaining ground in western Christendom. Its origins go back to the earliest attempts of Christian man to body forth a God in his own image, a reassuring image in times of spiritual anguish. It was with a similar intention that in the middle of the eleventh century the Patarenes of Milan turned their gaze towards the Cross, in which they saw a symbol of victory over death and the powers of evil. The pilgrims who soon after the year 1000 set out for Jerusalem, empty-handed, and whose quest blazed the trail for the crusades, also contributed to the emergence of the Gothic figurations of the Word made flesh. When, on their return from the Holy Land, these men gave eyewitness accounts of Judaea and the Lake of Tiberias and declared that they had touched Christ's tomb with their own hands, and even that they had seen Jesus himself, a tendency developed to impart, little by little, to the face of God the Father the features of the Son of Man, and to give the Son a larger place in the liturgies and chants of the cloisters. As early as 1100 the advocates of church reform had sought to replace the cult of the patriarchs of the Old Dispensation with that of the apostles, and drew spiritual nourishment from the Acts and the Gospel of St Matthew, where stress is laid on poverty. "The various paths to salvation mapped out by the friars, known as the Rules of St Basil, St Augustine and St Benedict, are not the parent stem of the religious life, but grafts inserted in it; not the roots, but foliage. There is but one rule of faith and salvation, a primordial, essential rule, from which all the others flow like streams from the same source, and this is the Holy Gospel which the apostles received from the Saviour Himself. Cling to Christ whose branches you are, and strive in so far as He gives you strength to do so, to conform to the teaching of His Gospel. Thus, when asked about your Rule, your Order, your vocation, answer that you obey the first and fundamental Rule of the Christian life, the Gospels, source and basis of all the Rules." The man who, round about 1150, drew up this prologue to the Rule of Grandmont was putting into words what the most enlightened knights and bourgeois felt, dimly perhaps as yet. Peter Waldo preached the doctrine of Christ as set forth in the Gospels and it was the Master Himself who bade St Francis discard all worldly goods and follow in His steps. Pope Innocent III was convinced that he had received his mandate from the very hands of Jesus and that his deeds were sanctioned by divine authority. The new, profound emotions that were stirring in the hearts of the Christian community—outcome of a raising of the cultural level and a heightened sensibility—account for the placing of the person of the Son of Man, God incarnate, in the forefront of the art of the cathedrals. Catharism may well have owed much of its success to the ambiguities of its vocabulary; its ostensible adhesion to the Gospel message tended to veil its blunt rejection of the Incarnation. By stripping it of such pretenses the Roman Church did away with its appeal to the masses and they now began to turn towards St Francis, who instituted the devotion of the Christchild's Crib *(presepio)* on the night of Christmas. Catholicism triumphed in the Christmas hymns.

In point of fact, however, the theologians who set the course of Gothic art did not visualize Christ as a child but as a king, ruler of the world. In the edifices in whose building the French kings co-operated He was represented as a crowned Doctor and soon was shown seated on a throne crowning the Virgin, his mother but also the Bride: a woman but also the Church. For the churchmen had ended up by justifying, in virtue of the part that Mary had played in the Incarnation, the high place the Mother of God had gradually won for herself in popular esteem during the twelfth century. They endorsed the placing of her image alongside that of Jesus in the heart of their theology, and likewise in the adornment of the cathedrals. And since in the first half of the thirteenth century it was no longer the great ladies of the courts who imposed his themes on the artist and he now conformed to the dictates of the Church, the

king, the bishops and the theologians, he did not express Our Lady's tenderness of heart or her sorrows, but her glory. Ceasing to be an occasion for public rejoicings, the Incarnation became a holy mystery. If sculptors and glass painters placed the image of the Virgin at the most conspicuous points, this was because she signified, for the schoolmen and doctors of the Church, the New Dispensation, fulfilment of the Old. In her person humanity linked up with God; she was the locus of the mystical marriage between the soul and its Creator. And she also gave concrete expression to the idea of a united Church, one and indivisible. For was not the spouse within whom God was made flesh, the Church herself, defender against heresy? Thus the "Coronations of the Virgin" in the cathedrals proclaim, with pomp and circumstance, the indisputable sovereignty of the Church of Rome.

Henceforth the evolution of the Marian iconography kept pace with the images of royal progresses and of the Church triumphant. In 1145 the Royal Portal of Chartres still celebrated the power and the glory of the Romanesque God who figured in the center of the porch, putting to flight the powers of darkness on the Last Day. But, challenging the rising influence of Catharism, it also declared that this God was made flesh, and one of the tympana flanking it contained Gospel scenes relating to the birth of Christ. If the first monumental image of the Mother of God made its appearance in the great city of the Beauce, it was because in this part of France the cult of the Virgin sprang from an ancient tradition going back to Carolingian times and was associated with that upsurge of spirituality in Neustria which had been promoted by the monks and the Frankish kings. Charles the Bald had presented the church of Chartres with some fine pieces of cloth brought from the East, said to be part of the garment Mary was wearing when visited by the archangel Gabriel. Bands of peasants and soldiers flocked to see this holy relic and knelt down before it in pious adoration. Next they were led down to the crypt where there was an effigy of the Virgin in majesty, seated on a throne. When, following Suger's precedent, the sacred relics were transferred from the darkness of underground shrines to the light of day, for all to see, the prelate who made the plans for the Royal Portal had a reproduction in stone of this reliquary statue installed at the center of the scenes of Christ's childhood on the tympanum of the west door. But these figurations were a mere accompaniment to the leading theme: the shepherds, humble compeers of the shepherds of the Ile-de-France, seem dazzled by the splendor of another vision, that of the Mother of God, a timeless, mysterious presence, hieratic here as at Torcello, but seated. For the Virgin also represents "the throne of Solomon, seat of Divinity" that Peter the Venerable was extolling at this very time. A little later the decorators of Laon Cathedral still utilized, in their celebrations of the Virgin, the symbols of the "concordances," Old Testament prefigurations of her immaculacy: the Burning Bush, Gideon's fleece, the Three Holy Children unscathed in the fiery furnace.

The cult of the Virgin was celebrated with an added fervor now that the Church tended more and more to see in her an image of itself. The final step was taken at Senlis in 1190—just when the Church was beginning to stiffen her resistance to heresy—by an emphatic restatement of the doctrine of the Incarnation. Here for the first time an entire cathedral porch was consecrated to the Mother of God. Even her funeral, or rather the transit of her earthly being to celestial glory, was represented. For according to the Oriental beliefs that had infiltrated Latin Christendom, the Virgin did not die but fell asleep, and angels carried her sleeping body up to heaven, sparing her the common lot of mortals. At Senlis Jesus and Mary figured side by side, enthroned, at the summit of the tympanum, and Christ has his mother on his right, signifying that she shares his royalty. Actually this sculpture was simply an illustration of two verses in the liturgy of the Feast of the Assumption: "The queen sits on his right, clad in golden raiment" and "He hath set on her head a crown of precious stones." Launched at the time when Pope Innocent III was claiming universal sovereignty for the Church, this imagery soon came into favor throughout western Christendom. At Notre-Dame in Paris, about 1220, it was given its most perfect interpretation.

Here too, however, it was still relegated to one of the sides of the porch. Thirty years later, when Reims Cathedral was completed, effigies of Mary figured in all parts of the edifice. The original plan drawn up by the master-mason Jean d'Orbais had provided for a porch whose central portion was to contain the patron saints of the cathedral. This plan was modified, these minor intercessors giving place to the supreme mediatrix, the Virgin. In the north portal, to which the patron saints are relegated, she figures in their midst, reinforcing their beneficent activities, and she reappears in the south porch, where her presence intensifies the mystical significance of the apocalyptic vision of the Last Day. Here, as at Senlis, the demonstration of the Christian verities on the front of the cathedral is centered on her person, and she reappears on the mullion of the central door. Monumental representations of the Annunciation, Visitation, Presentation in the Temple and that of King David, her ancestor, bear her company. The moldings of the arches illustrate her life on earth and are also decked with symbolic images of her virginity. Solomon and the Queen of Sheba prefigure her mystical union with Christ the King. To the rose window of the Creation corresponds the western rose depicting her Assumption. And, finally, at the summit of the gable we see Christ with his own hands bestowing on his mother the insignia of sovereign power, the new Adam crowning the new Eve, his spouse. For did He not by his Incarnation ensure the triumph of the Church in this world?

Adam and Jesus, his creator, are like each other. That question which from time immemorial had kept man in awed suspense, pondering on the mystery of the universe and the human predicament—that question "What is God's true visage?"—found an answer in the teachings of the theologians of France: "It is the face of man." In the Royal Portal of Chartres that answer had given rise to the first faint stirrings of life in those Romanesque faces which hitherto had been given an hieratic rigidity, the glacial aloofness of the supramundane. But now a smile rippled on their lips and their gaze lost its trancelike fixity. This new-won life proclaimed itself triumphantly; sculptors released bodies from the prisoning columns, and gave them the suppleness of natural attitudes under the folds of garments of the heavy cloth then being manufactured in Flanders for the princely courts.

Now that the cathedral porches were used as a stage setting for the liturgical drama and the number of personages figuring in it steadily increased, each had to be plainly recognizable. True, all had distinguishing marks, the attributes assigned by Christian iconography to each prophet, each precursor, every apostle. But a tendency developed to personalize their faces, to make them character-revealing. The vocabulary of the thirteenth-century literature read by the knights was quite inadequate in this respect. Joinville had a genius for describing battles and the brilliant life of royal courts, but grew sadly tongue-tied when it came to delineating a character. For practical purposes, in debates concerning the proper interpretation of feudal rights or details of dress—sometimes, too, in contacts with their confessors—the nobles had gradually sharpened their wits. The schoolmen, needless to say, were versed in self-analysis—this indeed was fundamental to Abelard's conception of morality. For all theology led up to a system of ethics; it involved soul-searchings and a close study of man's faculties and virtues. And since the doctors of the Church stressed the principle of the oneness of the universe, the intimate connection between the three parts of every human being—body, soul and spirit—, it followed that the traits of a man's face were a visible expression of his personality. Nevertheless the scholastic method aimed at resolving the idiosyncrasies of the individual into forms common to his species and made a point of differentiating between "types." As a result, it is types rather than individuals that the faces of the statues represent.

Many of the cathedrals were built very rapidly and so many figures had to be carved that the work was distributed among several groups of craftsmen. Some were headed by distinguished artists, others by lesser lights. The finest sculptural groups were probably made under the supervision of a master-mason who was responsible for all the building operations and co-ordinated the activities of his subordinates. It would seem that Jean de Chelles himself superintended the execution of the Presentation in the Temple, about 1250, in the porch of the north transept of Notre-Dame in Paris. To a group of sculptors working under Jean d'Orbais, first of the architects of Reims Cathedral, may be assigned most of the statues of saints, apostles and prophets subsequently installed in the large porch. They have affinities both with those in the north portal of Chartres and also—and here the link seems more direct—with figures made by Nicholas of Verdun between 1180 and 1205 for the Klosterneuburg altar, for the shrine of the Magi at Cologne and that of the Virgin at Tournai. Some of the statues, however—those of Mary and Elizabeth in the group of the Visitation, those of Gabriel and some prophets—, are treated in an unusual manner; their garments have just the same type of folds as those of the veils with which classical Greek sculptors draped their goddesses. Are we to assume that after the crusade of 1204 Hellenic models had a direct influence on the sculpture of the West? In point of fact the chief innovation here consists in the lifelike movement given the bodies, a movement like that of the Victories of Greek statuary, which dispenses with frontality and sweeps them forward. In the atelier of Jean Le Loup, between 1228 and 1233, were made the statues of the Virgin, of the Annunciation and the Presentation, of Solomon, the Queen of Sheba and Philip Augustus. They resemble those of Amiens, but are more expressive; they have an unwonted suppleness and grace, and the faces convey new shades of feeling.

About 1237 the layout of the Reims decorations was taken over in toto at Bamberg, where bishop Egbert, brother-in-law of King Philip of France, was starting building operations. On the choir screen of St George an unknown master represented Jonah and Hosea engaged in a heated controversy like two doctors of the Church. Rendered with a startling veracity, they seem charged with the dauntless energy of the pioneer explorers of the German backwoods, the missionaries and the early crusaders, inspired by the heroic faith of Parsifal.

THE PROPHETS JONAH AND HOSEA, ABOUT 1240.
RELIEFS ON THE CHOIR SCREEN OF BAMBERG CATHEDRAL.

THE PRESENTATION IN THE TEMPLE, ABOUT 1250.
SCULPTURE IN THE PORTAL OF THE NORTH TRANSEPT, CATHEDRAL OF NOTRE-DAME, PARIS.

ADAM, DETAIL OF A STATUE FROM BAMBERG CATHEDRAL. ABOUT 1240. DIOCESAN MUSEUM, BAMBERG.

JUDITH, STATUE ON THE NORTH FAÇADE (RIGHT-HAND PORTAL) OF CHARTRES CATHEDRAL. ABOUT 1210.

SAMUEL, DETAIL OF A STATUE ON THE NORTH FAÇADE (CENTRAL PORTAL) OF CHARTRES CATHEDRAL. ABOUT 1210.

MAIDSERVANT, DETAIL OF A STATUE ON THE FAÇADE OF REIMS CATHEDRAL. ABOUT 1240.

5

THE VIRGIN
AND THE RESURRECTED

Historians are at a loss for the underlying reasons of the change that took place when the martyrs and confessors to whom the cathedrals of France had formerly been dedicated were replaced by Our Lady, who thus became the sole and common patron of them all. There are grounds, however, for surmising that the sudden rise of the cult of Mary in the Gothic age—like the evangelical revival which had preceded it, like the eremitical monasticism of the first Carthusians, like the asceticism of Citeaux and so many other religious movements which since the end of the eleventh century had inspired new forms of imagery—was a result of the contacts of Latin Christianity with the East. For at this time the Byzantine establishment had more initiative, more creative energy, and more resources to draw on than that of France or Germany. All the great shrines of the Virgin were in the East. Embroidering on the rather scanty references to her in the Gospels and the Acts and eking them out with anecdotes of their own invention, Byzantine monks had built up an elaborate Marian iconography. It was there that the legend of the "Dormition" originated; Mary had not died, God would not let his spouse and mother suffer the indignity of physical decay. She fell asleep and her sleeping body was wafted to the celestial realm by a company of angels. Henceforth she sits enthroned in highest heaven on the right of God,

Son and Father. Thus she occupies an all-glorious place in the Kingdom of God, at the apex of the celestial hierarchy, immediately beside the Supreme Source of light and goodness. She is the highest dignitary in the court of heaven and Our Lord hearkens to her counsels. Full of loving-kindness for all men and compassion for their lapses, she pleads for them and welcomes them at their journey's end. Like her, all men and women will one day win through to the Light. Illustrated by the sculptors in Paris and Senlis, this tale of the Dormition encouraged preachers to stress the note of hope, that prospect of a glad resurrection of which her presence in the court of heaven gave a warranty.

People always felt death very near them in the thirteenth century. It is impossible for us today to form any clear idea of the fears that tormented the minds of all those peasants who never ate their fill and were forever at the mercy of epidemics or armed marauders. But we know more of the mentality of the nobility for whom courage ranked first in their code of honor and who were so often the prey of that most potent of emotions: fear. The knights took heart when they listened in some great hall to a minstrel singing the exploits of Roland or William of Orange, defender of the South against the Moslems, but they were full of dark forebodings when they embarked on ships sailing to the Holy Land or took part in tournaments where they had, turn by turn, to enter the lists and gallop at each other, lance in hand. The great advances made in the crafts of armor and fortification were an outcome of this fear, and it had a large part in the religion of the day. To how many of these men did church-going, touching sacred relics, joining in the liturgy, making the ritual gestures, mean more than palliatives of the haunting fear of death?

All were surrounded by the dead; the solidarity of a family was not embodied only in gatherings of the living members of the clan. The present generation felt itself linked to its innumerable forbears; their names and exploits were constantly recalled, and sometimes their phantasms visited the living in their dreams. Every knight was profoundly conscious of his lineage; the family tree had its roots in an array of tombs above which memorial services were regularly held. When he felt his end approaching, or when about to take part in some particularly dangerous venture, he gave thought to acts of piety and propitiation and donated to the priests and monasteries a share of his worldly goods, hoping to win the favor of the saints and make his peace with God. In short the chief concern of a man's life, the object of his most anxious thought and heaviest expenditure, was to forearm himself against the last enemy, death.

However the religion we see illustrated in the art of the cathedrals was not the religion of the masses. It was that of a small intellectual élite whose fervent faith enabled them to overcome their very human fears, to bathe their souls in the spiritual light, and to feel assured of a joyous resurrection. Christ had vanquished death—why then fear it? Each new dawn brought back the promise of the first Easter day when its rays fell on the tympanum where tier by tier the drama of the Last Judgment was enacted, a vision of all men rising from their graves, like the end of a bad dream. The shades of night fell from their faces and their eyes opened; casting off their shrouds, they bared perfect bodies to the rising light and entered into the true life.

When it became a practice to decorate the tombs of kings and prelates and to place on each an effigy of the dead man, the cathedral authorities insisted that this "likeness" should be sublimated, stylized. The tomb statues of Bishop Evrard de Fouilloy at Lyons and Henry the Lion at Brunswick might equally well have figured in the porches, among the effigies of prophets. The garments do not drape a corpse recumbent on a deathbed but a standing man, his eyes wide open, gazing at the celestial light. Like those of Solomon and King David, their faces are calm and confident, unwrinkled, without blemish. Had not St Augustine written "God made Himself man so that we men might become like gods"? In virtue of his Incarnation and Resurrection Christ himself had blazed the trail leading all mortals to the heavenly Father and, since death is only a passing phase and the tomb but a place of germination where each human being undergoes a transformation preparatory to the glorious after-life, the art of the cathedrals shows the dead Christian's body already invested with the perfect form it will have for all eternity in its celestial abode.

THE VIRGIN AND THE RESURRECTED

1. The Portal of the Virgin (tympanum of the left-hand door), 1210-1220. Notre-Dame, Paris.

2. Scenes of the Life of the Virgin, 1145-1150. South tympanum of the Royal Portal, Chartres Cathedral.

3. The Coronation of the Virgin, late 12th century. Tympanum of the west portal, Senlis Cathedral.

4. The Annunciation, about 1225. Statues in the west portal (right-hand door), Amiens Cathedral.

5. The Last Judgment, mid-13th century. Tympanum of the west portal (main door), Bourges Cathedral.

6. The Last Judgment, 13th century. Tympanum of the portal in the north front, Reims Cathedral.

1

2

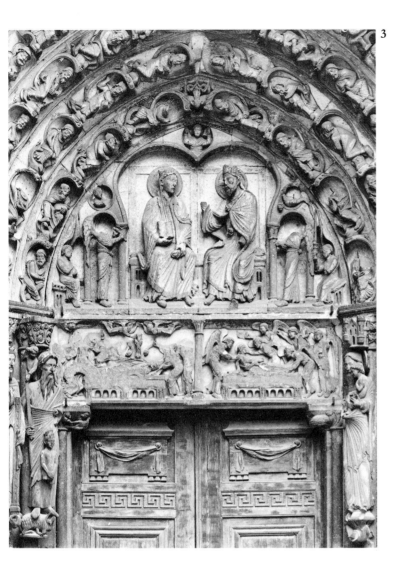

3

4

II. 156

THE REDEMPTION

In the image of the Creation and the Incarnation devised by the thirteenth-century theologians, the universe, ceasing to bear the stamp of guilt, had also ceased to terrify. It now seemed clear—anyhow to that section of the Christian community which was learning to profit by the new "enlightenment"—that sin could not be atoned for by rites apportioned to the gravity of the offence, just as that the miraculous decision of the "ordeal" was no sure test of the guilt or innocence of a man accused of a crime. The thirteenth-century Christian knew that salvation must be achieved by deeds and, still more, by intentions, by the love and understanding that made him feel he was at one with God, led him back to his Maker and to a more perfect imitation of Christ. True, sin still existed; it cast its shadow on all material things and obstructed the passage of the Light Divine. Jesus alone had vanquished it, and He alone could free man from its thrall. Therefore it was the Christian's duty to follow the Good Master and learn, like Him, to bear his cross.

This was the message broadcast by all the mendicant friars. "Do not speak to me," St Francis said, "of any other way of life than the one which Our Lord Himself has mercifully vouchsafed to show me. The Rule of the Friars Minor consists in obeying the Holy Gospels of our Lord Christ Jesus"—the Gospels in their stark simplicity, *sine glossa*, without any comment. St Dominic, too, claimed to be first and foremost "a follower of the Gospels." But the preaching of the Truth, though it now allowed for joy, laid stress on penitence. It urged the Christian to further his progress by accepting in his body the sufferings of the Passion. This was the lot of St Francis on Mount Alverno. "Some time before his death our brother and father was seen having marks on his body which were truly the Stigmata of the Crucified... At the first hour of the day Francis knelt down and stretching out his arms as on a cross and gazing towards the East, addressed this prayer to the Saviour. 'O Lord Jesus, there are two favors I beg Thee to grant before my death. First that, so far as this is possible, I may suffer the same pangs as thou, my gentle Jesus, didst suffer in thy cruel Passion. And, secondly, that I may feel, so far as possible, in my heart that boundless love which burnt in Thee, O Son of God, and which led Thee to endure willingly so many pains on behalf of us, miserable sinners.'" When fifty years later King St Louis wished to follow the same path, it was (as Joinville relates) "because he loved God with all his heart and imitated His deeds; this is proved by the fact that just as Our Lord died for the sake of His people, so our saintly king risked his life time and again out of love for his." For those who shared in the new affluence the thirteenth century was an age of spectacular progress, ever-increasing enjoyment of the good things of the earth. But calls to penitence, warnings not to stray from the path leading to the Promised Land, kept pace, step by step, with this advance. Like the guides of the crusaders, the sculpture in the cathedrals bore the sign of the cross. It teemed with images of the Passion. But this imagery also contained symbols of Christ's victory, proclaimed that God made man had Himself crossed the valley of death, and called on all mankind to follow Him to the abode of true joys, not to be found on earth.

In its glorification of a God who had suffered and died, Latin Christendom followed a trend of thought long current in the East. From the eleventh century on, Byzantine prelates had taught their flocks to see in the rites of the Mass a concrete reminder of Christ's death, burial and resurrection. The liturgy of the Eastern Church dramatized all the incidents of the Saviour's life. The Communion service was an epitome of the Gospel narrative, of which the Macedonian frescoes gave a visual transcription. Soon, too, reflections of these images made their appearance at Cefalù. The crusaders saw these figures on their way to the Holy Land, where they discovered a "real" Jerusalem, more immediately convincing than the eschatological symbols which had fired the imagination of the Western Christians in 1095. The storming of Constantinople in 1204 by Frankish warriors was an epochal event; it was hoped that the schism would soon be healed and the two severed portions of Christ's body reunited in a truly catholic church. What this victory actually did was to give the West an opportunity of seizing all the relics of the Passion preserved in the churches of Constantinople. Robert de Clary (chronicler of *La Prise de Constantinople*) gazed with awe-struck wonder at these treasures: fragments of the True Cross, the head of the lance that pierced the Saviour's side, two nails, the Crown of Thorns. And the sight of the instruments of the Passion lifted it out of a world of dreams into a vivid actuality. The knights bought or pillaged systematically all the precious relics; Count Baldwin of Flanders even brought back to his castle at Ghent some alleged drops of Christ's blood. For many centuries the West had cherished with naive faith the objects, often of dubious origin, preserved in abbey crypts. The authenticity of those brought back by the crusaders seemed better assured and they were given shrines in keeping with their unique sanctity. Old chapels were refurbished, new ones built. "King St Louis owned the Crown of Thorns and a large piece of the Holy Cross on which Our Lord was crucified; also the lance that wounded Him and many other sacred relics. To enshrine them he built the Sainte-Chapelle in Paris at a cost of over forty thousand livres minted at Tours. He decorated with gold and precious stones and other pieces of jewelry the places and the reliquaries containing the holy relics and it is said that these embellishments were worth a hundred thousand livres and more." Above each reliquary was a figurative ornament indicating the origin, significance and special properties of the sacred object preserved in it. Thus the vogue for decoration which developed in the first half of the thirteenth century was a direct outcome of the sack of Constantinople.

To do honor to the newly acquired relics, artists had to use their imagination. The art of Byzantium had employed type forms appropriate to the Old Dispensation. Now the emphasis shifted to the New and it was felt that the sufferings of Christ should be given less abstract expression. Accordingly the authorities drawing up the new artistic programs prescribed the use of themes of a more emotive order, culled from the Gospels. For the most urgent need was to convince the masses, and the Church

Militant, in its campaign against heresy, sought to strike home to the hearts of the populace at large. (A similar recourse to Gospel themes had been practised several generations earlier by the eastern artists.) Hence the frequent illustrations in sculpture and stained-glass of scenes of the Passion. In the sketchbook of Villard de Honnecourt we see Nicodemus unnailing the feet of Christ, and the original project for the Reims porch was modified to include —for the first time on a cathedral portal—a representation of the Crucifixion. For the same purpose the alterations made by Suger in the rendering of the Last Judgment were carried a stage further, with the result that its significance was totally changed. At Chartres the Christ of the Second Coming is not represented as a triumphant monarch, but given the humble aspect of a man who has greatly suffered; He displays His wounds and is surrounded by the instruments of the Passion, the lance, the crown of thorns and the beams of the cross. Nevertheless these instruments are not carried by His executioners or by Christ Himself, but by angels who hold them forth like holy relics and dare not even touch them with their hands—they are wrapped in fine linen. For the theologian who devised this scene did not aim primarily at stressing the Saviour's physical suffering, still less the mutilation of His body. For him the cross was not a gibbet, rather a sign of glory, and the wounds of Jesus do not betoken His agony. "They proclaim His strength," Thomas Aquinas said, "for He vanquished death."

At this time the doctors of the Church were less preoccupied with Good Friday than with the joyous victory of Easter. At Reims, at the back of the portal where windows were installed so that here too light should enter freely, the representations of the Redemption are surrounded by flowers and fruit and vineyards. The figures, too, are real persons, not symbols; however they are not just actors in a drama. The purpose of these statues is to represent the spiritual values of which the Crucifixion was the sign and to suggest its eucharistic correspondences. Since thirteenth-century Christendom was more than ever ecclesiastic and in its war against the heretics exalted the functions of the priesthood, and since Gothic art was, in fact, created by the priests, the statues of Reims were shown as celebrants of the Eucharist, the sacrament which elevated ministers of the Catholic Church far above the Cathar "Perfecti" and Waldensian preachers. They transposed that supreme event, the death of Jesus, into the eternity of the rites of the Church and a supernal peace. Above their serene company, at the level of the rose (where about 1260 the iconographic plan concluded), the row of kings provided for in the initial project was replaced, at the last moment, by another group, that of the persons who saw the risen Christ after His Resurrection. They proclaimed in the heights, at the climax of the upward-surging movement of the great cathedral, Christ's victory over death and bade all Christians rejoice in it. Implicit in their message was a promise of redemption. Well aware that even faithful Christians were haunted by a dread of the after-life, the Church assured them of their ultimate salvation. What was offered was something more effective than the Cathar rite of the *consolamentum*; for those who took refuge in the bosom of the Church the passage from darkness into light need have no terrors. St Francis had hymned the praises of "our sister, bodily death, which no living man can escape; unhappy are they alone who die in mortal sin, and blessed are those who have performed their Master's very holy will, for then the second death will not afflict them." In virtue of the Resurrection death has lost its sting.

The Church allowed the great men of the age to install their tombs in churches and to set up above them their likenesses in stone. Round about 1200 there began, in the oratory of the Templars in London, the long cortège of recumbent tomb effigies. At Saint-Denis St Louis decided to use Suger's basilica as a royal mausoleum enshrining the fune-rary monuments of his forbears, and gave Peter of Montreuil orders to this effect. With this in mind he arrayed the tombs in the transept crossing, like so many beds for lying-in-state. But he did not place on them effigies of corpses; instead, he set up column-statues with faces having the serene anonymity of those of the Kings of Judah. For in the timeless realm beyond the grave did not these French kings and queens have their appointed place in the "earthly" lineage of the Son of Man? And in the eyes of the Eternal Father to whom a thousand years are as a day, surely Christ's Passion and Resurrection signified but a phase of ever-rolling Time? For these were still prefigurations, incidents in the history of signs and symbols; the resurrection of all men existed for all eternity in its archetype, Christ's resurrection. The death of an individual man signalized no more than the return of light to its first principle, of the created being to its divine source. This is why the recumbent tomb effigies of the thirteenth century seem ageless, their faces so impersonal. Rid of all accidentals, they have reverted to the specific type-form, that of God incarnate; the ecstasy to which St Bernard aspired finds visible embodiment at last in these stately figures. At Reims the Resurrected, arising from their sepulchres charged with vibrant life, have the very aspect of the Son of Man, of Christ showing His wounded hands and side, yet resplendent with the light of godhead, of the Creator. Thus Man's destiny, his long progress, with its setbacks and its triumphs, culminates in the Redemption. But both the Redemption and the Creation are summed up in the Incarnation.

Within the cathedral the stained-glass workers transposed the didactic imagery of the porch into a world of light. The moment he crossed the threshold, the Christian drew a step nearer to an apprehension of the vera lux. *Become a son of God in virtue of the Incarnation, he shared in the heritage of divine illumination. He entered that interspace which, as Suger had pointed out, has its true being neither in gross earth nor as yet in the purity of heaven, but where already God speaks to man in a supernal radiance.*

Given the number of windows, the task of filling them with decorations in stained glass called for a large labor force. Many teams of workers were employed, not all of them up to the highest standard. Hence the occasional lapses in the quality of the composition and the sureness of the linework in the Sainte-Chapelle. But these flaws pass unnoticed, so potent is the magic of these richly glowing colors, so strong their grip on our emotions. Here we see put in practice the aesthetic of William of Auvergne. "This invisible beauty is a consequence either of the shape or the position of the parts within a whole; or else of the color, or else of two of these factors combined, whether by being juxtaposed, or in virtue of harmonious relations associating each with each." Colors are chosen not with an eye to faithfully copying natural appearances, but in view of their interrelations on the luminous ground forming their support. Like Pérotin le Grand's polyphony, the stained-glass window blends together an infinite variety of rhythms and modulations, often discordant inter se. *It effects a transformation of the visible, building up a world of strange enchantments.*

The lower stained-glass windows narrate; they supply the data of a doctrinal thesis on the lines of a professional lecture. The seminal text, the message, is located in the central medallion; beside and around it are subsidiary figurations culled from the Bible, which by an interplay of complementary allusions help the beholder to comprehend its purport, and to proceed from its literal to its mystical significance. And since this demonstration follows the rules of scholastic logic, the imagery proves, in visual terms, the strict coherence of the Christian dogma.

On the windows of the choir of Saint-Denis Suger had disposed a series of allegorical scenes, for understanding which "the anagogical approach" was essential. However, he had combined with these some easily understood scenes of the life of Jesus. In the twelfth-century cathedral the windows were filled even more profusely than the porches with an iconography immediately deriving from the Gospels. But they tell little of the public life of Christ and nothing of His miracles. Almost all the motifs relate to His childhood and Passion, as described in the Gospels of the Easter and Christmas services.

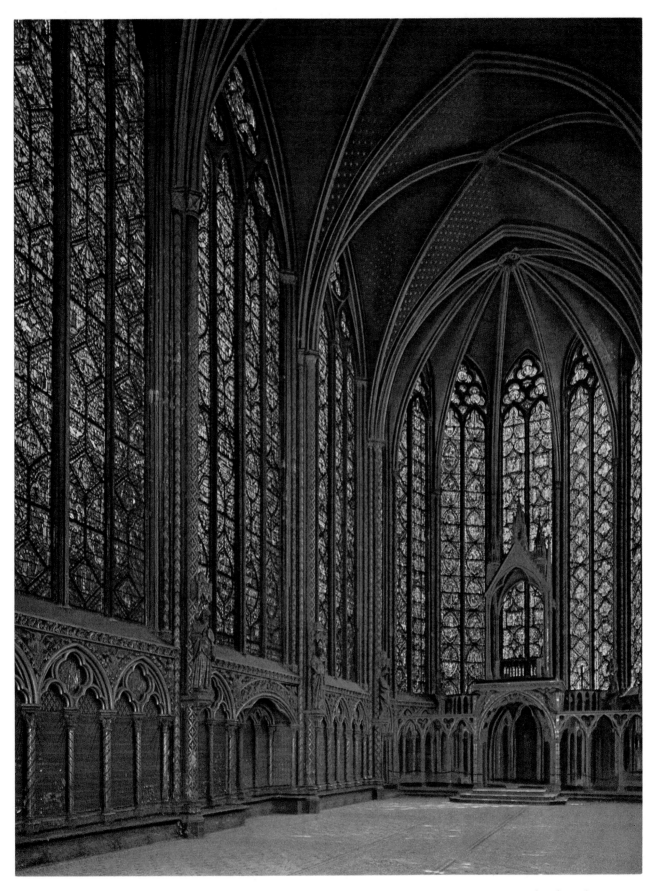

VIEW OF THE STAINED-GLASS WINDOWS FROM THE INTERIOR OF THE SAINTE-CHAPELLE, PARIS (1246-1248).

THE ANNUNCIATION AND THE NATIVITY, 13TH CENTURY. STAINED-GLASS WINDOW IN THE APSE OF THE CHURCH OF SAINT-JEAN, LYONS.

THE THREE MAGI AND THE FLIGHT INTO EGYPT, ABOUT 1215. STAINED-GLASS WINDOW IN THE APSE OF LAON CATHEDRAL.

At Bourges ten low windows arranged in pairs couple scenes with a didactic purpose: the demonstration of certain fundamental correspondences. Here with a wealth of colored signs the Passion confronts the Apocalypse, and the New Covenant the Last Judgment. In the upper part of the cathedral, however, large isolated figures occupy the bays. Arrayed around the choir a cortège of prophets on the north, of apostles on the south, converge on the image of the Virgin (standing for the Church) and proclaim, with a monumental simplicity, the unity of history and Christian dogma, and the concordance between the Old and the New Testaments. At Chartres the same prophets, surrounded by saints, carry on their shoulders the apostles. Daily the first rays of the rising sun bathe in light, above the darkness of the carnal world, these unsleeping guardians of the Faith. Here the almost garish profusion of colors investing the Gospel scenes and the complex figurations of analogies in the lower registers of the edifice is toned down. The figures in these austerely colored windows are the figures of men, men who had lived on earth but here are charged with power and majesty.

Most are the saints whose reliquaries were housed in the cathedral, where the store of relics had been recently enriched by a variety of holy objects brought from the East. In 1206 a portion of the head of St John the Baptist had been presented to Amiens and a stained-glass window was dedicated to him; he had another in the Sainte-Chapelle where the back of his skull was preserved. Chartres had a St Anne window, Sens a St Thomas à Becket window. Ferdinand of Castile presented Chartres with the St James window, St Louis with that of St Denis. These contained depictions of their coats-of-arms, and sometimes figures of the donors were included among the prophets. In the Reims windows Archbishop Henri de Braisne gave orders for the façades of his metropolitan cathedral and the seven provincial cathedrals to be represented under the images of Christ. Symbolic emblems associated these cathedrals with the "seven churches in Asia" mentioned in the Book of Revelation and with "the angels of the seven churches" who received Christ's message. The archbishop also had himself represented with his suffragans grouped around him as in a feudal court. At the very time when the Church was stressing the doctrine of the Incarnation and Gothic genius came to its full flowering, human pride was beginning to rear its head in the realm of the celestial glories, in the upper windows of the cathedral and, on its front, in the stately rows of kings.

ST DENIS HANDING THE ORIFLAMME TO CLEMENT OF METZ. 13TH CENTURY. STAINED-GLASS WINDOW IN THE SOUTH TRANSEPT OF CHARTRES CATHEDRAL.

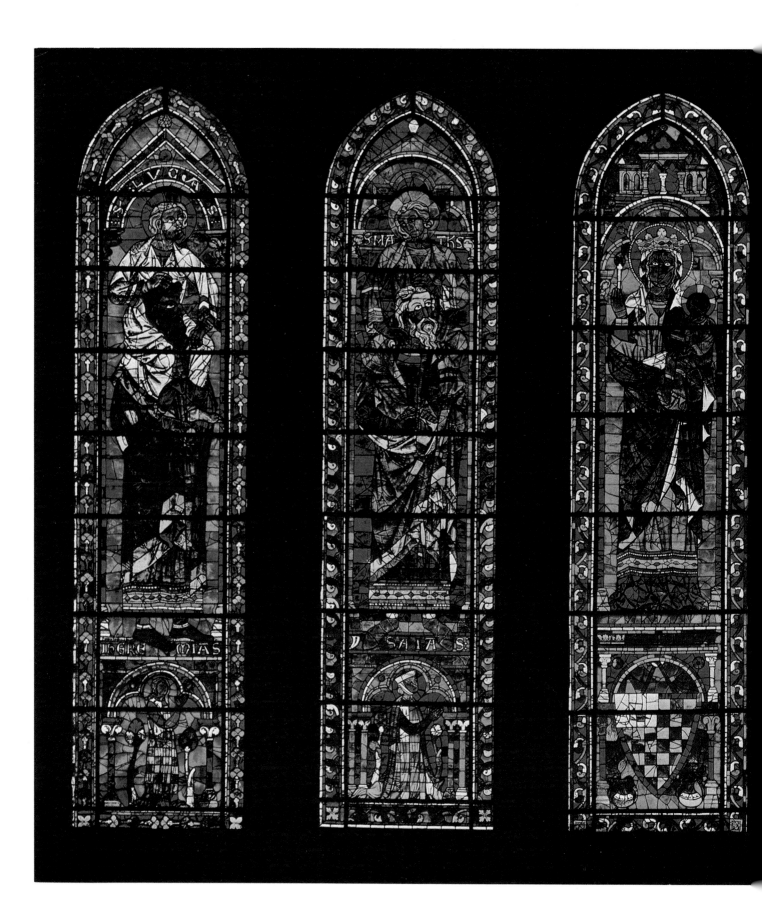

STAINED-GLASS WINDOWS UNDER
THE ROSE WINDOW OF THE SOUTH TRANSEPT.
13TH CENTURY. CHARTRES CATHEDRAL.

III

MAN
1250-1280

THE PERILS OF THE NEW AGE

It was in the university of Paris that the most effective weapons in the fight against heresy were forged. Most of the prelates of Christendom—the bishops of Scandinavia, of Hungary, of the Morea, St Jean d'Acre, Nicosia and many other parts of Europe—and the popes themselves, its patrons, were educated in this famous university. The students had joined the triumphal procession in which the prisoners taken at Bouvines were exhibited in cages to the exultant populace. After his resounding defeat of the Emperor, the King of France assumed the surname of "Augustus" and reigned supreme in the West. To the laurels of the French crown Louis IX added the aureole of sainthood. St Louis had an uncontested moral authority; he was the master of Languedoc and it was under his auspices that the inquisitors strove to eradicate the last traces of heresy in that region. His brother ruled Provence, Naples and Sicily and the thrones of Europe looked to him for guidance. He sought to give his nobles an example of the "new chivalry": of the ideal knight, valiant in battle, devout but capable of lighter moods and courteous to ladies. We get an idea of the king's face from the famous statue of a horseman at Bamberg. All the élite of Christendom aspired to speak his language. Meanwhile the sensuality of the troubadours, the extravagances of the Breton romances were giving place to the crystal-clear vision and gracious allegories of the first *Roman de la Rose*. Thanks to its famous university and sainted king Paris—and with Paris the art of France—held pride of place in thirteenth-century Europe.

This art had conquered new provinces, those which had been incorporated one by one in the royal domain (Normandy, Artois, Anjou) or, like Champagne, Burgundy and Flanders, had recognized the overlordship of the French king. The bishops had introduced at Trondheim, in Castile and in Franconia, notions in conformity with the tenets of the best contemporary theology; these they had acquired while studying in Paris. Dominicans and Franciscans had recently taken over the ideas originally formulated by the Cistercians and were giving them wide currency; the basilica at Assisi and the Minerva in Rome are Gothic churches. The struggle against heresy had broken down most of the barriers impeding the advance of the aesthetic of the French churches; imposed by force on the subjugated South, at Toulouse and Clermont, it was soon to make good in all the citadels of Catharism, at Limoges, Bayonne and Narbonne. Assimilating what was best in rival schools of art, French sculptors were adorning their works with these new-found acquisitions. In the statuary of Reims were forms borrowed from Roman sarcophagi, from Mosan baptismal fonts and from antique cameos, replicas of which were being produced in Paris. And today art historians are seeking to trace the debt these sculptors may well have owed to Greece herself.

Nevertheless from the middle of the century on, there was a feeling in Paris, headquarters of the now triumphant aesthetic, that a far-reaching change was impending, a change that was to transform the whole aspect of the visible world. Most of the work in the Sainte-Chapelle was terminated in 1248; on Notre-Dame in 1250; on Amiens in 1269; the large-scale sculpture at Reims was completed in 1260. And, as it so happened, this last-named year was precisely the one which according to Abbot Joachim of Floris in his prophetic *Expositio in Apocalypsin* was due to mark a turning point in history, and to usher in the Third Age of humanity. After the Age of the Father and that of the Son was to come the Age of the Spirit, when, as announced in the Apocalypse, the Eternal Gospel would prevail and a golden age begin in which all Christians would lead lives of joyous poverty and there would be no more need for a prelacy. Entirely consisting of monks and saints, the whole human race would form a new Church, purified, pervaded by the Spirit. Joachim's books were widely read and many began to see in St Francis the harbinger of this age of enlightenment. A Franciscan theologian, Gerard of Borgo San Donnino, lectured on the works of Joachim in the university of Paris. He had an opponent in another learned professor, Guillaume de Saint-Amour, who soon after 1250 wrote a treatise *Concerning the Perils of the New Age,* in which he denounced the preaching friars as "false prophets" wantonly competing with the lay teachers of the university, and even attacked the pope, patron of the mendicant Orders.

What Guillaume was expressing was in effect the reaction of the modern world to the Church's severe restrictions on progressive thought. This revolt took various forms, chief of them a protest against the tyranny of the papal "monarchy" and those who served it. The Holy See wished to dominate the world, to rule it with a rod of iron. It had already set upon the pope's tiara a second crown with fleurons, the crown of the kings of the earth, symbol of imperial power. For the Church claimed universal sovereignty as a legacy from Constantine the Great. Conquered Byzantium was garrisoned by Catholic knights and the pope had defeated the emperor Frederick II. When Frederick died, in 1250, the Curia did not appoint a successor and there ensued an interregnum. For the pope was determined to rule alone. He claimed unrestricted dominion throughout the length and breadth of Christendom, this being essential, he said, for the stamping out of heresy. In 1252 with this in mind Innocent IV authorized the use of torture by the inquisitors. Still, it was clear enough by then that the repression had done its work. Montségur had fallen, no avowed Cathar existed anywhere. The aim of this centralization of power in the Holy See was both to safeguard its temporal interests and to satisfy the worldly ambition of the cardinals. Surrendering to the materialist temptation against which St Bernard had warned her, Rome had become "the slave of Mammon." Some even saw in Rome the harlot of the Apocalypse, and Dante may have been thinking of this when he exclaimed (*Inferno*, XIX):

Ah, Constantine, how great were the evils mothered
Not by thy conversion but by that marriage-dower
Which the first wealthy pontiff got from thee!

Central to the millennial prophecies of Joachim was an abhorrence of the papal tyranny. The golden epoch he dreamt of and whose coming he predicted (for 1260) was to be the age of the Holy Spirit, when there would be no more need for priests. In 1252 the Holy See forbade the reading of *The Eternal Gospel.* But already in southern Christendom, where though the Cathar heresy had been eradicated, the ferment of the spirit of poverty still was operative, many Franciscans were beginning to rebel against the Roman hierarchy and to preach spiritual freedom and the imitation of the Poverello. At Hyères, on his way back from the crusade, St Louis had heard a mendicant friar declaiming against the monks who were leading pampered lives under the aegis of the royal court. Joinville was among the audience and he was equally against these "canting hypocrites" —though for different reasons. Because, for one thing, they chided him for his "vain display," and also because the bishop's men were enlarging their judicial powers at his expense, within his own domain. This antagonism to the established Church was developing chiefly in the vital centers of the kingdoms, the nationalistic States into which Europe was now in course of being divided. For, like the Italian communes and thirteenth-century Rome, Christendom as a whole was beginning to split up into self-contained, hostile units, fortresses from which every great power watched its rivals and made ready to attack them. The time of great wars was approaching, the unity symbolized by the "seamless garment" of the crowned Virgin in the cathedrals was coming to seem a myth and the New Jerusalem a shadowy hope having no real substance. Reality in 1250 was embodied in the secular State and its increasing horde of petty officials eager to defend the prerogatives of their employer since these ensured their own prestige. Among some of these servants of the princes one saw stirrings of the temerity which was soon to lead a man like Guillaume de Nogaret to slap a pope's face—on behalf of the king of France! Already in the mid-thirteenth century every monarch claimed to be master in his own house and mocked at the temporal pretensions of the papacy. Even St Louis, ready to serve Christ but not the bishop of Rome, espoused the cause of that arch-zealously anticlerical Frederick II and defended his own vassals against encroachments of the Church's jurisdiction.

The resistance of the contemporary world to ecclesiastical constraints was a result of the new, progressive spirit of the age and of the increasing prosperity of the West. There was also a revival of dissatisfaction with what remained of the old feudal system. While the poorer classes became more and more resentful of their lot, the well-to-do rebelled against the doctrine of abstinence from worldly joys preached by the Church. The messianic visions of men like Abbot Joachim and a vague hope of a golden age in which all men would regain the equality of the first days of the world were affecting the mentality of the submerged masses: workers in the suburbs of the larger cities (among whom heresy still lurked), the cloth-makers, the "blue fingernails" who in 1280 launched the first strikes known to history. Soon the movement spread to the depths of the country and there were sporadic outbreaks when some rebellious monk or fanatic visionary claiming divine inspiration mustered the forces of revolt. Bands of credulous peasants set forth in quest of a deliverer, an earthly incarnation of the Saviour, pillaging on their way the granaries of the Church. Such was the Shepherds' Crusade, a "religious Jacquerie" led by the so-called Master of Hungary, whose followers roved the countryside of the Ile-de-France, proclaiming their intention to rescue the good king of France from the hands of the infidels who had taken him captive. These vagrant, poverty-stricken hordes saw in the pope and the bishops, who blessed their persecutors and incited the knights to drown their revolt in blood and to destroy their vague but noble hope, the emissaries of Antichrist. Nobles, pope, bishops and even the mendicant friars regarded as mere trouble-makers these "Pastoureaux" who sought to rob well-born folk of the wealth which God had seen fit to bestow on them and who refused to be consoled for present ills by promises of a happy after-life. In one of the most charming of the romances of the period young Aucassin fears to be bored in paradise and to find in it no more pleasure than he does in the priests' litanies; if fair ladies have to go to hell, he prefers to follow them there!

Meanwhile another dream was being shattered by harsh reality: the dream of a coming millennium when the whole world was to be united in the Christian faith. All Europe, after the early successes of the war with Islam, had shared this dream—there was now a rude awakening. This disillusionment seems to have led to the most insidious malady of the age: the feeling that the images of a well-ordered Creation, conformant to God's plan, that figured in the cathedrals were not to be taken at their face value. Jerusalem, which meant so much to the crusaders,

had not been delivered; in 1190 they had failed to recapture the Holy Sepulchre. During the long siege of Acre they had learned that among the Saracens, too, there were "very parfit knights" and, saddest of all, they had returned in an inglorious plight, sick and empty-handed. They set forth again, but this time turned against fellow Christians, the "dissenters" of Southern France; then, guided by Italian traders, looted Constantinople. St Louis himself was captured and forced to pay a ransom; he was unable to complete his pilgrimage to the tomb of Christ. In 1261 schismatics expelled the Franks from Constantinople. St Louis tried once again to lead his vassals to the Holy Land. In the result the crusade came to nothing and St Louis sickened and died a month after it had started. "In my opinion," Joinville said, "all who urged the king to make this expedition were guilty of mortal sin." None the less Latin bishops, monks and colonists stayed on in the Levant and generations of knights were still to dream of new crusades. But the first fine zest had gone; the noble hope of a reunion of all the Christian nations at the Holy Sepulchre was ended. The armies of the West had ceased to advance. They were first held, then thrust back, by superior forces, one outpost after another was abandoned, and Europe herself imperilled. Western man was growing conscious of the immensity of Asia, the vast reservoir of man-power on which his enemies could draw and the ominous analogies with the age preceding the fall of the Roman Empire. He saw Mongol hordes pouring down from the steppes and when in 1241 and 1243 Polish and Hungarian Christians had to struggle desperately against these wild men with strange faces they thought to see in them the hosts of Gog and Magog or the Horsemen of the Apocalypse, harbingers of the day of doom.

The leaders of the Church were thus made aware that only a relatively small part of the world had been christianized; it was no longer possible to believe that it was only a question of time—perhaps a short time—for all mankind to be converted to the true faith. The culture of the thirteenth-century churchman was far ahead of that of his predecessors and he could not fail to recognize the fact that the created world was far vaster, more diverse and less docile than used to be supposed. It teemed with people who had never heard the word of God, who shut their ears to it, and conquering whom by arms was no light task. Henceforth there was no more talk in Europe of "holy wars." An age of explorers, traders, missionaries was now setting in. Why persist in fighting the infidels, doughty warriors all? Would it not be wiser to negotiate, to try to gain a foothold in those unconquerable kingdoms by peaceful trading, and on occasion preaching? In 1271 Marco Polo set out on the Silk Road, after getting from Venetian merchants, his compatriots, and from mendicant friars a description of the route to follow. The dynamism of the knights of France was replaced by the new dynamism of the Italian merchant-adventurers. Moreover a close study of the Gospels was making clearer every day how barbarous it was, indeed how contrary to Christ's teaching, to wish to exterminate the heathens or, as in the days of Charlemagne, to force them, under pain of death, to be baptized. No, the right thing was to talk to them, to familiarize them with the Christian way of life. The prelates had discarded Turpin's helm and many of them now wore the Franciscan homespun robe. At Damietta St Francis had seen for himself that, morally, the crusaders were little better than their adversaries and stood in no less need of being converted. With some of the Little Brothers he had ventured into the no-man's-land between the camps, got himself taken prisoner and openly preached the Gospel to the sultan—without any immediate success. But a new hope was dawning; it was learnt that Nestorian Christian communities still existed in little-known parts of Asia ruled by Tartar khans. Since the Mongols left the Christians in peace, they seemed more likely converts to the true faith than were the Moslems, the common enemy. They were regarded, in fact, as gentle savages; not as precursors of "the scourge of God" but as potential allies, who might help by taking the Moslem armies in the rear. A Franciscan mission actually set out to convert the "savages." St Louis sent the Asian chiefs "a set of vestments and altar-cloths in scarlet so as to win them to our faith. On these fabrics were images of the Annunciation, the Nativity, the Baptism of Our Lord, the entire Passion, the Ascension and the Coming of the Holy Spirit. Also the king sent chalices, books, all things needful for the service of the Mass, and two preaching friars to intone it in their presence." Europe was no longer sending out men of arms but the best of its preachers, and pictures to illustrate their sermons—all the new imagery of the cathedrals. Unfortunately these spiritual weapons were no more successful than the others. Christendom was still limited to a small portion of the world.

After 1250, at the very time when the western Christian was learning his relativity in space, he also discovered the relativity of Christian history. Until now Time had been conceived of as an homogeneous whole in which, conforming to the divine exemplar, past and future were coherent with the present, bound to it by some mystical relationship. *Sub specie aeternitatis* the moment of creation and that of the world's end were indistinguishable and the present moment was included in them. St Augustine and the Pseudo-Areopagite had expressed this view of Time. It was fundamental to Suger's "concordances," the Biblical paradigms of Peter "the Devourer," and the entire symbolic schema in which the art of the cathedrals reduced Time to the cosmic gyre of the rose windows. Past events do not explain the present but prefigure and complement it.

But in the second half of the thirteenth century there were signs that this conception of Time was losing its authority. Humbert of Romans, master-general of the Dominicans, was instructed by the pope to look into the history of the Greek schism. Plans were made for a council for reuniting the eastern and western churches, and the discussions were to be given an historical basis—a quite new departure. In his *Treatise in Three Parts* (1273) Humbert sought to discover reasons—not only supernatural reasons—for the present state of affairs. Ceasing to concentrate on the mystical correspondences assumed to exist between the facts of history and the contents of the Book of Revelation, he aimed at ascertaining the *real* relations between these facts, the links between them and their material and psychological context. Thus Humbert's attitude to history was diametrically opposed to that of Joachim of Floris; the Age of the Spirit was not to come in the future, it was over, and the present age pertained to the Church. This attitude clearly ruled out any conception of Time as a tissue of recurring patterns. The march of history was a constructive movement, guided by the urge which, in Humbert's youth, had activated culture and the building of cathedrals in the Ile-de-France. Humbert has much to tell of the optimism of the builders and architects, of the enthusiasm of the mendicant friars who, far from dreaming the hours away in a cloister, went out into the world, and even took to learning Arabic so as to convert the infidels of Islam. But the author was not blind to the difficulties and setbacks these missionaries would encounter. He had lived many years among the counsellors of St Louis, had witnessed the defeated king's return, the tragic issue of his new venture, the fall of the Emperor Frederick, then that of the Latin Empire of Constantinople. He goes so far as to say that the "Greeks" are not heretics but estranged brothers of the western Christians, and that not they alone were responsible for this separation. He has ceased to believe in the unity of Christendom, even indeed in its necessity; he sees it as contingent, relative, a purely human concept.

And, lastly, Humbert, like all the best thinkers of the day, was well aware that the eastern schism, Islam, the heathen peoples of Asia did not constitute the only coherent religious denominations outside the pale of the western Church. Confronted by Greek and Arab modes of thought, European intellectuals were compelled to recognize the relativity of their theology. Here was a disconcerting discovery and one which clearly, and in a fundamental manner, called in question the world of the cathedrals. The pontifical embargo on the study of Aristotle in the schools (except his works on logic) had proved ineffective. Albertus Magnus had no hesitation about lecturing on natural philosophy and in 1252 the English section included in the curriculum for a degree in arts the study of Aristotle's *De Anima*. Even the Dominicans—those who had settled in bishoprics in Byzantine lands still under the domination of the western Church—undertook the task of translating directly from the Greek the entire *Metaphysics*. And, from 1240 on, the influence of Aristotle's commentator Averroes had a yet more "subversive" effect. Of all the perils of the new age, most dangerous perhaps was the fascination this kind of philosophy had for the little world of professional thinkers, the men who supplied creative art with its intellectual paradigms. Forming as it did a coherent whole, it had to be accepted (or rejected) *en bloc*. It gave a total, intelligible explanation of the universe and its infinite diversity. At first, then, Aristotelianism had been welcomed as a serviceable instrument, the most efficacious means available for a proper understanding of the scheme of things. The Greek philosopher had proved to be a trusty guide in the exploration of the labyrinth of nature, he had helped to a logical classification of species and genera, assigned each to its due place—in a word had enabled man to draw nearer to the godhead. But closer study of his philosophy revealed the distasteful truth: that it was anti-Christian. Averroes

made abundantly clear the appeal of Aristotle's teaching to every thoughtful mind, but at the same time its total incompatibility with all the fundamental tenets of Christian theology.

According to Aristotle there had never been a Creation. From all eternity the movements of existing things had been inherent in God, Prime Mover of the celestial spheres; there had been no beginning of the cosmos in time. He had also ruled out any idea of man's freedom; no unique individual personality or destiny existed, only a human species. Like everything else, a man's body decays and dies; only his rational mind survives, but this spark of being is common to all and, parted from its fleshly shell, becomes submerged in the impersonal. In this bleak and abstract universe the Incarnation and the Redemption could have no place, no meaning. The trouble was that this philosophy commanded respect and as a whole seemed convincing. What hope was there of analysing it out into its elements, dissecting it, then overriding it? Logic, that new weapon given to Catholic dogma by the universities, had defeated Catharism. But how could it defeat Aristotle, when his philosophy relied on the same methods as those which, since the progress made in dialectics, had guided the doctors of the Church and even supplied the scaffolding of their theology? How harmonize this conception of a natural order of things, seemingly inviolable and invariable, with Holy Writ, with the teachings of St Augustine, the movements of efflux and return described by Dionysius? Needless to say, the influence of Aristotle and Averroes seriously affected only a very limited circle. But, as it was, this small circle was composed of the most advanced thinkers of the day, pioneers of the new culture. The younger men, students in the faculty of arts, accepted the new philosophy with neophyte enthusiasm, and there was no holding them. After 1250 the Church's worst enemy was not the Cathar "Perfectus" but the philosopher. Inevitably he became the target of attack. The papacy mobilized against him its militia, the mendicant Orders. It had already censured Joachim of Floris. In the universities it protected Dominicans and Franciscans against the attacks of Guillaume de Saint-Amour. In 1255 Pope Alexander IV ordered Albertus Magnus to refute the errors of Averroes, and three years later he appointed to the two chief chairs of theology in Paris Thomas Aquinas and Bonaventura: a Friar Preacher and a Friar Minor, both Italians.

The face of Jesus in the art of the cathedrals, guided by learned ecclesiastics, bore the stamp of intellect and reason. The populace, however, who no longer found in the old liturgic rites a remedy for their spiritual anxieties and, though more mentally alert than in the past, were still poorly educated and incapable of following the arguments of the professors to their conclusion, pictured to themselves another Christ, more fraternal, less aloof—the historical Christ whom Peter Waldo sought to evoke in his translations of the Gospels, who figured in the sermons of nonconformist preachers, and whom the Crusaders had glimpsed in Palestine. In Byzantium the Christian masses had felt a similar desire much sooner. But the Eastern Church had been untouched by the Gregorian reform. In it clerics and laymen were not so sharply differentiated and its married priests lived in closer contact with their flocks. It was accepted that every believer partook, after his fashion, in the divine illumination and that therefore the Church should countenance all the forms of spirituality that sprang up spontaneously among the population. Long before Roman Christendom, the Eastern Church included in its pastorals the Gospel anecdotes and pictorialized them. True, the figure of the Pantocrator still lorded it in Byzantine apses. And in the frescoes in the Serbian monastery of Mileseva, painted about 1230, the Virgin of the Annunciation, pure, apart and stately—like the Torcello Virgin—has the perfect, other-worldly form of her who was the instrument of God's incarnation. But in another fresco in the monastery we see a very different Mary, weeping on her Son's wounded hand. As at Nerez, fifty years earlier, on the first of the Pietàs.

The West became acquainted with these images, in which the divine was aligned to the human condition, largely as a result of the capture of Constantinople in 1204 and the spoils brought back by the crusaders. But there was an accessory cause: the development of trade routes along the Danube into the heart of southern Germany, whose merchant-adventurers roved the East and whose emperor had closer contacts than any other European monarch with the court of his colleague, the Byzantine emperor. In Swabian missals and psalters and in the Naumburg reliefs, the poignancy of the scenes of the Passion reflects that of the Byzantine Calvaries.

THE DEPOSITION, 13TH CENTURY. POLYCHROME WOOD. VOLTERRA CATHEDRAL.

THE BONMONT PSALTER: THE CRUCIFIXION, ABOUT 1260. FOLIO 15 VERSO, MS 54, BIBLIOTHÈQUE MUNICIPALE, BESANÇON.

Nowhere did Byzantine imagery have more influence than in Italy, where the preaching of St Francis was launching a great religious revival. The Poverello consecrated his life's work to the service of the humblest elements of the population and after his death crowds flocked to his tomb. The memoirs of his disciples, those who had known him in his lifetime, are full of naive anecdotes appealing to the simple folk for whom they were intended. The Fioretti *give us but a vague idea of the features of this uniquely Christlike saint. He figures in some pictures, but we must remember that Berlinghieri and the other Lucca painters did not cater for an élite but for a quite unsophisticated public whose emotions were easily stirred by reminiscences of the saint's life. The defects of these rather childish depictions are redeemed by their evident sincerity.*

At Pisa and other towns of Tuscany large painted wooden effigies of Christ Crucified had been made long before the days of Berlinghieri. They were suspended in churches, above the triumphal arch; their function was to proclaim to the congregation the victory of Christ, and also that of the Church whose face, identical with the Virgin's, was shown in a medallion affixed to the end of the right arm of the cross. But for the poor the crucifix had a different message; the body they saw was that of a man whose precious blood would wash them clean of sin. Had not St Francis, when gazing at one of these crucifixes, seen with his own eyes the Saviour bend towards him with a look of fraternal understanding and heard the divine voice bidding him expound, quite simply, to the people the meaning of His sacrifice and its redemptive power. By the time the rumor went round that St Francis himself had received in his hands and feet the marks of his crucified Saviour, the Tuscan crucifix had ceased to be an emblem of triumph and become one of suffering.

Around 1200 Pisan artists sometimes placed scenes of the Deposition, the Entombment, the Holy Women at the Sepulchre and the Resurrection on either side of the body of the Saviour. It was on His body that Giunta Pisano (active between 1236 and 1254) and Coppo di Marcovaldo (active between 1260 and 1276) focused their emotive effects, and soon in the art of Cimabue the tragedy of the death of God was summed up in an eloquent Crucifixion.

BONAVENTURA BERLINGHIERI (ACTIVE 1228-1274). ST FRANCIS AND SCENES FROM HIS LIFE, 1235. CHURCH OF SAN FRANCESCO, PESCIA.

CIMABUE (ACTIVE 1272-1302). WOODEN CRUCIFIX, LATE 13TH CENTURY.
MUSEO DELL'OPERA DI SANTA CROCE, FLORENCE.

NICOLA PISANO (ABOUT 1220-1278). THE CRUCIFIXION, 1260. DETAIL OF THE MARBLE PULPIT IN THE BAPTISTERY OF PISA.

REVELATION OF ITALY

Between 1250 and 1280 the economic prosperity of Europe made rapid strides, but gradually a change came over its orientation. The first advance, headed by the provinces best equipped for agriculture, was made in rural districts, with the Ile-de-France taking the lead. When its course was deflected to the towns, those in the wealthier provinces awakened from their age-old slumber. But while the great urban centers constantly expanded in the second half of the century, the peasants of northern France had reached the limit of their possibilities. All potentially fertile tracts had been brought under cultivation and no new land was being reclaimed. Here and there, indeed, the cultivators had carried their advance too far, into poor land whose resources were quickly exhausted. Disappointed, they abandoned it, let it run waste again, and there were signs of an agricultural recession. Productivity dropped in many places, since the soil had been overworked and no remedies for this exhaustion, in the way of new techniques, had been discovered. Yet the population went on increasing, and this increase led to a rise in the number of landless peasants who, finding no other employment, worked at starvation rates. The large landlords exploited the situation and, given the abundant supply of cheap labor, could sell their wheat at a handsome profit and so grew ever richer. But, as a corollary, many peasants suffered acutely from poverty and hunger. This overpopulation lay at the root of the widespread unrest, the outbreaks of revolt, and such hare-brained ventures as that of the Pastoureaux and the Children's Crusade. In the regions in which Gothic art was born a startling contrast existed between the state of affairs prevailing in the countryside, afflicted by shortages of food, epidemics and a constant sense of peril, and the towns secure within their walls, hives of ever-increasing activity, where men could eat their fill, drink wine, and money flowed freely. The wealth of the thirteenth century was in the hands of the townsfolk; of money-lenders and patricians who, having bought the estates of spendthrift nobles, squeezed the peasants, their debtors, and lured their sons to the town in order to pay lower wages to their employees. In Paris, in the cloth-making towns of Flanders and in the great markets of Champagne, businessmen made fortunes. The most successful tried to acquire a veneer of culture. Some married dowerless girls of noble birth. They aped the manners of the knights and they, too, patronized poets. For the entertainment of the Arras bankers, song writers and stage producers invented the comic theater. In France, however, at the close of the thirteenth century, the middle class were still relatively uncultured. Not so in Italy, *par excellence* a land of cities.

For some time wealthy traders from the north had been buying south of the Alps their most popular and profitable merchandise: spices, pepper, indigo, and the dainty fabrics sought after by royal princesses and archbishops: silks from Lucca, fine Florentine cloth. Most important of all, Italian mints provided much of the currency needed by commerce. The economic center of France lay in a part of the country where precious metal was still in short supply for purposes of coinage; most of it found its way into cathedral treasures or was converted into the personal adornments of the ruling class. Numbers of men from Asti and Piacenza carrying large money-bags traveled from fair to fair and set up their trestle tables in the marketplace. These Italian money-changers were at once envied and disliked (as much as Jews), but the prince protected them, since they kept him in funds. In Paris the Lombards had a street of their own near the river; they looked after the royal exchequer and directed the flow of capital in the city. When towards the middle of the century the minting of gold coins was resumed in Europe, most were made in factories at Genoa and Florence.

The fact that certain Italian cities had what was practically a monopoly in this field may well have been an indirect outcome of the crusades, which did so much to stimulate the taste for sea ventures in southern Europe. But it was also a result of the many pilgrimages made to the Holy Land, in the course of which the pilgrim ships put in at flourishing seaports in the eastern Mediterranean, where passengers and crews went on shore and visited the local bazaars, packed with tempting merchandise of all descriptions. In the eleventh century, when so many good Christians of the West had their eyes fixed on Jerusalem, Italian ship-builders were kept busy producing ships to convey the first bands of pilgrims towards the tomb of Christ. These men paid their fares; often they had scraped together the money by selling their estates to monasteries or mortgaging them. Some of this money found its way into the pockets of the shipmen who invested it in local produce, thus opening up commercial dealings with the Near East. Then came the crusade. Its huge armies followed the land route, but for the reconquest of Jerusalem they were helped by the fleets of Pisa and Genoa, which gladly put their shipping at the service of the Knights of Christ. In the thirteenth century most of the crusaders embarked at Pisa, Genoa and Venice on ships that were being constantly improved and built in larger numbers as the eastern trade grew more and more remunerative. Shipwrights and crews were quick to exploit this new source of wealth. The princes in command of the Christian expeditions not only left huge sums in their hands but gave them exclusive trading rights and exemptions from customs duties in the newly Christianized seaports. Sometimes, when the crusaders could not pay their fares in cash, they worked their passage by serving as ordinary seamen. The Venetians brought off the most skillful *coup* of all when, in order to safeguard their commercial privileges, they successfully diverted an entire crusade to Constantinople, richest city in the world, stormed and plundered by the crusaders in 1204.

The inhabitants of the cities from which they hailed supplied the sea-venturers with the capital they needed to open up trade with the Levant. There they speculated in the exchange and bought goods which fetched high prices in the French market. The pope placed an embargo on commercial dealings with the infidels, but they made light of it. Many lost their lives at sea or died of fever, but the others amassed fortunes which they invested, through their business associates, in the transmontane banks. In the mid-thirteenth century the Genoese took to building larger ships, equipped for longer voyages. In 1251 one of them conveyed to Tunis two hundred passengers and two hundred and fifty tons of freight. Another, in 1277, for the first time doubled the Spanish coast and contacted the ports of Flanders, thus opening up the new sea route which was, later, to spell the end of the great fairs of Champagne, and divert traffic from the commercial highways to which many regions of France still owed their affluence. This change of orientation, which had been gaining ground for two centuries, had ended in 1250 by placing Italian businessmen at the head of the world's economy. And gradually it also committed to their hands the direction of the cultural progress of the West. Thus at the very time when, everywhere else, there still was talk of the transfer of the native habitat of art and philosophy, first from Greece to Rome, then from Rome to Paris, a new mutation was getting under way. So far it was almost imperceptible and had made little obvious progress. For many years to come the university of Paris was to hold its dominant position and no contemporary Italian edifice could vie with Reims Cathedral. Nevertheless the great saint of the thirteenth century was not St Louis, King of France. He was the son of an undistinguished citizen of Assisi.

This upsurge of commerce in the Italian cities gave rise to a new social order. True, the townsfolk had, long before this, succeeded in restricting the clergy to their liturgical functions and in shaking off the domination of the barons. But whereas in French towns the commune was composed exclusively of bourgeois, in Italy it had remained aristocratic, the nobles had controlled it from the start. During the thirteenth century, however, in the newrich towns, the more active elements of the population began to challenge the power of the nobility and even to usurp it. In any case the class barriers, here, were less restrictive than those elsewhere between the knights and the commonalty. Now these barriers were still further lowered. Many noblemen, perforce or voluntarily, joined commercial firms, took a share in businesses or banks, while would-be patricians of the middle class adopted the way of life of the nobility, built towers on to their houses, bore arms and aspired to joining in the jousts of the knights. St Francis indulged in the recreations of a young nobleman in his early days. Already in 1200, in Italy, successful businessmen were beginning to live up to the standards of the aristocracy.

Such were the material and spiritual conditions under which arose a culture whose singularity became particularly apparent about 1250. One of its most striking characteristics was the cult of poverty, which (after a first brief deviation into heresy) was enthusiastically practised by the followers of St Francis. In the Italian communes, where the priests were less qualified than elsewhere to pose as models of sanctity, the clergy was looked askance at, and most of the cathedral schools stagnated. Thus those desirous of spiritual guidance turned instinctively towards the famous hermits who chanted Matins and Lauds in lonely grottoes, or towards the mendicant friars. Ardent though it was, religion in the towns had a poetic tinge; it was a matter of emotion rather than profound conviction. Intellectual activities found outlets outside the Church, in utilitarian disciplines: the study of law with an eye to the magistracy, or of mathematics, useful for the aspiring businessman. In the Mediterranean coastal towns the sons of merchants learnt Arabic. Some knew it well enough to read Arab manuals of arithmetic. In 1202 Leonardo of Pisa published his *Liber abaci*, which included a treatise on Moslem algebra. In practice these mathematical formulas were used more by accountants than by cathedral builders. For the new culture was slow to find expression in artistic forms congenial to it.

Capital circulated freely. Lent to the king of France and his bishops, it enabled them to build the transmontane cathedrals. But in the Italian cities little was as yet invested in works of art. For "squandering" of this kind was discouraged by the merchant class which now had a voice in municipal affairs, and also by the growing number of believers in a strict interpretation of the Gospel message. Though Dante was soon to trounce the excessive elegance of the Florentines, the amenities of town life in Italy (as everywhere else in Europe) were as yet of an extreme sobriety. For the churches hardly any new adornments were invented; mosaic workers and painters took guidance from Byzantine models; architects and sculptors, from Romanesque prototypes. The few faint stirrings of a new life that little by little modified their accents derived from St Francis and his conception of the holiness of all life. So far ancient Rome was not a source of inspiration; jurists were studying the maxims of Roman legislators, but the poets were little read and the wonders of Roman art still lost to view beneath successive layers of culture deposited by the intervening years, and thickened now by the renewed contacts with the East. Even in Rome herself the pope was a man, trained in Paris, to whose thinking it was the art of France that provided the best formulas for celebrating the power of the Church—and his own. Convinced that the art of the past had erred in glorifying the secular power of the emperors, rivals of the Church, he encouraged the use of the French art forms. This explains why the first resurgence of Roman forms did not take place in the cities of Tuscany or Lombardy, or even in Rome. There was, however, one part of Italy where the imperial power had held its own before succumbing to the attacks of the papacy. This was the kingdom of Sicily.

A little world apart. Could it even be regarded as included in Italy or as a Latin country? For Sicily lay beyond the boundary line which in antiquity had divided the Greek portion of the Empire from the Latin—a division which had been but little altered by the upheavals of the early Middle Ages. Situated at a junction of the newly opened sea routes, Sicily, Calabria, Apulia and Campania were still accessible in 1250 to the influences of all three Mediterranean cultures: Hellenic, Arab and West Christian. For a long while Byzantium had dominated this region. Part of it had been colonized by the Arabs. Then in the mid-eleventh century Norman adventurers had conquered Sicily. Their administrative organization was based on the feudal system, of lords and vassals subject to a royal suzerain, to which they were accustomed. But they were careful to maintain the methods of taxation, the prerogatives and regulations of the despotism they had superseded, and by these means built up the most powerful monarchy in Europe. The Norman rulers gathered round them priests and Latin monks and became the most loyal allies of the popes. None the less, even under the Norman yoke, the population of the island kept to their time-old way of life, their language and traditions. Though their kings kept open house to the troubadours, Greek and Arabic were written and spoken at their court. They followed the advice of Moslem doctors and astrologers. Far more than Regensburg, but also far more than even Antioch (whose rulers as it so happened were Sicilians), far more than the distant outposts of Genoa on the further shore of the Black Sea, more too than Venice, linked though it was with Byzantium, and more even than Toledo, Palermo was a place of curious and fruitful encounters where Westerners could indulge their taste for the exotic to their hearts' content. For there was no question of a few colonies violently implanted here and there in a hostile environment, of strongholds held precariously by bold adventurers, or of those favored cities to which warlike barons retired to take life easy between two successful forays. No, Palermo was the capital of a very ancient State, large and well established, opening with calm self-confidence on all the horizons of the sea. The benefactions of its rulers had enriched Cluny; the kings of Western Europe halted there on journeys back from the Holy Land. They felt at home there, among men who shared their faith and talked in the same way. Even so, this was the East. Like new Theodoras, the Sicilian princesses, scented, dressed in silk, lounged the hours away in sunlit orange groves. An East tuned to western ways, though retaining its peculiar glamour. Members of the royal household translated Hippocrates and Ptolemy into Latin and when, in the twelfth century, monasteries were erected for the Benedictine monks, their Romanesque arcades were promptly covered with a profusion of strange flowers and foliage and the walls submerged in a glittering haze of mosaics or by the decorative carving favored by the Moslem schools of theology.

At the beginning of the thirteenth century Frederick Barbarossa's grandson, when a mere child, succeeded to the throne of Sicily. Twenty-two years later the pope appointed him to the throne of Caesar. However Frederick II, though a Hohenstaufen, was no German, and with him the Holy Roman Empire reverted to the Mediterranean. St Louis, his contemporary and ally, was his cousin, but there could not be a greater contrast than that between these two men. Temperamental, physically a weakling— "in the slave market he would not have fetched two hundred sous"—but versatile and brilliantly intelligent, Frederick was often spoken of as a dangerous man. An implacable enemy of the papacy, several times excommunicated—but what did excommunication mean in those days?—he alone of all the Christian kings had succeeded in reopening to pilgrims the route to Nazareth and Jerusalem. *Stupor mundi et immutator mirabilis* was a contemporary description of this baffling and dynamic ruler, who even in his lifetime seemed a legendary figure. For the Guelfs he was an Antichrist, the beast of the Apocalypse "which rose out of the sea, like unto a leopard; his feet were as the feet of a bear and his mouth as the mouth of a lion, and he opened his mouth in blasphemy against God." The Ghibellines, however, saw in him the emperor of the end of time, and we can sense Dante's regret at having to place him in his Inferno. A legend grew up after his death that he still was sitting in a cavern in the Kyffhäuser mountain, before a stone table through which his beard had grown, waiting for the destined day when the need of his country should call him forth to restore to the Empire at long last a golden age of prosperity and peace.

Writing a hundred years after Frederick's death, Villani, the Florentine chronicler, described him thus. "A man of mark and sterling worth, of natural ability and all-embracing knowledge. He knew the Latin language, Italian, German, French, Greek and Arabic; was richly endowed with all virtues, liberal and courteous in giving, valiant and skilled in arms, and feared exceedingly. But he was dissolute and voluptuous, and had many concubines and mamelukes, after the Saracenic fashion. For he was addicted to sensual pleasures and led an Epicurean life, never giving a thought to any other life. He and his sons reigned in great glory but, for their sins, fell on evil days, and their lineage died out." True, Frederick II was an incorrigible amorist, but so were all the princes of the age—with the exception of St Louis. True, too, he had his chancellor's eyes put out, but there was no sadistic intent. Deriving from Byzantium, it was an accepted form of punishment in that part of Europe. He fraternized with infidels and his fortress at Lucera was garrisoned by Moors; he called Malik al-Kamil, Sultan of Egypt, his friend, exchanged gifts with him, and even knighted Moslem ambassadors. But there was no question here of unbelief or even lukewarmness; on the contrary his faith was absolute. He did not smile when leading the crusade. But he had an inquiring mind and liked having the God of the Jews and Mohammad's Allah explained to him. Just as one day he wanted to have a talk with St Francis. For the rest, he hounded heretics down ruthlessly, supported the Inquisition more strenuously than any other monarch of the age, and on his deathbed had himself clad in the Cistercian habit. A mass of contradictions, the Emperor seemed almost incomprehensible to the thirteenth-century theologians and chroniclers, whose minds were all of a piece. But then Frederick was a Sicilian.

More to the point for our present purpose is his thirst for knowledge. A knowledge somewhat different no doubt from that of the Parisian theologians. It stemmed not only from Aristotle, but from other books translated at the emperor's expense from Greek and Arabic. From personal experience, too; Frederick himself wrote a treatise on venery in which he minutely described the animals he hunted. The story went that one day he made a man die in an hermetically sealed jar so as to discover what became of the soul after death. For southern Italy was in the nature of a special case in the domain of scientific culture. In virtue of its prelates and inquisitors it belonged to the Catholic world and from its lawyers, trained in the schools of Bologna, it had learnt the disciplines of scholastic logic. All the same Euclid, Averroes and the accumulated wisdom of Greece and Islam were not like foreign bodies in Sicilian culture, but of a piece with it. The king presided at debates conforming, as at Oxford and Paris, to the strict rules of dialectics, setting forth the questions at issue and the conclusions arrived at. Problems of algebra, medicine and astrology were discussed at these reunions. Like the sultans, anxious to discover what the future had in store for him, Frederick consulted alchemists, mages, necromancers and horoscope casters, and in a Faustian desire to solve the riddle of existence steeped himself in the lore of Oriental occultism. Peter of Eboli, author of the *De Rebus Siculis Carmen*, composed for him a poem on the nature of the waters of Pozzuoli and their virtues; his shoeing-smith made for him a manual of farriery, and his astrologer brought back from Toledo Al-Bitruji's *Astronomy* and Aristotle's writings on zoology.

The Emperor and the savants at his court brought to the observation of natural phenomena the same lucidity as the Parisian masters. They were not, however, so much obsessed with a desire to orient their analysis of the created world towards its divine Maker; their physics was not tinctured with theology, but was a secular, autonomous discipline. Not that there was any doubt of their belief in the divinity of Christ and the efficacy of the sacraments. They regarded as "sinners" Aristotle, Averroes and all the Saracen or Jewish teachers who instructed them, looked after their bodies, read the stars for them. But their religion, like that of the towns of Tuscany, had something of the quality of poetry; it did not wholly dominate their intellectual researches or their probings into the mysteries of the visible world. When Reims and Chartres were being built the South Italians observed a cautious attitude towards the dogmas given visible embodiment in the cathedrals. Interested above all in reality, they applied themselves to detecting the forces at work in the growth of plants, the behavior of animals and the movements of the stars. In a purely detached manner, as in the schools of Islam. Perhaps because they tended to disregard the significance of the Incarnation and attributed to God the transcendence of the Moslem Allah, placing Him at an immeasurably far remove from the material world. This, anyhow, was the attitude prevailing in Frederick's entourage where for the first time in Christendom there arose a purely physical science unconcerned with the divine. Here that lively sense of concrete actuality developed which, a century and a half later, was to be reflected in the art of the Italian cities. This realism, so different from the realism of the Gothic cathedrals, owed its origin not (as is sometimes thought) to a new spirit awaking in the middle class, but to the direct encouragement of a king of whom it was said in the courts of Europe that he "lived like a sultan."

Along with St Louis this monarch was the greatest art patron of the period. When, after being chosen German king in 1218, Frederick II was crowned emperor two years later, he ordered his artists to break with the Byzantine traditions of his Palermitan ancestors. On his father's side he was a Swabian and he was backed by the Order of Teutonic Knights. Since an imperial art was what he wanted, he discouraged any sort of adaptation of the arts of France, which celebrated the glories of the Capetian kings and found favor with the Holy See. He preferred to patronize art forms that had recently sprung up on imperial soil, at Lucca and Modena: forms whose origins lay far away, in the primeval forests of Ottonian Germany. It was in the early years of his reign that the aesthetic of Lombardy succeeded in establishing itself in southern Italy. Figuring in the guise of a donor, the emperor had himself given the features of a Romanesque "idol" at Bitonto, and the columns of the royal basilica of Altamura carried zoomorphic capitals like those of Parma. But the young emperor took stock little by little of the prerogatives with which his coronation in 1220 had invested him. He heard much talk in royal circles of the might of "Caesar light of the world" and was attended by jurists who based their arguments on Justinian's Codex. When his troops had crushed the militias of the Lombard league, he had the trophies of his victory carried in triumph to the Capitol. His next step was to resuscitate the Roman eagles and fasces. The art of the bishops of Tuscany and Emilia could no longer celebrate his virtues now that he had ousted the papacy from Rome. Of a purely military and temporal order, his sovereignty had no need of religious rites. After 1233 he built no more churches; only castles, symbols of his might. Given an octagonal form, like the Carolingian chapel at Aix-la-Chapelle, Castel del Monte represents the imperial crown and at the same time the heavenly Jerusalem. But its eight walls—image of eternity in the mystique of numbers—did not shelter sacred relics or a chapter of canons intoning the liturgy. They demonstrated for all to see the might of the Christian Caesar, God's viceregent on earth, and in the decorative scheme the elegant precision of the art of Champagne replaced the visionary splendors of Romanesque. At the very time when St Louis was starting to build the Sainte-Chapelle, in homage to the Christ of the Gothic "coronations," Frederick had a statue of himself, as Caesar Augustus, erected at Capua. Thus ancient Rome was resuscitated, superb and victorious, from the dead past.

A short-lived reincarnation. In 1250 the great emperor died, and with him the grandiose reality of the Empire. Contemporaries saw in this collapse of the "imperial idea" one of the most striking indications of the dawn of a new age. Frederick's line died out. But Charles of Anjou, brother of St Louis, who, supported by the papacy, supplanted Frederick's offspring on the throne of Sicily, did not wholly obliterate the unique cultural flowering whose seeds had been sown in the island by the Hohenstaufen king and which the driving force of thirteenth-century Italy had brought to fruition. This prince, whose emblem was the *fleur de lys*, espoused all the ambitions of his predecessors, the Norman kings of Palermo, and their dreams of conquest on the three shores of the Mediterranean. He did not expel from his court the astrologers, physicians and translators. Peter of Maricourt, his "master of experiments," made astrolabes for him and soon his effigy in stone, invested with all the ponderous majesty of the Roman statues, lorded it in a public place. Charles wished to be acclaimed as a man of learning and a scientist, like his "opposite number" oversea, Alfonso the Learned, King of Castile, author of manuals of astronomy. So it was that the sculptors of Campania continued to borrow from ancient sarcophagi effigies of a majesty other than religious and these won general admiration. Indeed in central Italy they were felt to be better suited to the spirit of the time than were Byzantine or Romanesque symbols or the art forms of France. The decoration of Amiens Cathedral was still uncompleted when at Pisa Nicola Pisano carved the pulpit of the baptistery. Thus in an age of crisis and confusion the art of a new era took its rise at the southern extremity of Europe, on a soil prepared for it by Frederick II.

6

RESURRECTION OF ROME

It may seem strange that thirteenth-century Italy, despite the spectacular upsurge of prosperity that was soon to give it the lead on the economic plane of all the nations of Europe, failed to produce any works of art comparable to those of Chartres, Reims or Bamberg. The reason was that Italy did not constitute a State, but was divided into a great many autonomous political units. No sovereign concentrated in his hands the power of exploiting all the wealth of the country, no Italian court could vie with that of the king of France or even that of the king of Germany. Here the authority which in the past had enabled the monarch to promote the building and guide the destinies of the great cathedrals and monastic churches, had disintegrated. Established in Rome, the Pope claimed to govern the whole of Christendom, but the power he wielded was essentially spiritual; he had not as yet the fiscal machinery needed to fill his coffers, or funds for artistic ventures as prodigal and prodigious as those of St Louis. Theoretically all the central part of the peninsula was under his direct rule, but the pontifical agents were hampered by local town authorities and by the feudal nobility who, secure in their strongholds, flouted the Holy See. Similarly, the former ascendancy of the Lombard kings had lost much of its force, once they had become entangled with the kings of Germany over the claims the latter made for their "rights" in Tuscany and the Po valley—always in vain. For again and again when the German cavalry swept down through the Brenner, all they succeeded in extracting from the towns was a semblance of surrender. The Italians gave way for a moment, then waited for the plague and fever to decimate the Teutonic army and for its leader to beat an ignominious retreat, empty-handed. The communes in Lombardy and the valley of the Arno retained their independence, but their wealth was now split up, in small parcels, among a number of warring republics.

There was then only one well-established State in Italy, capable of financing large-scale enterprises, and that was the Kingdom ruled by the Princes of Palermo. They amassed enormous wealth and spent it freely on adorning their residences and churches. But the provinces they governed formed part of the eastern world, and it was Greek artists they called in to decorate with glittering mosaics their banquet halls and places of worship.

However, a radical change came over southern Italy when Sicily became incorporated in the Hohenstaufen heritage and Frederick II, once he had come of age, resolved to prove himself a worthy successor of the Caesars. This political change gave rise, in the only Italian court where there was scope for largesse on a truly regal scale, to a complete reversal of the then prevailing aesthetic, a return to Roman sources and the restoration, under the guidance of archaeologists, of classical art. Throughout the thirteenth century fantastic animals, dragons, hippocampi, deriving from Byzantine textiles, had wound their way into the ambos of cathedrals. The new art did not expel them, nor did it invade the churches; to begin with it was limited to civic monuments. Long before this, in the Lombard provinces, Romanesque aesthetic had struck root down to the deepest stratum, that of Roman antiquity. It excluded both the all-pervasive light and the vital impulse of the new French cathedrals. Like the ancient temples, the Romanesque church was shut-in, girdled with arcadings, and stability was the architect's prime concern. The Parma Baptistery rises skywards, but in the form of a cylinder, not a spire, and the statues ornamenting it have a family likeness to those of the gods and deified heroes on the gates of Latin cities, on their mausolea and triumphal arches. But it was under the aegis of Frederick II that Roman statuary was systematically resuscitated.

The castle of Capua, built between 1234 and 1240 —the years which witnessed the apogee of the statuary at Reims and Bamberg—contains some remarkable busts in which we see a reversion to Antiquity pure and simple, ungarbled by the liturgical allusions dear to the Romanesque sculptors. Indeed these effigies of the Emperor, of his counsellors, and of the civic virtues, might well have been brought to light by excavations on some ancient site. Soon they were copied by the decorators of religious edifices. In 1272, in Ravello Cathedral, the sculptor Nicola di Bartolomeo da Foggia, whose father had been employed by Frederick II, included a woman's head in the decoration of the bishop's throne. Was this a portrait of Sigilgaida Rufolo as some have thought? More probably an allegory of the Church; for in this face we surely have the visage of ancient Rome herself, reborn.

For some time the large cities of Tuscany had equalled in wealth the greatest princes of the land; but their citizens were then engaged in a struggle with the aristocracy, whose power they were gradually undermining. The leaders of the communes, who were in charge of the finances of these cities, were for the most part businessmen who had recently risen from the ranks and whose culture was only superficial. Still, some of them had taste and sense enough to purchase abroad (as did some New York bankers and Muscovite financiers at the turn of the last century) the finest extant works of art. But these were Byzantine ornaments and French illuminated books. These new men were well aware that the craftsmen of the Tuscan towns lacked both the imagination and the skill needed for creating the type of works on which their heart was set. Then Nicola Pisano came on the scene. Little is known of him except that he was born about 1220 and died in 1278. His statues (in stone) of Moses show the Lawgiver descending not from Sinai but the heights of Olympus. It was in 1260, year of the completion of Reims Cathedral, also the very year which according to Joachim of Floris was to usher in the Third Age of the world, that Nicola carved the famous Pisan pulpit, heralding the "new birth" of plastic art.

RESURRECTION OF ROME

1. Bust of the Emperor Frederick II. Mid-13th century. Museo Civico, Barletta.

2. View of Castel del Monte (Apulia), built by Frederick II in 1240.

3. Three pages from an illustrated manuscript of Frederick II's treatise on falconry *(De arte venandi cum avibus)*. 1220-1250. Vatican Library.

4. Base of a pulpit or paschal candlestick with four male figures. Emilia, 13th century. Museo Civico, Bologna.

5. Nicola di Bartolomeo da Foggia. Portrait bust of Sigilgaida Rufolo (?). 1272. Marble. Ravello Cathedral.

6. Bust of Pietro della Vigna, minister of Frederick II. 1239. Museo Campano, Capua.

7. Marble pulpit with mosaic decorations by Nicola di Bartolomeo da Foggia. 1272. Ravello Cathedral.

4

5

6

7

HAPPINESS

After the middle of the century the inventive powers of the artists employed on the French cathedrals began to flag. They made use of methods ever more logical, ever better calculated to flood the edifice with light, but these procedures were being drained more and more of their spiritual content. One of the reasons for this gradual despiritualization was the change in the system of education. The university devoted its energies almost exclusively to improvements in the mechanism of dialectics, and true culture was the loser in this process. The young men turned out by the schools were experts in the technique of reasoning and little else. Another reason was that fewer prelates took any real interest in creative art. More and more of them belonged to the mendicant Orders and many were of humble extraction. "Son of a churl and wife no better!" Thus Joinville described the Franciscan Robert de Sorbon who was annoying him, and went on to call him "a traitor to the candor of his forefathers." A good many of these prelates who, by way of the episcopate, had achieved the highest social rank became dazzled by their new eminence, addicted to luxurious living, and when it came to cathedral building interested chiefly in architectural *tours de force* and finished execution. The best of the clergy, those who kept faith with the spirit of poverty, were more concerned with preaching than with building, and when they struck out on new paths these led towards an ever greater humility, a more wholehearted devotion to the lesson of the Master. Monumental form meant little to them. St Bonaventura did not build cathedrals, he left that to the king of France, a truly saintly man, but not a professed theologian. So little by little the control of creative architecture passed into the hands of specialists, the "master-masons."

The status of these men had risen far above that of the artisans whose work they supervised. They were no longer expected, as in earlier times, to lend a hand in carrying stones or to carve these stones themselves. Experts in measurement, they submitted to the chapter a carefully worked out elevation, on parchment, of the projected edifice. "Some men," as a preacher of the time observed, "work with words. In the building of these large edifices there is commonly someone in charge who gives the others their orders by word of mouth and seldom or never stirs a finger. Compass and foot-rule in hand the master-mason tells his men, 'Make a cut here.' And though he does not do the work, he gets the highest wages." The master-masons knew all the secrets of their craft and were on easy terms with the doctors of the university who initiated them into the "science of numbers" and the lore of dialectics. But these men were not priests, they did not consecrate Christ's body, they had not spent long hours meditating on the Word of God and wrestling with its obscurities. They were executants, they did not draw inspiration, as Suger and Maurice de Sully had done, from a contemplation of the divine hierarchies, but applied themselves to solving problems of stresses and stability. When it came to invention, their approach was that of the technician, not the mystic; their business was that of handling raw material to best effect, not of elucidating mysteries. Those with a logical turn of mind gauged their success in terms of strict geometry. There were, however, some more sensitive practitioners whose ideal was not so much truth as beauty.

At Saint-Denis, around 1250, that great architect Peter of Montreuil did not innovate; he refined on what had been done before. He had a gift for exploiting to the full the aesthetic possibilities of an edifice; for arranging the disposition of light with a view to the pleasure of the eye as well as for homiletic ends. The two rose windows of the transept, one of them with its light converging centrally, the other radiating out in all directions, still conform—thanks to a strictly calculated mathematical formula—to that concept of a dual movement of efflux and return which, originated by Dionysius, was taken over by St Thomas Aquinas. But the careful balance between structure and ornamentation no longer exists. The functional values of the architectural masses are masked and elegance is Peter's prime concern. Similarly, though the statues in the Sainte-Chapelle are exquisitely proportioned they have lost their souls; superficially they resemble the Reims statues, but all the spirituality has gone out of them. When Gaucher, last of the great masters-of-works, installed in the portal the tall carved figures that had been made for it, he discarded the arrangement originally planned, guided by a purely doctrinal purpose. This meaningful arrangement, devised by theologians, seemed to him unsatisfactory. He placed each statue with an eye to its plastic values, no longer to its significance. The canons accepted his rearrangement, for they, too, were coming to like the new aesthetic. Already in the statue personifying the Synagogue the full weight of the body had rested on a single leg and there were intimations of that sinuous movement of the hips which gives fourteenth-century figures of the Virgin and female saints something of the lithe grace of dancers at the princely courts. This medieval "sway" can also be seen in the miniatures of illuminated manuscripts and in the stained-glass windows, where the elegance of the line evidences a desire to please the eye. Thus the Christian masses and the priests, their mentors, took to finding "beautiful" both the Living God and His Mother. This trend towards aestheticism may well have owed something to the crisis theological thought was undergoing in Paris, and to the underground movements that had occasioned it. At the bidding of the pope, St Thomas Aquinas and St Bonaventura led the campaign against the new deviations. The former took his stand on reasoning, entered the lists against Aristotle and his commentator, and set out to rout them in a dialectical tournament. But his Franciscan colleague saw in logic only a means for clearing the ground. "Philosophy is but a path to other forms of knowledge. He who lingers on it remains in darkness." Harking back to St Augustine, he distinguishes the empirical knowledge acquired through the senses, which only perceive appearances, from that deeper understanding which apprehends the glories of the world to come. His *Itinerarium Mentis ad Deum* sets forth the Christian's progress towards ecstatic union with the divine in an intense, all-consuming love. Why, then, waste time arguing with Aristotle? It is far better surely to advance along the path leading to the celestial heights. He warns the "intellectual" of his limitations. "Beware of thinking that you comprehend the incomprehensible." This teaching harmonized better than that of Aquinas with the spirit of the age, and had a direct appeal for those simple believers who in their quest of God trusted instinctively to the guidance of the Spirit. Hence Bonaventura's victory over Thomism, whose premises he controverted in his *Discourses on the Gifts of the Holy Spirit*. In 1270, alarmed by the extravagant claims of dialectics and mindful of the religious feelings of the masses, Catholic theologians deliberately entered on the path of mysticism.

But the mental climate of the Ile-de-France, of Paris prospering greatly in the reign of Philip the Bold, of the intelligentsia at the university and of the nobility, all for elegance and courtly manners, was little suited to any sort of mysticism. The religious zeal which had launched heavenwards the spires of Laon, Chartres and Reims had spent its force in the second half of the thirteenth century; it was shifting eastwards, towards the Rhine valley and the region in which small unorthodox communities such as the Beguines and Beghards were beginning to flourish. Commerce was thriving in Germany, new trade routes were being opened up, forests cut down to make room for towns. Albertus Magnus had left Paris shortly before 1250 and been given the post of lecturer at Cologne, where he expounded the Dionysian hierarchies and was the pride of the new Dominican study center. After him, another Dominican, Ulrich of Strasbourg, amplified and stressed that portion of his teaching which subordinated the techniques of rationalism to the mystique of illumination, thus blazing the trail for that first great speculative mystic, Meister Eckhart. It was the Germany of the Brethren of the Free Spirit and the Minnesingers that inherited the art of the cathedrals, and at Strasbourg that the last great Gothic workyards came into operation. The sculpture of Reims had a remoter offshoot at Naumburg in the heart of a world so far little touched by culture. Here, however, the artists, while taking much from Reims, tended towards expressionism; alongside scenes of the Passion, they set up statues of princesses in the flower of their beauty. In these backwoods, in an environment of visionary monks, the art of France lost much of its lucidity. It was invaded by a horde of monsters from the early Romanesque bestiaries, plunged into a world of phantasms and blind, irrational forces, peopled with those restless or oddly mannered forms into which Byzantine models had been transmuted by their Germanic imitators. Stripped of its logical premises, Suger's clear-cut aesthetic was dissipated in a haze of shimmering light and vague effusions centering on the cult of Mary. It was, in short, adapted to the taste of men who sought in emotion rather than in reflection an anodyne for their spiritual unrest.

In Paris the schoolmen were turning towards another path, still that of reason, but leading to happiness of a terrestrial order. Parisian intellectuals claimed more ardently than ever the right to philosophize and found encouragement in the new trend of theology towards mysticism. Since Christ came on earth and suffered for the salvation of all mankind and since all that the Christian needs for access to celestial joys is a full surrender to His all-embracing love, why should there be a ban on free discussion of secular matters and why deprive oneself of the pleasures of this world? The lay professors in the Faculty of Arts did not take part in theological debates; their task was limited to expounding Aristotle and their lectures on him were addressed to young students many of whom were to follow lay careers. They declared that the faculty of thought, of thinking freely, was essential to the dignity of man; that philosophy was the noblest discipline of all, and pointed the way to the supreme good. Was not its function the discovery of the laws of Nature, the true order of the scheme of things and, since Nature is the work of God, His instrument, a reflection of His mind and the work of His hands, how can it possibly be evil? By carefully exploring its secrets we discover the rule of a perfect life, in accordance with the divine plan. "Sin is in man, but righteous ways spring from the order of Nature. Therefore if man faithfully conforms to this order, he can be sure of pleasing God. And as a reward, he will live a well-balanced and joyous life on earth" (Boethius of Dacia). Thus the new school of thought showed the way to happiness.

A happiness which is the work of man alone and attainable by dint of his intelligence. For Lady Nature offers those who serve her well the gift of perfect bliss even in this earthbound life. That is the lesson of the second *Roman de la Rose* written about 1275 by Jean de Meung, an alumnus of the university of Paris. He denounces the many abuses that have tended to pervert the divine scheme: the lust for power, the meretricious arts of *courtoisie*, the hypocritical preaching of the mendicant friars. Then he evokes the perfect order of the primeval world. "Long ago, in the days of our remote forefathers, men and women, as the Ancients tell us, loved each other with a pure, abiding love, unsullied by gross desire or any sordid motive, and happiness reigned everywhere. Then land was not cultivated but left as God bedecked it; yet every man got from it all he needed." But now God's order had been ruined by Deceit, Pride and Double-dealing.

These ideas may be traced back to Averroes, but they also derived (and more directly) from the anti-heretical propaganda which, to confute the Cathars, insisted on the goodness of the created world. We can see these ideas in the iconography of the Creation figured forth in the art of the cathedrals. Nor did they conflict with that naive optimism of the early phase of Franciscanism which the Holy See, scenting danger, had forced the Minorites to abandon. They also harmonized with the common belief in an approaching millennium and with the aspirations of the underprivileged masses, who had been given to understand that God had created all his children equal. Thus the philosophy in vogue in Paris around 1270 may be regarded as a new phase in the progressive "discovery" of the Incarnation. A decisive forward step; it meant that the religious thought of the schools ceased to be esoteric, reserved to Initiates, and became accessible to laymen.

For, freed as it was from clerical restraints, this proposition of material happiness (the *Roman de la Rose* was written in the language of the courts) appealed to all the knights in love with life and their ladies, and to those who had refused to accompany Louis on his last crusade. ("There was no crusade in those times; none left his native land to go forth and explore foreign countries.") The joyousness of the courtly poems was transposed into another key. Men were invited to open their eyes to the beauty of all creatures and to rejoice in it. This new spirit found expression in the childish laughter of the Elect at Bamberg, in Rutebeuf's witty satires, and in the charming songs composed by the trouvère Adam de la Halle, simpler and more spontaneous than the scholastic polyphony of Pérotin le Grand. This had been the spirit of St Louis in his youth—before he had forgotten how to laugh. And it now lay behind the smiling anti-clericalism of the nobles of the French court and that of an entire generation of healthy-minded, clear-eyed young men for whom the false prophets, precursors of the Last Day, were not the dialecticians of the schools or the troubadours, but the preachers of repentance, canting bigots, who barred the way to the blithe freedom of a new golden age. The younger sculptors, all for grace and beauty, joined forces with them. It was they who provided the rich sap that fed the luxuriant flowers and foliage of the last capitals. And in the Bourges *Resurrection* it is a call to happiness, a glad tomorrow, that has summoned forth the women from their graves, their bodies invested with the grace of youth renewed. At Bourges we see the triumphant expression of that feeling for warm-blooded, truly human beauty which seemed to have died out in Paris in the art of Notre-Dame.

This philosophy of happiness was the outcome of three centuries of uninterrupted progress in the Ile-de-France. In Italy, that land of successful businessmen, it naturally enough was welcomed. But was there not a risk that in a country like Italy, where the ecclesiastical structure was less firmly established, Christianity might disintegrate completely and give place to paganism? Already Frederick II had been charged with impiety of this order. Benvenuto of Imola had this in mind when he said that "soon there were over a hundred thousand men of high estate who believed, like Farinata degli Uberti and Epicurus, that paradise must be sought for in this world and in this world alone." When Dante in the *Inferno* visited the circle to which were relegated

> Along with Epicurus all his followers
> Who hold that the soul dies with the body

it was Farinata who told him

> "With more than a thousand here I lie
> "And herewithin lies Frederick the Second."

Yet it was in his *Paradiso* that Dante placed "the eternal light" of Siger de Brabant, one of the leading Parisian philosophers and a moving spirit of the new school. In his description of the Orders of the world he ranges in two sequences, side by side but separate (as the masters of the Faculty of Arts had done), Church and State, Grace and Nature, Theology and Philosophy. He expressly declares the excellence and the autonomy of Philosophy—*Filosofia è uno amoroso uso di sapienza*—since it shows us

> After what manner Nature takes her course
> From the Intellect Divine and from its art.
> And if thy physics well thou studiest
> After a few pages thou shalt find
> That this thy art, so far as may be,
> Followeth Nature, as the disciple doth his master,
> So that thy art is, as it were, God's grandchild.

We might well regard the *Divine Comedy* as a cathedral, last of the great cathedrals. Dante based it on what he had learnt of scholastic theology from Dominican preachers at Florence who had studied at the university of Paris. For like the French cathedrals the poem leads us upward and onward by gradual degrees, corresponding to the hierarchies of light described by Dionysius, and through the intercession of St Bernard, St Francis and the Virgin, to the love "which moves the stars." Inspired by the Incarnation, the art of the great cathedrals had celebrated to wonderful effect the Body of Christ. That is to say the Church triumphant, the Church invested with worldwide dominion. But at the dawn of the Trecento, a tendency was developing in the western world to free the mind of man from the thrall of priestdom and to deflect his thoughts from the supramundane. Henceforth they were oriented in a different direction, towards "Nature, the art of God" (*Paradiso*, VIII). An art that could but point the way to happiness. Even Dante and his earliest disciples were conscious of this and set their course to a new bourne.

THE ROSE WINDOW

The art of the glass-worker was brought to perfection in the large rose windows which in the mid-thirteenth century were set up over the new transepts. These elaborate compositions signify at once the cycles of the cosmos, the merging of Time into Eternity, and the mystery of a God who is Light, of Christ the sun. Surrounded by apostles, prophets and saints, God is shown in the south rose of Notre-Dame in Paris and He shines forth in the midst of the music-making elders of the Apocalypse in the rose of the Sainte-Chapelle. The Virgin, i.e. the Church, figures in some rose windows. Circular, they demonstrate, in a whirl of rotating spheres, the identity of Aristotle's concentric universe with the centrifugal effusion described by Robert Grosseteste. The rose is also a symbol of love; it represents the fiery core of that divine love in which all human loves are consumed. And we also see in it a figuration of the labyrinth through which profane love gropes its way towards that sacred love which is its goal.

When around 1240 Guillaume de Lorris versified the courtly way of life in a poem embodying "the whole art of love," he named it Le Roman de la Rose. *The rose for him is the ideal lady, the flower the perfect knight passionately yearns to pluck. This he succeeded in doing in Jean de Meung's lengthy continuation of the poem, written some forty years later. Here the allegories are stripped of courtly affectation and given a natural, everyday presentment. Conscious of the cyclical recurrence of life, the ineluctable finality of individual death counterbalanced by the survival of the species, generation after generation, the poet sees in man's love of woman (that desire whose symbol is the rose) an elemental value poles apart from the love-play of the courts of chivalry. In this poem all those trivial, factitious graces are eliminated, man and woman join in a union that is simple, healthy, fecund. Thus the rose becomes an image of victory over death. A victory of Nature, that is to say of God, but also of mankind since all men co-operate in His creative plan. This will to life and the joy of living find superlative expression in the luminous polychromy of the rose window.*

ROSE WINDOW OF THE SOUTH TRANSEPT, WITH THE TRIUMPH OF CHRIST AND THE APOSTLES. ABOUT 1270.
CATHEDRAL OF NOTRE-DAME, PARIS.

ROSE WINDOW OF THE NORTH TRANSEPT, WITH SCENES FROM THE OLD TESTAMENT. ABOUT 1270.
CATHEDRAL OF NOTRE-DAME, PARIS.

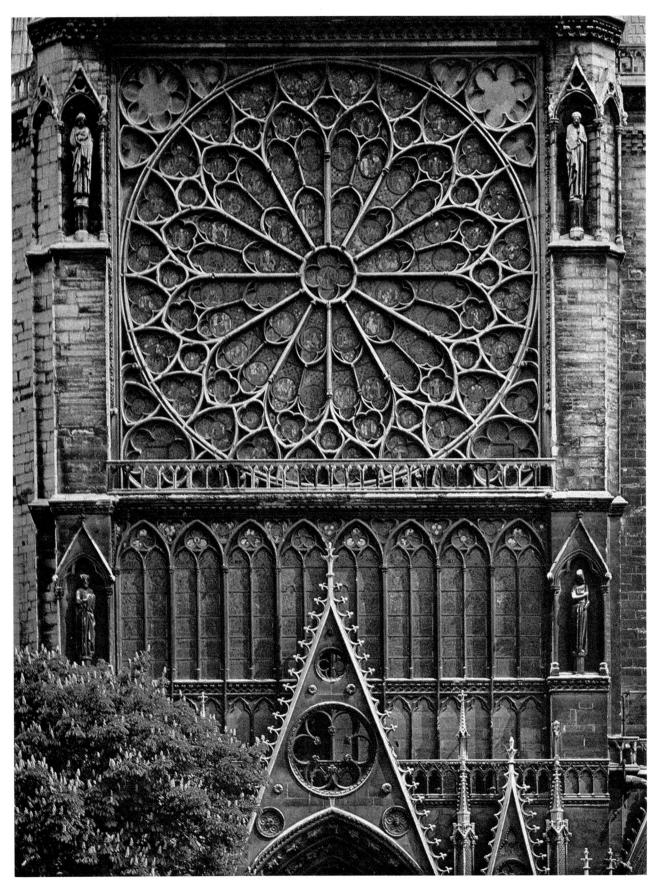

EXTERIOR VIEW OF THE ROSE WINDOW OF THE SOUTH TRANSEPT. ABOUT 1270. CATHEDRAL OF NOTRE-DAME, PARIS.

In the early thirteenth century the lords and ladies of the Ile-de-France were coming to appreciate the elaborate rules of courtly love-making and to find in them a fillip to their pleasures. For them was written the first Roman de la Rose. *However, the world of the courts still was organized in terms of lineage and feudal rights. This is why the knights and their kinsmen the canons never pictured the Virgin in the likeness of one of the damsels of the "garden of love," but as a mother and a great lady. There were of course frequent exchanges in this period between Marian poetry and courtly poetry, each contributing something to the other. But the progress of the cult of Our Lady and the simultaneous rise in prestige of the woman of high birth were separate phenomena; they did not follow the same rhythm, varied from province to province, stemmed from different levels of consciousness and answered to different urges. The image of Mary stood for a mysterious union of the values of virginity, fecundity and royalty that had no place in courtly love, anyhow in its early phase. On the Virgin all the primitive beliefs that had lingered on among the peasantry converged: beliefs that wavered between an atavistic dread of the Mother Goddesses of paganism and an equally superstitious veneration of the sacrosanct objects made by goldsmiths in which, in many monasteries, the relics of patron saints were enshrined. Until, about 1250, a Parisian master for the first time represented the Mother standing, with the Child in her arms, in a graceful attitude, with a slight sway of the hips—that of the figurations of the Church (with which Catholic theology was more and more identifying Mary)—the Gothic Virgin had always been shown in majesty, seated on a throne. This slightly mannered attitude was the one adopted by the wife of the lord at court ceremonies: the woman who had borne in her womb the hope of the line and the future of the House.*

But when the age of the great cathedrals was drawing to a close, a change took place, men's eyes were opening to the beauty of a perfect body, and sculptors began celebrating in large free-standing statues this new-won joy in life. It found elegant expression in the smiling angels of Reims, in a host of wooden angels, their brothers, and in the gracious body of the youthful Adam. It is now that statues of princesses make their first appearance: Yolande of Castile at Burgos, Uta at Naumburg. A habit had long prevailed among the populace of likening that very noble lady, their lord's wife, to the Queen of Sheba. And in Notre-Dame of Paris when the Virgin with the Child rises from her throne she becomes truly Queen of France. Sublimated like the august figures on the tombs, she embodies a perfection existent from all eternity in the mind of God. What she shows the world is still the ideal type-form of sovereignty, but with the added charm of a very lovely woman.

ANGEL. LAST THIRD OF THE 13TH CENTURY. WOOD CARVING FROM CHAMPAGNE. LOUVRE, PARIS.

ADAM. SCULPTURE FROM NOTRE-DAME, PARIS. LATE 13TH CENTURY. STONE. MUSÉE DE CLUNY, PARIS.

EKKEHARD AND UTA, 1255-1265. STATUES IN THE WEST CHOIR OF NAUMBURG CATHEDRAL.

HERMANN AND REGELINDIS, 1255-1265. STATUES IN THE WEST CHOIR OF NAUMBURG CATHEDRAL.

The choir of Bamberg Cathedral was dedicated to St George. This hero of the East, slayer of the dragon—i.e. error, misbelief and evil—who delivered from captivity the princess of Trebizond—i.e. the human soul—had also fought the good fight on behalf of his earthly lord and, more important, of Jesus the Saviour, freer of man, vanquisher of Satan and of death. In St George were incarnated the virtues of the miles Christi, *those of the crusaders who before and with St Louis had "put their bodies to peril" by the holy journey to Jerusalem. They were also the virtues of all the nobles whom the "sacrament" of knighthood had invested with the highest rank among the laity, imposing on them the duty of befriending the poor, safeguarding their bodily and spiritual welfare. These were virtues not of piety but of noble deeds, those of the man of noble note, the* prud'homme *("the name of* prud'homme," *St Louis told Joinville, "is so great and worthy that merely to speak it fills the mouth"); he was the paragon in whom wisdom, courage and loyalty joined forces with the love of God.*

In the first half of the thirteenth century, thanks to the progress of the western world, the feudal social order touched its zenith. It was led by two groups, the churchmen and the fighting men, both owing allegiance to the monarch in whose person the roles of priest and war lord coalesced; he was the guide, the pillar of light leading the chosen people to the Promised Land. Under the auspices of highly cultured prelates, the stately figure of the mounted knight, the "chevalier," was given a place in the iconography of the cathedrals. He is in the flower of his age, the age when a man takes over the management of his domain, the legacy of his ancestors and the destinies of his race, the age all men and women will have on the day of resurrection. Every inch a man, he is the standard-bearer of an essentially masculine society. Like the "Knight of May," symbol of the triumph of Spring, he gallops forth to conquer. He is like St Louis; also like Christ who created him in His image. In his eyes, lit with a gleam of other-worldly light, shines a will to grip the wide world in his embrace; but there is also something of uneasiness. For he is faring forth into the unknown, like the pilgrims, the crusaders, the protagonists of the scholastic tourneys, and the quest to which this man is dedicated will, ultimately, lead him to the discovery of—himself.

"THE KNIGHT OF BAMBERG," ABOUT 1235. BAMBERG CATHEDRAL.

INDEX OF NAMES

LIST OF ILLUSTRATIONS

PHOTOGRAPHS BY

Alinari, Florence (pages 133 lower left, 193-194 top, 195-196 bottom), Alinari-Giraudon (page 153 top), Anderson, Rome (page 93 bottom), Maurice Babey, Basel (pages 22, 23 top and bottom, 24-25, 27, 28, 31, 33, 34, 42, 43, 44, 45, 46, 47, 48, 53-54, 64, 65, 67, 74, 78, 80, 91, 93 top, 94 bottom, 108, 114-115, 116, 117 top and bottom, 118, 121-122, 123-124, 133-134 top, 134 bottom, 135 lower left, 136 right, 144, 145, 146, 147, 148, 149, 153, 154 right, 154 top and bottom, 155-156 top and bottom, 163, 164, 165, 167, 168-169, 179, 180, 183, 184, 204, 205, 206, 209, 210, 211, 213), Emil Bauer, Bamberg (page 81), Bibliothèque Nationale, Paris (page 76 top), British Museum, London (page 29), Fotofast, Bologna (page 195 left), Gabinetto Fotografico Nazionale, Rome (page 193 left), Giraudon, Paris (pages 32 and 123 top), Graphic-Photo, Paris (page 208), Hans Hinz, Basel (page 85), A. F. Kersting, London (pages 51 bottom, 51-52 bottom, 52, 77 top), Raymond Laniepce, Paris (page 75), Louis Loose, Brussels (page 12), Massitelli, Capua (page 196 upper right), Umberto Orlandini, Modena (page 117), L. Pers and M. Mackowiak by courtesy of the Polish Academy of Sciences, Institute of Art, Warsaw (page 109), W. G. Rawlings, Cambridge (pages 76 bottom, 77 bottom), Jochen Remmer, Munich (page 113), Umberto Rossi, Venice (pages 87, 133 lower right), Jean Roubier, Paris (page 51 top), Oscar Savio, Rome (pages 66, 86, 110, 111), Scala, Florence (page 84), Vatican Library (page 194 right), Yan, Toulouse (pages 92 top and bottom, 94 top, 124 top and bottom), Zacharias, Regensburg (page 82).

The bas-reliefs on the Portal of the Months of Ferrara Cathedral (pages 135-136 top) are reproduced by courtesy of Monsignor Vittorio Felisati; the photograph of the portals of Reims Cathedral (page 123 bottom), from the book "La Cathédrale de Reims," appears by courtesy of M. Hans Reinhardt and Presses Universitaires de France.

FOUNDATIONS
OF
A NEW HUMANISM

1280-1440

CONTENTS

I
VIA MODERNA

II
IMITATION OF CHRIST

III
POSSESSION OF THIS WORLD

I

VIA MODERNA

NEW MEN

During the fourteenth century the world of Latin Christianity showed a marked tendency to withdraw into its shell. It is true that the crusading fervor which had previously been the occasion for conquest had lost none of its compulsiveness and was still a guiding light both of ecclesiastical policy and of knightly conduct. But henceforward it was no more than a vision of what might have been. Between the years 1291, when Acre, the last Frankish possession in the Holy Land, was stormed, and 1396, when the Turkish army invading the Balkans routed the Crusaders at Nicopolis, there took place a gradual but unmistakable retreat from the eastern Mediterranean. After 1400 Byzantium was, in effect, a besieged and frightened outpost, doomed to succumb to the irresistible might of Asia and the Infidel.

This ebbing of the Western tide was due to the fact that the population of Europe, which for at least three hundred years had been steadily increasing, began to decline at the end of the thirteenth century. Before long the decline assumed disastrous proportions as a result of the Black Death in 1348-1350 and the numerous epidemics that followed it. By the beginning of the fifteenth century the population of many European countries was half what it had been a hundred years earlier. Countless fields lay fallow, thousands of villages were abandoned, and in most cities, as they shrank within their walls, whole districts fell into ruin. To this was added the tumult of war; for the aggressiveness which formerly had found vent in foreign conquest was now turned inwards. It led to constant clashes among States, great and small, by whose warring factions the unity of Christendom was shattered. Everywhere, in the open country and under the walls of besieged cities, the noise of battle could be heard. Armed bands of mercenaries and free companions looted and laid waste; brigands and freebooters made war their livelihood. The half-century on either side of the year 1300 witnessed one of the great reversals that have deflected, in physical terms, the course of

European civilization. The latter has followed two great rising curves, separated by a prolonged depression. The fourteenth century ushered in the era of stagnation and retreat that was to continue until about 1750.

This is no reason for echoing those historians who, unduly impressed by such evidence of recession, depopulation and strife, take an equally gloomy view of the history of thought, belief and artistic creativeness in the world of Latin Christianity. For there is no denying that cultural achievement in the fourteenth century, far from withering, was exceptionally prolific and progressive. The very decline and dislocation of physical amenities seem to have benefited cultural development in three ways.

In the first place, they altered the geographical distribution of wealth, thus creating new centers of intellectual and aesthetic activity. The effects of disease, battle and economic chaos were felt most severely in certain parts of Germany, in England and, doubtless more cruelly than anywhere else, in France, which had done especially well out of the earlier phase of expansion. Other regions, however, had emerged almost unscathed. In the Rhineland and Bohemia, in parts of the Iberian peninsula and above all in Lombardy, business was thriving, towns were expanding and a new spirit of curiosity and restlessness was abroad. As the seafarers from Genoa, Cadiz and Lisbon ventured further and further westwards, they began to shift the economic axis of Europe towards the Atlantic, thus making good all that had been lost in the Mediterranean.

Secondly, the misfortunes of the fourteenth century, especially the decline in population, were not invariably debilitating. They tended to concentrate wealth in fewer hands and to raise the general standard of living, thereby providing the means for more enterprising patronage of the arts and a wider diffusion of culture. At a time when successive disasters were scything away whole generations, men of substance seemed to be far thicker on the ground than they had been in the expansive calm of the thirteenth century, when the increase of wealth had not kept pace with that of the human race. As a result, more and more people began to indulge certain tastes and habits which formerly had pertained to the most select of the aristocracy. It became quite common for a man to drink wine or wear linen or read books; to decorate his house or his tomb, to appreciate a picture or a sermon, to commission an artist. Although production was stagnant and trade slumped, the love of luxury, far from weakening, was intensified.

Thirdly and above all, the collapse of the normal order of things eroded and undermined a number of values which had been the mainstay of Western civilization. Men's lives were in disarray, but they felt rejuvenated and, to some extent, emancipated. They were, indeed, exposed to greater suffering than their immediate forebears had known, but it was the stress and struggle of rejuvenation. The more percipient among them were struck, even dazzled by the feeling that they were living in a modern world and walking untrodden ways. They felt themselves to be new men.

Clear evidence of this sense of modernity may be seen in what happened to literary works composed around 1300, such as the second part of the *Roman de la Rose* or the incomparably more sublime *Divina Commedia*. Written in the vernacular for non-clerical readers, for whom they embodied all the learning and intellectual discoveries of the preceding age, these works helped to popularize culture, to broaden it down from schoolmen and clerics to intelligent laymen, especially those of the younger generation, who were eager to read and learn. They met with immense success. Expounded, discussed, read aloud in public, they became classics overnight. Their stock of knowledge and the way of life they portrayed became a yardstick for subsequent generations. They gave birth to literary criticism, which implied both aesthetic awareness and a feeling for the past, the sense of what had been and what was. At this time, in fact, every aspect of thought and sensibility underwent a process of renewal. It made itself felt in religion, for what came to be known, around 1380, as *devotio moderna* was the "modern" manner of approaching God. The constant, fundamental theme

of the new freedom consisted in opposition to the priestly hierarchy. In the fourteenth century European culture became popular and, *ipso facto*, secular. At this climacteric in the physical and spiritual history of Europe art kept up with the times by forsaking its emphasis on holy subjects. Henceforth its object was to provide men, in ever larger number, with the prospect or the recollection of pleasure.

*

Ars nova was the term used in the fourteenth century to designate certain types of music. Their main characteristics were profuse ornamentation, lack of didacticism, sheer aesthetic enjoyment and the attempt, accidental or contrived, to imbue sacred music with worldly delight. What happened was that instrumental flourishes were encroaching more and more on plainsong. Their burgeoning may be seen in the incidental music of Adam de la Halle or, much earlier, in the songs of the troubadours. Secular modes were invading the arcana of religious art, a process that was now being repeated in every realm of artistic creation.

No longer did architects, sculptors, goldsmiths, painters and those who employed them seek to swell the litany of the Incarnation which, during the thirteenth century, had gone forth from France throughout Europe, assigning to Man, Reason and Nature, those perfect expressions of God's presence, their true place in the harmony of creation. For these artists and their patrons, so determined to be modern, art was no longer, as it had been for the contemporaries of St Louis and as it would later become for the friends of Lorenzo the Magnificent, a means to lay bare the mysteries of the world and "our high-rais'd phantasie present." In their view art should merely depict, narrate, tell a tale. It should try to give a crystal-clear image of some story, or rather of a saga, not merely about God but also about the Knights of the Round Table or the Conquest of Jerusalem.

This was the essential change. The artist was no longer an acolyte, assisting the priest in his liturgical office. He had become the servant of ordinary men, men with eager eyes who wanted him to show them—not, indeed, everyday reality, for art became more than ever a means of escaping reality— but the world of their dreams. Hence the aim of fourteenth-century art was no longer to create a setting for prayer, ritual or Gregorian chant, but to capture dreams and make them visible. It was then that painting, since it could best give substance to a vision, won the primacy of the arts in Europe.

The motive power behind this profound transformation must be sought in the joint operation of three factors: social change, which affected the meaning and environment of artistry; change in beliefs and ideas, which affected the content and purpose of works of art; and change in the means of expression. Painters, like writers and philosophers, use a vocabulary inherited from the past and so deeply embedded in tradition that they can only break away from it slowly, painfully and with limited success. Something must be said, at the outset, about the nature of these three factors.

THE PATRONS

There is much to be said for beginning with the social aspects of art, for the new vitality and freedom of the fourteenth century were very largely the result of innovations in society. From the time when Europe became Christian down to the end of the thirteenth century, the major achievements in art, so vigorous that they endured and have left traces of themselves to the present day, were begotten of a single, very restricted class, whose members all shared the same outlook, education and aesthetic equipment. These men, who formed the exclusive coterie of the higher clergy, had been the true originators and unifiers of great liturgical art. After 1280, however, there was a considerable broadening of the social base of artistic achievement, which thus became more flexible, complex and heterogeneous. This process must be examined in some detail.

There was no marked change at this time in the artist's status. In the fourteenth century those who actually translated taste into works of art were all laymen; but so, for that matter, had been most of their predecessors in the twelfth and thirteenth centuries. They banded together in close-knit, highly specialized guilds, which became a sort of family, giving their members security, and helping them move from one town or place of employment to another, organizing meetings, training apprentices and propagating skills. They also, like all cliques, tended to become stereotyped and to be controlled by elderly men who looked askance at initiative. Such guilds already existed in the thirteenth century among goldsmiths and masons. After 1300 the system was simply extended to other crafts, such as painting. Sometimes it took the form of large, well-organized itinerant teams, artistic conquistadors, as it were, trained, led and inspired by a single chief in the person of a contractor who, like Giotto, sought commissions, made contracts and assigned jobs to his followers. Teams of this sort had, of course, worked long before on the building of cathedrals. It was only in the fourteenth century that the

leading works foremen, at the same time, indeed, as the *condottieri*, began to emerge from anonymity. They were asserting themselves and becoming known by name, which was the first step towards recognition of the creative personality. But even here the architects of the cathedrals had insisted on signing their work. Hence the only perceptible change consisted in extending a historical process which had also been shared by most types of craftsmanship. There was also the gradual rise in the status of painting, which was one of the major innovations in contemporary taste. The fact remains that until the end of the century, that is until the generation that reached creative maturity about 1420, the artist played second fiddle to his client. He was a manual worker of humble origin, generally one of the lesser townsfolk. His own skill was held in much lower esteem than the materials he worked in. Still, in the early years of the fourteenth century one begins to find artists of credit and renown who were eagerly courted and could sometimes pick and choose their clients. Such was Giotto, first of the great painters. Yet neither he nor even Ghiberti, a hundred years later, was wholly free. They were executants who could only deploy their skill in meticulous obedience.

One can, however, detect more definite changes in the relationship between the artist and those who paid him. At this time the art dealer made his first, hesitant appearance, in the sense that works were completed before being offered for sale. Shopkeepers would display them among their wares and leading Italian businessmen would make them known throughout Europe. This trade originated, no doubt, in articles like books, small ivory ornaments, devotional objects like traveling diptychs or gewgaws such as looking-glass covers or pouncet-boxes. There was even a trade in tombstones, for which Paris seems to have been the principal mart and place of manufacture. (But in Paris, too, in 1328 they were selling imported works of art, in the form of painted panels from Italy.) The steady boom in articles of virtu was stimulated by the fact that they were getting smaller and could more easily be transported. This in itself was only the corollary of a more fundamental stimulus: the fact that there was more money in private hands and that a growing number of citizens had the means and the inclination to buy things of beauty. No longer content with communal works of art, they wanted to have their own and to build up, for their enjoyment and credit, small-scale replicas of the treasures which formerly had been the prerogative of shrines and princes.

It was, in fact, this tendency to disseminate and secularize culture that made art a thriving business, and one can hardly exaggerate the part played by dealers in transforming the very conditions of artistic creation. Firstly, they brought a more rapid diffusion of methods and styles, with a resultant variety in contrast and cross-fertilization. But for the imported ivory figurines of Parisian workmanship, the sculptors, painters and goldsmiths of Central Italy would not have been so familiar with Gothic design. Secondly and above all, they set the artist free by transferring the initiative from client to creator. It must, however, be admitted that it was the lowest strata of creativeness that were thus emancipated. Only the seedier collectors went shopping, and what they found was the small change of art. There was little inventiveness in this reach-me-down stuff, where someone had dashed off a reproduction of a masterpiece, repeating it in a common accent. To reach the widest possible public, dealers sought primarily to lower the cost of production by speeding it up and using second-rate materials. When it came to turning out religious pictures, the fourteenth-century method was to strike them off by means of wood-engraving. Moreover, to attract and cater to these numerous purchasers, most of whom had little education, the retailers insisted on simpler, more obvious themes, with fewer demands on the intellect, greater appeal to the emotions and a larger element of story-telling. The part played by commerce in the art of this period was strictly that of making it popular. True creativeness found its stimulus elsewhere, in the activity of the patron.

Nowadays the really great artist, better off than any patron, has become his own patron. He composes and creates in total freedom, for his own enjoyment and as if for his own purposes. In these circumstances it is hard to realize how heavy was the yoke which, in the days of Cimabue, Master Theodoric or Sluter, the purchaser laid upon the artist. All major works were commissioned and every artist was rigidly subject to the will of his client, who might well be termed his master. This bond was of two kinds. Either there was a formal contract for a stipulated work, drawn up before a lawyer. This agreement specified, not merely the price and date of delivery, but the quality of the materials, the way in which the work was to be done and, last but not least, its general subject and layout, the colors to be used, the arrangement, gestures and appearances of the figures portrayed. Or else, in which case the loss of independence was more drastic and certainly more lasting, the artist spent some time as a member of his patron's domestic staff. Being part of his household and beholden to him for bed and board, or at best discharging the duties of a salaried employee, the artist was wholly at his patron's beck and call. This dependent status was, in fact, much sought after, for it freed a man from the restraints of belonging to a guild, a workshop or a team. Besides, it was the best way to make money. It put a man in touch with all that was most brilliant and up-to-date; it gave him access to the main centers of innovation, research and discovery; it set his feet on the ladder of social advancement. It is indeed in the aristocratic mansions of the early fifteenth century that one encounters a dawning respect for the artist's position and his freedom of action. Even so, the painter and sculptor, the carver of images and household goldsmith, even, in the grandest establishments, the overseer who directed the others and co-ordinated the work of embellishment, all bowed to the will of some lord. Can there conceivably have been any hint of give-and-take between him and the artist? Did Giotto argue with Enrico Scrovegni about any of the subjects for the Arena Chapel? Did the Limbourg brothers put before Jean de Berry their own designs for the calendar of the *Très Riches Heures*? The fact is that throughout the fourteenth century the meaning of an artist's work was wholly dictated, as a result either of his domestic status or of the terms of his contract, by the intention, taste or caprice of his patron.

The latter, of course, only imposed on the creative act its setting, theme and in a more limited sense, its mode of expression. The artist retained full control of his idiom, which had a life of its own, untrammeled by the dictates of patronage. This essential fact should be emphasized, for it emancipates the artist's work from its social context and explains why painters, sculptors and architects have always been discoverers and explorers of the universe. Like writers, scientists and philosophers, whom they sometimes anticipate, they have thus helped to give those who appreciate their work a new vision of the world. Needless to say there remained immense scope for individual inventiveness. Among all those captive artists there were many geniuses, and within the limits of their commission they gave free rein to their talents—more so, perhaps, than do modern artists who can choose their own subjects. The element of genius, of course, is impervious to analysis; but the aspects of a work of art that pertain to the history of taste and society were at that time controlled by its purchaser. He, therefore, is the proper object of this inquiry.

*

In the previous age art had flourished within a static, rigidly stratified society. The surplus wealth begotten of peasant labor flowed into the coffers of two restricted castes of nobility; one, warlike, and destructive, squandered its share in riotous living; that of the other, priestly and devout, was literally a sacrament to the greater glory of God. At the apex of these two élites stood the king, whose prowess in battle was combined, by virtue of holy unction, with the apostolic authority of a bishop. It was indeed the munificence of a king, St Louis, that brought the noblest art of the thirteenth century to its zenith. After 1280, however, the system began to break down. It is true that wealthy men were still addicted to habits of largesse and therefore to the patronage of artists, for oblations and rich gifts were doubly esteemed as symbolizing both power and humility. What changed was the character of patrons, and this was due in part to two influences.

The first of these trends consisted in a redistribution of wealth and a consequent dislocation and realignment of the ruling class which had the means to finance major artistic undertakings. There were two forces governing this trend. It resulted mainly from demographic change, especially the waves of high mortality that swept most of Europe in the second half of the century. In some areas epidemics,

beginning with the Black Death of 1348-1350, cut a swathe through the ranks of artists. In England the art of illumination, which up to then had been the country's outstanding and certainly most original achievement, suddenly deteriorated in the middle of the century and then went completely to seed. This was probably because the workshops were devastated by the plague and failed subsequently to repair their losses. Sometimes, therefore, high mortality may have had an immediate impact on the arts by annihilating the men who practised them. Yet it would seem that such a direct consequence was not usually widespread. No breach of continuity can be found in other sectors of English art, where the workers were doubtless more numerous and hardier. Thus the amazing originality of Gloucester Abbey flowered when the demographic disaster was at its worst. The death rate seems to have had a far deeper effect on the buyers of art and it was through them that it reacted on the themes and even the idioms of artists. For instance, there appears about 1350 an abrupt and striking change in the style of Central Italian painting. The stately elegance that lent such breadth and majesty to Giotto or Simone Martini suddenly vanishes and its place is taken by the comparatively vulgar mode of men like Andrea da Firenze or Taddeo Gaddi. There is no denying that work in the studios was disrupted by the sudden death of leading craftsmen and that it also suffered from the simultaneous upheaval in Florentine business, owing to the sensational bankruptcies that were the ruin of some and the making of others. The fact remains that the abrupt supersession of municipal authorities was unquestionably the decisive factor in the enervation of painting, its decline into prettiness, anecdote and gush. The plague of 1348, followed by recurrent epidemics, depleted the ranks of the upper class, who were already imbued with the humanist outlook. They were rapidly filled by jumped-up parvenus whose education was deficient, or at any rate markedly inferior, based as it was on the popular preaching of the Mendicant Orders. Art had to lower itself to their taste, with the result that, after 1350, the aesthetic standards of the Trecento in Tuscany, as indeed throughout Europe, declined in inverse ratio to the rate of social climbing.

Nor was plague the only cause of this scramble up the social ladder. It owed something to the fortunes of war, which at that time was endemic. It was not so much that the well-to-do suffered heavy casualties in battle, for they were adequately protected by the steady improvement in their armor. Besides, their opponents did not usually want to kill them but to take them alive. Fourteenth-century warfare was conducted with an eye to the main chance, in the form of ransom. Every knight who valued his fair name and put rank above the price of rubies secretly hoped, when he was taken prisoner, that his captor would set the ransom as high as possible. For such tangible proof of his consequence he would cheerfully undergo bankruptcy. Thus every battle and tournament involved large capital gains and losses. The victors, having done well out of their captures, often spent part of the windfall on artistic commissions. Lord Beaverly built his castle at Beverston with money wrung from French knights he had worsted in one of the big battles of the Hundred Years War. This particular English noble was already a wealthy man, and the fact that war, like the plague, opened the aristocracy to the low-born, sprung from a meaner, less cultivated class, was due to its becoming the business of professionals—captains, freebooters, *condottieri*, mercenary contractors of warfare. These people were quick to ape the manners and tastes of the nobility, but they made heavy weather of it in a plebeian, invariably ostentatious manner. Throughout the fourteenth century these two forces combined, by their exaltation of new men, to corrupt taste and lower aesthetic standards. Together they encouraged a general proneness to vulgarity.

The second major trend bore not on individuals but on society as a whole. Its effect was to change the circulation of property by upsetting the system of inheritance and causing the wealth necessary for patronage to flow into new channels. In the past all capital had consisted of land, in the shape of the rural manor yielding a fixed income. The most lucrative domains were, of course, those of the great religious houses, the monasteries, cathedral chapters and other ecclesiastical bodies who had promoted the highest achievements in art. After 1280 this scheme of things was disrupted by three factors. In the first place, the manorial system was affected by extensive changes in the farming economy which considerably impoverished the landowning aristocracy, and especially the old religious communities. Secondly, the royal States became much stronger and wealthier thanks to highly efficient fiscal innovations. About this time State taxation became the rule throughout Europe. By this means a large part of the currency in circulation was diverted to the royal coffers, where it provided the prince with luxuries, lined the pockets of his servants and financed the largesse to which he felt beholden not only by his own sense of dignity but also by the public image of Majesty which was now gaining ground. Thus while Christendom was contracting and growing weaker, the rare centers of great wealth constituted by royal courts could afford an increasingly brilliant display. This in itself favored yet a third tendency, whereby a number of big businessmen and financiers helped the sovereign with the levying of taxes and issue of currency. In this way they not only did well for themselves but contributed further to the glitter of the court. In most towns, which were losing their population, banking and commerce were on the wane; but they throve in the capitals and the principal marts where precious metals and luxuries were exchanged. Here the citizens of rank and fashion, enriched by services rendered at varying distance from the steps of the great thrones of Western Europe, acquired a taste for magnificence and largesse. At the same time they were becoming wealthy or cultivated enough to think of placing major commissions with artists.

These economic changes largely account for the fact that the Church's share in artistic activity steadily diminished during the fourteenth century. Ruined and exploited, crushed by royal and papal taxation, disorganized by changes in recruitment and the allocation of livings, nearly all the monastic and capitular communities ceased about this time to be major patrons of art. The only exceptions were a few churchmen and religious bodies, such as the Carthusians, the Celestines and the Mendicant Friars. Oddly enough, these were the most ascetic Orders, purporting to symbolize want and teach scorn for the flesh-pots. They ought seemingly to have condemned all forms of adornment and shown inveterate hostility to artistic creation. Some of them did. The Augustinian Eremitani who supervised Giotto's work on the Arena Chapel in Padua forced him to curtail his scheme of decoration and criticized him for doing many things "rather from pomp and self-seeking vainglory than for the glory and honor of God." Yet in the main the monasteries of the indigent Orders gave a great impetus to thirteenth-century art. There were two reasons for this. Being situated in or near large towns, they received lavish donations from nobles and citizens, for the abnegation and asceticism they exemplified won them the veneration of the inordinately rich, whose conscience was troubled by the life of ease and luxury they led. These communities, moreover, performed for society the important offices of preaching and burial, both of which called for a good deal of pomp and iconography. The fourteenth-century Church also produced individual patrons, such as abbots, canons, bishops, and, above all, cardinals and popes. In employing artists, however, these prelates did not act as ministers of religion or even as leaders of the community, but simply as men who wanted to cut a dash. In fact, they behaved exactly like princes. Apart from the indigent Orders, the Church's contribution to art was now in the hands of its most worldly, unspiritual members, those, in fact, who were already secularized. The bishops who beautified the cathedrals of England and France, though not princes themselves, were at any rate the servants of princes. They owed their wealth to the royal exchequer, just as the cardinals owed theirs to the papal treasury. They also inherited the tastes and ambitions of princes, especially the desire to exalt themselves by adding some signal and personal embellishment to their church. The lavish and fertile patronage of Boniface VIII at Rome or of Clement VI at Avignon, their encouragement of Giotto or Matteo da Viterbo were not intended so much to glorify God as to give spectacular and monumental evidence of their majesty in a State which was quite as much of this world as of the next.

Princes, in fact, took over from the Church the carrying out of major artistic projects, and their courts became the vanguard of creation and research. Of them all the most brilliant and powerful were those of the Pope, the King of France and the Emperor. They were, it is true, anointed rulers who since the dawn of Christian art had always been responsible for inspiring the finest artists. In the first place, however, it was during the fourteenth century that secular values began to prevail over religious in the interpretation of royal, papal and imperial authority, and that those who wielded it began to belittle their priestly function and to emphasize the *imperium*, that very concept of civil power which intellectuals were embracing as

they discovered the learning of ancient Rome. This was yet another facet of secularization. In the second place many of the wealthiest princes had never received holy unction and did not regard themselves in any way as priests. Such were the Duc d'Anjou, the Duc de Bourgogne, and the Duc de Berry who, as a result of the collapse of the French monarchy about 1400, had encouraged the revival of the Paris School; such too were the "tyrants" who had won control of the *signoria* in the great city-states of Northern Italy. In these courts, where men flocked and money flowed, with their travelers' tales and growing knowledge of the world, the social ladder could easily be climbed. They were the only place where the low-born could reach the highest rank, whether by military prowess, economic flair or clerical zeal. In these "households" and great families and courts, prayer was gradually giving way to policy, the spirit to the flesh. The new values were those of majesty and power, deriving in part from the Roman Law of jurists trained in the University law schools, partly from the Latin classics of scholars trained in the arts faculties. Even more conspicuous were the codes of chivalry and courtly behavior, products of the great development in social manners and observances which had begun with feudalism in the Middle Ages.

These scholarly and knightly values were adopted by the handful of prominent businessmen who in a number of towns, especially in Italy, were the only men outside the court and the cloister, capable of exercising a genuinely creative patronage. At that time the middle class in general did very little for the arts, and what it did was mainly on the lowest level of gimcrack production. Its patronage was organized communally through the innumerable brotherhoods to which the townsfolk belonged, their cultural activities being channeled into good works by the mendicant friars. It would be going too far, therefore, to claim that in the fourteenth century there was any middle-class art, or even middle-class taste. Only by rising above his class could the banker or merchant become a patron. This he did either by identifying himself with the court he served, or occasionally, in some of the great Italian cities, by helping to govern a municipal State and thus imparting to it not only the majesty and *imperium* of a prince but also the trappings of knightly decorum. All these men of substance, not to mention all sorts and conditions of townsfolk, were enthralled by what they glimpsed of courtly manners, with their combination of the ecclesiastical and aristocratic ideal. There was no "middle-class outlook," but rather a gradual permeation of a small group, sprung but emancipated from the middle class, by the courtliness of the knight combined with the humanism of the scholar. All this amounted as yet to a very slight broadening down but to a considerable degree of secularization.

One last consequence of social change must be stated. Wherever first-class art was appearing, whether in monastery, court or city-state, the new characteristics of fourteenth-century taste resulted in part from the greater initiative displayed by personal choice. This was true of objects bought in shops, ordered from a domestic artist or executed under contract. It was true even when the patron appeared to be a group, such as a civic guild, the chapter of York Minster, the Franciscans of Assisi or the Municipality of Florence. Always the decision turned on the purpose and taste of one man. When Giotto, in realizing the aesthetic ideals of the fourteenth-century Italian nobility, was at the height of his profession, he found himself confronted by a cardinal, Jacopo Gaetani dei Stefaneschi, and a pawnbroker's son, Enrico Scrovegni. He had to cope with them single-handed, and it seems unlikely, as we have pointed out, that he could bandy words. The artist nearly always had to serve one man, and a man with a far stronger personality than in the past and with far greater freedom to express it. This new-found freedom of self-expression, which pertained far more to the client than to the artist, is yet another facet of modernity.

The individual rather than collective origin of a work of art accounts for several characteristics that now began to emerge. In the first place, it showed much clearer evidence of personal affiliation. Even when it was public, in the sense of being offered to all and sundry, such as a stained-glass window or a statue over a church door, it always bore some outward stamp of having been made for this or that person. The ubiquity of heraldic symbols, the tendency of devotional paintings to include the figure of the donor, who presented them with a view to salvation for himself and his family, the attempt to make these figures true likenesses—all this is evidence of the patron's monopoly of the work he had initiated. The humbler his origins, moreover, the more jealous he was of his good name; and since the commission was a heaven-sent opportunity to show the world he had made good, he usually instructed the artist to be lavish in materials, layout and design. Fourteenth-century art, being dictated by private ambitions, tended to strain after effects and, in order to be more readily appropriated, to assume small proportions. Illuminated books, gold ornaments, jewels, valuable trinkets: such things could be handled, and by their costly materials they epitomized wealth and splendor. They appealed far more than a great statue or the vaulting of a nave to the taste of people who no longer wanted their aesthetic pleasures to be submerged in a community. Most of these objects now bore much more clearly the imprint of a personality. Usually it was that of the donor, who wanted to identify himself and to have certain details of his character brought out by the subject. Sometimes it was that of the artist, for the new patrons, who comprised fewer intellectuals than formerly, left greater initiative to the executant and allowed him more freedom of expression. Superficially, at any rate, the arts became more diversified, although at the bottom the artist's outlook, like that of his client, was still governed, throughout Europe and in every class, by certain cultural archetypes, common to them both.

In 1339 Jeanne d'Evreux, the widow of Charles IV of France, sought to acquire merit by making a benefaction to the royal abbey of Saint-Denis. She wanted her piety to take the form of a votive image of the Virgin Mother, standing in the traditional manner, with the Babe in her arms. The queen asked, however, that a more affectionate gesture by the infant Jesus should emphasize the Franciscan spirit of Love, and that her gift should be made of very costly material. The Parisian goldsmiths therefore made a small-scale model in silver-gilt, and they adorned the base, whose design gave a hint of church architecture, with a series of translucent, enameled scenes from the story of the Redemption. Personal ascription was modestly confined to a plain statement of the donor's name and rank, together with the exact date of her bequest.

About the same time Sir Geoffrey Luttrell of Inharm caused to be illuminated one of those psalters which corresponded in the devotions of the English aristocracy to the book of hours in France. On one page Luttrell appears himself in ceremonial guise. He has had himself portrayed in the rather crude trappings of knightly power, mounted for the tourney in a pose reminiscent of St George. He is attended by two fair ladies as evidence of his courtliness. The heraldic badge on his shield proclaims his prowess and that of his house.

In 1402 the humanist Pietro da Castelletto was commissioned by the heirs of that dashing prince, Gian Galeazzo Visconti, Duke of Milan, to write a funeral panegyric, which was illuminated by Michelino da Besozzo, pictor excellentissimus inter omnes pictores mundi. *The latter portrayed the dead man, surrounded by the abstract arabesques of courtly art, kneeling in his robes of State and bathed in the radiant presence of the Virgin and Child. Jesus himself is placing the diadem of the elect on his brow. The duchess, in a brocaded dress and holding a taper, stands in an attitude of mourning, while around her a group of fair maidens are in attendance upon Mary at the coronation. The gold background imbues the scene with the mystery of those dark, richly furnished closets where princes kept their treasure. Angels are holding aloft the various hatchments whose heraldic language proclaims the dead ruler's temporal power.*

By the end of the century donors were making their identity still more apparent by having effigies of themselves built into niches previously reserved for saints. They wanted to be recognized, for a good likeness immortalized their features and took the place of a mere symbol of ownership. About 1395 Count Pierre de Mortain gave a stained-glass window to the private chapel of the royal house of Navarre, in Evreux Cathedral. He is being presented to the Virgin by St Peter, his tutelary saint, and by St Denis, patron of the Kings of France, from whom he proudly claimed descent. He is fully armed, wearing his sword and the gilt spurs of knighthood. The surcoat of his cuirass is emblazoned with the insignia of his family. In order, however, that his features may be recognized, the artist has made them lifelike by transferring to glass the line drawing that would be used to illustrate a book.

Robert of Anjou made his oblation to the family saint, whose virtue had shed lustre on all the Angevin kings, and who afforded them from heaven his special protection. Here the living prince is glorifying his dead brother, who appears as a mightier prince than he. The bishop's throne has become a king's, and the penitential sackcloth worn by St Louis is almost hidden by a cloak as sumptuous as that of Robert himself. Angels are crowning the saint; the saint is crowning the donor. The path of intercession could not be more simply traced. The painting still displays the ancient hierarchy of worship. While it is true that Simone Martini has placed the two figures, one living and the other belonging to eternity, in the same majestic setting, it is evident that they come from different worlds. Later, however, when the Master of Flémalle was painting, realism had advanced so far that the picture had become a window, giving a glimpse of everyday life. One finds donors sharing the same surroundings and breathing the same atmosphere as figures from the other world. In the Annunciation *of the Mérode Altarpiece the donors are relegated to the courtyard, looking in upon the delightful abode of the Holy Family. For all their humility, there is something rather intrusive and tiresome about these bashful "extras." This, in fact, was the moment when the features of living men, which had entered into fourteenth-century religious art, began to withdraw from it and to emerge triumphant in the new-born art of portraiture.*

VIRGIN AND CHILD, 1339. SILVER-GILT STATUETTE GIVEN BY JEANNE D'EVREUX TO THE ABBEY OF SAINT-DENIS. LOUVRE, PARIS.

III. 23

VIRGIN AND CHILD WITH BISHOP BERNARD D'ABBEVILLE, ABOUT 1268.
STAINED-GLASS WINDOW, AMIENS CATHEDRAL.

III. 24

PIERRE DE NAVARRE, COMTE DE MORTAIN, KNEELING BEFORE THE VIRGIN, ABOUT 1395.
STAINED-GLASS WINDOW, EVREUX CATHEDRAL.

III. 25

LUTTRELL PSALTER: SIR GEOFFREY LUTTRELL MOUNTED, ARMED, AND ATTENDED BY HIS WIFE AGNES AND HIS DAUGHTER-IN-LAW
BEATRICE. ABOUT 1335-1340. FOLIO 202 VERSO, ADD. MS 42130, BRITISH MUSEUM, LONDON.

MICHELINO DA BESOZZO. THE CROWNING OF GIAN GALEAZZO VISCONTI (DETAIL). MINIATURE FROM THE FUNERAL PANEGYRIC
OF GIAN GALEAZZO VISCONTI BY PIETRO DA CASTELLETTO, 1403. MS LAT. 5888, BIBLIOTHÈQUE NATIONALE, PARIS.

III. 26

SIMONE MARTINI (ABOUT 1285-1344). ROBERT OF ANJOU, KING OF NAPLES, CROWNED BY HIS BROTHER ST LOUIS OF TOULOUSE, 1319-1320.
MUSEO DI CAPODIMONTE, NAPLES.

MASTER OF FLÉMALLE (ACTIVE 1415-1430). THE MÉRODE ALTARPIECE, ABOUT 1420. THE ANNUNCIATION (CENTER) WITH DONORS (LE

ST JOSEPH IN HIS WORKSHOP (RIGHT). THE METROPOLITAN MUSEUM OF ART, NEW YORK. THE CLOISTERS COLLECTION, PURCHASE.

THE WORLD OF THOUGHT

It is difficult and may well be impossible to determine precisely how changes in ideas, beliefs and social attitudes are related to new developments in art. In the case of the fourteenth century one is confronted by a mass of unknown quantities, for there was far less immediate connection between the two phenomena than there had been in the eleventh, twelfth or even thirteenth century, when the sole creators of great art had been learned men. It is evident that Saint-Denis faithfully reflects Suger's concept of the universe. The master-builders working on the abbey received explicit orders from him and it is fairly easy to see what he had in mind. In fact he expounded it himself, and there is no doubt that he planned and adorned the basilica just as he would have done a sermon and as, indeed, he planned and adorned his *Histoire de Louis VI le Gros*, using the same symbols, composing the same rhetorical and arithmetical harmonies, reasoning in a similar manner from analogy. On the other hand, while such pages from the *Très Riches Heures* as the *Garden of Paradise* undoubtedly reflect Jean de Berry's concept of the world, it is much harder to see how this happened. For one thing, the psychology of a French Prince of the Blood in 1400 is far more baffling than that of a twelfth-century Benedictine abbot. For another, his thought has undergone many subtle refinements.

It is true that much fourteenth-century art was intended to convey doctrine in a visual and intelligible form. This was true of all didactic pictures, especially the many paintings for which the Dominicans were responsible. The purpose of Andrea da Firenze's *Triumph of St Thomas Aquinas* in the Spanish Chapel at Santa Maria Novella in Florence, or Traini's painting of the same subject in Santa Caterina at Pisa, is not to depict Thomist philosophy and thereby restore it to public favor; it is rather to give people of average education a simplified version, all the more effective for being so easy to spell out, by reassuringly linking the philosophy, not only to

divine wisdom, but also to such familiar "fathers" as Aristotle and Plato, St Augustine and Averroes. It was, however, exceptional for works to be so rigidly planned. The new forms of patronage were no longer so prone to doctrinaire influence. In most cases they reveal no more than a certain correspondence between the artist's product and a more or less sophisticated philosophy, according to the donor's rank. The subject, moreover, is less concerned with thought, belief or learning than with expressing some social custom, convention or taboo. As a result of its tendency to become popular and secular, fourteenth-century art no longer tried to "point a moral or adorn a tale." Instead it reflected cultural patterns that were supposed to display and vindicate the status of a much larger and more variegated public who, as self-appointed leaders of society, commissioned works from architects, sculptors and painters.

All, whether prince, prelate or banker, adopted the same cultural patterns, based on two contrasting ideals, two exemplars of wisdom and conduct: the knight and the priest. Since the dawn of chivalry at the end of the eleventh century these two figures had stood at the poles of human endeavor. Much fourteenth-century literature, such as the *Songe du Verger,* still took the form of a dialogue or disputation between the paladin of the Clergy and the paladin of Chivalry, upholding contradictory ideals and principles. One of the new features of this period was, however, the mingling of these two cultures. This resulted from various tendencies, beginning with social change. In the fourteenth century a growing number of men belonged to both worlds. The secular activities of priests led them to adopt worldly habits which formerly had been confined to warriors. Conversely, there arose a class of *milites literati* or "lettered" knights who could master book-learning and were avid of scholarship. This fusion was yet another product of the royal courts, where knights and clerics, being entrusted with the same missions, were expected to possess similar skills. The union of the two cultures found expression in a new, courtly literature, designed both to entertain the monarch and, in a wider and deeper sense, "to benefit his subjects," a form of publicity which was now becoming an important attribute of the royal prerogative. These books, being designed for a literate but not exclusively clerical readership, were no longer written in Latin. They combined scholastic learning with use of the vernacular.

The invasion of the Court by Scholasticism is most clearly evidenced by the profusion of translations. In Paris at the end of the thirteenth century one finds a first attempt being made, in the entourage of the King of France, to bring the Latin writings of the Schoolmen within reach of men who were knights by training and vocation. About this time Jean de Brienne adapted the military treatise by Vegetius and called it, significantly, *The Art of Chivalry*. Philippe le Bel had the *Consolation* of Boethius translated. His wife did the same for a discourse on love written two generations earlier, and so did his daughter-in-law for Ovid's *Metamorphoses*. Here one can detect a threefold tendency: in the case of the king, still conscious of his priestly role, a work on religious ethics; in that of the nobleman, "a verray parfit gentil knight," a technical treatise on the pursuit of arms; in that of the ladies, the rules of courtly love and their best classical authorities. After the middle of the fourteenth century the same movement developed still further under the aegis of Jean le Bon, of Charles V and his brothers. The cultural trappings of the knights and ladies at the French court were enriched by selections from such great scholars as Livy and Petrarch, St Augustine, Boccaccio and Aristotle, who had described the "properties of things" and disclosed the secrets of nature. All this may have been meagre, superficial and fragmentary, consisting of such snippets of elementary knowledge as best suited the minds and outlook of fashionable people. It was nonetheless a notable advance, and it was accompanied by another gradual ascent in the same direction.

At the end of the fourteenth century the Valois court and its attendant aristocracy began to be frequented by a group of humanists who were graduates of the universities and thereby connected with the Church. They gathered round a number of influential men who were employed by great nobles as amanuenses. This post, which had been created fifty years earlier in the papal court at Avignon, was something quite new in Paris. It spread throughout the capitals of Europe and the city republics of Italy. Since the secretary's main task was to draft his master's writings, he had to be an accomplished Latinist, well versed in the classics. The purely temporal character of his duties led him to examine secular Latin texts from a critical, aesthetic standpoint. To him they were no longer liturgical exercises or means of interpreting the Word of God; they had become political precepts, evidence of a past whose historical meaning was just beginning to be grasped and, above all, sources of earthly bliss and models of earthly virtue.

This change of outlook at so exalted a level, with all that it implied in terms of education and mental discipline, opened the way to a general deconsecration of ecclesiastical culture. This happened just at the time when a number of works, hitherto reserved for clerical instruction, were gaining currency in fashionable society. By adopting a popular and secular tone, the charmed circle of the court, which was both the apex of society and the cynosure of citizens and churchmen alike, helped to assimilate the knightly to the clerical outlook in everyday life. Meanwhile a similar coalescence was taking place at a deeper level, owing to structural changes in the two cultural patterns.

*

As regards knightly culture, it was a case of emphasis rather than change, for by becoming more coherent, more refined it gained in persuasiveness and influence, so that its essential creed of joy and optimism came to be widely adopted. The code of chivalry, with its ideal of the perfect knight as pictured in medieval poetry, reached its apogee in the fourteenth century, although its various tenets had long been in the making. The earliest of them, the most ingrained and tenacious, had already taken root among the French nobility when feudalism was emerging early in the eleventh century. This original foundation consisted of purely masculine and soldierly qualities: physical strength, valor, loyalty to one's chosen leader, together with derring-do, that hall-mark of courage and technical mastery which stamped the "parfit knight." In the fourteenth century the essence of chivalry was still delight in battle and conquest, in displaying ascendancy and riding one's high horse. A further set of values had been adopted, beginning among the French aristocracy, as a result of women's emergence from their lowly state. This occurred about 1100 in southwestern France. The warrior caste was obliged to give woman her due, especially the baron's wife and the Lady of the manor. This gave rise to a new set of conventions, rules of courtesy which every knight who valued his honor and good name was bound to observe. Relations between the sexes began to be governed by the European concept of Love. This code of love and war may well be summed up in the title of a book of madrigals by Monteverdi, *Canti guerrieri e amorosi*. They show, incidentally, that it was still flourishing in the age of Baroque. It found expression partly in poems extolling heroism and love; partly in the strategy whereby a man was expected not merely to vanquish his opponent but also to win and retain the love of his rival's Lady. In both cases this strategy originated and developed as a sport, albeit one which was directed by rigid respect for a code of honor.

By the end of the twelfth century the code had been perfected, and the literature of subsequent generations disseminated its precepts throughout Europe, among men who wished to achieve distinction. Even before 1200 a number of major works had appeared, embodying such paladins of knightly legend as Perceval and King Arthur; but the height of their success and influence on society dates from the fourteenth century. It was at this stage in European civilization that the ruling class became intoxicated by knightly epics, which portray it at its most flamboyant by means of an increasingly stylized ritual, totally divorced from normal behavior. The fourteenth century was really an age of bloody warfare, arson, butchery and rape, when battlements bristled with spears amid a desolate, ravaged landscape, so brilliantly depicted by Simone Martini in the background to his equestrian portrait of a *condottiere*. The latter, however, fancied himself as a knight and pranced on the battlefield in all his finery. Yet at Crécy, Poitiers and Agincourt the nobles most wedded to chivalry made it a point of honor to fight in a courtly manner. Blind princes had themselves tied to the saddle and guided to the thickest of the fray, there to die gloriously like the heroes of Lancelot. At court even the most bloodstained mercenaries paid their suit to fair princesses. Just as

the old nobility were being ruined by economic change and their place usurped by self-made men who had done well out of war, business or service in some royal household, so the old prerogatives were being replaced by hollow, artificial replicas, which nonetheless kept the system in being. Such were the orders of chivalry founded in the fourteenth century by the kings of Castile, France and England, by the Emperor and the Dauphin of Vienne, as well as by many lesser princes, with a view to recreating King Arthur's Round Table. The new men could only become socially acceptable by showing how good they were at making love and war and how meticulously they observed the rules of the game. The real liturgy of the age, and the only one that still commanded respect, consisted in Courtesy and Prowess. They were displayed at galas and festivities, of which warfare was as much a part as any ball or tourney. That is why fourteenth-century art was no longer inspired by holy rubric but began to reflect these secular rites, giving them greater reality and enhancing their success. The sumptuous portrayal of knightly culture is, perhaps, the most striking innovation in art at this time.

From the outset chivalry had implied certain values that linked it to priestly culture. It had also, like all other social relationships, been subject in feudal times to evangelical pressure by the Church. A number of soldierly qualities, such as energy and prudence, had much in common with theological virtues. But churchmen went a good deal farther than this. Eleventh-century Christianity was so eager to trim its sails to the prevailing winds of society that it sanctified aggression. The Crusade was the Christian apologia for military prowess. Nonetheless, while the Church countenanced warfare, feats of arms and massacres, it continued to frown upon the pursuit of earthly joy, for which chivalry and courtliness were so largely responsible. The knight despised gold and commercial utility as heartily as any monk; but he did so in order to revel in waste, luxury and riotous living. Courtly love, of course, being rooted in adultery and lust, seemed no more compatible than military aggressiveness with Holy Writ. In this case, after some attempts to channel it in the direction of mariolatry, the Church refused its benediction. The literature of chivalry in the thirteenth century proclaimed the conflict between the exponents of ascetic and penitential Christianity, whom it denounced as canting sabbatarians, and the true knights, who sought to reconcile an easy-going belief in redemption with their love of life in this world. This contrast is made ironically in *Aucassin and Nicolette*, brutally in the songs of Rutebeuf, and with guileless freedom by Joinville.

At the same time, however, the knightly spirit of cheerfulness had worked its way into priestly culture. In one sector of Christianity it had sown the seed of revolutionary change. Before his conversion Francis of Assisi, the son of a prosperous citizen, had been steeped in the courtly ideal. Like other young men of his class, he had dreamed of knightly adventures and had written gay ditties. At the beginning of the thirteenth century, when, like a lovesick swain, he chose poverty for his Lady, he did so in the hope of attaining perfect bliss in accordance with the courtly code. Franciscan Christianity, more in keeping with the Gospel than any other, is fundamentally and deliberately optimistic. Triumphant and lyrical, it seeks the harmony of creation and proclaims the goodness and beauty of God in the love of all living things. The Franciscans accept all the most exacting demands of Christianity; yet they do not reject the world but go out to meet and conquer it. In this way they have adopted all that is most buoyant in the code of chivalry. The message of St Francis was too novel, too revolutionary to win complete acceptance from the Catholic authorities, and much of it was frittered away in the course of the thirteenth century. What remained, however, pervaded the world of religion, influencing the Church far beyond the Mendicant Orders and even winning over the rival host of Preaching Friars. In the fourteenth century, when theologians came to believe that every creature contained a spark of divinity and was worthy of love and consideration, they were following where the Poverello had led. So, too, was the Dominican, Heinrich Suso, when he extolled God in a paean of thanksgiving reminiscent of the *Laudes creaturarum*: "Most worshipful Lord, I am not worthy to adore Thee, yet my soul yearns for the heavens to sing Thy praises when they are lit in all their enchanting loveliness by the lamp of the sun and by the shining multitude of stars. Let the meadows extol Thee when high summer burnishes them in natural splendor, when they are enameled with bright flowers and attired in their own exquisite grace." Thanks to the teaching of St Francis, such feelings were brought into harmony with the code of chivalry and courtliness, which ceased to be merely the criterion of civilized behavior in Europe and set its seal on the new outlook of the Church.

*

The secular spirit entered the academic world of professional theology by a different channel. In the principal towns of Europe merchants had founded small grammar schools where their sons could be taught enough of the three R's to carry on the family business. Apart from these, teaching and learning were still clerical functions and the universities were in the hands of the Church, who claimed both students and masters for her own. Not all of them, however, intended to become priests, and some faculties, constituting the least clerical part of the university, trained men for lay professions. For at least two hundred years some of them—it was a speciality of the Bologna Law School—had offered facilities for reading and expounding Roman law. Here Scholastic logic could be applied to strictly temporal problems, those of government especially. These faculties forged the weapons of a political science unencumbered by theocracy, which asserted the secular supremacy of the Emperor and was inclined to contest the Church's claim to temporal sovereignty over the world. Since 1200 they had gradually been discovering ancient Rome, its laws, its symbols and some of its virtues. Owing to the increasing power of the state and its need for a larger and better trained staff of servants, the study of law became steadily more important, and with it that part of university life which was most attracted by secular modes of thought.

The biggest changes, however, occurred in those seats of Christian learning and nurseries of preachers and prelates, the Divinity Schools of Paris and Oxford. The vital stroke that was to free learning from its bonds was delivered in 1277, when an ecclesiastical ukase, first in Paris and then at Oxford, forbade the teaching of Averroes, the expositor of Aristotle, thereby condemning certain postulates of St Thomas Aquinas. This cast a slur on the efforts made during the past fifty years by the Dominicans of Paris to bring Aristotelian philosophy into line with Christianity, thus achieving the concordance of faith and reason which had been the goal of Latin Christianity since the end of the eleventh century. The Dominicans retorted at the General Chapters of 1309 and 1313, forbidding any departure by their members from Thomist doctrine. In 1323 they secured the canonization of St Thomas, and they sought by every means, especially painting, to vindicate him in the eyes of all men. They were successful in Italy, where throughout the fourteenth century the universities remained faithful to the teaching of Aristotle and the traditional methods of Scholasticism. In Paris and Oxford, however, their position was sufficiently undermined for the initiative in theological inquiry to pass, about 1300, to their rivals, the Franciscans. A revolution in Christian thought was accomplished by two Friars Minor, English scholars trained at Oxford, where for some time the emphasis in teaching had lain on mathematics and the observation of phenomena. Hitherto the aim had been to elucidate revealed truths by the rational methods of Aristotelian logic. Duns Scotus pointed out that only a very small part of dogma could be established by reason; the remainder must be taken on trust and no attempt should be made to prove it. After him, William of Occam really initiated the "modern approach." He stood in direct opposition to Aristotle, for he held that concepts were symbols and had no intrinsic reality, that cognition could only be personal and intuitive, and that the attempt to reach God or understand the world by means of abstract reasoning was futile. Man could only do so by two distinct paths: either by an act of faith, entailing acceptance of such undemonstrable truths as the existence of God or the immortality of the soul; or by logical deduction applied solely to what could be directly observed in the physical world.

Occamist doctrine went hand in hand with the tendency of civilization to become secular and thus inspired the whole of western thought in the latter part of the fourteenth century. It indicates two ways of evading the restraints of the Church. In the first place, by insisting on the non-rational character of dogma, it made possible an approach to God through love instead of reason. This released the powerful spring of mysticism which had welled up in Latin Christianity since the days of St Augustine, but which the triumph of Scholasticism had checked, forcing it back into the cloisters of Franciscan monasteries and small communities of ascetic penitents. It was thanks to this strain of mysticism that fourteenth-century Christianity made such a

wide and powerful appeal to the weak and ignorant, to humble folk and women. By substituting the individual for the community religion emancipated itself from the clergy. The supreme act of devotion now consisted in a loving quest for God, in the hope of union and fusion, of "marriage" between the quintessence of the human soul, the "ground" of Meister Eckhart, and the divine substance. In this private dialogue the priest had lost something of his liturgical function, for the believer could not authorize others to pray for him. He must himself attain gradually to the state of inward enlightenment, by means of spiritual exercises, immediate contact with Holy Writ and the daily imitation of Christ. It no longer behoved the priest to teach or expound; he was no more than a mediator, who should bestow sacramental grace and bear witness to Christ. On the other hand, more was expected of him and there was more awareness of anything in his attitude to "the pomp and vanity of this wicked world" that might seem inconsonant with his office. Occamism gave a foothold to those who attacked the Church for daring to poach on secular preserves; to those who sought to bridle its ambition and denounce clerics who were profligate or unchaste; and also to those who wanted the hierarchy to be amenable in disciplinary matters to the civil power and restricted by it to a purely spiritual role.

In the second place, when William of Occam encouraged men to unveil the mysteries of the physical world by reasoning from their experience, he was proclaiming the total freedom of scientific inquiry. Occamism consists above all in the rigid segregation of sacred and profane. The former is the province of the heart and should be under the spiritual direction of a purified Church. The latter belongs to the intellect and must be exempt from priestly interference. This doctrine not only secularizes knowledge but frees it from all metaphysics, especially from "Aristotle and his philosophye." It was not long before a Parisian scholar, Nicolas d'Autrecourt, could assert: "There is a degree of certainty that men can attain if they apply their minds, not to the Philosopher or the Commentator, but to the study of things." The new approach was immensely stimulating when it led to all strange phenomena being observed directly, critically and without reference to any preconceived system. It resulted in their being portrayed as they really were, in all their diversity, and in the replacement of the abstract, conceptual symbol by the true image of this or that creature. In this way Occamism gave an impetus towards realistic art. The growing realism of painting and sculpture in the fourteenth century should not be ascribed to the development of a mythical "bourgeois spirit." We have seen that the art of that time did not originate with the bourgeoisie. Realism in fact had its vanguard in the great aristocratic households, where the leading artists and scholars lived on intimate terms; and it kept pace with the most enlightened aspects of academic thought.

The development of philosophy had much in common with the propensity of chivalry no longer to belittle the tangible world and its phenomena, but to consider them excellent and worthy of notice. This characteristic shared by the two cultures required a more optimistic appraisal of creation, of a civilization which in the eyes of some was collapsing into ruin, and of a more variegated, fluctuating society where education and personal religious experience were rapidly gaining ground. The fourteenth century owes much of its modernity to this optimism and heightened awareness of things. It remained to find an idiom capable of expressing them.

1

THE SPIRIT OF CHIVALRY
AND THE CONCEPT OF SPACE

Like the liturgical world of the cathedrals, the world of chivalry was governed by myth and ritual. Prowess, largesse and courtesy were the values it set store by—values exemplified by King Arthur, Charlemagne and Godefroi de Bouillon. These paragons of the knightly virtues were not dream figures; they had once lived among men. Now, however, they no longer belonged to history but rather to legend, and the memory of their deeds set chronology at naught. They stood outside the pale of time. They figured regularly in the symbolic representations which accompanied the ordered rites of court ceremonial, coronation festivities, jousting and courtly love. In these plays they stood not only outside time but moved in an imaginary space, a fictive world without any limits or fixed dimensions. The central theme of the myth was the perilous adventure, the wandering quest, which led the heroes of chivalry—and the living actors who momentarily mimed their actions—into the indeterminate depths of the forest.

Of all the forms of nature, the forest offered the most favorable setting for the incidents of romantic fiction and the vicissitudes of clandestine lovers. Its shadowy glades and pathless depths conjured up an atmosphere of mystery and suspense which effectively blurred the dividing line between reality and fantasy.

The tapestries known in France as *verdures*, patterned with flowers and foliage, brought forest scenery into the halls of fourteenth-century castles and manor-houses. Similar designs, suggestive of the shifting, amorphous space of myth and romance, appeared in the ribs of Gothic vaulting and in the margins of illuminated manuscripts.

By about 1300 the ornamentation of the great cathedrals had been completed. Here the spirit of chivalry prevailed over the logic of the builders. Logic was lost to sight beneath an overlay of ornaments in which the fanciful and irrational were given free play. Thus in the central doorway of Rheims Cathedral the traditional scene of the Coronation of the Virgin stands detached from the façade; drifting away from the stability of the main fabric, it floats up into a dream-space. The natural upward thrust of Gothic churches is here released from measurable dimensions, soaring up in a profusion of flower and foliage ornament clinging to the edge of the gable. At the apex, borne on the wings of angels, the sun itself turns into a flower. These forms shoot up like the tree of the forest, like the flashing of light as it was conceived in the Franciscan cosmology of the Oxford schools. It was this vigorous burgeoning which, in the vaulting of Tewkesbury Abbey, in the octagonal crossing of Ely Cathedral and in the chapter house of Wells Cathedral, disrupted that ordered plenitude of space of which the master-builders of the thirteenth-century had found the principles in Aristotelian physics.

The illogical space of the forest, that ideal setting for knightly adventure and romance, also invaded the pages of English illuminated manuscripts, where it brought about a return to the fantasy of Celtic and Anglo-Saxon miniatures. Take, for example, the illustration to Psalm 109 in the psalter of Robert of Ormesby, a monk of Norwich. The large initial D encloses the symmetrical figures of God the Father and Christ the Son in a space which is still as rigorously ordered as that of a stained-glass window. But already in the foliage border surrounding the text the artist has given free rein to his fancy. The plant motifs, sprouting in all directions, teem with exquisitely rendered specimens of animal life, including the dragons which knights were always slaying in the recesses of the forest, though the stag was their usual game.

In Paris, however, the logic of the preaching friars of the University was still too strong for book illuminators to go as far as this. Produced about 1325 under Dominican influence, the Belleville Breviary illuminated in the workshop of Jean Pucelle has its margins sparingly decorated with leafy stems kept well under control, their pure arabesques standing out against the blank space around them. As for the decoration of initial letters, no great play is made with the abstract form of the letter. The essential thing is the scene it encloses within a pattern of sober lines where air circulates freely; this space is that of Giotto's pictorial staging. The painter who, half a century later, illuminated the *Grandes Chroniques de France* also placed the actors in the coronation ceremony on a kind of stage. But here it is the sinuous grace of the figures themselves that brings to mind forest trees and climbing plants.

Lorenzo Monaco, a Camaldulese monk, was at work in Florence at the very time, in the early fifteenth century, when Masaccio was painting his great frescoes in the Brancacci Chapel with their austere and stoic figures. Masaccio created a new language of art which few of his contemporaries could understand; whereas most of the Florentine patricians responded at once to Lorenzo's Gothic charm and courtly refinements. To the dramatic pathos of the Gospel story he gave an exotic appeal wholly in the spirit of the age of chivalry; his hallucinated Magi go riding through a rocky wilderness towards a land of dreams.

THE SPIRIT OF CHIVALRY
AND THE CONCEPT OF SPACE

1. Reims Cathedral: the Coronation of the Virgin, 1280. Gable of the central doorway of the west façade.

2. Tewkesbury Abbey: rib vaulting in the chancel, 1350.

3. Ely Cathedral: the octagon of the crossing. Late 11th to 15th century.

4. Wells Cathedral: the chapter house. First quarter of the 14th century.

5. Grandes Chroniques de France: the Coronation of Charles VI, about 1380. Folio 3 verso, MS. fr. 2813, Bibliothèque Nationale, Paris.

6. The Belleville Breviary (workshop of Jean Pucelle): Saul seeking to smite David with the Javelin, about 1325. Folio 24 verso, MS. lat. 10483, Bibliothèque Nationale, Paris.

7. Psalter of Robert of Ormesby: illustration to Psalm 109. Norwich, East Anglia, 1310-1325. Folio 147 verso, MS. Douce 366, Bodleian Library, Oxford.

8. Lorenzo Monaco (about 1370-1424). The Journey of the Magi. Drawing. Staatliche Museen, Berlin-Dahlem.

III. 39

1

III. 40

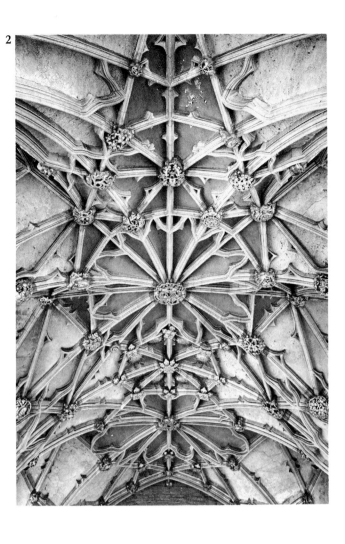

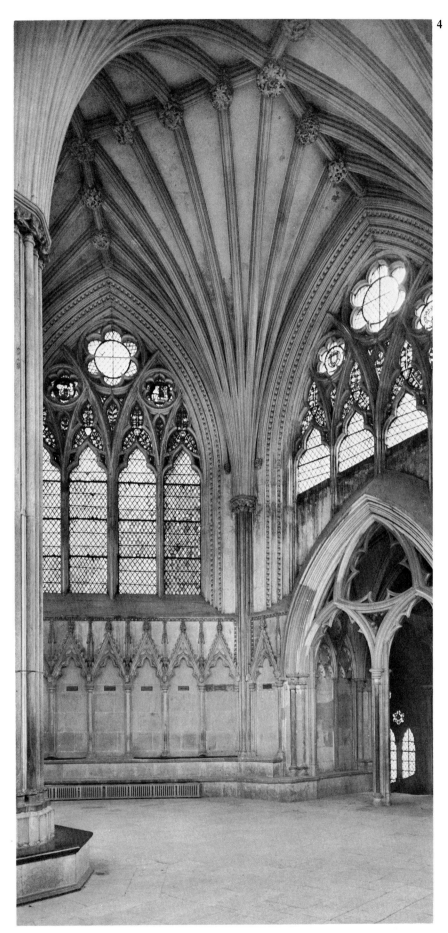

III. 41

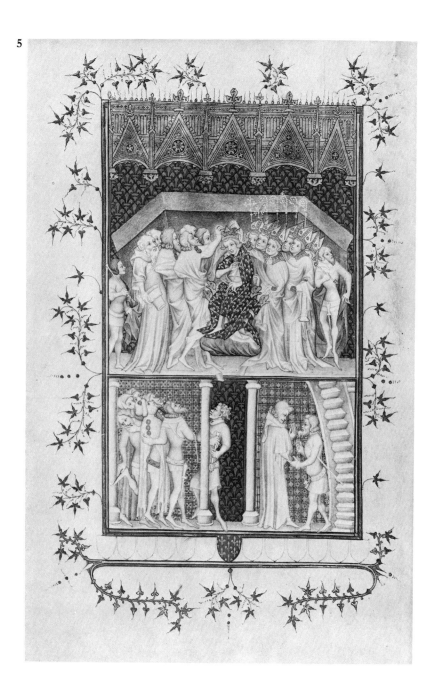

5

6

7

Having emerged triumphant at the end of the thirteenth century, the Popes were determined to lay their yoke on the Franciscans and bring them within the normal hierarchy. They therefore summoned the best artists in Italy to Assisi, so that the new message of the Friars Minor might be painted under the supervision of the Cardinals who were patrons of the Order. It was hoped that, if the main events of the Gospel story were thus brought to life, ordinary men and women would be stirred to the depths of their being. Cimabue, therefore, took the stiff, conventional figures of the Passion and filled them with a dramatic frenzy, whose daemonic power and anguish have only been enhanced for us by the ravages of time.

Then Boniface VIII wanted St Francis to be depicted in the Upper Basilica as the protector of the Roman Church. He summoned Giotto and told him to illustrate a number of passages from the Poverello's official biography. This the painter did by means of a frieze of separate but related scenes, cut off by a frame from their architectural surroundings. Later, in the Arena (or Scrovegni) Chapel at Padua, he used the same method to tell the life-story of Christ, the Virgin and Joachim.

In Giotto one finds none of the boundless horizons beloved of knightly romance. He divided space and time into strict compartments which, though also unreal, had the unreality of the theater. His settings were so designed as to leave room for actors to move freely, group themselves or give full rein to gesture and mime. In this way he created a space between the spectator and the backdrop of a classical proscenium, deep enough for the episode to be fully enacted. A little symbolic scenery provided a muted accompaniment, but what mattered was the action. The artificial setting removed the characters from their ordinary world to the empyrean of sacred drama. There they stood forth, St Francis and his friends, Joachim and the shepherds—and so did Mary and Jesus—depicted in the full reality of flesh and blood.

A hundred years later, a number of leading Florentine citizens came under the influence of humanists like Coluccio Salutati and Niccolò de' Niccoli. They spurned both the fevered effusions of mysticism and the dreamy make-believe of chivalry. With a Roman emphasis on the dignity of man, they aspired after a Christian faith no less deep and ardent, but sterner, untroubled by emotion and imbued with the sedate austerity of the Stoics.

Thus when Masaccio painted the Florentine chapel for whose decoration the silk-merchant, Felix Brancacci, had provided in his will, in 1422, he took his inspiration from Giotto. He created a space uncluttered by superfluous ornament and gave it depth by means of an architectural setting. There he placed the marmoreal figures of the apostles Peter and John, giving alms to the poor with the aloof deliberateness of human benevolence.

Between 1337 and 1339 Ambrogio Lorenzetti had the task of depicting, in the Council Chamber at Siena, the allegory of Good Government with its attendant Virtues, and of portraying the twenty-four City Fathers. He placed his figures, as it were, on the two tiers of a stage, and a very narrow one at that. Since he had a message to impart, he employed symbols and explanatory texts. The clearly demarcated space was itself symbolic of the new proselytizing zeal of the Preaching Friars. Beneath this imaginary scene, however, Ambrogio painted the vast expanse of Sienese contado, *without any artificial boundary—neither the architectural trimmings usually placed round Gothic pictures nor the little* trompe-l'œil *columns of Assisi. Ambrogio's space is as crowded as Aristotle's, for the landscape runs up to an excessively lofty horizon, practically shutting out the sky; yet it is a real landscape, for it was painted for a community of merchants and vine-growers, men who knew the price of a sack of corn or a bale of wool.*

There is no fear of those falconers getting lost in the greenwood. Every tree stands out by itself, as if it were the Idea of a tree. This is not the space of dreams or rites or the theater, or even that of idealized Virtues; it is the space of common sense, public policy and hard work. It was intended for men who built town clocks to divide up the day into hours, men who wanted to see where they were going and how much they were making.

CIMABUE (ACTIVE 1272-1302). THE CRUCIFIXION, ABOUT 1277. FRESCO, UPPER CHURCH OF SAN FRANCESCO, ASSISI.

VOLGETE GLIOCCHI A RIMIRAR COSTEI NO̅ GE̅ BOCCETO CHE QVI DIPI̅TA ZDISPO DELLA CORCORTE VIRATE S̅ PRACI

AMBROGIO LORENZETTI (ACTIVE 1324-1348). THE EFFECTS

GHERARDO STARNINA (ABOUT 1354-1413). ANCHORITES IN THE THEBAID (DETAIL).
UFFIZI, FLORENCE.

III. 48

...OD GOVERNMENT, 1337-1339. FRESCO, PALAZZO PUBBLICO, SIENA.

GIOTTO (ABOUT 1266-1337). ST FRANCIS RENOUNCING THE WORLD AND THE DREAM OF POPE INNOCENT III, 1296-1297.
FRESCO, UPPER CHURCH OF SAN FRANCESCO, ASSISI.

GIOTTO (ABOUT 1266-1337). JOACHIM WITH THE SHEPHERDS, 1305-1306.
FRESCO, ARENA CHAPEL, PADUA.

III. 50

MASACCIO (1401-1429). ST PETER AND ST JOHN DISTRIBUTING ALMS, 1426-1427.
FRESCO IN THE BRANCACCI CHAPEL, SANTA MARIA DEL CARMINE, FLORENCE.

NEW MODES OF EXPRESSION

In order to symbolize what was invisible, divine reason and the conceptual order of the universe, Latin Christianity had recently devised a language so splendid that it constituted a formidable obstacle to change. The works executed in thirteenth-century Paris by St Louis had perfected the art of translating the mystery of the Incarnation into stained glass and stone. Having reached its apogee, Parisian Gothic became crystallized in simple formulae, so satisfying that they discouraged all attempts at innovation and resulted in inertia. During the fifty years after the Sainte-Chapelle was completed, Parisian artists seemed to be imprisoned in a style which they were incapable of adapting to changes in thought and the outlook of civilized society. At a time when Boethius was being translated for Philippe le Bel, when Duns Scotus was teaching at Paris, when William of Occam was working out his system, the master-craftsmen, stone-cutters, glassmakers and illuminators continued to depict the messianic universe of Albertus Magnus, Perrotin, and Robert de Sorbon. Thanks to the influence of the University of Paris, where all professional thinkers were trained, the thriving trade in illuminated books and ivory statuettes carried these designs all over Europe. Yet the idea they gave of the world was already out of date.

At the beginning of the fourteenth century a modernizing current began to flow from two directions. French Gothic itself began to show a gradual but marked proclivity to mannerism. Patrons, becoming more susceptible to luxury and worldliness, began to insist on elegance. Artists tried to meet their wishes by diluting the pure Gothic style with a degree of concettism. They used costlier, more gratifying materials; they added frills to the sober masses of rational architecture; above all, they played tricks with design. By elaborating the arabesques that came from the partitioning of stained glass and from the clean lines of monumental statues, the blithe spirit of courtliness invaded and soon burst asunder the symmetry of liturgical art. Graceful and fine-spun, the arabesque used the swelling curves of statues or, still more freely, the lush foliation in the margin of illuminated books to interpret the rites of fashion which were gradually superseding those of divine worship. As a counterpart to the rhythm of rounds and virelays, to the preening of courtship, to the vicissitudes of the knight-errant's quest, these modulations reflected the dreams and various moods of courtly society, its desire for elegance, its gay pursuit of pleasure and adventure, its incipient frowardness in love. At the same time, to link this poetic fiction with reality, the breaks and flourishes of its design, like the harmonic breaks and intervals of the *ars nova*, must contain some identifiable and meticulously observed elements of reality. French artists, therefore, took example from sculptors who, on the capitals of cathedrals, had faithfully reproduced the foliage of gardens and coppices in the Ile-de-France. They also adapted the more recent experience of monumental masons whose clients asked that sepulchral effigies should be true portraits of the dead. Fully to express courtly fantasy, they had to combine symbol, allegory and an illusion of realism. By about 1320 they succeeded in eliciting from classical Gothic a lively, mannered style which by unexpected twists, like the discourse of a dream, wove fragments of plain truth against a background of myth and outlandishness.

At the same time, echoes of even more revolutionary changes were coming from Central Italy, whose merchants and bankers had got control of all the most lucrative business in Europe. Changes in Western economy had combined with the new system of papal taxation to make this region the financial power-house of the continent. Thanks to this accumulated wealth Paris was confronted by a rival in artistic creativeness and originality of expression. Although Italy had felt the preponderance of Parisian design, backed up by the expanding importation of French products, this subjection was more apparent than real. Her aesthetic tradition rested on two massive foundations. One was the bounty of the East, that glorious mantle of mosaics and icons which Byzantium had bestowed on Italy, layer upon layer, throughout the high noon of the Middle Ages and down to the twelfth century. It was still a living tradition, linked to its source by the trade-routes that ran between this part of Europe and Constantinople, the Black Sea, Cyprus and the Morea. The other foundation, deeper still, was indeed the bedrock of the Italian people: ancient Rome, whose ruins lay all around and many of whose buildings had survived. It might even be traced back to the remote Etruscans. Backed by the wealth of the Holy See and of the cardinals who patronized the order of St Francis and were themselves subsidized by the businessmen of Siena and Florence, the new artistic movement broke away from Paris. It rejected the alien and supposedly colonial influence of Byzantium and, striking down to the tap-roots of the Roman world, it proclaimed allegiance to the Italian motherland by reviving the forms of antiquity. It was indeed a Risorgimento, whose hero was Giotto. At the time when Dante was electing to write the *Divine Comedy* in Tuscan, it was Giotto who, according to the earliest critic of his art, the fourteenth-century Florentine painter, Cennino Cennini, changed "the art of painting from Greek to Latin." He changed it, that is, from a foreign tongue to an indigenous vernacular. Giotto had, in fact, been anticipated by sculptors who, working for Frederick II about the middle of the thirteenth century, had resurrected in Campania the style of imperial Rome. They were followed by the sculptors of Pisa, still rich from "holding the gorgeous East in fee," a city more imperial than Rome itself, where the German kings passed on their way to receive the imperial diadem in Rome. It was here that the Emperors fell foul of the Popes. Nicola Pisano, when decorating the pulpit of the Baptistery in 1260, designed a replica of an ancient sarcophagus. In the apse of the Cathedral, Pisa was placed in effigy as Queen Mother beside the Emperor, kneeling before the Virgin. Later, as the base of the pulpit he carved about 1310, Giovanni Pisano used a statue of the city, supported by four Virtues, facing one of the Emperor supported by the Evangelists. Civic pride united with devotion to the Empire to bring about a revival of Roman statuary.

Thus, early fourteenth-century art adopted two new modes of expression. In France it was all sunny charm, willowy grace and unconstraint, such as one sees in the *Eros* at Auxerre or the *Tempter* at Strasbourg. In Tuscany, Umbria and Rome itself, there was a sterner note of stateliness and secular power. Both made their first appearance in stone-carving; but since art was tending more and more towards narrative and description, they soon found their fullest expression in painting. Both reflected the intrusion of secular values. But the new Gothic style implied no more than a gradual change in conventions: the infiltration of knightly and courtly manners into regal and ecclesiastical ceremony; the permeation of worship by Franciscan gaiety and the steady renewal of respect for God's creatures. The Roman manner, on the other hand, represented a far more drastic departure. There was no gradual change in the triumphant Italy of Imperial Vicars and Princes of the Church; in the Italy of the *podestà* and the *condottiere*, of usurers and guilds and cities "branchy between towers" and hills that were becoming a vast amphitheatre of terraced fields, olive-groves and vineyards. Here the language of art underwent a seismic upheaval. The kings of Europe whose finery was supplied by Italian merchants; the pilgrims who flocked to Rome; the princes of France or Germany who went to Italy in search of fame and fortune: all experienced a far more blatant worldliness. In classical models Italian painters found the formula of a *trompe-l'œil* realism that accentuated the futility of symbols. The sculpture of Rome and her Etruscan ancestors was designed to extol and to lead the dead into a world that was frightening but not unfathomable. It spoke of Man's divinity and justified his conquest of power, wealth and the world. It bade him cease bowing down before priests and stand erect; not as yet to deny God, but to look Him in the face.

*

The idiom of the Pisans and of artists like Cavallini, Arnolfo, Giotto, Tino di Camaino expressed the hopes of the Italian Ghibellines and the straining of the great municipalities towards independence. It also helped Pope Boniface VIII to proclaim the majesty of the Holy See and its mission to dominate the world as the Empire had done. Likewise it enabled the cardinals directing the vast constructions at Assisi to tame and discipline the Franciscan form of worship, transforming the Poverello into a champion of Roman supremacy. Yet this language was too unwonted and uncompromising. It was not wholly intelligible to the new men whom the flourishing Tuscan economy was introducing to the fine arts. It was completely alien to nations beyond the Alps. Moreover, the prestige of Gothic was still too influential; the Roman manner was unsuited to courtly conventions; the secularization of art was accompanied by a tendency for it to become more popular, which meant that it must use more commonplace, less disturbing means of expression. All these factors prevented the fourteenth-century Renaissance from adopting this idiom, so that the new art-forms emerging in Tuscany and Rome about 1300 acted merely as a ferment on French style, helping it to free itself more rapidly from Central Italy, whose vitality was soon undermined by the transfer of the papacy to Avignon, the decay of Pisa, the failures of imperial policy, the convulsions that wrought havoc among the great banking families of Florence and, finally, by the ravages of the plague. Nor did the stimulus affect Paris, where the Gothic tradition was too deeply rooted, but only a number of princely courts, which by their mode of chivalry were more receptive to Italian inspiration and could thus play a part in forwarding the new aesthetic movement.

The French court in Naples was the first to do so. Cavallini and Tino had worked there, and it may have been there that Simone Martini came to enrich his drawing with the new techniques of courtly imagination. Not long after, Pope Clement VI embarked at Avignon on the most ambitious undertaking of the century, in which Italian decorators collaborated with artists from the north of France.

The papal court gave Matteo da Viterbo an even closer acquaintance with the fine points of chivalry than Simone Martini had acquired at Naples. About the middle of the century this painter achieved, with great facility, the first synthesis of the French and Tuscan manner. His work was exhibited in the main resort for all the princes and prelates of the world, who departed laden with *objets d'art* given to them by the Pope and his cardinals. The work of unification was thus begun by Matteo in Avignon, at the very center of Christendom and of the fourteenth century. Soon after there arose a magnificent patron in the Emperor Charles IV, heir to the Caesars but also, like his near relations the Valois Princes of France, wedded to Parisian taste. A lover of precious stones and bright ornament, he brought artists from Lombardy and the Rhineland to his court at Prague, where the Czech painters absorbed their teaching. Then, in the latter part of the century, the work of unification was taken up by the courts of Northern Italian "tyrants." These princes, who had usurped the sovereignty of the city republics, had close links with the court at Paris and were determined to be exemplars of chivalry and courtly elegance. Like the nobles north of the Alps, they were great horsemen, dog-fanciers and womanizers. Here the epics, romances and lyrical motifs imported from France flowered for the last time. But here, too, Giotto had painted, and Roman Italy was not far off. It was the painters employed by the lords of Milan and the patricians of Verona to illustrate their books who perfected the "Lombard style," uniting realism with the refinements of Gothic arabesque.

THE GREEK MODE

The frontier between the Greek and Latin provinces of the Roman Empire bisected the Italian peninsula, and during the earlier part of the Middle Ages the Emperors of Constantinople were bent on getting the whole of Italy into their hands. They proclaimed their might in Ravenna by the magnificence of their monuments, and Venice had long been subject to them. In the eighth century Rome and the South gave refuge to Byzantine monks who, persecuted by the Iconoclasts, brought with them their icons and illuminated manuscripts. Later, when merchants from the coastal towns of Italy ventured overseas they sought their fortunes in the Levant. At Byzantium and the cities of the Black Sea, even at Alexandria, they still encountered the Hellenic spirit. Finally, the Popes and the abbots of the great Italian monasteries constantly sought at Byzantium the craftsmen who could further their efforts to bring about an artistic revival. For all these reasons Italian art at the beginning of the fourteenth century was profoundly influenced by the Greek manner. This was true of all the decorative arts, painting especially.

The medium preferred was either mosaic or the illumination of small gilded panels intended to be placed side by side as in iconostases. Consequently one finds in Tuscan altarpieces that the story unfolds in a series of isolated episodes round the central hieratic figure of the Virgin or a Saint.

The Venetian-Byzantine tradition of craftsmanship was also faithfully observed when, about 1250, it was decided to clothe the vast interior of the baptistery at Florence in a gorgeous mantle of mosaic. This ubiquity of the Greek manner explains the astonishing way in which Duccio's scenes from the life of Christ, painted on the back of the Maestà which was borne triumphantly into the cathedral of Siena on June 9th, 1311, resemble frescoes painted a little earlier in Balkan monasteries, as well as contemporary mosaics in Byzantium.

THE DORMITION OF THE VIRGIN, ABOUT 1320. FRESCO, CHURCH OF GRACANICA (SERBIA).

DUCCIO (ABOUT 1260-1319). ALTARPIECE WITH THE MADONNA IN MAJESTY (MAESTÀ), 1308-1311. MUSEO DELL'OPERA DEL DUOMO, SIENA.

DUCCIO (ABOUT 1260-1319). SCENES FROM THE LIFE OF CHRIST ON THE BACK OF THE MAESTÀ, 1308-1311.
MUSEO DELL'OPERA DEL DUOMO, SIENA.

THE DESCENT OF CHRIST INTO LIMBO, RIGHT SIDE: THE RESURRECTION OF EVE, 1310.
FRESCO IN THE PARECCLESION, CHURCH OF ST SAVIOUR IN THE CHORA (KAHRIEH DJAMI), ISTANBUL.

DUCCIO (ABOUT 1260-1319). THE THREE MARYS AT THE TOMB (DETAIL), 1308-1311.
PANEL ON THE BACK OF THE MAESTÀ. MUSEO DELL'OPERA DEL DUOMO, SIENA.

Ihc salutat matrem suam cum osculo pacis dicens.

Salue mellica mea flostula virgo maria.

salbati aurea rutilacione resplenduit iuxta
quod psalmugraphus longe antea prophetauit
Nox inquiens sicut dies illuminabitur Et
sic facta est hec nox illuminacio mea fideli-
is meis quam subito michi dilectus filius asti-
tit et refulgente inhabitaculo lumine hiis
uerbis me dulciter salutauit. Aue inquit
mater mea aue. Quasi dicat ve iam merors
depone quia sine ve me in utero concepisti et
sine doloris molestia virgo permanens peperisti
plangere desine lacrimas absterge gemitus re-
pelle suspiria reice Iam enim implete sunt scripture quia oportuit me pati et a mortuis resur-
gere Iam prostrato principe mortis infernum
expoliaui potestatem in celo et terra accepi et
ouem perditam ad ouile pro humero repor-
taui quia hominem qui perierat ad regna
celestia reuocaui. Gaude igitur mater aman-
tissima quia facta es celi et terre regina
Et sicut morte interueniente obtinui dominium
inferorum sic ascensionis gloria refulgente
regnum accipiam super nos Ascendam igitur
ad patrem meum ut preparem me diligen-
tibus locum Tu autem surge dilecta mea co-
lumba mea speciosa mea electa michi et pre-
electa incipe iam in presenti gaudium tibi infu-
turo longe gloriosius eternaliter permansurus Isti-
mo in montem syon matre cum discipulis con

PASSIONAL OF ABBESS KUNIGUNDE: THE VIRGIN EMBRACING THE RESURRECTED CHRIST. PRAGUE, ABOUT 1320.
FOLIO 16 VERSO, MS XIV, A. 17, NATIONAL LIBRARY, PRAGUE.

III. 60

2

THE LATIN INTONATION

When in the arts of Central Italy the Latin accent again made itself heard, its return reflected a new trend in political thought and practice. During the twelfth century two powers struggled for the upper hand in Europe: the Roman Empire, which Charlemagne had revived as a challenge to the emperors in Constantinople, and the Roman Papacy, whose primacy the Greek Church had refused to recognize since 1054. Pope and Emperor were both eager to find some legal sanction for their claim to power. The professors of law at Bologna, whose business it was to expound the Code of Justinian, were accordingly invited to supply them with a clear notion, supported by scholastic logic, of what constituted the *imperium*—i.e. the legal right to command and enforce the laws. Here was an issue that at once evoked the glories of ancient Rome. Henceforth the Hohenstaufens, who were kings of Germany, and thereby "kings of the Romans" and candidates for the Empire, vied with the Popes, who were bishops and lords of Rome, for the privilege of assuming the attributes of Caesar. This competition, and the intellectual energies it galvanized, gradually cleared the way for that rediscovery of the Latin classics and the Roman world which we call Humanism.

Thus were revealed not only texts and formulas but a whole aesthetic which had once inspired the monumental setting of the imperial *auctoritas*. The emperor Frederick II, heir of the Hohenstaufens but an Italian by birth, culture and sentiment, was thus led to revive, in Campania in the second third of the thirteenth century, the large-scale political sculpture of ancient Rome. The real starting point of Renaissance sculpture is to be found here, on the confines of the Eastern Empire, of which Southern Italy had hitherto been one of the outlying provinces. It was not until 1260 however, in the Baptistery of Pisa, that Latin forms of expression impinged decisively on the style of religious art. The Western Empire had fallen apart after the death of Frederick II (1250). The Kingdom of Sicily, which Frederick had inherited from his mother, passed a few years later into the hands of a French prince, Charles of Anjou, brother of St Louis, and soon the graceful forms of Gothic art were being imported into Naples. The imperial spirit of enterprise, the sense of fidelity to the Roman past—these took root not in the South but in Central Italy, particularly at Pisa on the Tuscan coast.

Pisa had been enriched by trade with the Levant, and a large part of her wealth went to erect the splendid group of buildings—cathedral, baptistery, campanile and Campo Santo—which proclaimed the glory of the city. Lying on the main road by which the German kings traveled to Rome, Pisa gave them their first taste of a world where something of the grandeur of Roman antiquity lingered on. Pisa moreover was a Ghibelline stronghold, loyal to the Empire, cherishing the memory of Frederick II, eager to emulate the majestic monuments commissioned by Frederick at Capua. Nicola Pisano, a South Italian by birth, was schooled in the techniques of Campanian sculpture; he saw and studied the figure carvings on Late Antique sarcophagi; he made of St Peter a Roman hero, of the Virgin a Roman matron; he created the new style of Renaissance sculpture.

But Pisa, her fleet shattered by the Genoese, was on the decline. The overland trade route between Latium and the plain of the Po shifted from Pisa to Florence, and economic power passed into the hands of the Florentines. They too felt themselves to be ancient Romans at heart. About 1300 Nicola's son Giovanni Pisano, with his pupils Arnolfo di Cambio and Tino di Camaino, produced in the Roman spirit, at Pisa, Florence and Siena, the first pieces of large-scale sculpture which, since the decline of Romanesque statuary, could vie with the Gothic sculpture of the Ile-de-France. They have a rugged strength and majesty which the latter lacks: the Virgins of the Tuscan sculptors seem to be carrying not only the Christ Child but the weight of the world. Unlike the French cathedral sculptors, the Tuscans sought to convey an inner torment, the pathos of the Franciscan preachers. Their sensitive carving re-echoes at times the dramatic accent of Cimabue's great *Crucifixion* at Assisi; it recaptures the surging movement of the hunting scenes and renderings of such themes as the Crossing of the Red Sea carved on the sides of Late Byzantine sarcophagi.

Their success in the struggle against the emperors impelled the popes to adopt an imperial policy of their own. They called on the new school of Tuscan art to give tangible expression to their power and prestige for the benefit of pilgrims to the Holy City. As the Jubilee of 1300 approached, Rome saw an unprecedented concourse of architects and artists. It was now that, following that of sculpture, the language of painting, which had hitherto been Greek (i.e. Byzantine), was translated into Latin. In his mosaics at Santa Maria in Trastevere in 1291, then in his Santa Cecilia frescoes, Cavallini created a whole series of solid, majestic figures. It was Giotto, however, who led the movement to break away from the stereotyped forms of Byzantine art. Heir of the Tuscan sculptors, he painted some figures in grisaille which have all the plastic qualities of statuary. In his frescoes he went even further in the naturalistic delineation of man and the world. Thanks to Giotto, painting became the major art form of Europe, and has remained so during the six centuries since his death.

THE LATIN INTONATION

1. Giovanni Pisano (about 1248-1317). Allegorical Figure, 1277-1284. Marble. Museo di San Matteo, Pisa.

2. Giovanni Pisano (about 1248-1317). The Massacre of the Innocents, 1302-1310. Detail of the marble pulpit in Pisa Cathedral.

3. Arnolfo di Cambio (about 1245-1302?). The Virgin of the Nativity, 1296-1302. Marble. Museo dell'Opera del Duomo, Florence.

4. Tino di Camaino (about 1285-1337). A Counsellor of the Emperor Henry VII, 1315-1318. Marble. Campo Santo, Pisa.

5. Tino di Camaino (about 1285-1337). Caryatid personifying Faith, 1333-1337. Detail of the tomb of Mary of Valois. Marble. Church of Santa Chiara, Naples.

6. Giotto (about 1266-1337). Injustice, 1305-1306. Fresco in grisaille. Arena Chapel, Padua.

4

5

III. 66

At Avignon the Pope and most of the cardinals were Frenchmen from the Midi imbued with Gothic taste and the code of chivalry. Nevertheless, for the decoration of the palace which the Pope had just built to the glory of a second Rome, he commissioned a Sienese, Simone Martini, the most famous painter of the day. Simone had in fact been working for some time for the Angevin princes of Naples, for whom he had adapted the Tuscan style to suit the aristocratic languor and grace, as well as the affectation, of French taste. At Avignon, virtually nothing remains of the frescoes for which he was responsible; but his cartoons, or working drawings, traced out in Sinope red on the preparatory coat of plaster, have recently come to light on the walls of the Palace of the Popes. At the west end of the cathedral of Notre-Dame-des-Doms the artist made several sketches of Christ in Glory, with the Virgin seated on the ground "in all humility." They well reveal the elegance, strength of line and rhythmic power of his composition. The Ambrosian Library in Milan possesses a Virgil illustrated by Simone while at the papal court. One wonders whether the artist's adaptation of his pictures to the classical text was spontaneous or dictated by the humanist who ordered the work. No other painting of the Trecento is more akin to the ancients, either in conception or in the visual techniques employed.

Simone died in 1344. The bulk of the prodigious plan for decorating the court at Avignon was carried out between 1343 and 1368 by another Italian, Matteo Giovannetti da Viterbo, and his assistants. By this time creative artists were beginning to feel the lack of real stimulus which Central Italy, impoverished by financial crises and the exile of the papacy, could no longer provide. Meanwhile, Matteo found in the Rhone valley the first burgeoning of French art. The Pope and his cardinals, with a suspicious eye on the waywardness of Franciscan mysticism, welcomed the ostentation, finery and courtly manners that came from Paris. They allowed their artist complete freedom of invention, with the result that he merged Gothic lyricism with the broad spaciousness of the Tuscan School.

At the very time when Matteo and his assistants were at work in Avignon, Charles IV was seeking to restore the Empire and to build in Bohemia a capital worthy of its greatness. He founded the University of Prague in 1348, its organization being modeled on that of the University of Paris (where Charles had himself been a student); and he attracted to his court a host of architects, painters and sculptors, many of them from France. It was Mathieu d'Arras who designed the cathedral of St Vitus, whose pillared apse evoked the woodland groves of knightly romance. Descended from the Counts of Luxembourg, the Emperor was closely related to the royal house of France, and court life in Prague took its cue from Paris. From the court of Bohemia the refinements of Gothic art were diffused through Central Europe. Charles IV, however, was well aware of the dual character, at once Germanic and Roman, of the ancient empire over which he ruled; he had been crowned emperor in Rome and he realized that in Italy lay one of the sources of his power. It was only natural therefore that he should commission an Italian artist, Tommaso da Modena, to paint the altarpiece for the upper chapel at Karlstein. It was probably Nicolas Wurmser, a master from Strasbourg, who carried out the frescoes nearby, notably one in which the Emperor is seen as the servant of God, stooping over the reliquaries of the Passion. Thus the graceful style of the Ile-de-France, the Gothic traditions of the Rhineland and the plastic innovations of Northern Italy converged upon Prague from the opposite ends of the Empire; but the genius loci was wholly Czech and proved wonderfully rich in creative energy.

For at least a century past Bohemia had ceased to be a land of peasants and woodsmen; it had prospered, Prague had become the center of a vast network of trade relations, and wealthy princes and churchmen were surrounding themselves with precious objects and works of art commissioned from local artists and craftsmen. Throughout the fourteenth century prayer books were being illustrated with admirable miniatures, such as those in the Passional of Abbess Kunigunde which, however, still owe much to French models imported into Bohemia. Panel painters were active too. As early as 1350 the anonymous author of the Vysebrod Cycle had not only adopted and made his own the latest discoveries of Tuscan art, but had lent an added nobility to the narrative style of French stained-glass. By far the most striking products of Prague's golden age are the figures painted by the Bohemian, Master Theodoric, on the niches where relics were kept in the chapel at Karlstein. The features of his saints have a full-blooded eloquence far removed from the weak and willowy Gothic manner. This individuality was soon to be recaptured by the unidentified artist who painted the portrait of Rudolph IV of Hapsburg in the Diocesan Museum at Vienna.

SIMONE MARTINI (ABOUT 1285-1344). FRONTISPIECE OF PETRARCH'S "VIRGIL," ABOUT 1340.
MS A 79 INF., BIBLIOTECA AMBROSIANA, MILAN.

MATTEO GIOVANNETTI DA VITERBO (MID-14TH CENTURY). THE VISION OF ST JOHN AT PATMOS (DETAIL), 1346-1348.
FRESCO IN THE CHAPEL OF ST JOHN, PALACE OF THE POPES, AVIGNON.

MASTER THEODORIC OF PRAGUE (ACTIVE 1348-1367). ST JEROME. PANEL PAINTING FROM THE CASTLE OF KARLSTEIN.
NATIONAL GALLERY, PRAGUE.

NICOLAS WURMSER (ACTIVE MID-14TH CENTURY). THE EMPEROR CHARLES IV PLACING RELICS IN THE SHRINE OF THE CHAPEL OF THE HOLY CROSS, BEFORE 1357. FRESCO IN THE LADY CHAPEL, CASTLE OF KARLSTEIN, NEAR PRAGUE.

MASTER OF VYSEBROD (ACTIVE MID-14TH CENTURY). THE RESURRECTION, ABOUT 1350.
NATIONAL GALLERY, PRAGUE.

THE MISZLE VIRGIN AND CHILD, ABOUT 1330. POLYCHROME WOOD. NATIONAL GALLERY, PRAGUE.

THE TWO PATHS

It was about 1400 that the artistic developments which throughout the Trecento had been gaining ground in the entourage of the great princes of Europe found in Paris the ideal conditions for their completion and widest dissemination. From Paris the resulting synthesis of styles spread to all the aristocracy of the West—an aristocracy which, continually thrown together by their common pleasures and tournaments, their summer crusades in Prussia and incessant campaigning from one province to another, had been moulded into a homogeneous class, sharing the same parlance and outlook, the same ways and tastes. The long wars with England had come to an end, for the time being, and the advantage lay with the King of France. He stood now on a stronger footing; and, most important of all, he had grown richer, for the system of taxation wrought out in the stress of war was bringing into his coffers an abundant supply of gold which he could spend as he pleased. After the death of Charles IV the Empire had relapsed into impotence. The Papacy was divided against itself, with rival popes in Rome and Avignon. The hegemony of Europe thus fell to the King of France and to the sister courts of his uncles, the Dukes of Anjou, Berry and Burgundy. The sumptuous commissions of these princes caused artists from many parts of Europe to flock to Bourges and Angers, to Mehun-sur-Yèvre and the Chartreuse de Champmol at Dijon, but above all to Paris. Here the Lombard masters introduced the modernisms of illusionist painting, that concrete, sharply focused vision of the world which we find in the Veronese miniatures illustrating the *Tacuinum Sanitatis*. They introduced the techniques of *trompe-l'œil* to all the artists who came from the Netherlands in the wake of the sculptors of funerary effigies. These artists took them up and applied them less accurately but with a more vigorous and forthright touch, though rough and even uncouth at times. The art currents of North and South converged in Paris, mingling there with the elegance of the Gothic tradition; and thanks to the thriving trade in works of art, to their diffusion in the shape of gifts from one prince to another, and to the prestige of the royal court in Paris, the forms born of this union spread all over Europe.

Throughout this activity, and especially the synthesis in which it culminated, the prevailing mode of expression was French. This was only natural, for the secular power that dominated fourteenth-century culture was not Roman but chivalrous; and chivalry was French by origin and in its idiom, whether in Cyprus, Pampeluna or Windsor—or, for that matter, in Florence. The language that subjugated Europe in 1400, even including Tuscany, was therefore essentially Gothic. Artificial, two-dimensional, indifferent to the meaning of weight, mass and empty space, it had hardly accepted anything of the Roman renaissance, apart from a few of the techniques of realism. Patrons did not want their artists to produce monuments of stoic grandeur, but to portray the pleasure of living. In other words, they wanted reality to be translated into dreams and sport, in exactly the same way as society had long since adopted the make-believe of prowess and courtliness. Their requirements were met by an increasing resort to arabesque and *trompe-l'œil*. These two devices led to the fullest expression of courtliness in fourteenth-century art and, at the same time, severed its links with the divine and brought it down to the level of man. This is the heart of the matter. The new form of art, even when fulfilling a religious purpose, no longer spoke to priests but to men. When Giotto related the life of Christ, he presented it as a play, set on a stage with symbolic scenery. The world he portrays in his masque is not supernatural or liturgical but human. It tells a factual, human story, the tragedy of the man Jesus and the woman Mary. The other characters, on a par with them, are real men whom only the dignity of their bearing raises to the height of the living God. In a heroic, Roman manner Giotto has expressed what is, perhaps, the essence of the Franciscan spirit: the striving by Man to live like Jesus, like a god, like God Himself. A hundred years later, in the emotional technique employed by the Master of the Rohan Hours to depict "in the Gothic manner" the agony of Christ crucified, one finds the humanizing of divine figures carried to the opposite extreme. In both cases fourteenth-century art represents God and Man as brothers.

A mystic like Tauler believed that men could, through humility, come so near to God that they became "godly men." Such nearness to a God made flesh in the beliefs and sufferings of His creatures clearly put an end to many proscriptions, such as the Church's denunciation of human virtues and delights. The new men, freed from the priests, felt the urge both to commune more deeply with Christ and to enjoy the world. In daily life the twin courses of mysticism and naturalism, first charted by William of Occam, led to a double standard of behavior. Prince Louis d'Orléans and Queen Elizabeth of Bavaria "did all the pleasures prove." Yet he would make occasional retreats to a monastery, where he would hear five masses a day in his cell; while she had a meditation on the Passion of Jesus composed for her daily orisons. Karlstein, the fairy-tale castle built by Charles IV, opens onto the forests of Bohemia through courtyards designed for jousting and the meets of his hunt; but it also leads, by a plan that faithfully echoes the stages of mystical illumination, to a Sainte-Chapelle built for communion with the relics of Golgotha. The Lazarus with the body of Apollo, whom the Limbourg brothers caused to rise from the dead, displays to Jesus, his friend, the glory of his physical beauty. In art as in life, men divided their joy between imitating Christ and possessing the world.

The courtiers of Paris and Nicosia, of Windsor and Naples, danced on the rim of a volcano which they called Hell. They lived in a whirl of gaiety. They wore cloth of gold and rode blood stallions and made love to long-limbed girls. Yet they trembled in the knowledge that the life they clung to so eagerly was beset by darkness and horror and the threat of countless evils—plague, pain, the madness that turned kings into beasts, death and the unknown that lay beyond. Hag-ridden by their peril, they were driven to the extremes of asceticism or pleasure. The rather mawkish charm of early fifteenth-century art cannot quite conceal the black despair which causes the executioner to grin so horribly in scenes of martyrdom, or the Three Marys to wring their hands as they see the wounds of Christ. It is that despair which, at Barcelona, caused Bernardo Martorell to quicken the sense of pain and tragedy by lengthening out the body of the martyred St George along a tense diagonal. Princes in their anguish were obsessed by the Apocalypse, which revealed to them the flaws of creation.

After 1373 Nicolas Bataille, the most famous of Parisian weavers, was working for Louis, Duc d'Anjou, on his amazing portrayal in tapestry of the Revelation of St John the Divine. In this case the subject is rendered less disturbing by elegant draftsmanship and perfect harmony of colors. The Beast of the Apocalypse becomes part of the harmless ritual of chivalry, along with unicorns, gallant Hector and doughty Charlemagne.

Some years earlier, however, on the walls of the lady-chapel at Karlstein, an unknown hand had painted blind terror, the end of all things, the great spider and livid faces that come wheeling in a nightmare. Pisanello's St George, in the church of Sant'Anastasia at Verona, is no slayer of dragons, nor are his eyes on the princess. Is he not rather waking, dazed, from some hideous dream, against that background of storm, gallows and icing-sugar architecture?

NICOLAS BATAILLE (ACTIVE 2ND HALF OF 14TH CENTURY). THE ANGERS APOCALYPSE: "THE GREAT WHORE THAT SITTETH UPON MANY WATERS" (REVELATION, XVII, I). DETAIL OF THE TAPESTRY OF THE APOCALYPSE, 1373-1380. MUSÉE DES TAPISSERIES, ANGERS.

ANTONIO PISANELLO (1395-ABOUT 1455). THE LEGEND OF ST GEORGE AND THE PRINCESS (DETAIL), ABOUT 1435. FRESCO, CHURCH OF SANT'ANASTASIA, VERONA.

NICOLAS BATAILLE (ACTIVE 2ND HALF OF 14TH CENTURY). THE ANGERS APOCALYPSE: THE ASSAULT ON THE CITY OF GOD BY THE HOSTS OF GOG AND MAGOG AT THE INSTANCE OF SATAN (REVELATION, XX, 7-9). DETAIL OF THE TAPESTRY OF THE APOCALYPSE, 1373-1380. MUSÉE DES TAPISSERIES, ANGERS.

MASTER OF THE APOCALYPSE. THE DESTRUCTION OF THE CITY, ABOUT 1370. FRESCO IN THE LADY CHAPEL, CASTLE OF KARLSTEIN, NEAR PRAGUE.

III. 82

THE TRIUMPH OF DEATH

The fresco of the Triumph of Death *was designed for that most noble of cemeteries, the Campo Santo at Pisa, where it was accompanied by two others, depicting the* Last Judgement *and the exemplary life of the anchorites in the Thebaid. Like them, it was a summons to repentance and self-denial; but it also cried out to believers with a new accent of despair. The unknown artist had, in fact, exploited all the means of visual exhortation whereby the Mendicant Orders sought to edify the masses. It was the wealthy who stood in the direst peril, and they above all must be indoctrinated, weaned from fleshly delights and compelled to die in the faith. Two pictures were used, like successive arguments in a sermon, to drive the point home. In a leafy glade where knights and ladies were riding amid the flowers and the animals they knew so well, the artist set out the hackneyed parable of the* Three Dead *and the* Three Living, *with the sudden discovery of a corpse rotting in the sunlight. This well-worn theme, however, was greatly intensified by the adjoining picture, unprecedented in those days, of Death Triumphant, swiftly mowing down those who dallied in the garden of Love.*

The worldly-wise could not avoid the moral impact of such a vision. By dwelling on the beauties of this world—soft grass, rich dresses and sweet airs—the painter played upon man's dread of losing them. He took the tasteful designs with which Parisian craftsmen adorned the ivory toilet requisites of fashionable women and, with a turn of the screw, placed them on the walls of a graveyard. Over the main doorway of Leon Cathedral an earlier generation of sculptors had used a very similar gathering of courtly singers and musicians to exemplify the raptures of paradise; whereas the group at Pisa represent the guilty pleasures of this world, which man should renounce. He who relishes them sees in Death, Medicina di ogni pena, *the terrifying power that will snatch them away.*

The new teaching no longer offers men a gentle transition to assured, unearthly bliss. It is rooted in hard reality and the unconquerable fact of death. Knightly pleasures are extolled only that men shall be more aware of the final tragedy. Their faith must be nourished by consciousness of their own bleak destiny.

THE TRIUMPH OF DEATH, ABOUT 13

II

IMITATION OF CHRIST

THE LAYMAN'S CHRISTIANITY

The modernist tendency of the fourteenth century consisted very largely in a change of religious outlook and in "modern" forms of worship which were the result of the great conversion from medieval Christianity. By a very long process, beginning with the first mutterings of heresy in the eleventh century and reaching a sudden climax after 1200 with the preaching of St Francis of Assisi, the Christian religion had ceased to be ritual and sacerdotal. By the fourteenth century it had become the faith of the masses and priestly authority had been weakened. This age was no less Christian on that account than its predecessor; on the contrary, it was undoubtedly more so, for its faith was more personal, broader in scope and more firmly rooted in the Gospel. Hitherto the Christian life, to which Europe paid lip service, had only been lived fully by a small élite. As a result of this transformation Christianity became the religion of the people.

It also became more naïve. By assuming the homespun of a popular creed it was to some extent insured against doubt; for among the newly converted masses there was more credulousness and zealotry, a more benighted acceptance of the supernatural than there had been in cloister, chapter-house or quadrangle. The simple, fourteenth-century Christian was less exposed to the snares of unbelief; but he also went in greater terror of the Beyond, of those fearful powers, mysterious yet apparent, whom he must propitiate throughout life and especially at the dread moment of leaving it. The religion of the great thirteenth-century prelates, having overcome such terrors, developed in tranquillity, hopefulness and light; but the popular religion, which the Church accepted and tried to discipline, was a prey to darkness and fear of the occult. There emerged once more the demons which Gothic sunlight had driven into the darkest corners of cathedrals and which had hidden away in heretical sects or among magic springs and elf-haunted forests. Fourteenth-century laymen went in fear

of them, as of the pantocrator, and their religious life revolved round the daily act of pious prophylaxis which sought to exorcise the powers of evil and earn the compassion of God. In the new Christianity the layman was no longer, like his forefathers, the mute, uncomprehending spectator of liturgical rites; he now practised his religion according to his lights. This was true of rulers like Elizabeth of Bavaria, of Thuringian robber-knights, of scholarly women like Christine de Pisan and her fellow-countrymen, the Italian bankers, of Hanseatic merchants and wealthy farmers, down to the humble village hind. The work of art was one of the means whereby this practice found expression, whether it was a work of praise and fervor or of sacrifice and dedication of wealth; whether it was propitiatory or intended to prompt divine intervention. In every way it had come more than ever to fulfil a religious purpose.

The great change, however, was that art now obeyed the longings of the laity. Apart from all the economic and social changes that have been briefly examined, the relationship of the priest to his flock had been transformed. For centuries the Western Church had acted as a spiritual clearing-house. The clergy, both secular and monastic, prayed for the laity who supplied them with gifts, and their prayers obtained grace which was distributed among the faithful. By his alms and in accordance with a fixed tariff, every believer secured a portion of grace for himself and his family. This was expected to counterbalance his sins at the Last Judgement. On the threshold of great churches the image of St Michael weighing souls stood as a reminder of the redemptive power of this transaction. For the salvation of all, the clergy erected monuments of sacred art that were truly communal.

The disturbing successes of heresy, whereby a more educated laity sought release from its passive role and compensation for its repressions, led the

Church in the thirteenth century to renew its pastoral vocation. It could not depend upon the parish priests, ill-educated and often badly selected, who in any case tended more and more to live away from their cures and draw their stipend *in absentia*. Nor could it rely on the very humble men who actually did the work. It was the Mendicant Orders who, in the towns at least, took the lead and for this purpose developed methods of organizing and inspiring the masses.

With a view to co-ordinating the laity in a more dynamic body than the parish, the Friars Minor and Predicant enrolled among their Tertiaries all those who, without taking the tonsure, wanted no longer to see their faith through a glass darkly, but to live it. Many of these men had either embraced heresy or would have been constrained to do so. The less devout should at least unite in fraternities and guilds, in those associations for mutual benefit and occasional dissipation which the Church had long condemned for harboring pagan superstitions, but which in the fourteenth century it began to encourage, supervise and control. Grouped round an oracle, such as the image of a patron saint, endowed by the contributions of their members, these brotherhoods proliferated. There were craft, district and parish brotherhoods, hospital societies and charities, groups of penitents whose members ceremonially flogged one another, groups of worship, like the Italian *laudesi*, seeking to die in the odor of sanctity, whose main work consisted in edifying their members by "laudes," a form of community singing, and by staging, sometimes with considerable skill, scenes from the Gospel, such as the Nativity or the Road to Calvary. The Third Orders and the innumerable brotherhoods offered their members, who comprised the vast majority of town-dwelling laymen and a good many of those in the country, a spiritual life based on monastic practice: withdrawal into the cloister of silent prayer, the heroic struggle to win through to salvation, fasting, abstinence and daily spiritual exercises such as the chanting of psalms and recitation of canonical hours. The new administration bade the laity pray spontaneously, utter the words of Holy Writ and, if they could do so, read, mark, learn and inwardly digest them. It made the liturgy of convent and cathedral accessible to ordinary men and women in their everyday lives and in the privacy of their hearts.

In order that the people should receive instruction and the activities of the brotherhoods bear fruit, the missionaries of the Mendicant Orders fully exploited such means of edification as the pulpit and the stage, which were used in conjunction. When St Francis realized that it was not enough to attain his own salvation and that Christ commissioned him to broadcast His message, he did so by the spoken word. He was not a priest; so he sang of penitence, perfect joy and the love of God as a minstrel might have done, and the world heard him. Then he sent his disciples out along the roads and into workshops to use the same, very simple methods of persuasion. St Dominic founded his Rule for preaching. In order that the exponents of heresy, who lived with the people and spoke their language, might be beaten on their own ground, the Dominican intellectuals took the traditional homily of cathedrals and monasteries, which had only been addressed to churchmen, and made it a most effective weapon of propaganda. For this purpose they transposed the devout discourse of learned rhetoric into common speech and brought its argument down to the level of the least sophisticated audience. In the thirteenth century the sermon, like the prayer book, emerged from the cloisters and enclosed communities and was diffused among the people. After 1300 popular preaching gained steadily in influence.

The 1380's saw the beginning of the great missions and the campaigns of itinerant preachers. The fame of their mystical feats went before them and at the city gates they would be awaited by the whole municipality. Soon the squares would fill with listeners in a frenzy of enthusiasm. The crowd expected them to work miracles, dispel pestilence and, above all, show the way to a new life in this world and salvation hereafter. Of the Franciscan, Brother Richard, who preached at Paris in 1429, it is recorded that "he began his sermon about five in the morning. It lasted until ten or eleven and was heard every day by five or six thousand people. With his back to the charnel-house and facing the Charonnerie, the site of the Danse Macabre, he preached from a platform about a yard and a half high. The people of Paris were so moved to godliness that within three or four hours you could have seen more than a hundred bonfires, where they were burning gaming tables, backgammon boards, dice, playing cards, billiard balls and cues, in fact every sort of game that rouses men to anger and causes them to curse and swear like gamblers. That day and the next, women would burn their finery and maidens would sacrifice their peaked headdresses, their trains and all manner of fripperies." These agitators often stooped to catchpenny methods and sob-stuff. By reaching down into men's hearts they hoped to tap the deepest springs of emotion and thereby achieve mass-conversions. Wyclif denounced such ignoble tactics, and Chaucer's Pardoner is an evil charlatan. Yet their inexhaustible eloquence revealed and imparted to the people a brotherly, deeply moving image of Christ. It was the more convincing because their sermons were accompanied by a genuinely popular and festive show, which provided a setting of graphic paintings and sculptures, processions of singers and dramatic performances.

The theater, of course, originated in liturgy and as early as the tenth century was used to bring it within reach of the people. Like preaching, however, whose success it shared, it only became really popular and widespread in the fourteenth century. On the two great feasts of Christendom, Easter and Christmas, and on those of patron saints, the Italian brotherhoods performed countless *sacre rappresentazioni*. These were *tableaux vivants* which gradually became part of processions, were arranged in a series of scenes and acquired action, dialogue, music and fixed scenery. They were really private performances, reserved exclusively to members of a religious association whom they were intended to edify. But they acquired a deeper significance, for by miming the sufferings of Christ men could better comprehend the Passion and identify themselves with Him. By the end of the century, when the first great preaching missions were beginning, the theater had widened its scope and achieved its aim of becoming a huge, communal celebration. In Paris, London and other big towns the brotherhoods excelled in annual public performances of the Passion. Thus began the fifty most fertile years in the history of European religious drama.

The scene-shifting and make-believe, the chanting flagellants, the words and gesticulations from the pulpit were addressed not to the intellect but to the emotions. Their aim was to induce salutary feelings of pity and fear in every spectator. Whether in the midst of his fraternity or in the congregation at a sermon or in the audience at a mystery-play, each man felt himself involved. His soul and salvation were at stake; his responsibility and guilt were in the scales; the bell tolled for him. Deeply implanted in the emotions and quickened by the fear of God, this was a more disturbing, far more private Christianity. It took the form of dialogue: a dialogue between the penitent and his confessor in the secrecy of contrition, the whispered avowal of misconduct and absolution; a dialogue between the soul and God. By preaching and play-acting, by all the manœuvres of a direct approach, the Mendicant Orders stole converts from their rival, the secular Church. They also took over the anti-clerical tendencies of the heretical sects which they had originally been commissioned to lead back to the fold, and whose revival was now impeded by their activities.

All these movements swept through fourteenth-century Christianity and multiplied, sometimes to a dangerous extent. On the southern flanks of Europe, in Provence and Italy, where the Catharian and Waldensian heresies still exerted a strong residual influence, an entire branch of the Franciscan Order plunged into violent opposition to the Avignonese papacy. In claiming to be "spirituals," these "Little Brothers" were only showing devotion to their Founder; but they also expressed belief, founded on the works of the Calabrian hermit, Joachim of Floris, in the advent of a Third Age. After those of the Father and the Son, the teaching of St Francis had ushered in the Age of the Holy Ghost, in whose kingdom the intercession of the Church was no longer needed, since all true believers were filled with the Spirit, which the Roman Church was in fact betraying. These beliefs were echoed by the Rhenish communities of Beghards and Brothers of the Free Spirit. In 1326 they were hunted down and burned by the episcopacy because they, likewise, proclaimed the absolute freedom of the *perfecti* and the identification of the soul with God in mystic communion: "Feeling and possessing a natural state of inward peace, they believe themselves to be free and at rest, united to God without need of mediation, exalted above all the rites of the holy Church, above the commandments of God and above the law." Strange echoes of this pernicious doctrine could be heard in the Dominican convents where Meister Eckhart was teaching. In one of his sermons delivered in the vernacular he said: "Verily the power of the Holy Spirit takes what is most pure, delicate and sublime, the spark of the soul, and carries it up into the bright blaze of Love. So it is with a tree, when the sun takes what is purest and most sublime in its roots and carries it up to the branches where it becomes blossom. In the same way the spark of the soul is borne aloft to the light of the Holy Spirit and thus returns to its source. It becomes wholly one with God, so completely at one that it is more truly a part of God than food is of the body."

Later, at the end of the century, opposition to the hierarchy assumed harsher, more uncompromising forms in England and Bohemia. In the eyes of Wyclif, of the Lollard preachers and of the knights who heard them, the corrupt clergy were useless. The essence of religious life was to adore Christ the Brother and read the Gospel. The Word of God must therefore be translated into the common tongue, so that the people might hear it. These ideas were followed up by John Huss, who released the deepest springs of popular messianism. Briefly, before the outbreak of violence and slaughter, it succeeded in creating on a symbolic Mount Tabor an egalitarian family of the children of God, filled with the Holy Spirit and eagerly awaiting the imminent end of time. It was, however, in the Netherlands and in a far more restrained and submissive manner that the movement calmly attained its fullest expression by initiating what was rightly known as "modern worship." For some time laymen, priests and Dominicans had been founding on the Rhine little groups of "friends of God," who helped one another to adopt a rule of Christian brotherliness that should forsake the world and lead them to enlightenment. In his *Zierde der geistlichen Hochzeit* Ruysbroek urged his communities to practise complete self-denial in order to achieve union in Jesus. "A man who truly lives within himself suffices unto himself. He is freed from earthly cares and his heart opens reverently to the eternal goodness of God. Then the heavens are revealed and from the face of divine love a sudden light pierces his open heart like a thunderbolt. In that light the voice of God speaks to the loving heart: 'I am thine and thou art mine. I dwell in thee and thou in Me.'" In the Brotherhood of Common Life, founded by Gerhard Groot after he had long hesitated between the anchoretic life of Ruysbroek and the asceticism of the Carthusians, there was written before 1424 the devotional work which has enjoyed the most enduring success among the Christian laymen, the *Imitation of Christ*.

The priest still had a part to play in an act of meditation that did not attempt to fathom the mystery of God but to encounter Christ in His Humanity and gradually to blend with Him in inexpressible union. Since Jesus is nowhere more accessible than at the Lord's Supper, certain rites could not be dispensed with. The priestly office was rendered necessary by the essential meaning of the Mass, as a reconstruction of the Passion, at which men hoped to see, as long ago at Bolsena, blood ooze from the wafer or the figure of the Man of Sorrows rise from the chalice; or of the solemn, winding procession of Corpus Christi, when the body of Christ was displayed. Yet what mattered above all was "inward and spiritual grace," prayer, adoration by the soul and the gradual exaltation of its "ground." It was from these that the new forms of religious art took their fullest meaning.

THE CHAPEL

Fourteenth-century Christendom built many noble places of public worship. In those parts of Europe, such as England or Spain, where the landed gentry were still wealthy, abbots and canons sometimes renovated their churches. Elsewhere, religious houses received subsidies from a bishop, a patron or, as in the South of France, a Pope. In the case of monasteries, cathedrals and churches whose function was unchanged, there was no attempt at structural alteration. Innovations consisted either in some ornamental feature, an embellishment to the glory of its donor, or in enclosing the sanctuary by means of a rood-screen. That in the Capilla Mayor at Toledo forms a gorgeous but impenetrable barrier, enabling the celebrants to intone their office in seclusion and completely shutting out the congregation. Thus the final development of hieratic art emphasized the separation of liturgical tradition from the people.

Municipalities, meanwhile, were building churches for their townsfolk. They sought to glorify their city by erecting great parochial buildings, relegating the local tabernacles to the role of chapels-of-ease. These parish churches were intended to assemble the citizens, guilds and authorities in municipal ceremonies that were civic as much as religious. The big collegiate churches in Flanders, St Mary Radcliffe in Bristol, or Tinn, the merchants' church in Prague, could hold their own with cathedrals. They were proud and self-assertive, symbolizing power by means of lofty naves and steeples. Not far away another type of church was appearing, more spiritual in purpose and better suited to the new evangelical movement. These were the churches built by the four Mendicant Orders on the outskirts of every big town. The Austin friars, the grey Franciscans, the black Dominicans and the white Carmelites were all constructing immense halls for the new mode of worship, often designed with two naves, one for the Brothers and the other thrown open to the laity.

These churches exemplified self-denial, to which the Orders of poverty were beholden. Outside there were no buttresses but a severely plain, homogeneous mass, adapted in all respects to its function and on that account of great beauty. Within there was the same simplicity and unity. There might be several naves, but they were all the same height, for religious and laity are equal before God. They were only separated by a few slender pillars, with the aim of uniting in one body the people and the friars who led them. To ensure full participation by the laity, the new design was the absolute antithesis of the rood-screen. Everyone in the church must be able to hear the preacher, see the elevation of the Host, and even read a book. More glass was used, bays were widened and the gloom appropriate to tapers and chanting was dispelled. The Mendicants' design, huge, bare, sober, light and airy, soon to be adopted by collegiate churches and even cathedrals, provided a perfect auditorium for the spectacle that the public expression of piety had now become. Along the walls were placed rows of side-chapels for the private devotions of families and brotherhoods.

Originally the chapel had been regarded as an appurtenance of royalty, belonging to a sovereign endowed with charismatic and thaumaturgical powers. According to the ancient German belief, which lies at the root of the European concept of monarchy, the king held converse with the gods, officiated for his people and by his intercession secured victory and prosperity for them. In Carolingian times the ceremony of consecration christianized this magic office and brought it within the province of the Church. The sovereign was thus, like a bishop, the anointed of God. He had lost none of his religious attributes, but now he held them direct from God, whom he represented on earth in the conduct of temporal business. He was now responsible for the spiritual welfare of his people and bore witness of it before God. It was part of his calling that he always stood in immediate and personal relationship to the divine power. The king was the first layman, for a long time the only one, to pray as a priest. This accounts for the touching fervor with which Charlemagne spent sleepless nights wrestling with the alphabet. The royal household now comprised a staff of chaplains whose duty it was to encompass the monarch, like a bishop in his cathedral, with an uninterrupted act of worship. Its setting was the chapel, where the king had his throne, his episcopal *cathedra*. He was surrounded by his lieges and before him were displayed the holy relics of his treasury; for it behoved the sovereign, in order to enhance his powers of intercession, to collect as many fragments as possible of the saintliest bodies. The chapel was also, perhaps primarily, a reliquary: both a shrine and a monstrance for holy remains. The walls were lined with the most costly materials to provide a magnificent setting both for the relics and for the sovereign himself as he sat throned in majesty, bearing the symbols of his authority. Such was the chapel built by Charlemagne, on the lines of the oratories of the Eastern Roman Empire, for his palace at Aix-la-Chapelle. Such, too, was the Sainte-Chapelle in Paris, the supreme masterpiece of royal liturgical art, constructed by St Louis as a receptacle for the Crown of Thorns.

Throughout the fourteenth century European monarchs imitated this perfect example. Edward III of England, as soon as he had wrested power from his mother, determined to assert his youthful daring and vigor by proving himself equal to the King of France. At Westminster, close to the tomb of Edward the Confessor, whom he caused to be honored as a rival to St Louis, he built a chapel dedicated to St Stephen. When Charles IV of Bohemia sought to bring renewed lustre to the imperial diadem he had received, he constructed Karlstein. At the summit of this fairy-tale castle he placed a shrine inlaid with gold and bright jewels, its walls adorned with portraits of saints. This reliquary for the True Cross was, as it were, the mystical climax of the warlike and chivalrous virtues displayed in the lower courtyards. A long, heavenward ascent led to the chapel with its hidden precinct, jealously guarded by a series of ramparts and fragrant with the odor of sanctity, where the Emperor would be closeted with the crucified God whose Vicar on earth he felt himself to be.

Kings, however, were not the only men to build themselves sanctuaries in the fourteenth century, for unanointed princes also wanted to have theirs. A wonderful example is that at Bourges, where the Duc Jean de Berry placed the religious objects in his gorgeous collection of jewels. But the new trend in pious observances and the general dissemination of culture were most strikingly illustrated by the immense number of chapels owned by individuals and intended for their private use. Other chapels were not strictly personal but belonged to small groups, such as families, fraternities or permanent fellowships. Guilds, corporations and devotional societies needed a place for their occasional prayer meetings at which a priest officiated as their spiritual director. Since few of them had enough money to build their own chapel they would ask a church to house them and space would be reserved for them near one of the altars on either side of the high altar, where the public services were held. The latter were no longer so comprehensive as they had been, for each family and household wanted to worship in a private sanctuary. Great nobles had long been accustomed to equip their castles with oratories modeled on the royal chapels. This practice was growing, for the well-to-do wanted to live like lords, with the same food, drink, clothes and recreations. Every paterfamilias who could afford it employed a chaplain to say mass at home for himself and his family. Failing that, he sought, by means of a substantial donation, to secure a reserved space in church, either in the precincts of the choir or in one of the side-aisles. He hoped in this way to show that he had bettered himself and that his descendants would sit in the seats of the mighty. The Mendicant Friars did not object to selling space in their churches to the more prominent and bountiful members of their congregation. There were no fewer than twenty-five private chapels round the choir of the Cordeliers in Paris.

These family and fraternity chapels fulfilled a double purpose. The first, or external, function consisted in holding private services and saying masses for individual members of the group. They might be living but more often were not, for this function was essentially elegiac. Worship of the dead played a major part in men's instinctual religious feeling. As the Church adopted and formalized this spontaneous emotion, so there developed the Christian rites for the departed. At this time, membership of a fraternity meant above all that a man was assured of a decent funeral and that in subsequent generations fellow-members would pray perpetually for those who were dead. The descendants of a family felt similarly beholden to those who had gone before. As yet there was no waning of belief in the efficacy of rites performed by the living on behalf of the dead. On the contrary, there was a growing conviction that death was not the end.

The Pope at Avignon had proclaimed that a man's soul appeared before God immediately after death and received a first, beatific vision of Him; but between that brief encounter and the Last Judgement, separating the damned from the elect, there stretched the wastes of Purgatory. At this stage the soul could acquire merit that it still lacked for admission to Paradise, and a man's friends could credit his account with the benefits accruing from repeated commemoration of the divine sacrifice. Every testator, therefore, assigned a considerable share of his bequests to paying for a stately funeral service and, above all, for innumerable masses to be sung in perpetuity. Such legacies, whereby families often ruined themselves, were regarded as the best insurance against hell-fire. It was also believed that the nearer masses were celebrated to the remains of the person whose salvation was at stake, the greater was their redemptive power. The most effective arrangement, therefore, was to assemble in one place the tomb, the altar and the priest who was to perform the sacrament until the end of time. The Christian who was concerned for his own and his family's salvation endowed a private chapel as soon as he could afford it. This was no light matter, for it meant buying a place of burial, fitting it up appropriately and then providing capital for the perpetual maintenance of one or two resident chaplains, constituting the chantry. There was soon an entire ecclesiastical proletariat competing for these chaplaincies, which combined a good living with very little work. The chaplain in *Canterbury Tales* is the embodiment of easy sloth. Yet the abundant supply of priests eager for these sinecures could hardly keep pace with the demand, so inordinate were the requirements of the rich as they contemplated the grave. One Gascon noble, the Captal de Buch, provided in his will for fifty thousand masses to be sung in the year of his death, plus sixty-one perpetual anniversaries and eighteen chaplaincies. These practices deprived parishes of their working clergy and, by substituting selfish modes of worship, helped to destroy the Church's communal institutions.

These funerary rites were not, however, the only function of the chapel, which, with the increase in private worship, became in addition a place for the meditation and self-communion of a more exclusive religious life. In the oratory where he was wont to pray for the souls of the departed in his family or fraternity, the believer could also encounter God and gradually, in silent adoration, raise the "spark" of his soul towards Him. His chapel would be filled with objects conducive to such outpourings and tended, like the royal chapels, to become a reliquary. The more intelligible Christianity became the more credulous was belief in the redemptive power of saintly remains. In the twelfth and thirteenth centuries the sophistication of priestly culture in churches built and organized by the higher clergy had kept the veneration of relics within reasonable bounds. In the fourteenth century the influence of laymen swept away these restraints. Relics were considered the most valuable present one could give or receive, and they, like everything else, became vulgarized. Chapels, moreover, were adorned with images designed to fortify the soul or expose it to the light of the Holy Spirit. They filled the stained-glass windows and were mingled with symbols of ownership, such as the badge or motto or portrait of the Founder. Painted or carved in wood or alabaster, they were displayed on the panels of the reredos, a group of allegorical scenes which was normally kept folded and hidden from the public, and was only opened for the private use of its owners, who also owned the chapel. These images acquired an even more clannish atmosphere in the form of statues portraying the patron saints of the family or fraternity. They were kept in cupboards and only taken out by members of the privileged coterie, either for their private contemplation or to be paraded in public as evidence of prestige.

Things of this kind were not fixtures like a tomb or an altar but, being portable, could be removed from the chapel, projecting its mystical function into everyday life. Why should exercises in loving God be reserved to special times and places? The new Christianity purported to be coterminous with the believer's entire existence. One consequence of the fourteenth-century inclination to private worship was the use of small-scale devotional objects. They provided an even more personal counterpart to the chapel and could create, anywhere and at any time, an appropriate setting for deep and devout meditation. It now became fashionable for relics to be set in jewels and carried permanently on the person of him whom they were supposed to protect from harm and fill with grace. Little diptychs or triptychs were made of precious materials. They could be opened for prayer, like a reredos, before a battle or tournament, during a business journey or in the privacy of the closet. For many laymen the psalter and breviary, likewise, became a kind of portable chapel. Their illuminations, reproducing the subjects of stained-glass window or reredos, framed the sacred text in glowing pictures, more eloquent and emotive than the Latin words of prayer. Of all these objects the most valuable were probably those which have been preserved in collections to this day. They are lavishly designed and bear an odd resemblance to fashionable toys, for which they may sometimes be mistaken. Like chapels, they could be afforded only by the wealthiest men and women; but it is apparent from inventories, wills and family papers that less costly articles of the same kind were owned by people of moderate means, such as minor officials, knights of low degree and citizens of provincial towns. At the still humbler level of the masses, an equivalent commodity was being marketed very cheaply by the end of the century, in the form of woodcuts and illustrations which could be tacked to the wall, sewn on one's clothing or folded in a pocket.

In these prints, as in ivory diptychs, illuminations and jeweled reliquaries, the devotional image always has an architectural frame, the abstract symbol of a sanctuary. The constant use of arcading, pinnacles and gables is more than a vestigial reminder of the supremacy once enjoyed by the builder's craft. It shows that to the truly religious man these objects, better suited though they were to the modern form of worship, were nonetheless a substitute, not merely for the chapel where he sometimes knelt in prayer, but also for the cathedral he had abandoned. Amid the general surrender of the Christian religion into the hands of the laity, this phantom church still stood; partly as the enduring memory of an outworn rubric, partly as the palpable symbol of an inner faith, whose sanctuary was the heart of man.

THE HOUSE OF PRAYER

The fourteenth-century Christian regarded his priest, singing Mass in the parish church, mainly as the bestower of sacraments that conferred divine blessing. Now that his faith was wholly directed towards Christ's agony, the Mass came to appear as a symbolic paraphrase of the Passion. On the instructions of Jean Chevrot, bishop of Tournai, Roger van der Weyden minutely depicted the various sacramental rites on the side-panels of a triptych. The greatest of all sacraments is the Eucharist, which brings back the Real Presence of Christ on the Cross. The central panel, therefore, is devoted exclusively to the ceremony of consecration, represented by the scene on Calvary which dominates the foreground of the whole composition. The cross stands in a huge church, airy, gleaming and supported on slender columns. Light streams through delicately tinted windows, and the building is so designed that everyone can see the slow elevation of the Host. Indeed, the priest is showing us the Body of God as he stands in the center of the chancel, beneath a reredos of the Annunciation. Behind him, concealed by the rood-screen, canons are chanting their archaic plainsong.

In England, thanks to the enduring prosperity of its landowners, the great religious houses retained their wealth until the very end of the fourteenth century. Bishops and abbots lost no time in securing their profits against grasping monarchs by investing them in huge religious edifices, which also enabled them to indulge their fondness for display. In this way sacred art flowered nobly in the traditional forms of English architecture. These buildings were not public. Converging on the choir and cloister, they were intended exclusively for monastic devotions. In the covered walks of the cloister the monks could study and meditate; here the novices were given instruction and moral lectures were delivered. It was a place of mystical communion where those dedicated to the religious life advanced towards the knowledge of God and sought to identify themselves with the suffering Christ. Each of the arches bordering the cloister marked a step on the road leading to Calvary, to the Son of God suspended from the Cross. But all the members of the monastic community assembled at regular intervals within the church for the collective prayers and chants of the canonical hours.

Between *1337* and *1357* the great roof of the choir at Gloucester Abbey was built, in the words of the chronicle, "with the alms of the faithful who flocked to the tomb" of King Edward II, widely regarded in those days as a martyr. Technical advances made it possible to knock down the end wall and build the marvelous window through which the light of the Holy Ghost poured down upon the choir of canons below.

The Mendicant Friars, too, filled their churches with light, but for a different reason. They stood open to all, for they were built, not for private prayer or the bestowing of sacraments, but for pastoral teaching and guidance. They were great, unadorned barns, plain as the poverty they exemplified and perfectly attuned to the new, communal Christianity, the brotherhood of common men. In Florence, the single nave of the Franciscan church of Santa Croce consists of an immense bare space. At the exact center of the vast nave stands the Crucifix, dominating the church, attracting all eyes, reigning over all devotional attitudes. At the east end the high altar is flanked by a number of chapels, for there were many friars in residence and each of them had to sing Mass daily. Moreover, a number of leading Florentine families succeeded in having side-chapels assigned to them for their private devotions and for the burial of their dead. These chapels, on the fringe of the monastic community, became their property, maintained and embellished by their oblations. Here austerity was felt to be out of place: the prestige of the family was at stake, and each sought to outdo the other in the quality and extent of the frescoes which it displayed on the walls and ceiling of its own chapel.

The chantry built by the Earls of Warwick is none the less isolated for being set among the pillars of the choir at Tewkesbury Abbey. It was intended that the monks, assembled in prayer before the altar, should purvey their spiritual benison to the family vault; but the sepulchre is enclosed within a stone canopy, in the likeness of a church, which effectively marks it off as a place of private devotion for the House of Warwick.

THE CHOIR OF GLOUCESTER CATHEDRAL, WEST SIDE. 1337-1357.

CHOIR OF THE CHURCH
OF SANTA CROCE, FLORENCE.

ROGER VAN DER WEYDEN (1399-1464). ALTARPIECE OF THE SEVEN SACRAMENTS, CENTRAL PANEL: CRUCIFIXION IN A CHURCH,
WITH THE OFFERING OF THE HOLY EUCHARIST IN THE BACKGROUND, ABOUT 1445. MUSÉE DES BEAUX-ARTS, ANTWERP.

CLOISTER OF WORCESTER CATHEDRAL, 3RD QUARTER OF 14TH CENTURY.

CHANTRY OF THE EARLS OF WARWICK IN TEWKESBURY ABBEY, 1422.

THE USE OF IMAGES IN WORSHIP

The entire purpose of modern worship, of *devotio moderna*, was to prepare the soul for union with the Holy Spirit, leading it gradually on and, at the critical moment of death, securing it against the perils of its journey. It therefore bade the Christian draw near to the word of God and find in it the source of constant prayer and meditation. How should a man know the Father, the Son and the Holy Ghost, except through the Scriptures? To the fourteenth-century laity direct apprehension of Holy Writ became an essential part of the religious life, as it had been since the earliest days of Christendom for monks in the seclusion of Benedictine cloisters or in the cells of the Solitary Orders. It was no longer enough for the layman to listen passively to the reading or chanting of Biblical texts; he must understand them.

The rulers of the Church, suspicious and fearful of heresy, were not anxious that laymen should read the Bible on their own, so that translations of the Old and New Testaments did not bulk large in the efforts to make Latin ecclesiastical works available to the general public. About 1340 a Yorkshire hermit put the Psalter into vernacular Anglo-Saxon. Fifty years later a number of teachers at Oxford produced two versions of the Gospels, of which one was too scholarly for the uneducated and the other was more colloquial. These translators, however, being tarred with the brush of Lollardry, were regarded as radical opponents of the higher clergy. When Jean de Cy put the Bible into French and added a commentary, he was working for the King of France, Jean le Bon. His book, sumptuously got up, was a thing of great value in itself and by no means intended for popular consumption. By the beginning of the fifteenth century there was as yet nothing in French for the educated layman beyond short extracts from the Gospels, to be read on Sundays, and a few "edifying" passages adapted from the Bible. The latter reached him mainly in the form of sermons.

The preachers did at least endeavor to speak convincingly and make their audience grasp what they meant. By mime and gesture they tried to bring the Gospels home to the masses. They acted it themselves and caused the main themes of their sermons to be depicted in *tableaux vivants* or processions. They encouraged their listeners to enact the holy tragedy either in pageants or at the meetings of fraternities, or even in the privacy of their oratories. These sacred performances made it possible to reach the humblest of the laity, whose thick heads were impervious even to the most elementary arguments of the popular preachers. And they had a deeper purpose yet. The fact that members of the congregation were expected to play an active role by singing, or rather miming, would lead them actually to live events in the life of Christ and thus to be embodied for a moment in their brother, Jesus. Medieval piety had always sought to strengthen the willingness of the soul by giving it the support of the flesh. In Benedictine monasteries prayers were never silent but were shouted in unison by the whole community. The manipulation of parchment in transcribing a sacred text also involved physical effort, in which the wrist was as active as the mind. Strenuous reading aloud took the place of inaudible mumbling. By miming the Word of God a man could best make it his own and his faith a part of his life. The Dominican, Heinrich Suso, would walk at night from one pillar of his cloister to another, enacting the passion of Christ. These stations of the Cross would lead him to the crucifix in the chapel, where he would commune with the Virgin. Exercises such as this would bring him the moments of bliss that he has recorded: "It often seemed to him that he glided through the air, adrift between time and timelessness on the unfathomable ocean of God's mystery." Were all believers to do likewise, mustered and led by the Mendicant Friars, they too would walk the mystic road towards the radiance of salvation, in which death itself was but the narrow antechamber to deliverance. At times the entire population of a town would join in a huge communal performance. In 1400, during the three days of Pentecost, the craftsmen of Avignon staged a Passion play at their own expense. "Two hundred actors were needed, with a countless host of men armed and caparisoned. Many stands for men and women were erected in the square before the monastery of the Preaching Friars. Never had there been so princely a spectacle, or one that was seen by ten or twelve thousand people." Mystery plays, which were by no means confined to the fraternities, gave rise to a ubiquitous school of drama, where every Christian was to play a part in the daily performances of his private life.

This was how the image came to predominate, for it provided the most effective stepping-stone between the word of God and the passionate miming whereby body and soul were freed from their bonds, from all that impeded their progress "towards sublime contemplation on the heights of beatitude." The image helped the novice by setting his feet on the path. "Daughter," wrote Heinrich Suso, "it is time you took wing and left the comfortable nest that images prepare for the beginner." Preachers were well aware that they must appeal to the eye of the innumerable beginners who made up their congregations. But to have a more lasting effect they must also provide features and colors that would be engraved on the memory and give the faint-hearted a source of renewed fervor long after the missionaries' departure. Bernardino of Siena had used the symbol of Jesus' name, framed in a sunburst, not merely as an illustration but as the central theme of his preaching. At his request it was engraved upon the façades of patrician mansions. The effect of penitential sermons and *sacre rappresentazioni* could be thus prolonged by painted panels, polychrome sculpture and the dissemination of holy images by means of wood-engraving. In order to bring God within reach of the masses, who were equally prone to enthusiasm and apostasy, fourteenth-century religious art became essentially histrionic.

Giotto's renown rested on the fact that he succeeded better than any of his predecessors in splendidly reproducing the various scenes of a mystery play on the walls of churches. A producer of genius, he crystallized the flow of drama and provided exemplary concepts to those who sought

to love St Francis and St Joachim, Jesus and the Virgin, and who hoped by truly knowing them to apprehend their divine nature. The Friars, those educators of the baptized who strove to impart the New Testament to the very lowest strata of Christian society, believed the image to be a far more persuasive medium than reading the Bible or hearing it read. For the benefit of the laity the fourteenth-century Bible became "graphic," consisting in a series of stories as lively and enthralling as any of the popular myths or romances. For the illiterate, likewise, it assumed the narrative form of the "Poor Man's Bible," in which the gist of the story was broken up into a number of simple, expressive pictures. Those who led this new type of ministry believed, in the words of Eustache Mercadé, the author of a *Passion* which was performed about 1430 in the North of France, that "for some who do not understand the Scriptures it is better that they should be given examples, stories and paintings on the walls of monasteries and palaces."

These were the books of ordinary folk. As religion became more popularized, it naturally became more pictorial. "Stand on Calvary and fix the eyes of thy soul diligently on all that is being inflicted on thy Lord. Watch with the eyes of thy soul how some are planting the Cross in the ground, while others are preparing the nails and hammer." In the *Meditationes vitae Christi*, attributed to St Bonaventura but certainly written at the end of the fourteenth century by a Franciscan from Tuscany, all the metaphors and the whole drift of the work show how important a part was assigned to vision in developing a man's inner life.

In those days it was universally believed that vision engendered love and nurtured it. The fabric of affection was woven by light and the eyes were the windows of the soul. In the thirteenth century Robert Grosseteste, who founded the Oxford school of philosophy, had postulated, in opposition to Aristotle, a cosmogony based on light. He believed the universe to have originated in a sudden effulgence, which begot the spheres and elements, the shapes and dimensions of matter. This doctrine, as received and amplified by Franciscan scholars, led to a reinterpretation of natural philosophy through the study of optics; but it also coincided with the Neo-Platonist strain in Western Christianity, rivaling the rational theology of Aristotle and offsetting the appeal to the intellect by its encouragement of mysticism. Was not light, God-created and life-giving, the closest link between God and His creatures? By it the divine grace was diffused and the human soul enabled to behold the face of God.

These ideas led thirteenth-century thinkers to extol the eloquent use of light in the building of cathedrals. As time went on and Christianity became the affair of ordinary men and women, the learned theories of the Oxford Franciscans were easily wedded to traditional secular beliefs. For laymen, too, believed that a man must see in order to love, and that "eyes looked love to eyes that spake again." In the songs of thirteenth-century troubadours, the spark of love is transmitted by the eye to the heart, which it sets aflame, and by this stream of light two hearts are fused in one. Flame, heart, passion, spark: the same words are found in the sermons and instructions of mystics and in the erotic songs of chivalry. Sacred and profane love came together by the same process that united priestly and knightly codes of behavior. Just as the ardor of the courtly swain was kindled by the vision of his lady, so Heinrich Suso, miming the Passion of Jesus, was drawn towards the image of Christ crucified. In a late fourteenth-century manuscript illustrating allegorically the spiritual pilgrimage of Suso, his soul may be seen, at a moment of great stress, lying prostrate before an image of Jesus on the Cross. In the sculpted groups placed over tombs or in the panel paintings of commemorative altarpieces, the donors are portrayed kneeling before the divine Man and his Mother; and in their rapt gaze the light of sacred love seems to be flooding the depths of their being.

This accounts for the great part played by the monstrance in fourteenth-century ritual and for the long pause in the mass when the Host is elevated and displayed to the people, filling them with love. For the same reason reliquaries were designed as transparent containers in which the holy remains were visible. Everyone wanted to see the objects of his mystical yearning and found in doing so relief from anguish and food for hope. Piety at this degraded level reached the point of clothing images with magic powers. Was it not enough to look at a statue of St Christopher to be sure that one would not die in sin before the day was out? People there-fore insisted on the ubiquitous presence of these barely Christian effigies. That of the good giant Christopher kept watch over every crossroads and was placed on the west wall of churches so that the faithful, glancing up at him as they went out, might carry with them the reassurance of his protection. The ecclesiastical authorities, far from discouraging the popular tendency to worship images, in some cases guaranteed their supernatural powers. Indulgences were promised to those who uttered a certain prayer before the statue of Christ during the Mass of St Gregory, or who visited the Calvary in the Charterhouse at Champmol.

Some churchmen, however, wished to condemn this form of worship and placed a ban on allegedly miraculous images. A treatise was written "against those who adore images and statues," and further attempts were made by Gerson and Cardinal Nicholas of Cusa. An English writer stated the true doctrine in measured terms: "Images are designed by the Church as calendars for the laity and the ignorant, so that they may apprehend Christ's Passion and the good life and martyrdom of saints. But if a man renders unto lifeless images the worship he owes to God, or if he places in them the faith or hope that he could place in God, then he commits the gravest sin of idolatry." The most violent and uncompromising attacks came from certain heretical groups who clung to a truly spiritual faith, cleansed of all the defilements introduced by a corrupt, affluent, worldly-minded clergy. Images were included in their outcry against the pomp of the Roman Church. In 1387 two Lollards smashed a statue of St Catherine at Leicester. Soon after, the Bohemian Puritans of Mount Tabor objected violently to ornamental figures in churches. Iconoclasm, however, never amounted to more than an explosion of heretical violence. In the main fourteenth-century art, whether monumental or in the form of small objects of private worship, consisted in the expression of an unsophisticated faith.

Representational religious art was naturally related to the written word, such as extracts from the Bible or from the lives of saints, which were often copied directly onto phylacteries or along the edge of a painting. These sequences of pictures, which could be read like the illustrated strips of modern "comics," lent vigor to the message and ensured that it received wide and lasting publicity. Their function was to make belief tangible and visible. They resorted to symbol or, more often, allegory in order to clothe the invisible in familiar dress, with all the characteristics of earthly existence. These pictures set out to portray substance as well as meaning. Since they had to display the attributes of reality, the artists of that time borrowed from antiquity a number of illusionist devices. It was also necessary that sacred figures, whose function was to uplift the soul and release it from earthly trammels, should not rub shoulders with the profane. They must be set on a higher plane, even though painters and sculptors might well depict men face to face with God in the same imaginary setting. No one would ever mistake the donor for the Christ he is adoring, or even for the patron saint who stands protectively behind him. They belong to different worlds, separated by a barrier that can only be crossed at the fearful moment of death. To symbolize this paramount segregation, Giotto used certain theatrical effects, such as the abstract blue of his background in scenes that are outside the normal scheme of time. He also made great use of the stately manner which the rediscovery of Roman art had taught him. It is true that the characters in his solemn drama have the appearance of men. Joachim sleeps like any shepherd. Yet something undefinable would prevent one slapping him on the back—some invisible barrier like that which separates the actor from his audience, or the communicant from the priest carrying the Eucharist, or Don Giovanni from the statue of the Commendatore. Even in the most trumpery altarpiece, painted for some craftsmen's guild in a humble parish, figures from the Bible are never demeaned to the level of prosaic existence. In the religious art of this period there is always a point where unshaken belief in another world brings realism to a halt.

The hereafter, real but unseen, is disclosed, even before the dreaded revelation of death, by images presaging the radiance of divine love. For it is inhabited by a multitude of minor characters, the company of Saints. They, like the demons and evil spirits whom they harried, figured prominently in the religion of ordinary people. Despite their numbers, these mediators could be clearly distinguished from one another, and the more skillful artists, when portraying them in groups, tried to identify them individually. Each had his favorite habitat in this world, his abode in life and the resting-place of his mortal remains, and it was here that his miracles were performed. Each had his own powers, to be invoked in special circumstances, and his story was recorded in the great romance compiled for Christendom, Jacobus de Voragine's *Golden Legend*. The saints were recognized by their features, dress and symbolic accessories, so that Joan of Arc had not the slightest doubt which ones were announcing her vocation. The imagery, like the processions, of Christianity attached great importance to powers that warded off the more alarming forms of death, whether the recognized protector of a guild or class, such as the valiant horseman and lancer St George, the patron saint of knights, or the personal guardian to whom every Christian entrusted his body and soul. Images enabled the newly canonized, like St Thomas Aquinas or St Catherine of Siena, to attain celebrity, and the Church used its control over images to restrain the cruder forms of worship which grew up around these subordinate characters. The paintings at Assisi were so arranged as to place St Francis firmly within the official bosom of the Church.

The center of the devotional stage, however, was always occupied by the commanding figure of God: God in three persons, for many fourteenth-century fraternities took the Trinity as their patron, so that painters and sculptors were told to portray the three divine powers. Militant Christians, at their most enterprising, laid special emphasis on the Holy Ghost. Many of them believed, like the Little Brothers of St Francis, that His kingdom had come, and in the eyes of all Christians He determined the relationship between a man's soul and the Godhead. Yet in pictures of the Trinity the dove of the Holy Ghost always appears as an accessory, a sort of poetic hyphen. Even God the Father is relegated to the background as a symbol of majesty. The whole scene is dominated by the crucified Son. Prolonged Franciscan influence had resulted in fourteenth-century portraiture gravitating towards the source of love, the image of God made Man in the person of Jesus, brother and saviour. But which Jesus was this? In Romanesque tympana the Benedictines had portrayed Christ of the Advent coming at the Last Trump in the blinding radiance of His glory to judge the quick and the dead. Over the west door of cathedrals thirteenth-century philosophers had set Jesus the Doctor, book in hand as he expounded from his Chair. But the Christ adored by common men was Himself a man. He was a man who touched the heart, for the modern form of worship consisted in "a compassion that is close to tears." This was the Jesus whom the preachers described and the *sacre rappresentazioni* mimed, the Jesus of Christmas and Easter. He was a God of fable, a character in a story, this Christ who shared with poor men the helplessness of being a baby and the desolation of dying.

Christmas and Easter. The winter feast is one of joy, a cockcrow of hope at the blackest hour of the night. That joy, with its sweet message of comfort, pertains even more to the Mother than to the Child in the manger. As Christianity became more popular and more accessible to women, it developed rather sentimental variations on the Marian theme, which had in any case been thoroughly explored by the Church. First came Mary startled at her prayers by the angel of the Annunciation; then Mary kneeling before her new-born Son; then Mary watching Him at play among the smooth lawns and bright flowers of the Mystic Garden. Lastly there was the Virgin panoplied and raised in majesty above the company of Saints, assuming their protective role and, as sole Mediatrix, gathering all Christians beneath her blue mantle. Then, after the sackcloth and ashes of Lent, Easter was ushered in "with travail and holy sorrow." Only by untold suffering could Christ lead men to salvation. No spectacle in that age exerted a stronger appeal than the Passion; no symbol was more venerated than the Cross, the tragic kernel of a poor man's faith. Gradually the vision shifted, from Christ mocked and flogged to Christ nailed on the Cross, Christ dead. The Virgin was no longer the serene mother of the flowery meadows, of the Coronation or the Assumption; she was now the Virgin of pity, contributing to the act of redemption by the intensity of grief and the agony of love as she held in her lap the broken, lifeless body of her Son. The first representation of the Holy Sepulchre was carved in 1419 for the enactment of His burial on the stage. To mime the life of Jesus and behold its various episodes; "to watch with the eyes of one's soul how some were planting the Cross in the ground, while others were preparing the nails and hammer"; to become so rapt in this vision as actually to receive the Stigmata: all this was part of men's yearning to draw so near to Him that at last they might vanquish death as He had done. The imitation of Christ was wholly inspired by fear of eternal darkness and the hope of resurrection.

Since royal chapels were intended primarily to house the relics of saints, themselves encased in the most costly materials, they became repositories for jewelry and all manner of liturgical accessories. Every sovereign felt that he ought to bring his people nearer to salvation by adding to his collection. In the France of Charles VI, however, this aspect of royal piety was already tending towards mannerism, extravaganza and courtly display. Reliquaries became so ornate and were so artfully designed as to have a festive or theatrical air. One, for instance, is a glittering pyramid of gold, enamel and gems, displaying a host of tiny figures: God the Father, the Virgin in majesty, Jesus the Saviour and all their attendant apostles and tutelary saints. The increasing popularity of capitular art led to greater insistence on realism. The ordinary Christian wanted everything to be made plain. He expected the story of God and the saints to be told and illustrated so vividly that his own devotional response would be almost automatic. When the Florentine guilds decorated the new oratory of Orsanmichele, or when the people of Orvieto provided a splendid receptacle for their most precious relic, the Corporal, a piece of cloth stained with the blood of Christ, lifelike images combined with unstinted riches to enshrine the hallowed object.

Meanwhile the preaching friars were urging men to make spiritual exercises part of their everyday life. The tendency for prayer to become both personal and continuous led to a demand for smaller, more private objects. The Parisian workers in ivory produced miniature statues and altarpieces, in which the holy tragedy was enacted by a few figures in a diptych. To the devout this was as eloquent as the pulpit at Pisa, and it would go easily in a traveling-chest. By the end of the fourteenth century the triptych had become a locket. It provided the worthy Christian with a handsome ornament and enabled him to wear a relic on his person. When opened, it revealed an image of God in His suffering. This portable shrine, stamped with the symbol of the Passion, marks the end of a long process whereby, in the course of a century, the treasured objects of faith, once displayed to all in the Church's ceremonies, had gradually fallen into the strong grasp of the mighty who coveted jewels.

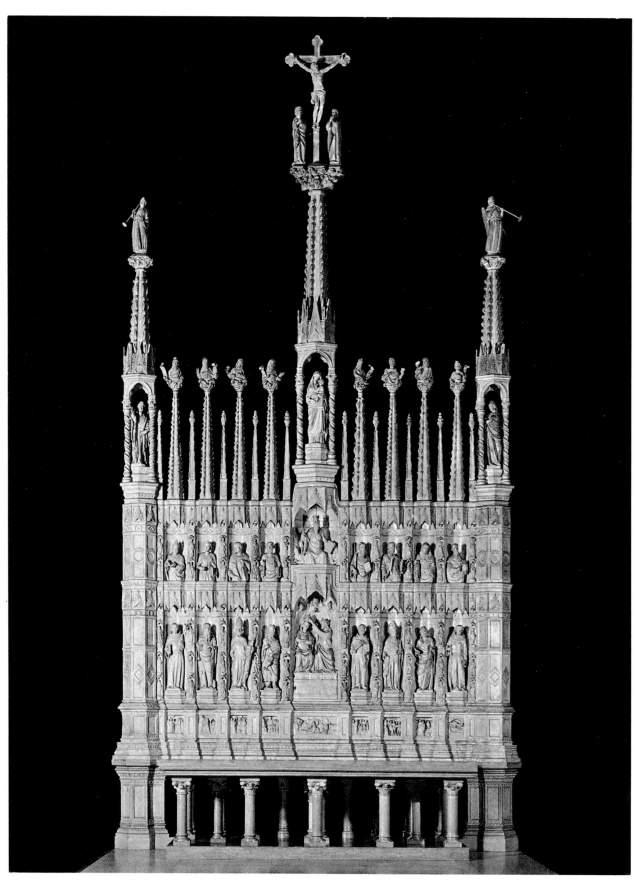

JACOBELLO (DIED ABOUT 1409) AND PIER PAOLO (DIED 1403?) DALLE MASEGNE. MARBLE ALTAR, 1388-1392.
CHURCH OF SAN FRANCESCO, BOLOGNA.

UGOLINO DI VIERI (ACTIVE 1329-1385). SILVER-GILT SHRINE OF THE CORPORAL, 1337.
CAPPELLA DEL CORPORALE, ORVIETO CATHEDRAL.

NICOLA PISANO (ABOUT 1220-BEFORE 1284).
PULPIT, 1260. BAPTISTERY, PISA.

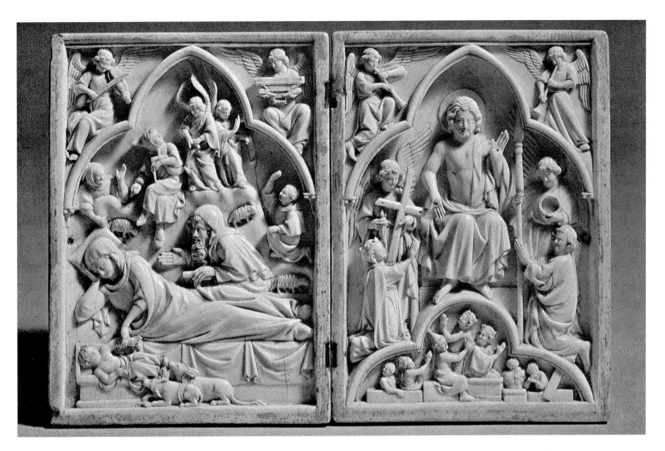

THE NATIVITY AND THE LAST JUDGEMENT. IVORY DIPTYCH OF THE FIRST HALF OF THE 14TH CENTURY.
FRENCH WORKMANSHIP. LOUVRE, PARIS.

LOCKET IN THE FORM OF A TRIPTYCH REPRESENTING CHRIST CROWNED WITH THORNS.
ABOUT 1400. SCHATZKAMMER DER RESIDENZ, MUNICH.

RELIQUARY OF THE CHAPEL OF THE HOLY GHOST. FRANCE, EARLY 15TH CENTURY. LOUVRE, PARIS.

Fourteenth-century piety reached an emotional climax when the suffering and death of Christ were portrayed in countless images of Calvary. In the imitation of Jesus Christ men were led to share His sorrows, witness His agony and thus to pass with Him through death and be raised by Him to glory. This was the one hope that enabled Christians in those days to look death in the face. Once Christianity became part of ordinary men's lives, both the Franciscans' call to repentance and the horror of the laity at seeing the flower of knightly zest fade and shrivel, combined to bring them to the foot of the Cross. Harshly it dominated the whole of religious symbolism.

The mode of portraying this tragic theme was formulated in the teaching of Assisi, where Pietro Lorenzetti was among the first to give it full expression. His painting shows the bare Cross, the torrents of blood, the wounded hands and side, the pincers that ripped the nail from His torn feet, and His poor, stark body, pathetically distorted. It was Lorenzetti who first depicted Mary and the disciples bending over the broken corpse and fervently kissing it.

When Philip Duke of Burgundy planned his own resting-place in the Charterhouse of Champmol, he commissioned a great crucifix in which painting and sculpture should combine to give the dead Christ every semblance of reality. Together, Claus Sluter and Jean Malouel strove to attain a degree of pathos to which the admirable head of Christ, no longer colored, still bears testimony. In this case the Cross was placed above a spring, the healing Fount of Life; and the prince's tomb, setting death at naught, blithely extolled the Trinity and almighty God.

In order to counteract the teaching of those heretical Franciscans who proclaimed that the kingdom of the Holy Ghost was approaching, the Church laid special emphasis on the mystery of one God in three persons. Thus the Holy Spirit was widely depicted in conjunction with the Crucifixion. God was seated in majesty on the "throne of salvation"; the dove of the Holy Spirit wore the countenance of the Son and upheld His Cross. In 1427 Masaccio painted this subject at Santa Maria Novella, placing it in the semblance of a chapel, with a masterly likeness of a skeleton beneath. The sublimity of the composition consists in the figure of Jesus on the Cross. The two donors are set apart, kneeling on either side of the picture, and their expressions deliberately exclude them from the world where the divine figures of the Virgin and

St John dwell in motionless eternity. Yet they are all drawn to the same scale and have the same monumental rigidity. In this way the donors are raised above the common level of mankind and are beatified by divine grace.

Meanwhile, Christ rose triumphant from the tomb. The power of the Resurrection required for its portrayal a dynamism which, it would seem, the patrons of that time seldom encouraged in their artists. Formerly religious art had strained after spiritual perfection, but the more humdrum piety of the fourteenth century was doubtless too down-to-earth to leap the grim abyss of death. The painters of chapels could do justice to the love and anguish of men, and their imaginative power enabled them even to imbue with grandeur their visions of the Last Judgement; but they were no good at portraying supernal bliss, and their scenes of Paradise were usually absurd.

There was one painter, however, who succeeded in endowing the Risen Christ with an invincible force, representing him as the dauntless hero of a victory over the powers of darkness and the fears that beset mankind: this was the unknown master of the Bohemian altarpiece from Trebon. This Christ might almost be the figurehead of that burning faith which was soon to inspire the Hussites. Nothing could contrast more strongly with the figure of the resurrected Lazarus in the Très Riches Heures. *The latter is truly a man, splendid of countenance and physique, with the clean-cut solidity of a classical bronze. Here the Limbourgs were holding out to the ageing Jean de Berry the traditional promise of knightly optimism, combined with the first-fruits of Italian humanism. In both cases it was an earthly promise.*

This concept could only have flourished in the hot-house, sophisticated atmosphere of 1400, when court life at Paris achieved an amazing brilliance, compounded of pomp, sensibility, eagerness and elegance, soon to be blighted by war. The ordinary man's attitude to death, not only that preached by the friars to their awestruck followers, but also the attitude of the stern, ascetic Christians for whom Masaccio worked, was one of terror or solemnity. A man's funeral did not portend his return to familiar pleasures; it was a farewell, a final rite for a corpse doomed to corruption. Only for the Virgin could it be a happy farewell, as angels decked her body with garlands for the coming Assumption. It was Mary rather than her Son whose death comforted the devout.

CLAUS SLUTER (DIED 1406). CRUCIFIX FROM THE CHARTREUSE DE CHAMPMOL (DETAIL), 1395-1399. MUSÉE ARCHÉOLOGIQUE, DIJON.

PIETRO LORENZETTI (ABOUT 1280-1348). THE DESCENT FROM THE CROSS, ABOUT 1329-1331.
FRESCO, LOWER CHURCH OF SAN FRANCESCO, ASSISI.

MASACCIO (1401-1429). THE TRINITY, WITH THE VIRGIN, JOHN THE BAPTIST AND DONORS, 1427.
BELOW, A SKELETON ON A SARCOPHAGUS. FRESCO, SANTA MARIA NOVELLA, FLORENCE.

LIFE AFTER DEATH

Fourteenth-century Christianity was more a matter of making a good end than of living a good life, and the chapel was the scene not so much of prayer and contemplation as of a funerary cult. Religious feeling, owing to its increasingly popular and secular nature, was overshadowed by the idea of death. As a result of showing the ordinary man's emotions and his dread of the unknown that lay beyond the grave, Christianity was bound to ask plain, disconcerting questions. What has happened to the dead? Where are they? Do not mysterious lights and unwonted sounds reflect their presence, separate and invisible yet close at hand and full of menace? Do they not crowd uneasily at the threshold of consciousness? Are they not in league with the powers of darkness and must they not, likewise, be propitiated by deference and dutiful oblations?

The teaching of the Church at its most exalted gave an answer that would dispel these fears. Death was but the strait through which man passed from his voyage on earth to reach his last haven. The day would come, and might come soon, when "time must have a stop." Christ would return in glory and man's body would be raised incorruptible. Then the good would be separated from the wicked and the resurrected host would make their way in two groups, one to eternal bliss, the other to eternal damnation. Meanwhile the dead would sleep peacefully in an abode of Elysian calm. This was what the burial service taught, and the medieval Church, at the zenith of its power, had persecuted and stamped out the pagan rites of sepulture. It had threatened with condign punishment those who persisted in taking food to the dead, and it had stripped tombs of jewels, clothing, weapons and all the elaborate furniture placed beside the dead man, to ensure that he enjoyed his ghostly existence and did not pester the living with his wants. Men went to their last sleep naked and destitute. An extraordinary restraint was observed. Not a single ornament or emblem was placed beside the Caro-lingian princesses interred beneath the foundations of the basilica of St Gertrude at Nivelles; and when archaeologists opened the only inviolate tomb of a French king, that of Philip I at Saint-Benoît-sur-Loire, they found nothing by the body but a simple covering of leaf-work.

The clergy, however, had to come to terms with popular beliefs that were too strong to be ignored. At Cluny, as early as the tenth century, they had begun to show greater latitude in the office for the dead, by permitting the living to bring them gifts in the form of prayers and expiatory rites. Gradually, moreover, they accepted the myth of an interval between death and the Day of Judgement, during which the souls of the departed, roused from their sleep, might lead a more active life. Those whom Dante visited were by no means wrapped in slumber. Under the hesitant supervision of the Church the domain of Purgatory was recaptured by pre-Christian attitudes to death. This was precisely the area that was extended in the latter part of the thirteenth century, when the priestly grip on religious observance was loosened and the devoted labors of the Mendicant Friars brought Christianity to the common man.

The Church's traditional reluctance to allow any but princes, prelates and saints to be buried within the sanctuary was gradually overcome by the people's determination that their dead should lie as near as possible to the altar. The obsequies of the wealthy were accompanied by every luxury that money could buy, for they must enter the kingdom of the dead with all the trappings of their rank. Since a man's power was reckoned by the number of his "friends"—those who were beholden to him and owed him allegiance—his bier was attended by his entire household, followed by the poor who had been his almsmen. Finally, his tomb was adorned with images, so that he might at least avoid total oblivion by surviving in effigy.

The determination, contrary to the Christian spirit of abnegation, to go on living within the tomb evinced a worldly, possibly more fundamental instinct; the desire to overcome the dissolution of the body and man's fear, not merely of the dead, but of his own death, of Death itself. From the beginning the Church sought to harness this instinct to its own ends and had always urged men to meditate upon the putrefaction of their bodies; for this revealed the hollowness and imperfection of the flesh, condemning the ephemeral pleasures here below and challenging men to renounce the world and follow the true path of God. The skeleton and the decomposing corpse were among the most eloquent symbols of preachers calling to repentance. A constant theme of the *laudi* sung by Italian fraternities was the desolation of the dead body, consigned to the worms, and darkness of the grave. This lesson was reinforced by imagery based on the poem of the Three Dead and the Three Living. It depicts three horsemen who come upon three open graves, and in the stench of their rotting corpses the living men are suddenly confronted by the vanity of this world. The putrefying flesh, crawling with worms, bore witness, firstly, to the close connection between sin and the flesh. It was believed that only the bodies of saints were incorruptible, and when the Preaching Friars opened the tomb of St Dominic they sniffed anxiously for the fragrant "odor of sanctity" that would prove the founder of their Order to have been truly one of the blessed. Secondly, the sight of decomposing flesh admonished the Christian to live prudently and maintain himself always, like the Wise Virgins, in a state of grace; for Death was an archer who fired without warning and struck his victim in an unguarded moment. Among the symbols of Christian ritual the vision of a decaying corpse constituted a sort of barricade against the insidious charms of a beguiling but accursed world.

The increasingly secular outlook of the early fourteenth century led to a complete reversal of this argument. The great fresco in the Campo Santo at Pisa places the picture of the Three Living and the Three Dead immediately next to that of the Triumph of Death, whose purport is the exact opposite. Death brandishing his scythe, swoops furiously down upon the pleasance where, amid all the refinements of courtesy, a group of fashionable ladies and gentlemen are extolling the delights of love and the good things of this world. He will cut short their revels and, like the plague or the Black Death, fling this gay company onto his growing heap of corpses. In this case the picture no longer symbolizes the vanity of mortal pleasures; it is man's scream of terror at the remorseless doom that awaits him. The startled horses, rearing away from the dead men in their open graves, are expressive of withdrawal and abnegation; whereas the heedless lovers, unaware of the whirling fury about to annihilate their bliss, are hungry for the sweets of life. For them, as for the troubadours to whose songs they dance, the world is a fine and pleasant place; it is unthinkable that they shall have to leave it. Death, Petrarch's *donna involta in vesta negra*, is portrayed at Pisa about 1350 as riding the wings of the storm; at Palermo a century later, as bestriding the skeleton of a mare. These portents of a dreaded, ineluctable triumph themselves reflect the triumphant lusting after fleshly happiness as fourteenth-century society discarded priestly ethics. When man rose from his knees he found himself facing Death no bigger than himself, the grim figure of his own death.

The new symbols appeared nonetheless on the walls of churches, for the preachers, in calling men to a devout life, were unable to quench their love of this world or to stem the strong current of optimism among the laity. They therefore attempted in their teaching to exploit the emotional flaw in this optimism, namely the horror of Death, who blots out all human joy. The frescoes at Pisa illustrate, as it were, a sermon purporting to strengthen an argument that had lost its force by means of another, infinitely more disconcerting because it explored the tragic depths of a keener sensibility. In this way a new form of the macabre came to dominate religious art by the end of the fourteenth century. About 1400 there appeared in Germany the first collections of prints entitled *Ars moriendi*. They depicted the various stages of a man's death-agony, when he is racked with regret for the world he must leave and beset by devils who make one last assault on him but are finally routed by Christ the Brother, the Virgin and the saints. It was about this time, probably in France, that the *Danse macabre* began to take shape. Popular superstition sometimes envisaged the triumph of Death as a magic flute-player whose artful piping swept away in an irresistible dance all sorts and conditions of men, young and old, rich and poor, popes, emperors, knights and princes. Preachers may have taught their listeners to enact this grisly tarantella of triumph, which was later incorporated into devotional imagery. In 1424 the new symbol of mortality was erected at Paris in the cemetery of the Innocents, not far from the group portraying the Three Living and the Three Dead, which had been placed there by the Duc Jean de Berry but had by now lost much of its effectiveness. The *Danse macabre*, expressing so vividly the anguish of man's destiny, soon made its impact everywhere, from Coventry to Lübeck, from Nuremberg to Ferrara. It gave a final turn of the screw to his foreboding, which no longer contemplated a remote and shadowy Day of Judgement but the present reality of "Death's pale flag." "Whoso dies, dieth unto grief." Death was not the drowsy calm of the seafarer coming safe to port; it was the yawning of a bottomless pit. The ascendancy of the macabre owed nothing to scourges of the age—war, pestilence or want; it was rather the outcome of two centuries during which Christian dogma had gradually come into line with the piety of simple men. Their fear of death did not mean that they had fallen from grace or faltered in belief, but rather that Christianity had grown less eclectic and now embraced humble folk who were steadfast in their faith but could not carry it into the realm of abstract vision. The *Danse macabre*, like the Italian concept of the Triumph of Death or the image of Christ lying dead in His Mother's lap, had little in common with the piety of monks or university professors; it expressed the religion of poor men who said their prayers among the tombs of chapels or Franciscan churches.

Once the idea of death at its crudest became the central and dominant feature of religion, it was natural that, through fear of dying and the yearning for resurrection, the imitation of Jesus Christ should concentrate mainly on His death. Hence, the tomb acquired great significance, and fourteenth-century patrons were mainly concerned with funerary display. This was the object of the most numerous and detailed commissions awarded to artists. All wills began by stipulating where the testator's remains were to lie buried until Judgement Day. People who intended to build a chapel, decorate it and provide capital for its maintenance regarded it as a place of burial rather than of prayer. It was customary to plan, build and adorn one's tomb long beforehand, and even to detail the arrangements for one's own funeral. The latter was regarded as the last and undoubtedly the greatest festival of a man's life. A festival was an occasion for lavish display, and the obsequies of those days were staged with a profusion of pomp in which money was no object.

"This is how the King (the unhappy Charles VI of France, in 1422, the lowest ebb of the Hundred Years War) was carried to Notre-Dame. Four of the bishops and abbots wore the white mitre, among them the new Bishop of Paris, who waited in the doorway of Saint-Paul to sprinkle the King's body with holy water before the procession started. All except him entered the church—the Mendicant Orders, the whole University and all the colleges, the Parlement, the Châtelet and the common people. Then he was taken from Saint-Paul and the attendants began to mourn loudly. He was borne to Notre-Dame *as the body of Our Lord is borne* on the feast of St Saviour. Six of those closest to the King carried a gold canopy above his body, which itself was borne on the shoulders of thirty of his servants. They may well have been more, for he was no light weight. He lay on a bed, wearing a gold crown and grasping in one hand the royal sceptre, and in the other the Hand of Justice. Its two gold fingers raised in blessing were so long that they almost touched his crown. Before him walked the Mendicant Orders and the University, the churches of Paris, then Notre-Dame and finally the Palace. They were singing, but no one else. All the people standing in the streets or at windows were weeping and crying out as if each one saw before him the dead body of his most dearly beloved. Seven bishops were present, and the abbots of Saint-Denis and Saint-Germain-des-Prés, of Saint-Magloire, Saint-Crépin and Saint-Crépinien. All the priests and clergy were in one body, and lords of the Palace, the Provost, the Chancellor and the rest, in another. Before them walked the poor serving-men dressed in black, weeping and wailing and carrying two hundred and fifty torches; and still further in front were eighteen criers of the dead. There were twenty-four holy crosses, preceded by men ringing handbells. Behind the body walked the Duke of Bedford, alone, unaccompanied by any of the royal princes of France. In this manner the dead King was taken on Monday to Notre-Dame, where two hundred and fifty torches were burning. The Office for the Dead was sung, followed early next morning by Mass. Thereafter the same procession was formed and he was buried beside his father and mother. More than eighteen thousand persons were there, of low and high degree. Each man received sixteen silver pence, and food was provided for all." This was, of course, the funeral of a very great prince, but in those days everyone longed to be able to command such a display for himself. The interest of this narrative is that it describes not only the ceremony but also the images with which royal tombs were now beginning to be adorned.

The main object of fourteenth-century funerary art was to perpetuate the religious drama that had been enacted round the dead man's body. His tomb, set against the wall or placed in the center of the chapel, was no longer a plain sarcophagus; it had become a replica of the state bed on which his corpse had been exhibited during the funeral. It bore a life-size effigy of the dead man, protected by a processional canopy like that carried above the Host at Corpus Christi. With a view to its prolonged exposure during the obsequies, the corpse had been embalmed and its viscera removed, frequently to be dispersed and interred in various sanctuaries. Sometimes the body itself was replaced by a facsimile in leather, or even by a living impersonator. The recumbent figure on the tomb had the air of a mummy, with its display of painted features and all the emblems of power. Beneath the arcature of a symbolic church, the funeral procession was reproduced on the sides of the tomb or on its enclosure: the officiating clergy, the family in mourning and crowd of poor men carrying lights as a token of fervent prayer, before receiving a last gift of alms in food and money. The dead man was indeed a prince who must show himself once more in majesty to his people and had therefore bidden them for the last time to a feast. His burial was also an act of propitiation, which the figures on his tomb were supposed to perpetuate. Finally, the prince became one with Christ, who at His second coming would lead him to eternal life. The iconography of his tomb, therefore, was completed by a symbol of redemption, sometimes the Easter Sepulchre but more often the Resurrection.

Very few Christians could appoint such monuments of luxury and ambition for their resting-place. Most of them ended in the anonymity of the charnel-house. Those with a little money ordered from funerary masons, who did a thriving trade, plain slabs on which the effigy was simply engraved and the liturgical text was reduced to a few phrases. But the prince's tomb, like his funeral, was what everyone would really have liked. It expressed and gave reality to the popular ideal of sepulchral pomp. In layout and design it gave a clearer image of death, whose novel features were gradually incorporated into funerary art.

When the former simplicity of tombs gave way to embellishments of this kind (a process which began in thirteenth-century England and Spain) for a long time the grand tradition of religious art was maintained. The clergy allowed recumbent figures but insisted that they should be hieratic and untroubled. The features of the French kings whom Louis IX caused to be sculpted at Saint-Denis are radiant with the serenity imparted by the last rites of the Church. Delivered from "the weariness, the fever and the fret," transfigured by the supernal beauty of a body prepared for Resurrection, they lie, open-eyed, in the sweet tranquillity of timeless sleep. They have passed through the waters of death and have reached the shores of eternity and peace. To the chanting of priests they have entered the rationally ordained realm of the supernatural as it was then conceived by Aristotelian metaphysics. The close of the thirteenth century witnessed the disruption of this composure by the influx of secular emotion. It destroyed the serenity of the dead, their impassive disdain for this world, and brought them back to the anguished reality of the living. It is true that in the Gothic North effigies on tombs long retained their marmoreal calm. Although that of Philip III of France, sculpted between 1298 and 1307, is to some extent a true portrait, the dead king is imbued with an aura of solemn majesty that is not of this world. In Italy, however, where recumbent figures had previously been unknown, a new approach can be seen in the first deliberately personified sculpture on a tomb. When, soon after 1282, Arnolfo di Cambio portrayed Cardinal Guillaume de Braye in the Dominican church at Orvieto, he visualized a more human, more earthly type of majesty, which became a model for later Italian sculptors. The art of Etruria and Rome, which they gradually revived, had itself been concerned mainly with the dead. But in this case the dead were not sleeping in a state of grace while awaiting resurrection; they wanted to live on in this world, surrounded by their temporal majesty. In Tuscany and Latium, at Naples, Verona and Milan, and later still in countries beyond the Alps, the tombs of secular and pontifical princes developed into elaborate mausoleums. The revival of the Roman cult, coupled with the ordinary Christian's horror of death, led to a number of variations on the central, liturgical effigy, stretched out on its catafalque: figures paralyzed with fear, for instance, or kneeling in prayer, or bravely mounted on a charger. That the dead should be portrayed in such attitudes as these shows how funerary art was being increasingly dominated by a purely secular mentality.

*

The hairy, rotting corpse of Cardinal de Lagrange or the meticulously anatomized skeleton painted by Masaccio in Santa Maria Novella revealed precisely what lay beneath the bedizened mummy on the tombstone. The image of *Memento mori* was still in the true tradition of religious thought. Like the Three Dead Men, it showed the hollowness of a world doomed to dust and corruption. Patrons who ordered such works undoubtedly wished, on the brink of the grave, to show their contempt for the flesh, their desire to rid themselves of it and make of their tomb an act of piety and humility, a call to repentance. The portrayal of corruption on tombstones merely echoed the Church's ancient bidding to renounce the vanities of this world; but it might also awaken in the beholder an obsession with the triumph of death. In this sense the image of abject fear was bound up with the grinning, nightmare procession of the *Danse macabre*.

Donors would sometimes ask the artist to portray them, no longer peacefully sleeping with the nameless multitude of the blessed, but in a more lifelike pose and with their own features delineated. Often they would not be recumbent on a bier but in the more active posture of prayer, or even, like the Emperor Henry VII on his tomb at Pisa, seated and holding court, surrounded by statues of his counsellors, who themselves were still alive. In this they were actuated by more worldly motives. They wanted, firstly, to focus attention on themselves. People must realize that it was not just anyone's grave, but theirs; for the building of a fine tomb in one's own lifetime was proof of social success, and the whole object of an artistic showpiece was to identify the man responsible for it. Besides, the tomb

was now addressed to the living. Its occupant demanded that the passer-by should pray for him and his salvation, and this selfish tendency in piety was also reflected by the desire to affix a personal seal to one's tomb. In most cases, where flatstones were bought ready-made from craftsmen who turned them out by the dozen, a name or heraldic symbol sufficed to identify the deceased. Important patrons, however, wanted to have recognizable effigies of themselves. When the tomb had not been prepared in its owner's lifetime, the sculptor's task was sometimes simplified by the death-mask used in the funeral procession. In this way the features of recumbent figures gave fourteenth-century artists a coveted opportunity to study adventitious details.

The desire to personalize one's sepulchral monument was accompanied by another purpose, less deliberate perhaps, but equally incompatible with the spirit of abnegation. If a man's countenance were carved in stone it would be immune to the ravages of death and he would win a lasting victory over the forces of dissolution. The same victory was proclaimed by the idealized features of thirteenth-century effigies; but in their case it belonged to the life hereafter, and men also wanted to survive in their mortal guise. Sometimes the living person of the deceased was recalled at his funeral by a kind of charade. When Bertrand Du Guesclin was buried at Saint-Denis "he was depicted as he had been in life by four men armed from head to foot and mounted on well-caparisoned chargers." The funerary portraits of fourteenth-century Christians came to assume something of the magic function ascribed to those of ancient Rome. The dead man would kneel in effigy on the massive tiers of his sepulchre; or he would be throned in majesty, like Ferdinand of Castile, in Seville, at the end of the thirteenth century; or later still, like King Robert of Naples at Santa Chiara, he would appear in his normal garb and likeness. In every case the image implied victory over the mortal fear it abjured.

These portraits became more and more common. Before long they were found not only on tombs but also on altarpieces where they stood beside God and the saints, only in a more lifelike and fleshly guise. Gradually they encroached on spaces hitherto reserved by liturgical art for sacred figures. The Emperor Charles IV decided to have his own portrait on the walls of the lower chapel at Karlstein

The Comte d'Evreux can be recognized in one of the finest windows of the Cathedral, a place where formerly the prophets had stood in unapproachable majesty. Statues of ordinary men were erected against the very walls of churches. To gratify his sovereign, Cardinal de Lagrange ordered for Amiens Cathedral images of King Charles V and his counsellor Bureau de la Rivière, of the Dauphin and the King's younger son, and of himself. On the façade of Bordeaux Cathedral the statues of Christ and the apostles were replaced by those of the Pope and his cardinals. Three hundred years earlier Cluniac monks, timidly and in fear of committing sacrilege, had ventured to place the awful countenance of the Lord at the entrance to sanctuaries. Now, on the threshold of such holy places as the Convent of the Celestines, the Collège de Navarre or the Charterhouse of Champmol, there appeared the benevolent features of princes and princesses—Charles V of France, Philip the Bold of Burgundy, and their wives. In churches the angels had to make way for the faces of mortals, especially of important men who were determined that a part of themselves should survive. The age of portraiture began with these new men and their discovery of the grimness of death.

There is not much likeness to the "tyrant" Can Grande della Scala in the heroically stylized knight who rides on the apex of his mausoleum at Verona; but the figure is an even more resounding manifesto of man's ascendancy and prestige. It was inspired by two ambitions that engendered the hope of earthly survival. The first was certainly of Roman origin. Already it had been the practice for professors who taught Roman law at Bologna, and were the first in the Middle Ages to kindle the flame of classical learning, openly to build themselves a sarcophagus, in the form of a stele, on unconsecrated ground. They sought to perpetuate their memory by having themselves portrayed in full panoply at their lecterns, presiding over their classes. The tone of an imperial triumph was echoed by the equestrian statue of Can Grande, copied by other members of the Scaliger dynasty and, after Milan's conquest of Verona, by Bernabò Visconti. The art of political magnificence, borrowed from the Caesars by Frederick II when he built Capua, culminated, among these municipal principalities and the public memorials to their lords, in the first monuments of the secular State. These princes secured temporal immortality in death. But on the marches of Roman Italy a torrent of knightly legend poured down from the Alpine passes. The valley of the Adige led by way of the Brenner to Bamberg, the seat of another Empire, Christian and Teutonic, chivalrous but feudal, still inspired by the heroes of the French "gestes," Roland, Oliver and Perceval. Can Grande and Bernabò wanted to be, not merely triumphant Caesars, but valiant knights. The victory commemorated in their statues was won in the tiltyard. Their knightly fame lives on in the echo, to be heard even in the boudoir, of their prowess and panoply of arms. They also wanted to be St George, spitting the dragon of death on their shining lances. In this new sepulchral art the recumbent figure of prayer and the dread warning of terror were challenged by the knight, flushed with his victory.

3

THE TOMB

For a long time it was the rule to allow none but saints to be interred within the church itself: the place of rest which the office for the dead besought God to grant to the mouldering flesh till the Day of Resurrection, had to be in the churchyard outside. But once the clergy had compounded with the common belief in an after-life, once it had admitted that after the death of the body the soul could still receive grace and reap spiritual advantage from periodic funeral services, it was clear to all that those souls fared best whose bodies lay closest to the altar, near the sacred relics, where they could get the full benefit of the church services. Prelates and grandees accordingly arranged to be interred inside the church. At first their tombs were inconspicuous. Then their sarcophagi and tombstones were embellished with inscriptions and ornaments; soon it was quite common for them to bear an effigy of the dead man, whose memory it was the artist's task to perpetuate. In the fourteenth century the creation of such works passed out of the Church's control altogether into the hands of laymen; more and more chapels were endowed and decorated by princes and lords, who vied with each other in ostentation; more and more concessions were made to popular superstition in which the preoccupation with death bulked large. As a result religious art tended to focus itself on the funeral monument.

The burial service sped the deceased on his way towards salvation. It had its natural counterpart in the Easter service—the rites that celebrate the glory and the resurrection of Christ, pledge of the believer's ultimate victory over death. Some private tombs in England are therefore combined with a symbolic representation of the Holy Sepulchre, at which mass was said each year at Easter time. In its earliest forms, however, tomb sculpture aimed primarily at perpetuating the funeral ceremony. It represented a festive gathering—the living assembled to pay homage to the deceased and escort him to the grave, or the priests ritually preparing the body for its eventual resurrection. Here the recumbent effigy of the dead man was the central figure on the decorated tomb, on which he lay in state till the end of time, surrounded by all the attributes of his temporal power. Here he reposed in peace—though in fact in many English tomb effigies the recumbent body appears to twitch and quiver, as if the will to live were too strong to be overborne. On the sides of sarcophagi, or those of the niche (often in the form of a chapel) in the wall of the church in which the tomb was recessed, Spanish sculptors were doubtless the first to represent the funeral procession. Assembled round the effigy of the Archbishop of Saragossa Lope Fernandez de Luna (who died in 1382), in his funerary chapel dedicated to the archangel Michael, are the twenty-four priests and monks who administered absolution, together with his three suffragan bishops and twelve of his noble kinsmen, all dressed in mourning.

In Central Italy the new sculpture was already voicing, in the accents of ancient Rome, the majestic spirit of the city republics. Its effect on the decoration of tombs was soon felt. In the church of San Domenico at Orvieto, on a sarcophagus discreetly inlaid with Cosmatesque designs, Arnolfo di Cambio carved for Cardinal Guillaume de Braye in the 1280s the first recumbent tomb effigy to appear in Italy. The monument is given, however, the characteristically Italian form of an arch of triumph. It rises up in tiers, like a series of stage-settings, and in one of the upper niches Arnolfo placed a second effigy of the Cardinal, now raised from the dead and kneeling beside his patron saints, who are commending him to the Virgin enthroned in the niche above. In Pisa Cathedral, for the tomb of the Emperor Henry VII, Tino di Camaino chose a similar arrangement, while modifying it in such a

way as to exalt the earthly glory of the Emperor and emphasize the concept of Empire itself. His figure of the risen Emperor is neither kneeling nor bowed in prayer: he is shown seated on his throne, as in life, surrounded by his counsellors.

At Naples, in the church of Santa Chiara, Tino executed for the Angevin kings a whole series of funeral monuments, culminating in 1343 in the imposing mausoleum of Robert the Wise. The recess in which the tomb stands is curtained like a baldachin and designed like the portal of a cathedral. Here are a host of figures, prophets, apostles, sibyls and saints of the Franciscan Order, all assembled round the culminating scene of Christ in Glory. More explicit tribute is paid on the side of the sarcophagus to the royal power of the House of Anjou: the dead king himself is enthroned in the center, flanked by the younger members of the family who will reign after him and maintain the glory of his race. King Robert is portrayed three times. He lies barefoot in the rough homespun which, as a Franciscan tertiary, he put on to die in; this is the image of humility. He is attended however by personifications of the seven liberal arts, for well before Charles V of France the Angevin king of Naples conceived of his earthly rule as the dominion of wisdom. On the dais above the tomb effigy, Robert sits enthroned; he has joined the Caesars in the immortality of civic triumphs. Above the dais Robert lives again, this time in the eternal abode of the devout Christian, praying to the Virgin and commended by his patron saints Francis and Clare. Here the funeral decoration conveys a dual message, political and spiritual. It becomes a simultaneous expression of proud glory and pious hope. The monument keeps alive the memory of a human achievement; at the same time, it extols the virtues of renunciation and proclaims an abiding faith in the powers of mediation vested in the Virgin and saints.

But at the beginning of the fifteenth century, in response to the new mood that had cast its pall over religious observances, another aspect of death appeared on tombs—its tragic aspect, calculated to induce loathing, fear and, in consequence, contempt for the weakness of the flesh. Cardinal de Lagrange, who died in 1402, had himself represented on his tomb as a decaying corpse, while for a patrician of Florence Masaccio painted, not the body, but the bare skeleton which, in Northern Europe, was already being swept up in the eerie round of the *danse macabre*.

THE TOMB

1

2

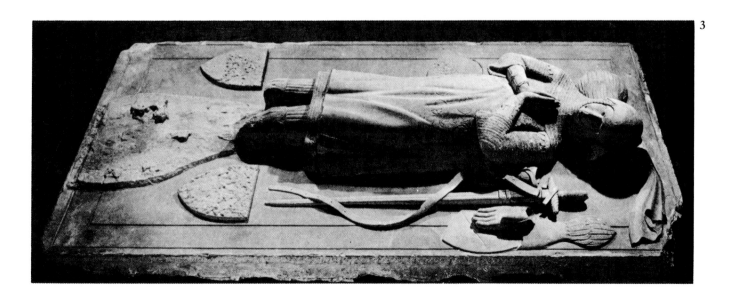

3

III. 131

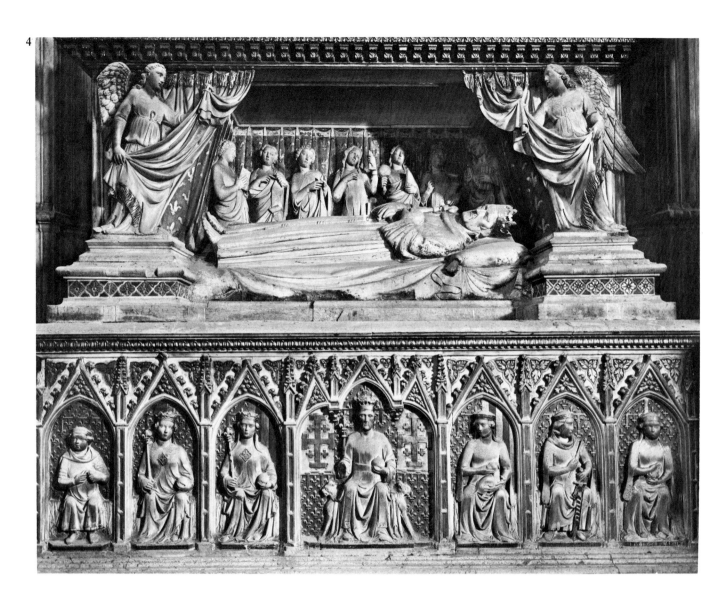

4

5

6

During the fourteenth century nearly every city in Italy bowed its neck to a tyrant. Either he ruled by force or the "seigniory" was conferred upon him by patrician families who, weary of ceaseless vendettas, conspiracies and tumult, hoped that the firm hand of a dictator might restore prosperity by imposing law and order.

Most of these jumped-up potentates, great and small, owed their success to the discipline and valor of the bands of mercenary troops which they employed; but they fondly imagined themselves "an antique Roman rather than a Dane," and expected their virtues to echo down the arches of the years. Nowhere in those times was a man's fame more loudly trumpeted than by the humanists in his pay who sang his praises and glorified his deeds in classical strains.

Verona and Milan were governed by men of ancient lineage and murderous temper. They lived like princes, drunk with absolute power, violent, greedy and shrewd. They were mighty hunters and renowned horsemen on the field of battle. Seeking to buttress their power by aping the deeds of the Paladins, they would come forth arrayed in the armor of Roland or Lancelot, cutting a brilliant figure at the head of their splendidly equipped companies of youthful knights as they rode out to tilt in tournaments or set off with fanfare on some campaign.

Yet they were still so insecure that they dare not perish, lest others should take their place. The usurper's act would not be forgotten in one generation, and the dead tyrant must therefore be transformed into a hero. At Verona, when a Scaliger died, his sons at first suppressed the fact, then erected his sarcophagus in the center of the town, in full view of the cowed inhabitants. Above the tomb an equestrian statue of the dead man symbolized his triumphant reign. Thus for all time Can Grande della Scala would gallop through the lists or ride in pursuit of a defeated enemy. At Milan, behind the high altar of San Giovanni in Conca, Bernabò Visconti stood motionless in his stirrups astride a great charger, unadorned and escorted only by figures symbolic of his alleged virtues. He had not crossed the threshold of death in order to kneel humbly at the gates of Paradise, but to remain a warrior and master of his city.

BONINO DA CAMPIONE (ACTIVE 1357-1388). MARBLE TOMB OF BERNABÒ VISCONTI, 1370. MUSEO DEL CASTELLO SFORZESCO, MILAN.

III. 136

FUNERAL MONUMENT OF CAN GRANDE DELLA SCALA, 1329. MUSEO DI CASTELVECCHIO, VERONA.

In the early Middle Ages the few gold coins to be found in circulation in Western Europe were stamped on one side with the head of the Byzantine emperor, a privilege he alone enjoyed as sovereign and leader of the Christian world. Frederick II in the thirteenth century was the first of the Western emperors to resume this right; he made full use of it and his fame was spread abroad by his gold "Augustales."

By the fourteenth century gold currency had become much commoner. It was the normal medium of trade, being minted by the principal banking and commercial cities of Italy, such as Florence and Genoa, and to some extent by kings. Such instruments of commerce and taxation, however, never bore the likeness of a prince. The human profile only appeared on medallions, which towards the end of the fourteenth century became collector's pieces. The older dies were much sought after by connoisseurs, who would then have them copied by their own artists. The treasury of Jean de Berry contained a superb collection of coins and medallions, all stamped, not with his own features, but with those of Roman emperors. As for the medallists of the French Court, they considered only the heroes of antiquity to be worthy of their art.

Once again the wind of change blew from Italy. Petty tyrants, political freebooters and the insignificant princelings of rocky Liguria and the Apennines sought every possible means of strengthening an authority that was continually threatened by conspiracy and the condottieri. *It was they who first ventured to substitute their own profile for those of emperors or deities, and they commissioned the best artists to depict their true likeness in gold.*

Painted portraits, like medallions, were symbols of majesty and pride. At first these portraits were confined to kings, and were generally executed in profile. Before long, however, members of the royal entourage, the family, friends and favorites of the king, and even some of the more prominent businessmen who had attracted his favorable notice, began to have themselves portrayed by painters in imperial attitudes.

ANTONIO PISANELLO (1395-ABOUT 1455). FOUR BRONZE MEDALS. MUSEO NAZIONALE (BARGELLO), FLORENCE.
UPPER LEFT: SIGISMONDO PANDOLFO MALATESTA, LORD OF RIMINI (1417-1468).
UPPER RIGHT: FILIPPO MARIA VISCONTI, THIRD DUKE OF MILAN (1391-1447).
LOWER LEFT: JOHN VII PALAEOLOGUS, EMPEROR OF THE EAST (1390-1448).
LOWER RIGHT: DOMENICO MALATESTA, MALATESTA NOVELLO, LORD OF CESENA (1418-1465).

JAN VAN EYCK (1385/90-1441). PORTRAIT OF GIOVANNI ARNOLFINI, ABOUT 1434.
STAATLICHE MUSEEN, BERLIN-DAHLEM.

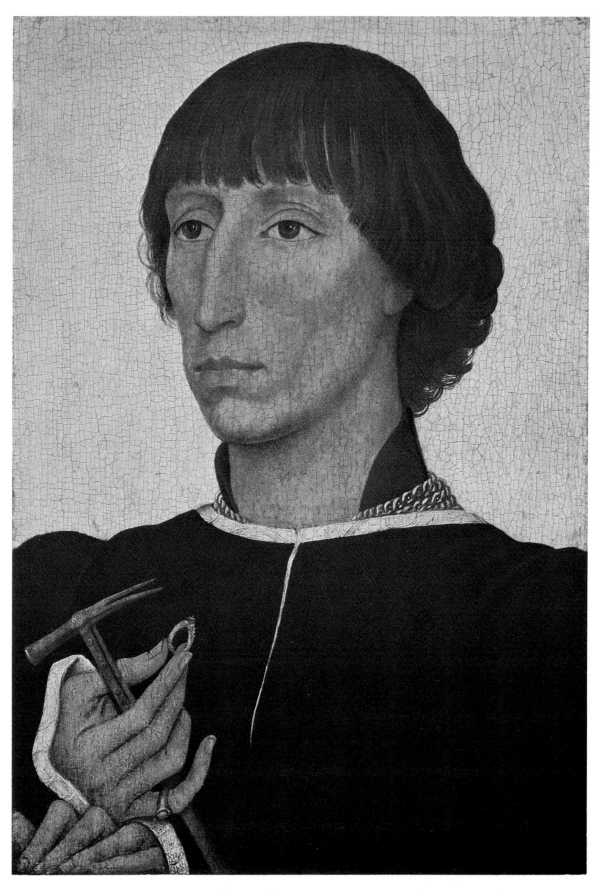

ROGER VAN DER WEYDEN (1399-1464). PORTRAIT OF FRANCESCO D'ESTE, ABOUT 1460.
THE METROPOLITAN MUSEUM OF ART, NEW YORK. THE MICHAEL FRIEDSAM COLLECTION, 1931.

4

THE PORTRAIT

A tomb is a personal possession. In the fourteenth century many a rich patron of the arts thought fit to impose on his sepulchre—as on his chapel, his armor and his home—a visible token of himself, in order to perpetuate his memory. For he thus made sure that throughout the ages all who came to pray beside his tomb would be reminded of the man he was. And since heraldic emblems, common to a whole lineage, did not seem to him sufficient for that purpose, he commissioned sculptors to make a real likeness of his face. Perhaps he also nursed a secret hope that by so doing he was neutralizing the dire processes of physical decay and ensuring his survival.

The idealization of the faces of thirteenth-century tomb effigies shows that this survival was to take place in the world beyond the grave, following on a glorious resurrection. The cathedral sculptures had represented bodies unsullied by the infirmities of their earthly lot, bodies in the prime of life and bearing the aspect in which, according to the teaching of the Church, they were to rise from their graves, summoned by the trumpet and bathed in the effulgence of the celestial light. But these abstractions had ceased to satisfy the man of the fourteenth century; he wanted to be recognizable. When he had his tomb built before his death, he posed for the sculptor and insisted on a good likeness. When the sculptor had to make an effigy of a man *post mortem*, he took guidance from the death-mask exhibited during the funeral procession. At Naples the artists commissioned to represent King Robert the Wise alive and seated on his throne made a plaster cast of the dead king's face and contented themselves with opening the eyes. The result was a terrifying effigy with a distraught gaze, that of a man roused from a nightmare and oddly resembling the wild-eyed Christ of the early Romanesque carvings.

Frankly expressionist, the art of the funerary portrait soon achieved an extreme verisimilitude. This can be seen in the recumbent tomb effigies of Wolfhart von Rot, bishop of Augsburg, Friedrich von Hohenlohe in Bamberg Cathedral and the Black Prince in Canterbury Cathedral. Son of Edward III of England, the Black Prince had come to be regarded throughout the western world, after his capture of the King of France at the Battle of Poitiers and his massacre of the inhabitants of Limoges in 1370, as the very incarnation of ruthless efficiency in warfare. The harshness and rude vigor of the carving match the personality of this grim warrior. The same style of carving serves to celebrate the pomp and power of the prince bishops and the prowess of dead knights. When, however, the sculptors were called upon to make the effigy of a dead woman, they employed a more elegant and appealing style, bringing out her physical attractions. Thus on the family tomb in Beverley Minster the face of Lady Percy, enshrined in an architectural setting "of imagination all compact," is invested with all the graces of courtly life. Cherubs bearing garlands hover round the recumbent body of the young wife of the tyrant of Lucca, Ilaria del Carretto, whose flawless beauty is immortalized by the art of Jacopo della Quercia.

When in the thirteenth century there was a revival of large-scale political statuary in Italy, the effigies of princes figured not above their dead bodies but on triumphal monuments. The earlier statues are still abstractions, not personal likenesses. The Emperor Frederick II and his chancellor Pietro della Vigna were portrayed at Capua with the features of Tiberius and Caracalla; the heroic symbolism of Roman busts was felt to be appropriate to such commanding figures, who had taken their place in history. But by the second half of the fourteenth century the old Empire was no more than a fading dream; Western Europe had been broken up into separate States and each ruler meant to be master in his own house. The attributes of supreme authority, like so many other cultural values, became vulgarized. Every European potentate desired to have his image made in painted stone, as the Emperor Frederick or Pope Boniface VIII had done before him. For he of course saw himself as the equal of these and meant to bequeath to posterity a lasting memorial of his reign. But he also wanted his features to be recognized in after times. For this purpose artists adapted the figures of cathedral sculpture, where Christ had long been represented as a king; indeed there was by now a tendency to clothe the bodies of Christ and the apostles in rich attire better suited to a social function, to show them in familiar attitudes and, generally speaking, to bring them down to the human level. All the sculptor had to do was to replace the face of a prince of the celestial hierarchy with the features of the earthly prince, his patron. Figures of this kind adorned the palaces and were often set up on the façades of churches. Philip the Bold of Burgundy commissioned from Claus Sluter a statue of himself in the attitude of prayer for the portal of the Charterhouse of Champmol; at Vienna an effigy of Duke Albert II of Habsburg, carved between 1360 and 1380, was placed in a triangular shrine at the top of one of the towers of St Stephen's Cathedral.

The new type of statuary made it easy for kings in stone to forgather with the prophets, now that the latter had almost entirely lost their aura of sanctity. Their wives, however, could not so easily mingle with the processions of female saints. For the growing spirituality of the cult of Mary then in the ascendant tended to preserve a greater distance between figures of the Virgin and those of ordinary women. The artist who carved the effigy of the French queen, Elizabeth of Bavaria, rigorously excluded any suggestion of the supramundane. The perfection at which he aimed was concerned with the beauty of the flesh alone; indeed this statue could be described as an apotheosis of the eternal feminine.

THE PORTRAIT

1. Tomb effigy of Bishop Wolfhart von Rot (died 1302). Augsburg Cathedral.

2. Lady Eleanor Percy (died 1328). Detail of the Percy Tomb in Beverley Minster, Yorkshire.

3. Tomb of Edward the Black Prince, 1376. Canterbury Cathedral.

4. Jacopo della Quercia (about 1374-1438). Tomb of Ilaria del Carretto (detail). 1406-1413. Lucca Cathedral.

5. Claus Sluter (died 1406). Philip the Bold, Duke of Burgundy, late 14th century. Portal of the Church of the Chartreuse de Champmol, Dijon.

6. Duke Albert II of Habsburg, 1360-1380. Statue from St Stephen's Cathedral, Vienna.

7. Bishop Friedrich von Hohenlohe (died 1352). Statue by the Wolfskeel Master of Würzburg. Bamberg Cathedral.

8. Elizabeth (or Isabeau) of Bavaria, Queen of France. Late 14th century. Palais Ducal, Poitiers.

3

4

III. 147

III. 148

7

III

POSSESSION OF THIS WORLD

THE MYTHS OF CHIVALRY

The horseman on Lombard tombs, clad in armor and rejoicing in his victories, took his place among the heroes. He joined the nine Paladins whom society had chosen to symbolize its virtues and love of life; Joshua, David and Judas Maccabeus; Hector, Alexander, and Caesar; Arthur, Charlemagne and Godefroi de Bouillon. These nine paragons had been painted by Giotto in the royal palace at Naples; they had figured in tapestries woven for princes; and about 1400 their statues formed part of the new décor in noble residences. All had been immortalized by history; the first trio by the sacred history of the Old Testament; the second by ancient history, now being revealed thanks to the vogue for translations of Latin literature; the third by history that had emerged in the form of a patchwork of incidents recorded in the *chansons de geste* and in the romances of the *matière de France* and the *matière de Bretagne*. The nine Paladins clearly reveal the foundations of chivalry. While some of its heroes were borrowed from the Church, the greater part had a secular origin. Rome lay in the center, with Jerusalem to the east and Aix-la-Chapelle, *douce France* and Windsor to the West. In the background were visions of Empire, of Crusading and the Orient. There was not a priest or a saint among them. These were men of the sword, kings and warriors victorious on the field of honor. They stood for might and valor. To portray the other face of chivalry, they were accompanied by nine Heroines, embodying the spirit of gallantry. They, too, came in groups of three from the Bible, from ancient history and from courtly love.

In the lives of the men and women whose love of pomp and pleasure is depicted in fourteenth-century art, imitation of the nine Paladins and their Ladies was a natural counterpart to the imitation of Jesus Christ. The deeds of the heroes should be re-enacted in life, just as those of the Saviour should be re-enacted in the anguished hour of death. Their exemplary conduct was exhaustively described in a mass of literary effusions, besides being portrayed symbolically at festivals and ceremonies. These mimes, however, never found their way into the theater, though they were often performed effectively as side-shows to entertain the company between the courses of a banquet. Their main setting was the absorbing ritual of the new orders of chivalry.

In 1344 the victorious King of England, Edward III, under the spell of the lengthy *Roman de Perceforest*, appropriated the project of his rival in courtliness, John Duke of Normandy, the future King of France. Froissart relates how "he formed the intention of rebuilding the great castle at Windsor, originally founded by King Arthur. This had been the birthplace of the mighty Round Table, whence so many valiant men had gone forth to perform heroic feats of arms. The King decided to create an order of knighthood comprising himself, his sons and the bravest men in the land. Forty in all, they would be called Knights of the Blue Garter. Every year on St George's Day they would hold a solemn festival at Windsor. The King of England began by summoning all his earls, barons and knights, telling them of his plan and his eagerness to institute such a festival. All agreed joyously, for they believed it would be fruitful of honor and love. Then they elected forty knights who were considered by esteem and renown to excel all the others in gallantry. To the King they swore an oath to maintain the Festival and the Order in the manner prescribed. The King built St George's Chapel at Windsor Castle and appointed a chapter, lavishly endowed in cash and kind, for the service of God. In order that the Festival should be made known in every land, the King of England sent his heralds to proclaim it in France, Scotland and Burgundy, in Hainault, Flanders, Brabant and the German Empire. To all knights and squires who attended it he granted a safe-conduct for two weeks after the Festival. The forty knights and their squires were to joust against all comers. The Queen of England would be present, attended by three hundred ladies and maidens, all of noble birth and similarly attired." This was to be a closed brotherhood, headed by the King, its members chosen for their valor and congregating, like all fraternities at that time, in a chapel. Their spiritual patron, St George, was the hero of victorious jousting, and their oath bound them to practise certain virtues for the rest of their days. They had a special robe, an emblem of valor, a motto and a yearly festival on the day of their patron saint, when the renown of their champions was celebrated in the presence of ladies. Thus the new secular liturgy was developed in a setting borrowed from the devotional societies. Courtly romance and skill in worldly pursuits took the place of Lauds and mortification of the flesh. The new orders of chivalry closely imitated the fraternities of *Laudesi* in trying to portray and vindicate a rule of conduct by means of regular communal performances. They, too, resorted to imagery in the form of charades and pictures. The rules of their code, moreover, were not confined to the closed circles surrounding kings and princes. They provided a way of life for all those who aspired to enter the nobility, or at least to be considered gentlefolk. Gentility means being of good birth, and it behove those who were not born to the purple, such as captains who had won lustre in battle or citizens who had made good, to excel in knightly conduct and courtliness. Patrons of the arts were drawn from the ranks of the well-to-do, who were constrained to believe the myths of chivalry and practise its observances in everyday life. In four-teenth-century art, therefore, the imagery of courtli-ness forms a pendant to that of worship.

Like the "Poor Man's Bible," the *Artes moriendi* or the frescoed chapels, these images served as moral examples and precepts. Their three main themes cor-responded to the three facets of knightly delectation. Most of the innumerable tapestries commissioned by Charles V of France and his brothers depicted religious scenes and were hung in chapels. The remainder comprised, firstly, pictures of the tented field or the tiltyard; Hector before the walls of Troy, the battle of Cocherel or the jousting of Saint-Denis. In the words of the *Songe du Verger*: "The knights of our time cause battles on foot and horseback to be painted in their halls, so that *by way of fantasy* they may take delight in *battles of the imagination*." Was it not the first calling and duty of a nobleman to fight in a good cause? A man of gentle birth, restrained by the code of honor, could find in battle an outlet for his combative spirit. A second feature of most secular tapestries was "verdure," whereby they obliterated the stone walls of a chamber and gave it "the fair and open face of heaven." The heroes of chivalry were also men of the countryside. They galloped through flowery meads, a sprig of may in their hand. If they started a hare, they would forsake fighting for the chase. Just as every romance was inevitably set amid the mystery and magic of a forest, so it was in the orchard that the nobleman loved to dally in his hours of ease. Lastly, there was the theme of courtly love. Around the year 1400, tapestries depicting the "Triumph of Love," the "Chamber of Love" or the "Goddess of Love," were ordered by various princes from the weavers of Paris, Arras or Mantua. They all extolled the stately concupiscence which rounded off the code of chivalry.

To these three sovereign values, all inspired by conquest—the joy of fighting, the joy of hunting, and the joy of wooing—there was added a fourth: the joy of amassing and possessing. It originated in the social upheaval which improved the status of businessmen and gradually admitted parvenus to the aristocracy. Its emergence was slow, furtive and unavowed; for chivalry took pride in being open-handed, magnificent and prodigal, and it poured scorn on stinginess. Nonetheless, secular morals were gradually tinged with gratification at one's own prosperity. This attitude first became apparent among upper-class townsfolk in Central Italy, where it conflicted with the Mendicant Friars' exhortations to poverty. Giotto is said to have written a scathing poem against those who preached abstinence, in which he substituted for complete destitution the ideal of balance and moderation. In the chapel at Padua, decorated for a man who had made a fortune in banking, the supreme Virtue, and the only one to be given a crown, is in fact Justice, namely the fair distribution of wealth. It is true that Petrarch applauded the austerity of Republican Rome, as did Boccaccio the unworldliness advocated by the Stoics he admired. It is true that the Mendicant Order of Jesuati was founded in 1360 by Giovanni Colombini, a Sienese businessman who had given all he had to the poor, and that the Florentines always turned in worship to Santa Croce or Santa Maria Novella, their two Mendicant churches. The princes of France, likewise, revered the strict poverty of the Celestines and Carthusians. By the end of the century, however, the Dominican, Giovanni Dominici, was beginning to make wealth respectable, by representing it as a condition to which some men might legitimately attain through the grace of God. He thus bestowed the accolade of the Church Predicant in rich cities on one Leonardo Bruni, secretary to the Florentine Republic, who invoked Cicero's *Tusculan Disputations* and Xenophon's *Oeconomicus* to support his contention that a man might surely acquire virtue by making money, so long as he earned it himself.

The secular ethic of enjoyment, with the concomitant pride in affluence that underlay its pursuit of pleasure, put a premium on all the good things of life that a man must leave at the end. Its values conflicted inexorably with those of piety, and their triumph in the fourteenth century showed that all the Church's efforts to christianize them had been in vain. It was all very well to portray affluence as the Lord's bounty or to affiliate a canonry to some company of knights and bestow blessings on their war-horses; it was all very well to point out that the beauties of nature merely reflected their Creator, or try to elevate a man's love for his lady into love of God. The upshot of all this was merely to give the proclivities of the age a veneer which in no way disguised their charms. The Church, in fact, surrendered to the irresistible influx of hedonism into a civilization that was becoming wholly secular. It was an age when the goldsmith's craft, at the behest not of bishops but of princes, reached new heights of magnificence. Its art, like that of the Carolingians, may be said to have been consummated in jewelry. For Suger, who loved precious stones, they enshrined the light of God and gave a foretaste of the true splendor that was to come, at present but dimly seen, and only to be unveiled on the Last Day. In the firm grasp of Jean de Berry, however, or of his cousin, Duke Gian Galeazzo Visconti of Milan, the jewel connoted earthly felicity, to be relished in all its fullness.

ARNOLFO DI CAMBIO (ABOUT 1245-1302?). STATUE OF CHARLES I OF ANJOU, KING OF SICILY, 1277. MUSEI CAPITOLINI, ROME.

In 1310 the court poet Jacques de Longuyon composed the elaborate Vœux du Paon in which he described the procession of the nine Paladins. According to Froissart they became the exemplar for every knight or squire who aspired to win fame by feats of arms. Just as the saints had fought the good fight of repentance and salvation, so these champions in armor became the heroes of knightly legend. Fashionable society modeled itself on the valor and "gentillesse" of the Paladin, whose deeds were evoked in mime and symbol. Jean, Duc de Berry, caused the nine heroes, whose statues already adorned one of the fireplaces of his palace at Bourges, to be portrayed in a series of hangings. By means of the lacy foliation of an architectural design, the tapestry conjures up an illimitable forest, through which scenes of music and merrymaking can be glimpsed at different levels. Julius Caesar is seated on the Imperial throne; with his crown, his plate-armor and flowing Carolingian beard, he belongs to no age but is endowed with the timelessness of courtly pageant.

History itself became a succession of warlike pageants. In battle men obeyed the rules of the tourney, and their tourneys often ended in battles. The knight went to war "neat and trimly dressed, fresh as a bridegroom," and after victory he would wait at table on his captives. Courtly art had no difficulty in combining reality with the supernatural. Every kind of painting served to show what men and women wore: scenes of coronations or illustrations for romances and love lyrics; religious subjects such as the Annunciation or, of course, the Adoration of the Magi, or even the Virgin of Sorrows. The aesthetic of chivalry required that not only its own legendary heroes but also Mary and the saints should be robed with a splendor once reserved for the most solemn rites of kingship and religion. This festal art consisted above all in shedding humdrum garments and clothing oneself in the raiment of fantasy.

After the close of the thirteenth century the new fashion began to appear in cathedral sculpture. At Strasbourg both the Tempter and the virgins he is about to lead astray are tickled by worldly pleasure. True, it is condemned by the artist, who covers the Tempter's cloak with slimy reptiles and gives the Foolish Virgins a somewhat wanton elegance. But the elegance is there, faithfully portrayed in all its lustrous charm.

NICOLAS BATAILLE (?). JULIUS CAESAR, DETAIL OF THE TAPESTRY OF THE NINE PALADINS, ABOUT 1385.
THE METROPOLITAN MUSEUM OF ART, NEW YORK. THE CLOISTERS COLLECTION, GIFT OF JOHN D. ROCKEFELLER, JR., 1947.

THE BLEST IN PARADISE. SCULPTURE ON THE TYMPANUM OF THE MAIN DOORWAY OF LEÓN CATHEDRAL, LATE 13TH CENTURY.

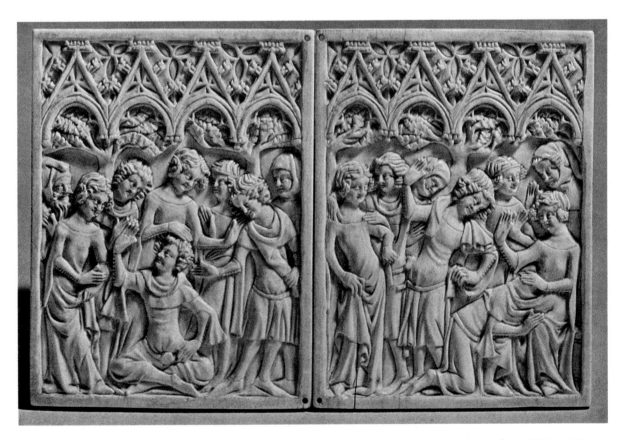

IVORY WRITING TABLETS REPRESENTING CHILDREN PLAYING AT HOT COCKLES, ABOUT 1375-1380. LOUVRE, PARIS.

III. 159

III. 160

THE TEMPTER, TWO FOOLISH VIRGINS AND A WISE VIRGIN,
ABOUT 1280. STATUES FROM THE FAÇADE
OF STRASBOURG CATHEDRAL.
MUSÉE DE L'ŒUVRE NOTRE-DAME, STRASBOURG.

III. 161

EROS

In the eyes of the knight and of the worthy burgess who aspired to gentility by aping him, the feast was a blazing pyre on which worldly wealth should be consumed. In feudal times pomp and extravagance had been the invariable accompaniments of government and war. The best ruler was the one who made the biggest show and shone in splendor without counting the cost. To command love and loyalty he must live in lordly style and from time to time invite all his friends to make merry with him, thus gratifying an increasingly sophisticated appetite for luxury.

Every incident in courtly life served as a pretext for a feast, and the ceremonial governing these orgies had a double purpose. Firstly, the feast was an occasion for ritual display. The lord appeared in the trappings of power and glory, laden with all the jewelry he possessed. He transferred something of his own glitter to those who had come at his bidding by presenting them with new garments. But the feast was also a ritual of destruction, a burnt-offering on the altar of hedonism. The lord solemnly sacrificed the goods painfully amassed by his toiling serfs. The junketings of the mighty mocked the poverty of the humble. By feasting the knight proved his superiority and towered contemptuously over poor drudges who labored under a heavy yoke. Let them scavenge while he caroused. By so doing he escaped the curse of Adam, condemned to eat bread in the sweat of his face. Illustrious and unconstrained, he vanquished Nature and robbed her with impunity. In death he presided at his ultimate feast, consisting in the pomp of his funeral, followed by a last banquet and a shower of gifts.

Fourteenth-century taste found its fullest expression in finery and display. Froissart's *Chronicles* were written to extol prowess, "a quality so noble and commendable that it should not be dismissed too briefly, for it is the very light and substance of a gentleman. As the log cannot burn without fire, neither can a gentleman attain perfect honor and renown without prowess." Froissart begins with a description of those sanguinary revels, the first major engagements of the Hundred Years War; he ends with the more elaborate and depraved orgies got up by Charles VI of France, who was mad. Paris in 1400 was the scene of knightly frolicking at its gaudiest. It seemed as if the spirit of carnival, in its determination to snap the bonds of daily life and escape from reality, had turned nature upside down. Darkness was banished, night and day became one and dancing went on till daybreak in the fitful, provocative gleams and shadows of torchlight. Men and women of noble birth enjoyed the freedom conferred by masks and fancy dress. In religious mimes they would act the part of the Good Thief or of Christ in agony. In dances they would become King Arthur or the wild man who slew the unicorn. And always, throughout the revels, they played at love.

The spirit of chivalry found disport in the wanton wiles of courtly love, which had beckoned the knight from the pages of every poem and romance during the past two hundred years. The clerks employed by princes had ransacked the archives of Scholasticism in order to draw up a code defining the elaborate ritual of a gentleman's relations with a high-born lady. The statutes of love appeared in the text and illustrations of books that were read aloud in the evenings to every nobleman and his household; and they were symbolized in ivory on caskets and mirrors. They were binding on any man who wanted to be received in genteel society. He must choose his Lady and serve her. Edward III of England put all the ardor and energy of youth into making himself the pattern of chivalry for his age. He was happily married. His Queen possessed all the qualities of a perfect wife and had given him two handsome children. Yet Edward went one day to the castle of the Countess of Salisbury, whose husband was his vassal, had been captured while campaigning for him and was even now held prisoner on his account. Edward wooed the lady and spent a whole evening, in the presence of her attendants, acting the part of a suitor enslaved by an invincible but hopeless love. Indeed, "Honor and Loyalty forbade him thus to perjure his heart in affronting so noble a lady and so true a knight as her husband. Yet Love spurred him so cruelly that he overcame and stifled both Honor and Loyalty." This may well have been the Lady for whom he founded the Order of the Garter, prescribed its ceremonial and chose its motto.

The ritual play of courtly love reversed the normal scheme of things. It freed a man from convention and by its essentially adulterous nature made amends for the restraints of wedlock. In feudal society marriages were contracted with an eye to the main chance. They were negotiated in cold blood and regardless of sentiment by the elders of the two clans, who concluded the bargain whereby the bride was handed over, to become her future lord's housekeeper, the mistress of his servants and the mother of his children. She had to be rich, well-born and faithful. Family law threatened with condign punishment both the adulterous wife and her would-be seducer; but it allowed the husband to fornicate and go a-whoring as he pleased. Every castle had its quota of eager damsels awaiting the knight-errant of courtly romance. This, indeed, was something more than mere dalliance, for it gave a man the option that marriage had denied him. Yet his choice never fell on a virgin, but on another man's wife. He took her not by storm but by blandishment, gradually sapping her resistance until she capitulated and granted him her favors. The whole campaign was conducted with a formal and meticulous strategy, reminiscent of the techniques employed in venery, jousting or siege warfare. Mythically, the pursuit of love became the hunt in full cry, the chosen lady a beleaguered citadel.

The knight's strategy, however, led him into bondage, for here too the normal order was reversed. In real life the lord "stoutly struts his dame before." In the game of love he must serve her, obey her lightest whim and undergo the ordeals she inflicted on him. Kneeling in adoration at her feet, in yet another reflection of the military world he adopted the posture of a vassal before his lord; for courtly language and behavior were wholly borrowed from the etiquette of vassalage. Principally there was the idea of service and all that it implied. The lover owed the same fealty to his mistress as did the liege to his lord. He had plighted his troth by an indissoluble bond. He must fight valiantly in his lady's name, for by his victories he would advance his suit. He must dance attendance on her and pay homage to her, just as feudal vassals did at their master's court. Like them, moreover, the lover expected his service to be rewarded in due time by successive gifts.

In this way the game of love sublimated and deflected sexual desire, without, however, seeking to become wholly chaste. In the thirteenth century the Church's efforts to subdue the spirit of courtliness did succeed in inspiring a number of poems which diverted the pursuit of love from a carnal to a mystic goal. This process of pious abstraction culminated about 1300 in the *dolce stil nuovo*. The ordinary swain, however, still hoped that his courtship would result in the lady's ultimate surrender, and for himself in a furtive and perilous defiance of the great taboo and of the punishment prescribed for adultery. All the same, during the period of waiting—and he was expected to wait a very long time—his lust went largely unrequited. The lover who hoped to win his lady had first to master himself. Of all the ordeals imposed by the code of love the one that best symbolized the stringency of this agreed delay was the "trial" extolled by the troubadours. The lady ordained that she and her knight should lie naked together and that he should contain his desire. Thus disciplined by the jejune pleasure of limited caresses, love would be strengthened and would attain a more emotional fervor. It would be a union of hearts rather than bodies. Thus, when Edward beheld Joan, Countess of Salisbury, he began to "ponder." Clerks in the service of feudal princes had used Ovid as a source of psychological euphemisms for physical love, and Western chivalry had adopted the code of courtliness just when Latin Christianity was being permeated with Mariolatry.

These two tendencies, making sex more spiritual and piety more feminine, intermingled and enhanced each other. Before long the Virgin became Our Lady, the paragon of her sex, to whom all men owed loving service. Her images, therefore, must be graceful, elegant and attractive. In order to captivate sinners, fourteenth-century Virgins were as exquisite in apparel and toilette as any princess. Some mystics, when they meditated upon the infant Jesus at his mother's breast, allowed their contemplation of her charms to lead them dangerously astray. Conversely, the inamorata expected her swain to voice his adoration in terms borrowed from the songs of mystic love. By becoming sentimental divine worship imparted an aura of sanctity to earthly raptures.

The fact remains that courtly love was always a game, to be played furtively with sly winks and carefully masked by a deceptive façade. It used the esoteric disguises of the *trobar clus*, of symbolic gestures and mottoes with a double meaning, of a language intelligible only to those in the know. Both in itself and in its manifestations it was, like the feast, simply a form of escapism. It was a thrilling but wholly inconsequent interlude, which no one took to heart. If those who played the game were sometimes taken in by it, they could pull themselves together by reading works that were a sort of antidote to erotic poetry. These satires and parodies, realistic and earthy, were just as popular as love lyrics. Jean de Meung's sequel to the first *Roman de la Rose*, in which his erotic allegories ended as a straightforward eulogy of physical love; the story of the Wife of Bath in *Canterbury Tales*; the bawdy anecdotes in the *Decameron*: after reading books like these a knight would drop the romantic mask and come down to earth—only to take wing again before long, for men could never decide between myth and reality. The latter, however, had no need of adornment. It was the world of feasting, illusion and romantic love that artists were expected to portray.

Courtly love was inspired and sustained by a vision. When Edward III entered the apartment of the Countess of Salisbury "everyone looked at her in wonder, and the King himself could not take his eyes from her. Then Dame Venus sent Cupid, the god of Love, to kindle the spark of passion, which burned long within him. The King, having gazed upon her, withdrew to a window, where he stood pondering deeply." Fourteenth-century art imbued clothing with poetic significance, for in order to attract attention and retain it one must make the most of one's appearance. Admission to the carnival was reserved to those whose apparel was worthy of the occasion and proved by its richness and superfluity the spendthrift extravagance of its wearer. In the illuminations of the *Très Riches Heures* the gorgeous profusion of hoods and cloaks is almost more bizarre than the ornamental diadem of beacons blazing from the castle towers. Since carnival was part of the courtly game and consisted in a formal dialogue between the sexes, women's clothes must be sharply distinguished from men's, and in fourteenth-century courts they did in fact reach the height of feminine individuality. By accentuating sexual charms they fulfilled the purpose of erotic display. They were not particularly close-fitting but acted rather as an enticement, artfully baiting the trap of seduction. Like stained glass, whose designs and colors inspired the Parisian fashion, clothes were intended to create an illusion of unreality. In the festival women were expected, with the help of slashed and padded gowns, horned headdresses and liripipes, to quit their ordinary personality and rise above it; just as in another, mystic festival the same fashionable women, moved by the call to repentance, would hasten to burn their paraphernalia at an auto-da-fé of renunciation. Those who illuminated the margins of psalters would insert fragments of real life among the abstract flourishes of their arabesques. In the same way artists who designed dresses for courtly festivities would permit glimpses of naked flesh among the artificial trappings of their creation; for they too were aiming at a poetic illusion.

The rites of love-making, however, allowed for further visions. It was a courtly convention that the lady, as one of the tokens she bestowed on her suitor, should let him, momentarily and from afar, see her naked. Thus the lover should always be obsessed by the true image of the loved one's body. It was quite common, moreover, for women to appear naked in the *tableaux vivants* presented on occasions of State or popular rejoicing. In courtly art, on the other hand, there seems to have been a strong and enduring inhibition from painting women in the nude. This did not apply to liturgical art, but there the body was portrayed in a state of *nature* in the theological sense, that is, untainted by sin and still possessing the perfection given it by God. In cathedral sculpture these images of physical perfection occurred mainly in two settings, the Creation of man and woman and the Resurrection of the dead. In both cases the flesh is seen in glory, either before Original Sin or in the shining liberation of the Last Judgement. It is probable that about the end of the thirteenth century stone-cutters were ceasing to sculpt the body without sentiment or any recollection of pleasures they had themselves experienced. Gradually the Idea was beginning to assume physical likeness. Both Eve and those risen from the dead began to display youthful charms. The fact remains that *gula* and *voluptas*, the living flesh "mounted for the hot encounter," still cowered under the shadow of anathema or were to be seen engulfed in hell-fire. Among the devils in the Arena Chapel Giotto painted the first erotic nude in European art. It may be that others, less stricken with guilt and remorse, have disappeared. It seems, however, that throughout the fourteenth century sexual taboos remained too strong for the laity to shake them off. Women's attire at the festivities of knights and princes continued to stop short of immodesty. When sculptors or painters portrayed nudity they felt obliged to make it sinful. A certain vexation of spirit is apparent in the angular, jerky style of the *Danses macabres*, giving the figures an air of wantonness. In the Gothic world woman's body was the last of all natural forms to obtain release from sin and the fullness of earthly joy.

Here, too, Italy led the way. The legacy of Greek and Roman statuary revealed the human body free from artificial adornment, unashamedly naked. Italian universities, emancipated from the Church, were already daring to dissect the dead, even at the risk of interfering with their resurrection. Before long sculptors began to draw inspiration from the freedom and realism of classical nudes for their own portrayal of the Creation and Last Judgement. Only at the very end of the fourteenth century did the Parisian school of painting produce a single torso with the serene innocence of antiquity and no trace of erotic sophistication; and it was that of Lazarus, a man raised from the dead. In Lombardy however, the home of chivalry, painters grew so bold as to depict Venus with nothing on, enjoying the sort of apotheosis hitherto reserved for God and the Virgin. They even showed gentlemen kneeling in adoration and receiving the spark of carnal love, much as St Francis had received the Stigmata—except that slight qualms of conscience made their hands tremble. It was not until the beginning of the fifteenth century, thanks to the patronage of Tuscan aristocrats, themselves freed by a Stoic Christianity from superstitious fear as well as from the need for erotic titillation, that woman's beauty could first be seen, after the stately Roman manner, in the perfection of bronze and marble. This was no resurrection; it was the genesis of Woman, bestowing on the New Man the gentle benison of her body.

Among all the Virgins and saints in what we still possess of fourteenth-century art there are very few portrayals of women in the nude. Although dalliance played a large and not always clandestine part in courtly etiquette, the figure of Eve was reviled. Only when religious art depicted sin or martyrdom was it permissible to hint at worldly licentiousness.

The most vivid illustrations of lechery were at first relegated to the marginal symbols on the periphery of major compositions, where the artist had always been allowed a comparatively free hand. This was the traditional setting for parables of vice and lust, which fourteenth-century art, obedient to the Church's teaching, represented by naked women. When Parisian craftsmen carved erotic scenes in ivory on the backs of mirrors or the lids of pounce-boxes, they boldly exploited these figures, which had supposedly been placed in churches to point a moral. About 1340 one of the stone-carvers at Auxerre gave a lascivious twist to his Gothic design, resulting in the superb sculpture of a naked girl crouched against a ram in an artfully seductive pose.

Many saints endured martyrdom by torture, a theme to which the artists who recorded their lives devoted meticulous attention. Paintings of blood and lacerated flesh reflected a fairly general taste for cruelty among those who commissioned them. About 1425 Master Francke was working for devotional societies in Hamburg and Lübeck. His clients were prominent citizens who had grown rich from trade in the Baltic and the North Sea. For all their uncouthness, these men appreciated the refinement of the Parisian aristocracy and, like the big merchants from Florence and Barcelona whom they met at Bruges, they were dazzled by it. Hence the sophisticated manner adopted by the artist in relating the life of St Barbara. Her executioners are arrayed like the Magi; the scene is made more violent by the steely, twisted drawing; and the princess herself is disrobed. Piety is mingled with fashionable sadism in this virgin body exposed to the lash and the knife.

About this time Ghiberti was designing for the Baptistery in Florence the bronze door on which he depicted the creation of Woman. Here Eve is floating upwards in the arms of that flight of cherubim which hitherto had borne heavenwards only one fleshly being, the Virgin of the Assumption. This is an Eve vindicated and redeemed, rejoicing in untroubled strength. There is no executioner to menace her, no fear to make her tremble. She is numbered among the pure and blessed. Beautiful and victorious over all affliction, she soars into the light of God.

MASTER FRANCKE (FIRST HALF OF THE 15TH CENTURY). THE MARTYRDOM OF ST BARBARA,
DETAIL OF THE LEFT WING OF THE ST BARBARA ALTARPIECE, 1420-1425. NATIONAL MUSEUM OF FINLAND, HELSINKI.

PERSONIFICATION OF LUST, MID-14TH CENTURY.
SCULPTURE IN THE SOUTH TRANSEPT, AUXERRE CATHEDRAL.

LORENZO GHIBERTI (1378-1455). THE CREATION OF EVE, DETAIL OF A PANEL ON THE PORTA DEL PARADISO, 1425-1447.
GILT BRONZE. BAPTISTERY, FLORENCE.

5

GLORIFICATION OF THE FLESH

As early as the beginning of the twelfth century Provençal poets had sung of the beauties of a woman's naked body—to begin with, in a frankly ribald tone. But soon the poets of courtly love sought rather to sublimate desire, to explore the possibilities of amorous suspense, to enhance it with sensuous imaginings and gracious imagery, and to invest the body of the beloved with an almost magical glamour. A perfect work of God, summing up in herself all the splendors of creation, this very lovely lady, whether seen in the flesh or glimpsed in dreams, inspired a passionate devotion. And one of the privileges of the "very parfit knight" was to contemplate the naked beauty of his lady love. An accepted practice in the medieval courts, this rite of homage had gradually made the more cultivated knights —those who could rid themselves of the crude licentiousness of military service—more susceptible to the graces of the body. All the same, over a long period a deep-rooted inhibition told against the representation in art of a woman's physical charms. When on rare occasions, in the heyday of the troubadours, artists ventured to transpose into painting or sculpture the vision of feminine beauty which haunted the minds of the poets and their audiences, this was done so furtively, and in forms which were thought so little worthy of survival, that no trace of them remains.

Artists felt qualms about making images of *voluptas*, which could not but be suggestive. But they were allowed in images of *natura*—of bodies, that is, unblemished by sin, as God had willed them to be when He created man and woman—to represent in a less clandestine manner, for all to see, the perfection of the human form. As early as the second third of the thirteenth century, in certain monumental figurations of religious art, sculptors attempted, timidly at first, to interpret the emotions aroused by the beauties of a woman's body. Some sacred themes lent themselves to this celebration of the flesh, without offending the pious-minded. One of them was that recurrent theme of Romanesque and Gothic imagery, the Last Judgement. The scene of dead men and women rising from their graves in all the fullness of life lent itself the more readily to the artists' new aspirations since the clergy commissioning such works were themselves beginning to appreciate the pleasures of earthly life and ceasing to reject so rigorously its allurements. Already on the tympanum of Bourges Cathedral, carved in 1275, the women rising from the dead seem quickened by the joyous breath of spring, burgeoning like young flowers amid the up-ended slabs of their tombs. Here—and this was a first, decisive step towards the inclusion of purely human emotion in a sacred scene —the sculptors frankly paid homage to the elegance of well-proportioned limbs and shapely bodies. The joy that emanates from these gracious nudes is chaste; they are invested with an ethereal purity, freed from evil and the fervors of profane love.

It was the rediscovery of the long-lost remains of Greco-Roman sculpture that did most to dispel the lingering effects of the religious and social prohibitions which had led to an obsession with sin, an aversion from all that savors of the flesh and a sense of guilt wherever pleasure was involved. Towards the close of the thirteenth century, motifs from an ancient intaglio representing Hercules and Eros sleeping under a tree had been carved on the base of the portal of Auxerre Cathedral. Here we find a feeling for physical beauty quite unaffected by the Christian mistrust of it. This new interest in the human form gained ground especially in Central Italy, where throughout the Trecento sculptors and painters came under French influence. But the Italians lived in much closer contact with the works

of classical antiquity. A growing interest in all that remained of ancient Rome led them to study the surviving statues and bas-reliefs and encouraged them to recapture so far as possible the spirit behind them. Already in the thirteenth century Arnolfo di Cambio's Madonnas were borrowing the stately forms of Roman matrons. Some late fourteenth-century drawings testify to a still more active and intensive study of the past. One of these, attributed to Gentile da Fabriano and now in the Louvre, represents a perfectly classical Venus, deriving from sarcophagus reliefs. But a new canon of the feminine body was developing. Though suppler and more graceful than that of the Roman marbles, it nonetheless diverged from the forms which, stemming from the aesthetic of the troubadours, had been perfected and refined in the courts of the Parisian aristocracy. Less flexible, more sensual, exempt from any qualms of conscience, it came to its full flowering in representations of the Creation of Eve on cathedral façades. The sculptor belonging to Lorenzo Maitani's workshop who decorated the façade of Orvieto Cathedral may well have worked previously on one of the great French cathedrals. He places his new-born Eve in the blithe setting of a French garden, while also giving her the strong, well-rounded forms of the ancient reliefs.

The painters patronized by the Duc de Berry successfully combined the elegant line of the Parisian artists with the graces of classical inspiration then in vogue in Italy. Thus in the scene of the paradise garden in the *Très Riches Heures* the Limbourg brothers celebrated in the lithe body of the youthful Adam and Eve's blonde beauty the joy of being alive and free in a "brave new world." In the Duke's collections there was also a medal representing Constantine the Great; on the obverse, beside a Fountain of Life surmounted by the Cross, are two figures, one of them a naked woman. The lithe, sinuous limbs, tiny breasts and supple curves reflect the mannered elegance of the Gothic courts whose highly refined art had imposed on women's bodies the fluent linearism and intricacy of the arabesque. How different from the Eve of Jacopo della Quercia, who saw her as an embodiment of strength, not of grace, a summation of the vital forces issuing from the earth, and imparted to her body the robust vigor of the goddesses of the ancient world.

GLORIFICATION OF THE FLESH

1. Personification of Lust, about 1290. Porch of the Cathedral of Freiburg im Breisgau.

2. Workshop of Lorenzo Maitani (about 1275-1330). The Creation of Eve, 1310-1330. Detail of the façade of Orvieto Cathedral.

3. Jacopo della Quercia (about 1374-1438). The Temptation of Adam and Eve, 1425-1438. Pilaster relief, central doorway, Church of San Petronio, Bologna.

4. Master of the Utrecht Life of the Virgin (?). Group of Fashionable Ladies and Gentlemen, about 1415. Silverpoint drawing. University Library, Uppsala.

5. Antonio Pisanello (1395-about 1455). Nude Figures with an Annunciation. Drawing. Boymans-van Beuningen Museum, Rotterdam.

6. The Limbourg Brothers. The Garden of Eden with the Temptation and Fall, about 1415. Miniature from the *Très Riches Heures du duc de Berry*. MS. 1284, Musée Condé, Chantilly.

7. Bronze medal from the collection of Duke Jean de Berry: Two Figures representing Paganism and Christianity. Early 15th century (?). Obverse of the medal of Constantine the Great. Münzkabinett, Kunsthistorisches Museum, Vienna.

1

III. 174

2

3

4

6

7

POWER

Since temporal possession meant, firstly, laying down the law, fourteenth-century civilization was epitomized by the prince, whose rule conferred peace and justice. The main secular purpose of European art, largely commissioned by princes, was to glorify power, which it did in the context of feudal tradition. Power had been symbolized for centuries by the image of the armed horseman. The lord, with his prerogative of command and chastisement, was primarily a warrior who lived in the saddle. In a society where every nobleman thought himself a St George, the horse preponderated in royal art. Even in Italy, where Rome had instituted other symbols of majesty, equestrian prowess continued for a long time to be emphasized by the rumps of rearing horses, whether in the battle-pieces of Uccello or in the frescoes at the Palazzo Schifanoia in Ferrara.

From the earliest feudal times, another unmistakable image of suzerainty in its warlike pride had been the tower. The fortified citadel was not merely the base of all military operations, the rallying-point for warriors and the last center of resistance; it was also the setting for courts of justice. Flaunting its strength like a banner, the tower was above all an emblem of power. It was only lived in as an after-thought.

The same was true of the fourteenth century. Once a man reached a position of authority he erected a tower at the same time as he ordered his tomb, so that the art of princes was mainly that of building castles. When Charles V had crushed the rising under Etienne Marcel and taught the Parisians that their king would brook no restraint on his sovereignty, he built the Bastille—just as William the Conqueror had built the Tower of London three hundred years earlier. A Marquis of Ferrara constructed the so-called Rebels' Tower with stone taken from the wrecked palaces of his defeated rivals. In the calendar of the *Très Riches Heures* every

landscape forms, as it were, a jeweled setting for one of Jean de Berry's castles. These battlements also served a practical purpose. In the fourteenth century warfare was endemic and its outcome depended less on pitched battles than on capture by siege or treachery of fortresses which in fact were more important strategically than ever before. Nonetheless, it was not solely for reasons of safety that rulers held court in their castles and performed within them both their ancient, liturgical office and their newer role as intellectual patrons. The prince's chapel and library were naturally placed within the walls, whose massive strength bore witness to his authority. Thus, Charles V placed his *librairie* in a tower of the Louvre, and at Karlstein the imperial chapel was encircled by battlements. At Avignon, where French bishops now occupied the Throne of St Peter, they built a fortified palace. Its two main centers, the pontifical chapel and the hall where His Holiness sat in temporal State, were locked away behind curtain-walls. Admittedly, the gold from papal offertories had to be guarded against the constant threat of marauding bands. The fact remains that the Pope and his cardinals wanted the headquarters of their alleged paramountcy over Christendom to be designed as a stronghold. Pope Clement, however, mitigated the grimness of the battlements with a few pinnacles, and in one of the towers he had a small, elegant suite fitted up for his own use.

Fourteenth-century princes were prepared to let a certain amount of cheerfulness break into the citadel of their might. This they did in two ways. If their home was to be a castle, let it at least be a comfortable one. Ever since the twelfth century the increasing part played by women in the world of rank and fashion had been gradually weaning their menfolk from the uncouth rusticity of fighting and hunting. As a result, they no longer wore armor all the time, and by the fourteenth century they had learned to make life agreeable indoors, even after dark and in winter, by means of torchlight and the glowing hearth. It behoved the prince, as a paragon of chivalry and "the mirror of all courtesy," to make provision in his home for the arts of conversation and love. Beside the great hall, therefore, where the men-at-arms congregated and the lord dispensed justice, newly-built or renovated castles contained a number of small apartments, to which fireplaces and tapestries added comfort and charm. It was in the fourteenth century that the prince's castle began to develop into a mansion. That of Saint-Paul, Charles V's favorite residence in Paris, had in its grounds several pavilions elegantly designed for recreation.

The second improvement was decorative. War itself was an occasion for display. It was the most stirring of all festivals, and the knight went forth to it in his bravest attire. Fourteenth-century battle-fields were strewn with gaudy surcoats, tatters of silken cloth, gold belts and a rich detritus of jewelry. The first duty of court painters was to embellish military equipment. In 1386, when the barons of France assembled in Flanders with a view to invading England, they wanted "their ships to be lavishly adorned and emblazoned with their badges." The Duke of Burgundy entrusted the decorating of his ship to his artist, Melchior Broederlam. According to Froissart, "Painters were in clover. There were not enough to go round, and they could earn whatever they asked. They made banners and standards from scarlet silk of surpassing fineness. Masts were painted from top to bottom, and some, in token of wealth and power, were covered with pure gold-leaf. Beneath was displayed the coat-of-arms of the noble to whom the ship belonged."

Since the ritual of war required all this parade of frills and furbelows, the baron's castle must also be adorned. Like his helm, it was crowned by an elaborate frieze, reproducing in stone the jeweled lattice-work of a reliquary and using the same Gothic arabesques in which the fantasy of courtliness found expression. Their convolutions reached the height of eccentricity in the roof of Jean de Berry's castle at Mehun-sur-Yèvre. Higher and higher rose these bastions and symbols of feudal power, with their banners and pennants streaming in the wind and their exuberant façades borrowed from rood-screens and the illuminations of missals, becoming in the end "such stuff as dreams are made on."

Europe, however, was beginning to embrace another concept of power, more ascetic and deriving from Roman law. Far more men were thinking about politics and the mechanics of power, largely because States themselves were growing stronger and better organized. Rulers had to employ officials of wider education, whose university training had accustomed them to reason methodically. National assemblies were convened at which representatives of the higher orders were asked to give advice on matters of State and even to debate policy. In the fourteenth century Europeans began to develop civic consciousness, and more of them were capable of conceiving power in abstract terms. About this time professional thinkers were bringing their minds to bear on the problems of government, for political science belonged to the realm of secular inquiry that William of Occam had thrown open to experiment and rational deduction. Scholars were at first preoccupied with the central conflict of medieval politics, namely, the ancient rivalry of Pope and Emperor, the twin potentates who, since the days of Charlemagne, had been dependent on each other and had both claimed to rule the world. That struggle had virtually ended in the middle of the thirteenth century with the triumph of the Holy See. But this in itself led to an argument about the origins of civil authority. While the jurists employed by the Pope used all the artillery of Scholasticism to win him a theocratic interpretation, those of Philippe le Bel, King of France, sought in Roman law the means to demolish the inordinate claims of Boniface VIII. In this they were allied to the Italian Ghibellines who, like Dante in his *De monarchia*, upheld the Holy Roman Empire. In this way the quarrel blew up again early in the fourteenth century. The transfer of the Papacy to Avignon made its worldly proclivities more apparent than ever. A German monarch invaded Italy in order to seize the imperial diadem. A large section of the Franciscan Order took issue with the Pope over the definition of poverty. At this moment two works appeared that were to inspire political philosophy throughout the fourteenth century.

When the Franciscan, William of Occam, wrote the *Dialogus*, after being prosecuted for heterodoxy by the Curia at Avignon and taking refuge with the Emperor, he continued to apply his basic principle of segregating the secular from the religious. In his rigid separation of Church and State he accorded the latter the exclusive right to political action. "The Pope," he said, "may not deprive men of liberties conferred on them by God or by nature." This enthronement of Nature beside God as a source of law implied far-reaching secularization of thought and jurisprudence. Meanwhile two professors at the University of Paris, Marsilio of Padua and Jean de Jandun, had previously published another work, *Defensor pacis*, which was far more subversive and uncompromising in the violence of its onslaught upon ecclesiastical authority. The Church had filched its temporal prerogatives from the Prince. It was wrong to suppose there could be any autonomous spiritual power, for there was no spiritual nature outside the laity. Hence, any special prerogative attaching to the Church must have been usurped and should be surrendered to the State. But how did the State obtain its authority? According to feudal tradition it was bequeathed by the sword, as a result of victorious warfare waged by the prince's ancestors. According to ecclesiastical Schoolmen it was a gift from God, who delegated His power to Kings—using, the Popes hastened to add, St Peter as His agent. The *Defensor pacis* had the downright audacity to attribute the origin of secular authority to the people, namely, "the majority of citizens who promulgate the law."

People, liberty, citizens, law, majority: such words, soon to be echoed by virtue, order, happiness, had the authentic ring of Roman maxims. Although they were still heard amid the din of war-cries, the voices were no longer those of Crusaders, but of legionaries and lictors. Marsilio of Padua gleaned them from the pages of Livy: Petrarch enriched them from his store of classical learning; and by the end of the fourteenth century Charles V of France was assuming the air of a Philosopher-King. He let it be known that he meditated in his book-room and frequented the company of scholars; that in winter "he would often read until supper-time the noble tales of Holy Writ, or the deeds of the Romans, or the moral teaching of philosophers." He had Aristotle's *Politics* translated, and the *Songe du Verger* gave him a theory of royal sovereignty wielded for the good of the *res publica* and guided by the advice of wise and moderate men. "When thou takest thy ease from the care and great thought thou givest to thy people and the common weal, then dost thou privily read or cause to be read some good writing and doctrine." The King no longer

led his army in battle but entrusted it to a High Constable. The Clerk had once more got the better of the Knight; but now he was a lay clerk, steeped in "the deeds of the Romans."

This new, civil authority, claiming to originate in nature and to rest on the people, required new emblems and symbolic figures. There was still room for the horse, provided it was that of Constantine or Marcus Aurelius, but no longer for the tower. In ancient Rome the sovereign was honored and set on a pedestal of power by other devices, whose remains Frederick II had unearthed and appropriated in Southern Italy. In the year 1300, when Pope Boniface had, by promising indulgences, lured all Christendom to the imperial and apostolic city, he caused the finest artists in Italy to place similar emblems around his throne, and he had statues of himself erected in cities that had been conquered on his behalf. The prince's power was manifested in his own lifetime by his appearance in triumphant effigy. Fourteenth-century magnates, accompanied by their household, were portrayed in majesty above the recumbent figures on their tombs, and they displaced prophets, apostles or the Queen of Sheba from the porticoes of churches. Among the first was the Emperor Henry VII whose effigy stood in the apse of Pisa Cathedral, while a little way off those of his four counsellors kept watch over his tomb. Charles V had himself portrayed, with his wife and sons, on the new staircase in the Louvre. The Kings of Bohemia stood sentinel over the Charles Bridge in Prague. Above the great fireplace in the palace at Poitiers, the lovely Queen Elizabeth of Bavaria looked down in regal distinction.

Opposite the Emperor's statue at Pisa there stood another, not of a lady but of an abstract, semi-divine power—the City herself. The city republics set out to glorify the civil attributes of power, as revealed by jurists in the laws of ancient Rome. Indeed the most advanced among them, in Central Italy, made great play with their Roman ancestry. Governed by sworn councils of citizens, who were theoretically equal and held office by turns, they pursued a martial, often aggressive policy, whose execution they entrusted to hired mercenaries. They believed law and order, on which trade and prosperity throve, to depend on internal harmony, freedom, loyalty and devotion to their city and to one another. They must unite for the greater glory of the city, which was reflected in massive buildings, constructed at public expense and designed by artists chosen competitively. Various symbols of military power survived amid these trappings of civic prestige. The campaniles of their collegiate churches stood ponderously foursquare, their façades, blank at the base, gradually becoming ornate towards the summit. These and the towering belfries of town-halls in Northern Europe had the fortified appearance of royal castles. The civic palaces of Tuscan *podestà*, those embodiments of imperial power, consisted of houses in the Roman style with inner courtyards, but transformed into fortresses and crowned by beetling towers. Moreover, every patrician family insisted on building a tower of its own. It was also thought fitting that victorious *condottieri* should be honored with statues, so that public squares and the façades of town-halls were soon teeming with feudal cavalry. In one respect, at least, this new municipal art did not favor war-like motifs. At the foot of the municipal tower public fountains gave a more peaceful air to the newly-built colonnades. Although in the last decades of the fourteenth century the loggia at Nuremberg was still adorned with the Nine Paladins of chivalry, the fountain which Nicola Pisano had constructed long before, in 1278, for the municipality of Perugia incorporated features of the new civic iconography. His patriarchs, saints, signs of the zodiac, symbols of the months and the liberal arts—all these obeyed the Scholastic traditions of the Church; but nearby he placed the She-wolf suckling Romulus and Remus, and the twin effigies of Perugia and Rome, *caput mundi*. Some years later, Labor and Good Government, the pillars of peace and order, were sculpted on the lowest tier of the campanile at Florence.

Nothing survives of the earliest Italian frescoes glorifying civic majesty, such as Giotto's horoscope of Padua, which he painted for the Palazzo Comunale in strict accordance with a plan scientifically worked out by a professor at the University. The oldest existing panegyric of this kind is that completed by Ambrogio Lorenzetti, between 1337 and 1339, on the instructions of the Republic of Siena. It is still the most consummate and expressive. The authorities had previously commissioned Simone Martini to decorate the outside of the town-hall with scenes from Roman history. To keep themselves in the path of righteousness they must also have constantly

before their eyes the virtues they should practise and the consequences of their administration. It was decided to give them food for thought in the contrasting allegories of Good and Bad Government. Ambrogio was directed to provide the Council Chamber with a convincing portrayal of the Aristotelian principles enunciated by the Schoolmen. In those days the lay mind could only grasp abstract ideas through the medium of allegory. If they were to be effective they must assume the form, countenance, dress and attributes of living men. That is why fourteenth-century didactic verse is filled with such a depressing phalanx of allegorical figures. Rubbing shoulders with the saints and dressed in much the same way, they made their inevitable appearance in every mime that tried to render a concept pictorially intelligible. They likewise cluttered up a large area of secular painting.

In the Council Chamber at Siena Bad Government is portrayed by the Prince of Evil, trampling Justice underfoot and escorted by the four powers of confusion—Disorder, Avarice, Vainglory and Wrath. Against them is set the triumph of Good Government, throned in majesty and clothed with the civil attributes of a sovereign. He has the bearded countenance of an Emperor. At his feet the She-wolf is suckling Romulus and Remus, and he is guarded by a troop of knights, their lances at the ready. In his splendor he emulates the Almighty, come to judge the good and the wicked. On his left, chained and captive, are the enemies of the City, the sowers of discord whom his victory has subjugated; on his right stand the twenty-four councillors, the serene masters of good doctrine. He, like St Thomas Aquinas in his Dominican apotheosis, is advised by allegorical figures—not the Nine Paladins, but the Nine Cardinal Virtues. In the sky, dominant but remote, are the three Theological Virtues. Around and a little below his throne, like the kings who in symbolic pictures of the Empire waited upon the Vicar of God, are seated in majesty the six Virtues of earthly life: Magnanimity and Strength; Temperance, Prudence and Justice. Lastly, "Sweet Peace sits crowned with smiles." A little way off, Justice is depicted again, in full face and enthroned with the same degree of stateliness. Inspired by Wisdom, she punishes the bad, rewards the good and, by giving and taking away, makes equitable distribution of worldly goods. (The fresco, after all, was commissioned by a Seigniory dependent on the *popolo grasso*, who regarded wealth fairly earned as lawful.) From the even scales of Justice hang two ropes which Concord is braiding in token of the friendship uniting the officers of State. In this way the abstract concept is given substance.

The impact of these Virtues, however, on Siena and its countryside is felt palpably in the humdrum events of daily life. These appear below the allegory, as if on a stage. They are no longer framed symbolically in the architecture of a chapel, for politics has no truck with liturgy. A whole people is working peacefully in pursuit of legitimate wealth. By their manifold tasks, depicted in minute detail, they earn enough to secure themselves from want and attain a greater measure of social justice. In the sweat of their face, moreover, do the peasant and merchant make possible the revels and recreations of the nobility, the butterfly dancing of maidens and the gallant cavalcades of falconry. Yet what finally emerges from this allegory of civil power is one of the finest portrayals of Nature in the whole of Western art. It is the first authentic landscape.

The fourteenth-century aristocrat's lust for power appears in the development of military architecture. It assumes two strikingly different forms in the ornate splendor of the château of Mehun-sur-Yèvre, near Bourges, one of Duke Jean de Berry's favorite country seats, and in the severely plain, slightly menacing architecture of the towered city represented by Ambrogio Lorenzetti in his Good Government fresco at Siena. (Something of the same contrast may be seen between the late medieval church spires of the German towns and the bristling towers of early Renaissance palazzi in Italy.)

The Limbourgs' miniature and Lorenzetti's townscape speak, as it were, two different languages. One has the ethereal dimensions of courtly myth, the vertical impetus of a mystical ascension; even the two peaks behind the castle (as well as the tree on the lower right) appear to be spiraling upwards, while the composition as a whole suggests the mazy convolutions of a poetic reverie. In the other a severe pattern of plain surfaces, staggered and interlocking, delineates a world of mass, density and depth.

The two works in fact represent two civilizations. The towers of the French prince's château are each capped by a hexagonal room as richly sculptured and traceried as a fairy-tale palace; the defensive apparatus is concealed beneath a riot of festive ornament. It is a setting fit for the fabulous adventures of King Arthur's knights as they roamed enchanted forests. A symbol of knightly lavishness, it glitters with the promise of treasure to be scattered far and wide. Such treasure, however, was jealously guarded from hostile neighbors by the towers of patrician families in Siena, or by that of the municipality at Gubbio. A few loggias were provided to admit fresh air, but the main purpose of these castles and palazzi was to unite kinsmen or townsfolk in a joint enterprise of economic rivalry and conquest. They were built to beat down competition.

THE LIMBOURG BROTHERS. THE CHÂTEAU DE MEHUN-SUR-YÈVRE, ABOUT 1415.
MINIATURE FROM THE "TRÈS RICHES HEURES DU DUC DE BERRY," MS 1284, MUSÉE CONDÉ, CHANTILLY.

THE SPIRE OF ST STEPHEN'S CATHEDRAL, VIENNA.

THE SPIRE OF ULM CATHEDRAL.

THE PALAZZO DEI CONSOLI AT GUBBIO (UMBRIA).

THE DUCAL PALACE AT MANTUA (LOMBARDY).

6

THE PALACE

In the fourteenth century the days of feudal independence were over; it had succumbed to the centralizing power of the monarchs. The world had grown smaller now that the crusades had come to an end and the military exploits of the knighthood were confined to the continent of Europe. A hundred years earlier the young King Edward III of England would, like his forbear Richard Cœur de Lion, have gone to the East in quest of glory; instead, he plundered nearby France. Henceforth the taste for military adventure found an outlet in the political field, as was indeed to be expected given the European situation. Christendom was now split up into separate States—a few great kingdoms, many minor principalities, and that host of small republics, fiercely competitive and at odds with each other, constituted by the towns of Italy and Germany. Everywhere the ruling princes and municipal magistrates had to cope with the unrest due to family feuds and rival factions. The western world resounded with the clash of arms throughout a century which witnessed an amazing development in military techniques and the art of fortification. Princes and towns saw to it that they were protected by stout walls. But the function of the castle was not merely to protect; it signalized the power of the kings and nobility. When, though perhaps less well off than some of his peasant neighbors, a country squire wished to ensure their deference, he built a turret on to his house, and it was more for reasons of prestige than of defense that royal palaces, like town halls, were given the air of fortresses.

Once it was clear that they would have to prolong their stay at Avignon, the Popes decided to build a residence befitting their hegemony. Benedict XII, who had been a monk, gave orders for the building of a papal palace laid out like a monastery near Notre-Dame des Doms. A narrow, austere edifice in the Cistercian style, it was flanked by bare ramparts giving it the look of a stronghold. Clement VI enlarged the palace and added a new unit centering on an immense courtyard suitable for receptions and parades. At the top of a staircase wide enough for ceremonial processions, he opened up a large decorated arch where the Holy Father could show himself to the public on solemn occasions. One of the towers contained a private apartment equipped with comfortable rooms and adorned with frescoes. But the exterior of the palace retained a forbidding aspect, like a clenched fist. This was not only to ward off the roaming bands of freebooters whose leaders threatened that one day they would carry off the Pope's gold, but also because the Pope was determined (to the dismay of the mystics) to lord it like one of the princes of this world, and to be if possible the most powerful of them all. Like Karlstein, like the old Louvre, like Bellver Castle built for the King of Majorca, the Palace of Avignon had in the heart of the building an open space, surrounded by loggias, where festivities were held. At the same time it safeguarded the person of the Pope with a cuirass of inviolable majesty.

Most of the cities of fourteenth-century Europe were dominated by a princely castle, a perpetual reminder of the overlordship of the State. At Prague, facing the merchants' quarter, the famous bridge built by the Emperor Charles IV to connect the left bank of the Vltava with the approach to his palace on the Hradcany hill was entered by a fortified gate. Serving less for defense than to glorify the royal house, it was adorned with monumental effigies of the kings of Bohemia. Some towns, however, had succeeded in securing for themselves a partial, sometimes a complete right of self-government, and they too sought to proclaim their autonomy by erecting grandiose buildings. For a long while these were always churches, and the towns that built and adorned them at their own expense competed with each other to raise the highest spire. From generation

to generation the local patricians added arcades, marble facings and pieces of sculpture, flaunting their wealth in the lavish decoration of their churches. In the churches, too, figured the first proud testimonies to the power and grandeur of the town itself. In 1310 the municipality of Pisa commissioned from Giovanni Pisano a symbolic effigy of the town. The artist gave it the form of a crowned caryatid feeding two children, as the Roman wolf had suckled Romulus and Remus. Likewise he endowed the figure with the ponderous majesty of the Roman tradition; it was upheld by the imperial eagle and escorted by the four cardinal virtues, one of them, Prudence, naked in the manner of a classical Venus. Nevertheless he placed this work in the cathedral, as one of the supports of the Gospel pulpit.

As early as the first half of the fourteenth century the free towns of Germany were financing the construction of town halls, seats of the local government, which, given the form of castles, resembled the residences of the nobility. Italian cities too were beginning to divert the sums raised by taxation from churches and chapels to public works of a purely civic nature. In 1334 Giotto was appointed city architect at Florence, superintending the work done not only on the cathedral but on the municipal palace, the Arno bridges and the city walls. The Campanile he designed belonged more to the Municipality than to the Church, and the sculptures at its base celebrated the Arts and Industries of the townsfolk.

The architecture of the city republics always contained a twofold central element: a castle and, beside it, a square. Like the kings, the local magistrates conferred in a tower overlooking an open space used for mustering the militia and for public meetings. The townsfolk of Gubbio built a handsome fortress-like *palazzo* for their consuls and, at the cost of tremendous efforts, flanked it with a lofty esplanade never used for trade or commerce. On this elevated platform, in the full glare of the Umbrian sun, the civic ceremonies took place. The people of Siena curtailed work on the huge cathedral planned by their fathers and, instead, erected in the semicircular Piazza del Campo a group of civic buildings, the first example of town planning in Christian Europe. The main unit was the Palazzo Pubblico, begun in 1298; on one side of it stands an elegant tower, the Torre del Mangia, which, despite its slenderness, served a military purpose and symbolized the city's proud intent to guard her independence.

THE PALACE

1

III. 195

III. 196

NATURE

Despite the tramping of men-at-arms and the ravages of plague, the fourteenth century was one of the great ages of song. Its lyrics, written to be sung in gardens, told of shepherds, the countryside and spring. Girls danced to them in meadows, and the roundelay of maidens in flowered dresses brought to the stony, angular Siena of Lorenzetti something of the smiling fields beyond the walls. Zest for life found fulfilment in the pure air of woods and fields. The art it inspired brought rustic pleasures indoors, transferring them to the walls of the closet or the pages of a book, where they conjured up dreams of roaming through field and forest, or recalled the familiar smell of grass and the hunter's prey.

Chivalry had originated in a society to whom towns were almost unknown. The lord of the manor owed his prosperity to land and the peasant who tilled it. Princes were always on the move from one estate to another, and they held court in completely rural surroundings. It is well known that St Louis loved to dispense justice beneath an oak, and much of the fourteenth-century knight's fierce relish for the fray consisted in the fact that warfare was, so to speak, an open-air sport. He charged through vineyards, skirmished along the edge of forests and laid about him amid the warm fragrance of freshly-turned earth. Battles began in the dewy dawn and waxed hotter as the sun rose in the sky. The castle, too, emerging from its battlemented seclusion, prepared a garden for the gentler pursuits of courtly life. At Avignon the Pope planted an orchard within the walls of his palace. Karlstein and Windsor were far from Prague and London. In Paris, since the old palace on the Ile de la Cité and even the Louvre were too remote from green fields, Charles V bought gardens in the Marais and there built his mansion of Saint-Paul. Every well-to-do merchant, aping the nobility, wanted to live in rural ease by acquiring land outside the city walls. Although Western society was becoming more and more urban in manners, tastes and occupations, it was so obsessed by the feudal lord as the embodiment of human happiness that it also succumbed to the charms of rusticity.

It so happened that Virgil had extolled those charms long ago, and the early Humanists, having rediscovered him, began to sing the praises of bucolic life, to point out how happy shepherds were and to bid their disciples exchange the tainted luxury of courts for the joys of pastoral simplicity. Countrified retreats became the setting for leisured converse. The convivial circle of the *Decameron* did not meet within the walls of Florence, and Petrarch forsook the bustle of Avignon for the lonely pool of Vaucluse.

It even became fashionable for worship to move out of doors. The only really religious characters in courtly romances were hermits, who shared with fairies the seclusion of thick forests. The sanguine spirit of Chivalry sought and found a God "who dwelt among the untrodden ways." For the believer who should forsake ritual and aspire after perfect love, "the radiance of God," said Meister Eckhart, "is everywhere, for all things give him the savor of God and reflect His image." Mystic ecstasy would convey the soul to an orchard, walled about but filled with flowers and birds and babbling brooks. The medieval church had crowned the Virgin and had shown her to the people as a queen enthroned amid angels and the solemn pomp of power. The fourteenth century brought her back among men. She shared the grief of atonement as they lay stricken before the dead body of their God; but she also partook of a woman's happiness. Rejoicing in the Visitation, or in the Birth and Childhood of Christ, the Virgin was embowered among the same garlands that Joan of Arc and her companions hung on summer nights from the trees where fairies lived. Seated on a grassy bank, she reigned over nature at peace.

To medieval monks and priests Nature had connoted the abstract idea of a perfection that lay beyond the senses. It was the conceptual form in which God manifested Himself—neither the tenuous chimera of sight, hearing or smell, nor the phantasmagoria of the world, but Eden as it had been before the Fall. It was a universe of peace, moderation and goodness, ordered by divine reason and as yet immune to the chaos and degradation wrought by sex and death. *Natura* stood in contrast to *gula* or *voluptas*, the warped nature of man, headstrong and disobedient to God's commands, and therefore abject, contemptible and damned. Twelfth- and thirteenth-century thinkers regarded Nature as something spiritual and incorporeal, whose mystery could not be discovered by the mere observation of phenomena, but only by proceeding in thought, from one deduction and one abstraction to another, until the ultimate divine reason was attained. Medieval physics was wholly conceptual, which was why it found Aristotle so congenial.

The Stagirite, it is true, based his physics on observation; but his path of inquiry wound upwards, in a manner identical to that of Scholastic logic, from the particular and fortuitous to the general, issuing finally in a concept. In this way knowledge gradually went beyond the shifting, ephemeral appearance of things in an attempt to reach the essential bedrock of all phenomena. By successive stages of abstraction it arrived at the Aristotelian forms of physics, mathematics and metaphysics. Physics, the knowledge of what is still subject to change, was thus rigidly separated from mathematics, the knowledge of what becomes fixed when the process of abstraction reaches the point where movement ceases. Aristotelian philosophy, once it had been translated from the Arabic, was enthusiastically espoused by masters and scholars of the Arts at the University of Paris. They were carried away by this complete, systematic, wholly rational cosmology, with its symmetrical counterpart in the microcosm of man himself.

This conceptual vision of the world made it all the easier to explain Nature as the embodiment of divine reason. Since art, moreover, was dominated by men who despised the sinful lusts of the flesh and, in their pursuit of knowledge, discarded observation and experiment in favor of the syllogism and pure logic, it was inevitable that Early Gothic, like Romanesque, should be abstract rather than representational. It did not depict a tree but the idea of a tree, just as it did not depict God, who was not apparent, but the idea of God.

Yet God had made Himself flesh. During the thirteenth century ecclesiastical art gradually moved from the essence of what it portrayed to its actual appearance. Before long it was possible to identify in the stonework of capitals the leaves of lettuce, strawberry and vine. The new Christianity preached by St Francis, whose optimism was akin to that of chivalry, urged that Brother Sun and other creatures of this world should be restored to honor, and its gradual propagation did much to revive men's interest in reality. The Friars Minor were numerous and influential at the University of Paris and the court of St Louis, and they spoke appreciatively of Nature as one of the glories of God in which the eye might take delight.

Even among Schoolmen some doubts arose as to the infallibility of Aristotle. Scholastic logic had itself been devised to expose and resolve conflicts between authorities. Before long it found that the Aristotelian cosmology did not quite agree with other systems, such as that of Ptolemy, revealed by translations of the *Almagest*. Only physical observation could eliminate these discrepancies and adjudicate between contradictory opinions. In the thirteenth century astronomers at Merton College, Oxford and at Paris University became the first Western scholars to make deliberate use of experimental method.

A more serious objection to Aristotelian physics was that it conflicted with Christian dogma. By imprisoning man in the cosmos it denied him free-will, and by postulating the indestructibility of matter it left no room for the Creation or the Crack of Doom. The exposition of Averroes made it brutally evident where peripatetic physics flew in the face of Christianity. In 1277, therefore, they were both solemnly condemned by Etienne Tempier, Bishop of Paris. This piece of intellectual tyranny had the effect of emancipating Western thought. By discarding a comfortable system which had an answer for everything, it plunged the world back into mystery and made scholars think for themselves.

Already the Franciscans at Oxford were beginning to blaze new trails. When Robert Grosseteste gainsaid Aristotle by his hypothesis that the substance common to the whole universe was light, man's concept of it was no longer "cabined, cribbed, confined," but flung open to the infinite. Since light could itself have been lit and might one day go out, one could imagine the world as having a beginning and an end. The new system, moreover, implied some form of calculus. Once the universe was interpreted in terms of light, physical reality could only be investigated by means of optical laws, which themselves were dependent on geometry and arithmetic. Mathematics were once more allied to physics and there was a strong inducement to calculate the size of the earth. The mystical tradition of numbers handed down by the Neo-Platonists could be harnessed to the new cosmogony.

As a result, exact science began to make rapid strides after the year 1280. According to Aristotle, the four elements were wholly abstract. The scholars of Oxford and Paris now sought to make them quantitative. Owing to the theory of light, implying scintillation, dynamism and thrust, the stable mathematics of the Greeks gave way to a mathematics of flux. Finally, the new doctrine illuminated the whole realm of knowledge by laying fresh emphasis on visual observation and giving it pride of place among methods of research.

At the end of the thirteenth century the vacuum created by the repudiation of Aristotle was filled when another Oxford Franciscan, William of Occam, convinced the Schoolmen that all abstract knowledge was illusory and that man's intellect could not penetrate the mystery of matter, which could only be apprehended sensorially in its external and fortuitous aspects. He thus restored the paramount importance of what men can touch and see. Thanks to the intellectual tide that reached the flood in Occamism and swept through the fourteenth century, the abstract in nature became concrete and things were once more what they seemed. This, combined with Franciscan joy and courtly exuberance, encouraged artists to open their eyes and behold "the many-splendored thing."

The world of chivalry, which now superseded the Church as patron of the arts, was inquisitive by nature and loved to see strange or exotic sights that gave free rein to fantasy. The knight-errant was by definition a vagrant and by predilection an explorer. The Crusades had furnished a pretext for travel on the grand scale, and few crusaders had been indifferent to the tourist attractions of the Levant. When books came to be written for this type of reader, they were mostly concerned with distant countries. Even in the early *chansons de geste* the pine and the olive stood as symbols for the recollection of bygone journeys and the yearning to set off once more. Tales of genuine travel competed with romances about knightly adventures in a world of myth and imagination. *Bestiaries, Lapidaries, Mirrors of the World, Wonder Books, Tales of Treasure Trove*: works like these, written in the vernacular for the courtiers of great noblemen, gave detailed descriptions of strange creatures which, unlike the unicorns and dragons, really existed. Every fourteenth-century ruler, partly for amusement but also because he wanted to possess the whole world, built up collections of curios which traders brought from the ends of the earth. In his gardens he kept a menagerie where live monkeys and leopards were on view.

There was also much speculation about the more humdrum aspects of nature, which nonetheless had their mystery and gave scope for fascinating discoveries. Hunting was in itself a form of conquest, for it enabled men in their daily lives to seize and subjugate the humbler creation. By means of the chase they became closely and accurately acquainted with the behavior and habitat of wild animals. Some of them, beginning with the Emperor Frederick II, embodied their experience in treatises. Together with love lyrics and chronicles of exploration, books on venery were among the earliest literary products of the knightly caste. They were the first writings on natural history, and they enjoyed a tremendous vogue. People were delighted when animals or plants they had observed in the hunting-field reappeared along the margins of their psalters or breviaries. Artists depicted them alongside fabulous beasts or wreathed in the trailing arabesques of imaginary flowers.

Taste in the age of chivalry required the portrayal of objects to be realistic but discrete, so that they should be individually identifiable and at the same time secluded and deeply interwoven with memory or poetic vision. The aristocracy made no attempt to display the whole pageant of nature: they merely selected a number of isolated features which were dotted about ornamentally amid the embroidered curlicues of their tapestries. These natural objects were pricked out against the abstract setting, such as a gold background or the red-and-blue checkerboard of stained glass, which was usually employed for ceremonial purposes.

Occamist physics had replaced the logical unity of a conceptual universe by a world consisting of disparate phenomena. Having destroyed the fullness and solidity of Aristotelian space, the Occamists had filled the vacuum with a gallimaufry of collector's pieces, which they tried to co-ordinate by means of the *impetus* or life-force, for which the Parisian scholar Buridan devised a mathematical rationale. Its movement resembled the swirling of the dancers' garlands in a roundelay, or the eddying of caparisoned horses in the vortex of the tiltyard. Although the Oxford scholars founded the science of optics, it was not from them that painters learned the laws of perspective. Nature as portrayed in the joyous art of chivalry had none of the structural solidity, based on mathematics, of the Romanesque basilica or Gothic cathedral. Spatially, it consisted in a series of piercingly vivid but unco-ordinated glimpses. The first attempts at constructing a landscape in paint were made in Italy.

Here the militant Franciscans extolled poverty of spirit and fulminated against scientific inquiry. Consequently the universities remained generally impervious to Occamism and continued to expound Aristotle and Averroes. The old philosophy lingered on until the teaching of Plato burst upon Florence with belated but devastating effect.

In the Italy of the fourteenth century, with the exception of medicine, all scientific achievements came from abroad. The intelligentsia consisted for the most part of bishops and Preaching Friars, who educated the upper classes and determined the iconography used in decoration. They retained the image of a unified, conceptual and wholly co-ordinated universe. Yet it was Italian artists, returning to the fountain-head of classical painting, who first rediscovered the ancient methods of creating illusion. Both the stately performances of civic ceremonial and those portraying the life of Jesus required no more than purely symbolic scenery and a few simple indications of time and place. They had therefore used the same abstract idiom as Roman or Byzantine art. The characters were surrounded by stylized trees and rocks, buildings and thrones. On the other hand, it was inherent in the dramatic quality of this art that the scenery should be arranged intelligibly within an enclosed space, and that the unreality of the setting should not clash too violently with the flesh-and-blood authenticity of the actors. On Giotto's majestic stage God and the saints were firmly delineated with all the massiveness and physical reality of statues. They had therefore to be given a certain amount of elbow-room. Giotto made no attempt to surround them with atmosphere or to pierce the wall behind them with a receding vista; but he did try, by means of a rather labored perspective, to ensure that the symbolic objects which showed where the action was taking place should appear to the spectator to exist in three dimensions. There was no occasion for crude realism in this transference from a liturgical to a dramatic mode of expression. Nonetheless, within the limits of an almost Aristotelian denial of chance and movement, it insisted that the optical laws governing illusion should not be ignored.

Giotto had no thought of being true to life. Yet only a few years after his death he was praised by Boccaccio for his skill in depicting reality. "Nature never made anything that he did not imitate or even reproduce in paint, so that men who see his work are often deluded into taking the painted for the real." Boccaccio's reality, of course, was not transcendent reality, and by nature he only meant outward appearance.

Meanwhile, Italian patrons had become inquisitive about the nature of things, and they now expected artists to give them a genuine illustration of reality. In this connection another attitude made itself felt. One could hardly call it bourgeois without slandering its most fervent hopes; yet it was an attitude common, not only to practitioners of medicine, law and government, but to all those who had done well in trade and had risen to power in the urban aristocracy. These patricians had not been to a university, but they had learned to use their eyes with the keenness essential for estimating at a glance the quality of the innumerable commodities of *mercatura*. The ramifications of their business compelled them to see the world plainly and to see it whole. They understood figures, and to them the word *ratio* also meant a bookkeeping transaction. Men like these wanted painted scenes to mirror reality more faithfully while preserving the logic, unity and spaciousness of the stage. Allegories of Good Government were, of course, conceptual and had an abstract setting; but at the lower and more prosaic level of vulgar curiosities, there appeared at Siena the first logically planned landscape. It was commissioned by a town council composed of merchants and businessmen just at the time when Giovanni Villani was using the accurate instruments of statistics to describe Florence.

After the plague epidemic of 1348-1350 had wrought its havoc, the Sienese landscape, as created by Ambrogio Lorenzetti in his frescoes in the town hall, was taken as a model by the image-carvers of Lombardy. Then, having traveled from Milan to Paris, it enabled the Limbourg brothers, who themselves had inherited the incomplete but more sensual realism of chivalry, to make a true portrait of the fair countenance of France.

The walls of royal apartments were concealed by tapestries or frescoes bidding the inmates go forth in pursuit of happiness, whether the zest of battle and the chase or the tranquil converse of an arbor. For his private rooms in the Wardrobe Tower at Avignon Pope Clement VI chose scenes of fishponds and the cool shade of noble trees. French painters were already working on these under the direction of Robin de Romans when, in 1343, Matteo Giovannetti da Viterbo was summoned to the papal court. While the Italian artist may have helped to complete these charming landscapes, it may well be that the great Sienese, Simone Martini, who was still living, was mainly responsible for them. The fresco is designed in successive planes, so that it recedes into a genuinely distant background. A little earlier Simone had used the same visual technique for the pastoral scenes of his Virgil *in the Ambrosian Library.*

Illustrators, in fact, were much given to depicting open-air life. Breviaries, especially, always began with a calendar of sacred festivals, which enabled artists to depict, month by month, the changing countenance of nature. The old, rural aristocracy of France regarded May as the month when the love of life was strongest and men shared in the triumphant rebirth of the countryside. May was the month of adventure, for then the grass was rich enough to provide pasture for lengthy forays. It was also the month of lovemaking, when village maidens would dance in the meadows. Elsewhere the Master of the Rohan Hours uttered the most pitiable of cries to lay bare all the suffering and sorrow of man; but for May he depicted the Heavenly Twins with the purity of a classical intaglio. This month was traditionally symbolized by riders on mettlesome steeds, and the horseman in the Rohan Hours *is the very incarnation of youthful gaiety as he canters into the greenwood, a spray of lily-of-the-valley in his hand.*

Man is not so closely wedded to nature in the landscapes by the Limbourg brothers. They are no longer depicted as a labyrinth, through whose web of mysterious apertures the eye is led from one discovery or surprise to another, until it encounters the blue, enclosing canopy of sky. Far from observing phenomena with the infinite detail of Occamist cosmogony, they present a vision of nature in its fullness, at once monistic and immeasurable. By their play of light the painters of the Très Riches Heures *have given their landscapes the authenticity of the world around them. It is a world no longer fragmented by abstract, analytical reasoning, but illuminated so that men may see it in the round.*

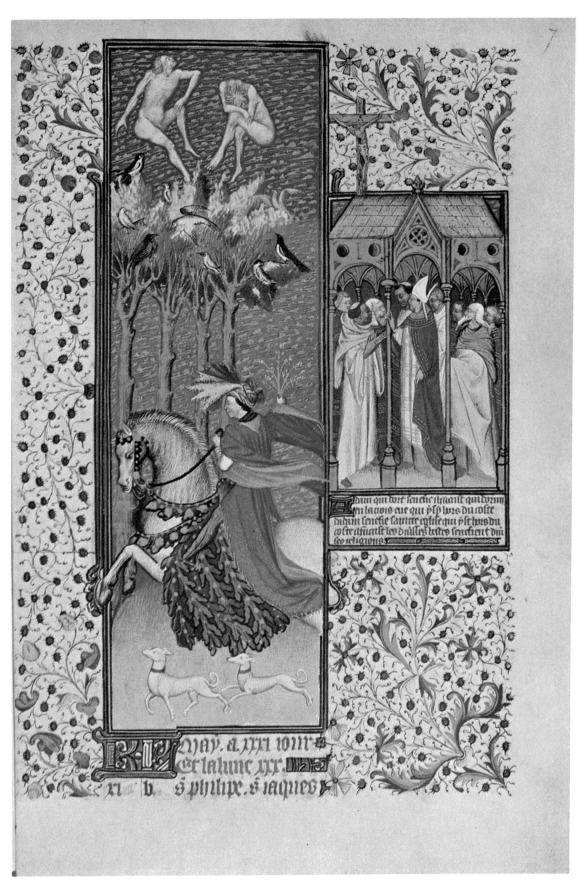

MASTER OF THE ROHAN HOURS. THE MONTH OF MAY, ABOUT 1418.
MINIATURE FROM THE CALENDAR OF "LES GRANDES HEURES DU DUC DE ROHAN," MS LAT. 9471, BIBLIOTHÈQUE NATIONALE, PARIS.

THE TRIUMPH OF DEATH, DETAIL: PARTY OF PLEASURE-SEEKERS IN A GROVE, ABOUT 1350. FRESCO IN THE CAMPO SANTO, PISA.

FISHING SCENE, 1343-1347. FRESCO IN THE CHAMBRE DE LA GARDEROBE, PALACE OF THE POPES, AVIGNON.

Cõment nature voulant orendroit plus
que onques mes reueler z faire essaucier
les biens z honneurs qui sont en amours
vient a Guille de machaut z li ordene z en
charge afaire sur ce nouueaux dis amou
reux. et li baille pour li conseillier z aidier
a ce faire trois de ces enfans. Cest asauoir
Sens. Retorique z musique. et li dit
par ceste maniere.

I E nature par qui tout est fourme
  Quanque a ca ius z sur terre z en mer
  Vueng et toy Guille. qui fourme
  Tu as part pour faire par toy fourmer
  Nouueaux dis amoureux plaisans
  Pour ce te bail et trois de mes enfans
  Qui ten diront la pratique
  Et se tu nes deux trois bien cognoistras
  Come sont. Sens. Retorique z musique

WORKS OF GUILLAUME DE MACHAUT: GUILLAUME DE MACHAUT RECEIVING "NATURE," ABOUT 1370.
FOLIO E, MS FR. 1584, BIBLIOTHÈQUE NATIONALE, PARIS.

III. 208

THE LIMBOURG BROTHERS. THE MONTH OF DECEMBER, ABOUT 1415.
MINIATURE FROM THE CALENDAR OF THE "TRÈS RICHES HEURES DU DUC DE BERRY," MS 1284, MUSÉE CONDÉ, CHANTILLY.

THE GENERATION OF 1420

At the approach of what the historians of European civilization call the Renaissance, both Paris and Rome were eclipsed by the new schools of artists in Florence and Flanders. At Rome the Papacy was floundering in the mire of schism, while in France the Valois court was convulsed and exhausted by family quarrels, civil disorder and war. These political vicissitudes did not emancipate the artist from his royal patrons, who continued to control him as firmly as they had done throughout the fourteenth century. It is true that Tuscany and Flanders now possessed the richest towns in the world; but in their heyday Paris, Avignon and Milan, the nurseries of courtly art, had been the most populous and thriving of great cities. Like the Limbourg brothers, Jan van Eyck was a court painter and body-servant to a prince. Though he sometimes worked for businessmen, they too belonged to a prince's household. They took pride in the fact and echoed their master's tastes. The Dukes of Burgundy, those princes of the royal house who had succeeded to the fame and fortune of the Kings of France, established themselves in Flanders, where they set up their court and attracted to it the finest artists who could no longer find work in Paris. It was thanks to their patronage that Flemish painting ceased to be provincial and suddenly took the lead in artistic discovery. The golden age of Florence began when the ravages of pestilence among her aristocracy had been repaired and her leading citizens, heirs to a culture inspired by knightly ideals, once more constituted a well-ordered society. The new forms of art germinated in Florence at the very moment when the Republic was imperceptibly turning into a principality; when the tyrant whose sons later tried to represent him as a paragon among patrons was already tightening his grip on the Seigniory. At Bruges and in Tuscany the Church was no less influential in 1420 than it had been in the past; but neither had its power increased, and art continued to be exactly what the monarch wanted. The geographical change, without implying any break in tradition, did put an end to the attempt at a uniformly Gothic style. Instead it revealed two divergent tendencies which from now on became sharply contrasted.

At the Burgundian court in Dijon and later in the Low Countries, sculpture took the initiative before painting. The same was true of Florence, where a hundred years earlier Nicola Pisano had led the way for Giotto. But it was the painters Van Eyck and Masaccio who completed the process. William of Occam's analytical vision, with its insistence on the discreteness of each object, received a razor-like trenchancy from the brush of Van Eyck. Yet he followed the Limbourg brothers in so focusing the objects he observed as to assemble these disparate phenomena within a cosmos unified by the Oxford theologians' principle of light. The dreamy fantasies of chivalry were dispelled by this light. It was the Pentecostal fire, the light which had illumined the mystics of Groenendael and which the Cologne school of painters had tried to reproduce in their mystical gardens. The surrounding wall of shadow; the flickering reflections of mirrors and precious stones in the peaceful seclusion of a closet; the iridescence caused by a shaft of light in the open air: by such means could reality be portrayed with harmony and truth. Masaccio, meanwhile, was reverting to the stately mode of Giotto in order to express an austere, Stoic Christianity, measured and self-controlled, for which neither fantasy nor mystic illumination would suffice. He eschewed the decorative profusion of arabesques and cared little about the appearance of things or the way they were lit. Tuscany was a land of architects, who loved the sobriety of plain surfaces and the chaste grandeur of stone, who measured not merely objects but the emptiness of space, which they shaped with geometrical simplicity. Like them, and like Donatello who invested the faces of his Prophets with all the torments of the soul, Masaccio depicted *virtus*, whose meaning the humanists had rediscovered in Roman literature and in the massive splendor of

Imperial sculpture. His reality, unlike Van Eyck's, was an abstract, Aristotelian vision of a rational universe, seen in the clear light of logic, proportion and mathematics.

There is nonetheless an awareness of man's nobility that is common to both the Occamist Van Eyck and the Peripatetic Masaccio. Each gave pride of place to man—the New Man, in the persons of Adam and Eve. Van Eyck imbued the body of Eve with the delectable sensuousness of physical reality. With his gently rolling hills clothed in rich woodland, he created a wonderful landscape, more captivating than that in his *Adoration of the Lamb*. Similarly, Masaccio chose for his devotional theme, instead of Jesus nailed to the Cross, the doleful figures of Adam and Eve cast out of Paradise.

Yet the real innovation at this moment in the history of art must be sought elsewhere. Hitherto Jan van Eyck had worked to order, doing portraits of canons, prince-bishops and the magnates like Arnolfini who ran the Bruges offices of Florentine banking houses. Then, one day he decided to paint his wife—not as a queen or as Eve or the Virgin, but just as she was. She was no princess, and her portrait had no value for anyone except the artist himself. On that day the court painter won his independence and was free to paint what he liked. And in Florence, where Ghiberti was about to write *Commentaries* on his work, as Caesar had done on the Gallic and Civil Wars, the artist's freedom was truly manifested when there appeared in the Brancacci Chapel frescoes, amid the apostles in the *Tribute Money*, the face of Masaccio himself.

By the end of the fourteenth century the wealthy men for whom artists worked insisted on being able to identify the objects in a painting. Occamist nominalism, moreover, taught that no one could hope to comprehend the universe except through sensory perception of individual phenomena. In the work of the Limbourg brothers the prolonged effort to reproduce tangible lineaments culminated in visual completeness. Light, striking through the veil of atmosphere, dissolved the old, theatrical backdrop and synthesized the formerly disparate elements of a painting. It now became possible to enhance this visual unity by the use of oils, so that two-dimensional painting superseded the art of illumination. In Eve's body, which Van Eyck painted as if it were an intricate landscape, the smooth flow of light into shadow lends greater distinctness to the texture of every part. Not only does the artist pay minute attention to physical substance; he also combines discrete sensory experiences in a coherent whole, embracing every dimension of reality. Thus did the Holy Ghost unite the souls of all men in bliss beyond compare; thus did the Light shine upon the face of the waters in the act of Creation.

In Masaccio painting has indeed become a mental process. His frescoes are the offspring of architecture, an abstract, numerical art, measuring and begetting space, subduing matter to the intellect, heedless of physical likeness. The architect employs logic and mathematics to give his concept reality. The new style of Renaissance architecture, initiated in Florence by Brunelleschi, discarded Gothic luxuriance and all extraneous ornament, reverting to the pure symmetry of the church of San Miniato. Masaccio, likewise, made of emptiness, of pure, abstract space the main element in his paintings. In it he placed Man, present in the flesh. "That flesh," as Leon Battista Alberti was soon to write in his Treatise on Painting, *"would crumble to dust; but as long as breath remained to it, whoever spurned the flesh would spurn life itself." Masaccio built flesh as if it were a temple or a monument. All his figures—like the faces of the statues carved by Donatello—are imbued with the seriousness of a steadfast faith, uncompromising, rational and resolute, calmly assuming the tragic burden of man's estate.*

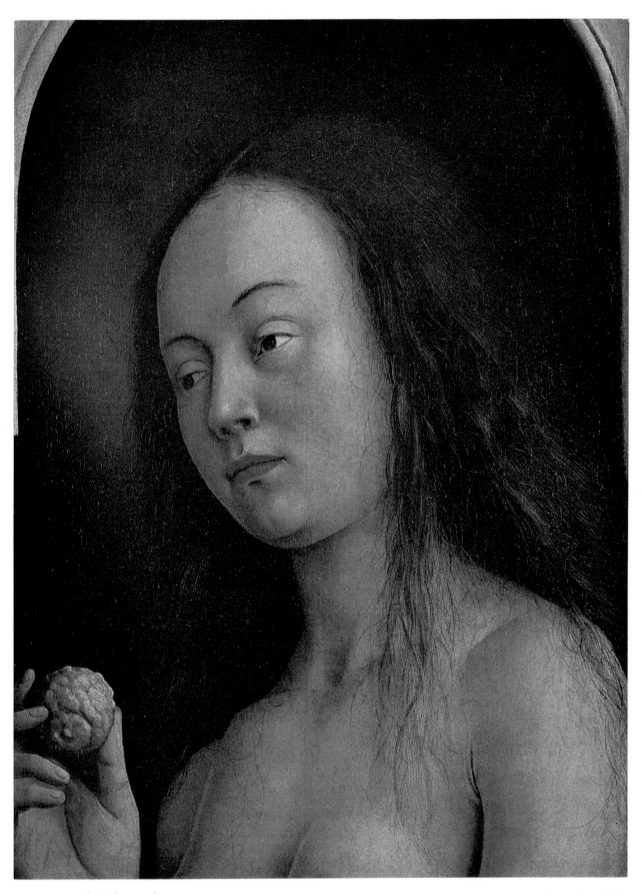

JAN VAN EYCK (1385/90-1441). EVE, DETAIL OF THE UPPER RIGHTHAND PANEL OF THE INTERIOR OF THE GHENT ALTARPIECE, 1430-1432. CATHEDRAL OF SAINT-BAVON, GHENT.

MASACCIO (1401-1429). ADAM AND EVE CAST OUT OF PARADISE (DETAIL), 1426-1427.
FRESCO IN THE BRANCACCI CHAPEL, SANTA MARIA DEL CARMINE, FLORENCE.

DONATELLO (ABOUT 1386-1466). THE PROPHET JEREMIAH (DETAIL), 1423-1436(?). MARBLE.
MUSEO DELL'OPERA DEL DUOMO, FLORENCE.

III. 215

INDEX OF NAMES

LIST OF ILLUSTRATIONS

PHOTOGRAPHS BY

Alinari, Florence (pages 65 right, 66, 131 top, 173/174, 174 upper right, 196), Alpenland, Vienna (page 147 right), Archives Photographiques, Paris (page 148 right), Maurice Babey, Basel (pages 27, 47, 48/49, 51, 57 top and bottom, 58, 59, 63, 64 top and bottom, 65 left, 81, 84/85, 111, 112, 117, 118, 119, 129, 130 bottom, 132, 136, 139, 145 left, 146 right, 156, 160/161, 168, 173 left, 188, 206, 214), Carlo Bevilacqua, Milan (pages 110, 189, 215), Henry B. Beville, Alexandria, Va. (pages 141,158), Bildarchiv Foto Marburg (page 148 left), Robert Braunmüller, Munich (page 113), Claudio Emmer, Milan (page 49), R. B. Fleming & Co, Ltd, London (page 145 right), John R. Freeman & Co, Ltd, London (page 26), Catherine Gardone, Dijon (page 147 left), Giraudon, Paris (pages 176 top, 185, 209), Hans Hinz, Basel (pages 48, 56), A. F. Kersting, London (pages 40 left, right, top and bottom, 99, 102, 103, 146 left), Raymond Laniepce, Paris (page 185), Louis Loose, Brussels (pages 101, 213), MAS, Barcelona (pages 130 top, 159), Karl H. Paulmann, Berlin (page 42), La Photothèque, Paris (pages 23, 24, 56, 60, 72, 73, 74, 75, 76, 80, 82 top and bottom, 113, 114, 131 bottom, 159, 167, 207), Luigi Rossi, Brescia (pages 194, 195), Rothier, Paris (page 39 left), Scala, Florence (pages 100, 137, 169), Yan, Toulouse (page 193), ZFA, Düsseldorf (page 187), and the photographic services of the following museums and libraries: Berlin-Dahlem, Staatliche Museen (page 140), Milan, Biblioteca Ambrosiana (page 71), New York, The Metropolitan Museum of Art (pages 28-29), Paris, Bibliothèque Nationale (pages 26, 41 upper right and upper left, 205, 208), Rotterdam, Museum Boymans-Van Beuningen (page 175), Uppsala, University Library (page 174 lower right), Vienna, Kunsthistorisches Museum (page 176 bottom), and by courtesy of Editions des Deux-Mondes, Paris (page 25), Oxford University Press (page 41 lower right) and Österreichische Fremdenverkehrswerbung, Vienna (page 186).

SKIRA

Text and colour plates printed by
IRL Imprimeries Réunies Lausanne S.A.

Binding by
H. + J. Schumacher A.G., Schmitten (Fribourg)

Printed in Switzerland